Internetware

Hong Mei · Jian Lü

Internetware

A New Software Paradigm
for Internet Computing

 Springer

Hong Mei
Peking University
Beijing
China

Jian Lü
Nanjing University
Nanjing, Jiangsu
China

ISBN 978-981-10-9646-4   ISBN 978-981-10-2546-4   (eBook)
DOI 10.1007/978-981-10-2546-4

Printed on acid-free paper

This Springer imprint is published by Springer Nature
The registered company is Springer Nature Singapore Pte Ltd.
The registered company address is: 152 Beach Road, #22-06/08 Gateway East, Singapore 189721,
Singapore

Foreword I

The Internet has become both the nervous system that coordinates our society and the brain in which all human knowledge is kept and accessed. It changed from being a network of networks enabling access to remote machines to a network of content, applications, people, and (software) services, thereby weaving itself into the fabric of today's global and interconnected physical world and society. The indispensable Internet poses many new challenges to software engineering; these challenges are becoming particularly acute with the emergence of computing applications that exploit the Internet in new ways. The emergence—and even the convergence—of mobile and cloud computing, sensor networks, cyber-physical systems, data analytics, and the Internet of Things is pulling software engineering further and further from the comfort zone of principles and techniques that have prevailed for decades.

This book presents results of an ambitious plan to meet the challenges paradigmatically, i.e., to systematically re-examine the fundamental aspects of WHAT-IS, HOW-TO-DO, HOW-TO-RUN, and HOW-WELL for software systems situated in the open and dynamic Internet environment. Prof. Hong Mei and Prof. Jian Lü led the research and coined the word "Internetware" to name the novel software paradigm for Internet computing. Technically, the paradigm is intended to support the construction, operation and evolution of software systems that consist of self-contained, autonomous entities situated in distributed nodes of the Internet and coordinators connecting these entities statically and dynamically in various kinds of interaction styles. These systems are also able to perceive the changes of open and dynamic environment, respond to changes through architectural transformations, and exhibit context-aware, adaptive and trustworthy behaviors in the Internet environment. The book gives a systematic and complete coverage of all the related aspects of Internetware, from the programming model to the engineering methods, to the runtime platforms, to quality assurance, and to the real-world practice and experiences. It also contains many timely and valuable new ideas, concepts, and technologies that will attract the interest of both academia and industry, fostering further advancement of research and developments in this area.

In addition to its technical contributions, the successful story of Internetware also exemplifies how original and systematic innovations can be achieved with deep insights, strong leadership, and persistent efforts. This is especially impressive considering the fact that Internetware was conceived independently in China 15 years ago when the software engineering community was predominantly representing professionals and researchers from Western countries.

This is an outstanding book on the new software engineering for the Internet computing: it is not only a summary of research efforts by the authors, but rather an accessible foundational reference book on software in the contemporary age.

Carlo Ghezzi
Politecnico di Milano
Milan, Italy

Foreword II

The convergence of various network technologies and applications, such as sensor networks, cellular networks, and social networks have pushed major Internet evolutions. Internet has evolved from a content delivery and resource sharing platform towards a ubiquitous infrastructure connecting human society, physical world, and massive computation resources and facilities. Software systems and applications running in such an "Internet-centric" environment are built upon highly virtualized computing environments, and have to continuously provide high-quality services and experiences for users who access applications from anywhere, at anytime, and by any device. As a result, software engineering development processes in all their phases and activities, such as software development, deployment, operation, maintenance, and evolution, are facing major challenges arising from the openness, situation-awareness, changeability, interactivity, adaptability, and evolutionary nature of the Internet-based applications. It is clear that addressing such challenges requires rethinking the principles and methods of software engineering.

A group of distinguished Chinese researchers proposed the term "Internetware" to refer to the new software paradigm for Internet computing environments. They devoted intense research efforts towards addressing significant fundamental issues for Internetware, including the autonomy of software entities, the openness of collaboration among software entities, the evolution and adaptation driven by context changing, and the trustworthiness of the system behavior. For almost 15 years, this group of researchers investigated approaches to address these issues with the sponsorship of National Basic Research Program of China ("973 program"). Their mission included studying, establishing and using systematic, disciplined, quantifiable approaches for software development, operation, and maintenance on Internet. Internetware is now consolidated as a quite full-fledged framework consisting of a new programming model, engineering approaches, runtime platforms, and quality assurance for software systems and applications running on the Internet.

Research on Internetware has resulted in numerous results recognized by premier conferences, top journals, real-world applications, and industrial solutions and products. This book, titled *Internetware: A New Software Paradigm for Internet Computing*, summarizes over 15 years of research around software engineering for Internet-based applications and the valuable results of this research. The book presents a core set of principles and methodologies for Internetware that will help engineers and designers in enhancing the effectiveness and productivity of the development processes for Internetware applications. The book also provides comprehensive guidelines and many representative real-world case studies that will be invaluable for software engineers in the development of Internetware applications.

This book also provides an important analysis of current research trends in modern software engineering in the Internet era. Many ideas and results discussed in the book represent important research directions that can be further extended and developed into more solid and theoretical foundations of software engineering for Internet computing.

I believe that this book is an important resource in the field of software engineering for everyone interested in novel trends, research, and methodologies in today software engineering.

Enjoy the book!!

Elisa Bertino
Purdue University
West Lafayette, USA

Foreword III

We are undergoing a tremendous change towards a new Internet-based and software-defined cyberspace, where our physical world and social communities can be virtualized by software technologies, delivered as software applications and services, and operated over an infrastructure that is Internet-based and globally networked. Cloud-based, mobile-oriented, and sensor-laden software applications and services establish the ubiquitous fabrics among every object in such a cyberspace, and have to adapt to ever-changing and on-the-fly requirements in response to instant feedback from this Internet-scale computing environment that is becoming more and more complex. As such, software engineering tasks are increasingly complex and highly challenging in view of unstable, noisy, and sometimes harsh environments. However, current software engineering approaches and techniques largely lack the capabilities to continuously explore the collaborative, situation-aware, adaptational, and evolutionary needs of software applications and services. Software engineering research needs substantial evolutionary or even revolutionary improvements.

The novel Internetware research in China is such an inspiring example. Led by Prof. Hong Mei and Jian Lü, as well as numerous other researchers in China, this area has made great efforts towards revolutionizing the emerging "Internet-based" and "software-defined" cyberspace in the past 15 years. The Internetware is proposed as a new software paradigm covering new programming abstractions, engineering approaches, runtime infrastructures, and quality assurance to make software applications and services collaborative, adaptive, evolvable, situational, emergent, and trustworthy. Internetware research has brought low-hanging fruits in premier academic conferences and journals. Meanwhile, some of the results have been successfully applied in real-world applications. In my opinion, Internetware research not only leads the pioneering software research and development in China, but also makes significant impacts on the software community worldwide.

This book provides to readers the authors' unique perspectives and efforts from the Internetware perspective, including the programming models, engineering approaches, middleware platforms and operating systems, measurements and quality-of-experience assurance, etc. This book also contains timely and valuable new ideas, concepts, and technologies for many application contexts such as cloud computing, mobile computing, social computing, cyber-physical systems, and so on.

It is my great pleasure to introduce this must-read book to faculty and students, researchers and practitioners, decision makers in charge of governmental research funding and other research & development executives who are interested in grasping and helping push the envelope of Internet-based computing technologies.

Carl Chang
Iowa State University
Ames, USA

Preface

To cope with new characteristics of software for the Internet computing environment, existing software paradigms need to be evolved to be a new one. Such a new software paradigm should be able to systematically support the development, deployment, operation, and quality assurance of software on the Internet. Around 2000, we coined a word *Internetware* from the two words "Internet" and "Software", to denote our visions of a new paradigm for software systems that are constructed, executed, used, and evolved in the open and dynamic Internet environment. Elaborately, these systems often need to be

Autonomous. Software entities are usually distributed, relatively self-contained, and independent. Software entities perform according to the composition or deployment strategies defined by their providers, and continuously satisfy the providers' requirements. A software entity can adapt itself when necessary, by sensing and collecting information on environment changes.

Cooperative. A set of software entities can collaborate with each other for the purpose of business or management. Often the collaborations are rather dynamic than static, to adapt to the user requirements and environments in an on-demand way. The collaboration mechanisms between software entities can be of various types, and can be changed if necessary.

Situational. Software applications can be aware of the runtime contexts and scenarios, including the underlying devices, operating platforms, networking conditions, application contexts, or the changes of other dependent applications, etc. Hence, both software entities (included in a software application) and their operating platforms might be capable of exposing their runtime states and behaviors in some way.

Evolvable. The structures and behaviors of software applications might dynamically change. Software applications usually consist of autonomous entities over the Internet, and provide online and continuous (e.g., 24 h * 7 days) services for a large number of users. Hence, software applications cannot be shut down during evolution. Software applications have to perform online evolution to accommodate new user requirements and environments. Possible evolutions can include addition/removal of software entities, changes of functionalities on-the-fly and just-in-time, changes of interaction styles between entities, change of topologies among entities, etc.

Emergent. Software applications can exhibit undesigned behaviors or undesired effects on runtime instances or interactions. Such nature might iteratively result in more and more changes of software application structures and behaviors to accommodate such emergences.

Trustworthy. Software applications should promise comprehensive tradeoffs among various quality attributes. As software applications serve a number of online users, the trustworthiness of the software applications should cover a wide spectrum, including reliability, security, performance, user experience, etc. Quality assurance can be relevant to various aspects, including autonomous entities, interaction styles, network environments, usage patterns, malicious attacks, software evolution, etc.

Since then, substantial efforts have been made on Internetware research and practices. Especially, two national projects have been carried out consecutively: the project *Research on Theory and Methodology of Agent-based Middleware on Internet Platform* (2002–2008) and the project *Research on Networked Complex Software: Quality and Confidence Assurance, Development Method, and Runtime Mechanism* (2009–2013). About 80 researchers from Chinese universities and institutes have participated in the projects, including researchers from Peking University, Nanjing University, Tsinghua University, Institute of Software of the Chinese Academy Sciences, the Academy of Mathematics and Systems Science of Chinese Academy Sciences, East China Normal University, and IBM China Research Laboratory. Since 2009, the Asia-Pacific Symposium on Internetware (http://sei.pku.edu.cn/~internetware), in cooperation with ACM SIGSOFT, has been held annually, attracting authors and attendees from China, USA, Europe, Australia, Japan, and Korea.

Internetware research gets funding support from various China's national research and development programs in the past 15 years. The preceding two projects are first sponsored by the Chinese National Basic Research Program (known as 973), which is one of the five major national programs in the national R&D program of China. After the first five years, some research topics identified for Internetware, are sponsored by the National Natural Science Foundation of China and the National High Technology Research and Development Program (known as 863). Some prototypes of Internetware operating platforms and development tools have been successfully transferred to commercial products and solutions under the support of the National Science and Technology Major Projects. In 2014, the *Research on Internetware: Theory, Approaches, and Technologies* was awarded by the *Top 10 Grand Progress of Science and Technology* awarded by the Ministry of Education of the PRC. In a word, the Internetware research community has been established and keeps increasing in the past a few years.

Book Overview

This book is organized to summarize and share the state-of-the-art efforts of Internetware research. More specifically, this book presents the efforts that address the challenges of software technologies in Internet computing environment, including the fundamental aspects of programming model, engineering approach, runtime operational platform, and quality measurements and assurance. In addition, this book also includes a number of real-world applications, experiences, and practices of Internetware. The book consists of five parts.

- *Part 1* gives an overview of a technical framework for Internetware. It takes a software architecture-centric viewpoint and organizes the framework as three connected aspects: system modeling, middleware support, and engineering method.
- *Part 2* presents a software model featuring environment driven adaptation for Internetware applications. Enabling techniques for the model, especially the modeling, management and utilization of environment information are discussed. An architecture-centric framework has also been built to prove the concepts and evaluate the techniques.
- *Part 3* focuses on the runtime support for Internetware application systems. The support covers various aspects of the execution and adaptation of software situated in the open and dynamic Internet environment.
- *Part 4* introduces the Internetware engineering approach. It essentially follows the core and underlying principle of software architecture throughout a whole-life cycle. This software architecture serves as a blueprint, and suggests or controls each phase in lifecycle for developing Internetware applications.
- *Part 5* describes how the Internetware paradigm is applied to real-world cloud and client applications. At the client side, applications on smartphones connect to the physical world and Internet by their built-in sensors and networking chips, respectively. At the cloud side, numerous computing platforms like virtual machines and middleware infrastructures are managed to run user tasks in a cost-effective way. We discuss how the Internetware paradigm is realized on the two sides, as well as how the two sides are connected and how applications can be diagnosed for energy efficiency.

Organizations of the Book

The book stems from a set of high-quality research papers that have been published on premier computer science conferences or journals. Indeed, there have been numerous efforts contributed to Internetware research in the past 15 years. Due to space limit, we have to select only some representative efforts that cover some typical Internet-based applications such as cloud/grid computing, services computing, mobile computing, Web, Internet of Things, and so on. These efforts are organized by the research framework of Internetware paradigm. When having acquired the copyrights of original publishers, the authors further make great efforts to revise and expand the original contents to better fit the goal of this book.

As mentioned previously, the Internetware research is a long-term and open study that involves hundreds of researchers with different background. Meanwhile, the understanding, synthesis, and scope of Internetware paradigm keep improving during our 15-year course of study. The selected efforts in this book were actually made at different time and from different perspectives. As a result, this book cannot comprehensively enforce the consistent understanding and representation of some aspects in Internetware. Indeed, it can reflect the history that we made substantive headway towards the essence of Internetware paradigm.

Audiences and Readers of the Book

This book can be a reference book to researchers and practitioners of software engineering, operating/network systems, programming languages, and so on. It can be also used as a textbook for graduate students and junior/senior undergraduate students who major in computer science.

Beijing, China   Hong Mei
June 2016   Jian Lü

Acknowledgments

We are deeply indebted to many friends and colleagues of the Internetware research group for their great efforts to promote the publication of this book. A discussion with Zhi Jin (Peking University), Tao Huang (Institute of Software, Chinese Academy of Sciences), Xuandong Li (Nanjing University), Daoxu Chen (Nanjing University), and Jianmin Wang (Tsinghua University) got the whole ball rolling.

Many thanks to our colleagues who made significant revision and extension of their previous work and provided reviews of the draft manuscript: Fuqing Yang, Gang Huang, Wei Zhang, Xuanzhe Liu, Yingfei Xiong, Haiyan Zhao, Yanchun Sun, Wenpin Jiao, Ying Zhang, Ling Lan, Junguo Li, Hui Song, Franck Chauvel, Xiaodong Zhang, from Peking University; Xiaoxing Ma, Xianping Tao, Feng Xu, Sanglu Lu, Chun Cao, Chang Xu, Wenzhong Li, Yu Huang, Ping Yu, Xiaoming Fu, Hao Hu, Tianxiao Gu, Linghao Zhang, from Nanjing University; Jun Wei, Guoquan Wu, Wenbo Zhang, Chunyang Yue, Hua Zhong, Hong He from the Institute of Software, Chinese Academy of Sciences; Jifeng He, Jing Liu, Xiaoshan Li, Zhiming Liu, from East China Normal University; Puewei Wang, Guangjun Cai from the Academy of Mathematics and System Science, Chinese Academy of Science; Lin Liu, Yang Chen, Xiaojun Ye, Yingbo Liu, from Tsinghua University.

Our colleagues, Tao Xie at University of Illinois Urbana-Champaign, Zhenjiang Hu at National Institute of Informatics (Japan), Shi-Chi Cheung at the Hong Kong University of Science and Technology, were exceptionally supportive throughout the writing of the text.

Meihua Yu helped establishing the online co-editing system to improve the work efficiency.

In particular, Gang Huang (Peking University), Xiaoxing Ma (Nanjing University), and Xuanzhe Liu (Peking University) made great efforts to help organize the compilation of whole book and identify the typos in early drafts.

Due to the limit of time, pace, our knowledge and experiences, some possible problematic issues are inevitable in this book. It would be highly appreciated that our audiences can help point out our mistakes and improve this book. Comments and suggestions can be sent to meih@pku.edu.cn or lj@nju.edu.cn. We would like to hear from you.

Thank you.

Beijing, China   Hong Mei
June 2016   Jian Lü

Contents

Acronyms

ABC	Architecture-Based Component Composition
ADL	Architecture Description Language
AEM	Application Execution Model
API	Application Programming Interface
BPEL	Business Process Execution Language
CBSE	Component-Based Software Engineering
CCM	CORBA Component Model
COM	Component Object Model
CORBA	Common Object Request Broker Architecture
CRC	Class Responsibility Collaborator
CSP	Constraint Satisfaction Problem
D2D	Device-to-Device
DFT	Dynamic Information Flow Tracking
DID	Destination Identification
DSL	Domain Specific Language
DSU	Dynamic Software Updating
DTN	Delay Tolerant Network
DUC	Data Utilization Coefficient
EJB	Enterprise JavaBeans
ESB	Enterprise Service Bus
FeatuRSEB	Feature Reuse-driven Software Engineering Business
FIP	Feature Interaction Problem
FORM	Feature-Oriented Reuse Method
GRASP	General Responsibility Assignment Software Pattern
GUI	Graphical User Interface
HTTP	Hyper Text Transfer Protocol
IIOP	Internet Inter-ORB Protocol
IOT	Internet of Things
J2EE	Java 2 platform, Enterprise Edition
JPF	Java PathFinder
JRMP	Java Remote Method Protocol
JSP	Java Server Page
JVM	Java Virtual Machine
LOC	Lines of Code
MAPE	Monitor, Analyze, Plan, and Execute
MDA	Model Driven Architecture
MOF	Meta Object Facility
OCL	Object Constraint Language

OOSE	Object-Oriented Software Engineering
ORB	Object Request Broker
Par-BCL	Parametric Behavior Constraint Language for Web Services
PKUAS	Peking University Application Server
PSM	Parameter State Machine
QVT	Query, View, Transformation
RDD	Responsibility-Driven Design
REARON	REquirement and ARchitecture ONtologies
REST	Representational State Transfer
RIM	Requirements Interaction Management
RMI	Remote Method Invocation
RSA	Runtime Software Architecture
SA	Software Architecture
SID	Source Identification
SM@RT	Software Model at Runtime
SOAP	Simple Object Access Protocol
SPS	Specification Pattern System
SWT	The Standard Widget Toolkit
TS	Timestamp
UDDI	Universal Description, Discovery, and Integration
UML	Unified Modeling Language
VANET	Vehicular Ad Hoc Network
WSDL	Web Services Description Language
XML	eXtensible Markup Language

Due to the open, dynamic, and ever-changing nature of the Internet computing environment, software on the Internet differs from traditional software in terms of forms, structures, and behaviors. Consequently, software applications (including software entities and their interactions) for Internet computing often need to be autonomous, cooperative, situational, evolvable, emergent, and trustworthy. This puts forward many technical challenges for software engineers.

We believe that, in addition to specific research for each concrete technical issue, a thorough re-examination of the fundamental software paradigm is needed. A software paradigm usually concerns with four main aspects: WHAT-IS, HOW-TO-DO, HOW-TO-RUN, and HOW-WELL. WHAT-IS refers to what is to be constructed and executed (software or program model). HOW-TO-DO refers to how to develop the required software applications including their constituent entities (development techniques, e.g., programming languages, engineering approaches, and supporting tools). HOW-TO-RUN refers to how to run the software applications including their constituent entities (runtime system supports, such as the operating systems or middleware platforms). HOW-WELL refers to how well the constructed and executed software applications can perform (promised software qualities, e.g., correctness, performance, reliability, user experiences, and their assurance mechanisms during software construction and operation).

One main objective of a software paradigm is to better leverage the underlying runtime environments such as hardware capabilities while offering a computing model that is sufficiently expressive and natural to characterize the application domain. A software paradigm evolves with the underlying runtime environments and the target application domains. For a software paradigm, WHAT-IS and HOW-TO-DO/HOW-TO-RUN are typically the first set of concerns to address and then HOW-WELL becomes a concern when the software paradigm is broadly applied in practice. Every shift of software paradigms (e.g., the shift from structured to object-oriented and then the shift further to component-based/service-oriented) typically brings significant challenges as well as tremendous opportunities to software technologies. After more than a decade of development and growth, the expanded runtime environments and application domains in the era of Internet call for a new shift on software paradigms to cope with new requirements on software for Internet computing.

In particular, a new software paradigm for Internet computing needs to satisfy the following requirements (organized along the four aspects; some of which are general to any software paradigm and some of which are specific to software for Internet computing):

• Software model (WHAT-IS). The software model should specify the forms, structures, and behaviors of software entities as well as their collaborations. These specifications will determine the principles and features of the corresponding software technologies (programming languages, development approaches, and runtime mechanisms). Basic software entities can be built upon current popular technologies, such as object-oriented technologies and service computing technologies. But new capabilities should be provided to enable on-demand collaborations among entities along with context-aware and situation-aware supports.

- Software operating platform (HOW-TO-RUN). The operating platform should provide a runtime space to operate software entities and their collaborations. To ease the migration of legacy software to software for Internet computing, the operating platform should be able to conveniently equip legacy software with new features added to satisfy the requirements on software for Internet computing. In addition, the operating platform should manage software applications and the platform itself in an intelligent and automatic manner.
- Engineering approach (HOW-TO-DO). The engineering approach should systematically control the whole lifecycle of developing software for Internet computing, including requirements specification, design, implementation, deployment, and maintenance.

- Quality assurance (HOW-WELL). Software applications on the Internet usually serve a large number of users in an online and simultaneous style. Both quantitative and qualitative measurement methods should be developed for various quality attributes such as performance, reliability, and usability, and for the comprehensive tradeoffs among these attributes. Assuring high quality requires quality assurance methods realized by engineering approaches at the development time (e.g., testing, verification and validation), and runtime mechanisms (e.g., online evolution and autonomic system management).

This part gives a brief introduction on the motivations and visions of the Internetware paradigm. After looking back on the driven forces behind pervious paradigm shifts in the history of software engineering, Chap. 1 discusses the need of a new paradigm in face of the challenges of Internet computing. It also proposes a roadmap towards this new paradigm. Chapter 1 gives an overview of a technical framework for Internetware. It takes a software architecture-centric viewpoint and organizes the framework as three connected aspects: system modeling, middleware support, and engineering method.

Internetware: A Shift of Software Paradigm 1

Abstract

Internetware is envisioned as a new software paradigm for resource integration and sharing in the open, dynamic, and autonomous Internet environment. In this chapter, we discuss our visions and explorations of this new paradigm, with focus placed on the methodological perspective. A set of enabling techniques on flexible coordination of autonomous services, automatic adaptation to the changing environment, and trust management-based assurance of system dependability are proposed to help the development of Internetware applications.

Keywords

Internetware · Software paradigm · Methodological perspective

1.1 Introduction

The Internet has become a new computing environment, in which software systems of new styles are developed, deployed, and executed. Tremendous amount and vast diversity of resources and services are emerging in this environment. Unprecedented potentials are seen through emerging approaches to the coordination and integration of these resources and services in

a global scale. Among these approaches there are Grid Computing [1], Service Computing [2,3], Ubiquitous Computing [4], and Cloud Computing [5], to name a few. Contrasting to its traditional counterparts such as stand-alone computers, LANs, and enterprise intranets, the Internet computing environment is much more open, dynamic, and autonomous. As a consequence, application systems in such an environment cannot be constructed in a tightly-coupled and once-for-ever manner as traditional ones often do. These new systems must respect the autonomy of the services they use, be capable of probing the changes of the environment and user preferences, and then adapt themselves accordingly to keep their service satisfactory with sufficient functionality, performance, and dependability.

Parts of this chapter were reprinted from Jian Lü, Xiaoxing Ma, Yu Huang, Chun Cao and Feng Xu. *Internetware: a shift of software paradigm*, In Proceedings of the First Asia-Pacific Symposium on Internetware © 2009 ACM, Inc. http://doi.acm.org/10.1145/1640206.1640213.

© Springer Science+Business Media Singapore 2016
H. Mei and J. Lü, *Internetware*, DOI 10.1007/978-981-10-2546-4_1

The challenges in developing such kind of applications not only lie in specific technical difficulties, such as inter-organization interoperation, runtime adaptation, decentralized authentication, *etc.*, but also come from the lack of suitable methods that can help developers to understand and manage the complexity of these applications. We believe that such challenges necessitate a major shift of software paradigm, because there is a mismatch between the assumptions of conventional software paradigms and the features of the open Internet environment. For example, conventionally, the decomposition of a system into computing elements could be totally under the command of its developers, but now the autonomy of resources and services in Internet must be respected; instead of assuming that the working environment would be the same as specified at development time, the system needs to deal with constant changes in the environment at runtime; moreover, rather than developed within a monolithic organization, the system is often based on independent services with different interests.

Reflections on previous shifts of software paradigm indicate that the balance of the forces from the problem, mental, and computing spaces is crucial to the success of a software paradigm. New applications in new open environments demand a new paradigm to rebalance the forces. In this chapter we discuss our visions and explorations of the *Internetware*, a new software paradigm envisioned for application systems situated in the open Internet environment. This new paradigm emphasizes the autonomy of the constituent entities of a system, the cooperation and coordination among the entities, as well as the situation-awareness, evolvability, emergence, and trustworthiness of the system [6–9]. Toward this new paradigm, a three-staged roadmap is proposed and adopted in our recent work. First, extending the mainstream Object-Oriented model, we propose a new structuring model for the coordination of autonomous services to satisfy particular demands in a flexible but disciplined way. Second, we give an environment-driven model to support the dynamic adaptation of systems to the changes in environment. Third,

we present a trust management-based model for evaluating and ensuring the dependability of systems built upon autonomous resources in the open Internet environment. A set of enabling techniques for these models are also briefly discussed.

The rest of this chapter is organized as follows. In Sect. 1.2 we discuss the rationale and architecting principles of the Internetware paradigm. Sections 1.3, 1.4, and 1.5 are dedicated to the open coordination model, environment-driven model, and dependability assurance model, respectively. Finally Sect. 1.6 summaries the chapter and briefly discusses directions for future work.

1.2 The Internetware Paradigm

1.2.1 The Need of a Paradigm Shift

A paradigm is an accepted model or pattern. Paradigms gain their status because they are more successful than their competitors in solving a few problems that the group of practitioners has come to recognize as acute. To be more successful is not, however, to be either completely successful with a single problem or notably successful with any large number [10].

Since the publishing of Kuhn's seminal book. *The Structure of Scientific Revolutions*, the importance of paradigms and paradigm shifts in scientific methodology is widely recognized. In his Turing Award Lecture, Floyd convinced us that paradigms of programming take an important role in helping the developers understand and manage the complexity in solving problems [11]. High level paradigms of programming-in-the-large are also called *software paradigms*. Various paradigms exist in software communities. Among them there are structured [12], object-oriented [13], component-based [14], and agent-oriented paradigms [15], to name a few. In his book [16], Kaisler discussed a set of widely used software paradigms and their associated techniques. A software paradigm provides a model of how software systems are developed, sometimes in the form of a metaphor. However it should be emphasized that behind the model there are a collection of assumptions, concepts, theories, and practices acting as the rationale.

With the transformation to the open, dynamic, and autonomous Internet environment, the following assumptions of conventional software paradigms become invalid more or less.

1. *Controllable computing elements.* All parts of a conventional software system are designed or adapted (in case of reusing existing components) to work together for a common purpose. There is no independent interest or decision of a single part other than what the system assigns to it. To develop such a system, it is convenient to decompose the application logic into the computing elements, in the form of, say, procedures or objects, and glue up these elements with predefined coordination mechanisms such as procedure calls or object method invocations. In open environments, systems are often built on third-party software entities, i.e., various resources and services, which may serve multiple applications simultaneously and have their own interests and decisions. Although these entities are, to certain extent, willing to collaborate, their *autonomy* must be respected. In this case the focus of application development has to be moved from computation to *coordination*, and traditional predefined coordination mechanisms may not suffice.

2. *Static environment settings.* Conventional software systems aiming at traditional environment settings are typically developed on the assumptions of invariant resources, such as available CPU, memory, underlying system calls, network bandwidth, and functionalities provided by other software systems. It would be feasible to make these assumptions when the environment was generally controllable. Such assumptions no longer hold for systems that rely on dynamic service integration over the open Internet environment. These systems are expected to be *situational*, i.e., capable of probing and understanding their runtime contexts and scenarios, and dynamically *evolvable*, i.e., capable of adapt their structures and behaviors at runtime to the changes in the environment they are situated in and the requirements must satisfy [3].

3. *Predefined behavior.* Conventional software development requires that delivered software products exhibit behaviors exactly conforming to their predefined specifications. However, in the open Internet environment, autonomous entities in the system may depend on each other, and thus can exhibit un-designed behaviors or unpredicted effects. Conventional software paradigms have no room to accommodate, or even exploit, such *emergences.*

4. *Directly verifiable trustworthiness.* The dependability of conventional software systems can be verified and validated using well-defined methods and techniques, such as testing, proving, and reviewing, provided that sufficient and reliable information about the software and its development process is available. This availability of information implies that the participants unconditionally *trust* each other. However, software systems in open environments may involve much more participants than traditional systems because they work in a truly decentralized environment. The independent interests of different participants and the dynamic environment make the trust relationships among them complicated and dynamic. In this situation, the dependability of a system should be highly affected by the trust relationships among the participants.

There already exist some related observations and proposals in the literature, e.g. System-of-Systems [17], Open Resource Coalitions [18], and Cyber-Physical Systems [19], but a new software paradigm that systematically addresses these requirements of the new application styles in open network environment is still missing.

1.2.2   Methodological Reflections

Generally speaking, software development is a mental process of devising a solution for a given problem, and it must be able to efficiently execute on a given computing platform. Observing software paradigms and paradigm shifts in the past decades, we can see a common scheme of successful paradigms—good balance of the forces from the problem space, the mental space, and the computing space.

The emergence of the structured paradigm in the 1970s was driven by the rapid development of the computing power and the need to alleviate software crises. At that time, the normalization of programming methods and language constructs to "structured" ones satisfied the need to manage the complexity of programming in the mental space with the now-affordable potential performance costs in the computing space, which well balanced the forces from the mental space and the computing space.

The Object-Oriented paradigm, maturing in the 1980s, is still the mainstream practice in today's software industry. As the scale and complexity of application problems increased continuously, the mental process of software development became more and more complicated with the regular but somewhat simplistic constructs of the structured paradigm, in spite of the advances in modularity, separation of concerns, information hidden, *etc*. The object-oriented paradigm brought a software structuring model well corresponding to the structure of the problem to be solved, which significantly eased the mental process. Moreover, the inheritance, polymorphism, and dynamic binding mechanisms implemented the mental process of classification and deduction efficiently in computing platforms. Thus a better balance of the forces from the problem space, the mental space, and the computing space was achieved again.

Based on the balance of forces from the three spaces, a software paradigm would provide a collection of tangible artifacts that can be directly used by developers to regulate their requirements, design their architectures, and implement their systems. Particularly, the following artifacts are necessary:

1. *Structuring model.* At the kernel of a software paradigm, there is a pattern about how systems are constructed from various software elements, i.e., what the form of computing compo-

nents is, what kind of coordination mechanisms are used to gluing up these components, and why desired system behavior can be achieved with these computing and coordination.

2. *Mechanism for flexibility.* As the "soft" part of computing, software is always expected to be flexible to certain extent. There must be some mechanism to support controlled adjustment of the behavior and/or the structure of the system to deal with the inevitable evolution of requirements. For example, in structured paradigm there are procedure encapsulation and data abstraction to facilitate replacements of procedures and data representations, whereas in the object-oriented paradigm there are inheritance and dynamic binding to support class extensions and polymorphism.

3. *Dependability assurance.* As one of the most complicated types of artifacts, software systems are prone to the loss of dependability. A software paradigm has a collection of associated mechanisms to systematically ensure system dependability. Generally, a set of dependability properties and metrics are first specified. Then, some validation and verification techniques are used to evaluate these properties. Finally, software improvement processes are carried out accordingly. The last two phases are iterated to keep the software system dependable in a specific context.

4. *Supporting tools and environments.* Reifying the models and mechanisms above, a set of languages, tools, and integrated environments are needed to help the developers follow the paradigm efficiently and correctly.

Collectively, these artifacts should answer the four fundamental questions in software development in a coherent manner: WHAT-IS (what is to be constructed and executed), HOW-TO-DO (how to develop the required software applications including their constituent entities), HOW-TO-RUN (how to run the software applications including their constituent entities) and HOW-WELL (how well the constructed and executed software applications can perform).

Last but not least, software paradigm shifts in the last decades showed that a successful paradigm needs to subsume and be compatible with existing mainstream paradigms, for social, psychological, economical, and technical reasons.

1.2.3   Architecting Principles for Internetware

The envisioned Internetware paradigm also needs to balance the forces from the three spaces. However, the forces are different from those of the object-oriented paradigm or the structured paradigm. Specifically, in the problem space, the trend is to move from solving specific problems in controlled environments to addressing flexibly scoped problems with the aim of satisfying different users in open environments. The focus is shifting from direct problem solving to resource sharing and coordination. In the mental space, monolithic view of individual developers or closely coupled developer teams is upgraded to a service-oriented view of multiple independent developers, and the focus is shifting from the computing logic on a specific computer for specific requirements to the coordination logic on a ubiquitous computing platform with autonomous services provided for requirements of an open group of users. In the computing space, the computing platform has evolved from a relatively closed and controllable base of standalone or networked computers to a ubiquitous computing platform in the Internet environment, and the focus is shifting from providing computing capabilities to enable and manage interactions.

In addition to the methodological considerations discussed above, we identify the following architecting principles for the Internetware:

1. *Programmable Coordination.* As discussed above, Internetware applications need to be built on autonomous resources and services that are provided "AS IS" by independent owners. Mechanisms should be provided to federate these autonomous software entities to satisfy specific demands, in a flexible but disciplined way. Thus the coordination aspect of programming must be explicitly addressed

[20]. Beyond providing the communication channel between services and adapting their interfaces, the mechanism should also support the explicit management of the interaction between the services, according to the application logic. Furthermore, to adapt to the changing environment and requirements, the coordination logic needs to be dynamically adaptable, or even evolvable at runtime.

2. *Situated in open environments.* Since Internetware application systems are working in an open, dynamic, and autonomous network environment, environmental issues are much more deeply involved in the construction of a system for Internetware than for conventional paradigms. On the one hand, the system must be able to deal with the changes of the environment at runtime; on the other hand, every participating component of the system has its own concerns on the computing environment and has to adapt to it accordingly. So the Internetware paradigm must explicitly support the probing, understanding, and reconciliation of environment and environment changes. Furthermore, the autonomy of the participating components and the locality of the environment of these components must be respected, which means that simply taking the perceived environment as system inputs may not work.

3. *Scalable with multi-level homeostasis.* To keep its service satisfactory, the system needs to adapt to changes of the environment. Thus, software homeostasis mechanisms are necessary to monitor system behavior and dynamically modify the system to repair abnormalities, or deviations from the expected behavior [18]. For Internetware, however, the homeostasis mechanism is more than a single monolithic close-loop control, which has limited scalability. Since an Internetware system is based on the coordinated collaboration of a group of autonomous components, there should be a multi-level mechanism that distributes the responsibility of homeostasis maintenance to different levels (e.g. system level, subsystem level, and component level) and different aspects of system (e.g. functionality, performance, and

dependability) according to their capabilities and responsibilities in the system.

4. *Dependable with explicit trust management.* To ensure the dependability of a system in open environments, it is unavoidable to deal with the complicated trust relationships among multiple independent participants, such as primitive service providers, value-adding service providers, brokers, and end users. Trust management mechanisms, which are originally proposed for decentralized authorization and authentication, could be brought to deal with the complicated trust relationships among participants. Combining trust management and conventional verification and verification techniques, a framework for the dependability assurance of Internetware applications should be provided.

1.2.4 Our Roadmap and Explorations

There is a long way towards a full-fledged Internetware paradigm. To achieve the final goal of shaping the complete methodology, building the comprehensive supporting environment and developing killer applications of Internetware, we need a stepwise roadmap in which a set of models, techniques, supporting facilities, and applications can be gradually developed following the identified principles (Fig. 1.1).

To this end, we first propose an open coordination model by extending the conventional object-oriented paradigm for a flexible and adaptive structuring technique. With the corresponding middleware, it demonstrates the coordinated application in open environment and lays the groundwork for Internetware research. A succeeding environment-driven model synthesizes the concerns about the coordinated software systems and the environment where they actually situate in and adapt to. Environment facilities are also developed to sense, monitor, and manage the environment. Cooperating with the mechanisms provided in the coordination middleware, the environment-interacting adaptive software systems can thus be realized. The dependability of the system is finally assured with a framework, which has certain trust management models, mechanisms, and facilitates to turn the systems into trusted ones. Although the three levels of the work are still preliminary, we hope they can illustrate our vision of the Internetware.

1.3 Open Coordination Model

1.3.1 Coordination Model for Internetware

The construction of Internetware software systems needs to primarily coordinate the existing

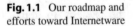

Fig. 1.1 Our roadmap and efforts toward Internetware

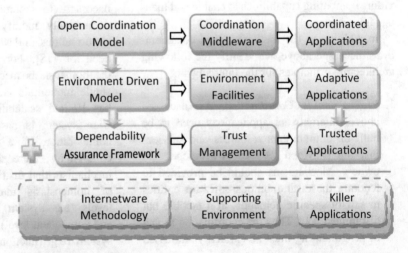

software entities and resources over the Internet. By the term of coordination model, it basically refers to the specification of inter-relationships among the computing entities and the regulations between their interaction [21]. To follow the principles and meet the challenges discussed in the previous section, a coordination model for Internetware is required to be in a position to accommodate to the high dynamism in the systems and facilitate the possible changes, either foreseeable or unforeseeable, to take place. At the same time, it should provide the developers and users a good understanding for the systems during the lifecycle of the systems. By such means, the complexities in the systems can be well controlled.

1.3.1.1   Classical Models of Coordination

There have been various coordination models proposed and they are briefly categorized as data-driven and control-driven [20]. Although the data-driven models, which usually advocate some shared data spaces, have be argued to be fit for the open systems [22], they have inherent short-comings, such as their insufficiency in isolating the computing and coordinating logic and indigestibility in specifying the system structure. In the models of the latter category, software entities, or say components, have well defined interfaces. The coordination is driven by propagating the state changes among components with some interacting mechanisms.

The object-oriented programming model introduces the classic control-driven coordination schema with the form of "O.m()". This object granularity model is also extended into the similar ones for the components [20,23] and services [24]. However, the core of the coordination is always reserved, which is to establish a fixed linkage between the objects with specific messaging facility. It is not difficult to see that this schema fits itself quite well in a closed computing environment with idealized assumptions, as argued before. As long as the computing entities are all under the control, the system can be modeled by this means and executed with no problem.

Nevertheless, the mechanism like "O.m()" consolidates the original coordination motivation and environment assumption [25]. Once these factors change, which are assumed to happen rarely, major re-organization of the coordination can be caused. However, the open environment of Internet breaks down those assumptions. The dynamism lying in all aspects of the system situated in such an environment needs to be fully considered into the construction of the system so that the changes can be effectively handled. Structurally, the inter-relationships of the entities within coordination could be more complicated than referring to each other directly and fixedly, and these relationships have to be determined on the runtime factors, such as availability and provision status of the software entities. And, the onefold interaction mechanism is also required to be enriched. Effective and dependable interactions should be achieved to respect the dynamic network environment where the software entities are situated and the autonomous interacting schema that they prefer.

1.3.1.2   Open Coordination for Internetware

Essentially, a coordination model for the software systems of Internetware paradigm should be of adaptability to the inherent dynamism of the systems to be modeled. Some techniques have already been developed to build the basic OO coordination mechanism with flexibility and adaptability, such as polymorphism [26] and some advanced communicating techniques [27,28], respectively. But ideally, the systems that are hosted in an open environment still need to be modeled with a unified model. From the study OO schema, the model should take an abstract and indirect way to shape the coordinating systems and organize the interacting entities. Thus the changes can be applied at some relatively high level of the model to avoid the massive modifications in the low level relations. Also, the interactions should also be modeled explicitly to enable the customization on the runtime communication among the coordinated entities. The actual execution of the system should be determined at runtime by investigating the onsite configuration of the coordination. Also, there are other conceivable advanced requirements on the coordination, such as the model level analysis and evaluation for the system non-functional qualities.

Overall, the coordination model as a kernel of the Internetware systems should carry enough information to put the system into execution, and more importantly, to get the adaptation of the system into effective operation. Beyond the conceptional modeling, a coordination supporting platform also needs the mechanisms to realize the potential adaptability brought by the model as a whole structuring of Internetware systems.

1.3.2   A Software Architecture Based Approach

Toward an effective open coordination model for the structuring of Internetware systems discussed in the previous section, we proposed a modeling approach based on software architecture. To put the coordination into execution, an intrinsic model implementation is introduced and adaptation facilitates are also advised.

1.3.2.1   Software Architecture Based Coordination Model

Software architecture "involves the description of elements from which systems are built, interactions among those elements, patterns that guide their composition, and constraints on these patterns" [29]. It is originally viewed as design specification and recently also employed in the research of software coordination [30–33]. With software architecture, the system components are organized and coordinated with connectors as inter joints. It offers explicit and programmable coordination logic. Especially, the connectors are treated as first class programming concepts. This allows connectors to be reconfigured dynamically to reflect coordination changes in addition to component adaptations. Software architecture supports the early analysis of system non-functional properties, which is one of its motivating benefits. Also there are various formal models and verification tools proposed to help the ensuring of architectural correctness. Software

architecture embodies essential information that should be held by the implementation to support and regulate future adaptation and evolution. These benefits make software architecture accepted as a relative ideal model for software coordination.

1.3.2.2   Intrinsic Coordination Implementation

To implement the coordination with the model of software architecture, techniques such as architecture refinement and explicit architecture maintenance, to name a few, are developed. These existing approaches share the issue that difficult and ad-hoc efforts are needed to maintain the consistency between a software architecture specification and the working system implementation.

Thereby, we propose an intrinsic approach to actually implement the coordination that software architecture models. The intrinsic mechanism fully integrates coordination into the programming model. The software architecture is encoded into some data structure and explicitly reified as a first class object, namely an architecture object, in the final implementation. The running components are glued with this object by delegating the runtime interpretation of object references and associated method invocations in the form of "O.m()" to the architecture object. In other words, the references and invocations are "functions" over the current software architecture configuration. By this means, the coordination concerns are separated from interacting component objects. The final coordination being carried out complies with the specified model of software architecture as the reified software architecture (which is implementation. And any change of the architecture object, in both the components and connectors, will immediately affect the runtime coordination process.

1.3.2.3   Supporting Dynamic Adaptations

Based on the intrinsic coordination implementation, it is natural to realize dynamic system adaptation as the reconfiguration behavior of the architecture object. Above the primitive adaptation actions, e.g., component add/remove and connector replacement, more sophisticated ones can be defined as the methods of the architecture object, by which means the concrete adaption process is specified for that type of the architecture. The implementation of these methods is mainly changing the topology with the facilities provided in base architecture class.

Also, there could be some system reconfiguration requirements gradually discovered after the system was put into operation. Common solutions for these unanticipated reconfigurations require a system restart. However, the stop of service could bring a high cost in some circumstance, esp. when there were valuable data not persistently stored. Our approach also provides a reasonable support for unanticipated dynamic reconfigurations. A new subclass of the original architecture class should be defined to implement new reconfiguration behavior. The consistency between the new and old architectures is ensured with the type consistence checking against the classes defining those architectures.

Summarily, the proposed software architecture based coordination model gives a unified approach to specify the interrelation of the components as well the interactions among them. The featured intrinsic implementation with the corresponding adaptation mechanisms provides the basis of the flexible and adaptable system structuring technique for Internetware systems. Besides, we also introduce an architecture checking technique based on graph-grammar [34]. A coordination middleware is also designed and implemented with some running cases. All these the works serve as the first step toward Internetware.

1.4   Environment-Driven Model

1.4.1   Structure and Dynamics

Internetware application systems run in the open, dynamic, and uncertain environment. For such a system, the runtime adaptation to frequent changes in the environment and users' requirements must be supported as an indispensable feature rather than handled as exceptions. Traditional software systems running in the principally closed, static, and controllable environment usually have their processing of the environmental information implicitly consolidated into the application logic. Such an approach cannot effectively cope with the dynamics of the open environment.

To adapt themselves at runtime in an environment-driven manner, Internetware application systems need to process the environment information explicitly and separately. Basically the environment context needs to be explicitly collected, understood, and utilized. However, if we monolithically divide the entire system into coordination of constituent components and explicit environment processing facilities, scalability of the system will be quite limited. We cannot effectively cope with the complexity of implementing, deploying, and operating Internetware application systems in the open environment. This is mainly because Internetware systems are the coalition of autonomous services in a large and fully-distributed environment. Such systems are commonly multi-level ones constructed from subsystems, and may have the fractal or self-similar characteristics. Different constituent components of the system have their own concerns of the computing environment and have to adapt to the environment independently.

Take the traffic control system as an example. In the district level, software entities for collecting and disseminating traffic information coordinate with each other to inform the drivers of the traffic information and instruct them to avoid the traffic jam in each district of the city. Traffic control systems in the district level coordinate with each other and form the traffic control system in the city level. Such system can further coordinate to form systems in upper levels of larger scale. The traffic control system in each level has similar structure.

Since the sub-systems in each level has their own concerns of the environment context, the environment processing facilities for Internetware application systems cannot be a monolithic software entity. It must also have the fractal characteristics, in accordance with the multi-level coordination of the Internetware application systems.

1.4.1.1   Multi-level and Self-similar System Structure

One constituent part of an Internetware application system consists of three parts:

- *Goal-driven adaptation logic.* Goal of the users specifies expected behavior of the coalition in given situations. The goal-driven adaptation logic decides how to change the coordination in different situations. A unified semantic framework for users' goal and the environment processing facilities is required for the logic reasoning. Customizable adaptation rules and reification mechanisms are also necessary for realizing decisions of the adaption logic.
- *Open coordination subsystem.* The open coordination subsystem is responsible for the business logic of the application. It also supports the dynamic reconfiguration of itself, in order to smoothly carry out the adaptation, as discussed in Sect. 1.3.
- *Environment processing facilities.* Expected behavior of the coalition corresponds to situation of the environment, which necessitates the explicit environment processing facilities. Such facilities are in charge of collecting,

understanding, and utilizing the environment information. They transform raw environment data to high-level representations of situations for the coalition.

The structure of the environment processing facilities has the fractal or self-similar characteristics, as shown in Fig. 1.2. For a specific part of the system situated in the environment, it has the environment-driven software structure discussed above. Subsystems further coordinate to form systems in a higher level, and the coordination in each level has similar software structure. We argue that such a fractal structure of environment processing facilities is a promising approach to achieve system scalability and cope with system complexity issues for Internetware application systems in the open environment.

1.4.1.2   Dynamic Maintenance of System Homeostasis

From the behavioral perspective, an Internetware application system can be viewed as a homeostasis of the coalition among services. Homeostasis is the propensity of a system to automatically restore its desired equilibrium state when changes in the

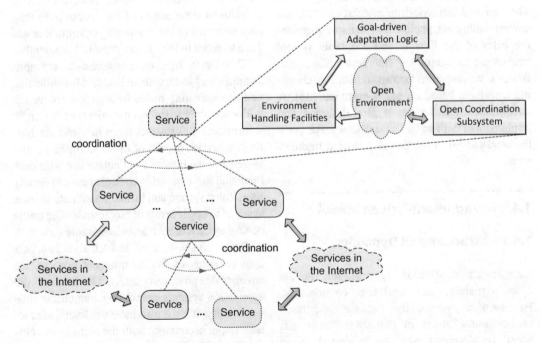

Fig. 1.2 Environment-driven software structure

environment may disturb this state [18]. Due to the fractal characteristic of Internetware application systems, the homeostasis is also achieved by multi-level coordination.

In order to achieve the homeostasis with respect to specific part of an Internetware application system, two different approaches can be adopted: prevention and repair. Prevention aims at taking advance measures to prevent deviation of the system behavior from the homeostasis. It is appropriate when the consequence of deviation from the homeostasis is high, but it may introduce great inflexibility and prohibitive overhead [18].

As for operation of an Internetware application system, the autonomy of services means that they may change while the coalition is running. So it is essential to take repair operations besides prevention. To repair the coalition when it constantly deviates from the homeostasis, mechanisms for online monitoring of the environment situation and system behavior, as well as mechanisms for adapting the coordination among the services are required.

In accordance with the self-similar structure of an Internetware application system, homeostasis of the whole system is achieved in a multi-level manner based on homeostasis of the subsystems.

1.4.2 Framework and Techniques

1.4.2.1 The REARON Framework

Each subsystem in a given level of an Internetware application system has the environment-driven software structure. To achieve the homeostasis of the subsystems situated in the environment, we need to interpret the context into some application goal-related events according to domain knowledge and application requirements. Moreover, following the architectural prescription rules, those events trigger architectural behaviors, which finally lead to the dynamic reconfigurations of the systems. So first of all, it is desirable to build a generic user-oriented description mechanism with some automatic reasoning ability to describe the application goals, environment context, and the architecture of the coordination systems. Upon this description mechanism, cus-

tomizable, scalable, and efficient transformation facilities are needed to fuse the knowledge of the three parties, evaluate the status of the running systems, and make appropriate orders to carry out system evolution processes.

We propose an ontology-based framework REquirement and ARchitecture ONtologies (REARON) to describe the requirement goals, environment context, and coordination among the services [6]. REARON is a framework which enables us to fill the gap between users' requirements, coordination of services, and the explicit environment processing facilities for the coordination. Base on this framework, we further study the ontology models for the environment context, as well as how to achieve online checking of environment situation.

1.4.2.2 Ontology-Based Modeling of Environment Context

Modeling the environment context is one of the essential issues in understanding the open environment. The dynamic nature of the open environment makes modeling of dynamic context a critical issue. However, there is little work on formal modeling of dynamic environment context. To this end, we proposed an enhanced ontology-based context model, which adopts static ontology to model static context, and adds timestamp and lifecycle description for dynamic context modeling [6]. Besides modeling the time information of dynamic context, there is also other important information to be modeled, such as behavioral patterns of the environment. Thus we further model time and dynamic context in the ontology level, and proposed a dynamic ontology-based context model [13]. We conceptualize temporal properties as the TemporalEntity class and its subclasses in OWL-Time, as well as the ConcreteEntity class and its subclasses in classic top-level ontology. We also conceptualize dynamic properties, including state, event, transition, condition, and operation, and conceptualize them as DynamicEntity and its subclasses. In the ontology model discussed above, we also propose corresponding semantic explanation and reasoning rules for the newly proposed concepts TemporalEntity and DynamicEntity.

1.4.2.3   Monitoring Situation of the Environment

One of the essential issues in achieving the homeostasis of Internetware application systems is to monitor the situation of the environment, i.e., to monitor whether the environment context bears specified property. The open environment is a truly distributed environment, but this characteristic is not sufficiently considered in the existing work. In asynchronous environments, the concept of time should to be reconsidered. In order to delineate and check temporal properties in the open environment, we reinterpret the temporal properties based on the causality between events induced by message passing. Then we delineate environment properties with predicates defined on the environment context. We achieve online checking of environment properties based on distributed predicate detection in asynchronous environments [35]. In order to effectively monitor the situation of the open environment, we also investigated enabling techniques such as context selection, context retrieval, and context privacy protection [6].

1.5   Dependability Assurance Framework with Trust-Management

1.5.1   A Trust-Based Approach

Dependability assurance is a fundamental issue in software development. As discussed above, the new features of Internetware applications and the open environment bring many new challenges. From the perspective of the problem space, the "dependability" of an Internetware application means much more than that of a conventional application because the former involves multiple participants with independent interests. Traditional software development follows a simple producer-consumer style: The user proposes his requirements, and the developer builds software to fulfill it. The trust between these two participants is simple and taken for granted. However, the separation of interests in a truly decentralized environment requires us to explicitly consider to what extent the participants are trustable and how the trustworthiness affects the dependability of the system constructed.

Consequently, in the mental space a systematic classification and analysis of different dependability-related relationships are needed to support the specification, evaluation, and improvement activities of dependability assurance. Concretely, three classes of relationships are identified [3]. (1) Trust relationships between principals describe to what extent a principle trusts another principle. For instance, a user trusts an independent service recommender. (2) Confidence relationships between principals and services indicate how confident a principal believes that a piece of software would satisfy his purpose. For instance, the company needs to be confident about the service before publishing it. Confidence on a local software entity can be evaluated with conventional V&V methods [36]. (3) Dependence relationships between software entities describe how a software entity is affected by other entities under certain coordination logic. Such kind of dependences are used in some recently developed dependability analysis techniques such as software architecture-based reliability evaluation and interface automata-based verification. The dependability of an Internetware application is often a combination of these different relationships.

Besides the trust-related issues discussed above, there are further difficulties to overcome in the computing space. In the open environment, available information about a non-local software entity (and its owner) is often incomplete and inaccurate, making it very difficult, if possible, to verify and validate the software component and system objectively and accurately in the same way as used before. Specifically, the autonomy and cost-of-use of software entities in open environment make white-box analysis and black-box testing on them generally infeasible.

Thus it is unavoidable to take a fundamentally different approach to the dependability assurance for the Internetware applications which features user-centric specification of dependability-related properties instead of developer-oriented metrics, and trust-based evaluation instead of testing and proving.

1.5.2 A Dependability Assurance Framework with Trust Management

There are some trust management [37] models originally designed for decentralized authorization and authentication, which deal with the trust relationships among security domains. Inspired by the idea of trust management, we give a dependability assurance framework with explicit consideration of the trust relationships among the participating principles. The framework includes three key elements: trust-based dependability evaluation of the software components, architecture-based dependability evaluation of the software system, and trust-based software component selection. The first two elements constitute a trust-based dependability verification and validation mechanism for software system in open environment, and the last one is a trust-based software improvement mechanism. The framework involves all three classes of relationships discussed above (Fig. 1.3).

Trust-based software component selection. Different from traditional software improvement techniques, component selection and substitution is a feasible approach to improve the dependability of the software system in open environment. The core idea of the trust-based selection mechanism is to rank candidate components according to direct or indirect experiences about them, which is collected and accumulated along a

managed trust network. A trust-based software services selection mechanism is given in [38].

Software Architecture-based dependability evaluation. Architecture-based dependability evaluation is similar with architecture-based reliability analysis. It is a white-box approach to evaluating the software dependability, and it takes into account the information about the architecture of the component-based software system. It is used to combine the local dependability information of components, which is obtained by trust-based dependability evaluation, into an evaluation of the whole system. There are three key steps involved in the architecture-based dependability evaluation. The first one is the description of the architecture with Petri-nets. The second one is the analysis of several typical control constructs. The last one is the computation of the whole dependability of the system synthetically. The approach is detailed in [39].

Trust-based dependability evaluation. Trust-based dependability evaluation consists of two elements, one is a trust-based information collection protocol, and the other is a trust-model to compute the dependability value based on the information collected. We provide a trust-based dependability evaluation mechanism in [40].

1.6 Conclusion

With the development of Internet technologies, the computing environment is becoming open, dynamic, and autonomous. Traditional software systems for the closed environment assume controllable computing elements, static environment settings, and directly verifiable trustworthiness. However, such assumptions no longer hold in the open environment. Thus we argue that a paradigm shift is necessary for the open environment. In this chapter, we have discussed our visions and explorations on the Internet paradigm for the open environment from a methodological perspective. We first discuss the architecting principles of this paradigm. Then we discuss our investigations on the open coordination model, environment-driven model, and dependability assurance framework.

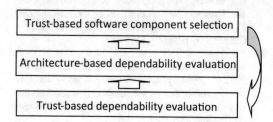

Fig. 1.3 The dependability assurance framework

It should be admitted that our work on the Internetware paradigm is still at a rather early stage. Though we have conducted separate case studies [3,6,25,39], killer applications in the open environment and systematic solutions following this new paradigm have not been fully developed yet. In our future work, we will conduct a comprehensive case study on how the new paradigm can improve the productivity and dependability of application systems in the open environment. We will also investigate key enabling technologies such as online evolution of application systems, asynchronous homeostasis maintenance, and social network-based trust management.

Acknowledgments This work is supported by National Grand Fundamental Research 973 Program of China (No.2009CB320702), National Natural Science Foundation of China (No.60736015, No.60721002), and "Climbing" Program of Jiangsu Province, China (No.BK2008017).

References

1. I. Foster, C. Kesselman, *The Grid: Blueprint for a New Computing Infrastructure* (Morgan Kaufmann, Amsterdam, Boston, 2004)
2. M.P. Papazoglou, D. Georgakopoulos, Service-oriented computing: introduction. Commun. ACM **46**, 24–28 (2003)
3. X. Ma, S.C. Cheung, C. Cao, F. Xu, J. Lu, *Towards A Dependable Software Paradigm for Service-Oriented Computing* (Springer City, 2009)
4. M. Weiser, Some computer science issues in ubiquitous computing. Commun. ACM **36**, 75–84 (1993)
5. B. Hayes, Cloud computing. Commun. ACM **51**, 9–11 (2008)
6. J. Lu, X.X. Ma, X.P. Tao, C. Cao, Y. Huang, P. Yu, On environment-driven software model for Internetware. Sci. China Ser. F-Inf. Sci. **51**, 683–721 (2008)
7. J. Lu, X. Tao, X. Ma, H. Hu, F. Xu, C. Cao, On agent-based software software model for Internetware. Sci. China Ser. E Inf. Sci. (Chinese Version) **35**(12), 1233–1253 (2005)
8. H. Mei, G. Huang, L. Lan, J.G. Li, A software architecture centric self-adaptation approach for Internetware. Sci. China Ser. F Inf. Sci. **51**, 722–742 (2008)
9. F.Q. Yang, J. Lue, H. Mei, Technical framework for Internetware: an architecture centric approach. Sci. China Ser. F Inf. Sci. **51**, 610–622 (2008)
10. T.S. Kuhn, *The Structure of Scientific Revolutions* (University of Chicago Press, Chicago, 1962)
11. R.W. Floyd, *The Paradigms of Programming* (ACM, City, 2007)
12. O.-J. Dahl, E.W. Dijkstra, C.A.R. Hoare, *Structured Programming* (Academic Press, London, New York, 1972)
13. G. Booch, *Object-Oriented Analysis and Design with Applications* (Addison-Wesley, Upper Saddle River, NJ, 2007)
14. C. Szyperski, D. Gruntz, S. Murer, *Component Software: Beyond Object-Oriented Programming* (Addison-Wesley, London; Boston, MA, 2003)
15. M. Wooldridge, N.R. Jennings, D. Kinny, *The Gaia Methodology for Agent-Oriented Analysis and Design.* Autonomous Agents and Multi-Agent Systems, 2000, pp. 285–312
16. S.H. Kaisler, *Software Paradigms* (Wiley-Interscience, Hoboken, NJ, 2005)
17. M.W. Maier, Architecting principles for systems-of-systems. Syst. Eng., 267–284 (1998)
18. O. Raz, M. Shaw, An Approach to Preserving Sufficient Correctness in Open Resource Coalitions, in *Proceedings of the Proceedings of the 10th International Workshop on Software Specification and Design* (IEEE Computer Society, 2000)
19. http://varma.ece.cmu.edu/cps/ NSF Workshop On Cyber-Physical Systems. City, 2006
20. G.A. Papadopoulos, F. Arbab, *Coordination Models and Languages* CWI (Centre for Mathematics and Computer Science, 1998)
21. T.W. Malone, K. Crowston, The interdisciplinary study of coordination. ACM Comput. Surv. **26**, 87–119 (1994)
22. T. Kielmann, Designing a coordination model for open systems, in *Proceedings of the Proceedings of the First International Conference on Coordination Languages and Models* (Springer-Verlag, 1996)
23. F. Arbab, Reo: a channel-based coordination model for component composition. Math. Struct. Comput. Sci. **14**, 329–366 (2004)
24. C. Peltz, Web services orchestration and choreography. Computer **36**, 46–52 (2003)
25. X. Ma, Y. Zhou, J. Pan, P. Yu, J. Lu, *Constructing Self-Adaptive Systems with Polymorphic Software Architecture* (City, 2007)
26. E. Gamma, *Design patterns: elements of reusable object-oriented software* (Addison-Wesley, Reading, MA, 1995)
27. M. Roman, F. Kon, R.H. Campbell, *Supporting Dynamic Reconfiguration in the dynamicTAO Reflective ORB* (University of Illinois at Urbana-Champaign, 1999)
28. J.P. Loyall, R.E. Schantz, J.A. Zinky, D.E. Bakken, Specifying and measuring quality of service in distributed object systems, in *Proceedings of the Proceedings of the The 1st IEEE International Symposium on Object-Oriented Real-Time Distributed Computing* (IEEE Computer Society, 1998)
29. M. Shaw, D. Garlan, *Perspective on an Emerging Discipline* (Prentice Hall, Software Architecture, 1996)

30. P. Ciancarini, Coordination models and languages as software integrators. ACM Comput. Surv. **28**(2), 300–302 (1996)

31. D. Garlan, S.-W. Cheng, A.-C. Huang, B. Schmerl, P. Steenkiste, Rainbow: architecture-based self-adaptation with reusable infrastructure. Computer **37**, 46–54 (2004)

32. M. Moriconi, X. Qian, R.A. Riemenschneider, Correct Architecture Refinement. IEEE Trans. Softw. Eng. **21**, 356–353 (1995)

33. C.N. Dellarocas, *A Coordination Perspective on Software Architecture: Towards a Design Handbook for Integrating Software Components* (Institute of Technology, Massachusetts, 1996)

34. X. Ma, C. Cao, P. Yu, Y. Zhou, A supporting environment based on graph grammar for dynamic software architectures. J. Softw. **19**, 1881–1892 (2008)

35. Y. Huang, X. Ma, J. Cao, X. Tao, J. Lu, Concurrent event detection for asynchronous consistency checking of pervasive context, in *Proceedings of the IEEE International Conference on Pervasive Computing and Communications* 2009 (PerCom 2009, Galveston, TX, 9–13 March, 2009)

36. R.S. Pressman, *Software engineering: a practitioner's approach* (McGraw-Hill, Boston, MA, 2005)

37. M. Blaze, J. Feigenbaum, J. Lacy, *Decentralized Trust Management* (Center for Discrete Mathematics & Theoretical Computer Science, 1996)

38. Y. Wang, F. Xu, H. Hu, J. Lu, A trust-based approach to select reliable components for internet coalition applications, in *Proceedings of the Proceedings of The Ninth IASTED International Conference Software Engineering and Applications* (Phoenix, AZ, USA, 14–16 November 2005)

39. F. Xu, J. Pan, W. Lu, A trust-based approach to estimating the confidence of the software system in open environments. J. Comput. Sci. Technol. **24**(2), 373–385 (2009)

40. J. Pan, F. Xu, X.L. Xin, J. Lu, A personalized trust-based approach for service selection in Internetwares, in *International Conference on Advanced Computer Theory and Engineering*, pp. 89–93 (2008)

Abstract

Being a new software paradigm evolved by the Internet, Internetware brings many challenges to the traditional software methods and techniques. Sponsored by the national basic research program (973), researchers in China have developed an architecture centric technical framework for the definition, incarnation and en-gineering of Internetware. First of all, a software model for Internetware is defined for what to be, including that Internetware entities should be packaged as components, behaving as agents, interoperating as services, collaborating in a structured and on demand manner, etc. Secondly, a middleware for Internetware is designed and implemented for how to be, including that Internetware entities are incarnated by runtime containers, structured collaborations are enabled by runtime software architecture, Internetware can be managed in a reflective and autonomic manner, etc. Thirdly, an engineering methodology for Internetware is proposed for how to do, including the way to develop Internetware entities and their collaborations by transforming and refining a set of software architectures which cover all the phases of software lifecycle, the way to identify and organize the disordered software assets by domain modeling, etc.

Keywords

Internetware · Component · Software architecture · Agent · Middleware

2.1 Introduction

Software is essentially a computer program modeling the problem space of the real world and its solution. Software can perform various tasks including controlling hardware devices, computing, communicating, and so on. It always pursues a computing model that is both expressive

Parts of this chapter were reprinted with kind permission from Springer Science+Business Media: <Science in China Series F: Information Sciences, Technical framework for Internetware: An architecture centric approach, volume 51, 2008, 610–622, FuQing Yang, Jian Lü and Hong Mei., figure number(s), and any original (first) copyright notice displayed with material>.

and natural. A basic software model comprises entity elements and the interactions among them. The model has evolved from the initial machine language instruction and the sequence and jump relationship, to high-level language statement and the three control structures, procedures and the sub-procedures relationship, object and message passing, to the currently popular model of components and connectors. The evolution of computing model greatly facilitates software construction and maintenance. On the other hand, software also pursues better utilization of hardware capabilities. Hardware devices are controlled by software, without which it is impossible for them to work efficiently and flexibly. For instance, operating systems are developed from the earliest boot programs for starting the computers, the simple device management programs, the multi-channel programs for efficiently utilizing the CPU and I/O, to resource management systems for efficiently utilizing both software and hardware. In that sense, the evolution of software technology and systems is mainly driven by the application domains and underlying hardware.

In the 21st century, Internet promotes the globalization widely and deeply and then brings new opportunities and challenges to the software applications. On the other hand, Internet is now growing up into a "ubiquitous computer" which consists of a great and growing number of computing devices. Internet provides much more powerful supports for problem solving than traditional computer systems. In order to cope with such evolutionary changes of application domains and underlying hardware, software systems need to be online evolvable, continually responsive and self-adaptive. Based on object oriented methods, software components and other techniques, software entities are distributed on the nodes of Internet as active and autonomic software services. These entities can collaborate with each other in various manners and thus form a software Web, which is similar to the World Wide Web, an information web. Such a new software paradigm evolved by Internet is called Internetware in this chapter [25].

Generally speaking, Internetware is constructed by a set of autonomic software entities distributed over the Internet, and a set of connectors enabling the collaboration among these entities in various manners. The software entities are capable of perceiving the dynamic changes of its environment, and adapting to these changes through architectural evolution (including the adding, deleting and evolving of software entities and connectors, as well as the corresponding changes of the system topology). Through such context aware behaviors, the system can not only satisfy user requirements, but also improve their experiences. The form of Internetware is very different with that of traditional software. From the micro perspective, software entities collaborate with each other on demand, and from the macro perspective, the entities can organize themselves into an application domain. Accordingly, the development of Internetware can be seen as the composition of various "disordered" resources into "ordered" software systems. As the time elapses, changes of resources and environments may "disorder" the existing software systems again, which will become "ordered" by composition sooner or later. The iterative transformation between "ordered" and "disordered" entities implies a bottom-up, inside-out and spiral development process.

Since traditional software engineering methods and techniques are originated from and more suited for a relatively static and closed environment, they are not appropriate for open, dynamic, ever-changing and decentralized Internetware. Basically, Internetware is still a natural evolution of traditional software over the Internet, and thus the characteristics, concepts, connotation and key techniques for Internetware can be seen as a general enough abstraction and specification of the software technology and methodology in the coming future. Aiming at Chinese software industry which should support modern service industries, researchers from Chinese universities and institutes (including Peking University, Nanjing University, Tsinghua University, Institute of Software of the Chinese Academy Sciences, the Academy of Mathematics and Systems Science of Chinese Academy Sciences, East China Normal University, Southeast University, Dalian University of Technology, Shanghai

Jiao Tong University, etc.) have proposed the project "Research on Theory and Methodology of Agent-based Middleware on Internet Platform" in 2002, sponsored by the National Basic Research Program (973). Currently, the research and practice outputs can be concluded as an architecture centric technical framework for Internetware, including the following three major aspects: For Internetware entity model, we separate an entity from the environments and other entities, and introduce decision-making capabilities into an entity to make it more autonomous. For the collaboration between Internetware entities, we address the shortcomings of object oriented methods such as the fixed message receiver, synchronized interaction and single implementation by the architecture-based programming for explicit, flexible and loose-coupled collaborations. For Internetware operating platform (i.e. the middleware), we use containers and runtime software architectures (RSA) to incarnate the Internetware entities and on-demand collaborations respectively, and use a series of key techniques, such as the componentized platform structure, completely reflective framework and autonomic management loop to achieve the self-organization and self-adaptation of Internetware. For Internetware development methodology, we propose the "software architecture across the whole lifecycle" to cope with the phenomenon that the main body of the development shifts from pre-software-release to post-software-release. We use an architecture centric composition method to support the development of Internetware entities and on-demand collaborations, and also a domain modeling method for organizing disordered resources into ordered ones.

2.2   Software Model of Internetware

Software model is the core of software methodology, i.e. how a special methodology, along with its supporting techniques, abstracts the elements and behaviors of a target software system. Being an abstraction of software systems running in the open, dynamic and decentralized Internet,

Internetware differentiates from classical software systems in constitution, operation, correctness, development, trustworthiness, lifecycle, etc.

- For the constitution, Internetware is open and reflective. Openness means that Internetware is constituted by a set of widely distributed, third parties provided, autonomous and service like software entities, which form a virtual organization by diverse connectors for the communication and interoperability. Reflection means that Internetware has two levels internally: the objective level and meta level. The objective level covers the scope of traditional software, as well as an explicit abstraction of the environment. And the meta level covers the context-aware mechanisms for external environment changes and evolution mechanisms for internal system behaviors.
- For the operation, Internetware can actively adapt to the context. The operation of the objective-level system is mainly to satisfy user requirements in the current period, and the operation of the meta-level system is to dynamically adapt the running system according to the environment changes so that the objective-level system can better satisfy user requirements in the next period. In that sense, the system in operation is evolving continuously. Furthermore, the software lifecycle of Internetware manifests as a dynamic model with emphasis on evolution.
- For the correctness, through the continuous evolution, Internetware seeks for variable and flexible user experiences instead of relative strict and static functionalities.
- For the development, developing Internetware is a process of looking for the best service and the value-added services. During this process, the incremental development approach supported by the autonomous software entities and on-demand collaborations essentially contains the principle of software reuse based on component composition.
- For the trustworthiness, besides the classical techniques for security and dependability, Internetware emphasizes a flexible mea-

Fig. 2.1 Software model
for Internetware

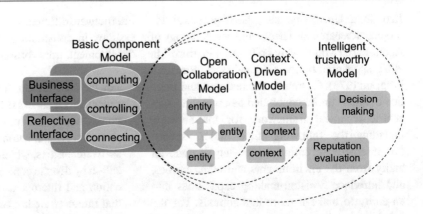

surement, deduction and application of trustworthiness, based on the historical information.

Emerging from the static, closed and controllable environment, the object-oriented (OO) software model has some inborn characteristics such as poor autonomy, fixed encapsulation, simple interaction, tight coupling, offline evolution, etc. Although there are some progresses on such areas as distributed object computing and aspect oriented programming, these inborn characteristics of OO model have not been changed fundamentally, and therefore it still cannot support the development of Internetware sufficiently and efficiently. As a result, on the basis of OO model, we propose an agent based, software architecture centric software model, as shown in Fig. 2.1 (technical details can be found in Refs. [1, 2, 11, 12, 14, 15, 24]).

2.2.1   Basic Component Model

First of all, the entity of Internetware is a component so that it can be deployed, executed and evolved independently. Like traditional software components, Internetware entities have the business interfaces to provide the functions of computation, control and connection. But different from traditional software components, Internetware entities have reflective interfaces to provide the capabilities for monitoring, analyzing, planning and adapting the business functions, so

that Internetware can be autonomous, evolutionary, cooperative, polymorphic, and context-aware. The heterogeneity of Internet determines that the Internetware entities do not have the same characteristics, and thus the Internetware component model has to be customizable and extensible. For example, software entities providing only business functions but none reflective capabilities can be seen as a basic type of Internetware entities. The software entities with the component meta model and reflective interfaces have the capability of self-awareness. The entities with the environment meta model and reflective interfaces have the capability of context-awareness. The entities with reflective interfaces for altering their states and behaviors have the capability of self-adaptation. The rationale and implementation of these Internetware characteristics are specified by the open collaboration model, context driven model, intelligent trustworthy model.

2.2.2   Open Collaboration Model

This model aims to provide a new interpretation for the core of OO model, i.e. the object-message structure, according to the open Internet. For the structure, the separation between software entities and their collaborations makes the collaborating logic explicit and independent entities based on software architectures. For the development, the software entities and their collaborations can be developed independently by service providers and service integrators, respectively. Service providers can develop the Internetware entities under the support of the mature object-oriented technology, and encapsulate those that use existing techniques like Web Services. Service integrators can design the collaborations using the techniques like the runtime software architectures, multi-mode interactions and collaboration-oriented service compositions. For the adaptation, software entities can be evolved or replaced by newly developed ones, while the collaborations can cope with changes by flexible service composition and layered evolution.

2.2.3   Context Driven Model

This model aims to build up a model to capture the features and changing modes of the context of the open collaboration model. These two models can interact with each other and evolve together by reactive service computing. To establish a context driven system, we need the awareness and analysis to the ever-changing interaction mode between the user and the environment of an Internetware system, and then, on the basis of such analysis to derive the context driven behavior mode and also to achieve the context awareness and the self adaptation based on the above framework and self-adaptive software architecture. The basic implementation techniques include agent-based contextual information collection and process, intelligent software architecture evolution, and so on.

2.2.4   Intelligent Trustworthy Model

This model aims to solve the problems derived from the open environment, such as the trustworthiness, personalization, self-evolution, etc. by combining the trustworthy computing framework and artificial intelligence on the basis of the context driven model. Based on the classical trustworthy computing techniques, which usually focus on single attribute in a developer-directed and specification-dominant manner, we develop more appropriate ones for Internetware, including taking multiple attributed into account, empirical and flexible assessment, etc. The support-

ing techniques include trustworthiness description and measurement frameworks specific to Internetware, agent-based trust management, trusted (semi) automatic composition and evolution, and so on.

2.3   Middleware for Internetware

Middleware is a special kind of distributed software that mediates between the application software and system software, enabling the interactions between distributed application software while hiding the complexity and heterogeneity of the underlying system software. Along with the rapid development and wide application of Internet, middleware technology, products, applications and standards are proliferating, and as a result, the connotation of middleware becomes much wider and can be considered as a new type of system software on Internet. The development of middleware has the following trends: (1) encapsulating more and more capabilities belonging to the tradition distributed operating systems for providing stronger runtime support; (2) becoming a ubiquitous operating platform for not only the traditional enterprise computing but also many new computing models, such as peer to peer computing, pervasive computing, grid computing and service oriented computing; (3) distilling more and more functions common to a special application domain besides those common to all applications; (4) putting more and more important impacts on the whole software lifecycle, including the operation, deployment, testing, implementation, and even design and analysis.

The proliferation and trends of middleware determine its role in Internetware technical framework, that is, an "operating system" for the deployment, operation and management of Internetware. Basically, the middleware for Internetware should have two capabilities. One is to support the incarnation of Internetware model, i.e. how to make the above mentioned Internetware entities executable and control their collaborations according to software architectures. The other is to enable the autonomic

Fig. 2.2 Model of
middleware for
Internetware

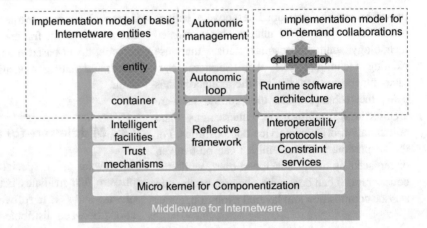

management of Internetware systems, i.e. how
to ensure the running Internetware system to
satisfy the expected functionality, performance,
reliability, security, etc. in the open, dynamic
and decentralized Internet. We establish a model
of middleware for Internetware as shown in
Fig. 2.2, and the technical details can be found in
Refs. [4–9, 16, 20, 22].

2.3.1 The Implementation Model of Basic Internetware Entities

The container is the runtime space of an Internetware entity, which is responsible for managing the entity's lifecycle (e.g. the class loading,
instantiation, caching, release, etc.), the entity's
runtime context (e.g. the invocation context and
database connections), and the binding between
entity's business functions and quality policies
(e.g. interoperability, security, transaction, persistence and rule reasoning). For a normal java
class which implements some business functions
and is deployed into a container, it can be bound
with various quality policies to implement various
advanced features, e.g. the interoperability protocols for allowing the invocation through RMI,
HTTP or SOAP, the constraint services for the
access control, data persistence and transactions,
the intelligent facilities for self adjustment of
prices based on rules, the trust computing mechanisms for the evaluation of users' reputation, and
so on. It should be noted that the implementation

of the business function, the quality policies and
their bindings can be adjusted online.

2.3.2 The Implementation Model of On-Demand Collaborations

Runtime Software Architecture (RSA) is a running entity provided by middleware, which has a
causal connection with the running system based
on the middleware's in-depth control of the whole
system. Such a causal connection ensures that
all the changes of RSA can immediately lead to
the corresponding changes of the running system, and vice versa. Every Internetware entity
can be abstracted as an RSA component, and the
interactions between entities can be abstracted as
RSA connectors. Thus the on-demand collaboration is incarnated by the RSA. From the macro
perspective, the collaborations between all Internetware entities form an internet-scale RSA. And
from the micro perspective, we can either adjust
a part of RSA to explicitly drive the collaboration between entities, or allow the entities to collaborate with each other autonomously, which is
still a part of RSA and then under the control of
RSA.

There are mainly two ways to establish the
causal connection between RSA and running systems: reflective programming model and reflective
middleware, each of which has its own advantages
and disadvantages. We use reflective middleware
as a basis, leveraging the reflective programming

model, to achieve a completely reflective framework, which improves the width and depth of the causal connection to support the on-demand collaborations.

2.3.3 The Autonomic Management of Middleware

The proliferation of middleware and the rich features of Internetware bring two challenges to the management of middleware. On the one hand, as its capabilities become diverse and complex, middleware becomes too complicated to customization, extension and quality control. On the other hand, as middleware is playing a more and more important role in the whole system, the management of middleware determines the users' confidence for the Internetware system, and thus, it is necessary to manage middleware in a systematic perspective. The flexible management objectives and environment changes further increase the complexity of middleware management. Consequently, autonomic management becomes a necessary capability for middleware, that is, middleware can manage itself with less or none human intervention.

Aiming at the three fundamental issues of middleware autonomic management, including the scope, operability and trustworthiness, we establish an architecture centric autonomic management loop for middleware. We model the software architecture of the middleware and its application to define the scope and connotation of middleware management, monitor and control the running system on the basis of RSA, and ensure the correctness and effectiveness through software architecture analysis and evaluation. For the key challenge of autonomic computing, i.e. analyzing and decision making, we first use software architecture and the formal description of decisions to make the knowledge explicit and well-formed. Here, we usually use architecture styles and patterns, domain-specific software architectures and application architectures to specify the common-sense, domain-specific and application-specific knowledge, respectively. For the adaptation plan, we can either use the imperative descriptions based on dynamic software architecture or the declarative descriptions based on self-adaptive software architecture. That is to say, middleware can automatically derive the adaptation plan using the given knowledge, e.g. use rules like <event, condition, action> to derive the proper actions under the give event and condition, refactor the partial software architecture by the knowledge derived from the description of bad patterns and the corresponding good patterns, and enhance the whole software architecture by merging a new style to the existing style.

2.3.4 Componentization of Middleware

The capabilities mentioned above require that the middleware has a fine and clear structure. For this reason, we make the middleware itself component-based by a micro kernel. The implementations for the middleware capabilities, such as containers, protocols, services, facilities, mechanisms and frameworks, are all encapsulated into platform components, and the micro kernel is for the customization, extension and autonomic management of these platform components. The micro kernel is mainly constituted by the following parts: registration and destruction interfaces for the dynamic insertion and removal of platform components, naming and searching interfaces for the selection of given platform components, bus mechanisms for the invocation of platform components through specific meta-programming interfaces, management mechanisms for the lifecycle of platform components, meta-data interfaces and meta-programming mechanisms. It should be noted that, unlike the micro kernels in operating systems, the micro kernel of middleware does not provide functions like memory management, inter process communication, I/O and interruption, for limiting the performance impacts.

2.4   Engineering Approach for Internetware

Due to the open, dynamic, and decentralized Internet, as well as the various user preferences, Internetware keeps evolving after it has been developed and deployed. When an Internetware is published, it is capable of perceiving the dynamic changes of its environment and evolves according to its functionalities and qualities so that it not only satisfies user requirements but also improves user experiences. Besides, the variation of user preferences and return of investment usually lead to a long-lived and ever-changing Internetware. Inevitably, the engineering of such Internetware faces the challenges from the development process, methodology and techniques. For these challenges, we propose a methodology for the engineering of Internetware, as shown in Fig. 2.3, and the technical details can be found in [3, 10, 13, 17–19, 21, 23, 26].

2.4.1   Software Architecture in the Whole Lifecycle

The classical software lifecycle emphasizes the development process from the requirements to the delivery. All efforts and challenges after soft-

ware delivery are simplified as "software maintenance". This is appropriate for engineering software systems under a relatively static, closed and controlled environment. However, it is not suitable for Internetware, because (1) the new software entities are usually assembled by the existing and reusable entities. Since all of these entities are relatively independent and there is no central control for them, it is hard to ensure that the assembled entities satisfy the required functionalities and qualities unless it starts to run; (2) the open, dynamic, and ever-changing environment requires Internetware entities and their collaborations to face with many changes. No matter whether these changes can be predicted or not exactly, the running system has to adapt itself continuously. As a result, software maintenance would become a relatively important phase; (3) Internetware provides services for the worldwide users. Furthermore, an Internetware usually consists of software entities which are distributed over the Internet and then has no chance to be shut down completely after it is deployed and starts to run. This implies that all maintenance activities, including debugging, optimizing and upgrading, have to perform online. All these activities also have the phases of analysis, design, implementation, testing and deployment, which cannot be controlled well by the concepts and techniques in the classical software mainte-

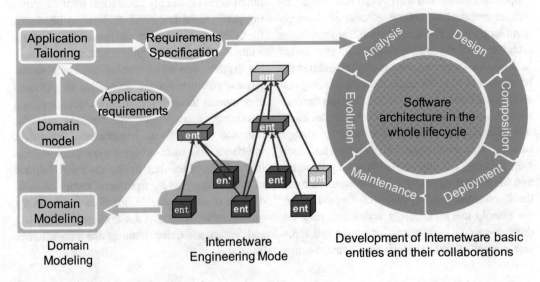

Domain
Modeling

Internetware
Engineering Mode

Development of Internetware basic
entities and their collaborations

Fig. 2.3 Internetware engineering approach

nance. For this reason, we propose the concept of software architecture in the whole lifecycle; that is, software architecture acts as a blueprint and plays a central role in every stage of Internetware lifecycle.

- Analysis (using concept view of software architecture). To narrow the gap between the requirements and design, we should use a structural method in the stage of requirements analysis to organize the problem domain and user requirements. We do not restrict a specific form for the artifact in this stage, so long as the artifact can be transformed into software architecture conveniently, naturally, and directly. For example, the analysis result from object oriented analysis, like class diagrams for a problem domain, can be directly viewed as a conceptual software architecture; the result from feature oriented requirement analysis, the feature model, can be used to generate the conceptual software architecture semi-automatically through a way similar to functional decomposition. There are also some architecture oriented requirement analysis approaches which can be used directly to obtain the conceptual software architecture.
- Design (using design view of software architecture). From the requirements specification of a software system, designers can make overall design decisions, refine the components and connectors of the conceptual software architecture and finally construct the static and dynamic software architecture models, including type diagrams, instance diagrams and process diagrams. During this process, designers or the development tools can maintain the traceability between the requirements specification and design model. It is worth noting that the philosophy of Internetware development is to reuse existing assets whenever possible. As a result, during this stage, designers should pay attention on the reusable assets, such as components, connectors, constraints, aspects, styles, patterns, etc.
- Composition (using implementation view of software architecture). This stage corresponds to the implementation stage in the

traditional software development. But unlike the implementation of traditional software architecture, which is achieved through programming according to the design, the basic functional units of Internetware are the existing and running Internetware entities, and thus the focus of Internetware development is not programming but composition. Here the composition means selecting the entities adapted to the software architecture and making all these entities collaborate according the specification in the software architecture. When the entities or collaborations do not fit the software architecture, developers need to do adaptation, and if such adaptation failed, they need to develop new entities to completely implement the target system.

- Deployment (using deployment view of software architecture). Internetware is usually running on a specific middleware platform and it should be deployed into the platform. Deployment involves a great deal of various data items which usually require deployers to configure manually. But actually, most information involved in the deployment already exists during the design and composition stages, and it can be used for the deployment after some kinds of transformation. On the other hand, the introduction of new entities or new interactions may require changing the organization of existing entities, and how to implement such organization is also the main task of the deployment. For these reasons, we define the deployment view of software architecture, which contains a lot of information inherited from the design and implementation views and also provides a visualized way for deployers to append extra information. This deployment view can also visualize the resource and load of the target environment, and support online changing the organization of running entities.
- Maintenance and evolution (using runtime view of software architecture). In a sense, Internetware development can be viewed as a continuous and iterative refinement, mapping and transformation of software architectures of the target system. After each refinement and transformation, the syntax and semantics of

software architecture become more accurate and complete. In the stage of maintenance and evolution, the runtime view reflects the actual runtime states of the system, and thus provides the most accurate and complete information of the system. This view is the runtime software architecture, which also supports the online maintenance and evolution without stopping the whole running system.

2.4.2 Development of Internetware Basic Entities and Their Collaborations

The two main tasks of Internetware development are the development of Internetware entities and the development of on-demand collaborations. Internetware entities are essentially the traditional stand-alone or intranet software systems, with extra characteristics like autonomous, evolutionary, cooperative, polymorphic, and context-aware. Therefore, the development of Internetware entities is actually to develop new traditional software systems with Internetware characteristics, as well as evolve existing traditional software systems to have Internetware characteristics. For supporting both types of the development of Internetware entities, we propose an architecture centric, component oriented software development method, called ABC (Architecture-based Component Composition).

Take the self-adaptation for example, for the application-specific self-adaptation, ABC leverages existing software architecture (SA) techniques in a systematic manner: SA models are used to analyze expected qualities for locating the part of SA models to be adapted at first; dynamic SA records what should be done at runtime to achieve the desired qualities; finally, the designed adaptation is executed by runtime SA without stopping the running system. For the general enough adaptation, domain experts can use bad architecture patterns to define the ill structures which may lead to quality problems, and provide the corresponding good patterns. The runtime software architecture can automatically detect if the running system has bad structures, and dynam-

ically refactor them into good structures. ABC also supports the introduction of rules into SA, and the entities governed by some rules can achieve rule-based self-adaptation by dynamically binding the containers with rule engines.

The on-demand collaborations of Internetware are controlled by runtime SA, that is, the development of on-demand collaborations is actually to develop the software architecture which controls Internetware entities. In that sense, ABC is still fit to the development of collaborations. But on the other hand, while the development of Internetware entities is still in the static, closed and controllable environment, the development of on-demand collaborations has to deal with the open, dynamic and decentralized Internet environment. As a result, different from developing Internetware entities by ABC, developing on-demand collaborations by ABC should take the characteristics of entities, e.g. distribution, autonomy and heterogeneity, as well as the characteristics of entity interactions, e.g. diversity, complexity and changeability, into account.

2.4.3 Domain Modeling for Internetware

Traditional software development processes are more suited for the relatively close, static and controllable environments. Most of them are top-down, that is, scoping the system border and using divide-and-conquer principles to make the whole process under control. However, the environment of Internetware has abundant resources and it is always open, dynamic, and ever-changing. The development over this environment can be seen as the composition of various "disordered" resources into "ordered" software systems. As time elapses, changes of resources and environments may "disorder" the existing software systems again, which will become "ordered" by the development sooner or later. The iterative transformation between "ordered" and "disordered" Internetware implies a bottom-up, inside-out and spiral development process. If only we can integrate these disordered entities during the development process and make them under "ordered" control, we can really achieve the development of entities and collaborations mentioned above.

As a systematic way to produce the reusable artifacts in a particular problem domain, domain engineering addresses the creation of domain models and architectures that abstract and represent a set of reusable assets within a domain through domain scoping, commonality and variability analysis and adaptable design construction based upon the study of the existing systems, knowledge from domain experts and emerging technology within a domain. Here, domain analysis refers to the process of identifying, collecting, organizing and representing the relevant information in a domain. In a sense, the domain analysis is a process in the bottom-up fashion, coinciding with the engineering of Internetware. Therefore, ABC adopts the methods and techniques of domain engineering to organize the underlying resources. We first construct the disordered resources over Internet as a domain model by domain scoping and analysis for representing high-level business goals of a set of Internetware systems; then generate the requirements specification for a new application by tailoring and extending the domain model; and finally implement the new entities and collaborations. When time elapses, the new application may be scattered somewhere on the Internet as a service and then becomes a new disorder resource. In turn, these new disordered resources can be added into the domain model by further domain analysis, and therefore the iterative process of disordered resources to ordered ones comes into being.

2.5   Conclusion

Internet brings new opportunities and challenges to the information technology, which therefore provides many new models and methodologies from different perspectives, such as grid computing, pervasive computing, service oriented computing, semantic web, web science, etc. Similarly, Internetware tries to investigate Internet from the perspective of software paradigm, that is, whether new or evolved software theory,

methodology and technology for the open, dynamic, ever-changing and decentralized Internet are needed or not. This chapter summarized the research and practice of Chinese scholars during the last five years, under the support of National Basic Research Program of China (973). Our achievements forms an architecture centric technical framework for Internetware, including a software model based autonomous entities and structured collaborations, a middleware implementing the software model and managing Internetware in an autonomic manner, and an engineering based on software architecture in the whole lifecycle.

Our future work will mainly focus on strengthening the current achievements in both depth and width. For the depth, we need to perfect the architecture centric technical framework, such as the intelligent trustworthy model, the autonomic management, the automation degree of engineering, etc. For the width, the future trend of integrating various networks will provide software a complex network environment, which consists of various heterogeneous networks like Internet, wireless networks, telecommunication networks, etc. Software running on such complex network environment is much more complex than that on Internet. However, we believe Internetware, though originated for Internet, and its technical framework provide necessary and efficient supports for such new environments.

References

1. J. Cao, X. Feng, J. Lu, H.C.B. Chan, S.K. Das, Reliable message delivery for mobile agents: push or pull? IEEE Trans. Syst. Man Cybern. Part A **34**(5), 577–587 (2004)
2. J. Cao, X. Ma, A.T.S. Chan, J. Lu, Architecting and implementing distributed web applications using the graph-oriented approach. Softw.-Pract. Exp. **33**(9), 799–820 (2003)
3. L. Hou, Z. Jin, W. Budan, Modeling and verifying web services driven by requirements: An ontology-based approach. Sci. China Ser. F: Inf. Sci. **49**(6), 792–820 (2006)
4. G. Huang, T. Liu, H. Mei, Z. Zheng, Z. Liu, G. Fan, Towards autonomic computing middleware via reflection, in *Proceedings of 28th International Computer Software and Applications Conference, COMPSAC'04*, 2004, pp. 135–140

5. G. Huang, X.Z. Liu, H. Mei, Online approach to fea-
    ture interaction problems in middleware based system.
    Sci. China Ser. F: Inf. Sci. **51**(3), 225–239 (2008)
6. G. Huang, Q.-X. Wang, D.-G. Cao, H. Mei, Pkuas: a
    domain-oriented component operating platform. Acta
    Electronica Sinica **30**(12A), 39–43 (2002)
7. G. Huang, H. Mei, F. Yang, Runtime software archi-
    tecture based on reflective middleware. Sci. China Ser.
    F: Inf. Sci. **47**(5), 555–576 (2004)
8. T. Huang, N.-J. Chen, J. Wei, W.-B. Zhang, Yong
    Zhang, Onceas/q: a qos-enabled web application
    server. J. Softw. **15**(12), 1787–1799 (2004)
9. T. Huang, X. Ding, J. Wei, An application-semantics-
    based relaxed transaction model for internetware. Sci.
    China Ser. F: Inf. Sci. **49**(6), 774–791 (2006)
10. S. Jiang, X. Baowen, L. Shi, An approach to analyz-
    ing recursive programs with exception handling con-
    structs. SIGPLAN Notices **41**(4), 30–35 (2006)
11. W. Jiao, H. Mei, Automated adaptations to dynamic
    software architectures by using autonomous agents.
    Eng. Appl. Artif. Intell. **17**(7), 749–770 (2004)
12. W. Jiao, H. Mei, Supporting high interoperability of
    components by adopting an agent-based approach.
    Softw. Qual. J. **15**(3), 283–307 (2007)
13. Z. Jin, R.Q. Lu, Automated requirements modeling
    and analysis: an ontology-based approach. Sci. China
    Ser. E **33**(4), 297–312 (2003)
14. J. Liu, J. He, Z. Liu, A strategy for service realization
    in service-oriented design. Sci. China Ser. F: Inf. Sci.
    49(6), 864–884 (2006)
15. J. Lü, X.P. Tao, X.X. Ma et al., Research on agent-
    based model for internetware. Sci. China Ser. F: Inf.
    Sci. **35**(12), 1233–1253 (2005)
16. H. Mei, D.-G. Cao, Abc-s (2) c: enabling separation
    of crosscutting concerns in component-based soft-
    ware development. Chin. J. Comput. Chinese Edition
    28(12), 2036 (2005)
17. H. Mei, J. Chang, F. Yang, Software component com-
    position based on adl and middleware. Sci. China Ser.:
    Inf. Sci. **44**(2), 136–151 (2001)
18. H. Mei, W. Zhang, H. Zhao, A metamodel for mod-
    eling system features and their refinement, constraint
    and interaction relationships. Softw. Syst. Model. **5**(2),
    172–186 (2006)
19. Y. Pan, L. Wang, L. Zhang, B. Xie, F. Yang, Relevancy
    based semantic interoperation of reuse repositories, in
    *Proceedings of the 12th ACM SIGSOFT International
    Symposium on Foundations of Software Engineering,
    FSE'04*, 2004, pp. 211–220
20. J. Shen, X. Sun, G. Huang, W. Jiao, Y. Sun, H.
    Mei, Towards a unified formal model for support-
    ing mechanisms of dynamic component update, in
    *Proceedings of the 10th European Software Engi-
    neering Conference held jointly with 13th ACM
    SIGSOFT International Symposium on Founda-
    tions of Software Engineering, ESEC/FSE'05*, 2005,
    pp. 80–89
21. G.-Z. Tan, C.-X. Li, H. Liu, W.U. Jian-Kun, Research
    and application of traffic grid. J. Comput. Res. Dev.
    41(12), 2066–2072 (2004)
22. Q. Wang, J. Shen, X. Wang, H. Mei, A component-
    based approach to online software evolution. J. Softw.
    Maint. **18**(3), 181–205 (2006)
23. Z. Wei, M.E.I. Hong, A feature-oriented domain
    model and its modeling process. J. Softw. **14**(8), 1345–
    1356 (2003)
24. W. Wu, J. Cao, J. Yang, M. Raynal, Design and perfor-
    mance evaluation of efficient consensus protocols for
    mobile ad hoc networks. IEEE Trans. Comput. **56**(8),
    1055–1070 (2007)
25. F.-Q. Yang, H. Mei, L. Jian, Z. Jin, Some dis-
    cussion on the development of software technol-
    ogy. Acta Electronica Sinica **30**(12A), 1901–1906
    (2002)
26. W. Zhao, L. Zhang, Y. Liu, J. Sun, F. Yang, SNIAFL:
    towards a static non-interactive approach to feature
    location, in *Proceedings of the 26th International Con-
    ference on Software Engineering, (ICSE'04)*, 2004,
    pp. 293–303

Part II
Internetware Software Model

In Part 1, we have already introduced the basic concepts of Internetware. As a software paradigm, Internetware aims to make software applications architected like the Internet, developed with the Internet, executed on the Internet, and provided as services via the Internet.

Software models are at the core of software paradigm. Software models should specify the forms, structures, and behaviors of software entities as well as their collaborations. An Internetware software entity has basic business functionality interfaces to enable collaborations. It has the capabilities to expose its own states and behaviors. It also has the capabilities to monitor and capture the environment information. Governed by a software architecture, the collaborations of entities can be globally planned and adapted.

This part discusses the environment model, software architecture model, and requirement model for Internetware, as well as their enabling techniques. The common theme behind these models is the goal to enable and manage flexible adaptations of an Internetware system to the constant changes in the environment it is situated and the requirements it has to satisfy.

Chapter 3 presents a software model featuring environment-driven adaptation for Internetware applications. Enabling techniques for the model, especially the modeling, management, and utilization of environment information are discussed. Prototype systems have also been built to prove the concepts and evaluate the techniques.

To support the online self-organization and self-adaptation of Internetware software applications, the software architecture implements and governs software entities and their on-demand collaborations. To better control the development process, the architecture organizes heterogeneous distributed resources for a specific domain according to domain modeling techniques. Chapter 4 discusses a software architecture-centric approach for Internetware's self-adaptation. In this approach the knowledge acquiring, organizing, and reasoning as well as the monitoring, analyzing, planning, and executing are all performed from the perspective of software architecture. A comprehensive case study is also given to demonstrate how the software architecture-centric self-adaptation approach increases system performance and reliability.

Internetware applications have to adapt quickly to the diversified and dynamically changing requirements in the physical, technological, economical, and social environments. The ability to dynamically combine contents from numerous web sites and local resources, and the ability to instantly publish services worldwide have opened up entirely new possibilities for software development. Chapter 5 proposes a requirement model-driven method for adaptive and evolutionary applications, providing high-level guidelines to meet the challenges of building adaptive industrial strength applications with a spectrum of processes, techniques, and facilities provided within the Internetware paradigm.

On Environment-Driven Software Model for Internetware

3

Abstract

Internetware is envisioned as a general software paradigm for the application style of resources integration and sharing in the open, dynamic and uncertain platforms such as the Internet. In this chapter, after an analysis of the behavioral patterns and the technical challenges of environment driven applications, a software-structuring model is proposed for environment driven Internetware applications. A series of explorations on the enabling techniques for the model, especially the modeling, management and utilization of context information are presented. Several prototype systems are also built to prove the concepts and evaluate the techniques. These research efforts make a further step toward the Internetware paradigm by providing an initial framework for the construction of context-aware and self-adaptive software application systems in the open network environment.

Keywords

Software engineering · Internetware · Context-awareness · Self-adaptation

3.1 Introduction

The rapid development and wide application of the Internet make it a new mainstream computing platform, on which software systems are developed, deployed and executed. In contrast to the relatively closed, static and controllable traditional computing platforms such as stand-alone systems, LANs and Enterprise intranets, the Internet platform is characterized by its openness, dynamism and uncertainty. To adapt to such a new platform, software systems must be more autonomous, more sensitive to context changes, more reactive, and more evolvable. Technically, there will be a tremendous number of autonomous software entities deployed as software services in the open Internet environment. In order to fulfill the application tasks, these services will connect

Parts of this chapter were reprinted with kind permission from Springer Science+Business Media: <Science in China Series F: Information Sciences, On environment-driven software model for Internetware, volume 51, 2008, 683–721, Jian Lü, XiaoXing Ma, XianPing Tao, Chun Cao, Yu Huang and Ping Yu, figure number(s), and any original (first) copyright notice displayed with material>.

to, and cooperate with each other to establish temporal or persistent coalitions with various coordination facilities. In such a way, a Software Web emerges, just as the WWW results from the web pages and hyperlinks between them. The openness, dynamism and uncertainty of the underlying network environment and the potentially boundless user preferences imply that application systems on such a Software Web cannot be constructed in a once-for-ever style as many traditional applications do. These new application systems must probe the changes of the environment and user preferences, and then adapt themselves accordingly to keep their service satisfactory with sufficient functionality, performance and dependability. Such a software paradigm is named the Internetware, which emphasizes the autonomy of the constituent services of a system, the explicit service coordination, and the reactiveness, evolvability and multi-goal of the system [1].

Against the requirements of the Internetware, the classic object-oriented software structuring model [2–5], originally developed in the relatively closed, static and controllable environments, has its own limitations. Adaptations of the basic model, development method, supporting techniques, run-time facilities are needed to directly and naturally support the construction, operation and maintenance of the applications in the open, dynamic and uncertain network environment. At the micro aspect, the traditional model supports only limited autonomy and fixed encapsulation of software entities and inflexible interactions among these entities. And at the macro aspect, the assumptions of environment are fixed and hidden in the design and implementation, the resulting system structures are tightly coupled, development processes are essentially centralized and top-down, and adaptations to the environment often mean redevelopment. In fact, to improve this situation, many new ideas, concepts, models, methods and techniques have been proposed in the literature. A survey has been given in [1], in which the trends of these developments have been summarized from a methodological viewpoint as follows: Overall, taking the open Internet environment as the computing platform, applications are

built as collations of autonomous services. Structurally, while the focus is not on the entities but the coordination among them, the explicit modeling of the environment must also be included as an integral part of the system. Behaviorally, the application systems have to be self-adaptive and self-managed, and achieve high dependability with trust management. Considering the development process, the specialization and cooperation are further deepened with the software-as-a-service model. Finally, the needs for middleware systems and other supporting systems of the new applications in the new environment are increasing.

Generally, software-structuring models, which decide how software systems are constructed, are at the kernel of a software methodology. Based on the considerations of the aforementioned Internetware characteristics and development trends, a research roadmap toward a methodology for the Internetware is designed with three major steps where three structuring models are developed in order [6]: Firstly, the open coordination model, secondly, the environment driven model, and finally the intelligent and trusted model. The open coordination model features its loosely coupled structure and distributed coalition of resources, which fulfils the needs of flexible coordination of various resources in the open network environment and dynamic adaptation of coalition systems. Based on the open coordination model, the environment driven model features its explicit handling of environment issues and self-adaptation to the change of the environment and user preferences. It provides a framework for the modeling and realization of various environment-system interaction patterns and supports online system evolution with self-adaptation and self-management mechanisms. Furthermore, the intelligent trusted model features its trustworthy services and intelligent decision making, which achieves high dependability and customizability with trust management and machine learning techniques. Eventually, a comprehensive software model for Internetware and associating principles, methods, techniques, and reference applications shall be provided.

In a previous paper [6], an agent-based approach to the open coordination model is proposed. Concentrating on resource sharing and service integrating in the open network environment, this approach improves the classic object-oriented approach with its direct and natural supporting at the following aspects: Firstly, at the structural aspect, the coordination logic is structured and separated from the software service entities; secondly, at the developmental aspect, the services used in a coalition application are provided by third-parties and the coalition is independently coordinated; thirdly, at the evolutional aspect, the coordination modes of the application systems can be reconfigured in a systematic manner, offline or online. Correspondingly, a programming model of agent-based coordination is devised. Also, an agent-based middleware for multi-mode coordination and a dynamic software architecture centric software coordination mechanism are provided. Such an open coordination structuring model lays a basis for our further research on the Internetware.

This chapter focuses on the environment driven model and corresponding enabling techniques. Addressing the problem of how to handle the openness, dynamism and uncertainty of the environment, we firstly analyze the behavioral patterns of interactions between Internetware application systems and their environments, and then present an initial structuring model with which the environment context information is explicitly modeled and well managed. The model also introduces a multi-layer interaction mechanism combining these environment handling facilities and the adaptable business system developed with the aforementioned agent-based open coordination model to support the construction of context-aware and self-adaptive software application systems in the open network environment. A set of enabling techniques, especially those about the context modeling, management and serving, are explored. Several prototype systems are also built to prove the concepts and evaluate the techniques. These efforts make a further step toward the paradigm of Internetware. The rest of the chapter is arranged as follows: In Sect. 3.2 we discuss the overall interaction patterns and the structuring model of environment driven software systems. Then in Sect. 3.3 we present our research on the enabling techniques on environment modeling and management. Section 3.4 is devoted to the problem of how to use the environment context information to drive the system adaptation. Several prototype supporting systems and an example application are presented in Sect. 3.5. Before concluding the chapter, some related work is discussed in Sect. 3.6.

3.2 An Approach to the Environment-Driven Model

Generally speaking, every software system runs in a certain environment for certain purposes of its user(s). The interactions among the three parties of the system, the environment and the user define the observable behavior of a software system. Under classic software structuring models, the user party is defined with the requirement specification, and the environment is often described with auxiliary documents. It is a basic assumption that these two parties will not change dramatically during the development and running of the software system. How to provide necessary flexibility to gracefully deal with requirement and environment changes is always a key problem in software engineering research. For example, the inheritance and dynamic binding mechanism of the object-oriented model can be used to build relatively stable structures for partially evolvable requirements. Also, agile methods such as Extreme Programming provide some flexibility in the methodological aspect. Despite these techniques, because classical software structuring models have been mainly used in traditional environments that are basically closed, static and controllable, their fundamental strategy for the handling of environment issues is implicit and inflexible, and adaptations to the changes often have to be realized with redevelopments and off-line upgrades.

Contrastingly, Internetware application systems are running in an open, dynamic and uncertain environment. For such systems much more frequent changes of the environment and requirements at runtime must be supported as required features rather than exceptions. To support these changes, it is necessary for the system to handle the environment issues explicitly and separately, and have the ability to dynamically adapt itself to the environment. This feature distinguishes the environment driven model from classical models. To develop such an environment driven model, observation and analysis of the overall interaction patterns, an experimental structuring model, and related enabling techniques are discussed in the following sections.

3.2.1 Overall Interaction Patterns of Environment-Driven Applications

An understanding of the interaction patterns between software systems and their environment is essential to the explicit handling of environment issues and constructing of adaptive systems. Some ideas and results in the fields of software agents and context-aware computing give us valuable inspirations on the understanding of the interaction patterns. But they must be reshaped before being used in the environment driven software model.

Some intelligent agent researchers describe the properties of the agent environment to include accessibility, deterministic, dynamism, continuity, etc. [7]. In the field of context-aware computing, there are different kinds of definitions of context. Early researchers often define context by enumerating various environmental elements. Dey [8,9] defined context from the developer's view-point as "any information that characterizes a situation related to the interaction between humans, applications, and the surrounding environment". More recently, Dourish [10] distinguished the understandings of context into representational and interactional. As a representational problem, the context is a set of information that can be understood, encoded and represented. With this understanding, the context is assumed to be delineable, stable and separable from the interaction activities. As an interactional problem, the

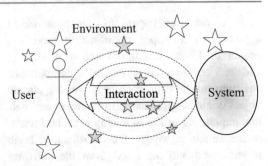

Fig. 3.1 Interactions among user, environment and system

context is viewed as the emergent feature of the interaction. With this understanding, "the contextuality is a relational property that holds between objects or activities", the context is dynamic, occasioned, and arises from the activity.

From a software engineering perspective, an environment driven application features the three-party interactions among the system, the user(s) and the related entities in the environment. "environment driven" means that the environmental entities and their status information are used to improve the quality of system's service for the user and the efficiency of interactions between the system and the user. The scenario is depicted in Fig. 3.1.

Elaborately, at the beginning, the user interacts with the system in the environment in a predefined way. After a period, it is observed that some environment entities have their influence on the interaction. And then these environment issues are taken into account and used to help the interaction and improve the service quality. Gradually, a relatively stable relationship among the user, system and environment can be delineated, understood, generalized and explicitly represented as the context model to direct the system's interactive behavior. Follow this process, the emergent interactive behaviors can be eventually solidified in the environment driven application system.

Therefore, it is possible to divide environment driven applications into three classes by determining to what extent the emergent relationships between the environment elements and the system-user interaction are supported. Applications in the first class directly support the emergent interactive behaviors constantly arising during their execution. The interaction pattern of this class is the loop of "Emergent behavior ⇒ New Emergent behavior". Unfortunately, necessary theories, methods and techniques for the systematic development of such applications are just under envisioning. On the contrary, applications in the second class only support the solidified environment-handling behaviors, which implies that the influence of the environment on the interaction between the user and the system will not change during system execution. The interaction pattern of this class is monotone and solidified. While the technology for this class of applications is relatively mature, this pattern is often unsatisfactory for the applications in the open network environment. The third class is a tradeoff between the two classes above. Applications in this class support intermittent emergence of new environmental influence on the user-system interactions. The interaction pattern of this class can be "Emergent behavior ⇒ Solidified behavior ⇒ New Emergent behavior" or "Solidified behavior ⇒ New Emergent behavior ⇒ new Solidified behavior".

3.2.2 A Structuring Model for Environment-Driven Applications

Based on the discussions above, a structuring model is proposed as an abstraction of the environment driven applications in the Internetware paradigm. With this model, a typical environment driven application system consists of the following three parts:

- The environment handling facilities deal with the modeling, probing, processing and management of environment context information and its dynamics, which covers the span from the low-level environment data to the abstract context representation.
- The open coordination subsystem is responsible for the business logic of the application. It must also support the dynamic reconfiguration of itself with a flexible coordination architecture so that the adaptation can be smoothly carried out when necessary.

- The goal-driven adaptation logic decides how to adapt the open coordination subsystem to the changes of the environment. A unified abstract semantic framework for the above two parts is required for such a logic reasoning, while reification mechanisms and customizable rules are also needed to realize the decision.

The framework is sketched in Fig. 3.2.

From a software developer's viewpoint, one of the fundamental difficulties is the huge gap among the users' goals, environment, and the system implementation. The users' goals are in the problem domain while the implementation is in the solution domain. The data about the environment by themselves cannot be understood and used to drive the system adaptation-they must be interpreted with the knowledge from the problem domain to be meaningful. In traditional software development process, the users' goals and environment assumptions are transformed gradually down to the implementation with various decomposition and refinement techniques, which is not applicable for the environment driven Internetware applications because the three parts must be bridged to each other during runtime.

With our model, the gap is bridged with three layers of interactions. Firstly, just like any distributed software systems, the application system makes use of the resources in the environment and acts upon the environment to do its current business. Secondly, the basic system consisting of functional components (or services) and connectors interacts with the built-in runtime software architecture object to support dynamic system reconfiguration reflectively. Finally, based on the semantic framework defined by application goals and domain knowledge, the runtime software architecture model interacts with the environment context model in a unified ontology space, which is driven by a set of automatic rules or manual directions.

Furthermore, with the evolution of the interactions among the system, the users and the environment, new environmental elements and their implications for the system behaviors may emerge. Therefore, all the three parts of the model must be dynamically extensible. New probes

Fig. 3.2 A structuring
model for environment
driven applications

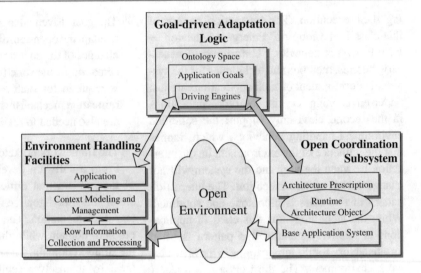

will be deployed, and new type of environment
information will be included to enrich the context
model. The built-in runtime software architecture
object can be upgraded polymorphically to
support unexpected dynamic reconfigurations.
Owing to the loose-coupled nature of the ontology space, it is also convenient to add/remove
ontology tuples and rules, and upgrade the
reasoning engines. With this openness, the model
is able to support the potential emergent behavior
of environment driven applications.

3.2.2.1 Environment Handling Facilities

All the elements outside a software system that
have their influence on the development, deployment, operation and maintenance of this system
form the environment of the system. In order to
understand the environment one must consider not
only its constitution but also its dynamics [1]. The
numbers and types of environment elements and
the relations between them may change at runtime.
Some of the changes are predictable, while others
are not. When an environment of a system is said to
be closed, static and controllable, we mean that the
environmental influence on the system's development, deployment, operation and maintenance are
predictable and controllable. Because the types
of the environment elements and their relationships are stable in the lifecycle of the system and
their value only changes in a predictable extent,

the software system can deal with the environment issues in a predefined manner. In summary,
the environment is "closed" overall, its constitution is "static", and content changes are "controllable" with the stable framework. For example,
a classical software system running on a standalone computer has its environment consisting of
memory capacity, CPU speed, input-output, user
preference, etc. During the lifecycle of the software system, the changes of these elements are
limited and predictable. Consequently, the environment is handled implicitly in the development
and hard-coded in the implementation. In contrast,
when an environment of a software system is said
to be open, dynamic and uncertain, we mean that
the elements that could affect the system's development, deployment, operation and maintenance
are, to a large extent, unpredictable and uncontrollable. The constitution of the environment is
dynamic, there will be new types of elements to
be taken into account, and changes of the content of an element can be beyond the predicted
extent. Therefore the system must rely on explicit
modeling and handling of environment issues, and
this modeling and handling must be able to be
enhanced at runtime to deal with unpredicted situations.

To bridge the gap between the scattered environmental data and the abstract user requirements
at runtime in the system, explicit handling of the

environment issues is needed, which consists of the following three layers. Firstly, the primitive environmental data are probed and processed, so that related attributes of environment elements are measured and events of interest of the environment changes are raised. All the information is represented with ad-hoc data structures in this layer. Secondly, based on the first layer, a context model is built with an ontology that provides the conceptualization of a common understanding of the domain [11]. With this formal model of the environment context, the context information is uniformly stored and well-managed, and some high-level processings such as conflict resolving, context fusion and reasoning are carried out to enhance its consistency, integrity and usability. Finally, with the application goals and domain knowledge that are also ontologically represented, the context information is translated to environment elements directly understandable in the current problem domain of the application, and encapsulated as directly usable services. By way of analogy, the tasks of the three layers are somewhat like the syntax processing, the semantic processing, and the pragmatic consideration of programming respectively.

With such a layered explicit handling of environment issues, we can get a consistent, complete and easy-to-use context representation and its interpretation under current application goals, which provides a basis for the decision of system adaptations. Detailed discussion on the environment handling techniques will be given in Sect. 3.3.

3.2.2.2 Open Coordination Subsystem

A software coordination system consists of a collection of autonomous software entities dispersed on the nodes over the Internet and a set of connectors to support the coordination by enabling the manifold interactions among them. Roughly speaking, such a system shall be aware of the changes happening in the external environment. Through the evolution in its architecture, including adding/removing/changing the software entities and/or connectors as well as transforming in the system topology, the coordination system is able to adapt itself to those changes so that it

can constantly fulfill the multifold requirements of the users. Apparently, the conventional object oriented technology featured with the object reference and object method invocation, written as "O.m()", can barely be enough to support such a software model. Therefore, we extend the original distributed object model by reifying software architecture into a runtime object explicitly. The introduced runtime architecture object also realizes a programming model for explicit and flexible coordination logic, which is carried out by software agents. This leads to an agent-based open coordination software model that supports multi-mode interaction, configurable coordination and the dynamic (expected or even unexpected) evolution. Please refer to [12] for details.

To bridge the semantic gap between user requirements and target implementation of the system, it is a reflective computing framework that becomes the essence of the open coordination model above, which is featured by the runtime architecture object. The reflective framework reifies the abstract architectural specification into an explicit object, which is causally connected to the real system. Thereby, the concrete system implementation and the abstract specification in terms of software architecture are virtually connected. However, the gap between architecture and requirements still remains. For this purpose, an ontological representation is further developed to describe architecture with respect to both the static configuration and the dynamic evolution processes, and declare both its description [13] and prescription [14]. This ontological representation is problem-oriented. However, what it describes is essentially the same as what the runtime architecture object reflects, and the evolution described with ontology can delegate the runtime architecture object to put into execution directly. We will discuss the techniques in Sect. 3.4.

Based on software architecture as a double-face abstraction mechanism, the problem-oriented ontologies can be developed, while at the same time the solution-oriented implementation can be naturally derived. Basically, the corresponding method for open coordination applications brings the flexible and dynamic adaptability into the environment driven Internetware systems. Also, it facilitates the abstract descriptions of system status and behaviors needed in the specification of adapting policies, which are the base for the design of goal-driven facilities.

3.2.2.3   Goal-Driven Adaptation Logic

With the work above, we can now put the description of both a coordination system and its external environment closer to the problem domain at some abstract level. In addition, with the conceptualization of the domain knowledge and application goals, a semantic framework enabling the communication among the users, system and environment can be developed. And with some automatic or manual reasoning under this framework, the control loop of required environment driven interactions is to be completed. Concretely, this technical route covers three major points. First, a common ontology description framework shall be constructed to maintain and manage the related knowledge about user requirements, the environment and the architecture. Second, a collection of transformation facilities shall be deployed to trigger appropriate evolution instructions by fusing the knowledge of those three parties and evaluating the current status of the environment and the system. Last, to support the solidification of emerging behaviors of environment driven systems, the three parts shall all be extensible to include new information, knowledge and capabilities at runtime.

We propose an approach based on an ontology space toward the above semantic framework. The ontology space covers both the problem domain and the solution domain, and depicts both the environment and the software architecture of the running system. Besides, additional requirement ontology is developed to capture the requirements from users in the framework uniformly. The idea of requirement ontology originates from the goal-oriented requirement engineering [15], which expresses user requirements in the form of a Goal Refinement Tree. As there can still be conceptual and semantic gap between the three ontologies, a set of transformation ontologies, which are somewhat like ontology mappings

[16], is further developed to glue them up. These ontology models will be detailed in Sect. 3.4.

Technically, OWL/RDF [17] is used as the ontology language in our approach. Ontology tuple instances are stored in an ontology space. A collection of reasoning engines is deployed upon the space and turns it into a blackboard system. The engines include standard OWL Description Logic reasoning engines, customizable rule-based adaptation engines and interfaces for direct user manipulations. With such a mechanism, the probed domain-independent information from environments, such as the five-seconded-average-responding-time of an online ticketing system, can be translated into an application-level one, say, not-a-satisfactory-responsivity. The application-level information can move forward to activate some application requirement, namely the improve-performance goal here, and further trigger some operation over the system architecture, like add-a-Slave-into-the-Master/Slave-architecture. Finally, the operation is to be carried out by the runtime architecture object against the system on the fly. With respect to the extensibility, this mechanism facilitates the online introduction of new domain knowledge, driving rules and reasoning engines into the ontology space. Moreover, the cognizance of the environment and new reconfiguration behaviors can also be injected by the expansion in ontology.

Figure 3.3 illustrates a structuring model for environment driven Internetware applications.

3.2.3   Model and System Characteristics

In order to adapt to the explicit, open, dynamic and uncertain environment, software systems based on the environment driven model differ greatly from traditional software systems in various aspects including system composition, operation, objective, development and lifecycle.

From the perspective of system composition, the differences between software systems based on the environment driven model and traditional systems can be studied from two orthogonal

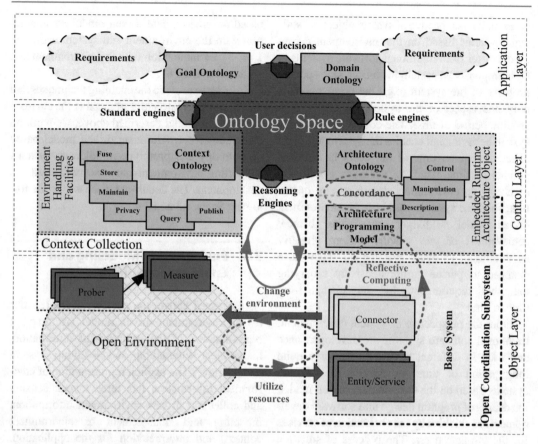

Fig. 3.3 Details of the structuring model for environment driven applications

views. From the horizontal view, software systems based on the environment driven model is a coalition of software entities, which are distributed in wide areas, provided by the third party and have the characteristics of autonomous services. These software entities are connected by collaboration connectors with different styles. From the vertical view, software systems based on the environment driven model mainly include three different layers: the object layer, the control layer and the application layer. At the object layer, we study the software system from the horizontal view. The control layer mainly focuses on how the software system evolves and adapts to changes in the environment. The environment and the system interact considering objectives of the application layer and the domain knowledge. Thus, the system achieves environment driven behaviors.

From the perspective of system operation, software systems based on the environment driven model greatly differ from traditional software systems in that they bear the characteristics of being environment driven. The system operation can also be viewed from two different layers. From the object layer, the system mainly focuses on satisfying users' requirements in a specific period of time. From the control layer, the system adapts its behavior to the changes in the environment and evolves according to users' requirements. Thus, the system can better satisfy users' requirements in the next period of time. Operation of the environment driven software systems as a whole can be regarded as an iterative process as follows: "Satisfying users' requirements in a specific period of time ⇒ Interacting with the environment ⇒ Adapting system behavior ⇒ Satisfying users' requirements in the next period of time".

From the perspective of system objective, software systems based on the environment driven model differ from traditional software systems in their emphasis on system evolution. One specific property of the system (e.g., the correctness) is only one aspect of the system objectives in a specific period of time. The control layer adapts system behavior and enables the system to satisfy different requirements of the users in different periods of time. Thus, in accordance with the emphasis on environment driven system operation, software systems based on the environment driven model no longer pursue the absolute achievement of one specific system property as traditional software systems do. They have changed to pursue comprehensively satisfying the users' requirements that may change from time to time.

From the perspective of system development, traditional software systems are developed once and used in different environments for a quite long period of time. In developing software systems based on the environment driven model, the details of program design and software development are shielded by the abstraction of services for the ultimate users. The process of software development has changed to that of continuously selecting the best service and acquiring the value-added services. In this process, the evolving paradigm of system development, supported by autonomous software entities and the separated coordination mechanism, is embedded in its own various software development techniques, including software reuse techniques based on component composition.

From the perspective of system lifecycle, software systems based on the environment driven model have lifecycles emphasizing on system evolution and adaption. They are quite different from lifecycles of traditional software systems, which are static and mainly focus on system development. One possible model might be: "Requirement analysis and prediction of possible changes + Analysis on system environment and its reduction $\Rightarrow$ Design of the objective system + Design of environment programs + Design of the environment-aware system + Design of control on system evolution $\Rightarrow$ system implementation based on environment driven model $\Rightarrow$ interaction with the environment and system evolution $1 \Rightarrow \cdots \Rightarrow$ interaction with the environment and system evolution n".

In order to provide the enabling techniques and middleware infrastructure supporting the environment driven model described above, we work on techniques for environment driven model based on ontology and prototype middleware systems supporting environment-aware software systems development. The details are discussed in the following Sects. 3.3 and 3.4.

3.3   Environment Modeling and Enabling Techniques

As discussed above, the primary characteristics of the environment driven model are "explicit representation of the environment information, hierarchical interaction and evolving system architecture". The explicit representation of environment information has three layers: sensing and collection of raw environment information, modeling and management of environment context, and interpretation for the application. Setting context modeling and management as the core and taking into account the lifecycle of environment information, the process of context processing and application can be described as in Fig. 3.4.

In the "initial state", the environment information is sensed and acquired by different kinds of software and hardware sensors, and becomes the "raw data". With the raw data, we conduct context modeling, decide the grammar structure and semantic information of the data, and model the raw data as explicit "context information". In general, context, which is based on fusing multiple sources of information and explicit logical reasoning, is called "high-level context". Otherwise, it is called "low-level context". Context information should be effectively stored and managed in the computer system. It should also be provided to the application as efficient, flexible, practical and accurate services. As the application proceeds and the environment changes, the context information might be frequently updated and replaced. If the

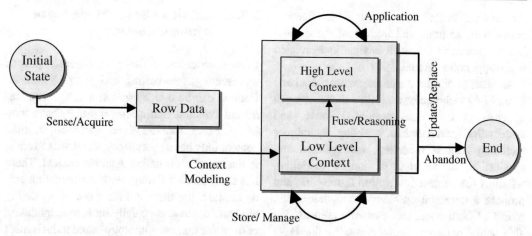

Fig. 3.4 Process of environment context processing and application

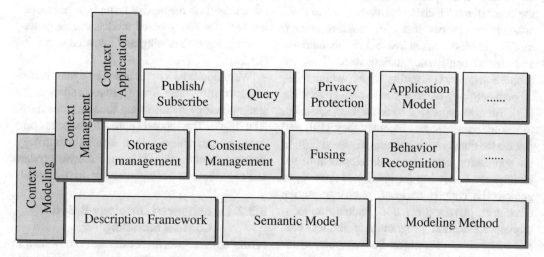

Fig. 3.5 Framework of key techniques for context processing

context information is not used by any application, it comes to an end.

3.3.1   Context Processing Framework

Analyzing the process of environment context processing and application from the perspective of software systems, the core requirements of explicit representation of context information are context modeling, context management and context application. In the light of this, a framework of enabling techniques for context processing can be described as in Fig. 3.5.

In the framework proposed above, context modeling is the basis for context information management and application. Context modeling usually has three aspects of techniques: description framework, semantic model and modeling method. The above context modeling forms the layer of context management. The context management layer involves context storage, consistency management, context fusion and other techniques, which provides important support for utilization of context information. On top of the framework is the layer of context application, which is supported by the layer of context management. It directly copes with the application and provides unified, effective, convenient, accurate and individualized context information service as well as techniques related to the application model.

In order to discuss the environment model and its enabling techniques, we follow the framework of enabling techniques presented above, and systematically researched enabling techniques including context modeling, management and application. In the layer of context modeling, we study the context description framework, and propose a universal ontology-based description model of both static and dynamic context. We also study ontology engineering. In the layer of context management, taking into account the context model discussed above, we explore enabling techniques including context storage model, context fusion/reasoning techniques, and context consistency maintenance. Then we propose an context reasoning engine, which relies on both ontology-based and rule-based reasoning [18]. We also propose a back-tracking approach to resolution of context inconsistency [19], and discuss the quality maintenance of context [20]. In the application layer, during development of the middleware FollowMe for intelligent spaces, we explore the context retrieval, publish/subscribe of context, privacy protection, middleware techniques, application programming model, etc., and make some progresses. For example, as for context retrieval, we propose a distance-based algorithm for context query optimization [21]. As for privacy protection, we propose an privacy protection method based on blurring degree [22]. As for context publication, we propose a context selection scheme based on negotiation [23]. As for the application programming model, we propose a pluggable programming model [18]. The research results discussed above cover different layers of the framework we propose. They constitute an infrastructure, which supports explicit representation of environment information. In the following section, we briefly introduce our work on ontology modeling, query optimization, privacy protection and context selection.

3.3.2 Ontology-Based Modeling of Dynamic Context

Context modeling is the most important part of representing, interpreting and utilizing context. Context can be divided into two categories: static and dynamic. Static context usually has a long lifecycle (e.g. Tom is a teacher). In contrast, some context only has a short lifecycle, such as "Tom is in the room". It is called dynamic context. There has been much existing work on modeling static context, but there is little work on modeling dynamic context, especially on formal modeling of dynamic context. Ontology-based models meet the requirements of context modeling better than other models in the field of formal context modeling [24]. Ontology-based models enable context sharing, logic reasoning and knowledge reusing [25,26].

We propose two approaches to dynamic context modeling. The first approach enhances the static ontology by attaching time features in the RDF triple. The second approach integrates time ontology and state machine with static ontology. Both approaches are used in our FollowMe system and contribute to our environment driven model.

3.3.2.1 Enhanced Ontology-Based Context Modeling

As discussed above, there exist static and dynamic environment contexts. Time information is essential to the dynamic context. However, static ontology-based modeling techniques and tools (e.g. Jena et al.) lack effective representation, management and application support for time information. Therefore, it becomes intuitive to enhance static ontology models with time information description and management, in order to model dynamic context. In this chapter, we propose an enhanced ontology-based context model, which adopts static ontology to model static context, and adds time stamp and lifecycle description for dynamic context modeling.

In detail, the static ontology model consists of top-level ontology and domain ontology. It mainly

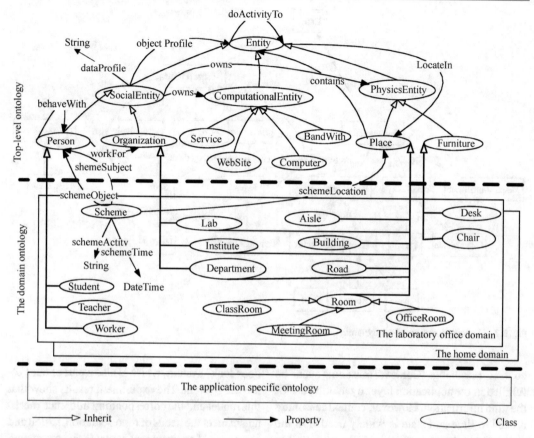

Fig. 3.6 Two-layer ontology structure

defines common concepts, domain specific concepts and their interrelations. Static ontology was represented by the RDF triple (subject, predicate, object), as shown in Fig. 3.6.

Based on the model discussed above, static contexts are organized as a set of static ontology instances, such as (Tom, type, teacher). From the aspect of the dynamic context modeling, we append the context lifecycle TTL and timestamp of context generation. TTL denotes the life period of a context while timestamp means the UNIX time when the context is generated or updated. The traditional RDF triple representation is extended to quintuple (subject, predicate, object, TTL, timestamp). Similarly, dynamic contexts are organized as a set of instances of the enhanced ontology, such as (Tom, locateIn, RoomA, 1200, 20071025034524).

In our smart space infrastructure FollowMe [18], we tried to apply the model described above

and research lifecycle management and conflict resolution of dynamic contexts, using the time information added in our context model [20]. The experiment results showed that the model proposed above worked well in static context processing, but it is still to be improved in dynamic context processing, especially in dynamic context fusion and reasoning.

3.3.2.2   Dynamic Ontology-Based Context Model

Besides modeling the time information of dynamic context, there is also other important information, such as changes of state (e.g. "Tom left RoomA") to be modeled. In a common sense, sensors can only provide the state of objects, but cannot provide the changes of states. For example, location sensors can detect people's location, but cannot detect changes of location. Thus, acquiring this kind of context relies on

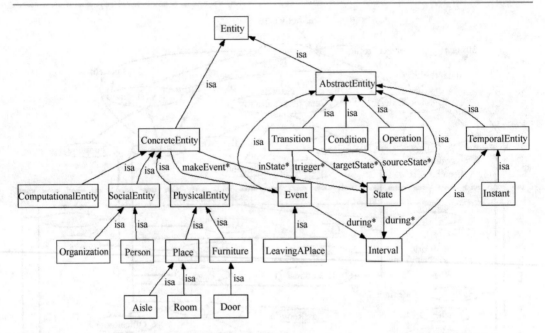

Fig. 3.7 Context model based on dynamic ontology

context reasoning. Context reasoning can be fulfilled in the application layer by making use of the time information. However, context reasoning related to time and state is widely needed in the environment driven applications. So we expect to model time and dynamic contexts in the ontology level, in order to benefit the applications.

In the light of the problem discussed above, we propose a dynamic ontology-based context model. Our model combines the W3C working draft OWL-Time (http://www.w3.org/TR/owl-time/) and UML state machine theory [27]. It also consists of the ontology level and the instance level. In the ontology level, especially in the top-level ontology, we introduce TemporalEntity and its subclasses in OWL-Time, as well as the ConcreteEntity and its subclasses in classic top-level ontology. We also design the DynamicEntity and its subclasses, including State, Event, Transition, Condition and Operation. The structure of the model is shown in Fig. 3.7.

In the ontology model discussed above, we also propose corresponding semantic explanation and reasoning rules for the newly designed TemporalEntity and DynamicEntity. In our experiments, we apply this method in an "environment driven

door-lock" system, which is also a part of our FollowMe System. The experiment results show that this model and the corresponding inference mechanism meet the needs of representation, fusion and reasoning of environment contexts that are related to time and state.

3.3.3   Logic Distance-Based Context Retrieval

Contexts in an open and dynamic environment are inherently distributed and are of huge volume. It thus becomes a critical problem on how to retrieve large amounts of context data efficiently in a distributed environment.

Existing work mainly used ontology-based semantic indexing to accelerate context queries [28,29]. However, the lack of a definitive ontology for this purpose makes it difficult to apply ontology-based semantic indexing in practice. In order to solve this problem, we define the logic distance between contexts from the perspective of the locality of context querying. We then propose a novel method of context indexing based on the distance between contexts. The rationale of the proposed method is as follows. We first give a formal description of contexts and define the context distance based on query patterns. Then we build logic clusters of contexts according to the distance metric we define. Finally, we optimize the performance of context query by making use of the logic clusters.

3.3.3.1 Formalization of Contexts

Assume that there are m different types of contexts $C_1, C_2, \cdots, C_m$ and a set of q different context-aware applications $A_1, A_2, \cdots, A_q$ in a large-scale smart environment. $C_i (1 \leq i \leq m)$ is defined as a q-dimensional vector:

$$C_i = (p_1, p_2, \cdots, p_q), \qquad (3.1)$$

where $p_j (1 \leq j \leq q)$ is the number of times A_j accessing C_i per unit time. Obviously, $p_j \geq 0$ for all j. This vector provides a formal description of the query pattern of C_i.

3.3.3.2 Distance Between Contexts

Given two types of contexts S and T (e.g., S is the light context and T is the temperature), let $S = (s_1, s_2, \cdots, s_q)$ and $T = (t_1, t_2, \cdots, t_q)$. Firstly we calculate the normalized inner product of S and T.

$$\cos(S, T) = \frac{\sum_{j=1}^{q} s_j t_j}{\sqrt{\sum_{j=1}^{q} s_j^2} \sqrt{\sum_{j=1}^{q} t_j^2}} \qquad (3.2)$$

Formula 3.2 presents the similarity of S and T from the perspectives of queries. Then, we give the definition of context distance between S and T.

$$D(S, T) = \sin(S, T) = \sqrt{1 - \cos^2(S, T)} \qquad (3.3)$$

It can be proved that the definition of D satisfies the nonnegative ($D(A, B) \geq 0$), reflexive ($D(A, A) = 0$), symmetric ($D(A, B) = D(B, A)$) and triangular ($D(A, B) + D(B, C) \geq D(A, C)$) conditions. Hence, it is a well-defined distance metric. Briefly speaking, if two types of contexts are often queried by applications at the same time, they tend to have small logic distance upon the definition above.

3.3.3.3 Context Clustering

We group "close-by" contexts into clusters based on the distance defined in formula 3.3. That is to say, the contexts in the same cluster have relatively similar query patterns. The clustering algorithm is based on k-means, and is described as follows:

(1) Randomly select k contexts as the centers of the clusters. (2) For each remaining context, assign it to the cluster whose center is the nearest to the context. The distance between a context and the center is calculated by the D function. (3) Compute the means of the new clusters and assign them with the new centers. (4) If there is no change, exit. Otherwise go to step 2.

This algorithm can be proved to be convergent. The value of k (number of clusters) should be decided before clustering.

3.3.3.4 Applying Clustering Results to Context Retrieval

Unstructured P2P network is a typical storage structure of distributed data and is also an important management environment for huge amount of contexts. We choose to apply our work in the unstructured P2P network *Gnutella*, and improve the flooding query method it adopts. Shortcuts are built (i.e. peer ID and IP address are cached) among peers that contain contexts of the same cluster. Therefore, when querying a context, it is only one hop away from the one that has been cached, and flooding is no more necessary. According to the clustering algorithm presented above, the smaller the k is, the more the shortcuts are built, and the smaller the average search path is, but the larger the cache space consumption and the maintenance cost for the change of network topology is. We should make trade-offs when deciding k in practice.

3.3.3.5 Performance Analysis and Comparison

We carry out evaluations on the performance of the context retrieval and distance metric we propose. Compared with the original Gnutella, when $k = 10$, and the number of peers is 1000, the average length of the search path is decreased by 20 %. When the number of peers is 10000, the search path is shortened by about 40 %. The performance improvement is obvious. The more the peers are, the greater the improvement is. When the number of peers is fixed, the smaller the k is, the shorter the average search path is, but the larger the cache space cost is. When k decreases, the improvement also decreases. The evaluation demonstrates that it is a good trade-off between the performance and the space cost to set k at 10 when the number of applications is 30 and the types of contexts is 128.

We compare the distance metric in formula 3.3 with the traditional Euclidian distance. The evaluation shows that the performance of our metric always outperforms that of the Euclidian distance, when the number of peers is more than 100.

As discussed above, the context clustering results can be used to improve the performance of context retrieval. It can also be applied to measure the semantics between two contexts. For example, if we execute our algorithm based on a large amount of queries that are collected from real-world context-aware applications, we can study semantic relations among contexts in the same cluster without any ontology interference. Since two words appearing frequently in the same web pages are proved to have some degree of semantic relations [30], it is conceivable that two kinds of contexts, which are often queried together, are also correlated in semantics. However, context clustering has many other applications that have not aroused our attention. This is among our future work.

3.3.4 Blurring Degree-Based Privacy Protection

Software systems running in an open and dynamic environment will continuously and proactively collect different kinds of environment information, especially information about the users. Protections of different kinds of private information are necessary in this process. Privacy deals with certain rights of individuals with respect to the collecting, processing and using of personal information [31]. Privacy protection focuses on the fundamental infrastructure, basic methods and tools to ensure the right of privacy.

Context publication in a computing environment involves three types of participants (Fig. 3.8): data owners, data collectors and data users.

Data collectors automatically collect context information from data owners. Data collectors keep context information in the database. Data users query data collectors for the context information. Data owners have the right to access specific data during the entire process. Context publication under privacy protection is to publish only the appropriate information to appropriate people in appropriate cases. That is to say, data owners hope to have more choices concerning what to disclose and how to disclose, so as to protect their privacy in different cases. Meanwhile, data users may also hope to protect their own privacy such as anonymity in using data.

Considering different kinds of data processing techniques [32–34], we propose our own privacy protection mechanism named Shadow, based on the definition of the blurring degree of context. This mechanism is partially implemented in the FollowMe [22] system.

Access control is often used to protect data owners' privacy. Data owners need to provide policies for publication of its context information and to indicate how to control the access to the data. So, data collectors are responsible for protection of the owner's context information according to the policies. A policy p can be represented as follows:

$$p = (subject, target, action, condition, dd)$$

For example, the policy

$$p_1 = (student, FollowMeGroup, faculty$$
$$.getLocation(), rest_time, 0.3)$$

means that if a student queries the location of a faculty of FollowMeGroup at rest_time, the blurring degree of this context should be less than 0.3.

Sometimes the system needs to generate new policies by itself based on historical information, since there might not exist any policy for a query. In the following new policy

Fig. 3.8 Participants in context publication

$a = (subject, target, action, condition, v_a),$

v_a can be defined as

$$v_a = k \sum_{k \in SP} v_i \frac{t(d(a, p_i))}{\sum t(d(a, p_i))} \qquad (3.4)$$

where SP is the set of historical policies, which have the same values of subject, target, action and condition with policy p_i, k is a normalized parameter, $t(\cdot)$ is a threshold function, and $d(a, p_i)$ stands for the distance between policies a and p_i.

When the data collector receives a context query, it should blur this context first and then return the blurred information to the inquirer according to the owner's policy. We propose an Ontology model-based blurring algorithm, as illustrated in the following example (Fig. 3.9).

For any attribute p, we define "$p.from$" and "$p.to$" to identify the range and domain of p. If $a = p.from$ and $b = p.to$, $b = a.child$ and $a = b.parent$, we can calculate the Blurring Degree (BD) of any entity in the model above by the formula below:

$$\begin{cases} BD(x) = \begin{cases} (ACC(x))^{-1} + \omega(x)DIFF(x), & if \ |x.child \neq 0| \\ 1, & if \ |x.child \neq 0| \end{cases} \\ \\ \omega(x) = \dfrac{\sum\limits_{x_i \in x.child} p_i BD(x)}{\sum\limits_{x_i \in x.child} BD(x)}, \\ \\ ACC(x) = MAXHEIGHT(x) + 1 - IMP(x), \\ DIFF(x) = (ACC(x) - 1)^{-1} - (ACC(x))^{-1} \end{cases}$$

$$(3.5)$$

where $IMP(x)$ is the maximum length of the paths from the root to node x. $MAXHEIGHT(x)$ is the height of the subtree X.

In Fig. 3.9, $MAXHEIGHT = 4$, IMP (*isolation booth*) = 4, and IMP (*hospital*) = 1. Then we obtain BD (*isolation booth*) = 1, BD (*sickbed* 375) = 1, and BD (*sickroom building*) = 0.42.

If a patient is in the "isolation booth" and his blurring degree is set at 0.5, any queries about his

location can only get "sickroom building". Location information "sickroom building" serves as a blurring of "isolation booth".

Besides, we consider two kinds of anonymity in the Shadow mechanism: anonymity for ID and anonymity for context. Anonymity for ID helps data users use pseudonym in a query. Anonymity for context hides the context information in an equivalence class of some indistinguishable attributes, such as K-anonymity [35], L-diversity [36] and T-closeness [37].

Traditional anonymity algorithm uses equivalence classes that contain unnecessary information, thus affecting privacy protection. The deficiencies of traditional anonymity algorithm are:

- Traditional anonymity algorithm uses obfuscation to protect the demanded record, but the record itself is still in the set. If an attacker can ignore some of the confusing candidates by some method, he might deduce the demanded information.

- Traditional anonymity algorithm involves other records in the database without extra data processing. An attacker might get unexpected information from the query.

- Every record of the context information in the equivalence class that a traditional anonymity algorithm returns exists in the database. That means once one certain record has been sensed, all other records in the same equivalent class can be inferred, which is also a kind of privacy disclosure.

- Traditional anonymity algorithm guarantees that the groups are constant. However, when the attribute of a data owner is changed, the attacker can immediately discover the change, for the answer set differs.

In summary, we improved the T-closeness algorithm and added some redundant information in the equivalent class returned by the algorithm [22].

Fig. 3.9 Part of ontology definition context structure for location in hospital

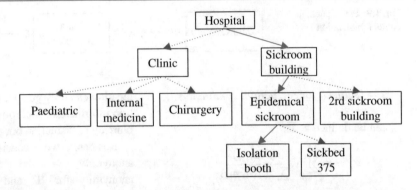

3.3.5 Negotiation-Based Context Information Selection

In the open environment context information is provided by different context providers with different qualities and may be conflictive [38]. So, when the requesters are unable to decide which information to select, negotiation among context providers is necessary.

We propose a reward-based negotiation model to deal with this problem. In this model, context providers negotiate with each other to decide who can provide appropriate context information and how they distribute the proceeds. The basic process is shown in Fig. 3.10.

As in Fig. 3.10, one application asks the Context manager for a specific type of context, the manager may find that providers A and B both satisfy the requirement. Then the manager tells A and B to negotiate with each other to decide which should provide the context information. Both A and B get their reputation information from the reputation database at the beginning of the negotiation process. When the negotiation is completed, the chosen provider will provide the context information to the Context manager. Then the Context manager delivers the information to the application and also stores this information in the Context Knowledge Database, where the current and historical context information is stored. The application also sends feedback information about the provided context. The Context manager will update the reputation information of the chosen provider according to the feedback information. Context manager also gives the proceeds to providers according to the feedback information.

During the negotiation, providers A and B convince each other by providing the reward of next negotiation [39]. Context providers' utility functions are used to evaluate offers and rewards.

The following is the utility function of provider A to evaluate the offer and reward at time t:

$$U_A(o, ep, t) = (w_1^A \cdot U_c^A(c) + w_2^A \cdot U_{ep}^A(ep)) \cdot \delta_A(t). \tag{3.6}$$

In the utility function, o means provider A's offer. Note that $o = (c, p)$, where c represents context information, p represents the percentage of proceeds which may be given, ep represents the percentage of rewards sent to persuade the opponent or given by the opponent in the next negotiation, t is the current moment, w_1^A and w_2^A are weights given to the proceeds and rewards respectively, and $w_1^A + w_2^A = 1$. Details can be found in [23].

The possibility that provider A is selected can be evaluated by the percentage of the proceeds A

$$U_c^A(c) = w_{c1}^A \cdot f_d(d) + w_{c2}^A \cdot f_{rep}(ref), \tag{3.7}$$

where the function $f_d(d)$ means the distance between the application and the context provider, function $f_rep(ref)$ represents the reputation of the context provider, w_{c1}^A and w_{c2}^A are weights given to the distance and reputation, and $w_{c1}^A + w_{c2}^A = 1$.

According to experiments, we find that:

- Normally, the context provider with lower distance and higher reputation gets more opportunities to provide context. The negotiator that failed gets a less portion of proceeds.
- Even when the context provider has a little longer distance or a little lower reputation than

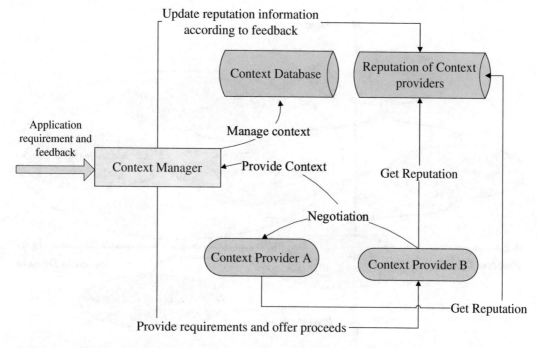

Fig. 3.10 Mechanism for context selection using a reward based negotiation

its opponent, it also has the chance to provide context, if it agrees to share more proceeds with its opponent or provide reward in the next negotiation.

- If other factors are similar, the context provider with higher initial reputation usually has more opportunities to provide context, and its reputation is enhanced when the task is finished.

3.4   Goal-Driven Adaptation and Rearon Ontologies

Taking an open, dynamic and uncertain execution environment into consideration, it becomes necessary for the software systems to exhibit some environment driven adaptation behavior to fulfill user's goals and guarantee the quality of services. By "environment driven" we mean that the system's capability of adapting both its structure and behavior according to the explicit context information from the external environment. The point here is to interpret the context into some application goal related events according to domain knowledge and application requirements.

Further, following the architectural prescription rules, those events trigger architectural behaviors, which finally lead to the dynamic reconfigurations of the systems. So first of all, it is desirable to build a generic and user-oriented description mechanism with some automatic reasoning ability to describe the application goals, the environment context and the architecture of the coordination systems. Upon this description mechanism, customizable, scalable and efficient transformation facilities are needed, in addition, to integrate the knowledge of the three parties, to evaluate the status of the running system and to make appropriate commands to carry out system evolution processes.

An ontology is an explicit and formal specification of the conceptualization of the common understanding in the knowledge of a given domain. It facilitates the interactions between different entities, including human beings and computing components, at a relatively high abstraction level. By applying some appropriate ontology description language, such as OWL-DL, it is also feasible to realize the automatic and efficient reasoning with some mature logic

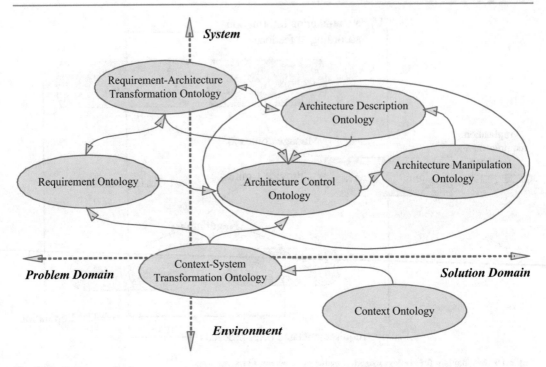

Fig. 3.11 Rearon ontologies

tools, for instance, the Description Logic. We design a series of ontologies based on OWL, named Rearon (Requirement and Architecture Ontologies), to describe the requirement goals, environment context and software architecture as well. In this section, we present Rearon first and then introduce the transformation facilitates designed for Rearon.

3.4.1 Rearon Ontologies

As shown in Fig. 3.11, Rearon consists of a set of ontology models, which cover both the problem domain and the solution domain, and depicts both the runtime system and execution environment. Roughly, Rearon can be divided into three sub-models: requirement ontology (RO), architecture ontology (AO) and context ontology (CO). On the respective boundaries of these three sub-models, the transformation ontologies (TO) are developed as the glue to get them connected. Currently TO includes requirement-architecture transformation ontology (RATO), requirement-architecture transformation ontology (RATO)

and context-system transformation ontology (CSTO).

3.4.1.1 Requirement Ontology

Requirement ontology is organized in three levels following the ideas from the field of requirements engineering [15,40]:

(1) Meta level ontology is the domain-independent abstract conception set, including Goal, Object, Agent, Action, etc.
(2) Domain level ontology is the common business conception set for some specific domain. For instance, an "online-traveling-service" application involves concepts of ticketing, planning, traveling, etc.
(3) Instance level ontology[1] describes specific instances for some given application domains. Following the above traveling application, One-Day-Beijing-City-Tour is an instance of the concept of traveling.

---

[1]In OWL instance data are also included in ontology.

Though RO is generally developed, it is not expected to be an alternative description tool for the goal-oriented requirement engineering, but rather the requirement specification of the adaptive behaviors of the environment driven software systems. Therefore, how to qualify the environment relevant requirements turns out to be the centric problem, which is solved using the Goal Refinement Tree [41] from the requirement engineering in our approach. On a Goal Refinement Tree, the higher level one node is located at, the more abstract it is and less operability it has. On the contrary, the lower level one is at, the more concrete it is and more operability it has. As the complete tree is more than enough for our purpose, only partial nodes are delivered. For example, taking an online ticketing system into account, its functional goals consist of querying, booking and so on, whilst the non-functional ones contain system responding interval, system security, etc. Generally, the former ones are relatively stable in a period whereas some of the latter ones could be varying constantly. For instance, as for the responding interval, it is decided by the networking situation and the running circumstance together. This goal, therefore, is divided into two sub ones: network latency and system responsivity. Furthermore, it is the latter that is relevant to the software system itself. This sub goal is thus chosen from the refinement tree as the one of the requirement elements for the development for the environment driven online ticketing application system. Please refer to [42] for the detailed describing syntax.

3.4.1.2 Architecture Ontology

As introduced in Sect. 3.2.2.2, the architecture ontology not only describes the static configuration but also the dynamic evolution of the software architecture of a system. Moreover, it specifies the control over the evolution processes targeting the requirement goals introduced above. Consequently, there are three architecture ontologies respectively: architecture description ontology (ADO), architecture manipulation ontology (AMO) and architecture control ontology (ACO). ADO corresponds to the general architecture description languages and mainly describes the static configuration of the architectures. AMO defines the actions to operate on the architectures. ACO associates AMO with ADO by specifying when to carry out the actions in AMO to manipulate the architectures described with ADO. AMO together with ACO achieve the dynamic management function over software architecture.

Besides, ADO and AMO also support architecture styles [43]. Architecture styles provide a terminological space for the software designers to communicate with each other and promote the reuse of the designs and the codes. So ADO and AMO are detailed into three layers, namely meta layer, style layer and instance layer respectively.

- ADO. The design of ADO takes ACME [44] as the reference. The details of its three layers are as follows:
(1) The meta layer has seven core concepts defined: Component, Connector, System, Port, Role, Representation and Rep-map. (2) The style layer defines the concepts for specific architecture styles. For instance, the Master/Slave style has the concepts of Master, Slave and so on. In addition to the attributes shared by all general components, they have some special ones adhered to the Master/Slave style. (3) The instance layer contains the description for a concrete architecture configuration, i.e., the instances of ontology. For example, in an online ticketing system designed and built in the Master/Slave style, aBusTicketService, aPlaneTicketService and aTrainTicketService are all instances of the ontology "Slave".
- AMO. AMO is applied to describe available reconfiguration actions for the architecture. Corresponding to ADO, AMO also has the three layers. Besides, the actions in these three layers can be further classified into global actions and partial ones respectively according to their working scope.
(1) In the meta layer there is a global action UpgradeArch as a upgrading function over the architecture. This action is a general abstract concept which is going to be reified into corresponding concrete one with respect

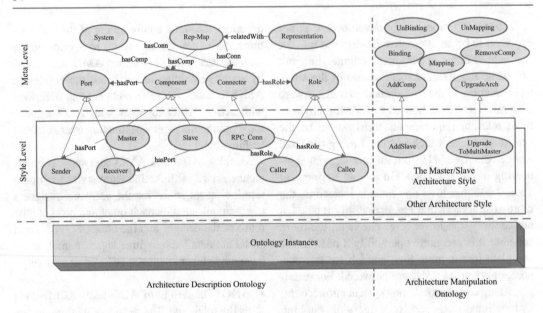

Fig. 3.12 ADO/AMO for the Master/Slave architecture style

to some specific style. There is also a set of primitive actions including AddComp, RemoveComp, AddConn, RemoveConn, Binding (bind ports and roles), Unbinding, Mapping (map architecture component such as a Slave to physical component such as an EJB) and Unmapping. (2) In the style layer there are style-specific actions. For example, respecting the Master/Slave architecture style, the global action of UpgradeToEMS can be defined to conceptualize the upgrading from the common Master/Slave style to the Extended Master/Slave style. And the primitive actions include AddMaster, AddSlave and so on, which interpret themselves literally. (3) Concrete actions specific to current applications are described in the instance layer. Figure 3.12 presents the ADO/AMO for the Master/Slave architecture style.

- ACO. ACO describes architecture dynamics, i.e., when an action or a sequence of actions defined in AMO should be carried out and what the intended consequence is. It often represents some essential properties for a certain architecture style. For instance, the rationale behind a Master/Slave architecture is that the performance capacity can be adjusted with addition/removal of slaves.

Information in ACO is merely triples of Condition-Operation-Consequence. Condition is the prerequisite of carrying out of Operation. Operation could be either a single action or a combination of multiple ones defined in AMO. Consequence is for the declaration of the effect of the Operation. It can be seen that neither RDF XML nor a graph can concisely describe ACO in terms of the readability. So the following intuitive approach is just taken.

Condition: ¬ satisfied (System.performance)
∧ full (Slave.capacity)
Operation: AddSlave
Consequence: ¬ full (Slave.capacity)

The primitive action shown in the above example demonstrates that an additional Slave is needed when every Slave's load reaches its capacity while the total capacity of the whole system is still expected to increase. After a new Slave is deployed successfully, all Slaves can be off the status of "fully loaded" again. The next example below is a combination of a global action and a primitive one. It depicts a solution, that is, to upgrade the common Master/Slave style into an EMS style, for the system performance issue when even the load of Master comes close to its capacity limitation. The EMS style has one more

Master than the original one. With the additional Master, the relation between Master and Slave as well as other system properties need to be reconsidered. Thus, the action UpgradeToEMS has to be executed in addition to the AddMaster action.

> Condition: ¬ satisfied (System.performance) ∧ full (Master.capacity)
> Operation: UpgradeToEMS, AddMaster
> Consequence: ¬ full (Master.capacity)

3.4.1.3 Context Ontology

Related techniques for the context ontology have been discussed in Sect. 3.3. Taking the application scenario of booking tickets online, the system responsivity is the main non-functional goal that is concerned. As argued above, it has two context items: UserExperiencedDelay, as the time interval from user request submitting to system response arriving, and NetworkLatency coming from some infrastructure which probes the networking situation between the users and the system. It is supposed to evaluate whether the system satisfies users by these two items.

3.4.1.4 Transformation Ontology

The well-designed RO, AO and CO can effectively describe the concepts within their respective domains. And they are good starts to glue software architecture with requirements/context. As we can see, there still are semantic gaps between above ontologies. So additional ontologies are developed to glue together concepts in different ontologies. So doing is somewhat like ontology mapping [16]. The mapping can be trivial for essentially coincident but differently represented concepts, or rather complicated with computations for related but different concepts.

Two ontologies are developed, namely Requirement-architecture transforming ontology (RATO) and Context-system transformation ontology (CSTO). RATO maps requirement concepts onto architecture concepts. And CSTO maps context items onto requirement concepts. As for our example of the online ticketing system, Responsivity_Goal in RO expresses the user requirement for the system responsivity with the property of rate while AO defines a performance property of system to label the system capability. At this very scenario, Responsivity_Goal.rate is essentially coincident to the System.performance. And such a coincidence is going to be caught with RATO. Similarly, the real responding time is the difference between the user experienced delay and the network latency. The conversion from UserExperience.interval and NetworkLatency.value into Responsivity_Goal.rate is done with CSTO.

3.4.2 Overall Interaction Patterns of Environment-Driven Applications

With Rearon ontologies, a unified knowledge model is proposed for the self-adaptive environment driven software systems. To achieve the desired adaptability against environment toward the application goals by utilizing the knowledge, appropriate transformation facilities should be built up. As Rearon applies OWL/RDF as its description language, the facilities are naturally a series of reasoning engines based on OWL/RDF. Though Description Logic is expressive, additional rules are still necessary to realize specific processing considering concrete applications in specific domains. Therefore, the transformation facilities contain multiple customizable rule engines besides standard reasoning engines for Description Logic.

Rearon ontology models together with the instances are stored at an ontology space in the format of RDF tuples (Fig. 3.13). A set of engines are deployed over the space to observe those RDF information. Also, each engine can generate new RDF information and inject, being regulated by a controller, them into the space. Or, they can also delegate the controller to remove some information out of the space. So actually, this is run as a blackboard system based on ontology. One Jena-based implementation of such a system is introduced in [45].

Four possible categories of the engines are enumerated as follows. The first is general OWL ontology reasoning engines, such as FaCT, RACE,

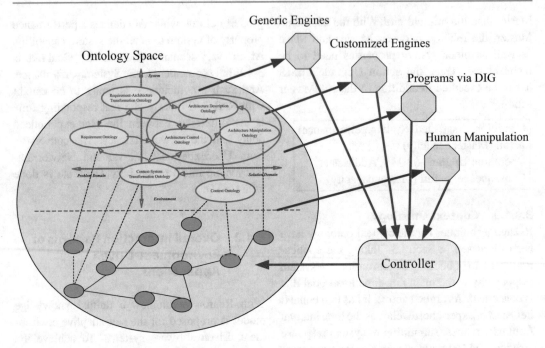

Fig. 3.13 Ontology space and engines

etc. The second is customizable rule reasoning engines. The rules are not limited with Description Logic or first-order logic, but can be like Event-Condition-Action or even specific Term Rewriting techniques, so that they are able to describe environment-adapting behavior directly and efficiently, which can support some complex and operational domain-specific processing. The third is programs directly accessing the ontologies via DIG interface. This category of engines is developed when automatic reasoning is not possible or the performance is the centric of concern. It can also be a communication channel between the system and the external to support the extending of system ontology. The last one is the user interface through which users can operate manually on the ontology space and adapting actions directly. In Refs. [42, 46], an adapting rule language is developed and the corresponding engine is proposed.

With Rearon and the transformation facilities upon Rearon, conceptually we bridge the gap between the environment context model and the adapting behavior of coordination systems with a problem domain oriented approach. Technically, we combine ontology-based reasoning and rule-based reasoning seamlessly and realize the triggering of the goal-driven evolution behaviors of application systems. The resulting architecture evolution actions can be put into execution by the runtime architecture objects introduced in the open coordination model on the fly [6]. By this stage, we build a generic and scalable framework to support the development of environment driven Internetware application systems.

3.5   Prototypes and Experiments

It has been several years since the emergence of applications that are self-adaptive to dynamic environmental changes. Such a kind of context-aware applications has experienced from non-organizational and ad hoc development methods (e.g. Active Badge [47], Cooltown [48]) to more principled methods which make good use of reusable toolkits (e.g. Context Toolkit [9]). Nowadays, most of context-aware applications depend on supports from the underlying infrastructure or middleware (e.g. Solar [49], SOCAM [26]), which can hide the heterogeneity of hardware and operating systems from upper layer applications and provide applications with execution and development environment. Based on some well-founded middleware, developers can construct and integrate complex applications in a more flexible and efficient way. According to the environment driven software model mentioned above, the coordination subsystem, environment handling facilities and goal-driven adaptation logic are essential in designing the supporting system for environment driven applications. In order to practise these three key techniques, we design and implemented some prototypes, i.e. Artemis-ARC, Artemis-MAC, Artemis-FollowMeLite and Artemis-FollowMeAgent (Fig. 3.14). Some environment driven applications are successfully developed based on these prototypes. These prototypes and applications promote to further study a more complete environment driven model and its corresponding middleware.

It should be noted that the aim of these prototypes is not to provide a complete supporting system and a killer application for the environment driven model but some initial proof-of-concepts for the aforementioned ideas and techniques. Although the Internetware paradigm as a vision for future software in the open network environment is increasingly evident, the full realization of this vision has two prerequisites that have yet to come now: there are massive autonomous software services deployed in the network, and there are

suitable business models for the industry of resource sharing and coalitions with sufficient satisfactory.

3.5.1 Artemis-ARC

The coordination subsystem is the central part of the supporting system for environment driven applications. It is the first step to realize self-adaptation according to runtime environment changes. Artemis-ARC designs and implements a coordination mechanism that introduces runtime software architecture object(s) to application systems. This object maintains the whole coordination structure of components/services. With this object, the interactions between components/services are decoupled and re-interpreted under a big picture of software architecture. The mechanisms from object oriented programming, such as inheritance and polymorphism, can be still applied upon the architecture objects to carry out a so-called software architecture oriented runtime evolution. Figure 3.15 shows the relationship among runtime software architecture, software specification, software implementation and external environment. The embedded runtime software architecture glues software specification with its implementation. A reflective architecture is established for system online evolution. Through modifying runtime software architecture, the system is evolved and the specification is updated synchronously [50].

Fig. 3.14 Some experimental prototypes for environment driven applications

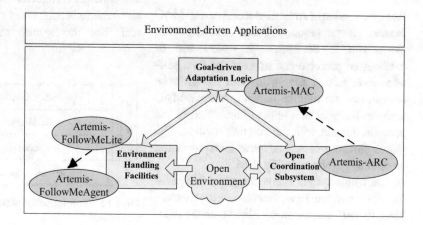

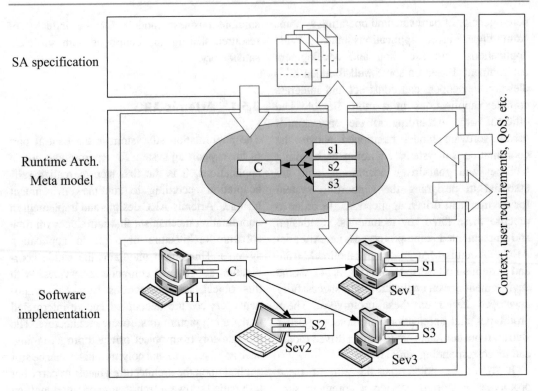

Fig. 3.15 DSA oriented Internetware coordination architecture

This runtime software architecture oriented Internetware coordination mechanism makes Internetware online evolution feasible. It provides supports for Internetware self-adaptation and environment driven online evolution. It is the basis of further development.

3.5.2 Artemis-MAC

As a new version of Artemis-ARC, Artemis-MAC focuses on the ontology based self-adaptation mechanism in Sect. 3.2.2. It makes use of ontology to perceive and express software self-adaptation related factors in both the problem domain and the solution domain. Artemis-MAC achieves the goal of a natural integration of the problem domain with the solution domain. The global structure of self-adaptive software based on ontology is shown in Fig. 3.16.

The whole system is constituted of five parts: the runtime system layer, the software architecture layer, the self-adaptation decision layer, the mon-

itor mechanism and the common services. The underlying supporting platform provides basic facilities, such as hardware, operating system, and network connectivity. The software architecture layer reuses the services of Artemis-ARC. It maintains current system configuration with a systematic global view, and observes some system properties. The software architecture layer consists of two parts: software architecture model and software architecture manager. The software architecture model takes charge of maintaining real time architecture information, including

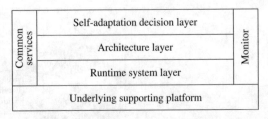

Fig. 3.16 Global structure of self-adaptive software based on ontology

system topology, component properties, etc. The software architecture manager is responsible of expressing the potential dynamic adaptations in software architecture layer according to adaptation decisions. It helps to indirectly adjust the runtime system structure and behavior. The software architecture manager implements the ontology-based adaptation executing engine for self-adaptive software and collects some information for monitors. The storage and usage of decision factors are separated from their producers and collectors. They are uniformly managed and manipulated by the newly added self-adaptation decision layer, which differs from other architecture based self-adaptive software.

The self-adaptation decision layer serves to maintain and manage decision factors and self-adaptation logics. It also chooses appropriate system adaptation strategies according to system real time status. The structure of this layer is shown in Fig. 3.17.

This layer treats decision factors and reasoning rules as input and system adaptation actions as output. From Fig. 3.17, we can see that this layer is made of three main modules: a decision factors management module, a self-adaptation logics management module and a self adaptation decision module.

- The decision factors management module is in charge of maintaining all decision factors of the whole system. This module receives decision factors from monitors. Ontology has prescribed a vocabulary to describe decision factors. These data will be stored into some database according to the properties of decision factors. Here we design two kinds of decision factors libraries: the standard and extended library. The standard library stores decision factors expressed in standard RDF tuples. The extended library stores other factors expressed in extended RDF. The extended library exists for processing those complex decision factors which cannot be easily expressed by standard RDF tuples.

- The self-adaptation logics management module maintains reasoning rules for adaptation strategies. The module receives user requirement specifications and validates these requirements with rule patterns. A rule pattern is used to ensure that input rules follow the pre-defined syntax. We classify rules into permanent rules and on-demand rules. Permanent rules participate in every time decision-making process; on-demand rules only take effect after their related factors change. This classification helps to reduce the scale of rule sets, and improves performance of reasoning.

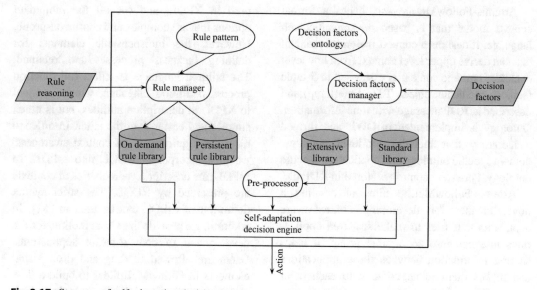

Fig. 3.17 Structure of self-adaptation decision layer

- The self-adaptation decision module includes a pre-processor and a decision engine. To guarantee the generality and efficiency of decision engine, it only supports reasoning standard RDF tuples. To deal with data in extended library, we design a pre-processor. This pre-processor can transform extended RDF data into standard ones according to pre-defined processing algorithm and transfer these data to the decision engine.

3.5.3 Artemis-FollowMeLite

In the lightweight platform Artemis-FollowMeLite, we practice some key techniques in environment handling facilities. OSGi techniques are employed in this platform to manage services flexibly and securely. We use semantic Web to establish an ontology based context model to support context sharing and reasoning. RDQL (http://www.w3.org/Submission/2004/SUBM-RDQL-20040109/) is chosen as context querying language. Workflow model is introduced to ease application development. Considering the multiplicity and instability of mobile device and wireless network, Artemis-FollowMeLite tries to proxy connecting service for different network connections. By deploying different components, it can adapt to multiple application environment.

Artemis-FollowMeLite establishes a formal context model that is based on semantic web language. It designs a context fusion mechanism that can derive upper level context from low level context. Dynamic context is expressed in 5-tuple (subject, predicate, object, TTL, timestamp) and described as RDF message with time information. Ontology is implemented in OWL and formed a hierarchy that includes top-level ontology, domain specific ontology and application specific ontology. Persistent context is stored in RDF file.

Artemis-FollowMeLite aims at creating a novel manner for developing context-aware applications. It tries to make scattered applications integrate into an organic group. It helps sharing information between these applications and makes them to negotiate with each other easily. We defined a specific workflow language to describe context-aware applications, named esPDL (Environment-sensitive Process Definition Language). Moreover, we design and implemented a workflow engine esWE (Environment-sensitive Workflow Engine) to parse esPDL and to support multiple context-aware application coordination.

- esPDL. esPDL is used to describe the business logic of context-aware applications. Each application is divided into multiple function modules (called processUnit), such as open-the-door, draw-the-curtain, and get-the-temperature-value. ProcessUnits can be shared by different applications, which greatly encourages the software reuse. The execution order and data exchange of prcessUnits are defined by esPDL. esPDL is written in XML-format, hence, the definition of application business logic is changed from hard-code to descriptive language. When developing a context-aware application, what we need to do is just giving an esPDL file and completing the processUnits that are needed. When we want to modify the business logic of the application, only the change of an esPDL file is necessary. Therefore, the easiness of software maintenance is greatly improved. esPDL is a tailored and modified XPDL. We omit the functions that are rarely used in XPDL, and cut off the redundant options that are complex and confusion-prone. However, the indispensable elements for defining business processes are retained. The tailored language is still a full-function process definition language, which is equal to XPDL in description abilities, but is much simpler and easier than the latter. In order to meet the requirements of context-awareness, we also incorporate RDQL into esPDL. In esPDL, the description and queries of contexts are presented by RDQL. The strict syntax definition of esPDL can be seen in [51]. In addition, we provide the visual toolkits for the development of context-aware applications. Users are allowed to drag and drop visual elements in FollowMeBuilder to build a flow chart of applications' business logic, which can be translated into esPDL file by the system automatically.

- esWE. esWE interprets and executes the business logic of context-aware applications defined in esPDL. esWE reads esPDL files and dispatches each processUnit to perform its work. Multiple applications can be run at esWE in a parallel fashion. The interactions between applications are also defined by esPDL and directed by esWE.

  esPDL supports the event mechanism. An important feature of context-aware applications is that they are triggered by events. For instance, an intelligent front desk system is triggered by the arrival of visitors; a guarding system is triggered by people's illegal entrance or exit; and the health care system for the old is triggered when the old has a fall or abnormal pulses occur. As our engine supports event mechanism, it simplifies the definition of business logic and improves the execution efficiency of context-aware applications. Moreover, esWE is able to interpret RDQL. As a result, it supports context communication among multiple applications, and bridges the context repository, context reasoning module and the applications.

- Pluggable programming model. Supported by esWE and esPDL, the development process of context-aware applications is simplified, and only an esPDL file and non-shared processUnits need to be written. In the Artemis-FollowMeLite system, each processUnit is a pluggable component (bundle) on the OSGi platform, and esPDL files (XML files) can be deployed dynamically. Therefore, the whole development process becomes a dynamic one. We call it a pluggable programming model. With this model, the complexity of application development decreases immensely, and the easiness of maintenance and flexibility of deployment are improved greatly.

3.5.4 Artemis-FollowMeAgent

Based on Artemis-FollowMeLite, we further studied how to enable user tasks to migrate in a per-

vasive computing environment in a "follow-me" style. The so-called "follow-me migration" means that user's tasks can move in the cyber space when user moves. All user task related information including application status, properties and context can simultaneously migrate and adapt to new available computing resources under the new environment. User can continue his tasks in his favorite manner at the new position [52].

FollowMeAgent platform is based on the service oriented infrastructure of FollowMeLite. It reuses most of OSGi services from FollowMeLite. The system architecture is shown in Fig. 3.18. The structure of the platform can be divided into physical layer, device access layer, service layer, agent layer and application layer. The physical layer consists of various hardware devices, such as communication devices like Bluetooth, GPRS, WLAN device, sensors and actuators, projector, printer, etc. This layer helps transform physical signals to computer readable data and transfer these data to device access layer. Device access layer integrates various devices in physical layer. These devices provide public interfaces in the form of OSGi bundle and further become services in service layer. Device access layer targets at supporting online pluggable devices. When necessary, it will download and install device drivers. Moreover it can automatically discover and integrate these new available devices into the FollowMeAgent platform.

Agent layer is the kernel layer in this platform. Agent containers with multiple agents run in the OSGi framework as bundles. The system assigns a customized agent for each user. This User Agent is responsible for responding to user's requirements, perceiving user's context, and capturing user's current computing task. Follow-me Agent is a specific user agent. It keeps sensing the user's position and has the capability of moving. Admin Agent provides user application management services, such as the life cycle management service, directory service, context management service, etc. The context management service is the critical service for follow-me migration. It fuses, classifies and reasons context from physical environment and users. System Service Agent provides some pluggable services and libraries. The appli-

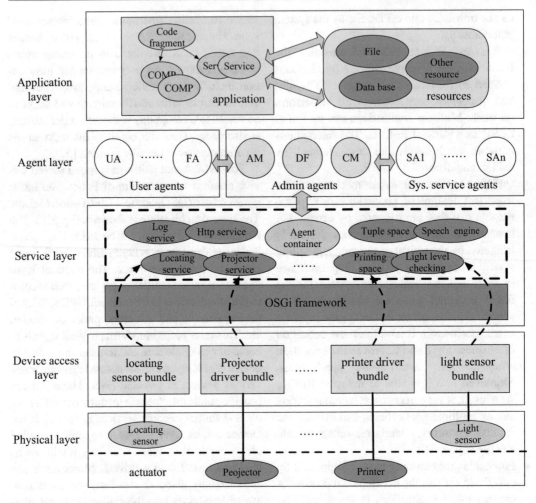

Fig. 3.18 Artemis-FollowMeAgent architecture

cation layer gets the services and libraries from the agent layer. The agent layer enables applications to migrate and re-configure.

3.5.5 Environment-Driven Applications

We developed a smart map application on Artemis-FollowMeLite prototype. It makes use of RFID technology to position object in a specific environment and dynamically establishes these objects on the map. When some object moves abnormally (for example, this object is stolen by somebody), the application will sound an alarm in time. Figure 3.19 describes system

physical deployment. Three RFID readers are deployed at corridor and monitored rooms. They frequently read information of RFID tags. RFID readers connect to computers, acting as context providers and send context information in specific format to context servers. Context servers are in charge of managing all context data in the environment. The servers can get high-level context through ontology and rules. When some context data, in which some applications are of concern, are created, the application can get concrete data by RDQL sentences or through event notifications. In order to accurately position objects, we deployed RFID readers with omni antennas in the rooms and RFIDs with beam antennas in the corridor. The terminal running

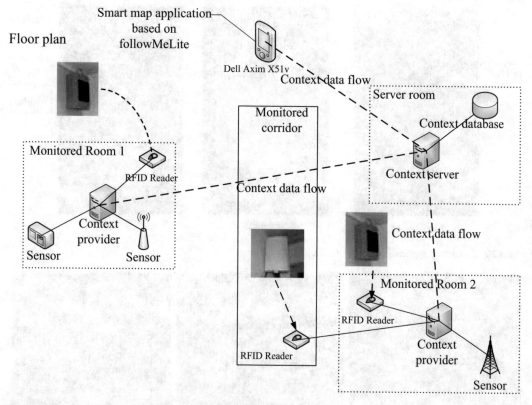

Fig. 3.19 Physical deployment of the smart map application

Artemis-FollowMeLite platform and the smart map application is Dell Axim X51v.

To facilitate integrating application logics and context information, we use esPDL files to describe the "smart map" application. Users trigger startup and shutdown of this application. When RFID tags are detected or found disappearing, the application can refresh tag contents according to real time context. Context servers deploy ontology and user defined rules set. All context information of this system will be passed to context server to reason. When reasoning module get the result of some object abnormal movement, the alarm will be sounded to show in the application GUI. Figure 3.20 shows the execution status of this map application running on Dell Axim X51v. At moment 1, IBM_T42 tag is shown in Room 510, tag txp is shown in the corridor. At moment 2, tag txp is shown in Room 510, and tag IBM_T42 is shown in the corridor. This time, the context server gets a reasoning

result that IBM_T42 abnormally moves from the rules: (1) tag IBM_T42 belongs to tag txp; (2) the safe domain of IBM_T42 is Room 510. When the workflow engine gets the message that tag IBM_T42 abnormally moving, it will trigger the alarm to notice the user as soon as possible.

Furthermore, we developed some "Follow-me" movable applications based on Artemis-FollowMeAgent platform, such as smart editor and smart media player. They both can migrate from PC or laptop to PDA or mobile phone, according to user position changes (Figs. 3.21 and 3.22).

By practicing these prototypes, we believe that an environment driven software model is feasible and effective. The ontology based context modeling technology and processing technology are feasible in achieving systematic, multi-layered and explicit environment processing. The dynamic coordination technology based on runtime software architecture can support

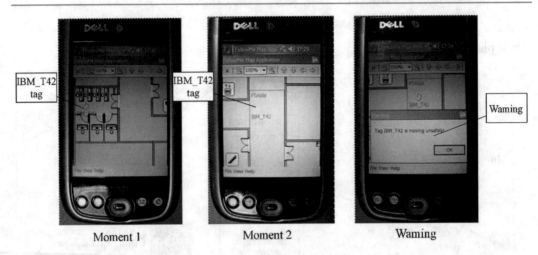

Fig. 3.20 Smart map application demonstration

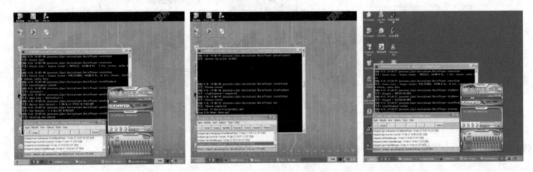

Media player running on laptop   When user leaves, pause the player   When user arrives at a new envi-
                                  and unload the application   ronment, the player migrates to
                                                                        the PC the users now uses, and
                                                                        resumes playing

Fig. 3.21 Migration of smart media player

system online adaptation. The ontology based technology and rule based reasoning technology can glue context model and architecture model together at a high level and thus get a complete software system with environment driven adaptation capability. We will try to assemble these prototypes in the next step and develop a relatively complete supporting platform for environment driven Internetware systems.

3.6 Related Work

It has become a great challenge, for more and more software systems, how to cope with open, dynamic and uncertain network environment.

There exists much related work addressing this problem. We discuss the representative work from the perspectives of key techniques involved in the Internetware-oriented environment driven model.

As for the explicit representation and processing of environment context, more attention should be paid to building formal and generic context models, and to developing context processing techniques for the environment driven model.

Concerning the explicit representation of environment context, the existing context modeling and processing techniques have evolved from proprietary processing to systematic modeling, from informal techniques to formal techniques, and

Editor running on PC   When user leaves, switch device   The editor migrates to a mobile
                                                                      phone with previous content

Fig. 3.22 Migration of smart editor

from processing static information to processing dynamic context. Context Toolkit [9] adopted
an informal context model, which models raw
context information by key-value pairs encoded
in XML. Context Fabric [53] defined a proprietary context description language to abstract context information. Ubi-UCAM [54], Browsing the
World [55], etc. used only a few terms to describe
the context information involved in the application. Meanwhile, Gaia [56] modeled context information by first-order-logic and represented context information by DAML+OIL. CoBrA [57]
used ontology to model context for an intelligent
space. The formal models described above have
greatly improved the context reusability, compared with the informal models. However, such
formal models mainly rely on the application logic
to model and process dynamic context information. They can be further improved concerning
the modeling and processing of dynamic context
information.

The existing techniques for context fusion,
retrieval and privacy protection are insufficient,
considering the requirements of environment
driven applications for systematic and high-
quality environment information services.
Existing techniques for distributed context
retrieval are mainly based on building indices for
context information using ontology. However, the
indices are built in an ad hoc way [29]. Existing
privacy protection techniques simply divide context information into two categories: accessible
and inaccessible [58]. This simple technique for

privacy protection lacks efficiency when applied
to large-scale context-aware systems.

Compared with the existing work, we set
system modeling as our research objective and
use ontology for building formal context models.
We use ontology to model time information
and dynamic context. Thus we obtain a context
model which achieves both static and dynamic
ontology engineering. We also make an attempt
to reason dynamic context. As for the related key
techniques, we measure the distance between
two pieces of context information from two
aspects: usage and query. Then we can cluster the
context information and improve the efficiency
of distributed context retrieval. By online calculation of the exposure of context information
based on the blurring degree, we adaptively and
efficiently protect privacy of context information.
We also address the issues related to handling
of dynamic context information, which are not
sufficiently addressed by the existing work.
Through modeling, management and application
of context information, explicit handling of environment from multiple perspectives is enabled,
and support for adaption of environment driven
systems is achieved.

As for the interaction between the software
system and the environment, the existing work
is mainly based on the principle called separation of concerns and decouples the processing of environment context and the application
logic. More attention should be paid to developing software models and enabling techniques with

which we can directly describe characteristics of the environment driven software systems. Part of the existing work focuses on supporting context-awareness in the middleware layer [9,59–62]. The collection and processing of environment context is managed by the middleware. The processing of context is made transparent to the upper-layer application, which enables the software developers to concentrate on developing the application logic. By processing context information in the middleware layer, we can develop generic context processing modules (e.g., context widget [9]). Such modules can be easily reused by dynamic reconfiguration of the middleware infrastructure.

Although processing context in the middleware layer liberates the application from the collection and management of context, it is still embedded in the application logic how to adapt the application behavior based on the context information. When developing context-aware applications in such a close-coupling way, the processing of context significantly complicates the development of systems. In the light of this, Martinez, Lopes et al. suggested that context should be handled in an upper layer and in an earlier phrase of application development. Martinez and Salavert [63] propose a conceptual model, which considers context-awareness as a newly added aspect of the software architecture. Components and connectors of the architecture can both explicitly collect and automatically process context information. Lopes and Fiadeiro [64,65] explicitly handled context- awareness as the first-class entity of software architecture. Thus, the software architecture could represent and organize context information involved in the system, and utilize context information in designing software components and connectors. In this way, the processing of context could combine and evolve with other components in the software architecture. Context processing and the application logic were separated in the software architecture. The techniques described above could work well with existing software architecture techniques.

Another kind of existing work focused on supporting context-awareness by the programming paradigm. When developers use traditional programming languages to develop context-aware applications, the handling of context spans across multiple functional modules of the program and is close-coupled in code of the application itself. Munnelly et al. [66] borrowed the idea of aspect-oriented programming and divided context information into fine-grained categories. Then, with regard to the fine-grained context information, fine-grained programming modules, which were easier to control, were developed. In this way, source codes for context processing were, to some extent, separated from the codes of the application itself. The understandability, maintainability and manageability of software were greatly improved. The work of Keays and Rakotonirainy [67] went one step further. They propose context-oriented programming based on the technique of code filling. In context-oriented programming, context independent part of the application was implemented as the skeleton, and the context dependent part as the stub. Different stubs could be filled into the skeleton based on changes of the context, which enabled context-awareness. In context-oriented programming, context is processed as the first-class construct, just like class in object-oriented programs.

The environment driven model proposed in this chapter processes environment information more explicitly and independently than existing work described above. Processing of environment information and the application logic itself are decoupled. In the layer of high level application objective and in domain knowledge definition, environment information and application logic are connected. Thus, they can evolve and be reused independently, in order to better satisfy the requirements of the open network environment.

3.7   Conclusion

In this chapter a software structuring model for environment driven systems is presented based on the observation and analysis of the behavioral patterns of Internetware applications. A set of related enabling techniques for the model, especially the modeling, management and utilization of context information, are developed. Several prototype systems are also built to give a proof-of-concept for the model and techniques. Surely these results are only an initial step toward the long-term objective of a methodology for environment driven Internetware applications. Future researches are planned to obtain a more mature and complete solution: On the aspect of environment modeling, the dynamism of context information should be directly modeled with formal tools such as temporal logic. The emergent environmental interaction behavior should be identified and managed to support the hybrid interaction pattern discussed in Sect. 3.2.1. The context fusion technique also has to be further enhanced for the highly open and heterogeneous environment. On the aspect of development methodology, the behavior patterns of various kinds of environment driven applications should be further understood so that abstract models and reusable implementations can be provided. Based on that, programming languages, methods and techniques can be provided to support the development of these applications in a disciplined and systematical manner. More realistic and non-trivial domain applications should be developed to validate the models and techniques. Last but not least, according to the roadmap to an Internetware methodology, it is also necessary to develop models and techniques for the evaluation and management of the trustworthiness of software entities and systems, and for the intelligent decision of how to maintain the sufficient satisfaction of system users, in the open, dynamic and uncertain environment.

Acknowledgments We thank Xu Feng, Hu Hao, Song Wei and Zhou Yu for their assistances.

References

1. J. Lu, X. Ma, X. Tao et al., Research and progress on Internetware. Sci. China Ser. E-Tech. Sci. **36**(10), 1037–1080 (2006) (in Chinese)
2. O.J. Dahl, K. Nygaad, SIMULA-an algol-based simulation language. Commun. ACM **9**(9), 671–678 (1966)
3. A. Goldberg, D. Robson, *Smalltalk-80: The Language and Implementation* (Addison Wesley, Reading, MA, 1983)
4. B. Meyer, *Object-oriented Software Construction* (Prentice Hall, New York, 1997)
5. G. Booch, *Object-Oriented Analysis and Design with Applications* (Addison-Wesley, Reading, MA, 1994)
6. J. Lu, X. Tao, X. Ma et al., On agent-based software model for internetware. Sci. China Ser. E-Tech Sci. **35**(12), 1233–1253 (2005) (in Chinese)
7. M.J. Wooldridge, *An Introduction to Multiagent Systems* (Wiley, Chichester, England, 2002)
8. G.D. Abowd, A.K. Dey, P.J. Brown, et al., Towards a better understanding of context and context-awareness, in *Proceedings of the 1st International Symposium on Handheld and Ubiquitous Computing* ed. by G. Goos, J. Hartmanis, J. Leeuwen. Lecture Notes in Computer Science, vol. 1707 (Springer-Verlag, Karlsruhe, Germany, 1999), pp. 304–307
9. A.K. Dey, D. Salber, G.D. Abowd, A conceptual framework and a toolkit for supporting the rapid prototyping of context-aware applications. Hum.-Comput. Interact. **16**, 97–166 (2001)
10. P. Dourish, What we talk about when we talk about context. Personal Ubiquitous Comput. **8**, 19–30 (2004)
11. T.R. Gruber, A translation approach to portable ontology specifications. Knowl. Acquis. **5**, 199–220 (1993)
12. X. Ma, Y. Zhou, J. Pan et al., Constructing self-adaptive systems with polymorphic software architecture, in *Proceedings of the 19th International Conference on Software Engineering and Knowledge Engineering*, ed. by S. Chang (Knowledge System Institute, Illinois, US, 2007), pp. 2–8
13. N. Medvidovic, R.N. Taylor, A classification and comparison framework for software architecture description languages. IEEE Trans. Softw. Eng. **26**(1), 70–93 (2000)
14. D.E. Perry, An overview of the state of the art in software architecture, in *Proceedings of the 19th International Conference on Software engineering* (ACM, Boston, 1997), pp. 590–591
15. A.V. Lamsweerde, Goal-oriented requirements engineering: a guided tour, in *Proceedings of the 5th IEEE International Symposium on Requirements Engineering* (IEEE Computer Society, Toronto, 2001), pp. 249-262
16. Y. Kalfoglou, M. Schorlemmer, Ontology mapping: the state of the art. Knowl. Eng. Rev. **18**(1), 1–31 (2003)
17. G. Antoniou, F.V. Harmelen, Web ontology language: OWL, in *Handbook on Ontologies*, ed. by S. Staab, R. Studer (Springer-Verlag, Germany, 2004), pp. 67–92
18. J. Li, Y. Bu, S. Chen, X. Tao, et al., FollowMe: on research of pluggable infrastructure for context-awareness, in *Proceedings of the 20th International Conference on Advanced Information Networking and Applications* (IEEE Computer Society, Washington DC, 2006), pp. 199–204
19. Y. Bu, S. Chen, J. Li, et al., Context consistency management using ontology based model, in *Current Trends in Database Technology*, ed. by H. Hopfner, C. Turker, B. Konig-Ries. Lecture Notes in Computer Science, vol. 4254 (Springer-Verlag, Berlin, Germany, 2006), pp. 741–755

20. Y. Bu, T. Gu, X. Tao, et al., Managing quality of context in pervasive computing, in *Proceedings of the Sixth International Conference on Quality Software* (IEEE Computer Society, Washington DC, 2006), pp. 193–200

21. S. Chen, T. Gu, X.P. Tao, et al., Application based distance measurement for context retrieval in ubiquitous computing, in *Proceedings of MobiQuitous 2007, Philadelphia, PA, USA*, 2007

22. W. Lu, *Shadow: Towards privacy protection in pervasive computing environment.* Master Thesis, Institute of Computer Software, Nanjing University, 2007

23. B. Shi, X.P. Tao, J. Lu, Rewards-based negotiation for providing context information, in *Proceedings of MPAC 2006, Melbourne, Australia*, 2006

24. T. Strang, C. Popien, A context modeling survey, in *Proceedings of First International Workshop on Advanced Context Modelling, Reasoning And Management at UbiComp 2004 Nottingham, England*, 2004

25. W.N. Borst, *Construction of engineering ontologies for knowledge sharing and reuse.* PhD Thesis. Enschede: University of Twente, 1997

26. T. Gu, H.K. Pung, D.Q. Zhang, Towards an OSGibased infrastructure for context-aware applications in smart homes. IEEE Pervas. Comput. **3**(4), 66–74 (2004)

27. J. Rumbaugh, I. Jacobson, G. Booch, *The Unified Modeling Language Reference Manual* (AddisonWesley Professional, 1998)

28. W. Nejdl, M. Wolpers, W. Siberski, et al., Super-peerbased routing and clustering strategies for RDF-based peer-to-peer networks, in *Proceedings of the 12th international conference on World Wide Web* (ACM, Budapest, Hungary, 2003), pp. 536–543

29. T. Gu, H.K. Pung, D.Q. Zhang, A peer-to-peer overlay for context information search, in *Proceedings of the 14th IEEE International Conference on Computer Communications and Networks, San Diego, CA*, 2005, pp. 395–400

30. F. Heylighen, Mining associative meanings from the web: from word disambiguation to the global brain, in *Proceedings of the International Colloquium: Trends in Special Language & Language Technology* (Standard Editions, Antwerpen, 2001), pp. 15–44

31. G.I. Davida, Security and privacy, in *Proceedings of the Fourth International Conference on Very Large Data Bases* (West Berlin, Germany, 1978), p. 54

32. M. Duckham, K. Mason, J. Stell et al., A formal approach to imperfection in geographic information. Comput. Environ. Urban Syst. **25**(1), 89–103 (2001)

33. M.F. Worboys, E. Clementini, Integration of imperfect spatial information. J. Vis. Lang. Comput. **12**(1), 61–80 (2001)

34. M.F. Worboys, M. Duckham, *GIS: A Computing Perspective*, 2nd edn. (CRC Press, London, 2004)

35. L. Sweeney, K-anonymity: a model for protecting privacy. Int. J. Uncertain. Fuzziness Knowl.-Based Syst. **10**(5), 557–570 (2002)

36. A. Machanavajjhala, D. Kifer, J. Gehrke et al., Ldiversity: privacy beyond k-anonymity. ACM Trans. Knowl. Discov. Data. **1**(1), 1–3 (2007)

37. N. Li, T. Li, S. Venkatasubramanian, T-closeness: privacy beyond k-anonymity and l-diversity, in *Proceedings of IEEE 23rd International Conference on Data Engineering*, 2007, Istanbul, 2007, pp. 106–115

38. C. Joelle, L.C. James, D. Simon et al., Context is key. Commun. ACM **48**(3), 49–53 (2005)

39. H. Raiffa, *The Art and Science of Negotiation* (Harvard University Press, Cambridge, MA, 2006)

40. A. Dardenne, A. Lamsweerde, S. Fickas, Goaldirected requirements acquisition. Sci. Comput. Prog. **20**(1–2), 3–50 (1993)

41. J. Castro, J. Kramer, From software requirements to architectures (STRAW01). SIGSOFT Softw. Eng. Notes **26**(6), 49–51 (2001)

42. J. Pan, *A design and implementation for a selfadaptive mechanism based on ontology.* Master Thesis (Institute of Computer Software, Nanjing University, Nanjing, 2007)

43. R.T. Monroe, A. Kompanek, R. Melton et al., Architectural styles, design patterns, and objects. IEEE Softw. **14**, 43–52 (1997)

44. D. Garlan, R. Monroe, D. Wile, Acme: an architecture description interchange language, in *Proceedings of the 1997 conference of the Centre for Advanced Studies on Collaborative research*, ed. by J.H. Johnson (IBM Press, Toronto, ON, Canada, 1997), p. 7

45. C. McKenzie, A. Preece, P. Gray, Semantic web reasoning using a blackboard system, in *Principles and Practice of Semantic Web Reasoning*, ed. by J.J. Alferes, J. Bailey, W. May, et al. (Springer, Berlin, 2006), pp. 204–218

46. Y. Zhou, J. Pan, X. Ma, et al., Applying ontology in architecture-based self-management applications, in *Proceedings of the 2007 ACM Symposium on Applied Computing* (ACM Press, New York, 2007), pp. 97–103

47. R. Want, A. Hopper, V. Falc et al., The active badge location system. ACM Trans. Inf. Syst. **10**, 91–102 (1992)

48. T. Kindberg, J. Barton, A web-based nomadic computing system. Comput. Netw. **35**, 443–456 (2001)

49. G. Chen, *Solar: Building a context fusion network for pervasive computing.* Ph.D. Thesis. (Dartmouth College, Dartmouth, 2004)

50. P. Yu, X. Ma, J. Lu, X. Tao, A dynamic software architecture oriented approach to online evolution. J. Softw. **17**(13), 1360–1371 (2006)

51. S. Chen, Y. Bu, Y. Li et al., Toward context-awareness: a workflow embedded middleware, in *Ubiquitous Intelligence and Computing*, ed. by J. Ma, H. Jin, L.T. Yang, et al. (Springer, Berlin, 2006), pp. 766–775

52. P. Yu, J. Cao, W. Wen et al., Mobile agent enabled application mobility for pervasive computing, in *Ubiquitous Intelligence and Computing*, ed. by J. Ma, H. Jin, L.T. Yang, et al. (Springer, Berlin, 2006), pp. 648–657

53. J.I. Hong, J.A. Landay, An infrastructure approach to context-aware computing. Hum.-Comput. Interact. **16**(2–4), 287–303 (2001)

54. S. Jang, W. Woo, Ubi-UCAM: a unified context-aware application model, in *Modeling and Using Context*, ed. by P. Blackburn, C. Ghidini, R.M. Turner, et al. (Springer, Berlin, 2003), pp. 178–189

55. G. Castelli, A. Rosi, M. Mamei, et al., A simple model and infrastructure for context-aware browsing of the world, in *Proceedings of the Fifth IEEE International Conference on Pervasive Computing and Communications* (IEEE Computer Society Press, New York, 2007), pp. 229–238

56. K. Henricksen, J. Indulska, A. Rakotonirainy, Modeling context information in pervasive computing systems, in *Pervasive Computing*, ed. by F. Mattern, M. Naghshineh (Springer, Berlin, 2002), pp. 79–117

57. H. Chen, T. Finin, A. Joshi et al., Intelligent agents meet the semantic web in smart spaces. IEEE Internet Comput. **8**, 69–79 (2004)

58. J.I. Hong, J.A. Landay, An architecture for privacy-sensitive ubiquitous computing, in *Proceedings of the 2nd International Conference on Mobile Systems, Applications, and Services* (ACM Press, New York, 2004)

59. M. Roman, C.K. Hess, R. Cerqueira et al., Gaia: a middleware infrastructure for active spaces. IEEE Pervas. Comput. **1**(4), 74–83 (2002)

60. P. Bellavista, A. Corradi, R. Montanari et al., Context-aware middleware for resource management in the wireless internet. IEEE Trans. Softw. Eng. **29**(12), 1086–1099 (2003)

61. T. Gu, H.K. Pung, D.Q. Zhang, A service-oriented middleware for building context-aware services. J. Netw. Comput. Appl. **28**(1), 1–18 (2005)

62. L. Capra, W. Emmerich, C. Mascolo, CARISMA: context-aware reflective middleware system for mobile applications. IEEE Trans. Softw. Eng. **29**(10), 929–945 (2003)

63. J.J. Martinez, I.R. Salavert, A conceptual model for context-aware dynamic architectures, in *Proceedings of the 23rd International Conference on Distributed Computing Systems: Washington* (IEEE Computer Society, DC, 2003), p. 138

64. A. Lopes, J.L. Fiadeiro, Algebraic semantics of design abstractions for context-awareness, in *Recent Trends in Algebraic Development Techniques*, ed. by J.L. Fiadeiro, P. Mosses, F. Orejas (Springer, Berlin, 2005), pp. 79–93

65. A. Lopes, J.L. Fiadeiro, Context-awareness in software architectures, in *Software Architecture*, ed. by R. Morrison, F. Oquendo (Springer, Berlin, 2005), pp. 146–161

66. J. Munnelly, S. Fritsch, S. Clarke, An aspect-oriented approach to the modularisation of context, in *Proceedings of the Fifth IEEE International Conference on Pervasive Computing and Communications* (IEEE Computer Society, Washington, DC, 2007)

67. R. Keays, A. Rakotonirainy, Context-oriented programming, in *Proceedings of the 3rd ACM International Workshop on Data Engineering for Wireless and Mobile Access* (ACM Press, New York, 2003)

On Self-adaptation Model for Internetware

4

Abstract

Being one of the basic features of Internetware, self-adaptation means that the software system can monitor its runtime state and behavior and adjust them when necessary according to pre-defined policies. Focusing on the three fundamental issues of self-adaptation, including the scope, operability and trustworthiness, a software architecture (SA) centric approach for Internetware's self-adaptation is presented in this chapter. All of the self-adaptive actions, i.e. monitoring, analyzing, planning and executing, are performed based on SA. In detail, runtime state and behavior of Internetware are represented and changed in the form of runtime soft-ware architecture. The knowledge for self-adaptation is captured, organized and reasoned in the form of SA so that automatic analysis and decision-making are achieved.

Keywords

Internetware · Self-adaptation · Software architecture · Middleware

4.1 Introduction

Internetware is a new software paradigm evolved by the Internet and it would be autonomous, evolvable, cooperative, polymorphic and context-

Parts of this chapter were reprinted with kind permission from Springer Science+Business Media: <Science in China Series F: Information Sciences, A software architecture centric self-adaptation approach for Internetware, volume 51, 2008, 722-742, Hong Mei, Gang Huang, Ling Lan and JunGuo Li, figure number(s), and any original (first) copyright notice displayed with material>.

aware [21]. One of the common technical challenges in the above characteristics is self-adaptability, i.e. Internetware is capable of perceiving the dynamic changes of its environment and adjust itself to meet its functionality, performance, dependability, etc. [17]. Though self-adaptation is not a unique issue in Internetware, whether the current research and practice results on self-adaptation can fit for Internetware is still unclear. To our point of view, to achieve systematic self-adaptation of Internetware, three fundamental issues should be addressed first:

- **Scope of Internetware self-adaptation**: i.e. what changes can be monitored and analyzed, and which adaptation can be executed? It is the primary issue that should be solved when trying to implement systematic self-adaptation of Internetware. Generally speaking, since Internetware belongs to artifacts, all changes in Internetware can be monitored and executed in some way. But the natures of Internet, such as openness, dynamicity and decentralization, limit the scope of Internetware's self-adaptation in practice.

- **Operability of Internetware self-adaptation**: i.e. how to achieve self-adaptation in a given scope, which is the core issue of Internetware self-adaptation? Taking Autonomic Computing [8] as an example. IBM presents an autonomic computing model from a practical view; that is, resources can be managed by monitoring, analyzing, planning and executing around some knowledge. According to the content of automation, Autonomic Computing is classified into five levels, from basic, managed, predictive, adaptive, to autonomic. Though the autonomic computing model and its classification levels present a general-enough operation framework for self-adaptation, they should be refined or specialized for Internetware, such as the concrete representation of knowledge, and the transformation between self-adaptation actions.

- **Trustworthiness of Internetware self-adaptation**: i.e. whether adaptive operations are correct and whether they can achieve anticipated results. It is the key issue to put Internetware self-adaptation into practice. The former needs to validate the functionality of Internetware after adaptive operations while the latter needs to evaluate the qualities such as performance, reliability and security (in fact, these qualities are the major objectives of self-adaptation). It should be noted that the scope of self-adaptation ensures that the trustworthiness of self-adaptation is a subset of that of the whole Internetware.

From a technical view, the above three issues can be considered as: how to understand the basic form of Internetware, how to monitor and analyze Internetware and make decisions, and how to evaluate the functionality and operational qualities of Internetware. In that sense, we argue that Software Architecture (SA) provides a feasible way to solve these technical challenges because:

- **SA provides a global, systematic and comprehensible model to confirm the scope of Internetware self-adaptation.** SA is the structure of a software system, described by a set of components, connectors and constraints [19]. SA can describe the basic form of Internetware, i.e. a set of agent-based software entities are running on different nodes of Internet, and a set of connectors enable the entities to interact with each other in multiple ways [12]. In that sense, Internetware self-adaptation is exhibited as the self-adaptation of the entities, interactions among the entities and the runtime environment. These elements can be modelled as the components, connectors and the constraints in SA.

- **SA supports the operability of Internetware self-adaptation**: First of all, the content of self-adaptation is decided by the acquisition (transforming implicit knowledge into explicit one), organization (transforming ill-structured or non-structured knowledge to well-structured one) and reasoning (transforming descriptive knowledge into reasoning one) of knowledge. As a kind of high-level, easy-to-analyze, easy-to-reason models, SA can represent knowledge of Internetware self-adaptation sufficiently and effectively. Secondly, being an important approach to analyzing and controlling the quality of a system, SA and its relevant techniques can directly support the monitoring, analyzing, planning and executing. Furthermore, performing these adaptive actions based on SA makes the entire self-adaptation process seamless and steady.

- **SA is helpful to the evaluation of the trustworthiness of Internetware self-adaptation**. In the traditional software development, SA is an important mechanism to guarantee the system qualities, including functionality, performance, reliability and security. SA provides supports for evaluating these qualities. As a natural extension of traditional software in Internet, Internetware can reuse or benefit from existing SA evaluation approaches and techniques. Along with the research on the SA model of Internetware [17], SA will play a more and more important role in the evaluation of the trustworthiness of Internetware self-adaptation.

Based on the above discussion, we propose a software architecture centric self-adaptation approach for Internetware in this chapter. The rest of the chapter is organized as follows: Sect. 4.1 gives an overview of the approach; Sect. 4.2 introduces the key techniques; Sect. 4.3 demonstrates the approach based on ECperf, a J2EE benchmark; Sect. 4.5 puts forward some related work and the last section concludes the chapter.

4.2   Approach Overview

SA centric self-adaptation is an approach that represents the knowledge by SA and adaptive actions are performed on SA. A self-adaptation model is shown in Fig. 4.1. In order to support the acquisition, organization and reasoning of knowledge, SA should provide four characteristics:

- **Reflective**: It means there is a causal connection between SA and the runtime state and behaviour of the target system. The changes of the target system will lead to the corresponding changes of SA and *vice verse*. Reflective SA is called RSA (Runtime Software Architecture) [9]. It confirms the scope of Internetware self-adaptation from a view of SA. It ensures that the analyzed changes and planed adjustments in the self-adaptation

are both accurate and consistent with the changes and adjustments on the target system. Furthermore, reflection of SA is a high-level abstraction of the management operations of the target system. Since it shields the details and heterogeneity of underlying management mechanisms in a certain degree, it makes our self-adaptation approach general enough.

- **Dynamic**: It means SA can accurately specify the changes and adjustments enabled by reflection, such as adding and deleting a component or connector, and modifying constraints. Dynamic SA (DSA) is a relatively new topic in SA research [14]. It is usually achieved by the predictions of designers and thus it is difficult to specify the runtime changes that are perceived by reflection. On the other hand, traditional DSA is usually supposed to be implemented by programming so that mismatches may occur between the adjustments described in SA and those performed by reflection at runtime. It makes adaptive planning incomplete or imperfect. So we provide a set of primitives to enhance traditional DSA from the view of reflection.

- **Reasoning**: It means that SA helps analyze the changes and obtain the corresponding adaptive adjustments by reasoning within a given scope. DSA must explicitly describe changes and corresponding adjustments (i.e. what-to-change and how-to-change), which can be automatically generated by reasoning on some rules (i.e. why-to-change). Reasoning is the key to implementation of the high level autonomic computing such as predictive, adaptive and autonomic. There are many types of reasoning rules and we now adopt three types: the ECA rules (Event-Condition-Action: for a given event, to decide the actions based on the condition), patterns (for a given pattern, to detect whether the pattern exists in the current system or not and transfer it to another pattern automatically) and styles (for a given style, to make the whole or part of the system manifest the style).

Fig. 4.1 Overview of
software architecture
centric self-adaptation
approach for Internetware

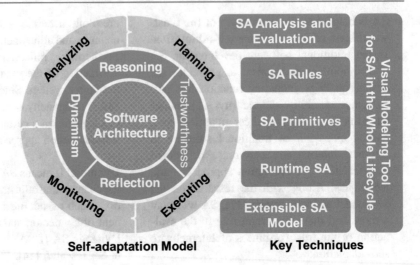

• **Trustworthy**: It means that the qualities of SA, such as the correctness of target system's functionality, performance, reliability and security, meet the requirements of users. Essentially, Internetware self-adaptation is a durative process to achieve or keep trustworthiness. The input of the process is an untrustworthy system and the output of the process is a trustworthy one. In other words, whether a system is trustworthy or not decides the start or stop of self-adaptation. Though trustworthiness evaluation and software self-adaptation are two relatively independent domains, we can reuse some existing results and experiences in SA validation and verification to solve the problems of self-adaptation's trustworthiness.

Based on the above four characteristics, the self-adaptive actions of Internetware can be performed automatically. In the monitoring, runtime state and behaviour of the target system are collected by RSA and described by DSA. In the analysis, the (static) SA of the target system together with the dynamic description generated in the monitoring is evaluated in terms of trustworthiness. If the target system is untrustworthy, planning activities are activated. Otherwise, the self-adaptation loop at this time is ended. In the planning, the source of untrustworthiness is identified and then a corresponding adaptation plan is generated by reasoning and described

by DSA. During the execution, the plan is transformed to operations of RSA which finally change the target system at runtime. These four phases make up of a self-adaptation loop and are processed circularly. It should be noted that people can participate in the loop to start or end it at any phase.

4.3 Key Techniques

4.3.1 Basic SA Model

Though there is no a standard SA model in the SA community, some widely accepted concepts on SA form the basic intension [14, 19]. We adopt the SA model defined by ABC/ADL [15] (Fig. 4.2) as a basic model for the SA centric self-adaptation because of the following reasons. Firstly, it defines all of key and common elements of SA, including components that encapsulate system's computing functionalities, connectors that enable interactions among components, a configuration that describes the topology of interacted components, and system-level constraints. Secondly, the SA model defined by ABC/ADL supports Internetware:

• Distinguishing the type and instance. Components and Connectors in Assets are type definitions whereas those in Instances element are

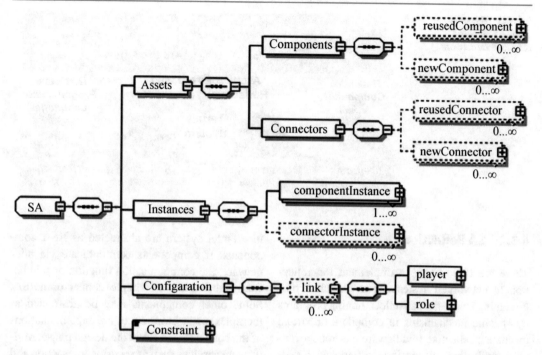

Fig. 4.2 The basic SA model defined by ABC/ADL

descriptions of component instances and connector instances. The separation between the type and instance makes SA model for Internetware a typed model, and as a consequence, architects can validate the designed model to ensure its correctness. Another advantage of the separation is that it helps reuse of component types and connector types.

- Distinguishing the reusable assets reuse and newly constructed assets. A newly constructed asset is different from reusable asset in that the former can be modified on demand, whereas the latter can only be used as a black box without any modification. So, it is necessary to distinguish between newly constructed asset (newComponent and newConnector) and reusable asset (reusedComponent and reusedConnector).

- Supporting simple yet effective configuration. A configuration decides the topology among component interactions. In order to cope with the diversity of interaction modes

among Internetware, ABC/ADL defines loose-coupled links to model these interactions. An analogue of link's semantic meaning is that a player plays a certain role. A player is corresponding to the computing functionality of a component, while a role is an abstract of communication functionality of a connector. Architects can specify the role of a component in the target system to fulfill requirements by a link definition.

- Supporting extensible constraint mechanism. One of the major reasons for the wide concern of SA in research and practice is that SA enables analysis at the early stage of system development. An architect tries to find the potential defects by such an analysis. The foundation of SA analysis is the constraint definition, such as the security, transaction and response time, in the SA model. Architects can extend the existing description to define, transform, guarantee and assess some special constraints.

Fig. 4.3 The software architecture based reflective framework

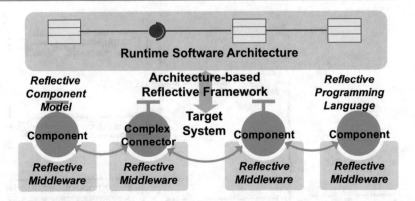

4.3.2 SA Reflection

There are three ways to implement the reflection in networked systems. The reflective programming languages can reflect running programs by specific mechanisms in compilers or virtual machines; reflective middleware can reflect running applications by specific mechanisms in middleware; reflective component models can reflect running components by pre-defined interfaces. Each way has its advantages and disadvantages. For example, the capability of reflective programming languages is the most powerful, but it is specific to languages and its abstraction level is too low and not systematic. The abstraction level of reflective middleware is higher, but its reflective capability is limited, in particular, it is difficult to reflect the details inside a component. The abstraction level of reflective component models is the highest and very close to SA, but its implementation depends on component developers and cannot reflect the environment of the component. In our approach, we use RSA to integrate all of the three ways while shield their heterogeneity and details to make the self-adaptation general enough.

As shown in Fig. 4.3, the main body of RSA is a reflective framework embedded in middleware [9]. The framework makes use of the reflective capabilities of both middleware and program languages. If a component deployed in middleware implements the interfaces defined by reflective component models, the interfaces can be invoked directly and thus the capability of reflective component models can be integrated. The components

in a target system are abstracted as RSA components. If components communicate via middleware, the communication function of middleware is abstracted as a (simple) connector in RSA. Some other components may be abstracted as (complex) connectors, if they are implementations of the connectors in SA at the design phase. Middleware services such as security, transaction and persistence are abstracted as constraints on components or connectors in RSA. The reflective capability provided by reflective component models is abstracted as the reflective interfaces of the components or connectors in RSA. The reflective capability of the programming language (i.e. Java) is utilized to implement or enhance the middleware-level and component-level reflection.

4.3.3 SA Dynamism

According to the elements in the SA model, dynamism in SA can be represented by three types of operational primitives on the SA elements, including entity primitive, relation (between entities) primitive and attribute (of an entity or relation) primitive, which can be formally defined as follows:

- An entity primitive is a 3-tuple R_E = (E, ID, OP), where E is the type of the changed entity (such as a host, service, component and call), ID is the unique label of the changed entity and OP denotes the operation performed on the entity (including "Add" and "Delete").

- A relation primitive is a 6-tuple $R_R = (E_1, ID_1, E_2, ID_2, R, OP)$, where E_1, ID_1, E_2 and ID_2 denote the type and label of the entities that the relation is associated to respectively, R is the unique label of the changed relation and OP is the operation, i.e. "Add" and "Delete".

- An attribute primitive is a 4-tuple $R_A = (E, ID, A, V)$, where E and ID denote the entity's type and label respectively, or E is NULL and ID denotes the relation's ID, and A is the name of the changed attribute and V is the attribute's value after change.

All changes that are monitored or performed by RSA can be described by the above primitives or their combinations. The set of operational primitives can be regarded as a kind of AML (Architecture Manipulation Language). Therefore, SA dynamism can be represented by the AML as a document independent of the other descriptions to make the SA models clear and flexible.

4.3.4 SA Reasoning

The knowledge for reasoning is often described as "IF THEN". We provide two types of reasoning knowledge representations in SA as discussed before: ECA (Event-Condition-Action) and SA specific representation, including patterns and styles. A pattern is an abstraction of a small part or fragment of an SA. Commonly used patterns include factory pattern, adaptor pattern, etc. A style is an abstraction of the whole, a big part or many fragments of an SA. Commonly used styles include pipes-and-filters style, three-layered style, etc. Structures abstracted as patterns or styles have positive or negative impacts on system's trustworthiness. And the self-adaptation in such a context can be classified into two kinds: eliminating those patterns or styles that have negative impacts, or incarnating those patterns or styles that have positive impacts. But in practice, only two types of self-adaptation are feasible: transforming negative patterns or styles to positive ones, or modifying the existing system to incarnate a positive style. As a result, there

are two types of pattern-based and style-based reasoning knowledge: one is "IF (there exists a certain pattern or style) THEN (transform it to another given pattern or style", and the other is "IF (the system satisfies some condition) THEN (modify the system to incarnate a given style)".

There are many description mechanisms for patterns and styles. To make the pattern-based and style-based knowledge easy-to-reason and easy-to-operate, we define a meta-model for describing the patterns and styles in our SA basic model, as shown in Fig. 4.4. *Component* element is used to describe different types of components in the system. *Connector* element is used to describe connectors among components. A *Component* instance can be linked to another *Component* instance in a *provide* or *require* relationship, while the linked *Component* instance act as the provider or consumer. *Service* element inherits from *Component* and *Service* instances stand for a kind of special components, i.e.. middleware services. *Host* element describes both hosts and middleware deployed on the hosts in a distributed environment. Two *Host* instances linked by a *connect* relationship stand for two hosts with some physical connection between them. The *Host* instance that contains a *Component* or *Service* instance implies that the component or service is deployed on the host. In addition, each type of entities in Fig. 4.4 has a set of properties to define the instance's states. Architects can not only model the application by *Component* and *Connector* instances and their relationships, but also model middleware capabilities by *Host* and *Service* instances and their relationships. The meta-model is also extensible in that architects can improve its modeling capability by extending the meta-model. Typical extended modeling capabilities include defining a specific type of component or defining a complex connector type. The dark elements in Fig. 4.4 are the extended elements from the core meta-model. *Method* element is used to specify the invocation between two component instances. A sequence of *Method* instances can be linked by *postInvoke* relationship to model an invocation sequence. *Proxy* is used to specify proxy components,

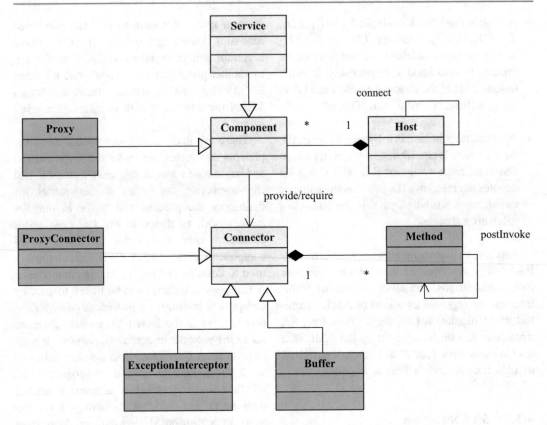

Fig. 4.4   The meta-model of software architecture's pattern and style

which are responsible for remote invocations in middleware. *ProxyConnector* is used to specify the links between ordinary *Component* instances and *Proxy* instances. *ExceptionIntercetpor* and *Buffer* elements are both complex connectors that help to specify exception-catching and request-buffering that will be used in the case study.

According to the patterns and styles specified by the above meta-model, the automated reasoning becomes possible, including (1) automatically detecting the given patterns or styles in a target system; (2) automatically generating a plan for transforming a negative pattern or style to a positive one, or at least, to that which has no negative impact on the system; (3) automatically generating a plan for modifying an existing system to incarnate a given style. We will give more details on these reasoning in the case study.

4.3.5   SA Trustworthiness

4.3.5.1   Correctness Evaluation

The correctness of Internetware self-adaptation includes two aspects: the target system is correct after adaptation and the adjustment operations can be executed accurately. Being a hot topic of SA research, SA V&V (validation and verification) usually add formal semantic models into the ADL (Architecture Description Language) and check some pre-defined properties or constraints by some formal methods. We integrate the V&V capability of ABC/ADL [1]: (1) The syntax-level V&V can check the matching of component interfaces and the topology properties of components and connectors; (2) The implementation-level V&V can check the compatibility with the target environment and type-matching of component invocations; (3) The semantic-level V&V can check some pre-defined constraints on system behaviors, such as dead-lock and live-lock, if some formal descriptions are available.

All adaptive operations are performed by reflection at last. But some operations should not or cannot be executed because of the limitations of the reflective framework, such as setting some values beyond the scope allowed by the underlying platform, accessing some resources protected by security mechanisms. In that sense, performing adaptive operations should not violate some constraints on relationships between the hosts and the components or services (e.g. the host should have enough resources for the components or services to be deployed), relationships between the components and services (the components have the right to access the services), and attributes (e.g. the value to be set is valid).

4.3.5.2   Effectiveness Evaluation

The target of self-adaptation is to guarantee the qualities. Before executing the adaptation plan, it is necessary to evaluate it to ensure that the adaptation will meet the users' anticipations. In current SA researches, there are a mass of algorithms to evaluate the qualities of a system and they can be reused in our approaches. In particular, the runtime environment should be taken into account so that the whole system can be evaluated in a systematic manner. For example, when using an algorithm for reliability analysis, data of both components and middleware services can be considered to evaluate the reliability of the whole system rather than only the application deployed onto the middleware [16].

On the other hand, quality evaluation is mostly carried out at design phase in traditional SA research and then some parameters are obtained by prediction. For instance, the time consumed in component operations or network transfers needs to be predicted when evaluating the response time of a system. Obviously, the evaluation results are not precise enough to reflect the realistic state of the target system. In our approach, the runtime information can be obtained by SA reflection on running system, and then the evaluation results become much more accurate.

4.3.5.3   Cost Evaluation

The cost of self-adaptation is the time and resources used to perform an adaptation plan. The cost should be predicted as exact as possible before performing the adaptation plan to ensure the cost-effectiveness ration is acceptable. Since the adaptation is performed at runtime in our approach, more time the plan consumes more impacts it may put. In that sense, the time spent during the plan execution can be regarded as the cost of the adaptation. The execution time of a plan is the sum of the time of all steps in the plan. Different plans have different steps, and then they will spend different time. We have presented a way to calculate the deployment time of different deployment plans in [23]. In that way, we concentrate on the time that all of the deployment steps consume. Based on it, a calculation of the adaptation time is provided as follows

$$
\begin{aligned}
Time_{refactor} = & \ T_{buffer} + T_{generate} + T_{transfer} \\
& + T_{deactivate} + T_{undeploy} \\
& + T_{deploy} + T_{activate}
\end{aligned} \tag{4.1}
$$

where $Time_{refactor}$ denotes the time which the adaptation plan consumes. Since the adaptation will consume some time, the user requests need to be saved in a buffer before the adaptation and be released after the adaptation. T_{buffer} denotes the time needed to buffer user requests and to release the buffered requests. $T_{generate}$ denotes the time needed to generate some assistant components for the adaptation, such as the interceptors. $T_{transfer}$ denotes the time needed to transfer the components or services to the target host. $T_{deactivate}$ denotes the time needed to deactivate the parts in the system which should be adjusted or replaced. $T_{undeploy}$ denotes the time needed to undeploy the parts which should be replaced. T_{deploy} denotes the time needed to deploy the new components or services. $T_{activate}$ denotes the time needed to activate the new components and services or update the configuration of the system. In this calculation, all possible steps in the adaptation are taken into account. But in a realistic system, most of the

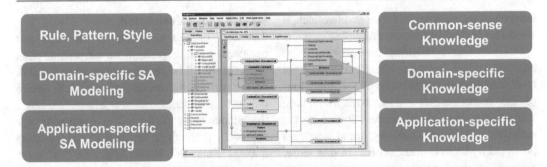

Fig. 4.5 An engineering approach to acquiring self-adaptation knowledge

adaptations only include a part of these steps. So we should select different steps for different adaptations when calculating the time. It is noticed that some of these steps can be performed parallelly, such as $T_{transfer}$, $T_{deactivate}$ and $T_{undeploy}$; that is, the new components or services can be transferred at the time when the old ones are undeployed or deactivated. It means that the factual cost may be less than the evaluation result in some cases.

4.3.6   A Tool for Modeling SA in the Whole Lifecycle

According to current experiences and achievements in the artificial intelligence and natural language processing research, it is impossible to implement a systematic self-adaptation without any human intervention in the coming future. Just as expressed in the Autonomic Computing levels, human intervention is inevitable for self-adaptation in practice. People can intervene the self-adaptation in two ways: the offline way is to participate in acquiring, organizing and reasoning the knowledge, while the online way is to participate in monitoring, analyzing, planning and executing the running system. In our approach, the knowledge is represented in SA and the self-adaptation steps are executed on SA. As a result, visualized modeling, monitoring and controlling of SA is a natural and user-friendly manner for human intervention in both offline and online ways. We employ ABCTool, a visualized SA modeling tool, to give a runtime SA view of the running system to facilitate online monitoring and controlling (Fig. 4.5) and to define SA models with reflection, dynamism and reasoning for Internetware at different lifecycle stages.

The major functionality of ABCTool is to provide supports for developers to model Internetware SA, including both domain-specific SA and application-specific SA, at each lifecycle stage. All these models and related activities contain the knowledge valuable to the self-adaptation. Let us take the classical SA design process as an example. An SA model would be continually refined until it passed the SA review. The classical SA design produces only one model that satisfies anticipated objectives. However, Internetware is multi-objective compatible and its objective is continually variable. It means that an SA model that does not satisfy the requirements at one time may satisfy the requirements changed in the future, while the current used SA model may not satisfy the future requirements. As a result, the SA model has to change time to time, which is a typical type of Internetware self-adaptation [24]. ABCTool can capture and store the engineering process of Internetware and corresponding artifacts, as shown in Fig. 4.5, which can be considered as an engineering approach for self-adaptation knowledge acquisition. It should be noted that the knowledge acquired by ABCTool can be divided into three types: the domain-specific knowledge acquired in the domain-specific SA modeling, the application-specific knowledge acquired in the application-specific SA modeling, and the common-sense knowledge such as the rules, patterns and styles.

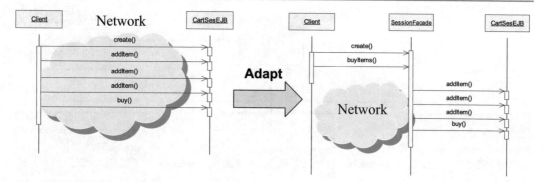

Fig. 4.6   The bad pattern in ECPerf and the adjustment

4.4   Case Study

ECperf is a standard J2EE performance benchmark from SUN Microsystems to measure the scalability, performance and cost of Java enterprise software systems. In this section, we will take ECperf as an example to demonstrate how the SA centric self-adaptation approach increases its performance and reliability. A reflective J2EE application server, PKUAS, is used as the supporting platform [9].

4.4.1   Pattern Driven Self-adaptation

As mentioned above, the trustworthiness of a system can be improved by transforming a negative pattern to a positive or harmless pattern. Such pattern driven self-adaptation is supported in our approach as follows: Firstly, administrators set up the pattern models using ABCTool, including the bad pattern models (describe the patterns with negative impacts) and the corresponding good pattern models (describe the patterns with positive impacts or harmless impacts); Secondly, the runtime information is collected and analyzed for discovering possible bad pattern instances in the target system; If some bad pattern instances are detected, the adaptation plan can be generated and described by the operational primitives mentioned above; Finally, the plan based on the SA model is mapped to the practical operations supported by the middleware, and then the actual adaptation is

performed. In this process, all steps can be fulfilled automatically except the first one, which should be finished by administrators.

4.4.1.1   Case Description

Imagine the following scenario in ECperf: as shown in the left part of Fig. 4.6, when a client wants to buy some items, we need to invoke the addItem() method to add the item to the shopping cart, and invoke the buy() method to commit the order. The problem with this scenario is that each call to the server is a remote call over the network, requiring the marshalling and unmarshalling, serialization and deserialization of parameters and return values, and data transmission through the network. Executing multiple network calls in this fashion will endow a significant negative impact on the performance. Therefore, these interactions are obviously qualified as a bad pattern, which is a kind of J2EE performance antipatterns named Fine-grained Remote Calls [5].

In order to eliminate the negative impact, the part of ECperf should be adjusted. One plan is to send the information of all of the items to Cart-SesEJB in a single bulk call. The classical EJB design pattern, Session Facade, can be applied in this situation. As shown in the right part of Fig. 4.6, a component named SessionFacade is added at the server side. The client invokes the buyItems() method to send the information of all items to the new component, and then SessionFacade invokes the corresponding methods of CartSesEJB.

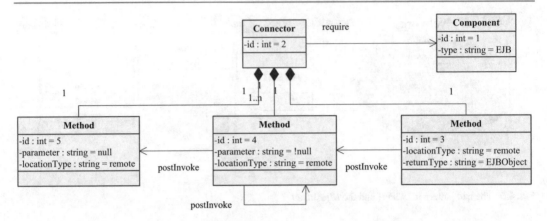

Fig. 4.7   The pattern model of Fine-grained Remote Calls

4.4.1.2   Detecting the Bad Pattern

In order to detect the bad pattern, administrators should set up the pattern model first. Figure 4.7 shows the bad pattern model in our case and it denotes a bad pattern: if an EJB receives a call sequence including a method call whose return value is EJBObject at first, followed by more than one method call whose parameter is not null, and ended by a method call whose parameter is null, it is a Fine-grained Remote Calls pattern instance.

During the detection process, the bad pattern model can guide the collection of runtime information. In this case, the information that needs to be collected is the method calls of all of the EJBs in the application, including the return value, the parameters and the call type (remote or local) of the method calls. After the information is collected, it is explored to match the bad pattern model and the result in this case is: CartSesEJB's call sequence create, addItem, addItem, addItem, buy, which denotes a Fine-grained Remote Calls pattern instance.

4.4.1.3   Building a Good Pattern Model

As shown in Fig. 4.6 we should change the source codes at the client side to get rid of the bad pattern. In order to transform the bad pattern into a good pattern by middleware adaptation without any modification on source codes, we need to set up a good pattern model as shown in Fig. 4.8.

In distributed computing systems, when calling a method of a component, the client never calls the method directly because the client and the component are running at different nodes. In fact the client will call the method in a component's interface implementation, called Proxy (also called Stub). When receiving a request, the Stub will delegate the request to the component in the remote server. There is also a Proxy at the server side (also called Skeleton). The Skeleton receives the remote requests and invokes the component at the server side after some preprocess (for example, unmarshalling the parameters). The Proxies are in charge of communication over the network, lying in the middleware layer and invisible to the application. They can be regarded as implementations of SA connectors. We can adjust the interaction between components by changing the Proxies. Compared to the bad pattern shown in Fig. 4.7, the good pattern in Fig. 4.8 adds two Proxies. The FacadeStub receives the request from the client and saves these requests until the whole call sequence is over, and it sends the information of all of the requests to the server. In fact, FacadeStub plays a role of adding the buyItems() method to the client. FacadeSkeleton plays the role of the Session Facade which is mentioned before. When receiving the requests from FacadeStub, it resolves these requests and sends them to CartSesEJB.

It is noticed that there are two views in this good pattern model: the part with solid lines is the application view, which describes the application only, and the one with dashed lines is the middleware view, which displays the actual behavior

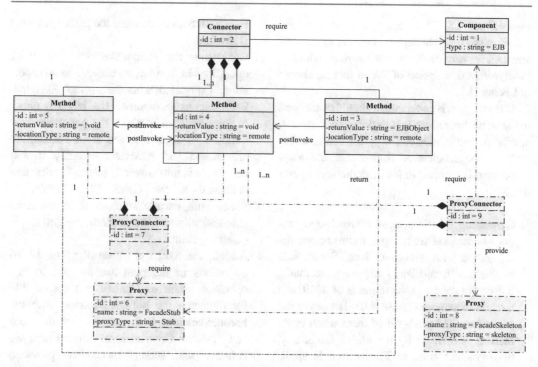

Fig. 4.8 The pattern models of Session Facade

```
1  1 : R_E ( Proxy , 6 , ADD ) ;
2  2 : R_A ( Proxy , 6 , name , FacadeStub ) ;
3  3 : R_A ( Proxy , 6 , proxyType , stub ) ;
4  4 : R_E ( ProxyConnector , 7 , ADD ) ;
5  5 : R_R ( Proxy , 6 , ProxyConnector , 7 , require , Add ) ;
6  6 : R_R ( Method , 3 , Proxy , 6 , return , Add ) ;
7  7 : R_R ( Method , 4 , ProxyConnector , 7 , composite , Add ) ;
8  8 : R_R ( Method , 5 , ProxyConnector , 7 , composite , Add ) ;
9  9 : R_E ( Proxy , 8 , ADD ) ;
10 10 : R_A ( Proxy , 8 , name , FacadeSkeleton ) ;
11 11 : R_A ( Proxy , 8 , proxyType , skeleton ) ;
12 12 : R_E ( ProxyConnector , 9 , ADD ) ;
13 13 : R_R ( Proxy , 8 , ProxyConnector , 9 , provide , Add ) ;
14 14 : R_R ( Component , 1 , ProxyConnector , 9 , require , Add ) ;
15 15 : R_R ( Method , 5 , ProxyConnector , 9 , composite , Add ) ;
16 16 : R_R ( Method , 4 , ProxyConnector , 9 , composite , Add ) ;
```

Listing 4.1 Pattern driven adaptation plan

of the middleware. From the application view, the model does not change but does change from the middleware view. It means that the adaptation can be achieved without modifying the application and all the changes in the middleware remain transparent or invisible to the application.

4.4.1.4   Planning and Executing

After the bad pattern instance is detected, the adaptation plan should be generated based on the SA pattern models. By comparing the bad pattern model and the good one, we can get a set of adjustment operations (i.e. the graph difference between

Figs. 4.7 and 4.8). These operations can be sorted based on the possible dependencies among them, and then we can get the adaptation plan, which is the dynamic description of SA in fact, as shown in Listing. 4.1.

Once the plan is generated, it should be mapped to the actual operations that middleware supports, and then the adaptation can be performed automatically by the middleware. In this case, the adaptation plan is mapped to four middleware operations:

1. Generating the FacadeStub: The 1–3 operations in the plan are mapped to this operation. Compared with a normal Stub, FacadeStub modifies both addItem() and buy() methods; it does not delegates the requests of addItem() method to remote CartSesEJB, but saves the parameters and sends all of them when buy() method is invoked by the client. Obviously, the implementation of FacadeStub is application specific, but the modifications on the methods are regular and they are pattern specific, and then the FacadeStub can be generated automatically. As a result, in order to execute the adaptation automatically, administrators should input the corresponding algorithms on the generation of the components for assistant after the pattern models have been set up. These algorithms are pattern specific and can be reused among different applications.

2. Adding the Stub Controller: The 4–8 operations in the plan are mapped to this operation. Stub Controller is responsible for replacing the normal Stub with FacadeStub and returning a FacadeStub instance when the create() method is invoked.

3. Generating the FacadeSkeleton: The 9–11 operations in the plan are mapped to this operation. Compared with the normal Skeleton, FacadeSkeleton modifies the buy() method. In this modified method, the parameters for multiple requests received from FacadeStub are parsed and refactored. Finally it will be divided into several method calls and delegated to the CartSesEJB. Similar to FacadeStub, FacadeSkeleton can be generated automatically and the generation algorithm is pattern specific.

4. Adding the Skeleton Controller: The 12–16 operations in the plan are mapped to this operation. Skeleton Controller is responsible for replacing the normal Skeleton with the FacadeSkeleton. It is noticed that the Stub and Skeleton Controllers mentioned here are common management mechanism provided by the middleware and can be used in different applications and different patterns.

4.4.1.5   Evaluating the Adaptation Result

Figure 4.9 shows the performance results before and after the adaptation. The details of runtime environment are described as follows: the BookEJB is deployed on a node with Pentium 4 CPU 2.8G and 1G memory; the web-tier components are deployed on a node with Pentium 4 CPU 2.4G and 256M memory; the database ECperf used is deployed on a node with Pentium 4 CPU 2.8G and 512M memory; the bandwidth of the network is 100M.

Fig. 4.9 Adaptation results of ECPerf

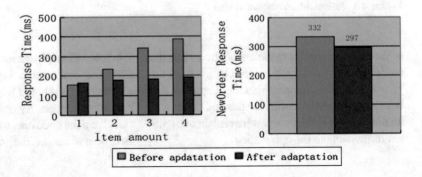

The left side of Fig. 4.9 shows a comparison of the response time of the call sequence "addItem*n, bu" before and after the adaptation. It can be concluded that after adaptation, the response time is decreased by 75 ms (millisecond) if the client adds one more item to the shopping cart. The reason is that one remote call will occur when adding a new item (i.e. the addItem() method is invoked once). A remote call mainly includes three more operations than a local call,: setting up the connection, transferring the data through the network, marshalling and unmarshalling the parameters and return values. When a remote call occurs, these operations will be performed and in this case they will consume about 70 ms. Multiple remote calls are replaced by only one remote call after the adaptation and the information required at the server side is sent in the bulk call, and then the cost on the network transfer decreases. The right side of the Fig. 4.9 shows the result from Order.summary, which is one of the formal reports of ECperf. The performance index here is the response time to create a new order, namely NewOrder Response Time. We can see that the response time decreases by nearly 10.5 %.

4.4.2   Style Driven Self-adaptation

Like the pattern, we can transform the negative style into a positive or a harmless one to improve system's trustworthiness. Unlike the pattern which abstracts a small part of SA and cannot be directly incarnated without changing the source codes, a style is a relatively global abstraction and then can be incarnated directly on running system without changing the source codes. In this section, we will take ECperf as an example to show how to incarnate a fault tolerance style in ECPerf directly by the self-adaptation.

4.4.2.1   Case Description
As a typical scenario in ECperf, ordering involves several activities in web browser as follows: a customer selects a product and its quality; adds the selected products to a shopping cart; clicked "order" button to summit the ordering request. The corresponding activities at the server

side include: OrderSes session bean invokes its newOrder method, in which a new OrderEnt entity bean instance will be created. The created OrderEnt instance is the corresponding object of a logical order entity. During OrderEnt entity bean's initialization, the customer's credit would be checked and various discounts are applied to the order. If all checks are passed, a new record would be generated and inserted into the database table. Most of these functions depend on the successful operation of J2EE data service. However, accidental network errors or transient database failures would make the data service unavailable, that is, the database connections managed by the data service become invalid, and all client requests using these invalid connections would fail.

To decrease the number of failed client requests during the data service failure, the data service should have capability of fault tolerance. In general, a fault tolerance mechanism includes two steps: error detection and recovery. The former aims to detect abnormal system states when faults are triggered. The latter tries to resume the system by recovering system states. Such fault tolerance mechanisms are usually orthogonal with the functions of the target system. This means that fault tolerance mechanism can be applied to the target system without impacting the functionalities. In that sense, fault tolerance mechanisms can be abstracted as fault tolerance styles, which can improve system reliability and availability if properly used [20, 22].

4.4.2.2   Defining Fault Tolerance Styles
Two classical fault tolerance styles are shown in Fig. 4.10a, b. The first style, exception-catching style, is used to detect errors based on the language level exception handling mechanism. It captures exceptions thrown at runtime and analyzes the exception trace to identify faults. The second style, buffer-redirector style, is used to recover faults. When a component failed, the style can recover system states by restarting the failing component and resetting its states. Meanwhile, all newly arrived requests would be buffered during the recovery and be redirected to the recovered component after its states

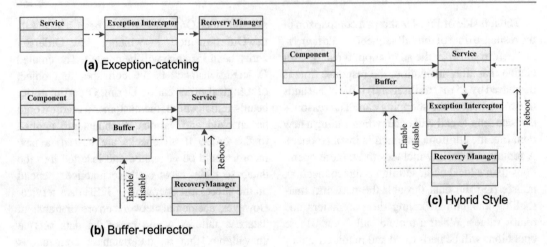

Fig. 4.10   A hybrid fault tolerance style of exception-catching and buffer-redirector

```
 1  1 : R_E ( ExceptionInterceptor , 5 , ADD )
 2  2 : R_A ( Exceptioninterceptor , 5 , name ,
        DataServExcepinterceptor )
 3  3 : R_A ( DataServExceptinterceptor , 5 , exceptionType ,
        SQLException )
 4  4 : R_R ( DataService , 1 , DataServiceExceptionMon , 5 ,
        thrownSQLException . ADD )
 5  5 : R_E ( Restartinterceptor , 6 , ADD )
 6  6 : R_A ( RestartInterceptor , 6 , name , ConnectionInterceptor
        )
 7  7 : R_R ( DataService , 1 , ConnectionInterceptor , 6 , restart ,
        ADD )
 8  8 : R_E ( ReqInterceptor , 4 , ADD )
 9  9 : R_A ( ReqInterceptor , 4 , name , ReqBufInterceptor )
10  10 : R_R ( DataServExceptinterceptor , 5 , RecoveryManager , 3 ,
        regFaultDetector , ADD )
11  11 : R_R ( RecoveryManager , 3 , RestartInterceptor , 6 ,
        regRecovery , ADD )
12  12 : R_R ( RecoveryManager , 3 , ReqInterceptor , 4 , callee , ADD )
```

Listing 4.2   SA Style Driven Self-adaptive Plan

were reset. To deal with the data service failure in ECperf ordering scenario, both exception-catching style and buffer-redirector style are needed. Figure 4.10c shows the resulting hybrid style.

4.4.2.3   Planning and Executing

To transform the original data service into a recoverable data service that satisfies the hybrid style, a set of adjusting operations are necessary. Comparing the structure of the original data service and that of the target one, a sequence of ordered operations can be generated as shown in Listing. 4.2.

Furthermore, the plan should be mapped into middleware management operations, which are responsible for changing the data service's structure at the implementation level. The following considerations should be taken. First, when database connections failed and as a consequence, the data service failed either, the data service would throw an exception to those entity beans that invoked the invalid database connections. From the view of SA, the exception will be propagated through the connector between the data service and the entity bean. Such exception propagation can be captured by an interceptor in the middleware. Second, restarting a component can be implemented by inserting an interceptor, which is responsible for updating database connections, into the data service. The interceptor stands between the data service and the database. At last, a new interceptor is inserted between the request redirector and component instance pool, not only blocking the allocation of component instances to new requests for OrderEnt session bean, but also resuming the allocation after recovery. A more detailed description of the above mapping of the plan is shown as follows:

1. Inserting a new interceptor (DataServExcept-Interceptor), which is responsible for capturing data service exceptions, into the EJB container interceptor chain (mapped by 1–4 operations in Listing. 4.2). The DataServExceptInterceptor implements handleException method and can capture all exceptions thrown by application components. In addition, the exception context would also be captured by the interceptor in order to justify whether the exception is caused by the data service.

2. Inserting a new interceptor (ConnectionInterceptor), which is responsible for recovering invalid database connections, into the data service (mapped by 5–7 operations). After database connections failed, the interceptor tries to obtain new database connections repeatedly. Once new database connections are obtained, invalid database connections would be substituted.

3. Inserting a new interceptor (ReqBufInterceptor), which is responsible for blocking the allocation of entity bean instances to client requests during the data service recovery, between the request redirector and component instance pool (mapped by 8–9 operations). Client requests in J2EE are processed only when it is allocated a component instance from the instance pool. As a result, blocking the allocation of entity bean instances ensures that no new request for the data service is processed. A filtering capability

makes the interceptor put little impact on the components that do not use the data service. After successful recovery of the data service, ReqBufInterceptor resumes the instance allocation.

4. Appending a recovery policy to the global RecoveryManager (mapped by 10–12 operations). The RecoveryManager is a fault tolerance framework for coordinated recovery of middleware services [11]. It is implemented as a middleware service and operates according to a set of recovery policies. Briefly speaking, the appended recovery policy can be described as: "if (DataServExceptInterceptor identified a data service exception) then (invokes ConnectionInterceptor to recover the data service and enables ReqBufInterceptor to block the instance allocation)". RecoveryManager operates as follows: (a) receives exception information from DataServExceptInterceptor; (b) starts ConnectionInterceptor to recover the data service after fault identification and enables ReqBufInterceptor to block the allocation of OrderEnt entity bean instances; (c) stops ConnectionInterceptor and disables the blocking of allocation after the data service is recovered.

4.4.2.4   Evaluating the Adaptation Result

We carry out a number of controlled experiments to validate the effectiveness of the fault tolerance style on middleware by self-adaptation. Fault injection, a widely used technique to simulate software faults, is used to trigger data service faults: a separate process stops the database periodically when the J2EE application server is processing customer's requests. At the same time, we use OpenSTA, an open source performance metric collector, to simulate a number of concurrent customer requests and collect runtime data. The number of requests that are successfully dealt with can be obtained and hence, the ratio of committed requests under data service failures can be obtained. Two recovery configurations are used, aiming at comparison: (I) only restarting the data service; (II) restarting the data service and enabling the buffer at the same time. To assess the performance impacts of different recovery con-

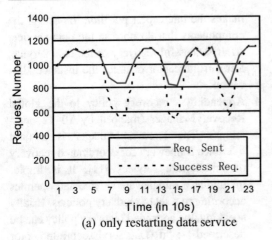
(a) only restarting data service

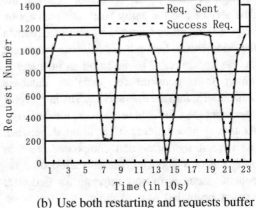
(b) Use both restarting and requests buffer

Fig. 4.11 Comparison of successful request numbers

figurations, the response time at the client side is recorded.

The fault injector injects database connection faults at the time of 60, 120, and 180 s to simulate transient database failures. The numbers of successfully committed customer requests are shown in Fig. 4.11, in comparison with the numbers of original requests. Style driven self-adaptation improves the reliability and availability of PKUAS data service from 55.04 % to 91.13 % and 99.38 %. In fact, higher ratios can be achieved by more complex fault tolerance styles, such as the coordinated recovery style [11].

Moreover, it should be noted that fault tolerance has a negative impact on the performance (Table 4.1). With style driven self-adaptation, the response time of ECperf in configuration I and II are increased by 1.5 % and 1.7 % respectively, when no data service failures happened. The performance impact comes from the recovery framework, i.e. RecoveryManager. When data

service failures happened, the response time in configuration I and II are increased by 12.5 % and 12.7 % respectively. The performance impact here comes from both recovery framework and blocked requests, because the requests that arrived during the data service recovery would be blocked until it is recovered. This would increase the average response time. As a conclusion, we find that different reliability and availability can be obtained under different fault tolerant styles, which have different performance impacts. Fault tolerance styles should be dynamically adapted according to runtime information in the context of Internetware. Moreover, reliability and availability improvement should not neglect the performance impact, and *vice versa*.

4.4.3   Performance Impact

In the above case study, we evaluate the performance impacts when executing the adaptation plans. Such performance penalty is inevitable and deserved because it only takes place during the adaptation and will bring significant positive results. On the other hand, monitoring probes the system operation and consumes extra resources and as a result, it will bring negative impacts on system performance. In particular, since monitoring is a continuous activity, its

Table 4.1 Average response time under different configuration(s)

	No Fault Tolerance	Configuration I	Configuration II
No faults	0.1021	0.1036	0.1038
Faults happened	0.1060	0.1193	0.1195

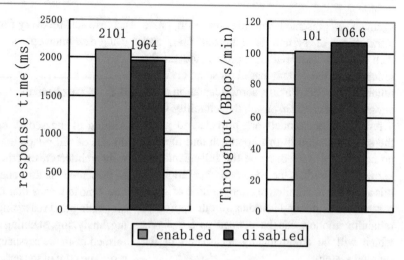

Fig. 4.12 Performance costs of self-adaptation

performance penalty lasts always and should be carefully controlled. Figure 4.12 shows that if the runtime information collection is enabled, the response time of ECPerf will increase by nearly 7 % and the throughput will reduce by about 5 %. The performance penalty is neither so heavy nor neglectable. Monitoring in our approach is usually done by the interceptors, which can be turned on/off and even installed/removed when necessary. Such configurability allows administrators to control the performance penalty of monitoring. It should be noted that monitoring system operation becomes a mandatory capability in more and more modern systems. It means that monitoring does not bring extra performance penalty which may be unacceptable any more but does contribute to the performance cost which is inevitable.

4.5   Related Work

At present, self-adaptation is a hot topic in the industry and some products or prototypes with self-adaptation have been developed. IBM, the advocator of autonomic computing, has gained some significant results. AutoTune is a typical instance of self-optimization [4]. It sets up the performance model between CPU, memory and two parameters of Apache server's configuration, and then Apache server can adjust the resource management policy automatically to meet the given goals of CPU and memory. LEO (Learning Optimizer) is a technique to increase the query efficiency of DB2 products [13]. It uses the optimization model to optimize the query, revises the model by the realistic query results and reaches the goal of self-optimization. Jann et al. did some work on dynamic reconfiguration of the physical resources such as memory, processors in IBM pSeries Servers, to get balance of the resources of multiple system instances and to achieve self-adaptation of the whole system [10]. Autonomic Computing techniques also experimented in the ANTS project of NASA [7]. In this project, runtime information is collected automatically, predictions on some performance goals are made by predefined algorithms, and finally relevant adjustments are performed. Although the approaches or techniques have the feature of self-adaptation, they all have some limitations. They always concentrate on the specific cases, specific products and specific environments. When these specific factors changed, the approaches or techniques become not applicable any more. In this chapter, the SA centric approach focuses on the common and fundamental issues in the self-adaptation including the scope, operability and trustworthiness. In particular, almost all knowledge and activities are based on the SA so that the approach is general enough.

Some researches apply the idea of model-driven approaches to self-adaptation. In ref. [3] a model driven approach for autonomic management is presented. In this approach, state information of system is collected first, and then analysis and predictions are made on the reliability of the system, based on some classical reliability models. Finally, some adaptation operations are performed to ensure the reliability. Only a few reliability models are provided to guide the self-adaptation in this approach and there is no common way to describe the self-adaptation knowledge. Further, the adaptation operations in this approach are limited to configuration of some parameters of the applications. In our approach, reliability models can be defined as SA styles which will be automatically incarnated in the running system.

Researchers on SA also concentrate on the self-adaptation. Taylor proposed an SA based evolution approach [18], that is, the SA of a running system can be optimized by the adjustments of the connectors. The adaptation operations on SA can be mapped directly to the applications that are developed with the specific programming framework, Java-C2. The Rainbow project proposed by Garlan separated the adaptation mechanisms from the applications to make them reusable and applicable in general while SA style is used as the knowledge to guide the self-adaptation [6]. Researchers in NanJing University provided an SA oriented self-adaptation system [2]. Two kinds of triggers are adopted during self-adaptation including the "IJEvent-Action-Rule" and the "IJActive Infinitive-Policy". And the self-adaptation operations are performed by RSA. All of the above approaches use SA to guide the self-adaptation at runtime. Compared with them, our approach has the following features: About the representation of the knowledge, our approach adopts three ways including ECA, SA patterns and styles. The latter two kinds of knowledge can be shown as graphs and are easy to define and reason; About the adaptation operations, our approach can not only change the applications, but also adjust the middleware context so that the scope of self-adaptation is wider and deeper. In the cases mentioned in this chapter, we can adjust the interaction between two components by changing the proxy components, and we can

achieve self-recovery for middleware services by using new interceptors.

4.6   Conclusion

Aiming at the scope, operability and trustworthiness of self-adaptation of Internetware, a software architecture centric self-adaptation approach is presented in this chapter. Software architecture centric means that the knowledge acquiring, organizing and reasoning as well as the monitoring, analyzing, planning and executing are all performed from the perspective of software architecture. The core of the approach includes a software architecture model with some new features such as reflection, dynamism and reasoning, a visualized modeling tool for software architectures in the whole lifecycle, and an architecture-based reflective middleware. The future work includes optimizing the prototype, improving the validation and verification, automating the acquisition of self-adaptation knowledge, and so on.

References

1. F. Chen, Q. Wang, H. Mei, F. Yang, An architecture-based approach for component-oriented development, in *26th International Computer Software and Applications Conference (COMPSAC 2002), Prolonging Software Life: Development and Redevelopment, Proceedings*, 26–29 Aug 2002 (Oxford, England, 2002), pp. 450–458
2. Y. Chun, M. Qian, M. Xiao-Xing, L. Jian, An architecture-oriented mechanism for self-adaptation of software systems. J. Nanjing Univ. Nat. Sci. Ed. **42**(2), 120 (2006)
3. Y.-S. Dai, Autonomic computing and reliability improvement, in *Eighth IEEE International Symposium on Object-Oriented Real-Time Distributed Computing (ISORC 2005)*, 18–20 May 2005 (Seattle, WA, USA, 2005), pp. 204–206
4. Y. Diao, J.L. Hellerstein, S.S. Parekh, J.P. Bigus, Managing web server performance with autotune agents. IBM Syst. J. **42**(1), 136–149 (2003)
5. B. Dudney, S. Asbury, J.K. Krozak, K. Wittkopf, *J2EE Antipatterns* (John Wiley & Sons, 2003)
6. D. Garlan, S.-W. Cheng, A.-C. Huang, B.R. Schmerl, P. Steenkiste, Rainbow: architecture-based self-adaptation with reusable infrastructure. IEEE Comput. **37**(10), 46–54 (2004)

7. M.G. Hinchey, Y.-S. Dai, C.A. Rouff, J.L. Rash, M. Qi, Modeling for NASA autonomous nanotechnology swarm missions and model-driven autonomic computing, in *21st International Conference on Advanced Information Networking and Applications (AINA 2007)* 21–23 May 2007 (Niagara Falls, Canada, 2007), pp. 250–257

8. P. Horn, Autonomic computing: Ibm\'s perspective on the state of information technology (2001)

9. G. Huang, H. Mei, F. Yang, Runtime software architecture based on reflective middleware. Sci. China Ser. F: Inf. Sci. **47**(5), 555–576 (2004)

10. J. Jann, L.M. Browning, R.S. Burugula. Dynamic reconfiguration: basic building blocks for autonomic computing on IBM pseries servers. IBM Syst. J. **42**(1), 29–37 (2003)

11. T. Liu, G. Huang, G. Fan, H. Mei, The coordinated recovery of data service and transaction service in J2EE, in *29th Annual International Computer Software and Applications Conference, COMPSAC 2005*, vol. 1, 25–28 July 2005 (Edinburgh, Scotland, UK, 2005), pp. 485–490

12. J. Lü, X.X. Ma, X.P. Tao, F. Xu, H. Hu, Research and progress on internetware. Sci. China (Ser. E) **36**(10), 1037–1080 (2006)

13. V. Markl, G.M. Lohman, V. Raman, LEO: an autonomic query optimizer for DB2. IBM Syst. J. **42**(1), 98–106 (2003)

14. N. Medvidovic, R.N. Taylor, A classification and comparison framework for software architecture description languages. IEEE Trans. Softw. Eng. **26**(1), 70–93 (2000)

15. H. Mei, F. Chen, Q. Wang, Y.D. Feng, ABC/ADL: an ADL supporting component composition, in *Formal Methods and Software Engineering, 4th International Conference on Formal Engineering Methods, ICFEM 2002, Proceedings*, 21–25 Oct 2002 (Shanghai, China, 2002), pp. 38–47

16. H. Mei, G. Huang, T. Liu, J. Li, Coordinated recovery of middleware services: a framework and experiments. Int. J. Softw. Inf. **1**(1), 101–128 (2007)

17. H. Mei, G. Huang, H. Zhao, W. Jiao, A software architecture centric engineering approach for internetware. Sci. China Ser. F: Inf. Sci. **49**(6), 702–730 (2006)

18. P. Oreizy, N. Medvidovic, R.N. Taylor, Architecture-based runtime software evolution, in *Forging New Links, Proceedings of the 1998 International Conference on Software Engineering, ICSE 98*, 19–25 Apr 1998 (Kyoto, Japan, 1998), pp. 177–186

19. M. Shaw, D. Garlan, *Software Architecture—Perspectives on an Emerging Discipline* (Prentice Hall, 1996)

20. J. Xu, A.B. Romanovsky, B. Randell, Coordinated exception handling in distributed object systems: from model to system implementation, in *Proceedings of the 18th International Conference on Distributed Computing Systems*, 26–29 May 1998 (Amsterdam, The Netherlands, 1998) pp. 12–21

21. F.-Q. Yang, H. Mei, J. Lv, Z. Jin, Some discussion on the development of software technology. Acta Electronica Sin. **30**(12A), 1901–1906 (2002)

22. L. Yuan, J.S. Dong, J. Sun, H.A. Basit, Generic fault tolerant software architecture reasoning and customization. IEEE Trans. Reliab. **55**(3), 421–435 (2006)

23. N. Zhang, G. Huang, L. Lan, H. Mei, Pattern-based J2EE application deployment with cost analysis, in *Proceedings of the Nineteenth International Conference on Software Engineering & Knowledge Engineering (SEKE'2007)*, 9–11 July 2007 (Boston, Massachusetts, USA, 2007), pp. 462–466

24. Y. Zhu, G. Huang, H. Mei, Quality attribute scenario based architectural modeling for self-adaptation supported by architecture-based reflective middleware, in *11th Asia-Pacific Software Engineering Conference (APSEC 2004)*, 30 Nov–3 Dec 2004 (Busan, Korea, 2004), pp. 2–9

On Requirements Model Driven Adaption and Evolution of Internetware

Abstract

Today's software systems need to support complex business operations and processes. The development of the web-based software systems has been pushing up the limits of traditional software engineering methodologies and technologies as they are required to be used and updated almost real-time, so that users can interact and share the same applications over the internet as needed. As a consequence, we are expecting a major paradigm shift in software engineering to reflect such changes in computing environment in order to better address the fundamental needs of organisations in this new era. Existing software technologies, such as model driven development, business process engineering, online (re-) configuration, composition and adaptation of managerial functionalities are being "repurposed" to reduce the time taken for software development by reusing software codes. In retrospect to the ten years applied research on Internetware, we have witnessed such a paradigm shift, which brings about many changes to the developmental experience of conventional web applications. Several related technologies, such as cloud computing, service computing, cyber-physical systems and social computing, have converged to address this emerging issue with emphasis on different aspects. In this chapter, we first outline the requirements that the Internetware software paradigm should meet to excel at web application adaptation; we then propose a requirement model driven method for adaptive and evolutionary applications; and we report our experiences and case studies of applying it to an enterprise information system. Our goal is to provide high-level guidelines to researchers and practitioners to meet the challenges of building adaptive industrial-strength applications with a spectrum of processes, techniques and facilities provided within the Internetware paradigm.

Parts of this chapter were reprinted with kind permission from Springer Science+Business Media: <Science in China Series F: Information Sciences, Requirements model driven adaption and evolution of Internetware, volume 57, 2014, 1-19, Lin Liu, Chen Yang, JianMin Wang, XiaoJun Ye, YingBo Liu, HongJi Yang and XiaoDong Liu, figure number(s), and any original (first) copyright notice displayed with material>.

Keywords

Requirements · Information system · Internetware · Adaptation · Evolution

5.1   Introduction

The term "Internetware" refers to a software paradigm that advocates the composition-based development of software systems from a set of software components distributed over the Internet [38–40,66]. The software components, or rather, Internetware, are autonomous, self-contained and distributed across the Internetwork. It is able to respond to the perceived changes in the environment by means of reconfiguration and reorganization. Internetware software collaborates with one another on demand, which adopts an iterative composition process turning various "disordered" resources into an "ordered" software system. Similar to the widely adopted component-based paradigm, the methodological framework of Internetware brings promptness, flexibility and reusability in building distributed software systems. As a new requirement emerges or a new software technology becomes available, existing requirements-solutions bindings can be adjusted for optimization purpose.

Internetware is an evolutionary product of the traditional software system due to the evolution of Internet from an information exchange platform into a software development and execution environment. It has many desired characteristics, such as autonomy, evolution, collaboration, polymorphism, reaction and so on. *Autonomy* of individual components refers to the capacity of a rational individual to make an informed, un-coerced decision, who determines the responsibility for the consequences of his own actions. Software components, equipped with a goal-environment modelling facility, are autonomous agents [16,58] which can determine what goal they pursue, and which action plan they may select, based on a set of predetermined strategic rules and criteria. (2) Internetware *collaboration* [14] means that the software entities are aware of the existence of others, and could collaborate to achieve a common goal. There are coordination mechanisms between them. The states of other components are observable by other components, as environment variables. (3) *Polymorphism* in Internetware refers to the capabilities of components to inherit a stable set of behaviour from its conventional software component ancestor, which exhibit different interfaces or quality level while needed. A switching mechanism is developed to match requirements with capabilities, and to select appropriate components. (4) Internetware entities should have the ability to sense the environment and provide useful information for *adaptation and evolution*. The run-time platform supports the monitoring of the environment variables. Adaptation requires modification of a software product performed after delivery to keep a software product usable in a changed or changing environment. It takes place when there is a known requirement for change. (5) The *evolution* property of Internetware requires it to observe changes in the environment and respond to the changes based on its current capabilities. The Internetware component could evolve dynamically according to the environment and user's requirements. The evolution occurs when the current functionality, performance, organization of Internetware cannot sufficiently satisfy the need of the environment. However, it is yet to be fully realised due to two major research issues: (1) there is no effective way to manage the diversity and constant changes of run-time requirements of Internetware; (2) users need an accessible supporting platform and evaluation environment for handling adaptation and evolution of Internetware system.

Conventional requirements activities are conducted before design. Once the system is deployed, requirements related activities become secondary ÍC handling change requests only. Today's web-based systems are required to keep evolving to cope with these run-time behaviours. Fickas and Feather [24] have studied the significance of monitoring requirements, based on the analysis of two commercial software cases; Jureta et al. [29] have proposed formalism in response to the emergence of services computing and its requirements for a transformation from static requirements to dynamic requirements. A more comprehensive probe into the research issues and challenges in this area is the research roadmap by Cheng et al. on software engineering for self-adaptive systems [15]. All these efforts agree on the importance of the research problem of requirements modelling, monitoring and evolution in an on-going basis for a running, live and ever-changing system, in the sense of self-adaption, automation and minimal disturbance to the running system.

This chapter introduces a requirements model driven adaptation and evolution in the Internetware setting. Section 5.2 describes the composition mechanism for Internetware systems, where details about the basic operations are given. Section 5.3 introduces the adaptation process and major algorithms. Section 5.4 uses a case study to illustrate and evaluate the proposed approach and the tools we have built to support the proposed process. Section 5.5 discusses related work and Sect. 5.6 summarises the contributions of the chapter.

5.2 Matching and Composing Internetware Components

There are a number of definitions on software components. In the context of component-based software engineering, software components are binary units of independent production, acquisition, and deployment that interact to form a functioning system [5]. Essential features of components include: (1) Components should be able to plug and play with other components so that they can be composed at run-time without compilation. (2) Components should separate the interface from the implementation so that they can be composed without knowing their implementation. (3) Components are designed on a pre-defined architecture so that they can interoperate with other components. (4) Component interface should be standardized so that multiple vendors can develop them and widely reused across the corporations. (5) Components can be acquired and improved though open market.

Internetware is developed based on the component-based development concept, the underlying component model is explained in Sect. 5.2.1. When feasible components implementing desired functions are chosen, component providers assemble the components into a coherent web-based system to fulfil user requirements. Usually, the chosen components should be composed according to certain business constraints and be executed in a pre-specified temporal order. The resulted system exhibits two perspectives: functionality and quality. The functionality of system describes what the system does and quality indicates how well the system performs its desired tasks. In particular, quality dedicates to the non-functional properties of system, such as cost, performance, reliability, security and so on. In this chapter, we assume that in an Internetware system, the qualities of a composite component are functions of the quality attributes of its component. For the quality attributes that are not compositional, we assume it is a required input parameter. If the quality of a component system satisfies the non-functional requirements of users, the system is suitable for the current context. Otherwise, it has to take adaptive actions according to the usersąí needs and the current state of the environment. To help effectively organize and compose components and build adaptive application, an adaptive composition framework is presented in this section, including a meta-model and a set of composition rules.

5.2.1 A Component Meta Model

The basic elements of the proposed adaptive composition framework are shown in Fig. 5.1. According to the meta-model, a component is characterized as a *component type* and a *component implementation*. A *component type* is the abstraction of the functionality and quality attributes of a group of concrete components, which can be either atomic or composite. All *concrete compo-*

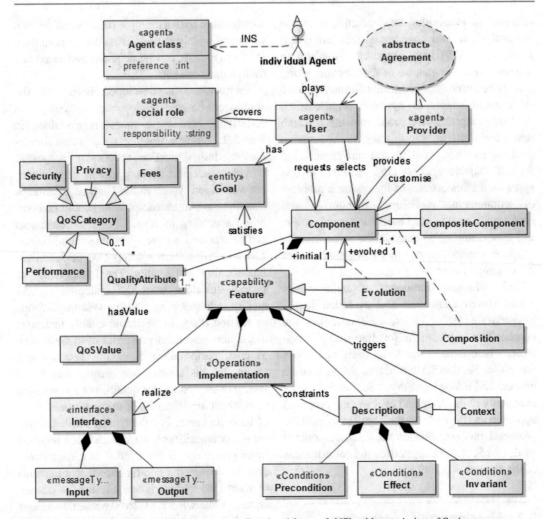

Fig. 5.1 A meta model of Internetware component. Reprinted from ref. [67], with permission of Springer

nents associated with a component type implement the same functionality but may have different component interfaces and quality levels.

The model also manifests that component functions has associated contexts and constraints. Quality of service (QoS) is used to satisfy quality constraints of users. The operational environment influences both the context constraints and the status of component. Such influences are further propagated to the component functionalities and quality constraints. To further explain the framework, Table 5.1 defines a set of functions and explains the relations among functionality, quality, quality constraints and context constraints. *"Function"* represents the functionality

of both component type (component class) and concrete component (component instance). If S is a component type and s_i one of its instances, then $Function(s_i) \models Function(S)$. That is to say, each concrete component provides the functionality that its corresponding component type declares. As in reality, it is not possible to specify all functionalities, qualities and constraints of components accurately by developers and users, we address this issue with the support of domain ontologies published online as well as common sense knowledge base.

We represent quality through using quality attributes and use the function *Quality* to values assigned for each quality attribute

Table 5.1 Major functions used in the meta model

Symbol of function	Meaning
$Function(s)$	The functionality of a component class or a component instance s
$Quality([q_{1...m}], s)$	A set of value or range measurements of component s on quality attributes $q_{i...j} (1 \leq i \leq j \leq m)$ The omission of quality attribute is defaulted as the complete set $q_{1...m}$
$Constraint([q_{1...m}], G_s)$	A set of derived quality constraints of a soft-goal G_s on specified quality attributes $q_{i...j} (1 \leq i \leq j \leq n)$ The omission of quality attribute is defaulted as the complete set $q_{1...n}$
Minimal Optimal $Maximal([q_{1...n}], G_s)$	User desired demand degree of soft-goal Gs on each specific quality attribute $q_{i...j} (1 \leq i \leq j \leq n)$ *The omission of quality attribute is defaulted as the complete set $q_{1...n}$*
$Constraint(s)$	A set of constraints imposed on component s áis operation environment

of concrete components. For example, if the average response time of component s is 1 s, then *Quality (average response time, s) = 1 s*. Multiple quality attribute constraints can be expressed as follows: $Quality(q_1 \ldots q_m, s) = \{Quality(q_1, s) \cup \cdots \cup Quality(q_m, s)\}$. We define $Quality(q, s_i) \models Quality(q, s_j)$ if component si has better performance on the attribute q than component s_j has. Based on this definition, we can deduce that $Quality(s_i) \models Quality(s_j)$ if on each attribute q_l of a fixed attribute set Q, $Quality(q_l, s_i) \models Quality(q_l, s_j)$ holds. It means that component s_i has better quality than component s_j. Meanwhile, each soft-goal G_s in the goal model is operationalized as a quality constraint through the symbol function *Constraint*. A concrete component s satisfies G_s on attribute q if $Quality(q) \models Constraint(q, G_s)$. E.g., soft-goal *responsiveness* could be stated as constraint "*response time < 2 s*", and a component s satisfies this soft-goal if *Quality (response time, s) = 1 s*, because "*response time = 1 s*" entails the constraint "*response time < 2 s*". Similarly, the annotation $Quality(s) \models Constraint(G_s)$ is used to represent that a component s is able to satisfy a soft-goal G_s. It is true if for each quality attribute q in the quality set Q we have $Quality(q) \models Constraint(q, G_s)$. It is common that a soft-goal needs the contributions from more than one component. Also, for each soft-goal related quality attribute, we define frequently used constraints, such as $minimal(q, G_s)$, $optimal(q, G_s)$, and $maximal(q, G_s)$, to express user desired demand

degree for soft-goal G_s on quality attribute q. In addition, components have associated context constraints on the expected value, or range for their operating environment. The function *Constraint* maps each concrete component to a set of associated constraints. For example, if the component "*Provide Video Tutorials*" only requires "*Network speed ≥ 50 kbps*", then *Constraint (Provide Video Tutorials) = Network speed ≥ 50 kbps*. The above evaluation process resembles the contracts-based development process proposed by Meyer [42]. Contracts have proved a powerful concept in software engineering, to the point where we have a well-regarded software development approach centred on their use, and native support in programming languages. In the Internetware setting, although we have not explicitly used the concept of contract, we include in the meta-model a concept "Agreement" to indicate that there at least some shared understanding about the requested functionality and quality and what the component can provide. The "agreement" shall include the propositions reflect the needs and capabilities from the two sides.

5.2.2   Component Lifecycle

Components are maintained in a component repository and monitored to ensure their quality requirements are met. Since the (concrete) components in the repository are the basic building blocks of component systems, they are

Table 5.2 The set of component manipulating operations

Symbol of Function	Meaning
New(s)	A new component instance s is added to the component pool
Availability(s)	A Boolean value indicating whether component s is available
Bound(s)	A Boolean assignment indicates whether a concrete component is bound to a component contract
Done(s)	A Boolean value indicates whether a concrete component has completed its execution
Remove(s)	Remove a component s from the component pool

Fig. 5.2 The lifecycle of a concrete component s. Reprinted from ref. [67], with permission of Springer

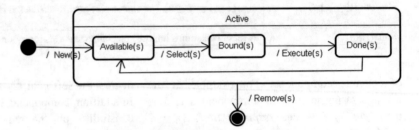

composed for fulfilling the users' goals and adapt to handle changes. To describe the lifecycle of components, a set of operations that could change the state of components are shown in Table 5.2: the status of a concrete component changes through $new(s)$ and $remove(s)$; the Boolean function $availability(s)$ to indicate whether or not the component s is available; the Boolean functions, $bound(s)$ and $done(s)$ to indicate whether a concrete component is bound to a component contract, or whether it has completed its execution. Figure 5.2 models the life cycle of concrete components in terms of a state transition diagram.

5.2.3   Component Composition Rules

Using requirement refinement techniques, we are able to derive alternative sets of tasks whose execution (in some unspecified order) fulfils a user target goal G. Each specification $S_p = \{T_0 \dots T_m\}$ has the property that $Sp \models G$. Each task in a specification can be mapped to an abstract component type, which is then instantiated at runtime by assigning a corresponding concrete component to it. Based on the refined goal graph structure and the hidden temporal/casual

constraints between all abstract components in specification S_p, we can derive an abstract component composition structure. Specifically, we use the following set of composition operators: $seq(s^+)$, $sel(s^+)$, $par\_and(s^+)$, $par\_or(s^+)$, where s denotes an atomic component, s^+ denotes a set of one or more components, and meanings of the operators are introduced in Table 5.3.

Functionalities are composed via composition operators: sequential $seq(s^+)$, conditional selection $sel(s^+)$, concurrent execution with complete synchronization $par\_and(s^+)$ and concurrent execution with 1 out of n synchronization $par\_or(s^+)$. Sequential composition $seq(s^+)$ and concurrent execution $par\_and(s^+)$ are derived from AND-decomposition of goals, while conditional selection $sel(s^+)$ and the other concurrent execution $par\_or(s^+)$ are derived from OR-decomposition of goals. When a user's requested quality exceeds the quality of any individual components of S_i, the system may run compose component (say s_{ij}, s_{ik}, s_{il}) concurrently (with complete synchronization) to meet the demand, by triggering $par\_and(s_{ij}, s_{ik}, s_{il})$ composition as described in Table 5.4.

When a user needs a high-reliability component, while existing component has a certain level of risk, the system may execute composite compo-

Table 5.3 Composition operators

Operators	Meaning
seq (s^+)	Sequential execution of atomic components s^+
sel (s^+)	Conditional selection of atomic components s^+
par_and (s^+)	Concurrent execution of atomic components s^+ (with complete synchronization)
par_or (s^+)	Concurrent execution of atomic components s^+ (with 1 out of n synchronization)

Table 5.4 The *par_and* composition

Operators	$Par\_and(s_{ij}, s_{ik}, s_{il})$
Precondition	$Constraint(s_{ij}, s_{ik}, s_{il})holds \wedge (Function(s_{ij}) \models$ $Function(s_{ik}) \wedge Function(s_{ij}) \models Function(s_{il})) \wedge minimal(throughput, G_s) \geq$ $Quality(throughput, s_{ij}) \wedge minimal(throughput, G_s) \geq$ $Quality(throughput, s_{ik}) \wedge minimal(throughput, G_s) \geq$ $Quality(throughput, s_{il}) \wedge available(s_{ij}) \wedge available(s_{ik}) \wedge available(s_{il})$
Trigger	$Throughput(Par\_and(s_{ij}, s_{ik}, s_{il})) \geq minimal(throughput, G_s)$
Effect	$Bound(s_{ij}) \wedge Bound(s_{ik}) \wedge Bound(s_{il})$

Table 5.5 The *par_or* composition

Action	$Par\_or(s_{ij}, s_{ik})$
Precondition	$Constraint(s_{ij}, s_{ik})holds \wedge (Function(s_{ij}) ==$ $Function(s_{ik}) \wedge Quality(reliability, s_{ij}) \leq$ $optimal(reliability, G_s) \wedge Quality(reliability, s_{ij}) \geq$ $minimal(reliability, G_s) \wedge Quality(reliability, s_{ik}) \leq$ $optimal(reliability, G_s) \wedge Quality(reliability, s_{ik}) \geq$ $minimal(reliability, G_s) \wedge available(s_{ij}) \wedge available(s_{ik})$
Trigger	$Quality(reliability, Par\_or(s_{ij}, s_{ik})) \geq Quality(reliability, s_{ij}) \wedge$ $Quality(reliability, Par\_or(s_{ij}, s_{ik})) \geq Quality(reliability, s_{ik})$
Effect	$Bound(s_{ij}) \wedge Bound(s_{ik})$

nent (for example, s_{ij} and s_{ik}) concurrently (with 1 out of n synchronization) to meet the demand, by triggering $par\_or(s_{ij}, s_{ik})$ in Table 5.5.

5.3 Components Adaptation

5.3.1 Adaptation Strategies

When a component system is built and put into operation, changes might occur to both the users' requirements and components operation environment. In order to provide satisfactory components to users, a component system should be aware of the requirements and environmental changes, and adapt to such situations. In response, adaptation

actions, strategies and processes need to be in place. Changes can originate from user requirements, especially their quality requirements. When user requirements change, the goal model and its refinement will be updated accordingly, and at last the lowest level of tasks will be updated: new task(s) are derived out, or existing task(s) are removed. As a result, the abstract components should be re-composed according to the new goal graph structure and concrete component will be revoked. For example, the users of *online shopping component* usually want the goods to be delivered quickly, but in some cases they desire the shipped goods be packaged well without damage during delivery. To resolve this problem, a new goal "*Good Shipping Quality*"

Table 5.6 Substitute operation

Action	$Substitute(s_{ij}, s_{ik})$
Precondition	$Constraint(s_{ik})holds \land (Bound(s_{ij}) \land (Function(s_{ik}) \models$ $Function(s_{ij}) \land (Quality(s_{ik}) \models Constraint(G_s) \lor \neg Available(s_{ij}))$
Trigger	$Quality(s_{ik}) \models Quality(s_{ij}) \land Available(s_{ik})$
Effect	$Bound(s_{ik}) \land Remove(s_{ij})$

and a new task *"Deliver with High Quality"* is added, and the *shipping component* will be selected.

Components are maintained in a repository and monitored to ensure their quality requirements are met. This is accomplished by monitoring component abnormal behaviour and performances (e.g. average user waiting time, response time, and the percentage of users being served) and environment (e.g. CPU utilization, memory usage, bandwidth availability, network stability, or number of concurrent online users). Component environment influences both the status of components and the user goals and their refinements. For example, if one of the constraints associated with component *"Provide Video Tutorials"* is *"Network speed ≥ 50 kbps"*, and environmental variable *"Network speed"* has a value that is less than 50 kbps, then the component is unavailable. The component repository would also change dynamically, such as adding a new concrete component, removing an existing component and recomposing a component. When changes occur, component system needs to perform adaptations to satisfy given requirements. Adaptive actions are needed to handle changes in user Quality requirements, environment variables, or components. Usually, such actions include reorganizing the structure of abstract component composition, reselecting and recomposing concrete component(s).

The composition actions shown in Table 5.3 could be reused in component adaptation.

Adaptive actions have associated preconditions, triggers and effects with usual semantics. All of them consist of propositions constraining environmental variables and the internal state of a component. E.g., for an abstract component s_i, when a new atomic component s_{ik} emerges, s_{ij} is an atomic component of a composite components that suddenly becomes not available, or waits to be executed at the moment, if $Function(s_{ij}) \models Function(s_{ik})$, and $Quality(s_{ij}) \models Quality(s_{ik})$, the system may take the *"Substitute"* action as shown in Table 5.6.

Based on the origin of changes, strategies are formed to decide what adaptive actions to be carried out, based on the user's goals to be satisfied, the environment conditions to be monitored and the component repository dynamically changing.

5.3.2   Adaptation Process

This section introduces a composite adaption process, which contains a feedback loop executed iteratively to satisfy the changes detected. The changes from user soft-goals, system operating environment or component repository are viewed as three possible triggers to the substitution or re-composition of components. Therefore, adaptation should be taken trying to keep the constant satisfaction of user requirements and the operations of composite system.

Algorithm 1: MatchGoalwithComponentFunction (ComponentRepository S, GoalGraph G,
GoalComponentMap GC_p)
Input: ComponentRepository S, GoalGraph G,
Output: a set of identified goal and component map GC_p

```
01      Goals G= ∅
02      GoalComponentMap GCp = ∅, Temp = ∅
03      Goals.add(G)
04      while Goals!=∅
05          Goal gt = Goals.get()
06          if ∃si ∈ S&Function(si) ⊇ Function(gt)
07              Goals.remove (gt)
08              GCp.add(< gt, si >)
09          else if gt is or-decomposed
10              for each gi ∈ or-decompose(gt)
11                  G= G.replace(gi, gt)
12                  MatchGoalwithComponentFunction(R, G, Temp)
13                  GCp = GCp ∪ Temp
14              end for
15          else if gt is and-decomposed
16              for each gi ∈ and-decompose(gt)
17                  G = G.add(gi)
18                  MatchGoalwithComponentFunction(R, G, Temp)
19                  GCp = GCp ∩ Temp
20              end for
21      end while
22      return GCp
```

Algorithm 2: SelectComponentInstance (ComponentRepository S, GoalComponentMap S_p,
Goals G)
Input: ComponentRepository S, GoalComponentMap S_p, Goals g_0
Output: a set of identified ComponentInstancesST

```
01      Components ST, DN
02      MatchGoalwithComponentFunction (ComponentRepository S, GoalGraph G,
        GoalComponentMap GCp)
03      for each g ∈ G
04          Si = GCp.getComponents(g)
05          for each sij ∈ Si
06              if Quality(sij) ⊨ Quality(g)
07                  ST.add(sij)
08              else
09                  DN.add(sij)
10          end for
11          if ST=∅
12              compose (Si, g0) by (seq(), sel(), par_and(), par_or()
13              if Quality(scomp) ⊨ Quality(g)
14                  ST.add(Scomn)
15      end for
16      return ST
```

Algorithm 3 describes the adaptation process, the input of which is Change (G, S, E), component Assembly is the major data object, both appears as an input, and also as a returned parameter, the algorithm captures changes, restructure and compose components processes to adapt to changes to ensure the effective execution of components.

Algorithm 3: Adapt (Goal G, ComponentRepository S, GoalComponentMap GC)
Input: ComponentRepository S, GoalGraph G,
Output: ComponentRepository S', GoalGraph G'

```
01    if new($g_n$)
02        G=G ∪ {$g_n$}
03        then MatchGoalwithComponentFunction (S, $g_n$, GoalComponentMap GC)
04        if ComponentInstances CI = SelectComponentInstance (S, GC, G) == Ø
05            S=S ∪ compose(S, $g_n$) using structure(Seq, Sel, Par_and, Par_or)
06            return
07    if remove($g_0$)
08        G=G\{$g_0$}
09        if ComponentInstances CI = SelectComponentInstance (S, GC, {$g_0$}) !=Ø
10            for ∀$s_i$ ∈ CI, if getGoal($s_i$, GC) \{$g_0$} == Ø
11                S=S \{$s_i$}
12            else S=S \remove( S, $g_n$)
13                if new($s_n$)
14                    MatchGoalwithComponentFunction ({$s_n$}, G, GoalComponentMap GC)
15                if Goals Gsn = GC.getGoal($s_n$) == Ø
16                    G = G ∪ Function ($s_n$) ∪ Quality($s_n$)
17                    return
18    if remove($s_0$)
19        S= S\$s_0$
20        Goals Gsn = GC.getGoal($s_0$) != Ø
21        if ComponentInstances CI =SelectComponentInstance (S, GC, Gsn)== Ø
22            G= G \{$g_{sn}$}
23        return
```

As shown in Fig. 5.3, the steps P_4, P_5, P_6 and P_7 form a feedback loop that executes iteratively to support run-time adaptation. Those changes on goals and component repository come from the user and the platform correspondingly, so they are not part of the feedback loop.

5.4   Internetware Testbed and Case Studies

5.4.1   Internetware Testbed

Web-based software applications have target users all over the world, so it is very difficult (if not impossible) to predict the access pattern before deployment. To cope with peak workload on demand or cater for potential high growth rates, service providers often over-provision their servers by as much as five hundred percent, which may lead to a considerable waste of resource for normal workload, not to mention the management cost spent on the over-provisioned infrastructure. Recent years, cloud computing emerges as a

new paradigm for hosting IT services over the Internet. The elasticity of cloud-computing infrastructure and the pay-as-you-go price model attract more and more enterprises to deploy their applications to a minimal set of cloud-computing infrastructures, which will later be scaled in or out to cope with the workload fluctuation. Cloud computing and dynamic resource provisioning has been a hot topic recently in both industry and academic fields. For examples, Amazon, Microsoft and Google all propose their own Cloud products and regard the infrastructure, the platforms and the software as services.

Based on the collaborative project teams' research results on Internetware theory and model and the run-time support environment, methodology, techniques and tools, a complex internetwork software deployment, simulation and evaluation platform is constructed, called Internetware Testbed. This Testbed is an environment in which software components conforming to the Internetware paradigm can be implemented. It is also an execution environment configured for Internetware function conformance test, various quality assurance test or the performance evaluation under configurable workloads. To construct the Testbed, project teams developed an instance of IaaS based on virtualization technology. The purpose of the Testbed is to support both Internetware innovation and Internetware applications research within a common experimenter platform. It can address the requirements of Internetware characteristics simulation such as autonomous, evolutionary, cooperative, polymorphic, and context-aware, as well as for Internetware conformance test, various QA test or the performance test under configurable workloads. The system architecture of this platform includes 4 physical clusters residing in four project partner organisations, connected locally via Local Area Network, via Wide Area Network between nodes, which is further extensible. The software systems architecture deployed is a heterogeneous cloud-computing environment with over 1000 virtual machines running in parallel across the network. Internetware development and management tools, as well as application prototypes in different domain are deployed in this environment, which can support more than a million system users working online at the same time.

5.4.2 Model-Driven Development and Evaluation of Internetware Applications

The application development and deployment tool set uses a collaborative adaptation model. We assume that the environment consists of software agents who have their own goals to fulfil, at the same time provide certain functionalities through which agents form a collaborative network to serve their goals collectively. As indicated in the above algorithms, we evaluate Internetware components from two perspectives: one is functional satisfaction of components, which involves the satisfaction of all alternative ways of delivering the services given functional and the other is the satisfaction level of non-functional goals. In each application domain, there can be several Internetware components offering similar functionalities.

Depending on their concrete implementation, this contributes to component consumer satisfaction differently, which in return impacts agents' decision. Accordingly, we need to evaluate the satisfaction degree of each component and rank them accordingly. Here, we introduce the steps of the functional satisfaction evaluation process. The $i*$ modelling language [65] is adopted to model and evaluate alternatives, and a simple logistics component example to illustrate our proposed method. *Step 1. Model the requirements of client-end application components.* In the Internetware environment, component delivery involves two kinds of agents: consumers, who need to achieve their goals, and suppliers, who can provide specific components to others. Requirements determine the functions that need to be bundled in a component, e.g., "Sell product", and for qualities that are expected by consumers, e.g., "Low cost". There are many factors that impact the final goal, functional or non-functional. Functional requirements indicate what the component provider needs to achieve. Non-functional requirements, on the other hand, indicate the criteria by which alternative components are evaluated. So, for candidates match the functions of a given goal, evaluation is mainly focused on non-functional properties. Figure 5.3 is an $i*$ SR model of a generic MRO application. User has goals, such as monitoring equipment, purchase supplies, locate tools and devices, issue repair requests, and also non-functional requirements such as purchase supplies at low cost, and timely, locate tools and devices accurately, issue repair request timely and accurately, etc. To achieve these goals, application developer needs to execute tasks, such as provide monitoring function, and make purchase order, tag tools and devices on map. There are dependencies between the two actors and other actors if external components are used or referenced. Figure 5.3 illustrates the relationship of these actors. To evaluate the satisfaction degree of each candidate, we should find out all the quality attributes concerned by the customer. Figure 5.3 shows the requirements of consumer, where we can find criteria for evaluating components. If there are plenty of quality attributes to be handled and they have

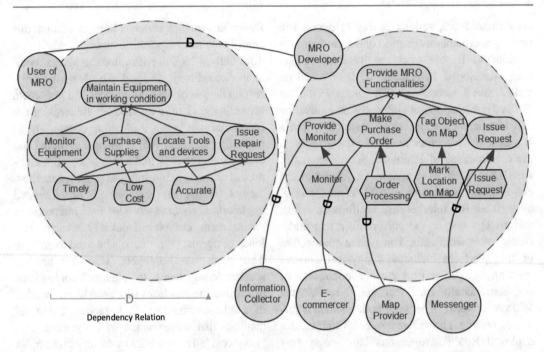

Fig. 5.3 Modelling MRO high-level requirements in *i**. Reprinted from ref. [67], with permission of Springer

non-trivial relationship to others, correlation analysis should be conducted to identify key factors. In our example, we consider three attributes contributing to component satisfaction: time, cost, and accuracy.

Step 2. Quantify the importance of each quality attribute.

There are different methods to quantify the weights of factors identified in the requirements model, such as the Delphi technique [19], Analytical Hierarchy Process (AHP) [57], Decision Alternative Ratio Evaluation (DARE), and Fuzzy Synthetic Evaluation. Among these methods, Delphi and AHP are best known. The general process for the Delphi technique includes several steps: a) a group of experts give their evaluation independently; b) evaluations are collected and sent out to experts; c) experts refer to other evaluation and re-evaluate; d) repeat step b) and c) when experts stop changing their attitude. The result has good reliability, but assumes expert availability, often a strong assumption. AHP works by comparing relative importance of every factor pair, followed by calculation of relative weights. It can be easily conducted and the process can be understood

not only by experts but also by general decision-makers. People can choose among these methods, or others. Once the chosen method has been applied, the weights of these four factors can be estimated.

Step 3. Evaluate candidates based on existing knowledge related to the quality contributions.

It is very hard to quantify satisfaction degree for these quality factors that are "soft" in nature. Domain expert knowledge is widely used in this situation and many algorithms are proposed based on experts' knowledge (such as set-valued statistics approach). Quality requirements are competing with each other when ranking candidates. There are a body of literature in the requirements engineering area that handles the trade-off between different optimization directions. For example, [59] provides both qualitative and quantitative approaches to evaluate goal models, and [33] provides a formal conceptual framework for handling non-functional requirements.

Step 4. Calculate the satisfaction degree of each candidate.

Given the weights of factors and component satisfaction for each factor, a straightforward way to evaluate the overall score is by their weighted sum. An algorithm proposed in [41] applies Ordered Weighted Averaging (OWA) Measure to Logic Scoring Preference (LSP) method. It solved the problem of dynamic returning aggregation function (at the same time, it represents factors' logic relations such as simultaneity and replaceability). This method also has been used for automated web services selection. If we add weights and evaluation values (the format is "weight: evaluation") on the model showed in Fig. 5.3 and mark the final score of candidate component (we use weighted sum based on data obtained from step 2 and 3). Following these four steps, we can evaluate the satisfaction degree of each candidate Internetware component.

5.4.3 Enterprise Applications Example

A case study of the Enterprise Product Lifecycle Management domain is used to further illustrate the proposed approach. Product lifecycle management is the process of an enterprise managing the entire lifecycle of a product from its conception, design, manufacture, to service and disposal. A typical PLM product supports for systems engineering, product and portfolio management, product design, manufacturing process management and product data management. There is a rich set of components for architects to choose from in order to form an integrated solution for an enterprise. While all systems are providing similar capabilities to organizations, there are also different ways to construct a specific system. All these differences can be traced back to the variations in customer requirements or constraints in the organizational environment. When project team receives customer requests, components are selected based on basic information about the usage context of the customer organization. For instance, the size of the enterprise, the industry sector the organization belongs to, the usual functionalities needed by the customer organization, and the amount of technical efforts and system expenses the organization can afford, etc. In order to make a rational selection among different design

alternatives and to identify a group of features that can best fit the customer aís needs, we have identified the following non-functional goals for these products: Fitness; Time-To-Market; Project Risk; Cost; Productivity; Rich Know-how; Quick Information Retrieval: the ability to retrieve information when needed; Customization cost; Integration cost; Training cost; Security Risk likeliness.

5.4.4 Experiment Scenarios on the Collaborations and Evolutions of Internetware Components

Taking the componentization of MRO System as an example, we adopt the mashup tool developed within the project team to wrap-up the existing product family into a set of Internetware components, so that the functionality of the current MRO system can be extended at run-time by the collaboration of MRO component with other components accessible within the platform. Assume that at the beginning of developing mashup system, there are 3 high-level goals: r_1, providing MRO management; r_2, Purchase materials on the Internet when needed and providing B2C service; r_3, integrating with Baidu.Map component and providing LBS Services.

$$(R, t_1) = \{r_1, r_2, r_3\};$$

$$Active\_queue : \{(r_1, t_1), (r_2, t_1), (r_3, t_1)\};$$
$$Inactive\_set : \{\};$$

At t_1, component s_1 satisfies r_1, while component s_2 and s_3 satisfies r_2 and r_3 respectively.

$$P(r_1, t_1) > P(r_2, t_1) = P(r_3, t_1); s_1(r_1, t_1);$$
$$s_2(r_2, t_1); s_3(r_3, t_1);$$

At the end of t_1, component s_1 is available, resulting in the high maturity of its corresponding requirement r_1. Due to the full completion and low priority at this moment, r_1 is picked out from the Active_queue, added into the Inactive_set. At the end of time t_1, the situation of requirements and components is as following:

$$M(r_1, t_1) > M(r_3, t_1) > M(r_2, t_1); P(r_2, t_1)$$
$$> P(r_3, t_1) > P(r_1, t_1);$$

$$Active\_queue : \{(r_2, t_1), (r_3, t_1)\};$$
$$Inactive\_set : \{(r_1, t_1)\}$$

Although Requirement r_1 is in Inactive_set, it will barely become a motive for system evolution ever since. Nevertheless, r1 is still equipped with the possibility for stimulating the appearance of new requirement. Requirement r_2 and r_3 are still pending for consideration. They both have the potential for further improvement, as well as stimulate new requirements.

Figure b. shows the goal model of requirements at t_2. Notice that a new sub-requirement appears. The new requirement r_4, comparing prices of materials among various B2C providers, is on the basis of component s_2. Treat r_4 as a sub-requirement of requirement r_2. It is obvious that r_2 is stimulated by component s_2, which shows that the requirement pyramid is influenced by the system component pyramid. On the other hand, component s_3 has not been completed at the end of Time t_1. The major target of s_3 in Time t_2 is for further improvement.

The initial state of MRO Mashup System in the beginning of t2 is as follows:

$$(R, t_2) = r_2, r_3; Active\_queue : (r_2, t_2),$$
$$(r_3, t_2); Inactive\_set : (r_1, t_1);$$

At t_2, component s_4 will satisfy the requirement r_2, while component s_3 satisfies requirement r_2.

$$s_3 \rightarrow (r_3, t_2); s_2, s_4 \rightarrow (r_1, t_1); P(r_2, t_1)$$
$$> P(r_3, t_1); M(r_3, t_1) > M(r_2, t_1);$$

At the end of phase t_2, component s_3 and s_4 are both fully completed, whereas neither requirement r_2 nor r_3 completed yet. r_2 and r_3 both have the potential for further improvement.

$$M(r_2, t_2) > M(r_3, t_2); P(r_2, t_2) > P(r_3, t_2);$$

$$Active\_queue : \{(r_2, t_2), (r_3, t_2)\};$$
$$Inactive\_set : \{(r_1, t_1)\}$$

Figure c. shows the goal model of requirements in Time t_3. Notice that in the beginning of t_3, there have been two totally new requirements. One is transaction requirement for smooth payment between different B2C providers, the other one is Weibo component requirement. It is obvious that transaction requirement is stimulated by requirement r_2. The initial state of MRO Mashup System in the beginning of t_3 is:

$$(R, t_3) = \{r_4, r_5\};$$

$$Active\_queue : \{(r_4, t_3), (r_5, t_3), (r_2, t_3),$$
$$(r_3, t_3)\}; Inactive\_set : \{(r_1, t_1)\}$$

At t_3, component s_5 will satisfy the requirement r_4, while component s_6 satisfies requirement r_5. Neither r_2 nor r_3 is completed totally, they have no improvement tasks in time t_3. As a consequence, r_2 and r_3 are both suspended in t_3 period. The completion of components and corresponding of requirement priority after second release of MRO Mashup System.

$$s_5 \rightarrow (r_4, t_3); s_6 \rightarrow (r_5, t_3); P(r_5, t_3)$$
$$> P(r_6, t_3); M(r_5, t_3) = M(r_6, t_3) = 0$$

At the end of time t_3, components s_3 and s_4 are both completed, whereas neither requirement r_2 nor r_3 are satisfied fully yet. r_2 and r_3 both have the potential for further improvement.

$$1 = M(r_4, t_3) > M(r_5, t_3) M(r_4, t_3) > M(r_3, t_2)$$
$$M(r_4, t_3) > M(r_2, t_2);$$

$$Active\_queue : \{(r_2, t_2), (r_5, t_3), (r_3, t_2)\};$$
$$Inactive\_set : \{(r_1, t_1), (r_4, t_3)\}$$

It is obvious that the higher-level requirements always depend on lower level requirements. Based on this, the evolution trend is somehow traceable and it is possible to make requirements prediction and components optimization. Suppose that engineers are developing system components according to the user requirements at a certain stage. If engineers can foresee the possibility of some evolving components, and undertake responding enhancement and optimization, the system is more likely to satisfy emerging requirements in the next stage, resulting in better user experience and shortened system development cycle. The system adapts to changes in the environments and evolves with higher efficiency and better quality.

5.5   Related Work

The importance of software adaptation and evolution is widely acknowledged by many researchers. This assumption has been adopted as the basis [8,10,13] of a refined taxonomy for maintenance changes. In the stage model proposed by Bennett et al. [8], maintenance refers to general post-delivery activities, and evolution refers to a phase that adapts the application to the constantly changing requirements and run-time environment. Nowadays in most of the literature, it is widely accepted that continuous changes are the key feature of evolution. It has been associated with the change of code [26,27,35], modules [2,62] or architecture [1,32,34] of a software system typically. In addition, there are also studies on reverse engineering [1,32] at the code and process level. At present, the state-of-the-art work focuses on capturing and handling the changes in requirements and the environment [21,30,56].

Internetware, as a new software paradigm, aims to make the process of adaptation and evolution automated by using software assets accessible in the open Internet environment. The most closely related literature is in the services computing domain, where services adaptation and evolution is a topic attract much interesting research work. Generally speaking, there are two perspectives on service evolution: macro and micro. [44,46] consider the problem from the perspective of a service system community, and apply evolutionary computing to simulate the biological evolution process; the rest concentrate on the micro perspective, i.e., the evolution of a composite software service, which is in line with the evolution of Internetware components.

In [48], Papazoglou interprets service evolution as the continuous development of a service through a series of changes through the service's different versions. The key challenge is the forward compatibility between different versions, which is further explained as: a guarantee that an older version of a client application should be able to interpret and use newer message/data formats of the provider. A few paper discussed the taxonomy of evolutionary changes [48,50,60], and there are more research efforts committing themselves to address the compatibility problem using different tactics, including versioning, design pattern/adaptor [25,31,60] and theory/model [3,4]. Two types of changes are introduced: shallow (confined to services or clients) and deep (leading to cascading and side effects) changes. Also, he proposes a contract-based approach and a change-oriented lifecycle methodology to address these issues. As for shallow changes, typically it could leads to two levels of mismatches [45]: (1) interface-level, i.e. structural (2) protocol-level (i.e. ordering mismatches between service interaction protocols). Most of the work currently focuses on WSDL services and their interface, and the evolutionary changes are further discussed on message, operation, service and binding [9]. In addition, change of QoS and the semantic has also been considered to the subcategory of service evolution [36,50,60].

Versioning is a traditional and practical way to address the above challenges. A common trait of them is maintaining multiple service versions for a specified interface. A simple naming scheme that appends a date or version stamp to the end of a namespace is suggested to ensure the uniqueness of the version identifier. At the technical level, they rely heavily on the SOA technology ÍC SOAP, WSDL and UDDI. Usually, it is used together with the design pattern and related tools [23,36,63]. Design pattern is a widely adopted and effective approach in practice. A typical class of approach is to maintain multiple versions of a service on the server side, and provide a proxy that enable dynamic binding and invocation for client applications [23,36]. In a similar spirit, Kaminski et al. [31] propose a Chain of Adapters (multiple service interfaces for one implementation version) and Frank etc. [25] suggest a service interface proxy (one service interface for multiple implementation versions) for dealing with the incompatibility. In addition, Le Zou [37,47] try to keep client applications synchronized with the evolved service through (semi-) automatic client side update. To address possible interface mismatches, Dumas etc. [22] introduces an algebra-based interface adaptation method, in which each interface is represented as an algebra expression that could be transformed and linked accordingly. Motahari Nezhad et al. [45] provide semi-automatic support for adapter generation to resolve the mismatches at the interface-level and deadlock-free interaction protocol level. Treiber in [60] proposes a Service Evolution Management Framework (SEMF) that relies on an information model (e.g. usage statistics, logging) to manage the web service changes on Interface, QoS and interaction pattern. Andrikopoulos et al. [3] develops a formal abstract service (service schema) model for service evolution management, which provides an understanding for change tracking, control and impact. In [27], an algorithm for automatically assessing the forward compatibility between two revisions of a service specification is proposed.

Besides structural evolution, service protocol [45,55], composition schema [49,51,52] and process [53,55] evolution has also been carefully studied. [7,51] are good examples in analysing and addressing service incompatibility at the level of interaction protocol. [49,51,52] focus on service equivalence and substitutability in evolving composition schema. In [53,55], the authors introduce business process evolution, of which the challenge is to dynamically migrate on-going instances into the new version of a process. [20,28] consider potential atomicity problems in service composition, which is also relevant to the content in this chapter. Also, there are some other interesting researches on service evolution. For example, [54,64] discuss about the two well-understood strategies: "just enough" (ignoring unknown content) and adding schema extension points, which could be helpful for the semantics of evolution. In [61], S. Wang proposes a quantitative impact analysis model based on inter- and intra-service dependency. [12,43] concentrate on whether the designed system covers the requirement and how human

intention drives the evolution of software system using the situ framework.

Service adaptation is also an important methodology to keep the system behave as expected under certain condition. It generally includes the following scenarios: the system may need to dynamically (re-)select candidate service when suffer from failure [6], (re-)composite services to fulfil changed business process [11,17], replicate and distribute more service instances to adapt to emergent work load [18]. Adaptation has much to do with evolution but also has subtle distinctions. Generally, the change of requirement and/or environment would not always lead to software evolution if the variation is within anticipation at design time. At the moment the system is able to adopt an alternative mechanism in response (adaptation). When the situation is new/unknown to the system, the software system has to evolve to handle this case. More specifically, adaptation is conservative which only takes advantage of existing building units to satisfy the changed requirements/environment; while evolution is aggressive which may change the system boundary, e.g. adding/removing/modifying a service in a system.

5.6 Conclusion and Future Work

The adaptation and evolution characteristics are two of the most prominent properties of Internetware components, as well as user requirements. Across the software life cycle, the evolution of Internetware system is driven by the need of requirements. In this article, we illustrate our understanding and practice on Internetware adaptation and evolution. First of all, we propose to model Internetware systems using a four tuple including goals, environments, processes and strategies. The four tuple covers the major properties required to represent the requirements and system behaviours in the process of Internetware adaptation and evolution. In particular, goals and environments are concepts capturing the problem space, processes and strategies are used to capture the solution space. Internetware components are the system entities implementing processes and strategies. Then we defined a typology of system based on the four-tuple model, so that the differences between conventional static systems, reactive systems, adaptive systems and compositional/collaborative adaption systems can be explicitly defined. Essentially the difference lies in the management of gradual changes in the goal model. Then we refined the four-tuple model into a meta-model for Internetware components and defined the algorithms for matching and composing Internetware components with the proposed requirements and system modelling elements. This further develops into the adaptation process through compositional actions. Examples in the enterprise application domain are used to illustrate the different steps in the components selection, evolution process. An experimental environment on the cloud is deployed by the project team to integrate and showcase the various tools and applications of the Internetware paradigm. The current case studies show that the requirements driven adaptation and evolution model of Internetware is feasible and effective to use.

In summary, user requirements and system component are both evolving continuously, in which they constantly influence the improvement of each other stepwise. User requirements have a direct impact on the design and development of system, while the implementation of system components would also stimulate the generation of new user requirements, either directly or indirectly. If we bear in mind a co-evolution model capturing the interaction between user requirement and system development. It can help extend the life cycle of software systems and achieve high quality and efficiency at the same time. This chapter proposes a requirements-driven evaluation framework for Internetware-based components, on both their functionality and quality. In particular, we offer an account of how to model these requirements, how to derive from them a space of component functionality alternatives, and how to select among these alternatives on the basis of desired qualities. In essence, the selection of component functionality is framed as a satisfaction problem for functional requirements, while component quality is addressed as an optimisation problem. The

research work shows that the Internetware paradigm presents a promising direction to compose software applications from existing software assets on demand. In the future, the proposed approach in this chapter can be further enhanced with other automated evaluation measures. Their efficacy in supporting components development and composition can be studied and evaluated. Another possible future line of research is to develop domain specific components selection knowledge base and integrate with widely used software development and deployment platform.

References

1. M. Alawairdhi, H. Yang, A business-logic based framework for evolving software systems, in *33rd Annual IEEE International Computer Software and Applications Conference, COMPSAC (2)* (Seattle, Washington, 2009), pp. 300–305
2. S. Ali, O. Maqbool, Monitoring software evolution using multiple types of changes, in *5th International Conference on Emerging Technologies, ICET 2009*, Oct 2009 (Islamabad, Pakistan, 2009), pp. 410–415
3. V. Andrikopoulos, A theory and model for the evolution of software services. Open Access publications from Tilburg University urn:nbn:nl:ui:12-4275071, Tilburg University (2010)
4. V. Andrikopoulos, S. Benbernou, M.P. Papazoglou, Managing the evolution of service specifications, in *Advanced Information Systems Engineering, 20th International Conference, CAiSE*, ed. by Z. Bellahsene, M. Lonard. Lecture Notes in Computer Science, vol. 5074, 16–20 June 2008 (Montpellier, France, 2008), pp. 359–374
5. M. Aoyama, Process and economic model of component-based software development, in *5th IEEE Symposium on Assessment of Software Tools (SAST)*, June 2007 (Pittsburgh, PA, USA, 2007), pp. 100–103
6. D. Ardagna, L. Baresi, S. Comai et al., A service-based framework for flexible business processes. IEEE Softw. **28**(2), 61–67 (2011)
7. K. Becker, A. Lopes, D. S. Milojicic et al., Automatically determining compatibility of evolving services, in *International Conference on Web Services (ICWS)* (Beijing, China, 2008), pp. 161–168
8. K.H. Bennett, V. Rajlich, Software maintenance and evolution: a roadmap, in *International Conference on Software Engineering, ICSE—Future of SE Track*, ed. by A. Finkelstein (Ireland, Limerick, 2000), pp. 73–87
9. M. Benhaddi, K. Baïna, E. Abdelwahed, A user-centric mashuped SOA. Int. J. Web Sci. **1**(3), 204–223 (2012)
10. J. Buckley, Requirements-based visualization tools for software maintenance and evolution. IEEE Comput. **42**(4), 106–108 (2009)

11. G. Chafle, G. Das, K. Dasgupta et al., An integrated development environment for web service composition, in *International Conference on Web Services (ICWS)* (Salt Lake City, Utah, USA, 2007), pp. 839–847

12. C.K. Chang, H. Jiang, H. Ming et al., Situ: a situation-theoretic approach to context-aware service evolution. IEEE Trans. Serv. Comput. **2**(3), 261–275 (2009)

13. N. Chapin, J. Hale, J. Fernandez-Ramil et al., Types of software evolution and software maintenance. J. Softw. Maintenance Evol. Res. Pract. **13**(1), 3–30 (2001)

14. F. Chauvel, H. Song, X. Chen et al., Using QoS-contracts to drive architecture-centric self-adaptation, in *Proceedings of the 6th International conference on Quality of Software Architectures: research into Practice—Reality and Gaps, QoSA'10* (Berlin, Heidelberg, 2010), pp. 102–118

15. B.H.C. Cheng, R. de Lemos, H. Giese et al. (eds.), *Software Engineering for Self-Adaptive Systems:A Research Roadmap*, vol. 08031 *Dagstuhl Seminar Proceedings*. Internationales Begegnungs- und Forschungszentrum fuer Informatik (IBFI), Schloss Dagstuhl, Germany, 13.1. - 18.1.2008, pp. 1–26

16. B.J. Clement, E.H. Durfee, Theory for coordinating concurrent hierarchical planning agents using summary information, in *Proceedings of the Sixteenth National Conference on Artificial Intelligence and the Eleventh Innovative Applications of Artificial Intelligence Conference Innovative Applications of Artificial Intelligence (AAAI/IAAI)* (Orlando, Florida, USA, 1999), pp. 495–502

17. M. Colombo, E. Nitto, M. Mauri, Scene: a service composition execution environment supporting dynamic changes disciplined through rules, in *4th International Conference on Service-Oriented Computing—ICSOC 2006*, 4–7 Dec 2006 (Chicago, IL, USA, 2006), pp. 191–202

18. C. Bunch, N. Chohan, C. Krintz et al., An evaluation of distributed data stores using the AppScale cloud platform, in *Third IEEE 2010 International Conference on Cloud Computing (CLOUD 2010)*, 5–10 July 2010 (Miami, Florida, USA, 2010), pp. 305–312

19. N. Dalkey, The Delphi method: an experimental study of group opinion. Futures **1**(5), 408–426 (1969)

20. C. Ye, S.C. Cheung, W.K. Chan et al., Atomicity analysis of service composition across organizations. IEEE Trans. Softw. Eng. **35**(1), 2–28 (2009)

21. N. Desai, A.K. Chopra, M.P. Singh, Amoeba: a methodology for modeling and evolving cross-organizational business processes. ACM Trans. Softw. Eng. Methodol. **19**(2), 1–40 (2009)

22. M. Dumas, M. Spork, K. Wang, Adapt or perish: algebra and visual notation for service interface adaptation, in *4th International Conference Business Process Management* (Vienna, Austria 2006), pp. 65–80

23. R. Fang, L. Lam, L. Fong, D. Frank et al., A version-aware approach for web service directory, in *International Conference on Web Services (ICWS)* (Salt Lake City, Utah, USA, 2007), pp. 406–413

24. S. Fickas, M. Feather, Requirements monitoring in dynamic environments, in *2nd IEEE International Symposium on Requirements Engineering (RE95)* (York, U.K., 1995), pp. 140–147

25. D. Frank, L. Lam, L. Fong et al., Using an interface proxy to host versioned web services, in *IEEE International Conference on Services Computing (SCC 2008) SCC (2)*, 8–11 July 2008 (Honolulu, Hawaii, USA, 2008), pp. 325–332

26. M. Godfrey, Q. Tu, Growth, evolution, and structural change in open source software, in *Proceedings of the 4th International Workshop on Principles of Software Evolution, IWPSE '01* (New York, NY, USA, 2001), pp. 103–106

27. S. Gala-Pérez, G. Robles, J.M. González-Barahona et al., Intensive metrics for the study of the evolution of open source projects: case studies from apache software foundation projects, in *The 10th Working Conference on Mining Software Repositories, MSR* (San Francisco, California, USA, 2013), pp. 159–168

28. C. Ye, S.C. Cheung, W.K. Chan et al., Detection and resolution of atomicity violation in service composition, in *The 6th Joint Meeting of the European Software Engineering Conference and the ACM SIGSOFT Symposium on the Foundations of Software Engineering (ESEC/SIGSOFT FSE)* (Dubrovnik, Croatia, 2007), pp. 235–244

29. B. Verlaine, E. Dubois, I. Jureta et al., Towards conceptual foundations for service-oriented requirements engineering: bridging requirements and services ontologies. IET Softw. **6**(2), 85–102 (2012)

30. L. Baresi, A. Marconi, M. Pistore et al., Corrective evolution of adaptable process models, in *Enterprise, Business-Process and Information Systems Modeling—14th International Conference, BPMDS 2013, 18th International Conference, EMMSAD 2013, Held at CAiSE 2013, BMMDS/EMMSAD*, 17–18 June 2013 (Valencia, Spain, 2013), pp. 214–229

31. P. Kaminski, M. Litoiu, H. Müller, A design technique for evolving web services, in *Proceedings of the 2006 conference of the Center for Advanced Studies on Collaborative research, CASCON '06* (Riverton, NJ, USA, 2006). IBM Corp

32. T. Kim, K. Kim, W. Kim, An interactive change impact analysis based on an architectural reflexion model approach, in *34th Annual IEEE International Computer Software and Applications Conference, COMPSAC* (Seoul, South Korea, 2010), pp. 297–302

33. S. Liaskos, S.A. McIlraith, S. Sohrabi et al., Representing and reasoning about preferences in requirements engineering. Requir. Eng. **16**(3), 227–249 (2011)

34. O. Le Goaer, D. Tamzalit, M. Oussalah, Evolution styles to capitalize evolution expertise within software architectures, in *22nd International Conference on Software Engineering and Knowledge Engineering, SEKE* (Redwood City, San Francisco Bay, USA, 2010), pp. 159–164

35. M. Lehman, J.F. Ramil, Software evolution—background, theory, practice. Inf. Process. Lett. **88**(1–2), 33–44 (2003)

36. P. Leitner, A. Michlmayr, F. Rosenberg et al., End-to-end versioning support for web services, in *IEEE International Conference on Services Computing (SCC 2008) SCC (1)*, 8–11 July 2008 (Honolulu, Hawaii, USA, 2008), pp. 59–66

37. Z. Zou, R. Fang, L. Liu et al., On synchronizing with web service evolution, in *International Conference on Web Services (ICWS)* (Beijing, China, 2008), pp. 329–336

38. Y. Li, M. Zhou, C. You et al., Enabling on demand deployment of middleware services in componentized middleware, in *13th International Symposium on Component-Based Software Engineering*, 23–25 June 2010 (Prague, Czech Republic, 2010), pp. 113–129

39. J. Lv, X. Ma, X. Tao et al., On environment-driven software model for Internetware. Sci. China Ser. F: Inf. Sci. **51**(6), 683–721 (2008)

40. H. Mei, G. Huang, H. Zhao et al., A software architecture centric engineering approach for Internetware. Sci. China Ser. F: Inf. Sci. **49**(6), 702–730 (2006)

41. W. Ma, L. Liu, H. Xie et al., Preference model driven services selection, in *Conference on Advanced Information Systems Engineering (CAiSE)* (Amsterdam, The Netherlands, 2009), pp. 216–230

42. Y. Wei, C.A. Furia, N. Kazmin et al., Inferring better contracts, in *The 33rd International Conference on Software Engineering, ICSE* (Honoulu, Hawaii, USA, 2011), pp. 191–200

43. H. Ming, C.K. Chang, K. Oyama et al., Reasoning about human intention change for individualized runtime software service evolution, in *Proceedings of the 2010 IEEE 34th Annual Computer Software and Applications Conference, COMPSAC '10* (Washington, DC, USA, 2010), pp. 289–296

44. D. Miorandi, L. Yamamoto, P. Dini, Service evolution in bio-inspired communication systems. Int. Trans. Syst. Sci. Appl. ITSSA **2**(1), 51–60 (2006)

45. W. Kongdenfha, H.R. Nezhad, B. Benatallah et al., Mismatch patterns and adaptation aspects: a foundation for rapid development of web service adapters. IEEE Trans. Serv. Comput. **2**(2), 94–107 (2009)

46. T. Nakano, T. Suda, Self-organizing network services with evolutionary adaptation. IEEE Trans. Neural Netw. **16**(5), 1269–1278 (2005)

47. M. Ouederni, G. SalaÃn, E. Pimentel, Client update: a solution for service evolution, in *IEEE International Conference on Services Computing (SCC)*, ed. by H.-A. Jacobsen, Y. Wang, P. Hung, 4–9 July 2011 (Washington, DC, USA, 2011), pp. 394–401

48. V. Andrikopoulos, S. Benbernou, M.P. Papazoglou, On the evolution of services. IEEE Trans. Softw. Eng. **38**(3), 609–628 (2012)

49. J. Pathak, S. Basu, V. Honavar, On context-specific substitutability of web services, in *International Conference on Web Services (ICWS)* (Salt Lake City, Utah, USA, 2007), pp. 192–199

50. S. Ponnekanti, A. Fox, Interoperability among independently evolving web services, in *Middleware* (Toronto, Ontario, Canada, 2004), pp. 331–351

51. S. Rinderle-Ma, M. Reichert, M. Jurisch, On utilizing web service equivalence for supporting the composition life cycle. Int. J. Web Serv. Res. **8**(1), 41–67 (2011)

52. S. Rinderle-Ma, M. Reichert, M. Jurisch, Equivalence of web services in process-aware service compositions, in *International Conference on Web Services (ICWS)* (Los Angeles, CA, USA, 2009), pp. 501–508

53. S. Rinderle, B. Weber, M. Reichert et al., Integrating process learning and process evolution—a semantics based approach, in *Business Process Management* ed. by W.M.P. van der Aalst, B. Benatallah, F. Casati et al., vol. 3649, Sept 2005 (Nancy, France, 2005), pp. 252–267

54. I. Robinson, Integrating process learning and process evolution—a semantics based approach, in *Business Process Management* ed. by W.M.P. van der Aalst, B. Benatallah, F. Casati et al., vol. 3649, Sept 2005 (Nancy, France, 2005), pp. 252–267

55. S.H. Ryu, F. Casati, H. Skogsrud et al., Supporting the dynamic evolution of web service protocols in service-oriented architectures. ACM Trans. Web (TWEB) **2**(2), 1–46 (2008)

56. M. Salifu, Y. Yu, B. Nuseibeh, Specifying monitoring and switching problems in context, in *15th International Requirements Engineering ConferenceRE* (New Delhi, India, 2007), pp. 211–220

57. T. Saaty, Decision making with the analytic hierarchy process. Int. J. Serv. Sci. **1**(1), 83–98 (2008)

58. J. Tang, Z. Jin, Assignment problem in requirements driven agent collaboration and its implementation, in *Proceedings of the 9th International Conference on Autonomous Agents and Multi-agent Systems: volume 1-Volume 1* (Toronto, Ontario, Canada, 2010), pp. 839–846

59. R. Sebastiani, P. Giorgini, J. Mylopoulos, Simple and minimum-cost satisfiability for goal models, in *Advanced Information Systems Engineering* (Riga, Latvia, 2004), pp. 20–35

60. M. Treiber, H.-L. Truong, S. Dustdar, On analyzing evolutionary changes of web services, in *Service-Oriented Computing-ICSOC 2008 Workshops* (Stockholm, Sweden 2009), pp. 284–297

61. S. Wang, M.A. Capretz, A dependency impact analysis model for web services evolution, in *International Conference on Web Services (ICWS)* (Los Angeles, CA, USA, 2009), pp. 359–365

62. Y. Wang, D. Guo, H. Shi, Measuring the evolution of open source software systems with their communities. ACM SIGSOFT Softw. Eng. Notes **32**(6), 7 (2007)

63. R. Weinreich, T. Ziebermayr, D. Draheim, A versioning model for enterprise services, in *21st International Conference on Advanced Information Networking and Applications Workshops, AINAW'07.*, vol. 2 (2007), pp. 570–575

64. E. Wilde, Semantically extensible schemas for web service evolution, in *European Conference on Web Services (ECOWS'04)*, Sept 2004 (Erfurt, Germany, 2004), pp. 30–45

65. E. Yu, Towards modelling and reasoning support for early-phase requirements engineering, in *Proceedings of the Third IEEE International Symposium on Requirements Engineering* (Annapolis, MD, U.S.A., 1997), pp. 226–235

66. L. Zheng, J. Tang, Z. Jin, An agent based framework for Internetware computing. Int. J. Softw. Inf. **4**(4), 401–418 (2010)

67. L. Liu, C. Yang, J. Wang, X. Ye, Y. Liu, H. Yang, X. Liu, Requirements model driven adptation and evolution of Internetware. Sci. China Inf. Sci. **57**(6), 1–19 (2019)

## Part III

Internetware Operating Platform

In Part 2, we have introduced the basic software model featuring the reflective interface beyond basic software components, and environment-driven adaptation for Internetware applications. Enabling techniques for the model, especially the modeling, management, and utilization of environment information. Around the software model, we present a software architecture centric framework to describe a high-level guideline for developing and operating Internetware applications. In Part 3 and 4, we will introduce how the technical framework is realized.

This part introduces the practices on the runtime support for Internetware application systems. The support covers various aspects of the execution and adaptation of software situated in the open and dynamic Internet environment. A key element of the support is the *runtime* model of software architecture reflectively connected to the actual runtime states of the structures and behaviors of the system. The idea of runtime software architecture has been realized in two different middleware systems. At a lower lever, to carry out adaptation of Internetware systems at runtime, it is crucial to support safe and efficient online update of running code. This requires advanced support for dynamic software updating in the programming language virtual machine. The runtime support for Internetware also goes beyond the system itself to the sensing and interpretation of the environmental situations, which include not only physical devices

but also software entities and services distributed in the open environment.

The key in architecture-based self-organization and self-adaptation is to recover software architecture from existing systems. Further, we need to change the system directly via manipulating the recovered software architecture. Chapter 6 presents an approach to recovering software architecture from component-based systems at runtime and changing the runtime systems via manipulating the recovered software architecture. Containing much more details than the designed software architecture, the recovered software architecture can accurately and thoroughly describe the actual states and behaviors of the runtime system. It can be described formally with the extension of traditional architecture description language, which enables the recovered software architecture to absorb the semantics embedded in the designed software architecture.

In order to support runtime software architecture, we need to maintain the causal connection between the architecture and the system, ensuring that the architecture represents the current system, and the modifications on the architecture cause proper changes in the system. The main challenge here is the semantic gap between the architecture and the system. Chapter 7 investigates the synchronization mechanism between architecture configurations and system states for maintaining the causal connections. We identify four required properties for such synchronization, and provide a generic solution to ensuring these properties. We provide a generative tool-set that helps developers implement this approach on a wide class of systems.

In software evolution, shutting down a running system before updating it is a normal practice, but the service unavailability can be annoying and sometimes unacceptable. Dynamic software updating migrates a running software system to a new version without stopping it. Chapter 8 presents a system that can support online update within very short interval. Instead of updating everything at once when the running application is suspended, the presented system updates only the changed code during the suspension, and migrates stale objects on-demand after the application is resumed. With a careful design, this lazy approach neither sacrifices the update flexibility nor introduces unnecessary object validity checks or access indirections. The system can reduce the updating pausing time by one to two orders of magnitude without introducing observable overheads before and after the dynamic updating.

To achieve situation-aware adaptation at runtime in a quite dynamic environment, an adaptation mechanism is usually expected to monitor environment changes, make appropriate decisions, and react accordingly. However, existing runtime monitoring solutions in service-oriented systems consider only the constraints on the sequence of messages exchanged between partner services and ignore the actual data contents inside the messages. As a result, it is difficult to monitor certain dynamic properties such as how message data of interest is processed between different participants. To address this issue, Chap. 9 propose an efficient, non-intrusive online monitoring approach to dynamically analyze data-centric properties for service-oriented applications involving multiple participants. By introducing a Parametric Behavior Constraint Language for Web services to define monitoring parameters, various data-centric temporal behavior properties can be specified and monitored. This approach broadens the monitored patterns to include not only message exchange orders, but also data contents bound to the parameters.

The open environment is intrinsically distributed and asynchronous. In asynchronous environments where different computing entities do not share the same notion of time, the concurrency property must be specified explicitly and detected at runtime. Chapter 10 applies the classical logical time to model behavior of the asynchronous environment. We give the formal syntax for specification of the concurrency property. We also give the semantic interpretation based on the modeling of asynchronous environment behavior. The CADA algorithm is proposed to achieve runtime detection of the concurrency property.

Runtime Recovery and Manipulation of Software Architecture of Component-Based Systems

Abstract

Recently, more attention is paid to the researches and practices on how to use software architecture in software maintenance and evolution to reduce their complexity and cost. The key in such architecture-based maintenance and evolution is to recover software architecture from existing systems. Almost all studies on architecture recovery focus on analyzing the source code and other documents. Such recovered software architecture can hardly capture runtime states and behaviors of the system. At the same time, current work pays little attention on how to change the system directly via manipulating the recovered software architecture. This chapter presents a novel approach to recovering software architecture from component based systems at runtime and changing the runtime systems via manipulating the recovered software architecture. Containing much more details than the designed software architecture, the recovered software architecture can accurately and thoroughly describe the actual states and behaviors of the runtime system. It can be described formally with the extension of traditional architecture description language, which enables the recovered software architecture to absorb the semantics embedded in the designed software architecture. The recovered software architecture can be represented as multiple views so as to help different users to control the complexity from different concerns. Based on the reflective ability of the component framework, the recovered software architecture is up-to-date at any time and changes made on it will immediately lead to the corresponding changes in the runtime system. The approach presented in this chapter is demonstrated on PKUAS, a reflective J2EE (Java 2 Enterprise Edition) application server, and the performance is also evaluated.

Parts of this chapter were reprinted with kind permission from Springer Science+Business Media: <Automated Software Engineering, Runtime recovery and manipulation of software architecture of component-based systems, volume 13, 2006, 257–281, Gang Huang, Hong Mei and Fu-Qing Yang, figure number(s), and any original (first) copyright notice displayed with material>.

Keywords

Software architecture recovery · Runtime system · Reflection · Component framework

6.1   Introduction

Recognized as a critical issue in the development of any complex software system, software architecture has become an important subfield of software engineering, receiving increased attention from both academic and industrial community. Software architecture describes the gross structure of a software system with a collection of components, connectors and constraints [32]. In general, software architecture acts as a bridge between requirements and implementation and provides a blueprint for system construction and composition. It helps to understand large systems, support reuse at both component and architecture level, indicate the major components to be developed and their relationships and constraints, expose changeability of the system, verify and validate the target system at a high level and so on [10,11]. Recently, software architecture is used to help maintenance and evolution [26,33,34] to reduce their complexity and cost that mainly result from the difficulty of understanding the large-scale and complex software [5]. Since that software architecture helps to understand large-scale software systems is well recognized, it is a natural idea to understand the system to be maintained and evolved through its architecture.

Obviously, the most important thing in such architecture-based maintenance and evolution is software architecture of the target system. Software architecture produced at design phase (called designed software architecture) seems able to be directly used in maintenance and evolution. Unfortunately, it cannot work well for three reasons. Firstly, the designed software architecture may be not available because the system is developed without an explicit architecting phase or the documents are lost. Secondly, the designed software architecture may have some differences or mismatch with the actual software

architecture built in the target system. Ideally, if the developers and maintainers always obey the strict principles of software engineering, e.g., update the design documents when any change is made in implementation or maintenance, the designed software architecture should correctly describe software architecture of the target system. But in practice, such work to keep the consistency among the documents and target system is too trivial, tedious and error-prone to be done seriously. Then, the differences or mismatch between the designed software architecture and the actual software architecture built in the system appear and become more when time elapses. Thirdly and finally, since different stakeholders have different requirements, the designed software architecture is for development and may not fit for maintenance and evolution. Typically, the maintainers require much more details about the system than the developers, e.g., internal structure of a component, details of a connector, and so on. Then, architecture-based maintenance and evolution should use software architecture recovered from the target system, instead of the designed software architecture.

Software architecture used in maintenance and evolution is usually recovered from the source code and other documents of the target system based on program comprehension, such as the work in [17,26,30,34]. Such recovered software architecture cannot capture some special details appearing at runtime, which are important to maintenance and evolution. For examples, the number of threads, size of buffers, number of network connections, use rate of CPU and memory, number of component instances, total number of invocations to a given component or its method, and other information related to workload are critical to tune performance; the exceptions occur at runtime help to correct errors; the account for invalid invocations may inform the maintainers that the security policy and mechanism may need to be changed; the maximum, minimal and average response time of a given method may identify that the algorithm in this method has to be re-implemented. Though these runtime details may be available in some special management tools, they are hard to integrate into software architecture recovered from the documents. Consequently, the maintainers cannot get all of their required information from the recovered software architecture.

After software architecture is recovered, the maintainers will observe and analyze the recovered software architecture and then maybe make decisions to adjust the system to meet some new requirements, achieve better performance, correct errors or faults, and so on. The maintainers can select and manipulate an appropriate management tool to adapt the system. Note that the tool is not designed for the recovered software architecture, and vice versa, the tool may be unable to perform the desired changes exactly, that is, the changes made on the system are less or more than the desired changes. Furthermore, as soon as the system is changed, the recovered software architecture has to be updated manually or to be recovered again. Recall the reason for the differences between the designed software architecture and the actual software architecture built in the system, the recovered software architecture seems to face the same mismatch problem. On the other hand, if the maintainers are allowed to adjust the system just via manipulating the recovered software architecture and promised that what you can change in the recovered software architecture is what the actual system allows to change, the above two problems will disappear.

In this chapter, an approach to online recovery and manipulation of software architecture is presented. Based on the reflection ability of the component framework, software architecture is recovered up-to-date from the runtime system that can be adapted through manipulation of the recovered software architecture. The recovered software architecture can be specified formally in architectural description language (ADL), which is extended from a traditional ADL via defin-

ing some new elements to accurately capture the actual states and behaviors of the runtime system. If the designed software architecture specified in the traditional ADL exists, the recovered software architecture can automatically retrieve semantic information in the designed software architecture and append them to itself. Almost all details in software architecture are recovered from the metadata in the runtime system and the complex architecture view can be automatically simplified with the help of special features of the ADL. To facilitate the observation and manipulation of the recovered software architecture, both API and GUI are provided.

The approach is demonstrated in a J2EE-compliant application server. Currently, there are three common component frameworks, including CORBA/CCM (Common Object Request Broker Architecture [4]/CORBA Component Model [3]), J2EE/EJB (Java 2 Platform Enterprise Edition [2]/Enterprise JavaBeans [1]) and .NET/COM (Component Object Model). Note that J2EE/EJB and .NET/COM are much more matured in technology and market than CORBA/CCM, J2EE/EJB and CORBA/CCM are much more open than .NET/COM, J2EE/EJB is compliant with CORBA/CCM and then the approach applied into one can also be applied into another with some modifications. Then, our approach is experimented on J2EE applications and some technical details in the rest of the chapter will be specific to J2EE/EJB. The results of performance test on this demonstration shows that the recovery and manipulation of software architecture have good performance and put little performance penalty on the runtime system.

The rest of this chapter is organized as the following: Sect. 6.2 gives an outline of our approach. Section 6.3 discusses what architecture recovered at runtime should be and how to describe it formally. Sections 6.4 and 6.5 present the details of recovery and manipulation of software architecture respectively. Section 6.6 evaluates the results of performance test. Section 6.7 introduces some related work to our approach and Sect. 6.8 summarizes the contributions and identifies the future work of this chapter.

6.2 Approach Overview

This section will discuss the role of the recovered architecture via comparing multiple architectures in the whole software lifecycle and the conceptual framework for recovering and manipulating software architecture from the component-based system at runtime.

6.2.1 Architectures in ABC

ABC is a software reuse methodology that supports the building of a software system with prefabricated components under the guide of software architecture [22]. It employs software architecture descriptions as frameworks to develop components as well as blueprints for constructing systems, while using middleware as the runtime scaffold for component composition. Previously, ABC focuses on software development and then did not address the role of software architecture in the post-delivery phases. Considering the work presented in this chapter, ABC is improved so that software architecture can guide all activities in the whole software life cycle, as shown in Fig. 6.1.

- Architecture-Oriented Requirement Analysis: In [21], an architecture-oriented requirements engineering approach is proposed to introduce concepts and principles of software architecture into requirement analysis and requirement specifications to achieve the traceability and consistency between requirement specifications and system design. In this phase, there is no actual software architecture but only the requirement specifications of the system to be developed, which are structured in the way similar to software architecture. It consists of a set of component specifications, connector specifications and constraint specifications and will be used as the basis for software architecting.

- Architecture Design: In this phase, architecture-oriented requirement specifications are transformed and refined in the architectural design of system, and some overall design decisions are made. In order to produce software architecture meeting functional and non-functional requirements of the target system, the architects may study the requirement specifications, transform and refine components and connectors in the problem space, create necessary artificial components and connectors, produce configuration of software architecture, build mapping relationships between requirement specifications and software architecture, check software architecture and so on. In order to improve the proportion of assets reused in the target system in the composition phase, the reusable assets library should be taken into consideration in this phase.

- Architecture-based Composition: In this phase, the components, connectors and con-

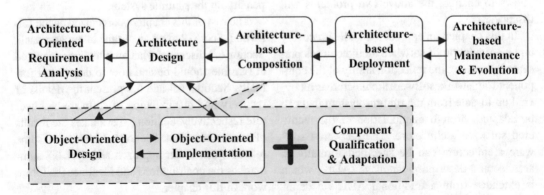

Fig. 6.1 ABC process model

straints[1] in the reusable assets repository will be selected, qualified and adapted to implement the logic entities produced in architecting. However, there are still some elements unable to be implemented by reusable assets. These elements have to be implemented by hand in object-oriented languages or other ones. Being implemented and tested, the elements will be stored into the repository and then composed into the target system as reusable assets. In that sense, the designed software architecture can be fully implemented by the reusable assets.

- Architecture-based Deployment: Component-based systems are usually implemented and executed with the help of some common middleware. Before the implementation of the system being executed, it must be deployed into the middleware platform. In this phase, software architecture should be complemented with some information so that middleware can install and execute the system correctly. Typically, the information includes declaration of required resources, security realm and roles, component names for runtime binding, and so on. For example, J2EE deployment description is a tool allowing J2EE applications to execute in J2EE application servers [2].

- Architecture-based Maintenance and Evolution: Usually, it is necessary to acquire information about the system as much as possible to achieve successful maintenance and evolution. Software architecture in this phase provides a framework to integrate all information collected from the runtime system, including details that are invisible in traditional architecture views. In other words, software architecture provides a high-level abstraction of the runtime system and a set of entries to observe and manipulate the runtime system in lower levels.

6.2.2 Conceptual Framework

Figure 6.2 shows how to recover software architecture from a runtime system and adapt the system via manipulating its architecture view. A set of runtime entities that represent basic elements in software architecture will be automatically created according to the runtime system. These entities reflect the runtime system, that is, changes occurring in the runtime system immediately lead to corresponding changes on these entities (shown as (1) arrow), and vice versa (shown as (6) arrow). Since basic elements in the recovered software architecture are mapped from the data encapsulated in the above runtime entities, changes in the runtime system will immediately lead to corresponding changes in the recovered software architecture (shown as (2) arrow), and vice versa (shown as (5) arrow). In other words, the recovered software architecture is always up-to-date and the runtime system can be adapted via manipulating the recovered software architecture. The architecture view consisting of the above basic elements may be too large and tangled to observe and manipulate. In the design phase, the complexity of architecture views is usually controlled by some special features, including composite component, complex connector and architectural style. Naturally, the recovered software architecture needs these special features to produce understandable views (shown as (3) arrow). One of the most important problems in the recovered software architecture is the lack of semantics, which is critical to understand the system and make decisions to change it. On the other hand, the artifacts in the development contain plentiful semantics, like the specification of the designed software architecture. Then, some special mechanisms enabling the recovered software architecture to absorb the semantic information in the design artifacts are needed (shown as (4) arrow).

6.3 Characteristics of Software Architecture at Runtime

The representation of the designed software architecture is not fit for the recovered software architecture because it cannot capture the actual states

---

[1]In ABC, the cross-cutting constraints, like security, transaction and persistency, are considered as aspects, which are implemented as independent entities and can be weaved together with components and connectors at runtime with the support of component framework. Then these aspectized constraints are also reusable assets.

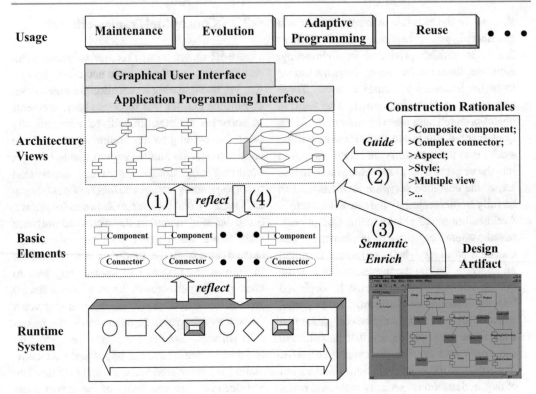

Fig. 6.2 Conceptual framework for online recovery and manipulation of software architecture

and behaviors of the runtime system. In other words, the recovered software architecture provides a novel view of the system, compared to the views provided by the designed software architecture.

6.3.1 Software Architecture at Design Time

To explain our approach more clearly, an example of an e-commerce system, as shown in Fig. 6.3, is used in the rest of this chapter. Software architecture in this diagram is a design view and its notations are defined by ABC/ADL (an Architecture Description Language in ABC) [9]. In the system, called eShop, customers can purchase computer products from Internet. OpShopping-Cart provides GUI to Client, who can access their

accounts represented by Customer, explore and buy products represented by Product, and review, change or delete their orders via OpOrder. Shop-pingCartLineItem represents one type of computer product and its quantity preferred by customer. ShoppingCart is responsible for creating, modifying and deleting a set of ShoppingCart-LineItems. OrderLineItem represents the type and quantity of one purchased product, and Order represents all OrderLineItem purchased at one time.

In the designed software architecture, components and connectors are usually considered as atomic or black-box entities. Consequently, one component or connector is observed and changed as a whole in maintenance and evolution. In particular, changes of software architecture can be divided into addition, removal, replacement and adaptation of components and connectors [29]. Considering the sample system, OpShoppingCart

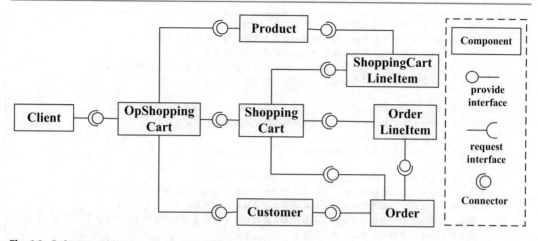

Fig. 6.3 Software architecture of eShop in ABC/ADL diagram

may be replaced to provide a better GUI to attract clients or be adapted to allow more clients to access simultaneously. New connectors supporting SOAP (Simple Object Access Protocol) may be attached to Customer, Product and Shopping-Cart so that eShop can be integrated with other e-commerce systems via Web Services. The connector between OpShoppingCart and Customer may be adapted to transport messages in a secure way, e.g., SSL (Secure Socket Layer).

6.3.2   Software Architecture at Runtime

In some component frameworks, including COR-BA/CCM and J2EE/EJB, components and connectors are instantiated and executed as composite or white-box entities. Listing 6.1 shows the details of the contract, implementation and constraints of an EJB. The contract of an EJB consists of a Home interface and a Component interface [1]. The Home interface defines the methods not specific to a particular EJB instance, such as to create, remove and find EJBs. The Component interface defines the business methods that specify the responsibility or functionality of the component. The implementation of an EJB has

no explicit relationship with the contract from the perspective of programming language. For example, CustomerBean is the implementation of Customer EJB. It does not explicitly implement Customer and CustomerHome interfaces in the class declaration and its methods can also be different with the methods defined in Customer and CustomerHome interfaces, e.g., the ejbCreate method of CustomerBean is the implementation of the create method of CustomerHome. Component framework will associate the implementation with the contract under the help of deployment descriptor that describes the structure of EJBs, their external dependencies and the application assembly information specifying how to compose individual EJBs into an application. Deployment descriptor also contains the constraints of an EJB specifying the non-functional requirements of the component, such as security, transaction, persistency and so on. For example, Customer EJB has a persistent attribute named customerID, a primary key that uniquely identifies particular instance of Customer and a secured method named findAllCustomers that can be invoked only by the administrator. Component framework will enforce the constraints with the help of common services, like security service and transaction service.

```
//One  part  of  contract  of  Customer  EJB.
interface CustomerHome extends EJBHome {
    Customer create(String name);
    Customer findByPrimaryKey(String key);
    Collection findAllCustomers();
...}
//Another part of contract of Customer EJB.
interface Customer extends EJBObject {
    String getAddress();
    void setAddress();
...}
//Implementation of Customer EJB.
class CustomerBean implements EntityBean {
    Customer ejbCreate(String name) {...}
    Customer ejbFindByPrimaryKey(String key) {...}
    String getAddress() {...}
    void setAddress() {...}
...}
//Constraints on Customer EJB in deployment
    description.
...
<cmp-field>customerID</cmp-field>
<prim-key-class>java.lang.String</prim-key-class>
<cmp-version>2.x</cmp-version>
...
<method-premission>
    <role-name>administrator</role-name>
    <method>
        <ejb-name>Order</ejb-name>
        <method-name>findAllCustomers</method-name>
    </method>
</method-permission>
...
```

Listing 6.1 Contract, implementation and constraints of Customer EJB

The component framework for EJB, that is, J2EE application server, has to make the contract, implementation and constraints work together while keeping them separate. As a result, a black-box component at the design phase becomes white-box at runtime in the viewpoint of component framework, as shown in Fig. 6.4. Meanwhile, a connector also becomes white-box, consisting of a client-side proxy (called stub), a server-side proxy (called skeleton) and a communication infrastructure compliant with some standard interoperability protocols, like IIOP (Internet Inter-ORB Protocol), SOAP and

JRMP (Java Remote Method Protocol). Since all of these runtime entities are usually independent of each other more or less, they are able to be observed and changed independently. For example, the implementation of Customer may be replaced because of changes to the database schema. It does not impact the external view of Customer, including the interface, constraints and clients. Then such change cannot be observed in traditional software architecture views. Furthermore, to perform such change in these views may be more complex and expensive, including to reload the interface classes, re-instantiate classes

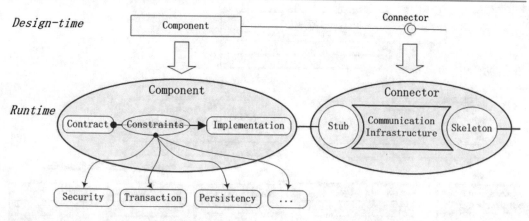

Fig. 6.4 Software architecture at runtime

enforced constraints, re-allocate resources, re-bind connections between the component and its clients besides to replace the implementation.

6.3.3 Description for Software Architecture Recovered at Runtime

Architecture Description Language (ADL) is proposed to provide formal notations for development and analysis of software architecture [32]. All existing ADLs focus on software development and cannot be directly applied into the recovered software architecture mainly because of the different perspective. In other words, existing ADLs have to be extended to describe the recovered software architecture. Considering the fact that the description in existing ADLs is the main artifact in architecture-based development, there are two advantages of the extension besides formal notations. One is that it enables the recovered software architecture to enrich the semantics from ADL descriptions, which will be demonstrated in the next section. Another is instinctive that it keeps traceability of software architecture in the whole software lifecycle.

ABC/ADL is an ADL supporting the design, implementation and deployment of component-based system in ABC [23]. The elements in ABC/ADL have similar definitions to those of the ADL Classification and Comparison Framework presented in [20]. As shown in Fig. 6.5,

the extension of ABC/ADL for the recovered software architecture includes the major elements as follows[2]:

- Runtime Software Architecture: it consists of all component and connector instances in the runtime system and extends Configuration in ABC/ADL. In the designed software architecture, a Configuration is a group of interconnected component and connector instances that comply with the constraints of architectural styles. It consists of the declarations of all instances of components and connectors used in the system and the topologic layout of these instances.

- Component: it represents a component instance in the runtime system and extends ComponentInst in ABC/ADL. In the designed software architecture, a ComponentInst only acts as a label to identify component types of the nodes in the layout. On the contrary, component instances are the first-class entities in the runtime system and then become the most important elements in the recovered software architecture. Considering the perspective of component frameworks mentioned above, the component contract is represented in Component Type in ABC/ADL, the component imple-

---

[2]Being an important element, Constraint is omitted in order to keep the figure simple and clear because the constraints can be contained in the whole architecture, single component, single connector, and even proxies.

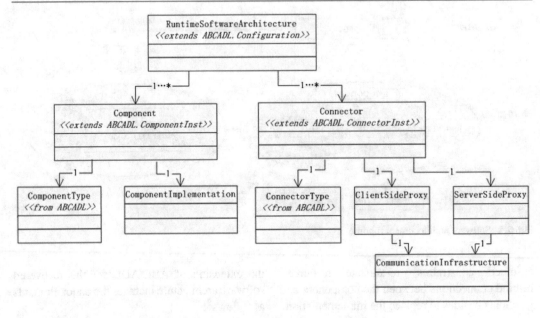

Fig. 6.5 Extension of ABC/ADL for describing the recovered software architecture

mentation is represented in Component Imple-mentation, and the component constraints are represented as a set of properties of Compo-nent.

- Connector: it represents a connector instance in the runtime system and extends ConnectorInst in ABC/ADL, like Component. It consists of a Connector Type, a Client Side Proxy and a Server Side Proxy, the later two of which have a Communication Infrastructure to describe the elements in the perspective of middleware.

In the above elements, the Runtime Software Architecture, Component Type and Connector Type can naturally inherit the semantics from the designed software architecture. The other elements are extended to accurately capture the states and behaviors of the runtime system.

6.4   Recovery of Software Architecture at Runtime

6.4.1   Overview of PKUAS

PKUAS (Peking University Application Server) is a J2EE-compliant application server [24], which

provides a deployment and runtime environment for several types of components, i.e., JSP/Servlet and EJB. Its internal functions are componentized into several loose-coupled system components, as shown in Fig. 6.6.

- Container system and container: a container provides a runtime space for the components in the deployed applications with lifecycle man-agement and contract enforcement [2]. PKUAS implements standard EJB containers for state-less session bean, stateful session bean and bean-managed entity bean [1]. One instance of a container holds all instances of one EJB. And a container system consists of the instances of the containers holding all EJBs in an applica-tion. Such organization of the containers facil-itates the configuration and management spe-cific to individual applications, such as security realm per application and architectural infor-mation of the application.
- Service: it provides the common functions, like naming, communication, security, transaction and log. The naming and communication services provide an interoperability frame-work that enables the components deployed in PKUAS to interact with each other and

Fig. 6.6 PKUAS
componentized
infrastructure

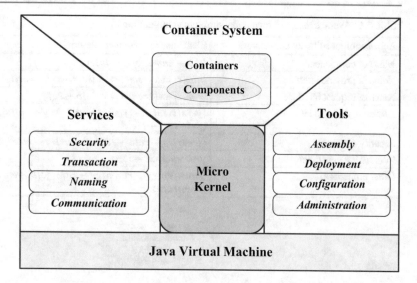

other components outside PKUAS through multiple interoperability protocols [15]. Currently, PKUAS supports IIOP (Internet Inter-ORB Protocol), JRMP (Java Remote Method Protocol), SOAP (Simple Object Access Protocol), IntraVM (optimized for two components collocated in the same JVM) and EJBLocal (supports interactions between EJBs collocated in the same JVM with the pass-by-reference semantics while the previous four supports pass-by-value semantics). From the perspective of software architecture, they implement main part of connectors, while other services are commonly used to enforce system-level constraints on components and connectors.

- Tool: it provides functions to facilitate the operation of PKUAS, such as deployment and management. In particular, the recovered software architecture can be observed and manipulated in the management tool.
- Micro kernel: it provides a registry and an invocation framework for the above system components and other management entities, like class loading, relation, timer and monitor. In fact, it is implemented as a JMX MBeanServer. JMX (Java Management Extensions) is a specification that defines the architecture, design patterns, APIs and services for application and network management and monitoring in Java

programming language [4]. In JMX, both managing components and managed components are implemented as MBeans, which support plug-and-play dynamically. The MBeanServer is a registry for MBeans and provides an invocation framework for MBeans in the same Java Virtual Machine (JVM).

The above system components identify which runtime entities should be considered in the recovery, and the metadata contained in PKUAS will identify what information can be recovered. Such metadata consists of the data derived from the deployment descriptor and that collected at runtime. A J2EE application is packaged and deployed as an archive with suffix of ".war", ".ear" or ".jar". Such archives typically contain interfaces and implementations of EJBs and deployment descriptors of EJBs and the application. The deployment descriptor describes the structure of EJBs, their external dependencies and the application assembly information, specifying how to compose individual EJBs into an application [2]. The deployment descriptor will be stored in the container system and containers at runtime. Table 6.1 shows some important information in software architecture that can be recovered from the metadata derived from the deployment descriptor. The detailed meaning of these metadata and the metadata collected at

Table 6.1 Average response time under different configuration(s)

Information in software architecture	Elements in deployment descriptor
Name of component	$\langle ejb-name \rangle$ in $\langle module \rangle$
Name of provide interface	$\langle home \rangle$ and $\langle remote \rangle$ in $\langle session \rangle$ or $\langle entity \rangle$
Name of request interface	$\langle home \rangle$ and $\langle remote \rangle$ in $\langle ejb-ref \rangle$
Persistency constraint	$\langle persistence-type \rangle$, $\langle prim-key-class \rangle$, $\langle cmp-field \rangle$, $\langle primkey-field \rangle$
Security constraint	$\langle security-role-ref \rangle$, $\langle security-role \rangle$, $\langle method-permission \rangle$
Transaction constraint	$\langle transaction-type \rangle$
Other properties	$\langle env-entry \rangle$, $\langle resource-ref \rangle$, $\langle ejb-class \rangle$, $\langle session-type \rangle$, $\langle reentrant \rangle$

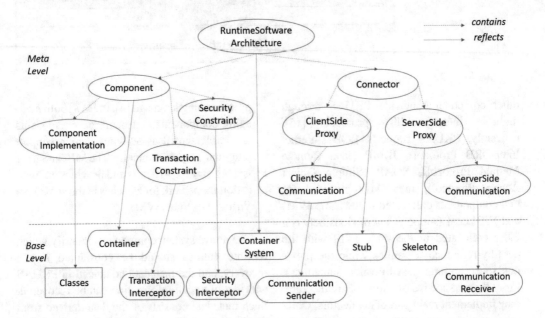

Fig. 6.7 Mapping between recovered software architecture and runtime system

6.4.2 Recovery of Basic Elements

In order to keep the recovered software architecture up-to-date and operable, the elements in the recovered software architecture are implemented as runtime entities and instantiated in PKUAS infrastructure. In terms of reflection, these runtime entities are meta-objects reflecting the base-objects that encapsulate the fundamental functions of PKUAS. Enforced by reflection mechanisms, changes occurring in PKUAS

runtime will be discussed in the details of the recovery later.

infrastructure and applications will immediately cause the corresponding changes in the recovered software architecture, and vice versa [16]. Then, to recover software architecture is to create these meta-objects and build connections with runtime entities in PKUAS infrastructure and applications, as shown in Fig. 6.7.[3] All instances of the containers in the corresponding container system will be queried through the micro kernel. Then the contract, implementation, constraints, connector instances and other details of a component can be retrieved from its container. More details of

---

[3]The meta-objects have the same name as the corresponding elements in the recovered software architecture.

the connector instances and some constraints can be queried from the communication service and other services.

The Runtime Software Architecture meta-object acts as a registry of Components and Connectors in the application held by a container system. It also contains some system-level properties, e.g., the references of common services used in the application. As the first meta-object created in the recovery, it will explore all containers in the given container system and then create corresponding Components. Currently, there are no special system-level constraints in J2EE applications.

The Component meta-object is responsible for creating Component Type meta-object, Component Implementation meta-object and Constraint meta-object and retrieving other information. The Component Type meta-object will retrieve the Home and Component interfaces of the EJB held by the given container and then retrieve the details of the methods via Java Reflective Facility [13]. The Component Implementation meta-object will retrieve the details of the implementation classes via Java Reflective Facility and analyze the dependencies among these classes to build a class diagram for component implementation. Component Implementation also has to retrieve the mappings between the contract methods and implementation methods mentioned in Sect. 3.1. In PKUAS, component constraints are enforced by the container with a set of interceptors, which are compliant with the "Interceptor" design pattern supporting to dynamically insert extra functions before and after the invocation of the target object, as shown in Fig. 6.8.

The enforcement of component constraints is usually supported by system services, which are invoked by PKUAS container with the help of the corresponding interceptors, such as skeleton interceptor, security interceptor and transaction interceptor. Some component constraints may be very simple and do not depend on system services, e.g., the limitation of the value range of the parameters. One Constraint meta-object will be created for one interceptor. There are little metadata for the interceptors except some standard ones, like security and transaction, which can retrieve metadata

from the deployment descriptor and their corresponding common services. Consequently, other Constraint meta-objects have no metadata more than the name and the order in the interceptor chain. More metadata may be complemented in the semantic enrichment discussed later or by the hands of users of the recovered software architecture.

Compared to Component, it is much more complex to create the Connector meta-objects, which has three steps. Firstly, when creating a Component meta-object, a set of Server Side Proxy meta-objects will be created according to the access points of the component. In PKUAS, an EJB can be accessed through multiple interoperability protocols and multiple addresses in the same interoperability protocol. Such information is specified by PKUAS-specific $\langle protocol \rangle$ elements in the deployment descriptor. The $\langle protocol \rangle$ element includes the name and address of the interoperability protocol and its JNDI name that is published into the naming service and retrieved by the client to access the component through the given protocol. Despite the $\langle protocol \rangle$ elements, an EJB at least supports IIOP because it is the standard interoperability protocol in J2EE. One Server Side Proxy meta-object will be created per access points. It holds the name of the component, the JNDI name and a Server Side Communication meta-object that holds the name and address of the interoperability protocol.[4] Secondly, when creating a Component meta-object, a set of Client Side Proxy meta-objects will also be created according to the metadata derived from $\langle ejb-ref \rangle$ and $\langle ejb-local-ref \rangle$ in the deployment descriptor that identifies which other components will be invoked by this component. The Client Side Proxy meta-object holds the name of the two involved components as the client-side and server-side component respectively and the JNDI name of the server-side component. Thirdly and finally, after all Component meta-objects are created, a Connector meta-object will be created per Client Side Proxy meta-objects. The Server Side

---

[4]As one ServerSideCommunication is usually shared by multiple ServerSideProxies and they have different abilities, we separate them into two meta-objects.

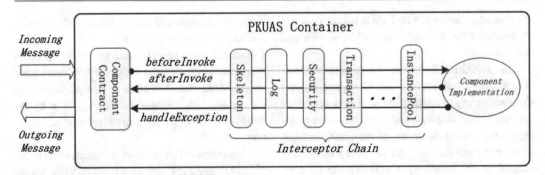

Fig. 6.8 Component constraint interceptors in PKUAS

Proxy meta-object of a Connector meta-object is that one holding the JNDI name specified by the Client Side Proxy meta-object. The Client Side Communication meta-object of the Client Side Proxy meta-object is created at this time and holds the same metadata of the Server Side Communication meta-object of the corresponding Server Side Proxy meta-object.

Though the fundamental elements in software architecture can be recovered mainly dependent on the metadata derived from the deployment descriptor, there are three important pieces of information to understand the runtime system missed. The first piece of information is the details of the methods (i.e., MethodDef in ABC/ADL) in the request interface. It is very important to keep the recovered software architecture integral because component A can provide an interface for another component B (or A can be connected to B through a connector) if and only if the MethodDef of the provide interface of A contains the MethodDef of the request interface of B. In PKUAS, the MethodDef of the request interface can be recovered from the metadata encapsulated by the log service (invoked by the log interceptor in Fig. 6.8), which can record all of the messages received or sent by EJBs. The outgoing messages contain the name and remote reference of the target EJB and the details of the invoked method. When all use cases of the runtime application are executed at least once, all of the MethodDefs of the request interfaces are recovered completely. Such mechanism also helps to recover the second piece of information. In the above recovery, the components invoked

by a given component are retrieved from the $\langle ejb - ref \rangle$ and $\langle ejb - local - ref \rangle$ in the deployment descriptor. But such elements only specify those components that will be invoked with the help of the naming service. Some other components may deliver their remote references to the component through parameters so that the component can invoke them without using the naming service. Consequently, some connector instances may be missed. Fortunately, such information can be retrieved from the log information of messages. The third piece of information is the dependencies between the MethodDefs of the provide interfaces and that of the request interfaces. It reveals which methods provided by other components are invoked by a component to provide a given method. In PKUAS, every incoming request message has a unique id that will be stored in the runtime context assigned to the invocation until the reply message is sent back. The log interceptor can be configured to record any outgoing message with the id. Then, for a given id, there are one or more incoming messages (one is the request of the invocation at least) and one or more outgoing messages (one is the reply of the invocation at least). Other outgoing and incoming messages are the requests and replies for invoking other components respectively, which indicate the information of the MethodDef dependency. Till now, the basic elements necessary to understand the runtime system are recovered and then the appropriate architecture views can be constructed. Considering the role of the recovered software architecture in maintenance and evolution, we found that other metadata collected at runtime is critical to make decisions. For examples, the Server Side Communication meta-object can count the number of the incoming messages through the access point; the Component meta-object holds the number of in-use, passivated and idle instances of component implementation. The details of these metadata will be discussed in Chap. 5.

6.4.3   Construction of Architecture Views

It is a consensus that software architecture should have multiple views for different users [14, 19, 33, 34]. Being the stakeholders that understand the system best, the designers usually produce multiple views of software architecture with some special features in ADL, such as composite component and architectural style. It implies that these special features can make the system understandable as much as possible at the architectural level. If the recovered software architecture can be represented in multiple views with these special features, its users may be able to understand the system better. In our approach, based on the above recovered elements, appropriate views of the recovered software architecture can be constructed with the special features in ABC/ADL, including the composite component, complex connector, aspect and architectural style [23]. The first two

features allow users to understand the system at different abstraction levels; the aspect supports to understand the cross-cutting non-functional properties of the system; and the architectural style helps to understand the whole or part of the system in a semantic way. Currently, some principles are defined to automatically identify the composite component and aspect, which will be discussed later. Other principles supporting to automatically identify the complex connector and architectural style are under development.

A composite component is a component that has its own interior architecture. At the design phase, this feature helps to refine the architecture gradually and make the design process more controllable. In the recovered software architecture, it helps to understand a set of coupled components at a higher level and decrease the complexity of a view through reducing its number of components. As shown in Fig. 6.9a, a composite component contains a set of components. Its provide interfaces and request interfaces are mapped to the corresponding interfaces of the internal components. Then, the messages received by the composite component will be delegated to the internal components, and the messages sent to the external components by the internal components will be delivered through the request interfaces of the composite component.

There are three principles to automatically identify composite components. The first principle is that a set of connected components can be a composite component if these components have

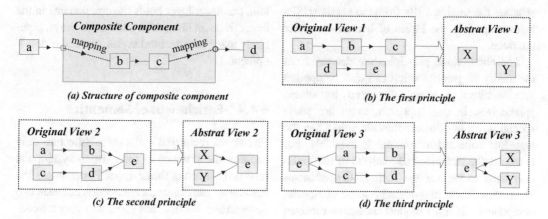

(a) Structure of composite component

(b) The first principle

(c) The second principle

(d) The third principle

Fig. 6.9   Abstraction of architecture views with composite components

no connection with other components, as shown in Fig. 6.9b. Considering the architecture view as a graph, this principle tries to decompose the view into connected graphs. It the connected graph contains more than one component, it becomes a composite component. This principle is very useful if the system has several sub-systems independent with each other. The new view generated by this principle is usually the highest abstraction level. The second principle is that if a set of connected components has a connection mediated by a component with another set of components and both component sets do not provide services to the mediating component, these two component sets can become two composite components respectively, as shown in Fig. 6.9c. This principle is very useful to separate business logics from business data or legacy if the mediating component is a wrapper of a legacy system or a set of data in a database. Typically, applying this principle into a J2EE application, the session EJBs that encapsulate the business logics can be grouped into composite components and then separated from the entity EJBs that encapsulate the backend database as a set of components. The third principle has a little difference with the second principle that the mediating component does not provide services to the two sets of connected components, as shown in Fig. 6.9d. It is useful to separate the representation logics from the business logics if the mediating component is responsible for interaction between the customers and the system. In a J2EE application, this principle helps to separate the session EJBs from the servlets/JSPs that encapsulate the logics of human computer interface.

The above three principles are derived from the theory of graphs, which can also be applied into architecture views recovered by others approaches. In our approach, there are some special principles that are feasible only when the metadata collected at runtime is available. For example, the statistics and analysis of the metadata used to recover the method dependencies mentioned above may identify some composite components. If most request messages received by one component are from another component,

they can be composed into a composite component. Likewise, if most request messages sent by a component are to another component, they can become a composite component.

Aspect is a way to encapsulate and modularize crosscutting concerns that used to be scattered over the whole system, such as security, logging, etc. [18]. ABC employs aspects to describe the cross-cutting constraints, which will usually be implemented as interceptors. Note that some simple interceptors may be only applied to a particular component, that is, such constraints are not cross-cutting. In PKUAS, only if an interceptor is applied to more than one component, its corresponding Constraint will become an Aspect. With the help of aspects, the non-functional properties related to multiple components in the recovered software architecture become much more comprehensive.

The layout of the recovered architecture view is very important to its understandability. Now, PKUAS can automatically generate the layout in two ways: the first is derived from the n-tier architectural style, that is, the view is divided into three parts horizontally, the left part is the representation tier that consists of servlets and JSPs, the middle part is the logic tier that consists of session EJBs, and the right part is the data tier that consists of entity EJBs; the second is based on the statistics and analysis of messages, that is, the view is divided into several parts vertically, the top layer holds all components involved in the most frequent invocation path that begins with the request messages received from the customers of the system, the lower layer holds the components in the fewer frequent invocation path. Other ways, especially using architectural styles, are under development.

6.4.4   Enrichment of Semantics

The above recovered software architecture only captures the structure of the existing system and misses the intent of the designer. For example, the maintainer can observe a connection between two components, but does not know why they are connected. Such software architecture that has poor semantics does little help to understand the software system. In other words, the above recovered software architecture has to enrich its semantics. In our approach, PKUAS can parse and analyze the specification in ABC/ADL and insert its semantic information into the recovered software architecture.

In ABC/ADL, the semantic description is not a standalone element, but scattered over every specification of elements, using Semantic Description keyword to mark [23]. The semantic description is trying to use formal methods to model, or, at least, use natural language to describe, the behaviors and features of the elements. Since the recovered software architecture is described in the extension of ABC/ADL, it is easy to copy the semantic description in ABC/ADL documents into the corresponding elements of the recovered software architecture. The ABC/ADL documents provide another important piece of information, that is, the layouts of architecture views produced by the designers. After reconstructing the views based on the recovered basic elements and the layout information in ABC/ADL documents, the maintainers can understand the intent of the designers and make best-of-the-breed decisions to adapt the runtime system.

6.5 Manipulation of Recovered Software Architecture at Runtime

As soon as software architecture is recovered, the runtime system can be observed, reasoned and adapted through its architecture views. Both based on the reflection, the recovery of software architecture utilizes the reflection in a bottom-up way, and its manipulation does in a top-down way. The mechanisms supporting to change the system at runtime, including the addition, deletion and replacement of the components and connectors as a whole, the replacement of component contract, constraint and implementation respectively, etc., are out of the scope of this chapter and can be found in [15,16,24]. Here, we only introduce what kind of manipulation can be made and how

to manipulate the recovered software architecture in a programmable and visible way respectively.

6.5.1 Manipulation via Reflection

Manipulation of the recovered software architecture can be divided into the following categories:

- Lifecycle Management: some runtime entities may have a manageable lifecycle. In PKUAS, the application, component, stub and skeleton can be started, stopped, suspended, resumed and re-started through manipulating the Runtime Software Architecture, Component, Client Side Proxy and Server Side Proxy.
- Add/Remove/Replacement: some runtime entities may be added, replaced and removed. In PKUAS, the component, component constraint, stub, skeleton and communication protocol can be added, removed and replaced through manipulating Runtime Software Architecture, Component, Connector and Communication Infrastructure respectively. The component type and implementation can only be replaced through manipulating Component.
- Statistics: some runtime entities may provide some statistics of their internal states and behaviors, which are useful to maintain and evolve the system, especially performance tuning. Typically, the statistics includes the number of threads in use, the size of buffer or memory footprint and the number of connections for a given application, the number of instances of a given component, the number of invocations for a given method or component, the maximum, minimal and average response time of a given method, and so on. In particular, the statistic ability of the runtime entities can be enabled or disabled through the corresponding elements in the recovered software architecture to make the best trade-off between performance and manageability.
- Business Invocation: some methods exposed by runtime entities can be directly invoked through the recovered software architecture.

For example, the maintainers of eShop can investigate the details of a given Customer through directly invoking its business methods, such as getName(), getAddress() and getBalance().

6.5.2 Programming Model

As shown in Listing 6.2, the APIs to access and operate the recovered software architecture are encapsulated in a stateless EJB, called MEJB. It has four advantages: firstly, the recovered software architecture becomes secure because EJB is protected by access control mechanism or secure transportation mechanism in EJB container, such as JAAS (Java Authentication and Authorization Service) and IIOP-SSL; secondly, the users can become familiar with the recovered software architecture quickly because it has the same programming model as J2EE; thirdly, the recovered software architecture can be accessed through multiple interoperability protocols because of PKUAS interoperability framework; Fourthly and finally, since MEJB also encapsulates the APIs of J2EE Management Specification [3] that is a standard to manage J2EE application server, it is enhanced to support the management of both J2EE platform and J2EE applications with the recovered software architecture.

6.5.3 Graphical Tool

As shown in Fig. 6.10, the maintainers can observe, reason and change J2EE platform and applications in the GUI tool, called PKUAS Management Tool. All actions in the GUI will be automatically transformed to the invocations to the above MEJB APIs. As a result, the maintainers can connect to any specified PKUAS instance and manage its deployed applications and equipped services in this tool. The components and connectors are shown as simple boxes and circles to keep the recovered software architecture simple and understandable. The details of selected component and connector are shown in two small windows below software architecture window. One small window figures the internal structure of component or connector from the perspective of middleware, while another lists the details completely. The changed layout can be saved into the deployment package of the application as an XML file. PKUAS Management Tool integrates the reusable asset repository to enable the maintainers to drag and drop components from the repository to the recovered software architecture so as to deploy new components or replace components in the runtime system.

For example, some clients of eShop may complain that they always take a long time wait for browsing the products. The administrator can use the management tool to activate the time

```
/* lookup MEJB and create an instance. */
Context ic = new InitialContext();
ManagementHome home = (ManagementHome)
    PortableRemoteObject.
    narrow(ic.lookup("ejb/mgmt/MEJB"),ManagementHome.
    class);
    Management mejb = home.create();
/* find RSA o eShop. */
ObjectName searchPattern = new ObjectName(
    "*:rsaType=J2EEApplication, name=eShop,*");
Set rsas = mejb.queryNames(searchPattern, null);
ObjectName eShopRSA = (ObjectName)rsas.iterator().nextElement();
/* explore components in eShop. */
Set components = (Set)mejb.getAttribute(eShopRSA,"AllComponents");
```

Listing 6.2 Sample code for accessing recovered architecture through MEJB

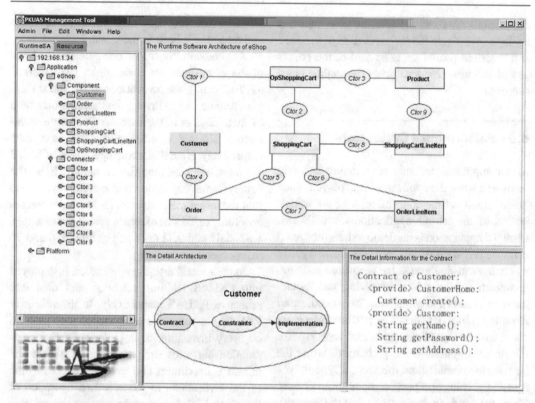

Fig. 6.10 Graphical window for observing and manipulating recovered architecture. It uses old notations of ABC/ADL and will update to new notations soon

statistics for the OpShoppingCart and Product component so that he could investigate the minimal, maximal and average response time of the two components which deal with the requests for browsing the products. After some new requests are processed, the results of time statistics reveal that the Product component consumes most response time. Then, the administrator reports the case to the vendor of eShop. The vendor may find that the implementation of Product does not optimize the query of database or does not make any cache for previous query results. Latter, a new version of Product is returned to the administrator. Compared to the old version, the new version has a much more efficient implementation and keeps other things, like the interface and constraints, unchanged. There are two ways to change eShop. One way is to replace Product as a whole, which will make PKUAS to reload the interface classes, re-instantiate classes enforcing constraints, re-allocate resources, re-

bind connections between the component and its clients and replace the implementation. Another way is to only replace the implementation of Product, which will make PKUAS to block the incoming invocations, buffer the old instances until its execution or transaction is over, create new instances of the new implementation and copy the unchanged attributes from the old instances (All technical details can be found in [16]). Considering that only the implementation of Product is changed, the administrator decides to replace the implementation only so as to limit the impact of the replacement. To perform the replacement, the administrator can double-click the implementation of Product to pop up its property window and set the location of the implementation classes. Once the administrator clicks the "Apply changes" label in the "Admin" label, the tool will invoke MEJB like "mejb.setAttribute (product, new Attribute ("implementation", newProduct. class))". After the replacement,

the administrator can activate the time statistics
again to investigate the response time of Product.
If the desired results are generated or the clients
accept the new response time, the maintenance
succeeds.

6.6   Performance Evaluation

In our approach, software architecture is firstly
recovered when the application is deployed. Such
initialization is time-consuming, e.g., the initialization of the sample application takes 180 ms.
Until the application is un-deployed, its recovered
software architecture will only be refreshed partly
by changes made through the recovered software
architecture, like adding, removing and replacing components and connectors, or data collected
at runtime, like statistics. The performance issue
about the first type of changes is how long to make
the runtime system actually changed, while the
performance issue about the second type is how
impact the collection puts on the runtime system.
Then, the test is to demonstrate that the recovery
and manipulation of software architecture at runtime have enough performance so as to be put into
practice and their supporting mechanisms do little
impact on performance of the runtime system. The
test application runs on a PC with PIII 800 MHz,
256M SDRAM and Windows 2000 Server with
Service Pack 3. It consists of a standalone Java
client sending a string in desired bytes and a state-

less EJB receiving the string, printing it in screen
and returning it back to the client.

As shown in Fig. 6.11a, compared to the invocation of business interfaces of an EJB (marked
as "EJB call"), the invocations to get and set single attribute and to invoke the business operation
of meta-objects in the recovered software architecture take 4.2 %, 4.5 % and 9.8 % more time
respectively. Note that, these operations of MEJB
are more complex than that of the test EJB. The
"queryNames" operation is also common in use to
find the target meta-objects. Its latency increases
according to the size of return values, for example,
5.82, 6.67 and 9.71 ms when getting 3, 8 and 30
meta-objects respectively.

In the second test, the application is deployed
into PKUAS without reflection and then into
reflective PKUAS respectively. In the reflective
PKUAS, the reflective computation may perform
on every invocation or not. The reflective computation performs time statistics to expose the
minimal, maximum and average response time
of the invocations to the specified operation of
the given EJB. When an invocation comes in, a
meta-object increments the invocation counter,
records two time-stamps when the invocation
comes in and its response goes out, calculates
their margin as the response time, add it into
the total time of all invocations and compare
it with the recorded minimal and maximum
response time to determine whether they should
be updated. As shown in Fig. 6.11b, the invoca-

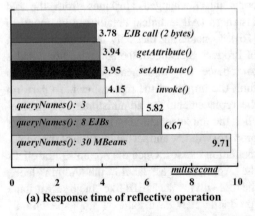

(a) Response time of reflective operation

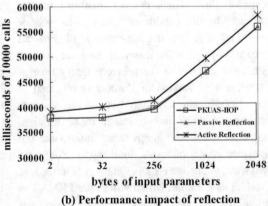

(b) Performance impact of reflection

Fig. 6.11 Comparison of latency in different runtime models

tion latency in PKUAS with passive reflection (marked as "Passive Reflection") is similar with that in PKUAS without reflection (marked as "PKUAS-IIOP"), and that in PKUAS with active reflection (marked as "Active Reflection") increases 3–5 %. Note that, the test EJB is so simple that its computation consumes very little time the meta-object of time statistics. In practice, an EJB will be much more complex and take more time to deal with invocations. Consequently, the percent of time cost in time statistics will decrease. Furthermore, the time statistics can be started and stopped whenever the maintainers need. Then, the performance impact is reasonable and acceptable in practice.

6.7   Related Work

In the past few years, software architecture recovery gets much more attention from the academic and industrial communities. Mendonça proposes X-ray approach to recovering software architecture from the source code of distributed systems [26]. The approach identifies components through analyzing the dependencies among the modules of the source code. It can identify connections possibly existing at runtime through pattern matching and structural reachability. In Dali proposed in [17], both source code and makefiles are analyzed and components are identified by architectural patterns step by step so that the abstraction level of the recovered software architecture can be controlled by the users. ManSART proposed in [34] can also recognize components from the source code and provide multiple views of the recovered software architecture through analyzing cross-cutting relationships among the artifacts recovered by different principles. Almost all of the work focuses on recovering software architecture from the implementation artifacts. They pay much attention on the identification of components and are poor of capturing runtime states and behaviors of the system. Furthermore, they do not address the problem of the adaptation of the system after its software architecture is recovered. In the approach presented in this chapter, the components, connectors and other runtime states

and behaviors can be recovered and manipulated based on reflection in the component framework. However, our approach can be only applied into component based applications which take middleware as the infrastructure, while X-ray, Dali, and ManSART can be applied into much more applications, especially the legacy systems developed without component technology.

Some researchers try to perform software maintenance and evolution with the designed software architecture. Oreizy et al. study how software architecture can support corrective, perfective and adaptive evolution at runtime and experiment on C2, a layered, event-based architectural style [29]. Garlan et al. use the gauges to collect the states and behaviors of the underlying system and adapt the system according to some special requirements at runtime [12]. Rosenblum et al. investigate the architectural concerns in the component interoperability framework and combine the JavaBean model with C2 style [31]. Bril et al. provide a toolset, called URSA, to support program understanding and complexity management in Philips [7]. In these approaches, the designed software architecture is used as a document at hand, that is to say, such software architecture cannot accurately and up-to-date describe the target system. And changes made on software architecture do not cause corresponding changes in runtime system until the maintainers explicitly manipulate runtime system in other ad hoc ways.

OpenORB [6] adds reflection ability into COM. It provides four self-representations, including software architecture of the whole system, the interfaces of components, the interception of components and resources. In fact, the complex self-representations provided by OpenORB and PKUAS are originated by the separation of concerns in reflection proposed by [28] and the architectural reflection proposed by [8]. But OpenORB and PKUAS have quite different implementations. Firstly, OpenORB represents the system in four independent views while PKUAS represents all information in software architectures. Secondly, OpenORB defines a set of reflective interfaces that the reflective COM objects have to implement. Then, the developers of application components have to be aware of reflection. In that sense, OpenORB implements architectural reflection in a reflective component model way, just like K-Components [10] and FORMAware [27]. On the contrary, PKUAS implements architectural reflection in a "pure" reflective middleware way, that is, does not define such interfaces so that the application developers are unaware of reflection. In our opinion, both ways have advantages and disadvantages on the runtime manipulation of software architecture. And a reflective EJB component model is under development to improve the reflective capability of PKUAS. More importantly, software architecture in OpenORB is produced at design and cannot be recovered at runtime.

6.8   Conclusion and Future Work

It is a feasible and attractive way to reduce the complexity and cost of software maintenance and evolution through software architecture recovered from existing systems. Current work on architecture recovery can hardly capture runtime states and behaviors of the system and does not pay attention on how the system can be changed when some decisions about maintenance and evolution are made after analyzing the recovered software architecture. An approach to recovering and manipulating software architecture at runtime is presented in this chapter. After analyzing the role of the recovered software architecture in software lifecycle, the differences between the recovered software architecture and designed software architecture are discussed and then a traditional architecture description language is extended to formally describe the recovered software architecture. In order to keep the recovered software architecture up-to-date at any time and change the runtime system via manipulating its recovered software architecture, the elements in the recovered software architecture are implemented as a set of meta-objects that are created at runtime and reflect other runtime entities internal of the system. It ensures that changes made on the recovered soft-

ware architecture immediately lead to corresponding changes of the actual states and behaviors of the runtime system, and vice versa. To manage the complexity of the recovered software architecture, some principles are defined, including composite component, complex connector, aspect and style. The approach is demonstrated in a reflective J2EE-compliant application server. In this demonstration, the recovered software architecture can be accessed and manipulated via both APIs and a GUI. Finally, the performance evaluation shows that the performance of this approach is acceptable and it puts little impact on the performance of the runtime system.

Future research will focus on the construction of architecture views and the practice in large applications. Some previous work on automatically generating multiple views of software architecture or class diagram will be investigated and experimented in our approach. The feedback of the customers of PKUAS may reveal which provided architecture views are most useful and which useful ones are missed. These practices may also reveal the activities in maintenance and evolution that can be automatically executed. In other words, based on the recovery and manipulation of software architecture and guided by some empirical rules, the runtime system may be able to maintain and evolve itself, which will reduce the cost of maintenance and evolution much more. On the other hand, we argue that the recovery and manipulation of software architecture will be more reasonable and effective if they are considered in software architecture at design. Some cases are studied in [25,35] while there are many open issues to be addressed when integrating the architecture recovery and modeling.

Acknowledgments   The authors would like to thank the referees, Dr. Lu Zhang and Dr. Wenpin Jiao for their thorough reviews, helpful comments, and corrections that have improved this chapter. They would like to acknowledge that this research was supported by the National Key Basic Research and Development Program (973) under Grant No. 2002CB312003; the National Natural Science Foundation of China under Grant No. 60233010, 60125206, 60403030, 90412011; and the IBM University Joint Study Program.

References

1. *Enterprise JavaBeans Specification.* SUN Microsystems (2001)
2. *Java 2 Platform Enterprise Edition Specification.* SUN Microsystems (2001)
3. *Java 2 Platform Enterprise Edition Management Specification.* SUN Microsystems (2002)
4. *Java Management Extensions Instrumentation and Agent Specification.* SUN Microsystems (2002)
5. R.D. Banker, S.M. Datar, C.F. Kemerer, D. Zweig, Software complexity and maintenance costs. Commun. ACM **36**(11), 81–94 (1993)
6. G.S. Blair, G. Coulson, A. Andersen, L. Blair, M. Clarke, F.M. Costa, H.A. Duran-Limon, T. Fitzpatrick, L. Johnston, R.S. Moreira, N. Parlavantzas, K.B. Saikoski, The design and implementation of open ORB 2. IEEE Distrib. Syst. Online **2**(6) (2001)
7. J.R. Bril, L.M.G. Feijs, A. Glas, R.L. Krikhaar, T. Winter, Maintaining a legacy: towards support at the architectural level. J. Softw. Maint. **12**(3), 143–170 (2000)
8. W. Cazzola, A. Savigni, A. Sosio, F. Tisato, Architectural reflection: bridging the gap between a running system and its architectural specification, in *Proceedings of 6th Reengineering Forum, REF'98* (1998)
9. F. Chen, Q. Wang, H. Mei, F. Yang, An architecture-based approach for component-oriented development, in *Proceedings of 26th Annual International Computer Software and Applications Conference, COMPSAC'02* (2002), pp. 450–455
10. J. Dowling, V. Cahill, The k-component architecture meta-model for self-adaptive software, in *Metalevel Architectures and Separation of Crosscutting Concerns* (2001), pp. 81–88
11. D. Garlan, Software architecture: a roadmap, in *Proceedings of the Conference on the Future of Software Engineering* (2000), pp. 91–101
12. D. Garlan, B. Schmerl, J. Chang, Using gauges for architecture-based monitoring and adaptation (2001)
13. J. Gosling, *The Java Language Specification* (Addison-Wesley Professional, 2000)
14. C. Hofmeister, R. Nord, D. Soni, *Applied Software Architecture* (Addison-Wesley Professional, 2000)
15. G. Huang, H. Mei, Q. Wang, F. Yang, A systematic approach to composing heterogeneous components. Chin. J. Electron. **12**(4), 499–505 (2003)
16. G. Huang, H. Mei, F. Yang, Runtime software architecture based on reflective middleware. Sci. China Ser. F: Inf. Sci. **47**(5), 555–576 (2004)
17. R. Kazman, S.J. Carrière, Playing detective: reconstructing software architecture from available evidence. Autom. Softw. Eng. **6**(2), 107–138 (1999)
18. G. Kiczales, J. Lamping, A. Mendhekar, C. Maeda, J.-M. Loingtier, J. Irwin, *Aspect-Oriented Programming* (Springer, Cristina Lopes, 1997)
19. B.P. Kruchten, The 4+1 view model of architecture. IEEE Softw. **12**(6), 42–50 (1995)
20. N. Medvidovic, R.N. Taylor, A classification and comparison framework for software architecture description languages. IEEE Trans. Softw. Eng. **26**(1), 70–93 (2000)
21. H. Mei, A complementary approach to requirements engineering software architecture orientation. ACM Sigsoft Softw. Eng. Notes **25**(2), 40–45 (2000)
22. H. Mei, J. Chang, F. Yang, Software component composition based on ADL and middleware. Sci. China Ser.: Inf. Sci. **44**(2), 136–151 (2001)
23. H. Mei, F. Chen, Q. Wang, Y. Feng, ABC/ADL: an ADL supporting component composition, in *Formal Methods and Software Engineering* (Springer, 2002), pp. 38–47
24. H. Mei, G. Huang, PKUAS: an architecture-based reflective component operating platform, in *Proceedings of 10th IEEE International Workshop on Future Trends of Distributed Computing Systems, FTDCS'04* (2004), pp. 163–169
25. H. Mei, G. Huang, W.-T. Tsai, Towards self-healing systems via dependable architecture and reflective middleware, in *Proceedings of 10th IEEE International Workshop on Object-Oriented Real-Time Dependable Systems, WORDS'05* (2005), pp. 337–344
26. C.N. Mendonça, J. Kramer, An approach for recovering distributed system architectures. Autom. Softw. Eng. **8**(3–4), 311–354 (2001)
27. R.S. Moreira, G.S. Blair, E. Carrapatoso, A reflective component-based and architecture aware framework to manage architecture composition, in *Proceedings of 3rd International Symposium on Distributed Objects and Applications, DOA'01* (2001), pp. 187–196
28. H. Okamura, Y. Ishikawa, M. Tokoro, AL-1/D: a distributed programming system with multi-model reflection framework, in *Proceedings of the Workshop on New Models for Software Architecture* (1992), pp. 36–47
29. P. Oreizy, N. Medvidovic, R.N Taylor, Architecture-based runtime software evolution, in *Proceedings of the 20th International Conference on Software Engineering, ICSE'98* (1998), pp. 177–186
30. C. Riva, Reverse architecting: an industrial experience report, in *Proceedings of the 7th Working Conference on Reverse Engineering, WCRE'00* (2000), p. 42
31. D.S. Rosenblum, R. Natarajan, Supporting architectural concerns in component-interoperability standards. IEE Proc.-Softw. **147**(6), 215–223 (2000)

32. M. Shaw, D. Garlan, Software Architecture: Perspectives on an Emerging Discipline, vol. 1 (Prentice Hall Englewood Cliffs, 1996)
33. A. van Deursen, Software architecture recovery and modelling: [WCRE 2001 discussion forum report]. ACM SIGAPP Appl. Comput. Rev. **10**(1), 4–7 (2002)
34. A.S. Yeh, D.R. Harris, M.P. Chase, Manipulating recovered software architecture views, in *Proceedings of the 19th International Conference on Software Engineering, ICSE'97* (1997), pp. 184–194
35. Y. Zhu, G. Huang, H. Mei, Quality attribute scenario based architectural modeling for self-adaptation supported by architecture-based reflective middleware, in *Proceedings of 11th Asia-Pacific Software Engineering Conference* (2004), pp. 2–9

Supporting Runtime Software Architecture: A Bidirectional-Transformation-Based Approach

7

Abstract

Runtime software architectures (RSA) are architecture-level, dynamic representations of running software systems, which help monitor and adapt the systems at a high abstraction level. The key issue to support RSA is to maintain the causal connection between the architecture and the system, ensuring that the architecture represents the current system, and the modifications on the architecture cause proper system changes. The main challenge here is the abstraction gap between the architecture and the system. In this chapter, we investigate the synchronization mechanism between architecture configurations and system states for maintaining the causal connections. We identify four required properties for such synchronization, and provide a generic solution satisfying these properties. Specifically, we utilize bidirectional transformation to bridge the abstraction gap between architecture and system, and design an algorithm based on it, which addresses issues such as conflicts between architecture and system changes, and exceptions of system manipulations. We provide a generative tool-set that helps developers implement this approach on a wide class of systems. We have successfully applied our approach on JOnAS JEE system to support it with C2-styled runtime software architecture, as well as some other cases between practical systems and typical architecture models.

Keywords

Software architecture · Bidirectional transformation · Runtime system management

7.1 Introduction

Nowadays, IT systems are required to be continuously available whereas the systems are running, their environments and user requirements are constantly changing. This calls for the system management at runtime to find and fix defects, adapt to the changed environments, or meet new requirements [10,18]. Currently, many mainstream platforms have provided management APIs for retrieving and updating the system state at runtime [26], but direct management upon these low-level APIs is not an easy task. First, the management API reflects the system in a solution space, requiring the knowledge of platform implementation. Second, the APIs are designed for general-purpose management, and thus are usually too tedious and complicated for a particular management activity.

To control the management complexity, many researchers propose to utilize software architecture for runtime management [11,22,26]. They represent the running system as a dynamic architecture model, which has a *causal connection* with the system state. That means if the system state evolves, the architecture configuration will change accordingly. And similarly, if the architecture configuration is modified, the system will change accordingly, too. Thanks to this causal connection, management agents (human administrators or automated management services) can monitor and control the system by reading and writing this abstract architecture model, utilizing mature architecture-based techniques (such as architecture manipulation languages and architecture analysis [2]) to make high-level management decisions at runtime. We name such architecture models as *Runtime Software Architectures* (RSA, [13]).

There are many approaches to RSA-based runtime management. These approaches reveal the usage and advantage of RSA, but their mechanisms for maintaining causal connection are tightly-coupled with the target system, requiring the systems to be implemented according to specific styles [4,22] or instrumented with specific management capabilities [11,13]. Due to the tight coupling, these approaches cannot be directly applied on the existing systems that are already implemented without consideration of RSA, because it is tedious and error-prone to instrument them with RSA-enabling code.

In this chapter, we focus on providing RSA support to the existing systems. The key issue is to maintain the casual connection based on the general-purpose management API provided by the target system. We sum up this issue as a *synchronization* between architecture model and system state, and identify four required properties for such synchronization, namely *consistency*, *non-interference introspection*, *effective reconfiguration*, and *stability*. These properties are necessary for management agents to use the synchronized architecture model for monitoring and controlling the system.

However, there are some challenges to implement such synchronization.

1. There is an abstraction gap between the system state and the architecture model. The system state is determined by the implementation of the target platform, located in the solution space, while the architecture model is determined by the management requirements, located in the problem space. To represent the system in the proper perspective, the architecture model and the system state usually have heterogeneous forms and asymmetric contents, and thus it is not easy to determine the effect of architecture changes on the system side, and vice versa.
2. Since the architecture and the system are changing simultaneously, the synchronization has to deal the conflicts between architecture modifications and system changes.
3. The system modifications through the API do not always lead to the expected effects. The synchronization needs to handle such modification exceptions properly, in order to prevent the management agents from getting the inaccurate information for the running system and thus making wrong decisions.

In this chapter, we present a generic approach to synchronize architecture models and running systems, satisfying the above properties. To address the above challenges, we use bidirectional model transformations to propagate changes across the abstraction gap between architecture and system, employ a two-phase execution to filter out conflicts in the changes, and employ a three-way check to identify modification exceptions. We provide a generative tool-set to assist developers in implementing this approach on a wide class of systems. Developers need only provide high-level specifications about the system and the required architecture style, including two meta-models to specify what constitutes the architecture model and the running system, a model transformation to specify their relation, and a declarative specification about how to retrieve and update the system state, and our tool-set automatically generates the required synchronizer to support RSA on this system. The contributions of this chapter can be summarized as follows.

- We formalize the generic synchronization between architecture models and running systems, and define a set of required properties for such synchronization.
- We provide an architecture-system synchronization algorithm based on bidirectional transformation, satisfying the above requirements.
- We provide a generative tool-set to assist developers in implementing the approach on a wide scope of systems, supporting RSAs on them.

We have applied this approach to several practical systems, including JOnAS/JEE and PLASTIC.[1] These case studies demonstrate the feasibility, efficiency and wide applicability of our approach and tool-set.

This work is based on a series of our earlier approaches. We utilize the code generation approach for wrapping low-level management APIs [27,29]. The idea of using model transformation to achieve synchronization was discussed in [34].

The rest of this chapter is structured as follows. Section 7.2 illustrates the basic concepts of RSA. Section 7.3 discusses the synchronization for maintaining causal connection. Section 7.4 presents our synchronization approach based on bidirectional model transformation, and Sect. 7.5 introduces our generative tool-set to help implementing this approach. Section 7.6 describes our case studies. Section 7.7 summarizes related work and Sect. 7.8 concludes this approach.

7.2 Runtime Software Architecture

7.2.1 An Illustrative Example

The right part of Fig. 7.1 shows a simple mobile computing system for file transmission, which we construct upon the PLASTIC Multi-radio Networking Platform [16]. As shown in the figure, three devices are currently registered on a central desktop, which pushes files into these devices via different types of connections, including Wi-Fi, Bluetooth and wired cable. At runtime, the administrator may wish to *monitor* what devices are registered, and how they are connected. He also needs to *reconfigure* the system, e.g. when the Wi-Fi signal is too weak for the first device, he could switch the connection into Bluetooth.

The left part of Fig. 7.1 is an architecture model conforming to the Client/Server architecture style [11]. The `Clients` stand for the devices, the `Server` stands for the desktop computer, and the `Links` stand for the connections between them. Administrators could add or remove clients, change connection types. If they find a client that needs further maintenance, they add a be-careful mark on it.

To support the management activities mentioned above, the architecture model must have a *causal connection* [4] with the running system. The architecture model must change as the system changes. For example, if a device unregisters itself, the corresponding `client` element in the architecture will disappear. Similarly, the architecture modifications must cause correct system changes. For example, if the administrator switches a link type, the real network connection will be reset.

---

[1]The tool-set and the artifacts used in the case studies can be found in our project website: http://code.google.com/p/smatrt.

Fig. 7.1 A client/server styled runtime architecture for a PLASTIC-based mobile system

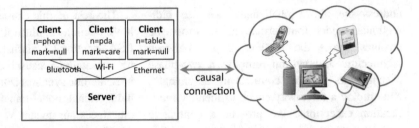

7.2.2   A Formal Description of Runtime Software Architecture

The above example illustrates three elements of RSA, i.e., the architecture model, the system state, and the causal connection. This section discusses these elements in detail, with the help of a simple formal description.

7.2.2.1   Architecture Models

Architecture models are constituted of a set of model elements (like clients and servers). These elements have attributes, and refer to other elements. The types of architecture elements in our example are shown in the left part of Fig. 7.2: A root element typed as `Structure` contains several `Servers` and `Clients`, which connect with each other through `Links`. An architecture configuration is a set of element instances conforming to these element types. Model manipulations (like adding a component or changing an attribute value) change the model from one configuration to another.

We use A to stand for the set of all possible architecture configurations (which is determined by the meta-model), and use $\Delta_A \subseteq A \times A$ to denote all possible changes from one architec-

ture configuration to another. Following [1], we present the model changes as a composition of primitive model modifications, including creating or deleting an element, and getting or setting a property. From this point of view, model differ $(- : A \times A \rightarrow \Delta_A)$ finds a set of primitive modifications to represent the changes, and model merge $(+ : A \times \Delta_A \rightarrow A)$ execute the modifications to get a new model. For architecture models, the effect of modifications is predictable, i.e., $\delta = a' - a \Rightarrow a + \delta = a'$.

7.2.2.2   Runtime System States

According to [26], a running system is constituted of system elements, like the devices and the desktop computer. The system elements may have local states (like the connection type), or be associated with each other. The type of system states (like what elements exists, their local state values, and the references between them) can be also defined by a meta-model, as shown in Fig. 7.2. Similar to architecture models, we use S and Δ_S to stand for the system meta-model and all possible changes. The changes may be caused by the system itself, or by manipulations from outside.

For the above example, reading and modifying the system state can be performed through the

Fig. 7.2 The definition of architecture and system elements for the running example

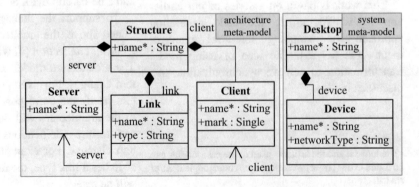

Fig. 7.3 The relation between architecture and system

```
transformation CS2PLA(arc:CS,sys:PLASTIC){                              relation
  key Structure{name};... key Device{name};
  top relation StructServer2Desktop{
    tmpName:String;
    enforce domain arc strt:Structure{name=tmpName,
      server=svr,clien t=clnt:Client{},link=lnk:Link{}};
    enforce domain arc svr:Server{name=tmpName};
    enforce domain sys dsktp:Desktop{name=tmp Name, device=d vc:Device{}};
    where{ClientLink2Device(svr,clnt,lnk,dvc);}; }
  relation ClientLink2Device{
    tmpName:String; tmpType:String;
    enforce domain arc svr:Server{};
    enforce domain arc clnt:Client{name=tmpName};
    enforce domain arc lnk:Link{client=clnt,server=svr,type=tmpType};
    enforce domain sys dvc:Device{name=tmpName, type=tmpType};} }
```

PLASTIC API. To see all the devices from the desktop computer, we could invoke the API on the desktop to get all registered `MNClients`, each of which stands for a device connected to this desktop. We can invoke `getActualNetworkQoS` on a `MNClients` to see its connection, and invoke `activateBestNetwork` on it to change the type.[2]

Unlike architecture models, manipulations on running systems are *not always predictable*, i.e., $\delta = s' - s \nRightarrow s + \delta = s'$. The modifications may have *no effect* or *side effect*. For example, if we modify a device's network into Bluetooth but the device is suddenly outside the coverage of the desktop's Bluetooth signal, then this manipulation has *no effect*. If we delete (disconnect) the network between the desktop and the first device, then the device itself is also unreachable from the desktop, and thus the resulting system changes also include a *side effect* that is a deletion of the device. The reason for this is that the APIs usually do not reflect the complete system state. We abstract a running system as a tuple: (S, E, σ), with S, the system meta-model, E, the set of environment (e.g. the device is out of the Bluetooth range), and σ, the state transition function: $\sigma : S \times E \times \Delta_S \longrightarrow S$,

standing for the system logic (e.g. if a network-link is removed, the device also disappears). For a current state $s \in S$, in the current environment $\varepsilon \in E$, and after the execution of a manipulation $\delta \in \Delta_{S_M}$, the result $\sigma(s, \varepsilon, \delta)$ is the subsequent state of this system.

7.2.2.3 Causal Connections

[7] and [26] refined the concept of "causal connection" into the following two requirements.

- **Correct Introspection**. No matter how system changes, the management agents could always get the *correct* system state through the architecture model.
- **Correct Reconfiguration**. Management agents could directly modify the architecture model, and the modifications will dynamically cause the *correct* system change.

Here the *correctness* depends on a given relation between the architecture configuration and the system state $R \subseteq A \times S$. When $(a, s) \in R$, we say that architecture a and system s are *consistent*, or a is a *reflection* of s. For our illustrative example, this consistency relation embodies the information like "if there is a device in the system, there must be a client in the architecture model with the same name, and vice versa". We illustrate this relation using a QVT transformation as shown in Fig. 7.3. It defines that the `Structure` and the `Server` together map to the `Desktop`; A `Client` and its connected `Link` together map to a `Device`.

---

[2]Originally, PLASTIC only open the interface for resetting networks according to a set of QoS requirements. To simplify our example, we altered it a bit to open the capability for switching networks directly by types.

7.3 Maintaining Causal Connections by Architecture-System Synchronization

We defined the Architecture-System Synchronization (ASS) according to a relation R, for a system σ, and under the environment ε, as a function:

$$Synch_{(R,\varepsilon,\sigma)} : A \times A \times S \longrightarrow A \times S$$

The first two inputs are architecture configurations before and after management agent's modification. The third input is the current system state. The outputs are the synchronized architecture configuration and system state.

7.3.1 The Four Properties

In order to satisfy the two requirements above (i.e. introspection and reconfiguration), we use a series of *properties* to constrain the synchronization behavior. Specifically, for any $(a_o, a_c, s_c) \in A \times A \times S$ if

$$Synch_{(R,\varepsilon,\sigma)}(a_o, a_c, s_c) = (a_s, s_s)$$

then we require the results (a_s and s_s) to satisfy the following propositions.

Property 7.1 (Consistency)

$$(a_s, s_s) \in R$$

First of all, we require the synchronized architecture configuration (a_s) and system state (s_s) to be consistent, so that Management Agents (MAs) could use the resulted architecture configuration to deduce the current system state and the modification effect.

Property 7.2 (Non-interfering introspection)

$$a_o = a_c \implies s_s = s_c$$

Consistency alone does not ensure correct introspection. For example, suppose that in a_o and a_c, the types of the first links are all $\mathtt{Wi-Fi}$,

and in s_c, the corresponding connection type has changed to $\mathtt{Bluetooth}$. In this situation, the ASS could choose to change the real network type back to $\mathtt{Wi-Fi}$. Although this result satisfies *consistency*, the MA will not get the *genuine* system state, but the one polluted by ASS. Therefore, we require that if the architecture is not modified, the ASS cannot change the system.

Property 7.3 (Effective reconfiguration)

$$a_c - a_o \subseteq a_s - a_o$$

Similarly, *consistency* is not enough for correct reconfiguration. For example, if the MA modifies the link from $\mathtt{Wi-Fi}$ to $\mathtt{Bluetooth}$ and in the current system the connection is still $\mathtt{Wi-Fi}$, then to satisfy *consistency*, the ASS could ignore the architecture modification and leave the current system unchanged (that means the result is (a_o, s_c)). To ensure correct reconfiguration, we require that all the MA's modifications (i.e. $a_c - a_o$) *remain* in the final architecture change (i.e. $a_s - a_o$).

Property 7.4 (Stability)

$$(a_c, s_c) \in R \implies a_s = a_c \wedge s_s = s_c$$

Finally, we add an extra property to guarantee that, when the current architecture model and system state are already consistent, the ASS leave them unchanged. This property prevents irrelevant system changes from interfering the architecture model. It also allows the MAs to record some extra information on the architecture model. For example, the MAs could change the layout of the architecture model or mark some part of it to make it more intuitive, and since this change does not have any relation with the running system, this property ensures that the synchronization does not break the layout.

7.3.2 The Challenges

There are several challenges to implement an architecture-system synchronization that satisfies the above properties.

First, the architecture model and the system structure are *heterogeneous* and *asymmetric*. *Heterogeneity* means that the relation between architecture and system is not a simple one-to-one mapping between architecture and system elements. In our example, the link elements in the architecture model do not have corresponding system elements. They just represent of the connection type of the devices. *Asymmetry* means that the architecture and the system may all contain some information which is not relevant to the other side. For example, the "be careful" mark on the client elements does not have any counterpart in the real system. Due to the heterogeneity and asymmetry, it is challenging to propagate changes correctly from the system to the architecture and vice versa. And moreover, according to the *Stability* property, we also have to identify the irrelevant information and keep it unchanged during the synchronization.

Second, the architecture and system changes may happen *simultaneously*, and thus these changes may conflict. For example, if the MA changes the type of the first link, and in the meantime, the first device is closed. Then if the ASS still propagates the architecture modification, it will invoke the management API to reset the network of this inexistent device, and cause unexpected results. If such conflicts are not properly handled, the synchronization may even cause harmful invocations to the management API.

Third, the system modifications are not predictable for the ASS, because it cannot get complete system information from the management API. If the exceptions are not properly handled, the synchronization results may be inconsistent. For example, if the MA changes the first link to `Bluetooth`, the proper system change is to switch the connection type of the first device. If this switching operation fails, to ensure consistency, the ASS should catch the exception and roll back the modification of link type.

7.4 Architecture-System Synchronization Based on Bi-transformation

This section presents our approach to implementing architecture-system synchronization. Aiming at the three challenges discussed in the last section, our main ideas can be summarized as follows.

- We utilize bidirectional transformation and model comparison to translate changes between architecture and system.
- We employ a *two-phase execution* to filter out conflicting changes, preventing them from harming the system.
- We add a *validating read* after changing the system to get the actual effects of the system modifications, in order to construct a consistent architecture model even in the presence of modification exceptions.

In this section, we first introduce the enabling techniques of our approach. Then we explain the algorithm on our illustrative example. Finally, we evaluate the algorithm according to the four properties (Sect. 7.3.1).

7.4.1 Enabling Techniques

Bidirectional transformation. Bidirectional transformation uses *one* relation between two sets of models (i.e. two meta-models) to derive two directions of transformations between them. Formally speaking, according to [30], for two meta-models M and N, and a relation $R \subseteq M \times N$, the bi-transformation is constituted of two functions:

$$\vec{R} : M \times N \longrightarrow N$$
$$\overleftarrow{R} : M \times N \longrightarrow M$$

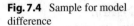

Fig. 7.4 Sample for model difference

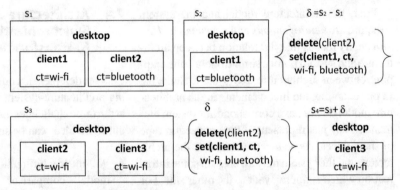

"$\vec{R}$ looks at a pair of models (m, n) and works out how to modify n so as to enforce the relation R: it returns the modified version. Similarly, $\overleftarrow{R}$ propagates changes in the opposite direction." [30]. Note that the transformation requires two parameters, because the relation between the two models is not bijective, i.e., for $m \in M$, there may exist more than one $n \in N$ satisfying $(m, n) \in R$. This is because each of the models may contain the information that is not reflected in the other one. Detail discussions and examples could be found in [9].

Model difference and merge. Model difference denoted by "−" compares two models to get the difference between them, i.e. $- : M \times M \longrightarrow \Delta_M$. It represents the calculated difference as a set of primitive model operations [1]. Model merge denoted by "+" executes the difference into a model to get a new model, i.e. $+ : M \times \Delta_M \longrightarrow M$. For example, the top half of Fig. 7.4 shows two models and the difference between them, and in the bottom half, we merge this difference with another model: the `delete` operation eliminates `client2`, but the `set` operation has no effect, because the target element `client1` does not exists in this model.

System-model adaptation. The model transformation and difference techniques are based on standard models, usually the models conforming to the OMG's MOF standard [20]. We assume the architecture models already conform to MOF standard, because more and more people choose MOF-based languages, like UML, to describe architecture models, and there are tools to convert architecture models in other languages into MOF-compliant ones [8]. But for system state, since most systems only provide ad hoc management APIs, we need a *system-model adapter* to support reading and writing the system state in a model-based way. Specifically, when reading, this adapter returns a MOF-compliant model that reflects the current system state. By contrast, when writing, it generates the proper invocation of the management API according to the model operation, changing the system state.

7.4.2 The Synchronization Algorithm

Algorithm 7.1 shows our algorithm in pseudo-code. It takes two architecture configurations before and after modification (a_o and a_c, respectively) as inputs. It propagates the architecture modifications into the current system, and reflects the new system state as the output architecture configuration (a_s). This algorithm has four steps. We first calculate what the architecture modifications mean on the system side. Then we use a two-phase execution to filter out conflicting changes, and execute the valid ones on the system. After the execution, we fetch the result system state, and feed it into the architecture. Finally, we check the result to see if all the MA's architecture modifications are successfully executed.

To explain this algorithm intuitively, we use a synchronization scenario on our mobile computing system, as shown in Fig. 7.5. The top half of this figure illustrates the evolution of the architecture configuration during the execution of this algorithm, and the bottom half illustrates the evo-

Input: a_o and a_c, the original and current architecture model
Output: a_s the **synchronized** architecture, and δ_l the failed modifications
Side-effect: changing system state from s_o into s_c
Modification recognition
$s_c \xleftarrow{read} adapter$; *get the system's "current state"*
$s'_o \leftarrow \overrightarrow{R}(a_o, s_c)$; *get system model reflecting the original arch.*
$s'_c \leftarrow \overrightarrow{R}(a_c, s_c)$; *get system model reflecting the modified arch.*
$\delta_d \leftarrow s'_c - s'_o$; *the "desired system change" reflecting MA's modification*
Two-phase execution:
$s_d \leftarrow s_c + \delta_d$; *attempt to execute the change" to the static model*
$\delta_v \leftarrow s_d - s_c$; *the "valid change" that passes the attempt*
$adapter \xleftarrow{write} \delta_v$ *executing the valid change to the system*
Result feedback:
$s_s \xleftarrow{read} adapter$ *retrieve the synchronized state* $\quad (s_s = \sigma(s_c, \varepsilon, \delta_v))$
$a_s \leftarrow \overleftarrow{R}(a_c, s_s)$; *get the "final architecture"*
Effectiveness Check:
$\delta_m \leftarrow a_c - a_o$; *get the MA's "modification"*
$\delta_a \leftarrow a_s - a_o$; *get the "actual arch change" after synchronization*
$\delta_l \leftarrow \delta_m - \delta_a$; *get the "lost change", and warn the MA*

Algorithm 7.1 Synchronization algorithm

lution of system state. The original architecture model a_o contains one server and three clients. The MA resets two links into Wi-Fi, and add a be-careful mark on a client. The modification result is a_c. In the meantime, the system has changed into s_c, with one device disappearing (shown by dashed lines and grayed text). Note that the architecture modification and the system change conflict, i.e., the MA changed the type of the third link, but the corresponding device (tab) does not exist in the system any more. We expect the resulting architecture model (a_s) to reflect the system change (a client deleted) and keep the non-conflicting architecture modifications (the type of the first link and the mark of the second one). The resulting system state (s_s) contain the effect of this architectural modifications (i.e. having the first network changed into Wi-Fi).

Step 1: Modification Recognition. Our first step is to recognize the meaning of the MA's architecture modifications on the system side. We first read the system-model adapter to get the current system state and preserve it as a system model s_c

(as shown in Fig. 7.5, marked as s_c). Then, we use this system model as a reference to transform the original and modified architecture models (i.e. a_o and a_c, respectively) into two system models (s'_o and s'_c). These two system models are not the representations of the real original and current system states, but the images of the two architecture models. We compare these two images, and get the difference as follows:

```
[ set(phone, network,
    bluetooth, wi-fi),
  set(tab, network, cable, wi-
    fi) ]
```

This difference is the meaning of the MA's architecture modifications (resetting two link types) in the system side, and we name it as the *desired system changes* (δ_d) by the MA.

Step 2: Two-phase execution. Our second step is to execute the desired system modifications into the running system. Due to the conflicts between architecture and system changes, the desired modifications may contain some invalid modifications, like setting the network type

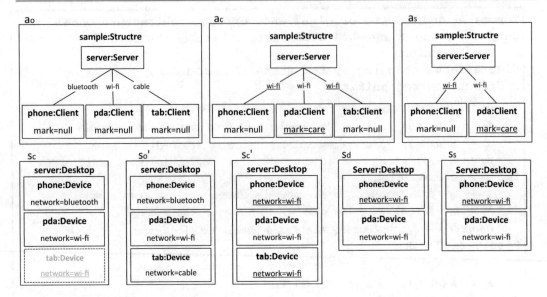

Fig. 7.5 Sample architecture model and system state

of the `tab` device. We cannot directly execute these modifications into the system, and thus we employ a "two-phase" execution: the first phase filters out the invalid modifications, and the second phase executes the valid ones. Specifically, in the first phase, we execute the desired modifications on the system model s_c. Since this execution is not performed on the real system, the invalid modification does not harm the system. Moreover, according to the behavior of the model merge [1], this modification does not change the model. After this "fake" execution, we get a system model which records the desired and valid system state by the MA (see s_d in Fig. 7.5). We compare this model with s_c again, and get the valid modifications, i.e.

```
[ set(phone, network,
    bluetooth, wi-fi) ]
```

Finally, in the second step, we invoke the system adapter to execute this valid modification (δ_v) into the real system. Notice that currently we check the validity in a simple way: Checking if the modifications are syntactically meaningful to the current system state. We plan to introduce OCL into system meta-model to specify semantic constraints, in the future.

Step 3: Result feedback. Our third step is to propagate the original system change (the disappearance of the `cable` device) and the actual effect of the system modification (setting `phone`'s network to Wi-Fi) into the architecture model. We use the adapter again to read the system state. This state is the real modification result determined by the system state before synchronization (s_c), the system logic (σ) and the current environment (ε). If this modification is executed successfully, the retrieved system model is like s_s in Fig. 7.5. Then we use the backward transformation to transform this final system state into the architecture side, as the resulted architecture model. In order to preserve the irrelevant architecture modifications (like marking the "pda" client), we use the modified architecture model (s_c) as the basis to perform this transformation.

Step 4: Effectiveness check. We cannot always ensure the *effective reconfiguration* property (we discuss this later in Sect. 7.4.4). So we employ an extra step to check what architecture modifications have not been successfully propagated. We first compare a_o and a_c, and the difference is constituted of the original architecture modifications from the MA (δ_m).

```
[ set(link1, type, bluetooth,
   wi-fi),
  set(link3, type, cable, wi-
   fi),
  set(pda, mark, null, care) ]
```

Then we compare a_o with a_s, and the difference reflects the actual architecture evolution (δ_a).

```
[ set(link1,type, bluetooth,
   wi-fi),
  set(link3, type, cable, wi-
   fi),
  delete(tab) ]
```

Finally, we calculate the *relative complement* of δ_a in δ_s, to see which expected modifications do not remain in the actual effect:

```
[ set(link3, type, cable, wi-
   fi)]
```

We warn the MA about this "lost modification", so that the MA could choose to re-try this modification or to find a substitute solution.

7.4.3 Assumptions

Our algorithm depends on the following assumptions.

First, we assume that a pair of forward and backward transformations $\overrightarrow{R}$ and $\overleftarrow{R}$ satisfy two basic properties of bi-transformation [30]. The first property is *Correctness*. That means the relation R holds on the transformation results: $(m, \overrightarrow{R}(m, n)) \in R \land \overleftarrow{R}((m, n), n) \in R$. The second property is *Hippocraticness*. That means the transformations do nothing for the already consistent models: $(m, n) \in R \implies \overrightarrow{R}(m, n) = n \land \overleftarrow{R}(m, n) = m$.

Second, we assume the model difference and merge (like Line 14 or Line 7, but not for the reading and writing on system states through adapters) to be deterministic [1]: $\forall m, m' \in M, \delta \in \Delta_M . \delta = m' - m \implies m' = m + \delta$ In addition, we also require the modifications to be idempotent, i.e. $\forall m \in M, \delta \subseteq \Delta_M . m + \delta + \delta = m + \delta$. For MOF-based models, to satisfy idempotency, we require the multiple properties to be unique and unordered [33].

Finally, we assume that the environment does not change during a synchronization process.[3] This assumption is not difficult to satisfy in practical situations. On the one hand, most system changes concerned by MAs do not happen frequently, like components added or parameter changed. On the other hand, as a fully automated process, the synchronization spends much less time, comparing with the time for MAs to make their management decision. For the systems where the casual violation of this assumption is not acceptable, developers could utilize an environment lock before each synchronization process. This assumption does not prevent multi-objective management: Different management agents could utilize different RSA of the same system, and perform management activities simultaneously, providing that the synchronization processes do not overlap.

7.4.4 Discussion About the Algorithm and the Properties

We evaluate this algorithm according to the four properties we discussed before. In summary, this algorithm satisfies three properties *in any situations*, and satisfies "effective reconfiguration" *when the MA's modification intention is reachable at the current system*.

The algorithm satisfies Consistency, i.e. $(a_s, s_s) \in R$. After the final backward transformation (Line 12), a_s and s_s has the following relation: $a_s = \overleftarrow{R}(a_c, s_s)$. According to the "Correctness" property of bi-transformation, $(a_s, s_s) \in R$.

It satisfies Stability: $(a_c, s_c) \in R \Rightarrow a_s = a_c \land s_s = s_c$. Since a_c and s_c are consistent, i.e. $(a_c, s_c) \in R$, the "Hippocraticness" property of bi-transformation ensures that the forward transformation (Line 4) results $s'_c = s_c$. δ_d changes some state into s_c (Line 5), and thus executing δ_d on some state will also return s_c, so finally, $\delta_v = \phi$. Since we assume that the environment

---

[3]A duration after the MA modifies the architecture and launches the synchronization, and before they get the resulted architecture configuration. We do not require the environment to be stable during the time when MA modifies the architectures.

is stable, executing an empty modification will not cause the system to change, and thus we get $s_s = s_c$. For the other part of *Stability*, since $s_s = s_c \wedge (a_c, s_c) \in R \Rightarrow (a_c, s_s) \in R$, the "Hippocraticness" property also ensures the backward transformation does not change the architecture, and thus we get $a_c = a_s$.

It satisfies Non-interfering Introspection: $a_o = a_c \Rightarrow s_s = s_c$. $a_o = a_c$ means that the two transformations in Lines 2 and 3 has the same inputs. The deterministic transformation produces the same outputs, i.e. $s_o = s_m$, and thus in Line 5, $\delta_d = \Delta(s_o, s_m) = \phi$. Similar to the above discussion, this empty change will cause no effect on the current system, and so $s_s = s_c$.

It satisfies Effective Reconfiguration, *if the MA's desired system modification is reachable for the current system.* We first explain the premise. The desired system modification (δ_d in Line 5) is the intention of MA's architecture modification. We say the desired system modification is *reachable for the current system*, if we can successfully effect this modification in the current system. Formally, a reachable modification $\delta \in \Delta_S$ for the current system (s, ε, σ) must satisfies $\sigma(s, \varepsilon, \delta) = s + \delta$.

Due to space limitation, we give only an informal proof for this theorem. We divide MA's architecture modification ($\delta_m = a_c - a_o$ in Line 14) into two parts, say $\delta_m = \delta_{ms} \cup \delta_{mi}$. δ_{ms} is significant to the system (like changing the link type), and the desired system modification δ_d is the image of δ_{ms} in the system side. According to the premise, after the adapter reading and writing, the δ_d will be merged into the current system, and is contained in the resulted system state s_s. In the backward transformation, a_c contains δ_{ms} and a_s contains its image. This implies that the transformation does not need to break δ_{ms} to make a_s consistent with s_s, and thus a_s still contains δ_{ms}. The other part, the δ_{mi}, is insignificant to the system (like marking a device). These modifications will never break the consistency between architecture and system. According to the "Hippocraticness" property, the backward transformation will keep this modification in a_s. As a result, the whole δ_m remains in the resulted architecture a_s, and thus $a_c - a_o \subseteq a_s - a_o$.

In practical situations, we cannot ensure that the MA's modification is always reachable for the current system. First, MA needs a relatively long time to make modification decisions. During this time, the system may change and making the MA's modification outdated. Second, for some specific system logic and environment, the modifications will fail or cause side-effects, and MAs cannot predict that. It is usually a big burden if we constrain the MA to only perform reachable modifications. As a result, in this paper, we choose a simpler solution: we allow MA to perform any modification, and after synchronization, we inform them about the violations to this property (the "effectiveness check" step). Such violations help MAs understand the current system, and find reasonable modifications through attempts.

7.5 Generating Synchronizers for Legacy Systems

We developed a tool-set named SM@RT to help developers in implementing our synchronization approach on different systems to provide runtime software architectures for them. As a generative tool-set (shown in Fig. 7.6), from the developer's specifications about the system and the architecture (Layer 3), the tool-set (Layer 2) automatically generates the synchronizer (Layer 1) to maintain causal connection between the architecture and the system at runtime (Layer 0). We design this generative tool-set in two steps.

First, we provide a generic implementation of the synchronization algorithm discussed in Sect. 7.4. This engine is independent of architecture styles and running systems. To make this generic engine works for a specific legacy system and a specific architecture style, we need to customize it with the following artifacts (recall the algorithm in Fig. 7.1):

1. the architecture and system meta-models that guide model comparison,
2. the relation between them to guide the transformations,
3. the system adapter for manipulating the system state, and

Fig. 7.6 Overview of
SM@RT toolset

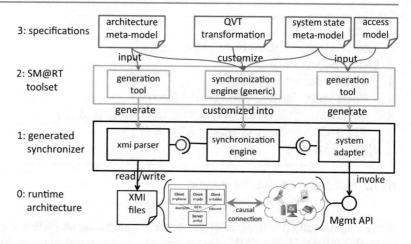

4. the XMI parser to read and write the architecture model.

Our second step is to assist developers in providing these customization artifacts. For the first two artifacts, we choose the MOF model and the QVT transformation language for developers to specify the meta-models and the relation, respectively. But since writing the adapters and the parsers from scratch is tedious and error-prone, we provide further assistance for the last two artifacts. We automatically generate XMI parsers from the architecture meta-model, and automatically generate the adapter from the system meta-model and a declarative specification of the management API, which we name as "access model".

In summary, the SM@RT tool-set has two main parts: a generic synchronization engine, and two generation tools. It also contains some auxiliary tools, like the graphical editor for specifying MOF meta-models and the textual editor for the access models. In the rest of this section, we briefly present our implementation of the two major parts.

7.5.1 Implementing the Generic Synchronization Engine

We implement the synchronization algorithm in Fig. 7.1 using a set of existing model processing tools based on Eclipse Modeling Framework (EMF: [6]), which can be regarded as an implementation for Essential MOF (EMOF: [21], a core subset of MOF standard).

We choose an open source QVT transformation engine, the mediniQVT [15], to implement the bidirectional transformations. mediniQVT is implemented on the EMF framework, and uses the EMF generated Java classes to manipulate models. It is a complete QVT implementation, supporting the expressive power defined by QVT language, and satisfying the properties we require as assumptions.

We apply a model comparison engine that we have developed before [33] to implement the model different and merge. This comparison engine is also implemented on the EMF framework, conforming to the definition by [1]. As an experimental tool, our comparison engine has some constraints on the meta-models, i.e. any classes must have an ID attribute and the multi-valued references are not ordered.

To work for a specific system, this generic implementation can be customized by two meta-models defining the architecture and system, and a QVT transformation specifying their relation. The meta-models and the QVT transformation for our running example are shown in Figs. 7.2 and 7.3. The attributes marked with stars are the IDs of the classes.

7.5.2 Generating Specific XMI Parsers and System Adapters

The generator for XMI parsers takes the architecture meta-model as an input, and produces the

```
1  @Map
2  @MetaElement=Device::Network
3  @Manipulation=Get
4  @CodeFragment=@Begin
5    MNClient mnc=(MNClient)$core;
6    QoSInfo qos=mnc.getActualNetworkQoS();
7    $result=qos.getNetworkType();
8  @End @EndMap
```

Fig. 7.7 Excerpt of access model for PLASTIC

parser automatically. We implement this generator by directly reusing the EMF code generation facility.

The generator for system adapters takes as inputs the system meta-model and an "access model", and produces the adapter. This generator is an achievement of our previous work [29], and in this paper, we just briefly introduce its input and output.

To generate the adapter for a specific system, we require developers to provide an "access model" to specify how to invoke the system's management API. An access model is a set of items, each of which defines a piece of code that implements a primitive manipulation operation (get, set, create, etc.) on a specific kind of system data (Device, Network, etc). Figure 7.7 shows one of the items in the access model for PLASTIC, defining how to "*get* a *device's connection type*". The meta element (Line 2) indicates the type of target system element. The manipulation (Line 3) indicates the primitive operation, and the Java code (Lines 4–8) shows how to invoke the API. The logic for this API invocation is as follows: We get the instance of `MNClient` for this device, retrieve its QoS information, and return the network type from the information.[4]

From the access model, our generator automatically produces the system adapter. The adapter maintains an EMF compliant model at runtime, and external programs (like our synchronization engine) use the standard operations to manipulate this runtime model, like copying the runtime model to a common static model (the `read` operation in the algorithm in Fig. 7.1), or executing the modifications to the runtime model (the `write` operation). In the background, the adapter synchronizes the model state with the system state at real time, so that the external programs could always get the current system state, and their modifications on the runtime model will immediately be executed to the real system. More details about this low-level real-time synchronization could be found in our previous paper [29].

7.6　Case Studies

We have applied our approach on several practical systems, providing RSA support for them. These cases illustrate its feasibility and validity, as well as the development efficiency for implementing it. In the following of this section, we first describe a C2-JOnAS case in detail. Then we present other cases briefly, and summarize all the cases.

7.6.1　C2-JOnAS

Our first case study is to provide C2-styled runtime architecture for JOnAS. Here JOnAS [24] is an open source JEE application server, while C2 [22] is an architecture style aiming at the runtime evolution of UI-centric systems. Since many JEE applications are UI-centric, it is a natural idea to

---

[4]As mentioned before, we revise PLASTIC a bit to add "network type" as a new QoS value, and let the PLASTIC framework to choose network directly by type. Note that this revision is not a necessary part for applying our approach. We did it just for making *this example* straightforward.

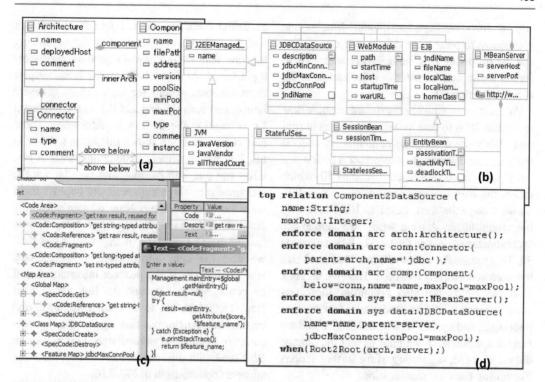

Fig. 7.8 Specifications for generating C2-JOnAS synchronizer

use C2-styled architecture models for managing JOnAS-based systems.

We prepare the four inputs as shown in Fig. 7.8, to let the *SM@RT* tool-set generate the synchronizer. We defined the *architecture meta-model* (Fig. 7.8a) following the description of C2 style [22], where `Architectures` contain several `Components` and `Connectors`, which link to each other through `above` and `below` associations. We defined the *system meta-model* (Fig. 7.8b) according to the JOnAS document. We care about the `EJBs`, `JDBCDataSources` and `WebModules` running on a system, and a set of their attributes. We defined the *access model* (Fig. 7.8c) by studying the sample code for using JOnAS management API [12]. We wrapped the Java code for deploying and un-deploying EJBs, data sources and web modules, and for getting and setting their attributes. The pop-up diagram shows a sample item for invoking `getAttribute` method of JMX to get all kinds of attributes. Finally, we defined a *QVT transformation* to connect the architecture and

system meta-models. We use five QVT relations to reflect all types of management elements to components. Figure 7.8d shows one of these relations. It specifies that a `Component` maps to a `JDBCDataSource`, if and only if they had the same name, and the `Component` links to a `Connector` named "jdbc".

The generated synchronizer maintains a C2-styled runtime architecture for a JOnAS system. For this case, the target system is a JOnAS server deployed with a Java Pet Store (JPS) application [31]. We launch the synchronization engine with an empty model as the initial architecture. After the first synchronization, we obtain an architecture model showing the current structure of the running JPS. The left snapshot of Fig. 7.9 shows this model opened in a graphical C2 architecture editor, after a manual adjustment of the layout. At this time, the area inside the red dashed frame is empty. This system contains one component (`HSQL1`) to provide the data, several other components to organize and aggregate the data (such as `CatalogEJB` and ShoppingCartEJB), and finally one component to present the data (petstore). We use the following two management scenarios to further show how to use the RSA and how the synchronizer works.

We first use a simple experiment to show how to use this RSA to tune system parameters at runtime: We write a script to continuously request the SignOn component, and we soon notice that the Pool Size of HSQL1 becomes 50, which means the data source's connection pool is full. So we change the Max Pool to 100 and launch the synchronizer. After a while, we launch the synchronizer again, and the Pool Size exceeds 50. That means the database's maximal pool size has been successfully enlarged. Then we set Max Pool to 20000, but after synchronization, this value becomes 9999 (the upper limit of connection pool supported by this version of HSQL), and we receive a notification warning us that the change did not succeed, suggesting us for further actions like rolling back the modification.

Our second scenario simulates the runtime evolution case used by [22]. We want to add RSS (Really Simple Syndication) capability into JPS at runtime to support subscription of pet information. Following the typical C2-based

evolution scenario, we add ProductArtist and ItemArtist components for organizing the raw data as *products* (a product represents a pet breed [31]) and *items* (same breed of pets from different sellers are regarded as different items), respectively, and add the rss component for formatting the data as an RSS seed. These new components are shown inside the red box in Fig. 7.9. We implement these components as two EJBs and one web module, and then launch the synchronizer, which automatically deploys them onto the JOnAS server. Now we can subscribe an RSS seed with all *items* via "http://www. localhost/rss" (top-right of Fig. 7.9). After that, we find the item information is too tedious, and want to see if the product information will be better. We just change the link above rss from ItemArtist to ProductArtist, and launch the synchronization again. The system behavior is changed immediately, and we get an RSS seed with different contents, from the same address (bottom-right of Fig. 7.9).

7.6.2 Client/Server-JOnAS

The second case study is a combination of the first one and the running example. We provide

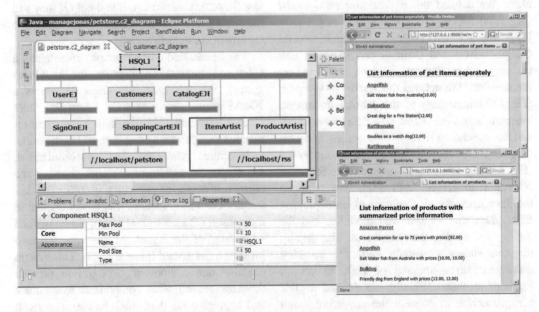

Fig. 7.9 Snapshots of C2-based JEE management

a Client/Server-styled RSA for JOnAS, where the server represents the data source and the clients represent the EJBs interacting with this data source. The server and the clients all have a `resource` attribute, which represent the data source's max connection pool and the EJB's instances amount, respectively. This RSA is useful for database administrators to see how the data source interacts with other components.

To construct the synchronizer, we directly reuse the meta-model we have defined for Client/Server style (Fig. 7.3), and the meta-model and access model for JOnAS (Fig. 7.8). We write a new QVT transformation to specify that `Server` maps to `J2EEDataSource`, and `Client` maps to the `EJB` that depends on this data source, and their attributes map correspondingly. This QVT transformation has 56 lines in total.

We perform a self-adaptation scenario on this RSA, imitating the one presented by [11]. We specify the self-adaptation rule using an extended version of OCL [28].

```
context Server do let
sum:Real=self.link->
        collect(e|e.client.consumption)->sum()
in sum > self.resource => self.resource <- sum
```

At the architecture level, this rule means that if a server's resource is less than the sum of all its clients' consumption, then enlarge this server's resource. We input this rule to the extended OCL engine, and execute "synchronize, OCL-execute, synchronize" every five minutes. The effect on JOnAS system is automatically enlarging the data source's connection pool, when the sum of EJB's instance size (an instance implies a potential database connection) exceeds the data source's maximal connection pool size.

7.6.3 Other Case Studies

Besides the running example on PLASTIC, and the above two cases on JOnAS, we also performed several other cases on different platforms, implementing different kinds of RSAs. We perform these cases based on the system adapters we have generated in our earlier work [29].

Jar-UML. We wrap the BCEL (Byte Code Engineering Library, http://jakarta.apache.org/bcel/) API to reflect the class structure inside a Jar file, and write a QVT transformation to map this Java-specific class structure with the UML class diagram. This case is a reproduction of the Jar2UML tool (http://ssel.vub.ac.be/ssel/research/mdd/jar2uml). It is a weakened case of RSA, since it only supports the introspection of class structures, without reconfiguration.

Eclipse-GUI. The target system for this case is any Eclipse window (views, editors, dialogs, etc.). We generate a system adapter to reflect the SWT widgets (buttons, text box, containers, etc.) constituting the window. The architecture model is a generic GUI model constituted of components connected with composition relations. Using this RSA, developers can change the attributes of the widgets dynamically, such as the text, the background color, etc. They can also add or remove widgets into the window at runtime.

7.6.4 Summary and Discussion

Table 7.1 lists all the cases we have introduced in this paper. In this section, we summarize these cases to evaluate and discuss our RSA approach in three aspects. We first discuss the application scope of this approach, including what target systems it applies to and what kind of RSA usages it supports. Then we evaluate how this approach supports these RSA usages on the target systems, emphasizing on how the four properties (Sect. 7.3.1) are embodied in these cases. Finally, we show its practicability, i.e. it is easy to implement this approach on different systems, and the implementations have acceptable performance.

7.6.4.1 Application Scope

This approach applies to a wide range of target systems. According to Table 7.1, we have applied it on four different kinds of systems, covering enterprise (JOnAS), desktop (SWT), and mobile computing systems (PLASTIC). Actually, whether it applies to a particular system depends on whether we can construct the adapter for this system, and

Table 7.1 Summary of the cases. For each target system, we list the platform name, the size of system meta-model (the total number of model elements, including classes, attributes, associations), and the size of access model (lines of code). For the architecture, we list the name of style or ADL, and the size of architecture meta-model (for the last two cases, we reuse the existing ADL and tools, without defining meta-models). Then we list the size of QVT (lines of code), and the approximate upper bound of time spent (in seconds) for a single synchronization. Finally, we briefly describe the type of management activities we have tried on these RSAs

#	Target system			Architecture		QVT	Time	Usage
	Platform	mm	Acc	Style	mm		Max	
1	PLASTIC	6	547	C/S	15	15	0.5	Dynamic configuration
2	JOnAS	61	237	C2	29	157	2	Runtime evolution
3	JOnAS	61	237	C/S	17	56	1	Self-adaptation
4	BCEL	29	124	UML	–	139	6	Reverse engineering
5	SWT	43	178	ABC	–	104	1	Dynamic configuration

[29] has revealed that we can generate adapters for a wide range of systems.

This approach supports typical RSA usages. The above cases reproduces several typical RSA usages presented in classical literatures (like the runtime evolution in [22], and the self-adaptation in [11]) and the ordinary usages (like reversing the class structure of jar files or dynamically configuring the GUI). With this conclusion, we can expect that this approach has the potential to support a wide range of RSA usage.

The usage of RSA depends on the capability of the management API. We realize runtime evolution and self-adaptation on JOnAS, because its JMX API supports deploying components and configuring their parameters at runtime. On the contrary, we do not support changing the UML model reflected from Jar files, because BCEL does not support changing the class structures. That means the RSA usage is mainly limited by the capability of the management APIs. This limitation is reasonable, for the current goal of this approach is to help management agents to utilize the existing management capabilities of the target systems in an RSA-based way, but not to instrument the systems with new management capabilities. Actually, the usage is also influenced by the adapter and the QVT relation. However, we have showed that we can generate the strong enough

adapters to wrap all the provided management capabilities [29], and we also believe that as the standard transformation language, QVT is capable of relating the system with any architecture model (this could also be demonstrated weakly by the cases, because we define all the required relations as QVT rules, in very small sizes).

7.6.4.2 Evaluation About the Four Properties

This section evaluates if we provide the right RSAs for runtime management. We have define the *right RSA* by four properties, and proved that our approach satisfies these properties. The cases further demonstrate that these properties are necessary and important for RSA-based runtime management.

Obviously, in all the cases, the synchronization satisfies *Consistency*, otherwise the reasoning upon the RSA is meaningless. Notice that even the modification has exceptions, like we assign a too big value to the pool size in case #2, the resulted architecture is also consistent with the resulted system state. This ensures the management agents always plan their activities based on the genuine current system state.

Non-Interfering Introspection ensures that all the system changes are reflected immediately. Therefore, in the self-adaptation case (#3) the adaptation engine observes the situation of too many resource consumptions *on time*, to make proper changes.

The synchronizer satisfies *Effective Reconfiguration* for the *reasonable* architecture modifications, like the change of maximal pool size to 100 and the addition of components. But the change of maximal pool size to 20000 is not effectively reconfigured to the system. This is not the fault of the synchronizer, but because we, as the administrator, performed an invalid modification. The synchronizer raises a warning to help us notice and analyze this failure.

Finally, the synchronizer satisfies *Stability*, and thus the tuning on the architecture layout (case #2) is preserved after the synchronizations. This property also allows the management activities to be performed step by step. Take the evolution scenario in case #2 as an example, we can first add a component without connecting it with any connectors. At this step, the relation is not broken, and thus we can still execute the synchronization to see the system changes, before we go on to finish configuring this new component.

7.6.4.3   Implementation Efficiency and Execution Performance

This section discusses how much effort is required to implement RSA on a particular system, and how it works in practical environment.

The major benefit of our approach is that it enables developers to *efficiently* implement runtime architecture on existing systems. The case studies highlight this benefit. The RSA we provide for JOnAS is not a trivial one: It reflects 6 kinds of management elements (supporting adding and removing most of them) and 54 kinds of attributes (with 12 of them writable), but to implement it, we only defined four model-level specifications (as shown in Fig. 7.8), with 90 model elements and 394 lines of code in total. The whole work takes us only 2 full days, from study, specification to debugging. The generated code contains 27024 lines of code. The other cases also use inputs in small sizes to generate complex code. By contrast, a case study in the Rainbow project costs 102 K lines of manual code [11], and the case in C2 project costs 38 K lines of code [22]. Although the

cases and the contrasts are not directly matched, the code size at least reveals that our generative tool-set could save developers' effort. The efficiency depends on the complexity of RSA usages, as well as the type of the target platform. For commercial solutions, like JOnAS and SWT, we write small code for a big architecture meta model (bigger architecture supports more powerful management capabilities), in contrast with the academics prototype platform like PLASTIC.

The cases also reveal the potential of reuse supported by our approach. For case #3, we reuse the system specifications on JOnAS (case #2), and add only two attributes on the C/S architecture meta-model (case #1). Reuse will further increase the efficiency to implement our approach.

The performance of this synchronizer is *acceptable* for human participant runtime management. We define *acceptable performance* with the reference to the existing and widely used runtime management tools. For JOnAS, the official runtime management interface is a web-based management console, the `jonasAdmin`. Using this default console, after each modification, the administrator has to wait about 1 s (depending on the environment) before the page is refreshed. For Java class structure, using eclipse JDT, it also takes about 1 s to expend the full structure of a medium-sized package (1000 classes). Since these tools are already widely used in practical runtime management, and also considering the delay of human decision, we regard the synchronization time around 1 s as *acceptable* for manual runtime management. From this point of view, case #1, #2 and #5 are acceptable. For case #1 and case #5, the average synchronization time for all kinds of architecture changes is 0.31 and 0.85 s, respectively. For case #2, the synchronization time varies for different kinds of architecture changes. For example, changing the pool size and adding the RSS components (case #1) take 0.75 and 1.37 s in average. Case #4 takes longer time: Constructing the UML model from scratch for a large Jar file (`bcel.jar` itself) with 1155 classes takes 5.62 s on average. The good news is that for such reverse engineering task, we do not often need to construct the system architecture. However, for automated management, like case #3, the performance is not ideal: The self-adaption loop takes 0.81 s in average. That means the self-adaptation loop has to be performed in a much longer interval, in order to avoid too heavy system burden. So currently, our approach is only proper to the automated management scenarios which handle the not-so-frequent system changes.

There are complex factors that affect the performance of synchronizers.

First, the execution time of synchronization process is constituted of the time spent on QVT transformation and the API invocations. The latter plays the leading role in the current cases. For example, the difference of the two scenarios in case #1 (0.75 s vs. 1.37 s) is caused by the fact that deploying an EJB costs 0.6 s while setting an attributes is almost transient. Similarly, case #4 takes so much time mainly because it had to invoke the BCEL for so many times to collect the information about the one thousand classes. Alternatively, the time spent by the model transformation is almost constant for the existing cases (between 0.5 and 1 s).

Second, the performance is affected by both the complexity (the size of meta-models and the QVTs) and the scale (the size the final architecture model for a specific scenario) of the RSA. The current cases show that the scale is more important (case # 4 takes much more time than others). We have tested mediniQVT with complex QVT rules, and found that the execution time becomes unacceptable when the QVT rules reach 1000 lines. But so far, the RSA cases do not require so complex relations.

7.7   Related Work

Using software architecture for runtime management is a hot topic in the recent decade, and much work has been devoted to the high-level representation and utilization of RSA, and the low-level mechanisms for maintaining causal connection between an architecture model and a running system.

For the representation and utilization of RSA, [19] first propose to represent system structures

as *nodes* and *links*, and allow people to manage the system by adding, removing or replacing these nodes and links. Oreizy et al. [22] propose a layered architecture style named C2 to support runtime evolution of GUI-centric systems. Garlan et al. [11] propose using RSA for policy-driven self-adaptation, and their policies originate from the design time architecture constraints. [23] surveyed many relevant approaches, and summarized several typical architecture styles. [14] also surveyed several approaches, focusing on the ones that use RSA for self-adaptation. In this chapter, we do not focus on a specific representation or usage of RSA, but the generic approach to implement RSAs in different styles, supporting different usages.

Current approaches employ different mechanisms to maintain the causal connections between architecture models and running systems. We roughly classify the mechanism into three kinds, according to their degree of coupling with the target systems. First, some early approaches require the target systems to be developed with built-in RSA support. For example, [22] require their target systems to developed under the Java-C2 framework. To use Fractal architecture at runtime [5], the system classes must implement the interfaces defined by Fractal. This requirement limits their applicability in practice. Second, some approaches allow the target systems to be developed under industrial standards, but enhance their runtime platforms (middlewares) with RSA mechanisms. These approaches are also known as "reflective middleware", covering many mainstream component models, like DynamicTAO [17] and OpenORB [3] for CORBA, and PKUAS [13] for JEE. The problem here is that these platforms are not yet well accepted in practice, and thus few existing systems are constructed on them. Third, some researchers try to insert probes and effectors into existing systems to collect runtime data, organize them as architecture model, and effect architecture modifications [11,25]. But since most existing systems are not designed for code-level evolution, inserting code into them, if possible, is usually tedious and unsafe. Our approach is close to the third type in that we also seek to provide a generic mechanism for existing systems, but we choose a safer way, utilizing the low-level management APIs provided by the existing systems.

Another advantage of our approach is its ease of application: To bridge the abstraction gap between architecture and system, developers only need to provide a declarative specification about their relation. Some approaches embed similar ideas. [7] allow developers to map detailed system events into abstract architecture events using a simple event composition language, and [25] develop a more sophisticated language to map events. Taking the specification, their event transformation engines causally connect the architecture and system during runtime. In this chapter, we choose model transformation language for specifying state-based (not event-based) relations between architectures and systems, which is proper to the way of manipulating system states through active APIs invocations (not by passive event notifications).

Our general solution for architecture-system synchronization has its root in the research on bidirectional transformation [9] and model synchronization [32]. We applied this technique to a novel field, i.e. synchronizing a common model (the architecture) with a dynamically changing model (the system), and thus we meet some new challenges like conflicting changes.

7.8 Conclusion

In this chapter, we presented a synchronization approach to maintaining runtime software architectures for a wide range of existing systems. We applied bidirectional model transformation to bridge the abstraction gap between architecture models and system states, and adapted bi-transformation to handle conflicting changes and identify modification failures. This approach satisfies a set of well-defined properties, i.e. *Consistency*, *Non-interfering introspection*, *Effective reconfiguration*, and *Stability*, which ensure the validity of the RSAs for runtime management. We also provided a generative tool-set to assist developers in implementing this approach on different running systems. We applied our approach to provide RSAs for some practical systems.

Our approach requires the target systems to have low-level management capabilities, usually some kinds of management APIs. It could also utilize other forms of management capabilities, such as configuration files, system commands, etc. provided that people could define how to manipulate them as pieces of code. But in this chapter, we use only management APIs as examples. Since runtime management becomes an important concern for modern systems, more and more systems provide such low-level management capabilities. Our approach is an effort to link such existing low-level management capabilities with the research on architecture-based runtime management. An issue here is how to help developers determine if the management API is sufficient for a particular architectural adaptation. We have an approach to analyze the capability of system API [27], and we plan to provide a QVT analysis support to find out if the architecture operations used by the architecture adaptation is included in API capability.

Currently, our approach cares only about the structural part of RSA. That means after each synchronization, the resulted architecture configuration is a snapshot of the current system state. In future, we will investigate how to analyze a series of such snapshots to obtain the behavioral models for the system.

References

1. M. Alanen, I. Porres, Difference and union of models, in *Proceedings of the 6th International Conference on the Unified Modeling Language, Modeling Languages and Applications, UML 2003*, San Francisco, CA, USA, 20–24 Oct 2003, pp. 2–17 (2003)
2. G. Blair, N. Bencomo, R.B. France, Models@ run.time. Computer **42**(10), 22–27 (2009)
3. G.S. Blair, G. Coulson, L. Blair, H. Duran-Limon, P. Grace, R. Moreira, N. Parlavantzas, Reflection, self-awareness and self-healing in OpenORB, in *Proceedings of the First Workshop on Self-Healing Systems, WOSS 2002*, Charleston, South Carolina, USA, 18–19 Nov 2002, pp. 9–14 (2002)
4. G.S. Blair, G. Coulson, P. Robin, M. Papathomas, An architecture for next generation middleware, in *Proceedings of the IFIP International Conference on*

Distributed Systems Platforms and Open Distributed Processing, ICODP 1998 (1998)

5. E. Bruneton, T. Coupaye, M. Leclercq, V. Quema, J.B. Stefani, I. Rhone-Alpes, An open component model and its support in Java, in *Proceedings of the 7th International Symposium on Component-Based Software Engineering, CBSE 2004*, Edinburgh, UK, 24–25 May 2004, pp. 7–22 (2004)

6. F. Budinsky, S.A. Brodsky, E. Merks, *Eclipse Modeling Framework*. Pearson Education, project address, http://www.eclipse.org/modeling/emf (2003)

7. T.S.A. Chan, S.-N. Chuang, MobiPADS: a reflective middleware for context-aware mobile computing. IEEE Trans. Softw. Eng. **29**(12), 1072–1085 (2003)

8. J.S. Cuadrado, J.G. Molina, A model-based approach to families of embedded domain-specific languages. IEEE Trans. Softw. Eng. **35**(6), 825–840 (2009)

9. K. Czarnecki, J. Foster, Z. Hu, R. Lämmel, A. Schürr, J. Terwilliger, Bidirectional transformations: a cross-discipline perspective, in *Theory and Practice of Model Transformations* (2009), pp. 260–283

10. R. France, B. Rumpe, Model-driven development of complex software: a research roadmap, in *Proceedings of the International Conference on Software Engineering, ISCE 2007, Workshop on the Future of Software Engineering, FOSE 2007*, 23–25 May 2007, Minneapolis, MN, USA, pp. 37–54 (2007)

11. D. Garlan, S.W. Cheng, A.C. Huang, B.R. Schmerl, P. Steenkiste, Rainbow: architecture-based self-adaptation with reusable infrastructure. Computer **37**(10), 46–54 (2004)

12. J. Hanson, Pro JMX: Java Management Extensions (2004)

13. G. Huang, H. Mei, F. Yang, Runtime recovery and manipulation of software architecture of component-based systems. Autom. Softw. Eng. **13**(2), 257–281 (2006)

14. M.C. Huebscher, J.A. McCann, A survey of autonomic computing-degrees, models, and applications. ACM Comput. Surv. **40**(3), 1–28 (2008)

15. ikv++. medini QVT, http://projects.ikv.de/qvt (2009)

16. IST STREP Project, PLATIC Multi-Radio Device Management—Developer Guide, http://www.ist-plastic.org/ (2008)

17. F. Kon, M. Roman, P. Liu, J. Mao, T. Yamane, C. Magalhã, R.H. Campbell, Monitoring, security, and dynamic configuration with the dynamic TAO reflective ORB, in *Proceedings of the IFIP/ACM International Conference on Distributed Systems Platforms, Middleware 2000*, New York, NY, USA, 4–7 Apr 2000, pp. 121–143 (2000)

18. J. Kramer, J. Magee, Self-managed systems: an architectural challenge, In *Proceedings of the International Conference on Software Engineering, ICSE 2007, Workshop on the Future of Software Engineering, FOSE 2007*, 23–25 May 2007, Minneapolis, MN, USA, pp. 259–268 (2007)

19. J. Kramer, J. Magee, The evolving philosophers problem: dynamic change management. IEEE Trans. Softw. Eng. **16**(11), 1293–1306 (1990)

20. OMG, Meta object facility (mof) core specification. Available specification, OMG, Oct 2006

21. OMG, Catalog of OMG Modeling and Metadata Specifications, http://www.omg.org/technology/documents/modeling_spec_catalog.htm (2008)

22. P. Oreizy, N. Medvidovic, R.N. Taylor, Architecture-based runtime software evolution, in *Proceedings of the 1998 International Conference on Software Engineering, ICSE 98*, Kyoto, Japan, 19–25 Apr 1998, pp. 177–186 (1998)

23. P. Oreizy, N. Medvidovic, R.N. Taylor, Runtime software adaptation: framework, approaches, and styles, in *Proceedings of the 30th International Conference on Software Engineering, ICSE 2008*, Leipzig, Germany, 10–18 May 2008, Companion Volume, pp. 899–910 (2008)

24. OW2 Consortium, JOnAS Project. Java Open Application Server, http://jonas.objectweb.org (2008)

25. B. Schmerl, J. Aldrich, D. Garlan, R. Kazman, H. Yan, Discovering architectures from running systems. IEEE Trans. Softw. Eng. **32**(7), 454–466 (2006)

26. S. Sicard, F. Boyer, N. De Palma, Using components for architecture-based management: the self-repair case, in *Proceedings of the 30th International Conference on Software Engineering, ICSE 2008*, Leipzig, Germany, 10–18 May 2008, pp. 101–110 (2008)

27. H. Song, G. Huang, Y. Xiong, F. Chauvel, Y. Sun, H. Mei, Inferring meta-models for runtime system data from the clients of management APIs, in *Proceedings of the 13th International Conference Model Driven Engineering Languages and Systems, MODELS 2010*, Oslo, Norway, 3–8 Oct 2010, pp. 168–182 (2010)

28. H. Song, Y. Sun, L. Zhou, G. Huang, Towards instant automatic model refinement based on OCL, in *Proceedings of the 14th Asia-Pacific Software Engineering Conference (APSEC 2007)*, 5–7 Dec 2007, Nagoya, Japan, pp. 167–174 (2007)

29. H. Song, Y. Xiong, F. Chauvel, G. Huang, Z. Hu, H. Mei, Generating synchronization engines between running systems and their model-based views. in *Proceedings of Models in Software Engineering, Workshops and Symposia at MODELS 2009*, Denver, CO, USA, 4–9 Oct 2009, Reports and Revised Selected Papers, pp. 140–154 (2009)

30. P. Stevens, Bidirectional model transformations in QVT: semantic issues and open questions, in *Proceedings of the 10th International Conference Model Driven Engineering Languages and Systems, MoDELS 2007*, Nashville, USA, 30 Sept–5 Oct 2007, pp. 1–15 (2007)

31. Sun, Java PetStore, http://java.sun.com/developer/releases/petstore/ (2002)

32. T. Vogel, S. Neumann, S. Hildebrandt, H. Giese, B. Becker, Incremental model synchronization for efficient run-time monitoring, in *Proceedings of Models in Software Engineering, Workshops and Symposia at MODELS 2009*, Denver, CO, USA, 4–9 Oct 2009, Reports and Revised Selected Papers, pp. 124–139 (2009)

33. Y. Xiong, Z. Hu, H. Zhao, H. Song, M. Takeichi, H. Mei, Supporting automatic model inconsistency fixing, in *Proceedings of the 7th Joint Meeting of the European Software Engineering Conference and the ACM SIGSOFT International Symposium on Foundations of Software Engineering, 2009*, Amsterdam, The Netherlands, 24–28 Aug 2009 (ACM, 2009), pp. 315–324

34. Y. Xiong, H. Song, Z. Hu, M. Takeichi, Supporting parallel updates with bidirectional model transformations, in *Proceedings of the 2nd International Conference on Theory and Practice of Model Transformations, ICMT 2009*, Zurich, Switzerland, 29–30 June 2009, pp. 213–228 (2009)

Low-Disruptive Dynamic Updating of Internetware Applications

8

Abstract

In this chapter, we present Javelus, a Java HotSpot VM-based DSU technique for Java-based system with very short pausing time. Instead of updating everything at once when the running application is suspended, Javelus only updates the changed code during the suspension, and migrates stale objects on-demand after the application is resumed. With a careful design this lazy approach neither sacrifices the update flexibility nor introduces unnecessary object validity checks or access indirections. Evaluation experiments show that Javelus can reduce the updating pausing time by one to two orders of magnitude without introducing observable overheads before and after the dynamic updating. Our experience with Javelus indicates that low-disruptive and type-safe dynamic updating of Java applications can be practically achieved with a lazy updating approach.

Keywords

Dynamic software updating · JVM · Lazy updating · Low disruption

8.1 Introduction

Software is always evolving to new versions in order to eliminate defects and meet new requirements. Normally, software updating should follow the well-known shutdown-patch-restart scheme to

get the new version working. For mission critical systems with high availability requirements, such as those used in financial truncation processing, transportation management and medical life supporting, service downtime is unacceptable or prohibitively expensive. Even for those everyday software systems such as Microsoft Windows and Office, the disruption of software upgrading could be at least annoying. In addition, when debugging a complex software system, frequent restarts for code modification could be tedious and time-consuming. Dynamic Software Updating (DSU) can alleviate these problems by updating a

---

Parts of this chapter were reprinted from Information and Software Technology, Volume 56, Tianxiao Gu, Chun Cao, Chang Xu, Xiaoxing Ma, Linghao Zhang and Jian Lü, Low-disruptive dynamic updating of java applications, Pages No. 1086–1098, Copyright (2014), with permission from Elsevier [OR APPLICABLE SOCIETY COPYRIGHT OWNER].

running software system without having to stop and restart it.

In recent years, DSU has been extensively studied [5,12,16,18,30], although the idea of dynamically modifying running programs is not new—it can be traced back to dynamic linking, which was systematically supported in MULTICS [8]. Specifically, for updating Java programs at runtime, it is natural to extend the Java Virtual Machine (JVM) with DSU support [10,31,33]. In JVM a Java program at runtime consists of a set of classes, a set of heap objects instantiated from the classes and a set of thread stacks storing frames of active methods. To update a running program, one must replace the classes with their new versions and transform their objects accordingly with user provided or default *transformers*. To keep system consistency, DSU systems usually suspend the execution and apply updates when no method-to-update is active.

Most of existing proposals of DSU for Java take an eager approach. They locate *stale objects* (i.e., objects instantiated from old versioned classes) and update them all at once [31,33]. Stale objects are detected by traversing the whole heap. Objects with increased sizes cannot be updated in-place, so all references to them, including stack variables and object fields, must be adjusted to point to the new locations. Generally, these tasks are fulfilled by exploiting the garbage collection facilities provided by the virtual machine. The garbage collector used here must be forced into the stop-the-world mode and make a full-heap collection, even if it itself were a concurrent and incremental collector. The program is unable to proceed during this process, and the pausing time can be up to seconds long. Although this time is usually much shorter than that of doing shutdown-and-restart, it is still not acceptable for many applications that require very short response time, such as high-performance Web servers and interactive applications.

We take a lazy approach to DSU to cut down the pausing time. It is motivated by following two observations. First, for most updates, as only a small portion of all objects are affected, traversing the whole heap is unnecessary. Second, many updated objects would not be used immediately or even not used any more. Our lazy approach updates objects on-demand. Each stale object is updated on the first access to it. In this way, we eliminate expensive whole-heap traversing, avoid updating useless objects and disperse the effort of object transformation to later program executions.

However, lazy object updating is not without challenges. A naïve implementation would bring unwanted overheads at execution time because (1) accesses to objects would need to be trapped with validity checks and (2) references to objects whose sizes are increased have to be made indirect. In addition, in a lazy DSU, object transformers are invoked concurrently with application methods. So it could be extremely tricky to program these transformers correctly unless we provide a reasonable semantic guarantee on the updating process.

This chapter presents the design and implementation of Javelus,[1] a lazy DSU system for Java based on the OpenJDK Java HotSpot VM.[2] It supports arbitrary changes to Java classes and provides an easy but powerful model for programmers to write transformers. Its overhead during steady-state executions is negligible. In addition, Javelus guarantees that no stale code will run after the updating is triggered and no stale object will be accessed by any updated code. With a carefully optimized object validity checking strategy and a novel object allocation model, Javelus achieves very short pausing time without sacrificing updating flexibility and system efficiency. In comparison with existing eager approaches, the pausing time can be tens to hundreds times shorter.

The main contributions of this work are an efficient lazy object updating mechanism and an implementation of this updating mechanism on an industry-strength Java HotSpot VM. The work was initially reported in [14], and the current chapter has been completely rewritten and reorganized to give a more complete and clearer presentation of the work. Critical enabling techniques such as how we use versioned class hierarchies to ensure type safety and how we deal with type

---

[1]The source code of Javelus and the applications used to evaluate it can be found at http://artemisprojects.org/projects/javelus.

[2]http://openjdk.java.net.

narrowing are presented for the first time. In addition, we improved our evaluation of Javelus by adding new application subjects and making direct comparisons between lazy and eager approaches.

The rest of this chapter is organized as follows. We first discuss the general requirements of, and approaches to, dynamic software updating in Sect. 8.2 and then give an overview of Javelus in Sect. 8.3. The following three sections are dedicated to explain how to prepare dynamic updating, how Javelus dynamically updates code and how it lazily updates stale objects, respectively. In Sect. 8.7, we evaluate Javelus with a micro benchmark and also real version updates of Tomcat and H2 server applications. We summarize related work in Sect. 8.8 and conclude the chapter in Sect. 8.9.

8.2 Dynamic Updating: Eager Versus Lazy

A Java program statically consists of a set of classes with inheritance and association relationships between them. Dynamically, in addition to the reified representation of these classes (called *metadata*), a runtime image of a running program also contains a stack (or stacks) of active method frames and a set of objects instantiated from the classes. To update a running program, one must not only refresh the class metadata to the new version but also rebuild the whole runtime image satisfying the following properties:

- *Type safety*: The program can continue to execute without type errors.
- *Semantic continuity*: The states in the current image are preserved as many as possible.

Generally, it is impossible to automatically ensure the semantic correctness of a dynamically updated program [15]. It is DSU users' responsibility to maintain the semantic correctness in addition to type safety and semantic continuity.

A practical DSU system should also fulfill the following requirements [16,31]:

- *Efficiency*: There should be no overhead before and after the updating.
- *Flexibility*: It should allow most kinds of changes happened in real-life software evolution.
- *Low disruption*: The interruption of service caused by the dynamic updating should be minimized.
- *Timeliness*: Updates should be applied as soon as possible.

Dynamic updating can be done eagerly or lazily. As shown in Fig. 8.1, in an eager approach all updating work is carried out when the program is suspended at some safe point.

Fig. 8.1 Eager versus lazy updating. **a** Time-line of eager updating; **b** time-line of lazy updating

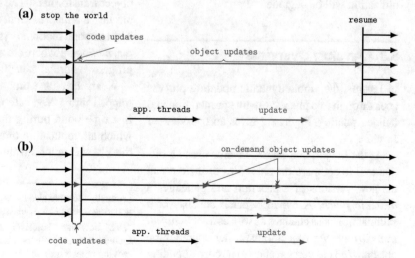

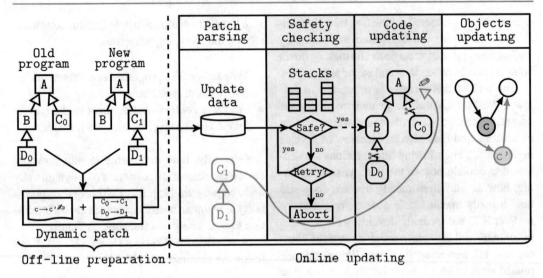

Fig. 8.2 System overview

In a lazy approach, the program is allowed to resume immediately after refreshing the class metadata, and some stale objects in the heap would be updated later in an on-demand way. Eager approaches are usually believed to be more efficient but, meanwhile, more disruptive than lazy ones. However, lazy approaches can create overheads during a program's execution in that the program must be instrumented to trigger on-demand updating of stale objects and references. Besides, lazy approaches often use indirections to update objects with increased sizes, and require additional spaces to store *forward pointers*. Hence, the efficiency and space utilization will be degraded.

8.3 Javelus: Overview

In Javelus, the whole dynamic updating process goes through two phases: off-line preparation and online updating. Figure 8.2 gives an overview of Javelus.

At the preparation phase, Javelus uses an off-line tool to compare the class files of the old and the new versions of a program and generates a *dynamic patch*. A dynamic patch consists of a summary of class changes as well as a set of *object transformers*. An object transformer upgrades the objects of an old version class to its corresponding

new one.[3] Developers need to manually fill transformation logics in transformer templates if their default ones are inappropriate.

After all transformers have been prepared, the dynamic patch is ready to be delivered to dynamic updating. Developers initiate a dynamic updating request by sending the patch to Javelus via a provided invoking interface. The whole online updating phase involves four steps: dynamic patch loading, safe point checking, code updating and object updating.

After receiving an updating request, Javelus first loads in the dynamic patch and prepares metadata for the new version classes and corresponding object transformers. The new version classes are put into a *temporal dictionary* for later querying. The temporal dictionary is separated from the *system dictionary* where classes are loaded during the program's normal execution.

Next, Javelus waits for the program to be trapped into a VM safe point. A VM safe point is a time point during the program execution at which all application threads are suspended.[4] At the VM safe point, Javelus checks all stack frames

---

[3] Actually there are also *class transformers* responsible for updating static fields of classes.

[4] JVM now can exclusively carry out its internal work including, among others, critical GC operations such as moving objects around.

to determine the safety of the following updating phases. If there is no active *restricted method*, i.e., the method whose frame is inconsistent with the new code, the VM safe point is indeed a DSU safe point [16] and it is safe to start updating code without any need for updating stack. Otherwise, Javelus would wait for a certain time interval and then retry, or just abort the updating process after a number of failed retries.

Then, Javelus updates all changed classes at the DSU safe point. All expired code of these classes, including those compiled and inlined elsewhere by the Just-In-Time (JIT) compiler, will be refreshed according to the new version of classes.

Finally, the program is resumed after all code has been updated. Javelus intercepts all accesses to potentially stale objects during the remaining execution. Once a stale object is detected, the thread accessing this object will be trapped into an object updating routine. Any access from other threads to the object will be blocked until the routine has finished. To avoid costly pointer updating, Javelus first attempts to update the stale object in-place. If the size of the object is increased, Javelus will create a mixed object for it. A mixed object uses two physical objects to simulate one logical object and only the newly added fields have to be accessed indirectly. Eventually these two physical objects will be merged into one object after a compacting garbage collection that will be invoked later. The routine will also initialize the new object with the state of the stale object by calling the corresponding object transformer.

8.4 Dynamic Patch Generation

Javelus uses dynamic patch to specify what have changed and how to apply them. A dynamic patch is composed of a sequence of *changed classes*. It may cover more changed classes than a static patch. For static updating, we only need to consider one class's own implementation individually without considering those of its super-classes, as changes of super-classes will naturally propagate to sub-classes which have already been loaded during execution. However, in the case of dynamic updating, changes from super-classes will not propagate to sub-classes if we pay no attention to the latter. This is because sub-classes may have been loaded before changed super-classes are updated. Objects instantiated by sub-classes contain fields and methods inherited from super-classes. Therefore, we have to update such sub-classes as well and treat them as directly changed classes.

To generate a dynamic patch, Javelus first identifies a set of changed classes and determines their updating types at class-level and class member-level (methods and fields). A changed class has an *old* version and a corresponding *new* version. A *deleted* class can be viewed as a changed class without a new version and a newly *added* class can be viewed as a changed class without an old version. Then, Javelus generates a set of transformer templates for *type changed classes* (this will be explained in Sect. 8.4.2). After transformers have been prepared by DSU users, the generated dynamic patch can be delivered to dynamic updating.

8.4.1 Identifying Changed Classes

Javelus maps classes between two versions of a program by their identifiers. Every class has a unique identifier in the scope of a single version. At development time, the identifier is the qualified class name. At runtime, the identifier is composed of a class loader and the qualified name [20]. To map classes at runtime, Javelus defines a name space for a class loader in the dynamic patch. Changed classes loaded by the class loader are grouped into the corresponding name space. Javelus also has provided an interface for programmers to resolve the class loader of each name space at runtime. By comparing the identifiers, Javelus can easily figure out *deleted* and *added* classes. A class that has changed its identifier will result in a deleted class and an added class in the dynamic patch. For mapped classes, Javelus further figures out *changed* classes and determines their updating types.

More specific updating types of classes are investigated against their members. A class member, i.e., a field or a method, is identified by

Table 8.1 Changed classes listed by updating types and updating actions

Updating type		Updating action
added		define
deleted		undefine
changed	type changed	redefine
	method body changed	swap
	indirectly changed	relink

its name and descriptor in the scope of a class [21]. A class member is marked as deleted if its *identifier* or *modifier* has changed. For mapped methods, Javelus further compares and analyzes their method bodies to determine their updating types. There are two method-updating types: body changed and indirectly changed. Body changed methods have changed their byte-code. Indirectly changed methods have not change their byte-code but have links to old class members.

Thus, Javelus classifies changed classes into five updating types in a dynamic patch, as shown in Table 8.1. They are,

- *Added*: According to whether added classes are required by loading of other new classes, the added classes will be *defined* into the JVM eagerly by the Javelus updating subsystem or lazily by executing code. In the Java HotSpot VM, *defining* a class means adding the class metadata into the system dictionary and then the class can be queried and used by other classes.
- *Deleted*: The deleted classes will be naturally collected by garbage collection once all objects instantiated by them are collected. Javelus *undefines* them and makes their methods obsolete and non-executable. *Undefining* a class means removing the class metadata from the system dictionary and then the class must not be used by any other class any more. More details will be discussed in the Sect. 8.6.1.3.
- *Type Changed*: There are many reasons why a class is classified as type-changed, such as inheriting a type changed class, implementing a type changed interface, adding or removing class members, adding or removing super types. Javelus will *redefine* these type changed

classes, i.e., to *undefine* their old versions and then *define* their corresponding new versions again. As the types have been changed, objects instantiated by old versions must be updated.

- *Method Body Changed*: Method body changed classes only contain changes of method byte-code in class files. Javelus will load new versions and swap new methods of new versions into old versions. Redefining these classes is unnecessary. So, their types remain the same at runtime. Objects instantiated by these classes are assumed not to be updated. They may only have semantic changes, which can only be determined by programmers.
- *Indirectly Changed*: Indirectly changed classes have no changes in class files, nor are their super-classes type-changed. They just contain indirectly changed methods. Javelus will remove links to old class members and new links will be built again during execution.

8.4.2 Default Transformation and Custom Transformers

Once a class is identified as a type changed class and to be updated, all its objects become stale and need to be transformed to the new type. In Javelus the transformation of a stale object is triggered by the first access to it after the class updating. Such transformation includes two phrases: first, reallocating space for the new object; and second, assigning valid values to fields of the new object. The first phrase is done internally by Javelus. Although some deliberated rearrangements of the layout of fields may happen here (see Sect. 8.6.3 for details), these rearrangements are completely transparent to application code. For the second

Fig. 8.3 An example of transformer templates

```
1 class User{
2    String userName;
3    String password;
4    String[] forwardAddresses;
5 }
```

(a) v0

```
1 class User{
2    String userName;
3    String password;
4    EmailAddress[] forwardAddresses;
5 }
```

(b) v1

```
1 void defaultTransformer(User_v0 v0, User v1){
2    v1.username = v0.username;
3    v1.password = v0.password;
4    v1.forwardAddresses = null;
5 }
```

(c) a transformer template

```
1 class User{
2    String userName;
3    String password;
4    EmailAddress[] forwardAddresses;
5    public void updateObject(
6      @OldField(name="forwardAddresses",desc="[String;",clazz="User")
7      String[] p1){
8      final int length = p1.length;
9      forwardAddresses = new EmailAddress[length];
10     for(int i=0;i<length;i++){
11       forwardAddresses[i] = new EmailAddress(p1[i]);
12     }
13   }
14   public static void updateClass(){}
15 }
```

(d) a transformer template

phrase, Javelus performs default transformation, and invokes custom transformers if any, to convert states of stale objects into proper ones of new objects, so that the application can continue to run correctly in the new version.

Javelus' default transformation logic just copies values of unchanged fields from a stale object to its corresponding new object and assigns a default value to each newly added field. Here, default value is decided based on the type of a field, e.g., 0 for an integer field and null for a reference field. Figure 8.3 uses a piece of Java code to show what the default transformer actually does, where v0 refers to a stale object and v1 refers to its corresponding new object.

By providing default transformation, Javelus rids programmers of writing tedious routine transformation code. According to our experiences, default transformation is able to successfully update many real-world applications. However, sometimes default transformation may not be sufficient for establishing a correct state for a new object. For the example shown in Fig. 8.3, the new field forwardAddresses must be assigned with an array of EmailAddress if the

old forwardAddresses in the stale object is not null. This kind of custom transformation logic is application dependent and must be provided by users with *custom transformers*. Javelus automatically generates *transformer templates* for type changed classes to facilitate the development of custom transformers.

A transformer template of a type changed class contains four essential parts as described in the following.

Declared fields   A template class re-declares all fields of the new version, so that its object transformer method can access them freely. Deleted fields are passed to the transformer method as annotated parameters.

Object transformation method   The object transformation logic is specified in a method named as updateObject. Programming the object transformation logic is quite similar to programming a constructor. In the body of this method, this is referring to the to-be-transformed new object, and the value of each deleted field is provided by Javelus through an annotated method parameter.

Class transformation method   The class transformation method, named as `updateClass`,
is similar to the object transformation method,
except that it works on static fields. Again, the
value of each deleted static filed is provided as
an annotated method parameter.

Super Types   When the super-class of the current type changed class is also type-changed,
the corresponding transformer class for the
super-class needs to be inherited as a superclass. If there is an object transformation
method defined for the super-class, Javelus
automatically calls it at the beginning of the
object transformation method for the current
class.

Transformer developers are quite free in
writing the transformation code in Java language.
However, they must be aware that class updating
can happen at any DSU safe point and object
transformation is triggered on-demand after class
updating. To ensure semantic correctness, a deep
understanding to the application logic and to the
difference between two versions are necessary.
Fortunately, in most cases, the difference is
quite small (otherwise it is not meaningful to
update *dynamically*) and the transformation
logic is usually straightforward. For the example
shown in Fig. 8.3, the semantics of the class is
not changed but the representation of the field
`forwardAddresses` is changed from an array
of strings to an array of wrapper classes.

Programming transformers could be tricky if
the application logic is significant changed. Two
rules of thumb are: (1) never using locks in transformation code to avoid potential deadlocks, and
(2) never accessing values other than the local state
of the current object unless you know what you are
doing.

An effective strategy to simplify programming
transformers is to restrict *when* the DSU happens
to only those periods during which behaviors of
old and new versions "converge". To restrict the
time points of DSU, one can manually include
some methods in the set of *restricted methods*
(see the next Section) so that DSU will not happen when these methods are active. However,

one should be aware that this restriction can also
reduce the timeliness of dynamic updating.

8.5   Updating Code

8.5.1   Reaching a DSU Safe Point

The running program needs to reach a DSU safe
point to update. DSU safe points are stricter VM
safe points where none of the application thread
stacks contains any frame of active restricted
methods. There are four types of restricted
methods: (1) deleted and body changed methods;
(2) methods pointing to an object instantiated by a
type narrowed class (see Sect. 8.6.1.2); (3) methods that have been overridden and their receivers
are stale objects as a new method will be dispatched after the receivers have been updated; (4)
methods that have been blacklisted by DSU users.

Note that for those methods of changed classes
whose byte-code is unchanged, Javelus does not
include them as restricted methods but automatically repairs corresponding method frames in
stacks. In this way Javelus can still reach a DSU
safe point despite the activeness of these methods.
This technique greatly improves the timeliness of
dynamic updating.

If no restricted method is found, a VM safe
point is also a DSU safe point and Javelus can proceed to update classes. Otherwise, Javelus inserts
a *return barrier* [31] in the frame of the deepest
restricted method for each thread and interrupts
the updating process. Once the restricted method
has returned, the updating process is resumed by
the return barrier. If a certain number of retries
still fails, the updating process may be aborted.

8.5.2   Updating Classes

Javelus reads a dynamic patch and loads all new
classes and interfaces in an order that supertypes
should be loaded first. For method body changed
classes, their types remain unchanged and their
objects are still valid in the new version. Only
the method body in corresponding class meta-

data must be updated. Note that we cannot simply remove metadata objects of old classes and create corresponding new metadata objects. This is because the address of a class's metadata object has been used in every object of this class as its type identifier, and the identifier must be kept the same before and after the updating to avoid unnecessary object updating. Javelus uses a technique that swaps the contents between old and new metadata objects to keep such type identifiers the same. For type changed classes, their old versions are undefined to keep type consistency and their corresponding new versions are defined. Values of unchanged static fields are copied from old versions to corresponding new versions by the default transformation.

For new defined classes, the class initialization method is replaced by the class transformer. Javelus leaves new classes in an uninitialized state and class transformers are executed for initialization upon the first access to the class during the remaining execution.

Javelus repairs frames of active unchanged methods in old classes. All compiled methods are forced for recompilation. For active compiled methods, the Java HotSpot VM interprets them after de-optimization. After code updating, the JVM turns into running in the interpreted mode for a moment.

8.6 Updating Objects

The program is resumed immediately once the class updating is finished. Stale objects will be updated in an on-demand way during the remaining execution. Javelus must guarantee that

- no stale object would be used as an instance of the new version of the class without being upgraded first, and upgraded objects should inherit their original roles,[5]
- no old code would be executed any more, and
- no type error would be caused by dynamic updating.

To this end, Javelus has to insert additional checks for all potential violations of these properties. At the same time, the amount of these checks must be kept minimal to reduce overhead. Javelus first makes a safe estimation of the scope of references to stale objects by analyzing their types affected by the updating (Sect. 8.6.1). This analysis is done at an offline preparation phase. At the updating phase Javelus also optimizes the object validity checking in various aspects (Sect. 8.6.2).

To reduce the performance penalty caused by size-increased objects, Javelus uses a novel object allocation model that realizes in-place upgrading where access indirections are kept minimal (Sect. 8.6.3). The model is fully transparent to program code and is compatible for the Java HotSpot VM.

8.6.1 Affected Types

Objects in the Java HotSpot VM are accessed directly through references. A stale object would not cause any problem unless it is referenced. A reference has a static type declared in the code, and a dynamic type determined by the runtime object it points to. If the dynamic type is *not* a subtype[6] of the static type, dereferencing will cause a type error.

In Javelus, the static type of a reference is updated when the corresponding class is refreshed, but the dynamic type can still be invalid if the object it references is a stale one whose defining class is no longer a subtype of the refreshed class. To avoid blindly checking all accesses to all objects, Javelus identifies a set of *affected types* and only intercepts dereferencing of references statically typed with those affected types. A type is affected if a reference of this type points to a stale object and we call this reference *mismatched*.

8.6.1.1 Versioned Class Hierarchy
A versioned class hierarchy is a combination of class hierarchies of different versions of

---

[5]This means that *all* references to a stale object should be redirected to the same upgraded object.

[6]Note that the subtype relation is reflexive.

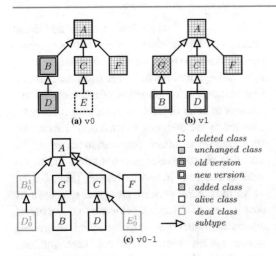

(a) v0   **(b) v1**

〔〕	*deleted class*
☐	*unchanged class*
▣	*old version*
▢	*new version*
▨	*added class*
☐	*alive class*
☐	*dead class*
→▷	*subtype*

(c) v0-1

Fig. 8.4 **a** Class hierarchy of v0; **b** class hierarchy of v1;
c versioned class hierarchy from v0 to v1

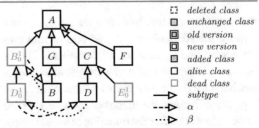

〔〕	*deleted class*
☐	*unchanged class*
▣	*old version*
▢	*new version*
▨	*added class*
☐	*alive class*
☐	*dead class*
--→▷	*subtype*
--→▷	α
···▷	β

Fig. 8.5 Versioned class hierarchy with α and β edges

programs.[7] Figure 8.4c shows a versioned class hierarchy that contains classes from two versions, namely v0 (see Fig. 8.4a) and v1 (see Fig. 8.4b). Every class in the class hierarchy is annotated with the version where it was born (i.e., defined) and the version where it died (i.e., be undefined). For example, B_0^1 is defined in version v0, which is indicated by the subscript 0, and undefined in version v1, which is indicated by the superscript 1.

When a class is said to be *alive* or *dead*, it is with respect to the *current* version after possibly a series of updating. Since dead classes are no longer used in the updated code, affected types must be alive classes.

A newly updated class must be counted as affected, together with all its super-classes in the new version. In the above example, B, G and A (because of B_0^1), and D, C and A (because of D_0^1) are affected. On the other hand, alive super-classes of the old version must also be counted in. For example, A (because of B_0^1 and D_0^1) is affected.

To mark stale objects that may be pointed to by references of the new version, we introduce the *super-class-by-updating* relation between old and new versions. In short, we name this relation as α, e.g., $B_0^1 \xrightarrow{\alpha} B$. Note that the tail of an α edge

must be an old version. Super-classes reachable by following a path contains a α edge are called *induced super-classes*. For example, as shown in Fig. 8.5, G is an induced super-class of B_0^1.

All alive classes reachable from the old version following any subtype and α edge are marked as affected. In the example in Fig. 8.5, only F is unreachable from the old version and is thus not affected. All other classes are affected.

8.6.1.2 Type Narrowing

Type errors could still occur even if every stale object had been updated. For example, suppose that there is a reference statically typed in B. It may point to a stale object of D_0^1 before updating and then point to an object of D after updating. However, D is not a subtype of B in the current version. Besides, a reference value typed in B can be passed to a reference typed in G without any type checking. This makes class G possibly point to an object instantiated by D, although a reference typed in G cannot point to an object instantiated by D before updating.

In the aforementioned example, the most notable distinction is that not all supertypes (i.e., super-classes and implemented interfaces) of D_0^1, including those induced by α edges, are part of supertypes of D. We say that D is type narrowed, using the definition in [34]: *a type is narrowed if one of its original supertypes is no longer a supertype in the new version of the type.*

We have to amend the definition in [34] as Javelus, as we have pointed out, uses a lazy approach. First, we introduce the *sub-class-by-updating* relation between new and old versions. In short, we name this relation as β, e.g., $D \xrightarrow{\beta} D_0^1$. Note that the tail of the β edge

---

[7]We omit interfaces in the versioned class hierarchy, as in our implementation, interface types never violate type-safety (see Sect. 8.6.2.1).

Fig. 8.6 An example for common super-classes

```
class Main{//main class
    void main(){
        Shape shape = new Circle
            ();
        /* dynamic updating
            happened */
        shape.draw();}}
abstract class Shape{// super
        class
    abstract void draw();
    abstract void draw(Canvas
        canvas);}
class Circle{// old version
```

```
    void draw(){
        draw(Canvas.getDefault())
            ;}
    void draw(Canvas canvas){
        /*code draw a circle*/}}
class Circle{// newversion
    Canvas canvas;
    void draw(){draw(this.
        canvas);}
    void draw(Canvas canvas){
        /*code draw a circle*/}}
```

must be a new version. A new versioned class is *narrowed* in Javelus if there exists an alive type which can be reached from the new version *only* in a path beginning with a β edge. References statically typed with these alive types are subject to *type narrowing checking*.

8.6.1.3 Deleted Classes

Stale objects instantiated by deleted classes should not be used any more after the deleted classes have been undefined. However, they can still be accessed via references typed in alive super-classes, and methods of deleted classes may be executed even after code has been updated. For example, an object instantiated by E_0^1 may be pointed to by a reference typed in C.

Currently, Javelus treats such stale objects as they were instantiated by alive super-classes. Conceptually, one can think of these objects being updated to new versioned classes identical to the alive super-classes. We believe this is a reasonable choice to preserve semantic continuity. For example, the object instantiated by E_0^1 is used as an instance of C. Users can change this behavior by defining specific object transformers for deleted classes. For method invocations dynamically dispatched to the method defined in deleted classes, Javelus would redirect them to the corresponding method in super-classes.

8.6.1.4 Common Super Classes

Intercepting all dereferencing of references of affected types could still be expensive, and should be avoided unless it is necessary. We have observed that old and new versions of a class often have unchanged common super-classes. For

example, the Object class in Java is the *common super-class* (CSC) of all other classes. Accessing stale objects through references typed in common super-classes never causes type errors. Fields in CSC are assumed to be valid by default unless users explicitly include them in object transformers. So we can avoid intercepting accesses to these fields even though the concerned object is stale.

However, semantic problems may arise when a virtual method of the common super-classes is called. For example, as shown in Fig. 8.6, suppose that the dynamic updating happens at Line 4. Then, shape at Line 5 is pointing to a stale object. Calling the draw on it will lead to the old method started at Line 10, whereas the valid result should be the new method started at Line 16. Javelus solves this problem by implementing implicit checks at the beginning of old methods. Calling such virtual methods on stale objects will trigger such validity checks but not on new or updated objects. After stale objects have been updated, Javelus forces the caller to call the method again. Therefore, explicit checks for CSC are not necessary.

8.6.2 Optimizing Object Validity Checks

8.6.2.1 Optimistic Checks

Valid checks can be done pessimistically or optimistically. One may pessimistically check target objects before every dereferencing, or optimistically assume that target objects are always valid and rely on some roll-back mechanism to fix the problem in case of illegal accessing. Apparently, the optimistic strategy can be more efficient if illegal accessing is rare. In well-designed Java programs many references are statically typed with interfaces.[8] Javelus piggybacks the mechanism of interface method dispatching to implement an optimistic check strategy.

In the Java HostSpot VM, dispatching an interface method takes two steps. The JVM first checks whether the receiver implements the interface (an exception will be thrown if not). Next, the method with the given method symbol is looked up. Suppose that Javelus dispatches a method of an interface I to a stale object. I must be implemented either by the old or by the new version of the class of this object.

If I is implemented by the old version, the situation is very similar to that of common super-classes. The updating will be triggered by the code inserted in the beginning of an old method. If the new version class implements I, the method invocation will be re-dispatched to the new version. Otherwise an exception will be thrown due to type narrowing.

If I is only implemented by the new version, an exception will be raised immediately. Instead of throwing the exception to program code, Javelus will intercept the exception and check the receiver, update it if possible, and then dispatches the method again.

8.6.2.2   Eliminating Redundant Checks

Javelus can eliminate redundant validity checks, i.e., those checks on the same reference for successive dereferences. We implemented this optimization by piggybacking on the null pointer elimination algorithm of the JIT compiler. During the analysis of the JIT compiler, Javelus adds information to each reference to indicate whether it may be mismatched. Hence, validity checks on any known matched reference can be eliminated. Note that accesses via mismatched references to valid members of common super-classes can also be eliminated.

The above optimization will only work on DSU-free code blocks, as dynamic updating will kill all known matched references. Note that new compiled methods after classes have been updated are indeed DSU-free, as Javelus will recompile all methods and de-optimize the active compiled methods. The only case that dynamic updating can happen inside a compiled method is the on-stack-replacement of a long running loop. On-stack-replacement of the Java HotSpot VM ensures that an interpreted frame that contains a long running loop can be transformed into a compiled frame on-the-fly. In this case, the loop body is DSU-free and the optimization is still effective.

8.6.2.3   Other Optimizations

We have also optimized validity checks in the interpreter. In the Java HotSpot VM, programs are executed in a mixed-mode: some methods are interpreted directly by the interpreter while other methods are compiled to native code by the JIT compiler. There are also interpreted frames and compiled frames co-existing in thread stacks. Passing control from interpreted callers to interpreted callees is performed by common *method entries* while to compiled callees is by *adapters*. Javelus creates another set of method entries and adapters that contain validity checks. Consequently, checks before a method call are unnecessary unless the method is virtual. Checks before virtual method dispatching is necessary because the new virtual method table could be larger than the old one and dispatching a method not in the old virtual method table would cause an error.

8.6.3   Mixed Object Model

One major challenge in implementing a lazy approach is to update objects in-place even though their sizes are increased, because otherwise we have to update all references targeting at a object moved to somewhere else. Note that in the Java HotSpot VM objects are directly pointed to by references.

Javelus uses an object allocation model called *Mixed Object* to solve this problem. A mixed object is a logic object implemented with two physical objects, viz. *in-place object* and *phantom*

---

[8] A principle of reusable object-oriented design is "Program to an interface, not an implementation" [11].

Fig. 8.7 Integrating mixed object model with a mark-compact garbage collector

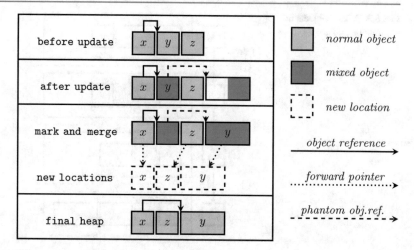

object, respectively. The in-place object takes the space of the stale object, and the phantom object is allocated somewhere else to hold fields that cannot fit into the space of the in-place object. A phantom object is only referenced by its corresponding in-place object. Any access to a mixed object must take its in-place object as the entry point.

To implement this model, Javelus leverages the *abstract fields* of objects. In JVM, every object is allocated with some abstract fields to facilitate JVM functions such as locking, default hash code and garbage collection. In the 32-bit Java HotSpot VM, 64 bits are used for these fields [28]. Javelus defines a new pattern of these abstract fields to indicate whether the current object is a mixed object and encode the address of its phantom object if any. The pattern takes the space of the original abstract fields, which are moved to the phantom object. Note that mixed objects are only used for transforming objects whose sizes are increased in updating. Objects directly instantiated from the new versioned class are allocated normally. To support the transparent accessing to fields in phantom objects, Javelus intercepts all accesses to these fields and makes redirection if the target object is a mixed object.

In principle Javelus does not depend on any specific garbage collection algorithm. However, it can leverage the garbage collector to convert mixed objects to normal objects, so that the overhead caused by access indirections and loss of memory locality is eventually eliminated.

Figure 8.7 shows how a mixed object is eliminated by a mark-compact garbage collector. There are three objects, x, y and z, in the initial heap. After updating, a mixed object is created for y. During garbage collecting, y's in-place object is merged with its phantom object and a normal object is formed. Then the in-place object can be freed. References to y (e.g., the one in x) are eventually updated to y's new location when the object is compacted.

8.6.4 Transforming Objects

Javelus generates a set of transformer templates for type-changed classes. As Javelus performs a *default* transformation first, users only need to write transformers for classes that really require custom transformation. The default transformation will update the type (identifier) of an object, retain values for unchanged fields, and initiate newly added fields with default values.

Once a stale object is detected, the current thread accessing the object will be trapped into an object updating routine. If the object is being updated by another thread, the current thread will be blocked until the updating is finished. Currently, Javelus uses a global lock to schedule all updating routines. Although this policy might cause bottlenecks for multi-threaded applications, it provides an easy sequential programming model for object transformers.

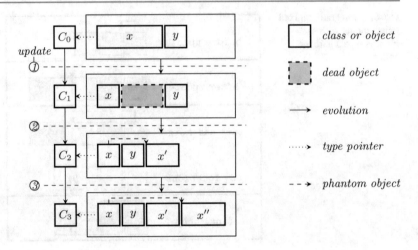

Fig. 8.8 Mixed objects in continuous updating

The process of object transformation is as follows. At the beginning, a stale object is typed in the old version. Javelus first backs up values of deleted fields to a special data structure and copies values of unchanged fields to a prototype object. Next, Javelus allocates the new object in-place, using the mixed object model if the object size is increased. Now the object is typed in the new version of the class. Then Javelus copies all unchanged fields back from the prototype object. Finally Javelus invokes the object transformer to complete the transformation.

In Javelus, transformers can directly access fields defined in the new version of classes. Fields defined by old classes are passed to transformers as parameters. Normally a transformer only reads from and writes to the fields of the current object and will not cause any data race with program code. However, sometimes a transformer needs to access other objects, and users should be aware that this could occur concurrently with the execution of other threads of the program.

8.6.5 Continuous Updating

Javelus supports continuous updating, i.e., the next updating can be performed immediately following the previous one. Since Javelus uses a lazy updating strategy, continuous updating implies that objects in different versions can coexist in the heap. Nevertheless, at any time, only the latest version of the program can be executed in Javelus, and stale objects are upgraded before use.

Our mixed object model also facilitates continuous updating. In this case mixed objects can also be stale, but in-place objects are always allocated at the same positions no matter how many times updating has happened.[9] Fields in phantom objects are decided by comparing their offsets with the *smallest* object sizes among all related versions.

As shown in Fig. 8.8, object x has a large space initially. In the first updating, the space is contracted. In the second updating, a phantom object x' is created for object x. Note that we cannot assume the unused space after x is still there because garbage collection may occur at any time. For example, as shown in Fig. 8.8, the unused space has been collected by the garbage collection that occurs before the second updating. In the third updating, a new phantom object is created and replaces the old phantom object. Finally, object x is typed in class C_3.

8.7 Evaluation

We evaluate Javelus by measuring updating disruption and performance of steady-state execution. For practical reasons,[10] we do not directly

---

[9]Unless they are moved by the garbage collector.

[10]Most Java DSU systems, including Jvolve [31], JDrums [2] and DVM [24], are built on research or early JVMs,

Table 8.2 Micro benchmarks

Base	Increase	Reorder	Decrease
`class C{`	`class C{`	`class C{`	`class C{`
`    int i1;`	`    int i1;`	`    int i3;`	`    int i1;`
`    int i2;`	`    int i2;`	`    int i1;`	`    int i2;`
`    int i3;`	`    int i3;`	`    int i2;`	`    Object o1`
`    Object o1`	`    int i4;`	`    Object o3`	`    ;`
`    ;`	`    Object o1`	`    ;`	`    Object o2`
`    Object o2`	`    ;`	`    Object o1`	`    ;`
`    ;`	`    Object o2`	`    ;`	`    void`
`    Object o3`	`    ;`	`    Object o2`	`        touch`
`    ;`	`    Object o3`	`    ;`	`        (){`
`    void`	`    ;`	`    void`	`        o2=o1;`
`        touch`	`    Object o4`	`        touch`	`        o1=o2;`
`        (){`	`    ;`	`        (){`	`        i1++;`
`        o2=o1;`	`    void`	`        o2=o1;`	`        i2++;`
`        o3=o2;`	`        touch`	`        o3=o2;`	`    }`
`        o1=o3;`	`        (){`	`        o1=o3;`	`}`
`        i1++;`	`        o2=o1;`	`        i1++;`	
`        i2++;`	`        o3=o2;`	`        i2++;`	
`        i3++;`	`        o4=o3;`	`        i3++;`	
`    }`	`        o1=o4;`	`    }`	
`}`	`        i1++;`	`}`	
	`        i2++;`		
	`        i3++;`		
	`        i4++;`		
	`    }`		
	`}`		

compare Javelus with other Java dynamic updating systems, but instead we implement an eager updating mode in Javelus for the purpose of comparison.

To perform eager updating, after all classes have been updated, Javelus scans the heap to collect all stale objects, transforms all stale objects,

and then forces a full heap compacting garbage collection immediately. Note that all check related flags are not set in this mode and thus there will be no updating relevant check in later executions.

In our evaluation, all experiments were conducted on an Intel Core i7-2600 CPU (@3.40 GHz) with 4 GB RAM. The operating system is Arch Linux with kernel version 3.9, and the JRE used is 1.6.0_45-b06 build.

8.7.1 Experiments with Micro Benchmarks

We first experimented with the same micro benchmark used to evaluate Jvolve [31] and DCE VM [33]. Table 8.2 lists relevant classes used in the benchmark. The benchmark program creates

---

(Footnote 10 continued)
which are much slower than the modern Java HotSpot VM, so it would be meaningless to compare disruption and performance across these different JVMs. DCE VM could be a suitable rival for Javelus since they both build on the Java HotSpot VM. Unfortunately, DCE VM has to run in debugging mode to support dynamic updating, and this makes its performance seriously degraded. For a fair comparison, we tried but failed to extend DEC VM to support dynamic updating in normal mode. According to the updating mechanism and performance data reported in [33], it is not very different from Javelus in eager mode, which is used in our evaluation.

Fig. 8.9 DSU pausing
time of micro benchmarks

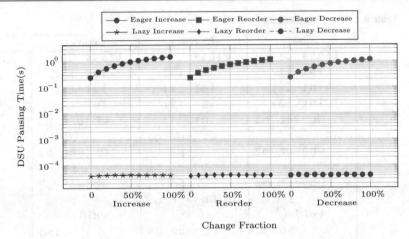

Fig. 8.10 Average
accessing time

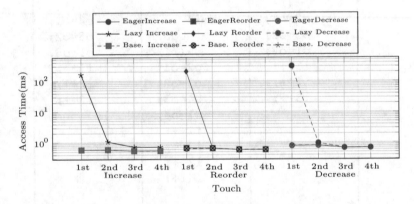

4,000,000 objects, of which 0–100 % are to be updated in different runs.

Figure 8.9 shows the mean pausing time of 20 repeated runs. The disruption of lazy updating (about 0.04 ms for each configuration) is four order of magnitude less than that of eager updating (ranging from 298 to 1825 ms). Note that according to [31], Jvolve's pausing time ranges from 618.7 to 2627.9 ms, and according to [33], DCE VM takes more than 400 ms, although their configurations (OS and machine) of experiments are different from ours.

Figure 8.9 also confirms that the pausing time of eager updating is proportional to the number of affected objects, while that of lazy updating remains stable when the number of stale objects increases.

To measure the overhead of post-updating execution, we used a `touch` method that reads and writes each field of an object being updated and counts the execution time of this method. All objects were touched four times after updating. The first touching triggered the lazy object updating. After the second touching a garbage collection was explicitly invoked. The second and third touching were used to measure the performance before and after mixed objects have been merged.

Figure 8.10 shows the average accessing time to updated objects. Note that in the figure "Base." means the accessing time measured on the baseline JVM without dynamic updating. For lazy updating, accessing to stale objects at the first time is expensive, but the cost quickly decreases in following accesses. There are three factors contributing to the cost of the first access: (1) the JVM has to warm up again; (2) Javelus has little optimization for lazy updating in the interpreter; (3) all updating actions are triggered by optimistic checks and the recovery from illegal states takes time.

Fig. 8.11 DSU pausing time for DaCapo benchmark

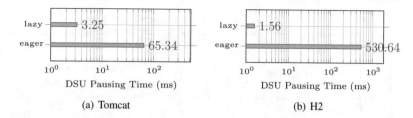

(a) Tomcat

(b) H2

Accessing *Increased* objects at the second touching is slower than that of *Reorder* and *Decrease*. This is because *Increased* objects require mixed object redirections. With mixed objects being merged, this overhead decreases gradually. Nevertheless, as mixed object checks still exist, the accessing time can be a little bit larger than that of eager updating, but this extra overhead is generally unobservable in practice.

8.7.2 Experiments with Tomcat and H2

We also evaluated Javelus with real updates of the Tomcat application server[11] (from 7.0.3 to 7.0.4) and the H2 database management system[12] (from 1.2.125 to 1.2.126). The dynamic patch generated for Tomcat contains 318 changed classes, and the patch for H2 contains 267 classes. We used the Dacapo [7] benchmark to drive the two servers in our experiments. Since DaCapo verified responses, these experiments also tested the correctness of Javelus's dynamic updating.

Figure 8.11 shows the pausing time for updating Tomcat and H2, respectively. The results have been averaged over 20 runs. The eager approach is 20 times (for Tomcat) to 300 times (for H2) disruptive than the lazy approach, respectively. The difference is smaller than that in the earlier micro benchmark because in this set of experiments changed objects are only a few hundreds.

To investigate dynamic updating's impact on application performance, we used JMeter[13] to measure Tomcat's response time when the server is dynamically updated from 7.0.3 to 7.0.4. In experiment, JMeter was configured with eight

concurrent threads. Each thread repeatedly sends a set of requests to the Tomcat server. Figure 8.12 shows the response time of each request sent during the timespan from 500 to 4000 ms (the first 500 ms is omitted as it is the warm-up phase). A dynamic updating request was issued at 2000 ms.

With the eager approach, there are a few requests with a response time more than 80 ms, which is about 10–20 times larger than normal. On the contrary, with the lazy approach (i.e., Javelus's normal setting), the largest response time is only 9 ms, as the cost of dynamic updating is distributed more evenly. We also calculate the maximum, minimum, mean and variance in eager (with and without outliers), lazy, and baseline settings. From the Table 8.3, we can observe that the lazy approach has a similar maximum and minimum in comparison with those of the baseline. This indicates that the lazy approach does not introduce signification overhead in normal application execution.

8.8 Related Work

Updating software system at runtime has been extensively studied in the literature. In this section we first discuss dynamic updating systems for Java, which are close to Javelus, and then briefly overview some dynamic updating systems for other programming languages and those for component-based systems.

8.8.1 Dynamic Updating Systems for Java

Dynamic updating systems for Java can be classified into two categories: VM-based systems and transformation-based ones. VM-based systems

---

[11] http://tomcat.apache.org/.

[12] http://www.h2database.com/.

[13] http://jmeter.apache.org/.

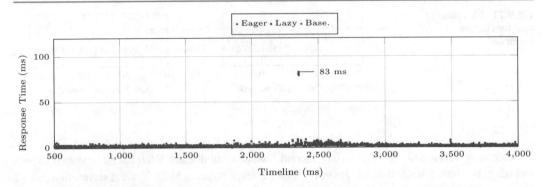

Fig. 8.12 Tomcat response time

Table 8.3 Statistics of Tomcat response time

	Max (ms)	Min (ms)	Mean (ms)	Var. (ms^2)
Eager	83	0^a	2.07	16.28
Eager (w/o outliers)	8	0	1.87	0.61
Lazy	9	1	2.43	1.01
Base.	8	1	2.21	0.49

^{a}JMeter reports response time in millisecond, and in this case the response time is too small to measure

have their advantages in flexibility and efficiency, as changes are made to runtime states in the JVM directly. However, they often heavily depend on specific implementations of JVMs, and tightly couple with these JVMs' facilities such as dynamic class loading, garbage collection and just-in-time (JIT) compilation components. On the other hand, in theory transformation-based approaches can be VM-independent, although in practice many of them such as those proposed in [29,30] depend on the HotSwap mechanism, which may not be available in some JVMs. Besides, transformation-based updating systems have to introduce wrappers to trigger updating as well as indirections to bring new objects into effect. Gregersen concluded that eventually supporting dynamic updating in JVMs is a better choice [13].

8.8.1.1 VM-Based Systems
JDrums [2] and DVM [24] built on early JVMs. Both of them update objects lazily but this works only on classic JVMs, in which Java programs run in interpretation mode and objects are referred indirectly through handles. Therefore, their techniques can hardly be applied to modern JVMs where JIT compilation is enabled, objects are

directly accessed, and various types of garbage collectors are used.

Dmitriev [10] introduced HotSwap as part of debugger interfaces of the Java HotSpot VM. HotSwap can only support swapping method bodies, but Dmitriev has proposed many extensions on supporting more flexible changes [9]. Subramaniam et al. implemented Jvolve [31] on top of the JikesRVM.[14] Jvolve is more flexible than HotSwap: it can support all changes except changing super-classes or interfaces. Würthinger et al. [33] extended HotSwap and developed DCE VM, which supports arbitrary changes of classes. Both Jvolve and DCE VM require the underlying JVM to be configured with a simple modified garbage collector such that objects can be updated eagerly through a stop-the-world garbage collection.

8.8.1.2 Transformation-Based Systems
PROSE [27] aimed at replacing method code at runtime. In other words, it does not support class schema changes. PROSE updates code in a controlled and systematic way and the control logic is also written in Java. DUSC [29] creates several

---

[14]http://www.jikesrvm.org.

auxiliary classes to simulate one original class at load time. DUSC requires more space and cannot change public interfaces. JavAdaptor [30] is based on HotSwap and can update class schemas by class renaming and caller updating. JRebel [17,18] is a relatively flexible and efficient transformation-based approach. It can be well integrated with existing Web servers, and it helps to prove that a less flexible DSU system is also useful. JRebel has proved to be adapted to at least three JVM implementations at least [18]. DUCS [3] was first presented by Bialek et al. as a framework for updating component-based systems and was extended for updating class-based Java programs [4]. DUCS first partitions class-based programs into larger modules. These modules are used as basic updating units. Hence, classes within the same module can be accessed directly.

8.8.2 Dynamic Updating Systems for Other Programming Languages

Neamtiu et al. developed Ginseng for dynamically updating C programs [25,26]. However, this work has some limitations. For example, in order to add new fields, heap data must be allocated with additional space. Every access to a field must be trapped with a version check in order to trigger updating, and this can be time-consuming. Besides, Ginseng requires that updating points must be inserted into source code first and the program being updated should be compiled by a special compiler.

Chen et al. presented POLUS for C-like programs [5,6]. By using a *relaxed consistency model*, changed code can be updated even when they are active. In POLUS, different versions of a program can be executed simultaneously. To ensure system consistency, POLUS requires programmers to write special methods to convert states bi-directionally between old and new code. However, POLUS cannot update heap data. Mariks et al. [23] implemented UpStare to support immediate updating by reconstructing stack. Nevertheless, programmers have to write valid transformers for such stack reconstruction, which is a non-trivial task.

8.8.3 Dynamic Updating for Component-Based Systems

DSU can also be carried out in a granularity coarser than class. To update a component in a (distributed) component-based software system, normally one would not trouble himself to deal with internal logic of a component, but drives the component into a steady state before upgrading it. The problem is how to ensure the correctness of ongoing activities on other components depending on the to-be-updated component. In a seminal work, Kramer and Magee proposed a *quiescence* criterion for safe updating [19]. However, the approach could be disruptive. Vandewoude et al. relaxed this condition to a *tranquility* criterion to reduce disruption [32], but it cannot guarantee consistency. Ma et al. used *version consistency* to achieve low-disruptive updating without sacrificing consistency [22]. Ajmani et al. [1] introduced a model that allows different versions of components to serve at the same time so that the updating can be gradually done.

8.9 Conclusion

This chapter presents Javelus, a DSU system which is implemented on top of the industry-strength Java HotSpot VM. Javelus supports arbitrary changes of Java classes and can achieve low updating disruption without sacrificing efficiency. We have also conducted experiments on real updates of software widely used by industry to evaluate Javelus. The experimental results have shown that Javelus is low disruptive yet efficient.

Although Javelus's current implementation depends on facilities provided by the underlying JVM, we believe that many of the techniques discussed in this chapter, such as mixed object model and techniques on reducing validity checks, can be adapted to other JVM implementations.

On the other hand, better integration with a modern JVM may further improve the performance of dynamic updating. For example, we plan to investigate how to reduce the disruption caused by the re-compilation of updated code, and this would require a deeper involvement of the HotSpot technology. We are working along this direction.

Acknowledgments We thank the anonymous reviewers for their detailed and helpful comments and suggestions. This research was partially funded by the 863 Program (2013AA01A213) and National Nature Science Foundation (61100038, 91318301, 61321491, 61361120097) of China. Chang Xu was also partially supported by Program for New Century Excellent Talents in University, China (NCET-10-0486).

References

1. S. Ajmani, B. Liskov, L. Shrira, Modular software upgrades for distributed systems, in *Proceedings of the European Conference on Object-Oriented Programming. ECOOP'06* (Springer, Berlin, 2006), pp. 452–476

2. J. Andersson, T. Ritzau, Dynamic code update in JDRUMS, in *Proceedings of the ICSE Workshop on Software Engineering for Wearable and Pervasive Computing* (2000), pp. 1–9

3. R. Bialek, E. Jul, A framework for evolutionary, dynamically updatable, component-based systems, in *Proceedings of the 24th International Conference on Distributed Computing Systems Workshops—W7: EC (ICD-CSW'04)—Volume 7. ICDCSW'04* (IEEE Computer Society, Washington, DC, USA, 2004), pp. 326–331

4. R.P. Bialek, E. Jul, J.G. Schneider, Y. Jin, Partitioning of Java applications to support dynamic updates, in *Proceedings of the Asia-Pacific Software Engineering Conference* (2004), pp. 616–623

5. S.M. Blackburn, R. Garner, C. Hoffman, A.M. Khan, K.S. McKinley, R. Bentzur, A. Diwan, D. Feinberg, D. Frampton, S.Z. Guyer, M. Hirzel, A. Hosking, M. Jump, H. Lee, J.E.B. Moss, A. Phansalkar, D. Stefanović, T. VanDrunen, D. von Dincklage, B. Wiedermann, The DaCapo benchmarks: Java benchmarking development and analysis, in *OOPSLA '06: Proceedings of the 21st Annual ACM SIGPLAN Conference on Object-Oriented Programming, Systems, Languages, and Applications* (ACM Press, New York, NY, USA) (2006), pp. 169–190

6. H. Chen, J. Yu, R. Chen, B. Zang, P.C. Yew, POLUS: a powerful live updating system, in *Proceedings of the International Conference on Software Engineering. ICSE'07* (IEEE Computer Society, Washington, DC, USA, 2007), pp. 271–281

7. H. Chen, J. Yu, C. Hang, Yew PC, Dynamic software updating using a relaxed consistency model. IEEE Trans. Softw. Eng. **37**(5), 679–694 (2011)

8. R.C. Daley, J.B. Dennis, Virtual memory, processes, and sharing in multics. Commun. ACM **11**(5), 306–312 (1968)

9. M. Dmitriev, Safe class and data evolution in large and long-lived Java applications. Ph.D. thesis, Department of Computing Science, University of Glasgow (2001)

10. M. Dmitriev, Towards flexible and safe technology for runtime evolution of Java language applications, in *Proceedings of the Workshop on Engineering Complex Object-Oriented Systems for Evolution* (2001)

11. E. Gamma, R. Helm, R. Johnson, J. Vlissides, *Design Patterns: Elements of Reusable Object-oriented Software* (Addison-Wesley Longman Publishing Co., Inc, Boston, MA, USA, 1995)

12. A.R. Gregersen, B.N. J.rgensen, Dynamic update of Java applications—balancing change flexibility vs programming transparency. J. Softw. Maint. Evol.: Res. Pract. **21**(2), 81–112 (2009)

13. A.R. Gregersen, D. Simon, B.N. J.rgensen, Towards a dynamic-update-enabled JVM, in *Proceedings of the Workshop on AOP and Meta-Data for Software Evolution. RAM-SE '09* (ACM, New York, NY, USA, 2009), pp. 2:1–2:7

14. T. Gu, C. Cao, C. Xu, X. Ma, L. Zhang, J. Lu, Javelus: a low disruptive approach to dynamic software updates, in *Proceedings of the 2012 19th Asia-Pacific Software Engineering Conference—Volume 01. APSEC '12* (IEEE Computer Society, Washington, DC, USA, 2012), pp. 527–536

15. D. Gupta, P. Jalote, G. Barua, A formal framework for on-line software version change. IEEE Trans. Softw. Eng. **22**(2), 120–131 (1996)

16. M. Hicks, S. Nettles, Dynamic software updating. ACM Trans. Program. Lang. Syst. **27**(6), 1049–1096 (2005)

17. J. Kabanov, JRebel tool demo. Electr. Notes Theor. Comput. Sci. **264**(4), 51–57 (2011)

18. J. Kabanov, V. Vene, A thousand years of productivity: the JRebel story. Pract. Exp. Softw. (2012)

19. J. Kramer, J. Magee, The evolving philosophers problem: dynamic change management. IEEE Trans. Softw. Eng. **16**(11), 1293–1306 (1990)

20. S. Liang, G. Bracha, Dynamic class loading in the Java virtual machine, in *Proceedings of the ACM SIGPLAN Conference on Object-oriented Programming, Systems, Languages, and Applications. OOPSLA '98* (ACM, New York, NY, USA, 1998), pp. 36–44

21. T. Lindholm, F. Yellin, *Java Virtual Machine Specification*, 2nd edn. (Addison-Wesley Longman Publishing Co., Inc, Boston, MA, USA, 1999)

22. X. Ma, L. Baresi, C. Ghezzi, V. Panzica La Manna, J. Lu, Version-consistent dynamic reconfiguration of component-based distributed systems, in *Proceedings of the 19th ACM SIGSOFT Symposium and the 13th European Conference on Foundations of Software Engineering. ESEC/FSE '11* (ACM, New York, NY, USA, 2011), pp. 245–255

23. K. Makris, R.A. Bazzi, Immediate multi-threaded dynamic software updates using stack reconstruction, in *Proceedings of the Conference on USENIX Annual Technical Conference* (2009)

24. S. Malabarba, R. Pandey, J. Gragg, E. Barr, J.F. Barnes, Runtime support for type-safe dynamic Java classes,

inProceedings of the European Conference on Object-Oriented Programming (2000), pp. 337–361

25. I. Neamtiu, M. Hicks, Safe and timely updates to multi-threaded programs, in *Proceedings of the ACM SIGPLAN Conference on Programming Language Design and Implementation. PLDI '09* (ACM, New York, NY, USA, 2009), pp. 13–24

26. I. Neamtiu, M. Hicks, G. Stoyle, M. Oriol, Practical dynamic software updating for C, in *Proceedings of the ACM SIGPLAN Conference on Programming Language Design and Implementation. PLDI '06* (2006), pp. 72–83

27. A. Nicoara, G. Alonso, T. Roscoe, Controlled, systematic, and efficient code replacement for running Java programs, in *Proceedings of the ACM SIGOPS/EuroSys European Conference on Computer Systems. Eurosys '08* (ACM, New York, NY, USA, 2008), pp. 233–246

28. Oracle (2006), The Java HotSpot performance engine architecture, http://www.oracle.com/technetwork/java/whitepaper-135217.html. Accessed 01 June 2013

29. A. Orso, A. Rao, M.J. Harrold, A technique for dynamic updating of Java software, in *Proceedings of the IEEE International Conference on Software Maintenance* (2002), pp. 649–658

30. M. Pukall, C. Kästner, W. Cazzola, S. Götz, A. Grebhahn, R. Schröter, G. Saake, JavAdaptor—flexible runtime updates of Java applications. Softw.: Pract. Exp. **43**

31. S. Subramanian, M. Hicks, K.S. McKinley, Dynamic software updates: a VM-centric approach, in *Proceedings of the ACM SIGPLAN Conference on Programming Language Design and Implementation* (2009), pp. 1–12

32. Y. Vandewoude, P. Ebraert, Y. Berbers, T. D'Hondt, Tranquility: a low disruptive alternative to quiescence for ensuring safe dynamic updates. IEEE Trans. Softw. Eng. **33**(12), 856–868 (2007)

33. T. Würthinger, C. Wimmer, L. Stadler, Dynamic code evolution for Java, in *Proceedings of the International Conference on the Principles and Practice of Programming in Java* (2010), pp. 10–19

34. T. Würthinger, C. Wimmer, L. Stadler, Unrestricted and safe dynamic code evolution for Java. Sci. Comput. Program. **78**(5), 481–498 (2013)

Specification and Monitoring of Data-Centric Temporal Properties for Service-Based Internetware Systems

9

Abstract

Service-based systems operate in a very dynamic environment. To guarantee functional and non-functional objective at runtime, an adaptation mechanism is usually expected to monitor software changes, make appropriate decisions, and act accordingly. However, existing runtime monitoring solutions consider only the constraints on the sequence of messages exchanged between partner services and ignore the actual data contents inside the messages. As a result, it is difficult to monitor some dynamic properties such as how message data of interest is processed between different participants. To address this issue, we propose an efficient, non-intrusive online monitoring approach to dynamically analyze data-centric properties for service-oriented applications involving multiple participants. By introducing Par-BCL—a Parametric Behavior Constraint Language for Web services—to define monitoring parameters, various data-centric temporal behavior properties for Web services can be specified and monitored. This approach broadens the monitored patterns to include not only message exchange orders, but also data contents bound to the parameters. To reduce runtime overhead, we statically analyze the monitored properties and combine two different indexing mechanisms to optimize monitoring. The experiments show that our solution is efficient and promising.

Keywords

Runtime monitoring · Web services composition · Temporal property

Parts of this chapter were reprinted from Journal of Systems and Software, Volume 85, Guoquan Wu, Jun Wei, Chunyang Ye, Hua Zhong, Tao Huang and Hong He, Specification and monitoring of data-centric temporal properties for service-based systems, Pages No. 2738–2754, Copyright (2012), with permission from Elsevier [OR APPLICABLE SOCIETY COPYRIGHT OWNER].

9.1   Introduction

Service-oriented architecture (SOA) is an emerging software engineering paradigm to develop dynamically evolving applications. In this paradigm, service providers develop Web services, and publish them at service registries. Service consumers can then discover the required services from the service registries and compose them to create new services. Process based composition of Web services has recently gained significant momentum for inter-organizational business collaboration. WS-BPEL [34] now represents the de-facto standard for Web services composition, in which a central node called composition process usually coordinates the interactions of distributed, autonomous Web services. An instance of process is an actual running process that follows the logic described in the process specification.

Due to the frequent changes of business and environmental requirements, service-based systems are usually required to be self-adaptive. For example, to adapt to market changes, a service-based travel agency application may dynamically select and compose the airline services that are best beneficial to customers. Moreover, due to the dynamic network situation, the quality of service (QoS) that a service provider delivers may change from time to time. Therefore, systems need to adjust their behavior dynamically according to the perception of environmental changes (e.g., substitute a new service). In the past decade, scientists and engineers have made significant efforts to design and develop self-adaptive software systems. Many researchers advocate to incorporating an external feedback control loop into the system [15,37]. To build self-adaptive software systems in practice, Garlan et al. [21] propose Rainbow, an architecture-based adaptation framework, which uses a reusable adaptation infrastructure and system-specific adaptation knowledge to support self-adaptive software systems. In the area of service-based systems, a lot of works adopt similar approach to achieve self-adaptation [7,16,36,40].

The correctness of service-based systems is an important concern but usually cannot be determined statically [32,39], as both the agents interacting with the system and the individual third-parties that constitute it may change or behave unpredictably. There is an increasing interest towards self-healing service-based system, which can detect faults and errors instantly and then contain their effects within defined boundaries [7,30,38]. In practice, continuous monitoring is usually deployed to assure whether the runtime behavior of the system complies with specified properties. In this way, systems can be recovered immediately (e.g., by terminating the execution or trying to restore the systems to an error-free state) once serious problems are detected.

The need to monitor service-based systems has inspired many research projects in recent years [5, 6,10,32,39]. However, most existing works focus on monitoring properties related to the control flow of the system. These constraints are expressed in terms of messages names and only the sequence of messages exchanged between services is considered. As a result, some dynamic properties such as how data inside the messages is processed between different participants are not supported. For example, in an online shopping system, to constrain the running behavior of a customer who has made a commitment to one transaction, a property specifying that the purchased items should eventually appear in the final payment bill is needed. In this chapter, we refer to this class of properties as *data-centric temporal properties*. In Sect. 9.2, we will illustrate the need and the usage of such properties.

To validate data-centric temporal properties at runtime, existing monitoring approaches [5,10, 39] rely only on one unique identifier (e.g., process instance ID or session ID) to dispatch system events to right monitor instance. However, this is not adequate when multiple data of interest inside a message need to be monitored: these data may flow through different activities that are within or across different process instances.

To address these limitations, we proposed a non-intrusive online monitoring approach [46] to dynamically analyze data-centric temporal properties for service-based systems, from the point of the view of a composition process. We introduce Par-BCL—a Parametric Behavior Constraint

Language for Web service—to specify various data-centric temporal properties. Specifically, parameters are introduced to specify a set of message data that needs to be monitored during the system execution. In addition, Par-BCL extends Specification Pattern System (SPS) [20] with first-order quantification over message data and introduces parameterized event to support the expression of temporal behavior constraints that are related to a set of message data. To validate data-centric properties, we proposed an optimized online parametric monitoring approach, which overcomes the limitation of existing works and can detect dataflow within or across different process instances. The novelty of the proposed monitoring approach lies in that the introduction of parameters broadens the monitored patterns to include not only message exchanged, but also the data contents bound to the parameters. In this way, as system runs, the dataflow information among different partner services can be tracked timely to detect whether the specified property is violated or not.

With respect to our previous chapter, this chapter makes the following extensions and contributions: (1) we extended the syntax of Par-BCL notation to express some complex properties that not only concern dataflow related constraints, but also require the monitored data to satisfy some constraints; (2) we designed new index mechanism and monitoring algorithm, which can locate the monitor instances more efficiently; (3) we proposed a new filtering mechanism, which can reduce the overhead caused by message data extraction; (4) we conducted more comprehensive experiments to evaluate the effectiveness and efficiency of our solution.

9.2 Motivation Example

To investigate the necessity of monitoring data-centric behavior properties in service-based systems, we introduce two representative scenarios: car rental application and supply chain application. More such properties can be seen in the literature [27,28].

9.2.1 Car Rental Application

This example is taken and adapted from the work [32]. Two processes are deployed in a car rental application. The diagrams in Fig. 9.1 show the high level steps that are executed to provide car rental services for customers. The CarRequest process is responsible for renting cars to customers and the CarReturn process collects cars returned from customers. Both processes interact with the following four partner services to provide the required functionalities:

Car Information Service (CIS). This service maintains the registry of all the cars and allocates cars to customers. It also provides operations to check and update the stock of cars.

Sensor Service (SS). This service tracks cars in the park automatically. When a car is parked or leaves, the sensor service will report the information to CarRequest and CarReturn processes.

User Interaction Service (UIS). This service is responsible for interacting with customers.

Payment Service (PS). It is responsible for transferring money between the car rental company and the customer.

In a typical car rental scenario, a new CarRequest process is launched when a car rental request is received from UIS. Then the process checks whether the requested cars are available by invoking CIS. If all cars are available, it will ask for confirmation by producing a bill. At this step, the customer can make a commitment to rent at least one car in advance, and the system will offer a corresponding discount. Also, the customer has the opportunity to cancel the whole order. If receiving a positive confirmation message, the process proceeds to cash transfer. This is achieved by providing an account number. Alternatively, a cancellation message listing some cars removed from the bill can be sent before the final payment. The process releases keys to the customer after successful payment. When any car is found to leave the park, the sensor service will inform the CarRequest process to invoke CIS to update the status of these cars.

A new CarReturn process is started when it receives a car return message from the customer. The process then inquires the customer whether he/she

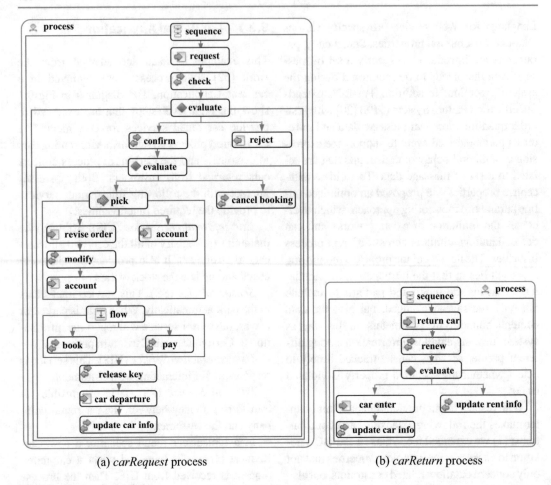

(a) *carRequest* process   (b) *carReturn* process

Fig. 9.1 Car rental application

needs to re-rent the car. If so, it only needs to up-date the status of rented cars. Otherwise, when re-ceiving the message from the sensor service which indicates that the returned cars have been parked in place, the process invokes the car information service to update the status of the car.

In this chapter, we assume the local workflow of business process is correct and the interaction with external partners may cause application in-consistency [24,45,48]. For example, due to mal-functioning of a sensor service, it may miss the departure of a specific car from the park and thus does not report it to the CarRequest process. As a result, the availability status of this car is not up-dated timely. This may cause application inconsis-tency because another CarRequest instance may wrongly accept a rental request and allocate this

car to a new customer before this car is returned (by starting a new CarReturn instance). To avoid this situation, the following data-centric property can be specified and monitored at runtime:

Data-centric property 1. *For each rented car, there must be a departure event between two con-secutive entrances to the parking lot.*

This is an inter-process constraint involving two processes: CarRequest and CarReturn. It ap-plies the universal temporal constraint to monitor each rented car moving in and out of the park. Figure 9.2 shows the message definition of sense-Car and the typical message transmitted at run-time.

Besides the properties related to system cor-rectness, some business related policies are also data-centric. For example, in above scenario, one

(a)

```
<message name="senseCar">
  <part name="sensor" type="tns:departure" />
  <part name="session" type="xsd:integer" />
</message>
<complexType name="departure">
  <sequence>
    <element name="parkInfo" maxOccurs="unbounded" />
      <complexType>
        <sequence>
          <element name="carID" type="xsd:string"
                   maxOccurs="unbounded" />
          <element name="parkID" type="xsd:string"/>
        </sequence>
      </complexType>
    </element>
  </sequence>
</complexType>
```

(b)

```
<senseCar>
  <sensor>
    <parkInfo>
      <carID> c1 </carID>
      <parkID>p1</parkID>
    </parkInfo>
    <parkInfo>
      <carID>c2</carID>
      <carID>c3</carID>
      <parkID>p2</parkID>
    </parkInfo>
  </sensor>
  <session>10001</session>
</ senseCar >
```

Fig. 9.2   senseCar Message

(a)

```
<message name="requestedCar">
  <part name="cars" type="tns:carInfo" />
  <part name="account" type="xsd:string" />
</message>

<complexType name="carInfo">
  <sequence>
    <element name="car" maxOccurs="unbounded">
      <complexType>
        <sequence>
          <element name="model" type="xsd:string"/>
          <element name="amount" type="xsd:integer"/>
        </sequence>
      </complexType>
    </element>
  </sequence>
</complexType>
```

(b)

```
<requestedCar>
  <cars>
    <car>
      <model>m1</model>
      <amount>a1</amount>
    </car>
    <car>
      <model>m2</model>
      <amount>a2</amount>
    </car>
  </cars>
  <account>u1</account>
</ requestedCar>
```

Fig. 9.3   requestedCar Message

can specify a constraint to define the expected running behavior of a customer who has made a commitment, that is, before the end of the transaction, the customer will eventually rent at least one car in the final payment, as shown in the following data-centric property:

Data-centric property 2. *For the cars rented by the customer who has made the commitment, there must exist a car in his billing information,* *which will eventually appear in the final payment confirmation.*

This property is intra-process as it is only related to the CarRequest process. It involves the data user account, rented cars and bill, and specifies the existential temporal constraints for the rented cars. Figure 9.3 shows the message definition of requestedCar and typical message content.

Fig. 9.4 Supply chain
application

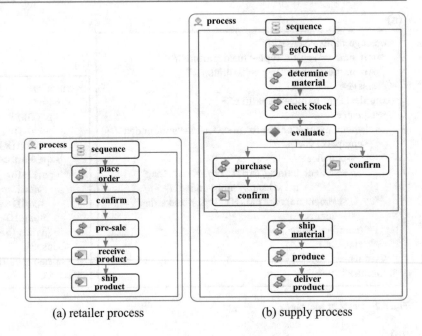

| (a) retailer process | (b) supply process |

9.2.2   Supply Chain Application

This example is taken and adapted from the work [4,48], where the supply process interacts with six partner services: Retailer, LocalSupply, Wharehouse, Vendor, Transport and Manufacture to provide their products to customers. Figure 9.4 shows the high level steps of Retailer process and Supply process and some details are omitted to improve the readability.

As depicted in Fig. 9.4, when receiving an order request from the retailer, the supplier first invokes LocalSupply service to determine the resources that are needed to produce products. Then it queries the stock to determine whether all required resources are available. If stocks of some resources are low, the process will purchase these resources from external Vendor service and put them into the Warehouse. When receiving the confirmation message from Retailer, the process will notify Transport service to ship all required resources to the manufacturer. The manufacturer begins to produce products after receiving a notification message from the supply process. Then, the retailer can pre-sell the products and deliver them after receiving the products from the supplier.

In this example, concurrent supply process instances may interact implicitly as they share the same warehouse. The execution of these instances can lead to application inconsistency. For instance, suppose process instance p1 buys some resources and puts them into the warehouse. Then, process p2 queries the stock and uses up these resources to produce products in another collaboration. As such, the activity produce in p1 will fail because the resources it purchased have been used by p2. Therefore, the collaboration between the retailer and p1 will fail and lead to application inconsistency as retailer has pre-sold the products.

One way to solve this problem is to add locks between the activity check stock and produce to prevent the resource from being used by other concurrent process instances during this duration. However, since services are reusable components, adding locks will seriously compromise the performance of the supplier's services because it may hold the locks for a long time in each of its collaboration. Also, not all collaboration with supply chain service would lead to failure caused by such implicit interaction. Based on the def-use relations among activities, we identify such afflicted implicit interaction by analyzing their potential affected activities in a service composition [48], and apply the following behavior constraint to guarantee the application consistency of this collaboration:

Data-centric property 3. *For the resources which are purchased by one process instance, after they are shipped to the manufacturer for production, they cannot be used by another different process instance.*

This property applies universal behavior constraint to the resources purchased from external service. It is an inter-proc property, as it involves two concurrent supply process instances.

Also, we can specify the following property to guarantee the manufacturing process can be done successfully.

Data-centric property 4. *For the received order, all required resources must be shipped to the manufacturer before production. Moreover, for each resource, the shipped amount must be greater than the required amount.*

This property is intra-proc as it only considers the constraint within one supply process instance. Different from property 3 which only concerns the behavior constraint related to the resources, we need to further specify the constraint on the monitored data, that is, the shipped amount must be greater than shipped amount for each resource.

To check behavior correctness properties at runtime, there are already a lot of works in the area of dynamic analysis of service-based system [5–8, 10,32,39]. However, most existing property specifications abstract away the actual data inside the messages and define the properties concerning only the temporal relation of the messages. They are propositional and not adequate to express data-centric properties mentioned above.

To express properties that are related to data contents inside the message, in recent years, Hallé and Villemaire [26] proposed LTL-FO+, an extension to Linear Temporal Logic with first order quantification over the message data. Although one can extend LTL-FO+ to express data-centric properties in Web services compositions, we find that it is difficult to write these properties correctly, especially when multiple related data elements inside a message are involved (e.g., to express property 2, in which both data car and

park inside the entrance and departure message need to be extracted). We will discuss this in detail in Sect. 9.7. To check these properties, Hallé and Villemaire proposed an online monitoring approach. However, it is mainly suitable for client side enforcement. For service side program, this non-optimized monitoring approach will incur great performance overhead, because there will be a large number of concurrent process instances at runtime, and each message may contain a lot of data that needs to be monitored.

To address these limitations, we propose an efficient monitoring approach to dynamic analysis of data-centric properties which are expressed in Par-BCL. In the next section, we first introduce the specification of Par-BCL.

9.3   A Language for Specifying Data-Centric Properties

9.3.1   The Syntax of Par-BCL

Our approach to defining data-centric properties builds upon the property Specification Pattern System (SPS) proposed by Dwyer et al. [20]. It is a pattern-based approach to representing, codifying, and reusing property specification. We choose SPS to specify the temporal relation of the events, as it is easier to understand and write compared to some formal logic (e.g., LTL, QRE), and has been shown to capture a majority of system properties [38].

Based on SPS, Par-BCL further allows first-order quantification over the message data. In addition, it introduces the concept of parameterized event, and can define properties in the form for a set of message data, parameterized properties cannot be violated at runtime in a declarative way.

An example of data-centric property 1 expressed in Par-BCL is shown in Fig. 9.5. *rent, initial_enter, depart* and *again_enter* are the symbols representing the messages of interest. Parameter $car and $park store the message data that need to be monitored at runtime. "scope=inter-proc" means that the monitored data may flow across different process instances at runtime. The last part specifies that for each rented car ($car),

```
1 Monitor Car_Behavior($car, $park){
2 scope = inter-proc;
3 event rent : ?CIS.book binding<$car> with($msg.sensor//carID);
4 event initial_enter : ?Sensor.enter
5     binding<$car, $park> with($msg.sensor//carID, $msg.sensor//parkID);
6 event depart : ?Sensor. depart
7     binding<$car, $park> with($msg.sensor//carID, $msg.sensor//parkID);
8 event again_enter : ?Sensor.enter
9     binding<$car> with($msg.sensor//carID);
10
11 forall ($car,$park)
12     between_and(seq(rent<$car>,initial_enter<$car,$park>),again_enter<$car>)
13     exist(depart<$car, $park>);
14 }
```

Fig. 9.5   Data-centric property 1

<Specification> → **Monitor** <Head> <Body>

    <Head> → <Name > (<Parameters>)

      <Body> → <Scope> <EventDecl>*

                 <Quant> ! <Parameters>"

                 <Range > <Pattern>

    <Scope> → **Scope** = [**inter-proc**| **intra-proc**];

<Parameters> → <Para> [,<Para>]*

      <Para> → <Var>

  <EventDecl> → **event** <Symbol>: <Event > [<Binding>]

    <Binding> → **binding** ! <Para> [,<Para>]*" **with** (<DataQuery>, [,<DataQuery>]*);

   <EventRef> → <Symbol>|< Symbol> (<Var>[,<Var>]*)

    <Symbol> → <Identifier>

     <Event> → [! |?] <Partner>.<Operation>[&&<FilterCondtion>]*

     <Quant> → **forall** | **exist**

    <Pattern> → (**absent** (<Tracecut>)| **occurs** (<Tracecut> [, **at least** |**at most**, <n>])

             | **precede** (<Tracecut>, <Tracecut>) | **leadto** (<Tracecut>,<Tracecut>)) [&&<Assertion>]*

     <Trace> → (<EventRef> | **seq** (<Tracecut> [, <Tracecut>]*)

             | **all** (<Tracecut> [, <Tracecut>]*) | **any** (<Tracecut> [, <Tracecut>]*))

  <Assertion> → <Para> (!= | == | > | < | ≥ | ≤) <Para>

     <Range> → **global** | **after** (<Tracecut>) | **after_until** (<Tracecut>, <Tracecut>)

             | **between_and** (<Tracecut>, <Tracecut>) | **before** (<Tracecut>)

Fig. 9.6   Semi-formal syntax of Par-BCL

if it is sensed to enter a parking lot ($park) and later this car ($car) is sensed to enter a parking lot again, a departure event must occur between these consecutive entrance events.

Figure 9.6 presents, in a semi-formal way, the syntax for the proposed Par-BCL language. In the following, we will explain the meaning of the main elements in Par-BCL.

Event. As service providers may not release the details of their services, runtime monitor-ing of service-based systems is usually based on the messages exchanged between involved ser-vices. The event in Par-BCL is thus defined based on the WSDLs of all involved services. To ease the presentation, we use the following notation "? Partner.operation" to represent that process re-ceives an invocation request (denoted by opera-tion) from the Partner, and "! Partner.operation" to represent that process sends an invocation request (denoted by operation) to the Partner. Expression

"< *FilterCondtion* >" can be used to specify conditions on the attributes inside the message to monitor the message of interest only.

Parameter&Binding. Parameter keeps message data that needs to be monitored. Since the same data can be expressed differently in different messages, to track the flow of a set of message data across different participants, Par-BCL uses parameter binding "*binding* << *Para* > [, < *Para* >]∗ > *with*(< *DataQuery* > [, < *DataQuery* > ∗])" to bind the message data to the parameters. At runtime, these parameters will be instantiated and the "behavior" of each group of the data values will be monitored.

< *DataQuery* > here represents a query language to extract the monitored data inside the message. As the interaction between the composition process and partner services is based on xml message, currently, XPath [47] is used as query language to extract the message data. We use variable $msg to denote the exchanged message and a special attribute processid in $msg is used to represent the process instance that a message belongs to.

Scope. The scope defines how specified properties will be monitored. It can be two values: *intra-proc* and *inter-proc*. *intra-proc* means the monitoring only needs to track the dataflow within individual process instance, while *inter-proc* needs to track dataflow across different process instances.

Body. The body part of Par-BCL is based on SPS, which allows expression of properties in the form "*pattern of interest can't be violated within a range*". Patterns in SPS are generally classified into five kinds: *leadto*, *precede*, *exist*, *bounded exist* and *absent*. The definition is briefly described as follows:

leadto: it specifies that a event must eventually be followed by another event. In essence, it specifies the cause-effect relation of events;

precede: it specifies that an event must always be followed by another;

absent: it restricts an event does not occur;

exist: it states an event must occur;

bounded exist: it extends exist pattern with lower and upper bounds on the number of event occurrence.

Each pattern has a range. Range includes global, before, after, between-and after-until. The corresponding definition is defined as follows:

global: it refers to the entire history of the system execution;

before R: it concerns the initial portion of the history up to first execution of the specified event *R*;

after Q: it concerns the portion after the first occurrence of the specified event *Q*;

between (Q, R): it concerns any part of the execution from one event *Q* to another event *R*;

after-until (Q, R): it is like between range but the designated part of execution continues even if *R* does not occur;

Although there already exists some SPS based property specifications in the area of service based systems [31,42], they are all propositional and not suitable to express data-centric properties. We extend SPS with first-order quantification over the parameters. To describe the behavior of a group of data across different partner services, we introduce the concept of parameterized event to express the operation of the partner service on the message data.

Consider the property forall ($car, $park) in φ. Figure 9.5 (φ here represents the expression "**between_and(...) exist(...)**"). This property is true *iff* for all the groups of $car and $car value, φ is not violated. The event in φ can be a non-parametric symbol, called *base event* or a symbol with parameters, called *parameterized event*. Event *initial_enter* $car, $park is parametric in both $car and $park. This parameterized event is generated when car ($car) enters the parking lot ($park) from the received entering message.

Tracecut. Based on primitive event, we define three composite event operators: any, seq and all to capture complex events during the process execution. Tracecut addresses the SPS limitation by supporting the specification of concurrent and sequential behaviors that can be applied to the behavior patterns. Also, more complex events can be defined based on the combination of these operators.

- *any operator*. This operator takes a set of trace-cuts as input. The complex event is captured when any event of them occurs.
- *seq operator*. It takes a list of n (n > 1) tracecuts as its parameter, such as $seq(< E_1 >, < E_2 >, \ldots, < E_n >)$. It specifies an order in which the events of interest should occur sequentially.
- *all operator*. This operator takes a list of trace-cuts as input. If all specified events occur, the complex event is captured. This operator does not specify the order of events occurrence.

Assertion. It specifies the assertion to the parameters. For some data-centric properties (e.g., property 4), apart from the constraints on the sequence of events, we need to further require that the monitored data from different messages satisfies some constraints. Note that, this is different from $< FilterCondition >$, which is to filter the message.

Currently, Par-BCL only considers how to express data-centric behavior constraints. It can also be extended to specify corresponding recovery strategies. Thus, when the property violation is detected at runtime, recovery actions can be enforced timely to heal from such failure. We plan to support this feature in the future work.

9.3.2 Par-BCL for Data-Centric Properties

By extending SPS, Par-BCL provides an easy and intuitive way to specify data-centric properties. Figures 9.7, 9.8 and 9.9 gives the Par-BCL representation of property 2–4.

Figure 9.7 specifies that for the cars that a customer has committed to rent, there must exist at least one car, which will appear in the final payment confirmation. Intra-proc means that in this property, the monitored data flows within individual process instance. Condition *msg.result = true* means that this customer commits to rent the car in the transaction.

Figure 9.8 specifies that for the resources (denoted by resource type $type and resource identifier $resource) that one process ($process) purchases, after they are shipped to the manufacturer,

these resources cannot be used by another different process instance ($process').

Figure 9.9 shows the property 4 expressed in Par-BCL. It specifies that for the resources that are needed to produce products, if the user confirms the order, all of them must be shipped to the manufacture. Also, to guarantee the manufacturing process can be done successfully, assertion "amount <= amount" specifies that the shipped amount of each resource must be greater than the needed amount.

9.4 Monitoring Model of Par-BCL

Par-BCL can monitor the behavior of each group/set of related message data in the binding parameter at the same time. The execution trace against which the various properties are checked is extracted from the running process as a sequence of events. Events carry sufficient information about the message data for the monitor to correctly check the property. We propose a parametric monitoring model to verify data-centric properties. It consists of three orthogonal mechanisms: filtering, parameter binding and verification. Figure 9.10 shows the monitoring model adopted by Par-BCL.

9.4.1 Filtering

First, filtering mechanism observes the current trace and extracts property-relevant events. As XPath is currently chosen as the message data query language, intuitively, we can use XPath engine to extract the message data that needs to be monitored. However, we abandoned it for the following reasons: firstly, as stated by Charfi and Mezini [16], using XPath engine to navigate xml document is time-consuming; secondly, if a message has multiple parameters to bind, it will be evaluated more than once, making the extraction more time-consuming; finally, the extracted data elements may not preserve the same relation as they are in the original message after filtering. For instance, to evaluate senseCar message (see Fig. 9.2) with binding clause "**binding** <$car,

```
 1 Monitor Customer_Behavior($account,$car,$bill) {
 2 scope = intra-proc;
 3 event request : ?UIS.requestCar
 4     binding<$car, $account> with($msg.cars//model,$msg.account);
 5 event commit: ?UIS.commit && $msg.result = true
 6     binding<$account> with($msg.account);
 7 event billing: !UIS.confirm
 8     binding<$car,$bill> with($msg.cars//model,$msg.bill);
 9 event pay: !BANK.pay
10     binding<$car,$bill> with($msg.cars//model,$msg.bill);
11
12 exist($account, $car, $bill)
13     after(seq(request<$account,$car>,commit<$account>)
14     leadto(billing<$car,$bill>,pay<$car,$bill>);
15 }
```

Fig. 9.7 Data-centric property 2

```
 1 Monitor Resource_Constraint ($type,$resource,$process,$process') {
 2 scope = inter-proc;
 3 event buy: ?Vendor.Purchase
 4     binding<$type,$process> with($msg.resources//type, $msg. processid);
 5 event ship: ?Shipper.Ship
 6     binding<$type,$resource, $process> with($msg.resources//type,$msg.
             resources//id, $msg.processid);
 7 event produce:!Manufacturer.produce
 8     binding<$resource,$processâĂŹ> with($msg.rescources//id,$msg.processid);
 9
10 forall($resource,$type, $process, $process')
11     after(seq(buy<$type, $process>,ship<$type, $process, $resource>)
12     absent(produce<$resource, $process'> && ($process !=$process'));
13 }
```

Fig. 9.8 Data-centric property 3

```
 1 Monitor Shipper_Constraint ($type, $resource, $amount, $amountâĂŸ) {
 2 scope=intra-proc;
 3 event determine: ?LocalSupply.determineMaterial
 4     binding<$type,$amount> with($msg.resources//type,$msg.resources//amount);
 5 event confirm: ?Retailer.confirm
 6 event ship:?Shipper.Ship
 7     binding<$type,$resource,$amount> with($msg.resources//type, $msg.
             resources//id,$msg.resources//amount);
 8 event produce: !Manufacturer.produce
 9     binding<$resource> with($msg.resources/id);
10
11 forall($type,$resource,$amount,$amountâĂŹ)
12     leadto(seq(determine<$type,$amount>,confirm),ship<$type,$resource,
             $amountâĂŹ>)&&(amount<=amountâĂŹ)
13     before produce<$resource>;
14 }
```

Fig. 9.9 Data-centric property 4

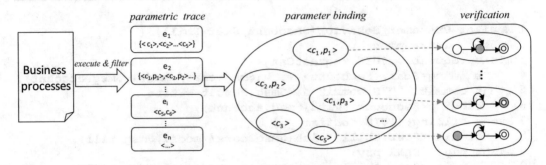

Fig. 9.10 Monitoring model of Par-BCL

$park>$ **with** ($msg//carID, $msg//parkID)", if data values inside msg are extracted respectively, $c1, c2, c3$ will be returned for XPath expression "$msg//carID$", and $p1, p2$ will be returned for "$msg//parkID$". Based on $c1, c2, c3$ and $p1, p2$, it will be difficult to maintain the same relation of ci and pi as they are in the senseCar message.

To extract the monitored data efficiently, we adopt the path sharing approach proposed by Diao et al. [19], which encodes multiple path expressions using a single NFA and can provide tremendous performance improvements. After filtering, an event containing a set of k-tuple data (k is the number of parameters that need to be bound for a message of interest) will be returned, and these k-tuple data can preserve the same relation as they are in the message. Figure 9.11 shows an NFA representation to extract data carID and parkID of senseCar message. After filtering, the set of k-tuple data $< c1, p1 >, < c2, p2 >, < c3, p2 >$ can be correctly returned. Here, we simplify the representation of k-tuple data by hiding its parameter name, e.g., $< c1, p1 >$ means $< (car, c1), (park, p1) >$.

9.4.2 Parameter Binding

After filtering, the events will construct a parametric trace. Our approach to monitoring parametric trace against data-centric properties is inspired by the observation of Chen and Rosu [13] that "each parametric trace actually contains multiple non-parametric trace slices, each for a particular parameter binding instance". Whenever a parameter is bound more than once in a trace (by the same or different events), the parameter is not rebound to a new set of data. Rather, this step checks, for each group of old data that the parameters were bound before, whether there is data in the new binding which is equal to the old one. If this is not the case, the new event symbol is ignored for this particular trace. In other words, an execution trace is defined to match the behavior pattern when there exists some set of binding values that can be consistently bound in such a way that the execution trace of process instances can match the specified behavior property according to different sets of binding values.

For example, for the event ei with data $< c5 >$, $< c6 >$ in Fig. 9.10, as the sub-trace that $< c5 >$ represents has already exists (created by event e1), ei will not create a new sub-trace but be appended to the sub-strace of $< c5 >$. For the $< c6 >$, as the corresponding sub-trace does not exist in the former parameter binding, ei will create a new sub-trace represented by $< c6 >$.

$carID : $msg.sensor//carID
$parkID : $msg.sensor//parkID

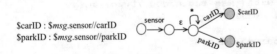

Fig. 9.11 Message data extraction based on path sharing

9.4.3   Verification

The verification mechanism checks whether each sub-trace obtained after the parameter binding violates the specified property. As sub-trace has already no parameter information, this step is the same as the ordinary event pattern matching.

To enable automated online monitoring, we need to formally define the semantics of tracecut, pattern and range operators. In our approach, we choose finite state automata (FSA) as their underlying semantics representation since it is easily understandable, mathematically well defined and can be directly used for online trace matching.

As Par-BCL first declares the messages of interest before specification of the constraint, which is very similar to pointcut in Aspect-oriented Programming [25], here we give its FSA notation based on exact-match semantics (where every relevant event must be matched) shared in the AOP community [2]. Although Smith et al. [41] have given the FSA representation of SPS, its skipping semantics (where any event may be skipped during the match) is generally favored by runtime verification community. An important difference between the two is that under the exact-match semantics, taking the regular expression 'AB' as an example, it means "A implies next B", while under the skipping semantics, it means that "A implies eventually B".

Figure 9.12 gives the FSA notation of pattern and tracecut operators based on filtering seman-tics (P, Q here is the symbol which represents base or parameterized event, and violation state is not shown for brevity). To tracecut operator any, seq and all, as the constructed complex event is equivalent to regular expression, it is possible to detect complex events using FSA. To identify $any(E_1; E_2; ...; E_n)$ and $all(E_1; E_2; ...; E_n)$, we first construct automata A(Ei) for each event Ei, then a product automata is built based on the Cartesian product of each A(Ei). For instance, Fig. 9.12(i) shows the FSA of tracecut $any(E_1; E_2)$ and $all(E_1; E_2)$. The final state is the set $\{01, 10, 11\}$ for $any(E_1; E_2)$ and $\{11\}$ for $all(E_1; E_2)$. Note that, in accordance with the filtering semantics, for $seq(< E_1 >, < E_2 >, ..., < E_n >)$, we restrict that an arbitrary number of events specified in $< E_1 >, < E_2 >, ..., < E_n >$ cannot be allowed to appear between two events addressed by consecutive parameters.

A range is applied to a pattern by adding additional states called range states and by adding transition between range states and the states of the FSA that represent the pattern. When applying range to pattern, we must determine at each state of pattern FSA, what the effect will be when encountering range event at the point in the event sequence. Details about how to apply the range state to pattern automata can be seen in the work [41].

For the complex behavior constraint, a tree structure is adopted to organize the relationship of multiple automata. We do not construct a single

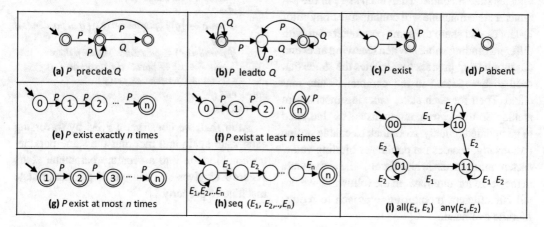

Fig. 9.12   FSA of pattern and tracecut operator

automaton as it may destruct the filtering seman-tics of each sub-automaton. Using the tree struc-ture, each automaton in the non-terminal node can still obey the filtering semantics, as the automaton is interested in only the events that the incoming edges represent [44].

9.5   Efficient Monitoring Process

As mentioned above, matches with different pa-rameter bindings should be independent of each other. This means that a separate monitor instance is required for each possible parameter bindings. At runtime, hundreds of thousands of monitor in-stances will be generated. Monitoring such prop-erties efficiently is a non-trivial issue. Also, in the monitored properties, some events may con-tain partial information about parameters, mak-ing it more difficult to locate relevant parameter bindings [11,13]. For example, in the property 2, when a billing<$car, $bill> event is received, we need to find rent<$account, $car> event with the same binding for $car, and transitively, com-mit<$account> event with the same $account as the rent. In this section, we introduce our efficient monitoring process to reduce runtime overhead.

We proposed an efficient monitoring process. The basic idea is to divide the parameter binding instances of step 2 according to different parame-ter combinations. We compute the possible para-meter combinations for a specified property, and maintain their association through building a pa-rameter state machine. Then each state in the pa-rameter state machine will contain lots of monitor instances that share the same parameters but with different binding values. When receiving an event, our monitoring process first locates the states that need to be updated in the parameter state ma-chine. Then for each state, indexing mechanism is adopted to locate monitor instances that need to be updated quickly. Note that, to enable online monitoring, besides the parameter binding value, each monitor instance also records the active state in the behavior automata. In the following, we de-tail our efficient monitoring approach to reduce runtime overhead.

9.5.1   Parameter State Machine

To find possible parameter combinations, our approach fully utilizes the specified properties through static analysis of the monitored property. By traversing the constructed behavior automata, we build a Parameter State Machine (PSM), in which each state (called parameter state) stores one possible parameter combination, except the initial state with null value. The transition between parameter states is triggered by event symbol. Thus PSM describes the transition of the possible parameter combinations for a specified property.

To build a corresponding PSM, we maintain a parameter set for each state in the constructed behavior automata. Parameter set stores the pos-sible parameter combinations that can appear at specified state. Algorithm 1 shows the algorithm of computing parameter set for each state. We can regard the behavior automata as a graph and each event represents an edge. Then the algorithm tra-verses the set of edges from initial state to the final state and computes parameter set for each state. The condition "$if\ enable(s') \subset enable(s') \cup temp$" ensures that we only call the recursive step on line 9, if new possible parameter combination can be added. This algorithm is bounded above by the number of one cycle paths through the graph.

Algorithm 1 *compute_parameter_set*
Input: *paraSet$(s) \leftarrow \phi$ for any state $s \in S$*
1: **for all** *defined transition $s = \delta(s,e)$* **do**
2:      **if** *paraSet$(s) == \phi$* **then**
3:          *temp $\leftarrow$ parameter(e)*
4:      **else**
5:          *temp $\leftarrow \{q \cup \{parameter(e)\} | \ q\ in\ paraSet(s)\}$*
6:      **end if**
7:      **if** *paraSet$(s') \subset$ paraSet$(s') \cup temp$* **then**
8:          *paraSet$(s') \leftarrow$ paraSet$(s') \cup temp$*
9:          *compute_parameter_set(s')*
10:     **end if**
11: **end for**

After that, we construct a PSM by traversing each state again and merging the same parame-ter combination into a separate parameter state. Figure 9.13 gives an example of parameter state machine of property 1.

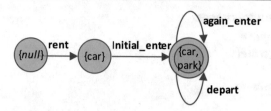

Fig. 9.13   Example of PSM

Table 9.1   Index table

Key	Parameter state list
rent	null
initial_enter	car
depart	car, park
again_enter	car, park

To locate parameter states that need to be updated quickly, based on constructed PSM, we further build an index table which uses event symbol as key, and returns a parameter state list. Table 9.1 shows the index table built from PSM of Fig. 9.13.

9.5.2   Monitor Instance

At runtime, each parameter state may contain a large number of monitor instances, making it time-consuming to locate monitor instances that needs to be updated. To locate monitor instances efficiently, we use the partition technique proposed by Avgustinov et al. [2] for indexing monitor instances. Generally, for each parameter state, the strategy for choosing index parameters is found by intersecting the corresponding parameter set with the parameters that event binds to benefit as many outgoing transition as possible.

For example, to parameter state car, park in Fig. 9.13, the set of parameters that can be used as index is found by intersecting {car, park} with {car} and {car, park}(for event against_enter and depart respectively). Therefore, monitor instances at this state would be indexed by their binding for car. If the result of intersection is null, we can mark some event as "frequent", and repeat above process by just using the "frequent" event to find parameters that can be indexed.

9.5.3   Monitoring Algorithm

Using the proposed static parameter state indexing and dynamic monitor instance indexing mechanism, we present an efficient monitoring algorithm (see Algorithm 2).

For a received event $< e, d >$, firstly, function $query\_parameter\_state$ (line 1) will query the index table of parameter state using e as a key, which returns a list of parameter states that needs to be updated. For each data element u in d, the algorithm traverses each possible parameter state s and computes next state s when e occurs (line 2–4). If s is initial state and e is a start event, it will create a new monitor instance and the active state is updated according to behavior automata (line 5–8). When a violation state is entered, an ERROR_EVENT_BINDING exception will be thrown (line 10).

If s is not the initial state, function $look\_up$ uses internal index tree to locate all monitor instances that are associated with data element u (line 15). If s is not transferred to a new state $s'(s = s')$, then for each monitor instance β, its active state will be updated according to the behavior automata (line 17). If a new parameter state s' is entered, the binding value and active state of β will be updated (line 19–20). After that, the instance will be appended to the monitor instance list that the monitor of state s' manages and removed from state s at the same time (line 21–22). Then the algorithm will check the active state of β. If a violation state is entered, an ERROR_EVENT_BINDING exception will be thrown (line 25).

Note that, during the phase of building index for parameter state, when a new state is needed to add, it should be inserted into the head of list. Thus we ensure the monitor instances are updated correctly. For example, consider the following situation: when an event $< e, (v = 1, i = 2) >$ is received, according to the parameter state list of event e (see Fig. 9.14), both monitors of state {u, v} and {u, v, i} need to be updated. However, if the monitor of {u, v} is updated first, according to the algorithm, it can cause the creation of new monitor instance $< u = 3, v = 1, i = 2 >$. When the

Algorithm 2 *Locate and update monitor instances*

Input: *e: event symbol; d: set of k-tuple data*
```
 1:  List states ← query_parameter_state(e)
 2:  for all state u ∈ d do
 3:      for all parameter state s in states do
 4:          s' ← s.transition(e)
 5:          if s is initial state and e is a start event then
 6:              create monitor instance m
 7:              m.binding_value ← u
 8:              update active state of m according to behavior automata
 9:              if active state is violation state then
10:                  throw ERROR_EVENT_BINDING
11:              else
12:                  add m to the monitor instance list of s
13:              end if
14:          else
15:              for all monitor instance β in s.lookup(u) do
16:                  if s' == s then
17:                      update active state of β according to behavior automata
18:                  else
19:                      β.binding_value ← β.binding_value ∪ u
20:                      update active state of β according to behavior automata
21:                      remove β to the monitor instance list of s
22:                      add β to the monitor instance list of s
23:                  end if
24:                  if active state is violated then
25:                      throw ERROR_EVENT_BINDING
26:                  end if
27:              end for
28:          end if
29:      end for
30:  end for
```

monitor of {u, v, i} is updated, the new monitor instance < u = 3, v = 1, i = 2 > created by the monitor of {u, v} will be updated again, which can incur wrong result.

9.5.4 Management of Monitor Instances

Another performance-related concern in our proposal is the memory overhead. As stated above, a large number of monitor instances will co-exist at runtime and become very large in the end. However, monitor instances can be no longer

used when it is transferred to the new parameter state. To avoid memory leak, the data structure of monitor instance list should be carefully designed further.

We use an array structure to store monitor instances, as shown in Fig. 9.15. To manage these monitor instances, a new column pointer is introduced for each monitor instance. Using this index, a free list is maintained, as shown in Table 9.1. Initially, the list is traversed sequentially and the index of each element is assigned the subscript value of next element. The head of free list is assigned 0, the subscript of first element. With free list, new monitor instance can be created by visiting the

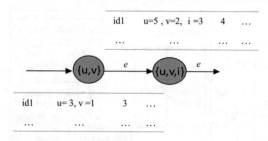

Fig. 9.14 Segment of a PSM

	parameter binding	active state	pointer
	u = 1, v = 2	3	1
	u = 2, v = 3	4	2
	…	…	…

free 0

Fig. 9.15 Monitor instances list

head of this list and allocating corresponding entry to it. When the monitor instance is no longer used, it is inserted into the head of free list.

9.5.5 Architecture and Implementation

In the previous section, we elaborate the design of proposed Par-BCL language. To monitor data-centric properties, we present an implementation of runtime framework through an aspect oriented extension to WS-BPEL engine. In this solution, business process logic and properties are defined and treated separately, since we advocate separation of concerns, which facilitates both the process design and later management. Figure 9.16 shows its overall architecture based on our developed OnceBPEL engine [14]. Similar extensions can be considered for other engines. In what follows, we describe the core components:

Aspect Manager. It represents the main advice that is weaved into the execution environment. As the implementation of WS-BPEL engine revolves around the runtime visitor design pattern and it also maintains an internal AST (abstract syntax tree), after a thorough study, we define our point-cuts using AspectJ [25] as (1) after the engine visits a Receive node; (2) before and after it visits an Invoke node; (3) after it visits a Pick node and (4) before it visits a Reply node, to capture the message interaction between the process and partner services.

After weaving, this component has direct access to the context information of current activity. Before or after a message activity is executed, aspect manager is inserted that defers the execution to the aspect runtime infrastructure. It looks up the matched event in the configuration manager based on the current execution context.

Configuration Manager. It's a persistent component in which we store the basic description information about the property, such as the events of interest, the binding clause, and optional filtering condition. At runtime, the aspect manager will query this component to extract the property-relevant events and send it to monitor manager.

Monitor Manager. This module constructs corresponding behavior automata when a property is deployed. As a side-effect, PSM will be constructed. Based on PSM, an index table is further built. After filtering, an event containing the monitored data will be sent to the monitor manager, which then executes the algorithm provided in Sect. 9.4 to locate and update relevant monitor instances efficiently.

Note that, for *inter-proc* properties, one PSM is maintained to track dataflow across different process instances. For *intra-proc* properties, as it only checks dataflow within individual process instance, one PSM is generated for each monitored process instance. In order to unify the monitoring approach, for *intra-proc* properties, we can choose process ID as an additive index for each parameter state. As a result, only one PSM is enough to monitor *intra-proc* properties.

When a monitor instance enters the violation state, monitor manager needs to further decide whether the specified property is violated. For the universal quantifier, if any monitor instance enters the violation state, the property is violated. For the existential quantifier, our approach maintains a bit vector to record whether the monitor instances created by a start event are violated. Each monitor instance makes a reference to the corresponding entry in the bit vector. When a monitor instance

Fig. 9.16 Overall architecture

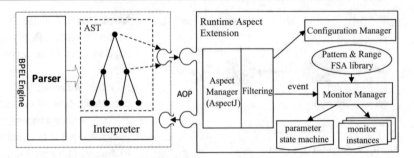

needs to bind more parameters (i.e., a new monitor instance is generated and the old monitor instance is deleted), the reference will also be modified. At runtime, if all monitor instances that the bit vector represents enter the violation states, the specified property is violated.

For the property which has assertion expression, to determine whether it is violated, monitor manager will first check the temporal relation of events. If this step fails, the property is violated. Otherwise, monitor manager will further check the assertion expression. If the assertion does not hold, the property is also violated.

When monitor manager detects that a received message violates the specified property, the default behavior is to block the execution of process instance that produces this message and report the violation. Alternatively, some recovery strategies can be applied timely. This is out of the scope of this chapter and we plan to support this functionality in the future. Interested readers can also be referred to the work done by Simmonds et al. [38].

9.6 Experiments

To evaluate the feasibility and effectiveness of the proposed parametric monitoring approach, we conducted a series of experiments by using car rental application and supply chain application as a case study, in which runtime properties 1–4 were evaluated.

9.6.1 Violation Detection

We begin by first checking whether the violations of specified properties can be detected at runtime.

In the experiment, through analysis of the events in properties 1–4, we used a simulator to generate 50 message traces of length ranging from 10 to 200. Each trace ends up with a termination symbol. These traces were then checked by the runtime monitor. At the same time, we analyzed each trace through manual analysis. By comparing the two results, we conclude that all violations can be correctly checked by proposed monitoring approach.

9.6.2 Performance Evaluation

In the second experiment, we evaluate the performance of the proposed monitoring algorithm. Hallé and Villemaire [26] proposed an online monitoring algorithm to check temporal properties with data parameterization. Here, this algorithm is used as a baseline in the comparison. We implemented it by using javaCC to parse LTL-FO+ expression. When receiving an event at runtime, a module which implements the functionality of Watcher [27], updates the internal state of the formula according to predefined decomposition rules. We compared the processing time per message required by Par-BCL and LTL-FO+ respectively.

By traversing possible execution paths of property 1 and 2, we used a simulator to generate 50 traces of length ranging from 10 to 500 events, respectively. For property 1, each event manipulates 20 cars from a pool of 5000 possible car IDs and 1 park from 250 park IDs. For property 2, each event manipulates 10 cars from a pool of 500 possible car models and 1 billing from 50 billing IDs. The experiments were run on Windows XP with P4 2.53GHZ and 1GB RAM. For each trace, the

Fig. 9.17 Performance evaluation

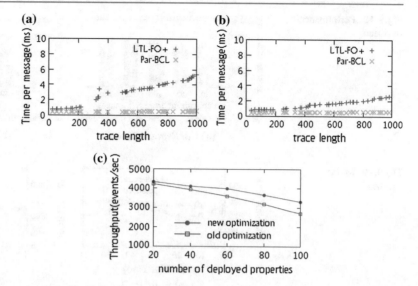

total processing time was recorded. Figure 9.17a, b show the processing time per message of two algorithms for various trace lengths.

We can see that our algorithm to process each message has a lower overhead. The processing time per message is under 0.3 ms using our algorithm, while the time is about 2ms using the algorithm proposed by Hallé and Villemaire [26]. We think the main reason is that in our work, the behavior automata is constructed completely when the property is deployed, while in LTL-FO+ [26], the automata to check the property is computed and generated at runtime. Also, using our monitoring algorithm, the length of event trace does not impact the performance due to the adoption of index mechanism. However, using non-optimized algorithm in LTL-FO+ [26], processing time per message grows, as a large number of "monitor instances" will be generated with the increase of trace length, which makes it time-consuming to locate monitor instance.

As Par-BCL is mainly used for server side monitoring, in the third experiment, we aim to evaluate the throughput (event/second) of the monitor with different number of properties. To show the efficiency of our new index and monitoring algorithm, we compared with our previous work [46], where parameter names are used as key to index

parameter states based on multi-level index tree, and inverted index list is adopted to locate monitor instances.

In this experiment, each property contains 3–8 parameters. By analysis deployed properties, we use a simulator to generate 1000 different traces, which are made up of 50000 events. Each event contains 5 groups of data elements and the domain of each element is 2000. The event stream is loaded into memory before the experiment to make sure that the events are delivered as fast as our monitor can process them. Figure 9.17c shows the throughput with varying number of deployed properties using different monitoring approaches. We can see that the new monitoring algorithm has better throughput. Even for 100 properties, the throughput using new algorithm is about 3300 events per second, while the throughput is about 2750 events per second using old monitoring algorithm. The main reason is that: (1) parameter state location based on multi-level index tree costs more time than the index table adopted in this chapter; (2) although the location of monitor instance based on inverted index list is quick, its maintenance is time-consuming especially when an item needs to be updated. In addition, as expected, the more monitored properties, the lower the throughput.

Fig. 9.18 Performance overhead

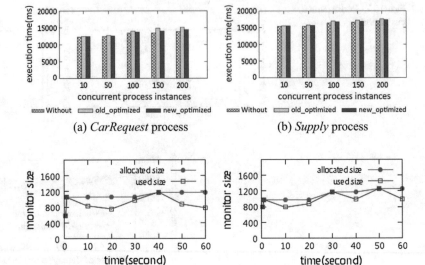

(a) *CarRequest* process   (b) *Supply* process

Fig. 9.19 Memory overhead

(a) property 3   (b) property 4

9.6.3   Overhead Evaluation

The above experiment mainly evaluated the performance of parametric monitoring algorithm (the filtering step is ignored). To evaluate the overall overhead incurred by proposed monitoring approach, we implemented the car rental application and supply chain application using WS-BPEL respectively. The processes were deployed at a Windows server 2003 with P4 2.8 GHZ and 2G RAM. The partner Web services were implemented to simulate the functionality of partner services, which were deployed at Windows XP with P4 2.8 GHZ and 500 MB RAM. These machines were connected by a 100 MB LAN.

For the car rental service, we measured the average execution time for different concurrent process instances. In this experiment, properties 1–2 were deployed. The parameter for generating event is the same with experiment 2. Figure 9.18a shows the average execution time of process CarRequest from the perspective of the client using the round Trip Time (in milliseconds) for varying number of process instances.

The first column in each set shows the execution time of process CarRequest without monitoring. The second column shows the execution time of process CarRequest when using old monitoring approach. The third column shows the ex-

ecution time of process CarRequest when using the monitoring approach proposed in this chapter. Clearly, the monitoring approach proposed in this chapter incurs lower overhead. In the second configuration, the average execution time of Car-Request process is about 8 % higher, while in the third configuration, the average execution time is under 5 %. Obviously, the results are affected by the scalability of the WS-BPEL engine itself. We can see that the execution time grows linearly with the number of concurrent process instances.

We also evaluated the performance overhead using the supply chain application as a case study (see Fig. 9.18b) and gain similar results. The experimental result shows that overhead incurred by monitoring is very low (<5 %) and can be negligible.

In last experiment, we evaluate the memory overhead of our approach. As the number of monitor instances is proportional to the amount of memory used by monitor, this value hence can be used as a measure of memory overhead. In this experiment, we used loadrunner to generate 200 concurrent process instances for the supply chain application. The whole testing time is 1 min. During the process execution, for each monitored property, we recorded the allocated size for monitor instances and the number of live monitor instances. Figure 9.19a, b show the memory overhead of property 3 and property 4 at different time. It shows that at first these two numbers increase quickly, as a large number of monitor instances are generated. Then, the allocated size grows slowly as some monitor instances are destroyed and the free list can be used to create new monitor instances.

9.7 Discussion

As far as we know, the work done by Hallé and Villemaire [26–28] is the most similar to ours. Hallé and Villemaire present LTL-FO+, an extension to traditional Linear Temporal Logic that includes first order quantification over the data inside message, and an online algorithm for runtime monitoring of message contracts with data parameterization. We think Par-BCL has similar expressive power as LTL-FO+, as SPS [20] adopted by Par-BCL can capture most propositional behavior property in practice. Although LTL-FO+ allows unrestricted use of universal and extensional quantifier with message data, while Par-BCL only allows quantification outside the property operator for consideration of efficient monitoring, we find that all properties listed by [26,27] can be expressed in Par-BCL.

Moreover, Par-BCL presents an intuitive way to express such properties, as it is based on SPS [20]. Compared to LTL(which LTL-FO+ is based on), SPS is easier to understand and write. Also, the concept of parameterized event facilitates the specification of data-centric property for Web services composition. For example, for the property "a shopping cart created with an item should contain that item until it is deleted" given in the work [27], the corresponding LTL-FO+ representation is $G(\forall_{(CartAdd/Items/item/ANSI)} i_1 : (\forall_{(CartAdd/CartID)} c_1 : \sigma(c_1, i_1) \text{ W } \varphi(c_1, i_1))))$, where $\sigma(c_1, i_1) = \forall_{(CartGetRsp/CartID)} c_5 : (c_1 = c_5 \rightarrow \exists_{CartGetRsp/items/item/ANSI} i_5 : i_1 = i_5)$ and $\varphi(c_1, i_1) = \forall_{CartRemove/CartID} c_4 : (c_1 = c_4 \rightarrow \exists_{CartRemove/items/item/ANSI} i_4 : i_1 = i_4)$, while using Par-BCL, this property can be directly translated as **forall** ($item, cart$) **after_until** (CartAdd($item,cart$), Remove-Cart($item$, $cart$)) **leadto**(ReqCart($cart$), RspCart($item$, $cart$)).

Currently, Par-BCL has some limitations: (1) it does not support to express some properties with time interval, e.g., the property event E precedes E at least c time units; (2) it does not consider some composite patterns [49], which are the composition of pattern properties using boolean logic operator; (3) Tracecut in Par-BCL now only supports to capture three simple composite events, and it can be extended to specify more complex events using regular expression. For example, * is used to specify that event can occur zero and more times, and + is used to specify that the event can occur one or more times. We plan to support these functionalities in the future work.

9.8 Related Work

Runtime monitoring of system executions against expected properties plays an important role in the deployed system as a mechanism to achieve self-adaptive software and increase system reliability. The problems that we tackle in this chapter have also been studied in different context, more notably in the area of self-adaptive system [21,29,30], object-oriented systems [1,9,12,13,23,33] and Web services [5–7,10,32,39]. In this section, we first discuss our work in the context of engineering self-adaptive systems. Then we will review existing works on runtime monitoring of Web services and discuss some recent efforts on parametric trace monitoring in OO systems. In the following, we position our work with respect to the above-mentioned efforts.

9.8.1 Engineering Self-adaptive System

Service-based systems are often developed by dynamically selecting and assembling a set of loosely coupled Web services. These services may change at runtime in their function or delivered QoS. To deal with such dynamics, systems must be self-adaptive (i.e., optimize performance, recover from runtime failures).

Several frameworks have been proposed for constructing self-adaptive software systems. Some serve as a conceptual reference model. For example, IBM's MAPE-K model [30] describes the different stages of self-adaptation: monitoring, analyzing, planning and executing functions, with the addition of a shared knowledge base. Our work concentrates on the first two stages in this model. Specifically, it supports to specify and analyze data-centric behavior properties. Kramer and Magee [29] propose a three-level reference model for self-management, which includes component control, change management and goal management. Our runtime monitoring framework provides mechanism to monitor process state, and this framework can also be easily extended to enforce some recovery actions. Others adopt an implementation perspective. For example, Oreizy et al. [35] provide an architectural based approach to self-adaptive software, which supports two simultaneous processes: evolution management and adaptation management. Currently, our work focuses on adaptation management, particularly, evaluating and monitoring, and it provides an efficient monitoring approach to detect data-centric property violations.

To gain a better understanding of developing self-adaptive systems, Weyns et al. [43] propose a formal reference model for self-adaptation, which allows engineers to effectively specify, compare, and evaluate alternative design choices for self-adaptive systems. We plan to apply this formal model to self-adaptive service-based systems in the future work.

9.8.2 Runtime Monitoring of Web Services

Baresi et al. [6] propose an assertion-based approach to monitoring WS-BPEL processes, where the monitors are specified as assertions that annotate WS-BPEL codes, which are then automatically translated to monitored processes. They further propose a validation framework [7] that supports static and dynamic analysis of Web services. Properties are expressed in ALBERT language, which introduces formulae, such as until and be-

tween, to specify invariant assertions. Operators forall and exists are mentioned in the language syntax and can be used to fetch and memorize elements.

Simmonds et al. [39] propose a framework for runtime monitoring of Web services conversations as a means to check behavior correctness of the entire system. They use UML 2.0 Sequence Diagram as a specification language to capture properties that depend only on the order and occurrence of system events.

Based on SPS, Li et al. [31] introduce a declarative approach to specifying the interaction behavior of Web services as Interaction Constraints. A tool support for monitoring these constraints is also given. However, they do not support the specification of concurrent and sequential behavior.

Barbon et al. [5] propose an event based monitor language for the specification of both instance and class monitors. The instance monitor can deal with the execution of a single BPEL process instance, while class monitor supports checking the behavior of all the instances of a deployed process.

All above these works cannot support the monitoring of data-centric properties. Mahbub et al. [32] develop a framework for monitoring requirements of WS-BPEL processes. Their approach uses Event Calculus (EC) to specify the requirements that need to be monitored. During the execution, all process events are generated and transformed to events in EC. Run-time checking is interpreted as integrity constraint checking in a temporal deductive database. This approach is less intrusive because the monitoring proceeds in parallel with the execution of the business process and has a lesser impact on performance. It also leads to a less responsiveness in discovering erroneous situations.

To detect inconsistency failure caused by implicit interactions among concurrent process instances, previously, we propose an approach to specify inter-process behavior properties related to shared resources and verify such properties with the aid of a parametric stateful aspect extension to WS-BPEL [45]. This work has two main limitations: firstly, it assumes the shared process data extracted by XPath expression is a single value. However, in practice, the result of data extraction is usually a set of multiple values; secondly, it requires the start event of the property will bind all the parameters in order to simplify the implementation. This work overcomes these limitations.

Also, there are some recent works which aim to validate data related Web services properties through static analysis. For example, Hallé et al. [28] present CTL-FO+, an extension over computation tree logic that include first order quantification on message content, to express data-aware behavior constraints. Gerede and Su [22] propose ABSL (artifact behavior specification language), another extension of CTL that includes a form of first-order quantification to express artifact related behavior constraints.

9.8.3 Parametric Properties Monitoring for OO Systems

There are a very large amount of works which aim to build feasible monitoring solution for object-oriented language and systems [18]. More recently, monitoring parametric properties has received increasing interest as it provides an effective and natural means to describe object oriented system behaviors, where the parameters are typed by classes and bound to object instances at runtime.

Several approaches were introduced to support the monitoring of parametric properties, including Eagle [9], Tracematch [1,2], PQL [33], PTQL [23] and JavaMOP [11–13]. Barringer et al. [9] describe an algorithm for rule based runtime monitoring, where the rules are temporal fixpoint functions that can include data arguments. Program Query Language (PQL) allows programs to express design rules that deal with sequence of related objects. Both static and dynamic tools have been implemented to find solutions to PQL queries. Program Trace Query Language (PTQL) is a language based on SQL-like relational queries over program traces. The current implementation can instrument java program to execute the relational queries on the fly.

To deal with parameter bindings, Tracematch and JavaMOP both use multi-level trees (implemented using hashmaps) for indexing, but they differ in structure of the trees. The tracematch system has a tree for each automaton state, and the leaves of each tree are variable bindings associated with that state. In contrast, JavaMOP has a tree structure for each symbol, and the leaves of the tree hold sets of automaton instance. Although the initial design of JavaMOP does not support partial binding, their further work [11,13] propose a general algorithm for slicing parametric traces. In order to optimize the monitoring, they utilize static knowledge about the property to construct an enable set for each event. A thorough evaluation shows that the adopted technique outperforms other state-of-art techniques optimized for particular logics or properties.

Inspired by JavaMOP, we propose an efficient monitoring approach for data-centric Web services properties. However, the indexing technique and memory leak elimination based on weak reference that JavaMOP adopts are not suitable in our environment. JavaMOP generates one aspect file for each specification and then weaves all aspect files into the original system. Hence, it's possible to use the indexing technique [12] to implement all the mappings of the proposed monitoring algorithm [13], whereas in our implementation, only aspect manger (written in aspectJ) is weaved into the WS-BPEL engine and it cannot construct an indexing tree for each parameterized event declaration. To reduce runtime overhead, our optimization mechanism also makes use of the knowledge about the monitored property. However, different from the enable set for each event [13], we construct a parameterized state machine from the behavior automata and use two-layer indexing mechanisms to locate the monitor instances that need to be updated quickly.

9.9 Conclusion

Runtime monitoring is a key aspect to develop self-adaptive service-based systems. In this chapter, we proposed an efficient online monitoring approach that is non-intrusive, and allows for dynamic analysis of service-based system involving multiple participants. Particularly, a Parametric Behavior Constraint Language for Web service is introduced, which enables specifying various data-centric behavior properties. To reduce runtime overhead incurred by monitoring, we statically analyze the monitored properties to generate parameter state machine from the event pattern automata to optimize monitoring. The experiments show that our work introduces low overhead to the system performance. We plan to conduct more experiments to further check the feasibility of our approach and more real-life case studies to understand its applicability in practice.

In the future work, we aim at supporting self-healing service-based systems. Our online runtime monitoring techniques have constituted a solid basic for dynamic recovery of service based system: the recovery strategies can be enforced as soon as errors are monitored and detected. We plan to extend the Par-BCL language and study corresponding recovery strategies that can recover the systems from various runtime failures. We also plan to investigate techniques that can help to locate the causes of failures by mining the execution logs of the systems.

References

1. C. Allan, P. Avgustinov, A.S. Christensen, L. Hendren, S. Kuzins, et al., Adding trace matching with free variables to AspectJ, in OOPSLA'05, (2005), pp. 345–364
2. P. Avgustinov, J. Tibble, O. de Moor, in Making trace monitors feasible, in *OOPSLA'07* (2007), pp. 589–608
3. P. Avgustinov, O. Lhoták, O. de Moor, J. Tibble, On the semantics of matching trace monitoring patterns, in *Workshop on Runtime Verification (RV'07)* (2007), pp. 45–46
4. I.B. Arpinar, U. Halici, S. Arpinar, A. Dogac, Formalization of workflows and correctness issues in the presence of concurrency, in *Distributed & Parallel Databases*, vol. 7, no. 2, Apr 1999, pp. 199–248
5. F. Barbon, P. Traverso, M. Pistore, M. Trainotti, Runtime monitoring of instances and classes of Web service compositions, in *ICWS'06* (2006), pp. 63–71
6. L. Baresi, S. Guinea, Towards dynamic monitoring of WS-BPEL processes, in *ICSOC'05*, pp. 269–282
7. L. Baresi, S. Guinea, P. Plebani, Policies and aspects for the supervision of BPEL processes, in *CAiSE'07*, pp. 340–354
8. L. Baresi, D. Bianculli, C. Ghezzi, S. Guinea, P. Spoletini, Validation of web service compositions. IET Softw. **1**, 219–232 (2007)

9. H. Barringer, A. Goldberg, K. Havelund, K. Sen, Rule-based runtime verification, in *VMCAI'04* (2004), pp. 44–57
10. C. Beeri, A. Eyal, T. Milo, A. Pilberg, Monitoring business processes with queries, in *VLDB'07* (2007), pp. 603–614
11. F. Chen, P.O. Meredith, D.Y. Jin, G. Rosu, Efficient formalism-independent monitoring of parametric properties, in *ASE'2009* (2009), pp. 384–394
12. F. Chen, G. Rosu, MOP: an efficient and generic runtime verification framework, in *OOPSLA'07* (2007), pp. 569–588
13. F. Chen, G. Rosu, Parametric trace slicing and monitoring, in *TACAS'09* (2009), pp. 246–261
14. W. Chen, J. Wei, G.Q. Wu, X.Q. Qiao, Developing a concurrent service orchestration engine based on event-driven architecture, in *OTM'08* (2008), pp. 675–690
15. B.H. Cheng, R. de Lemos, H. Giese, P. Inverardi, J. Magee, Software engineering for self-adaptive systems: a research roadmap, in *Software Engineering for Self-Adaptive Systems* LNCS 5525 (2009), pp. 1–26
16. A. Charfi, M. Mezini, AO4BPEL: an aspect-oriented extension to BPEL. J. World Wide Web **10**(3), 309–344 (2007)
17. A. Charfi, T. Dinkelaker, M. Mezini, A plug-in architecture for self-adaptive web service compositions, in *ICWS'09* (2009), pp. 35–42
18. N. Delgado, A.Q. Gates, S. Roach, IJA taxonomy and catalog of runtime software-fault monitoring tools. IEEE Trans. Softw. Eng. **30**(12), 859–872 (2004)
19. Y.L. Diao, M. Altinel et al., Path sharing and predicate evaluation for high-performance XML filtering. ACM TODS (2003)
20. M.B. Dwyer, G.S. Avrunin, J.C. Corbett, Patterns in property specifications for finite-state verification, in *ICSE'99* (2004), pp. 411–420
21. D. Garlan, S.W. Cheng, A.C. Huang, B. Schmerl, P. Steenkiste, Rainbow: architecture-based self-adaptation with reusable infrastructure. IEEE Computer **37**, 46–54 (2004)
22. C.E. Gerede, J.W. Su, Specification and verification of artifact behaviors in business process models, in *ICSOC'07* (2007), pp. 181–192
23. S.O. Goldsmith, R. Callahan, A. Aiken, Relational queries over program traces, in *OOPSLA'05* (2005), pp. 385–402
24. P. Greenfield, D. Kuo, S. Nepal, A. Fekete, Consistency of Web services applications, in *Proceedings of 31st VLDB Conference* (2005), pp. 1199–1203
25. K. Gregor, L. John, M. Anurag et al., *1997* (Aspect oriented programming, ECOOP, 1997)
26. S. Hallé, R. Villemaire, Runtime monitoring of message based workflows with data. EDOC **2008**, 63–72 (2008)
27. S. Hallé, R. Villemaire, R., Runtime enforcement of Web service message contracts with data, in *IEEE TCS*
28. S. Hallé, R. Villemaire, O. Cherkaoui, Specifying and validating data-aware temporal Web service properties. IEEE Trans. Software Eng. **35**(5), 669–683

29. J. Kramer, J. Magee, Self-managed systems: an architectural challenge, in *FOSE '07: 2007 Future of Software Engineering* (IEEE Computer Society, 2007), pp. 259–268

30. J.O. Kepbart, D.M. Chess, The vision of autonomic computing. Computer **36**(1), 41–50 (2003)

31. Z. Li, J. Han, Y. Jin, Pattern based specification and validation of Web services interaction properties, in *ICSOC'05* (2005), pp. 73–86

32. K. Mahbub, G. Spanoudakis, A framework for requirements monitoring of service based systems, in *ICSOC'04* (2004), pp. 84–93

33. M. Martin, V.B. Livshits, M.S. Lam, Finding application errors and security flaws using PQL: a program query language, in *OOPSLA'05* (2005), pp. 365–383

34. OASIS. Web services business process execution language (ws-bpel) v2.0 (2007). http://docs.oasis-open.org/wsbpel/2.0/wsbpel-v2.0.pdf

35. P. Oreizy, M.M. Gorlick, R.N. Taylor et al., An architecture-based approach to self-adaptive software. IEEE Intell. Syst. **14**, 54–62 (1999)

36. H. Psaier, L. Juszczyk, F. Skopik, D. Schall, S. Dustdar, Runtime behavior monitoring and self-adaptation in service-oriented systems. SASO **2010**, 164–173 (2010)

37. M. Salehie, L. Tahvildari, Self-adaptive software: landscape and research challenges. ACM Trans. Auton. Adapt. Syst. **4**(2), 1–42 (2009)

38. J. Simmonds, S. Ben-David, M. Chechik, Guided recovery for web service applications, in *FSE'10* (2010), pp. 247–256

39. J. Simmonds, Y. Gan, M. Chechik et al., Runtime Monitoring of Web services conversation. IEEE TSC. **2**(3), 42–57 (2009)

40. J. Siljee, I. Bosloper, J. Nijhuis, D. Hammer, DySOA: making service systems self-adaptive, in *ICSOC'05* (2005), pp. 255–268

41. Smith, L. Rachel et al., Propel: an approach supporting property elucidation, in *Proceedings of the 24th International Conference on Software Engineering* (ACM, 2002)

42. Q.X. Wang, J. Shao, F. Deng et al., An online monitoring approach for Web services requirements. IEEE TSC **2**(4), 338–351 (2009)

43. D. Weyns, S. Malek, J. Andersson, Forms: unifying reference model for formal specification of distributed self-adaptive systems. ACM Trans. Auton. Adapt. Syst. **7**(1) (2012)

44. G.Q. Wu, J. Wei, T. Huang, Flexible pattern monitoring for WS-BPEL through stateful aspect extension, in *ICWS'08*, pp. 577–584

45. G.Q. Wu, J. Wei, C.Y. Ye et al., Detecting data inconsistency failure of composite Web services through parameteric stateful aspect, in *ICWS'10* (2010), pp. 68–75

46. G.Q. Wu, G.Q., Wei, J., Ye, C.Y., et al., Runtime monitoring of data-centric temporal properties for Web services, in *ICWS'11* (2011), pp. 161–170

47. W3C, XML Path Language (XPath) Version 1.0 (1999). http://www.w3.org/TR/xpath/

48. C.Y. Ye, S.C. Cheung, et al., Detection and resolution of atomicty violation in service composition, in *ESEC-FSE'07* (2007), pp. 235–244

49. J. Yu, T.P. Manh, J. Han, Y. Jin, Y. Han, Pattern based property specification and verification for service composition, in *WISE'06* (2006), pp. 156–168

Runtime Detection of the Concurrency Property in Asynchronous Pervasive Computing Environments

10

Abstract

Context-awareness is an essential feature of pervasive applications, and runtime detection of contextual properties is one of the primary approaches to enabling context-awareness. Existing property detection schemes implicitly assume that contexts under detection belong to the same snapshot of time. However, this assumption generally does not hold in pervasive computing environments, which are characterized by the asynchronous coordination among computing entities. We argue that in pervasive computing environments, the concept of time needs to be reexamined. Instead of assuming the availability of global time or synchronous interaction, we rely on logical time in detection of contextual properties. Toward this objective, we first discuss how to model states and temporal evolution of the asynchronous environment. The key notion is the lattice structure among all meaningful observations of the environment. Then we propose the Concurrent contextual Activity Detection in Asynchronous environments (CADA) algorithm, which achieves runtime detection of contextual properties. We show the correctness of CADA based on the lattice of meaningful observations. We also analyze whether CADA accurately detects contextual properties in time. CADA is implemented over MIPA—the open-source context-aware middleware, and extensive experiments are conducted. The evaluation results show that CADA accurately detects contextual properties even when faced with dynamic changes in asynchrony of environment, duration of contextual activities and number of context collecting devices.

Parts of this chapter were reprinted from © [2011] IEEE. Reprinted, with permission, from Yu Huang, Yiling Yang, Jiannong Cao, Xiaoxing Ma, Xianping Tao and Jian Lü. *Runtime detection of the concurrency property in asynchronous pervasive computing environments*. In IEEE Transactions on Parallel and Distributed Systems (TPDS), Volume. 23, No. 4, pp. 744–750. April 2012. DOI:10.1109/TPDS.2011.176.

© Springer Science+Business Media Singapore 2016
H. Mei and J. Lü, *Internetware*, DOI 10.1007/978-981-10-2546-4_10

Keywords

Concurrency property · Context-awareness · Asynchronous environment

10.1   Introduction

Pervasive computing creates environments that embed computation and communication in a way that organically interacts with humans to enhance or ease their daily behavior [1–4]. Contexts refer to the pieces of information that capture the characteristics of computing environments, and context-awareness allows applications to dynamically adapt to pervasive computing environments [5–9].

Context-aware applications need to detect whether contexts bear specified properties, in order to adapt their behavior accordingly. For example, in a smart office [10], the application running on the user's smart phone may specify property C_1: *location of the user is the lecture room and a presentation is going on in the lecture room*. Thus the application can adaptively turn the phone to vibration mode when C_1 is satisfied. Moreover, contexts are often error-prone due to noises [11,12]. Users may specify properties which accurate contexts must obey based on their understanding of mathematical and physical laws. Thus, noisy contexts which violate such properties can be eliminated [9,13,14]. For example, users may specify that C_2: *no one appears in two different places at the same time*, to make sure that the location context is correctly collected.

Detection of contextual properties has been recognized as an important approach to enabling context-awareness in pervasive computing and software engineering communities [9,13–17]. Existing detection schemes implicitly assume that contexts under detection belong to the same snapshot of time. Refer to the examples above. Consider two pieces of location context: *the user is in the lecture room* and *a presentation is going on in the lecture room*. Only with the assumption that these two contextual activities take place at the same time, can the application detect that C_1 is satisfied. We can also see that similar assumption must also hold for C_2.

However, the assumption on the availability of global time or synchronous interaction does not necessarily hold in pervasive computing environments [5,18–22]. Specifically, context collecting devices may not have synchronized clocks and may run at different speeds. They heavily rely on wireless communications, which suffer from finite but arbitrary delay [20,21]. Moreover, due to resource constraints, context collecting devices (usually resource-constrained sensors) often employ periodic or adaptive schemes to schedule the dissemination of context data. Different context update rates also result in asynchrony, which cannot be easily synchronized by existing clock synchronization schemes [19].

We argue that in pervasive computing environments, the concept of time must be reexamined [18,23]. Often, we cannot assume the availability of global time or synchronized coordination in detection of contextual properties. Faced with challenges induced by the asynchrony, the contribution of this paper is three-fold:

- We model states and temporal evolution of the asynchronous environment based on the 'happen-before' relation resulting from message passing and its on-the-fly coding by logical vector clocks [23–25]. One key notion of our model is the lattice structure among all meaningful observations of the environment [26–28].
- We propose the *Concurrent contextual Activity Detection in Asynchronous environments* (CADA) algorithm, which achieves runtime detection of contextual properties. We derive the design of CADA and show its correctness based on the lattice of meaningful observations.
- We analyze whether CADA correctly detects contextual properties in time. We further implement CADA based on MIPA—the open-source context-aware middleware we developed [29], and extensive experiments are

conducted. The evaluation results show that CADA accurately detects contextual properties even when faced with dynamic changes in asynchrony of environment, duration of contextual activities and number of context collecting devices.

The rest of this paper is organized as follows. Section 10.2 discusses our model of environment behavior. Section 10.3 presents the design of CADA. Sections 10.4 and 10.5 present performance analysis and experimental evaluation respectively. Section 10.6 reviews the related work. Finally, Sect. 10.7 concludes the paper with a brief summary and the future work.

10.2 Property Detection for Pervasive Context

In this section, we first describe how we model states and temporal evolution of the pervasive computing environment. Then we discuss the specification of contextual properties. Notations used in our model are listed in Table 10.1.

Detection of contextual properties assumes the availability of an underlying context-aware middleware [13,15,16,30]. The middleware accepts contextual properties specified by the application, detects at runtime whether the properties are satisfied, and informs the application of the results (see more discussions in Sect. 10.5.1). Specifically, in order to detect contextual properties, a collection of *non-checker processes* $P^{(1)}$, $P^{(2)}$, ..., $P^{(n)}$ are deployed to monitor specific regions of the environment. Examples of non-checker processes are sensor agents manipulating physical sensors. One

checker process P_{che} collects context information from non-checker processes, and achieves runtime detection of contextual properties. P_{che} is usually a third-party service deployed on the middleware.

10.2.1 Asynchronous Message Passing and Logical Time

We model all processes involved in the detection of contextual properties as a loosely-coupled message passing system, without any global clock or shared memory. Communications suffer from finite but arbitrary delay. Dissemination of context data may be delayed due to resource constraints.

We assume that no messages are lost, altered or spuriously introduced. Though we do not assume that the underlying communication channel is FIFO, we use message sequence numbers to ensure that P_{che} receives messages from each non-checker process in FIFO manner [31–33].

We re-interpret the notion of time based on the classical Lamport's definition of the *happen-before* relation (denoted by '$\rightarrow$') resulting from message causality [23], and its "on-the-fly" coding given by Mattern and Fidge's vector clocks [24,25].

10.2.2 Consistent Global State (CGS) and the Lattice Structure Among CGSs

In a run of the system, each $P^{(k)}$ generates its trace, which consists of a series of *local states* connected by *contextual events*:

Table 10.1 Notations in our model of environment behavior

Notation	Explanation
n	Number of non-checker processes
$P^{(k)}/P_{che}$	Non-checker/checker process ($1 \leq k \leq n$)
$s_i^{(k)}, e_i^{(k)}$	Local state and contextual event
$\mathcal{G}$	Global state (either consistent or inconsistent)
$\mathcal{C}, \mathcal{C}[k]$	CGS, kth constituent local state
$\phi^{(k)}$	Local predicate on $P^{(k)}$
ϕ	CGS predicate, which is the conjunction of $\phi^{(1)}, \phi^{(2)}, \ldots, \phi^{(n)}$

"$s_0^{(k)}, e_0^{(k)}, s_1^{(k)}, e_1^{(k)}, s_2^{(k)}, e_2^{(k)} \ldots$". A *global state*

$$\mathcal{G} = (s^{(1)}, s^{(2)}, \ldots, s^{(n)})$$

is defined as a vector of local states from each $P^{(k)}$.

A key notion in describing state of the environment is the *Consistent Global State* (CGS). If the constituent local states of a global state $\mathcal{C}$ are pairwise concurrent, $\mathcal{C}$ is a CGS, i.e.,

$$\mathcal{C} = (s^{(1)}, s^{(2)}, \ldots, s^{(n)}), \forall i, j : i \neq j :: \neg(s^{(i)} \rightarrow s^{(j)})$$

The CGS denotes a meaningful observation of a distributed and asynchronous environment [26,28].

It is intuitive to define the *precede* (denoted by '$\prec$') relation between two CGSs: $\mathcal{C} \prec \mathcal{C}'$ if $\mathcal{C}'$ is obtained via advancing $\mathcal{C}$ by exactly one local state on one non-checker process:

$$\mathcal{C} \prec \mathcal{C}' \equiv \exists k, \text{ such that } \mathcal{C}'[k] \text{ is the first local state after}$$
$$\mathcal{C}[k] \text{ on } P^{(k)}, \forall l : 1 \leq l \neq k \leq n :: \mathcal{C}[l] = \mathcal{C}'[l]$$

The *lead-to* relation (denoted by '$\rightsquigarrow$') between two CGSs is defined as the transitive closure of '$\prec$', i.e.,

$$\mathcal{C} \rightsquigarrow \mathcal{C}' \equiv \mathcal{C} \prec \mathcal{C}' \text{ or } \exists \mathcal{C}'', \mathcal{C} \rightsquigarrow \mathcal{C}'' \rightsquigarrow \mathcal{C}'$$

The run of the system can be viewed as the advancement between CGSs with the '$\prec$' relation. The set of all CGSs with the '$\rightsquigarrow$' relation define a lattice [27,28,34], as shown in Fig. 10.1. The lattice structure among all CGSs serves as a key notion in the specification and detection of contextual properties in this work.

10.2.3   Specification of Contextual Properties

Contextual properties are specified via logical predicates defined over states of the environment. Specifically,

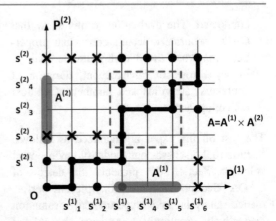

Fig. 10.1 The lattice among CGSs

- *Local predicates* are specified over local states on non-checker processes. The value of a local predicate only depends on information local to the corresponding non-checker process.
- *CGS predicates* are specified over CGSs to delineate global properties of the environment. CGS predicates consist of local predicates (defined on constituent local states) connected by binary logic connectors $\wedge, \vee$ and $\Rightarrow$ (imply).
- *Predicate transformers* $Def(\cdot)$ and $Pos(\cdot)$ are applied over CGS predicates [35,36]. The predicate transformers are necessary because from local states observed by non-checker processes, we cannot decide how the computation actually proceeds. We can only know that the computation proceeds along one of the multiple possible paths (sequences of CGSs connected by '$\prec$') in the lattice. Predicate transformers make CGS predicate meaningful over multiple possible paths of computations.

In the rest of this work, we focus on how to detect conjunctive predicate $Def(\phi)$, where $\phi = \phi^{(1)} \wedge \phi^{(2)} \wedge \cdots \wedge \phi^{(n)}$. We adopt predicate transformer $Def(\cdot)$ because the context data is intrinsically noisy and error-prone in pervasive computing environments. We use $Def(\cdot)$ to ensure that the activity of interest to the context-aware application actually happened. We focus on conjunctive predicates because other types of CGS predicates can be easily detected if we can detect conjunctive predicates [31,32].

In the next section, we discuss how to detect $Def(\phi)$ in asynchronous pervasive computing environments.

10.3   Concurrent Activity Detection in Asynchronous Pervasive Computing Environments

In this section, we study how to detect conjunctive predicate $Def(\phi)$, as specified in Sect. 10.2.3. We first build the connection between $Def(\phi)$ and concurrent contextual activities. Then we derive design of the *Concurrent contextual Activity Detection in Asynchronous environments* (CADA) algorithm.

10.3.1 $Def(\phi)$ and Concurrent Contextual Activities

We first interpret the meaning of $Def(\phi)$ over the lattice of CGSs. By *contextual activity* on $P^{(k)}$, we mean the longest period (consisting of consecutive local states) in which the local predicate of concern is true, i.e.,

$$A^{(k)} \equiv [s_{i_1}^{(k)}, s_{i_2}^{(k)}, \ldots, s_{i_l}^{(k)}], \forall s \in A^{(k)}, \phi^{(k)} \text{ holds on } s$$

To ease the discussions below, we define four local states and two contextual events concerning $A^{(k)}$. Their meanings are intuitive, as shown in Fig. 10.2. $A^{(k)}.first$ defines the first local state in $A^{(k)}$. $A^{(k)}.prev$ denotes the last local state before $A^{(k)}$. The contextual event connecting $A^{(k)}.prev$ and $A^{(k)}.first$ is denoted as $A^{(k)} \uparrow$. The definitions of $A^{(k)}.prev$, $A^{(k)}.first$ and $A^{(k)} \uparrow$ are

duals of $A^{(k)}.next$, $A^{(k)}.last$ and $A^{(k)} \downarrow$ respectively.

On a given CGS $\mathscr{C}$, if conjunctive predicate ϕ holds, $\phi^{(k)}$ is true on every local state $\mathscr{C}[k]$, i.e., $\mathscr{C}[k]$ is within some activity $A^{(k)}$. Thus, $\mathscr{C}$ satisfying ϕ is inside the n-dimensional rectangle $A = A^{(1)} \times A^{(2)} \times \cdots \times A^{(n)}$ in the lattice. Furthermore, predicate $Def(\phi)$ means that, no matter how the computation proceeds, it always passes at least one CGS inside A.

Discussions above explain the meaning of $Def(\phi)$. However, they do not imply how $Def(\phi)$ can be efficiently detected at runtime. This motivates us to interpret $Def(\phi)$ from another perspective. Specifically, we can also view an activity as an interval on the time axis. Intuitively, predicate $Def(\phi) = true$ means that no matter how the computation proceeds, the corresponding intervals always overlap.

The overlapping can be easily determined using the following criteria [32]:

$$\forall i, j : 1 \leq i \neq j \leq n :: A^{(i)} \uparrow \rightarrow A^{(j)} \downarrow \tag{10.1}$$

As an example, the concurrency between two activities is shown in Fig. 10.3.

From the discussions above, we derive the following theorem

Theorem 10.1 $Def(\phi)$ *is true, if and only if the contextual activities satisfy Eq. (10.1).*

Theorem 10.1 explains the main rationale behind the CADA algorithm. CADA actually detects the concurrency among contextual activities. Theorem 10.1 ensures that CADA equivalently detects $Def(\phi)$. We prove Theorem 10.1 by proving the following Lemmas 10.2 and 10.4. Rationale of the

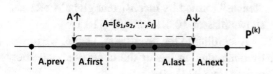

Fig. 10.2 States and events concerning an activity

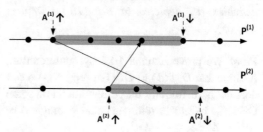

Fig. 10.3 Concurrency between two intervals

proof is explained via the example in Fig. 10.1. In this example, $A^{(1)} = [s_3^{(1)}, s_4^{(1)}, s_5^{(1)}]$. $A^{(2)} = [s_2^{(2)}, s_3^{(2)}, s_4^{(2)}]$. $A = A^{(1)} \times A^{(2)}$ is highlighted by the dotted-line square.

10.3.1.1 Concurrency Among Activities Implies $Def(\phi)$

Given that Eq. (10.1) holds, in order to prove $Def(\phi)$, we need to show that the computation will definitely go through A. In our example, we instantiate Eq. (10.1) as: $s_2^{(1)} \to s_5^{(2)} \wedge s_1^{(2)} \to s_6^{(1)}$.

Since $\forall k < 2, s_k^{(1)} \to s_2^{(1)} \to s_5^{(2)}$, we have that:

$$\forall 0 \le k \le 2, (s_k^{(1)}, s_5^{(2)}) \text{ is not a CGS}$$

This means that none of the global states in the horizontal line segment between global states $(s_0^{(1)}, s_5^{(2)})$ and $(s_2^{(1)}, s_5^{(2)})$ is a CGS, as denoted by the upper horizontal line of crosses in Fig. 10.1.

Similarly, since $s_{21} \to s_{16}$, we have that:

$$\forall 0 \le k \le 1, (s_6^{(1)}, s_k^{(2)}) \text{ is not a CGS}$$

This means that none of the global states in the vertical line segment between global states $(s_6^{(1)}, s_0^{(2)})$ and $(s_6^{(1)}, s_1^{(2)})$ is a CGS, as denoted by the vertical line formed by crosses in Fig. 10.1.

Since the computation can only proceed through a sequence of CGSs connected by '$\prec$', we know that the computation can never go across the lines of inconsistent global states. Thus, as shown in Fig. 10.1, it is obvious that the computation will definitely pass the square of A, as forced by the "fences" formed of inconsistent global states. According to the discussions above, we derive the following lemma:

Lemma 10.2 *Concurrency among contextual activities (as depicted in Eq. (10.1)) implies $Def(\phi)$.*

Proof We prove Lemma 10.2 by contradiction. Assume that $Def(\phi) = Def(\phi_1 \wedge \phi_2 \wedge \cdots \wedge \phi_n)$ does not hold. Initially, the computation is at some CGS $\mathscr{C}_{ini}$ before the n-dimensional rectangle $A = A^{(1)} \times A^{(2)} \times \cdots \times A^{(n)}$, i.e.,

$$\forall i, \mathscr{C}_{ini}[i] \to A^{(i)}.first$$

The computation will eventually reach some CGS $\mathscr{C}_{evt}$ after A, i.e.,

$$\forall i, A^{(i)}.last \to \mathscr{C}_{evt}[i]$$

Since $Def(\phi)$ does not hold, we have that,

$$\exists \mathscr{S} : \forall \mathscr{C} \in \mathscr{S}, \mathscr{C} \notin A.$$

Here $\mathscr{S}$ is a sequence of CGSs connected by '$\prec$'. The first and last CGSs in $\mathscr{S}$ are $\mathscr{C}_{ini}$ and $\mathscr{C}_{evt}$ respectively.

As the computation proceeds over $\mathscr{S}$, assume that the computation has passed through $A^{(i)}$, and is still before $A^{(j)}$, i.e. the computation has arrived at some CGS $\mathscr{C}$ such that

$$\mathscr{C}[j] = A^{(j)}.prev \text{ or } \mathscr{C}[j] \to A^{(j)}.prev$$
$$A^{(i)}.next = \mathscr{C}[i] \text{ or } A^{(i)}.next \to \mathscr{C}[i] \tag{10.2}$$

According to Eq. (10.1), we have that:

$$A^{(j)}.prev \to A^{(i)}.next \tag{10.3}$$

According to Eqs. (10.2) and (10.3), we have that

$$\mathscr{C}[j] \to \mathscr{C}[i]$$

This contradicts with the fact that $\mathscr{C}$ is a CGS.

Thus, if there exists some non-checker process $P^{(i)}$ such that $P^{(i)}$ has not entered $A^{(i)}$ ($\mathscr{C}[i] = A^{(i)}.prev$ or $\mathscr{C}[i] \to A^{(i)}.prev$), none of other non-checker processes $P^{(j)}$ can go beyond $A^{(j)}$. This contradicts with that the computation does not intersect with A and eventually arrives at $\mathscr{C}_{evt}$.

Note that the discussion above is the formal description of the fact that the computation must go across A as forced by the horizontal/vertical "fences" formed by inconsistent global states, as shown in Sect. 10.3.1.1 and Fig. 10.1.

According to the discussions above, we prove by contradiction that if the contextual activities satisfy Eq. (10.1), $Def(\phi)$ holds.

10.3.1.2   Early Detection

From Fig. 10.1, we can see that if $s_2^{(1)} \to s_2^{(2)}$, we have that none of the global states between $(s_2^{(1)}, s_2^{(2)})$ and $(s_0^{(1)}, s_2^{(2)})$ is a CGS, as shown by the lower horizontal line segment of crosses in Fig. 10.1. In this case, the computation is restricted to a narrower region. Obviously, $Def(\phi)$ still holds. This more stringent requirement corresponds to the following equation:

$$A^{(1)} \uparrow \to A^{(2)} \uparrow \wedge A^{(2)} \uparrow \to A^{(1)} \downarrow \quad (10.4)$$

Given that Eq. (10.1) already guarantees $Def(\phi)$, why should we propose this more stringent requirement? This can be explained by Fig. 10.4. If Eq. (10.4) holds, the concurrency among activities can be decided with only 3 timestamps of $A^{(1)} \uparrow$, $A^{(2)} \uparrow$ and $A^{(1)} \downarrow$. Since the concurrency can be decided without $A^{(2)} \downarrow$, CADA has chances to detect concurrency earlier. We call this case *early detection*.

In the general case, Eq. (10.4) is extended to:

$$\exists i :: (\forall j : j \neq i :: A^{(j)} \uparrow \to A^{(i)} \uparrow \wedge$$
$$A^{(i)} \uparrow \to A^{(i)} \downarrow) \quad (10.5)$$

Based on the discussions above, we have the following corollary:

Corollary 10.3 *If there exists one activity which satisfies Eq. (10.5) while other activities satisfy Eq. (10.1), $Def(\phi)$ holds.*

The proof of Corollary 10.3 is trivial since the requirement of early detection is more stringent than Eq. (10.1).

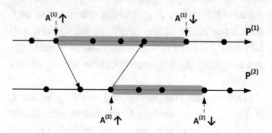

Fig. 10.4 Early detection

Discussions in Sects. 10.3.1.1 and 10.3.1.2 motivate the design of CADA, as presented in detail in Sect. 10.3.2.

10.3.1.3 $Def(\phi)$ Implies Concurrency Among Activities

Given that $Def(\phi)$ holds, we need to prove that no matter how the computation proceeds, Eq. (10.1) holds. We show this by contradiction. If Eq. (10.1) does not hold, we have that:

$$\exists i, j, \neg(A^{(i)}.prev \to A^{(j)}.next)$$

In our example, this could be instantiated as:

$$\neg(s_2^{(1)} \to s_5^{(2)}) \; or \; \neg(s_1^{(2)} \to s_6^{(1)})$$

We focus on the first case, and arguments for the latter case are similar. Given that $\neg(s_2^{(1)} \to s_5^{(2)})$, we need to consider two cases:

- If $s_5^{(2)} \to s_2^{(1)}$, we have that the ending of $A^{(2)}$ happens before the beginning of $A^{(1)}$. Thus it is certain that $A^{(1)}$ and $A^{(2)}$ do not overlap, which contradicts with that $Def(\phi)$ holds.
- If $\neg(s_5^{(2)} \to s_2^{(1)})$, we have that $(s_2^{(1)}, s_5^{(2)})$ is a CGS. Thus, the computation can possibly pass $(s_2^{(1)}, s_5^{(2)})$. Once the computation arrives at $(s_2^{(1)}, s_5^{(2)})$, it will definitely circumvent A. This also contradicts with that $Def(\phi)$ holds.

According to the discussions above, we have the following lemma:

Lemma 10.4 *$Def(\phi)$ implies Eq. (10.1).*

Proof We also prove Lemma 10.4 by contradiction. Assume that Eq. (10.1) does not hold, i.e.,

$$\exists p, q, \neg(A^{(p)}.prev \to A^{(q)}.next)$$

which is equivalent to two cases: (i) $A^{(q)}.next \to A^{(p)}.prev$; (ii) $A^{(p)}.prev \|$ $A^{(q)}.next$.

Case (i) means that the ending of $A^{(q)}$ happens before the beginning of $A^{(p)}$. Obviously this contradicts with the fact that $Def(\phi)$ holds. So we focus on Case (ii) below. We need to prove that there exists some CGS $\mathscr{C}$ such that

$$\mathscr{C}[p] = A^{(p)}.prev, \mathscr{C}[q] = A^{(q)}.next$$

i.e., for any other non-checker process $P^{(i)}(1 \le i \le n, i \ne p, i \ne q)$, we need to find local state s on $P^{(i)}$, such that $(s||A^{(p)}.prev) \wedge (s||A^{(q)}.next)$.

For the initial local state $s_0^{(i)}$, we have that $\neg(A^{(p)}.prev \to s_0^{(i)})$ because according to our system model, nothing happens before the initial state. Furthermore,

- if $\neg(s_0^{(i)} \to A^{(p)}.prev)$, we have already found $s_0^{(i)}$ such that $s_0^{(i)}||A^{(p)}.prev$.
- otherwise if $s_0^{(i)} \to A^{(p)}.prev$, we consider the next local state $s_1^{(i)}$. Apply the arguments for $s_0^{(i)}$ again, we have that $s_1^{(i)} \to A^{(p)}.prev$ must hold.

According to the discussions above, we have that if none of local states on $P^{(i)}$ is concurrent with $A^{(p)}.prev$, there are infinite local states which happen-before $A^{(p)}.prev$. This contradicts with the axiom of finite causes [27]. Thus we prove that there must exist some local state on $P^{(i)}$ which is concurrent with $A^{(p)}.prev$. Similarly, we can prove that there must exist some local state on $P^{(i)}$ which is concurrent with $A^{(q)}.next$. Thus, we prove that there exists CGS $\mathscr{C}$ such that:

$$\mathscr{C}[p] = A^{(p)}.prev, \mathscr{C}[q] = A^{(q)}.next$$

For the computation which passes $\mathscr{C}$, since $\mathscr{C}[p] = A^{(p)}.prev$, we have that the computation has not entered A yet. Meanwhile, since $\mathscr{C}[q] = A^{(q)}.next$, we have that the computation will never pass A in the future. This leads to contradiction with that $Def(\phi)$ holds.

According to the discussions above, we prove by contradiction that if $Def(\phi)$ holds, the contextual activities satisfy Eq. (10.1).

10.3.2   Design of the CADA Algorithm

CADA runs on both the non-checker process side and the checker process side. Non-checker

processes send *control messages* among each other, in order to build the happen-before relation required by Eqs. (10.1) and (10.5). The checker process collects logical timestamps in *checking messages* from non-checker processes and detects specified contextual properties.

10.3.2.1   CADA on the Non-checker Process Side

Non-checker processes are in charge of collecting contextual events and checking local predicates. They also proactively send control messages among each other upon the local predicate becomes true. This builds the happen-before relation required in Eqs. (10.1) and (10.5).

We denote the vector clock timestamps of $A^{(k)} \uparrow$ and $A^{(k)} \downarrow$ by lo and hi respectively. The initial timestamps of the interval $A^{(k)}$ is $[null, null]$. In order to possibly achieve early detection, logical timestamps $[lo, null]$ and $[null, hi]$ are sent right after contextual events $A^{(k)} \uparrow$ and $A^{(k)} \downarrow$ respectively. The $flag\_msg\_act$ is used to reduce redundant checking messages. Pseudo codes of the CADA algorithm on the non-checker process side are listed in Algorithm 3.

10.3.2.2   CADA on the Checker Process Side

Design of CADA on P_{che} is derived from the discussions in Sect. 10.3.1. Specifically, P_{che} maintains a queue of timestamps $Que^{(k)}$ for each $P^{(k)}$. Upon receiving a timestamp, P_{che} first checks whether this timestamp should trigger comparison of timestamps. When this timestamp is appended in some non-empty queue, non comparison is triggered. Otherwise, P_{che} checks whether the logical timestamps at the heads of the queues satisfy Eq. (10.1) or (10.5). Timestamps which cannot establish the required relations are iteratively deleted.

During the comparing and deleting process, if Eq. (10.1) is satisfied, we detect concurrent activities. Moreover, we use Num_{null} to denote the number of queues which has $[lo, null]$ as its head element. When $Num_{null} = 1$, i.e., exactly one $Que^{(k)}$ has $[lo, null]$ as its head element,

Algorithm 3 $1:$ **Upon** $A^{(k)} \uparrow$
 $2:$ $send\_ctl\_msg(VC^{(k)})$ to each $P^{(i)}(i \neq k)$;
 $3:$ $lo := VC^{(k)}$;
 $4:$ **if** $flag\_msg\_act = true$ **then**
 $5:$ $send\_chk\_msg([lo, null]^{(k)})$ to P_{che};
 $6:$ **else**
 $7:$ store $[lo, null]^{(k)}$ in $MsgQue^{(k)}$; /* queue of messages to be sent */
 $8:$ **end if**
 $9:$ $++VC^{(k)}[k]$;

 $10:$ **Upon** $A^{(k)} \downarrow$
 $11:$ $hi := VC^{(k)}$;
 $12:$ **if** $flag\_msg\_act = true$ **then**
 $13:$ **if** $MsgQue^{(k)} \neq empty$ **then**
 $14:$ restore $[lo, hi]$;
 $15:$ $send\_chk\_msg([lo, hi])$ to P_{che};
 $16:$ clear $MsgQue^{(k)}$;
 $17:$ $flag\_msg\_act := false$;
 $18:$ **else**
 $19:$ $send\_chk\_msg([null, hi])$ to P_{che};
 $20:$ $flag\_msg\_act := false$;
 $21:$ **end if**
 $22:$ **else**
 $23:$ clear $MsgQue^{(k)}$;
 $24:$ **end if**
 $25:$
 $26:$ **Upon** $receive\_ctl\_msg(VC^{(j)})$
 $27:$ **for** $i = 1$ **to** n **do**
 $28:$ $VC^{(k)}[i] := max\{VC^{(k)}[i], VC^{(j)}[i]\}$;
 $29:$ **end for**
 $30:$ $flag\_msg\_act := true$;

this timestamp has chances to enable early detection. P_{che} checks whether this timestamp satisfies Eq. (10.5) while other activities satisfy Eq. (10.1). If these two requirements are satisfied, P_{che} achieves early detection. Pseudo codes of the CADA algorithm on P_{che} are listed in Algorithms 4, 5 and 6.

10.3.3 Discussions

On P_{che}, the number of comparisons is $O(n^2 p)$, where n is the number of queues each of length at most p. On each $P^{(k)}$, the number of message

activities is $O(p)$. The space complexity is $O(n)$, for recording the vector clock.

Note that the message complexity of CADA is mainly due to building the happen-before relation between beginnings and endings of contextual activities when there is no global clock. Existing work may impose less message complexity. However, they cannot work in asynchronous pervasive computing environments.

In asynchronous environments, it is possible that CADA does not correctly detect the concurrency among contextual activities. This problem is discussed in detail in the following Sect. 10.4.

Algorithm 4   *1:* **Upon** *receiving a checking message;*
2: *flag_trigger_checking :=*
      whether_trigger_checking(); / Algorithm 3 */*
3: **if** *flag_trigger_checking = true* **then**
4:   *do_checking(); /* Algorithm 4 */*
5: **end if**

Algorithm 5   *1:* **Upon** *receive_ctl_msg(Msg) from $P^{(k)}$*
2: *result := false;*
3: **if** *Msg = [lo, hi]* **then**
4:   *$Que^{(k)}$.enqueue([lo, hi]);*
5:   **if** *head($Que^{(k)}$) = [lo, hi]* **then**
6:   *result := true;*
7:   **end if**
8: **else if** *Msg = [lo, null]* **then**
9:   *$Que^{(k)}$.enqueue([lo, null]);*
10:   **if** *head($Que^{(k)}$) = [lo, null]* **then**
11:   *result := true;*
12:   **end if**
13: **else if** *Msg = [null, hi]* **then**
14:   *combine [null, hi] with [lo, null] at the end of $Que^{(k)}$, and obtain [lo, hi];*
15:   *replace [lo, null] with [lo, hi] in $Que^{(k)}$;*
16:   **if** *head($Que^{(k)}$) = [lo, hi]* **then**
17:   *result := true;*
18:   **end if**
19: **end if**
20: **Return** *result;*

Algorithm 6   *1:* **if** *$Msg = [lo, null]^{(k)}$* **then**
2:   **for** *i = 1 to n, i ≠ k* **do**
3:   **while** *head($Que^{(i)}$).hi ≠ null and ¬(head($Que^{(k)}$).lo → head($Que^{(i)}$).hi)*
         do
4:   *delete_head($Que^{(i)}$);*
5:   **end while**
6:   **end for**
7: **else if** *$Msg = [null, hi]^{(k)}$ or $Msg = [lo, hi]^{(k)}$* **then**
8:   *changed := {k};*
9:   **while** *changed ≠ φ* **do**
10:   *newchanged := φ;*
11:   **for all** *i ∈ changed, 1 ≤ j ≤ n* **do**
12:   **if** *head($Que^{(i)}$).hi ≠ null and ¬(head($Que^{(j)}$).lo → head($Que^{(i)}$).hi)*
         then
13:   *newchanged := newchanged ∪ {i};*
14:   **end if**
15:   **if** *head($Que^{(j)}$).hi ≠ null and ¬(head($Que^{(i)}$).lo → head($Que^{(j)}$).hi)*
         then
16:   *newchanged := newchanged ∪ {j};*
17:   **end if**

10.4   Performance Analysis

In the previous section, we present the design of CADA. However, does CADA work well in pervasive computing environments? Specifically, can CADA achieve accurate detection of concurrent activities? What are the odds of CADA achieving early detection? We investigate these issues in this section. We first analyze what factors make CADA falsely detect contextual activities. Then we quantify the probabilities of correct detection and early detection of sensed activities. Finally, we discuss the discrepancy between sensed and physical activities.

10.4.1 The Causes of Faults

To analyze the causes of faults, we investigate in detail the process of contextual property detection. In different phases of the detection process, the notion of contextual activity has different meanings. Initially, activities of interest to the context-aware application take place in the physical environment. We denote them as '*physical activities*'. Then, the physical activities are sensed by non-checker processes. We denote them as '*sensed activities*' (i.e. $A^{(k)}$ in Sect. 10.3). Finally, logical timestamps of sensed activities are sent to the checker process, which detects at runtime whether the contextual properties are satisfied.

In the ideal case, the application is accurately aware of the physical activities in time, and achieves accurate detection of contextual properties. However, in reality, there may be faults in different phases of the property detection process. We investigate each phase in detail. Specifically, we investigate:

- whether P_{che} correctly detects the concurrency among sensed activities (Sect. 10.4.2).
- whether the sensed activity accurately depicts the physical activity (Sect. 10.4.3).

10.4.2 Concurrency Among Sensed Activities

There does not exist an algorithm which always achieves correct detection of concurrency among sensed activities in asynchronous environments [37,38]. Thus we study the probability of correct detection, as well as the probability of early detection in the following Sects. 10.4.2.1 and 10.4.2.2. In the analysis of this section, we mainly focus on the case of two activities. Detailed investigation of

the more general case is left to the experimental evaluation.

10.4.2.1 Probability of Correct Detection

To quantify the probability of correct detection, we first analyze when and how CADA falsely detects the concurrency among sensed activities. Observe that CADA is never false positive, i.e., when CADA detects concurrency among sensed activities, the intervals definitely overlap. This is because CADA detects concurrency only when it guarantees that Eq. (10.1) is satisfied.

However, CADA could be false negative, i.e., when CADA does not detect the concurrency, it is possible that the sensed activities are actually concurrent. For example, intervals of two sensed activities do overlap as shown in Fig. 10.5, but if $P^{(1)}$ receives the message from $P^{(2)}$ (denoted by $msg^{(2)}$) later than $A^{(1)} \uparrow$, P_{che} will not detect that $A^{(1)}$ and $A^{(2)}$ are concurrent.

CADA correctly detects overlapping intervals if and only if $msg^{(1)}$ and $msg^{(2)}$ are received in time. Formally, the probability of correct detection is:

$$P_{corr} = P(x, y, z) = Pr\{msg^{(1)}.delay \leq y + z\}$$
$$Pr\{msg^{(2)}.delay \leq x - z\}$$

Here we define random variables X, Y and Z, whose values are x, y and z respectively, as shown in Fig. 10.5. The expected probability of correct detection is:

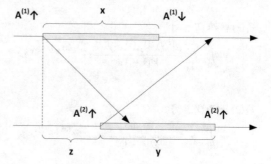

Fig. 10.5 False negative detection of concurrency between sensed activities

$$E[P_{corr}] = E[P(x, y, z)] = \int_0^\infty \{ \int_0^\infty [\int_0^x P(x, y, z)$$
$$dF_3(z)] dF_2(y) \} dF_1(x)$$
$$(10.6)$$

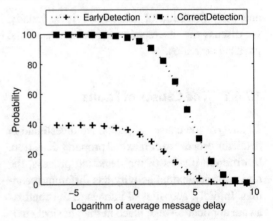

Fig. 10.6 Probabilities of sensed activity detection

Here, the probability functions $F_1(x) = Pr\{X \leq x\}$, $F_2(y) = \{Y \leq y\}$, $F_3(z) = Pr\{Z \leq z\}$.

To further investigate $E[P_{corr}]$, we model intervals on $P^{(i)}$ based on the queuing theory [39,40]. Specifically, a queue of intervals with Poisson arrival rate $\lambda^{(i)}$ is adopted. The duration of intervals follows the exponential distribution of rate $\mu^{(i)} (\frac{\lambda^{(i)}}{\mu^{(i)}} \leq 1)$. We also need to model the message delay, which greatly affects $E[P_{corr}]$. The distribution of message delay is affected by implementation of the underlying layers of network (e.g., the MAC or routing layer), and greatly varies in different scenarios. Although it is doubted whether there exists a universal model of message delay, the exponential distribution is widely used and also evaluated by both simulations and experiments [41]. In our analysis, we adopt the exponential distribution to model message delay. Note that our analysis is also applicable when message delay follows other types of distributions. With the models we adopt, the probability of correct detection is:

$$P_{corr} = P(x, y, z) = (1 - e^{-\lambda(y+z)})(1 - e^{-\lambda(x-z)})$$

According to [40], the probability function of the interval length is:

$$F_1(x) = Pr\{X \leq x\}$$
$$= \int_0^x \sum_{k=1}^\infty \frac{\mu^{(1)}(\lambda^{(1)}\mu^{(1)}x^2)^{k-1}}{k!(k-1)!} e^{-(\lambda^{(1)}+\mu^{(1)})x} dx$$

$$F_2(y) = Pr\{Y \leq y\}$$
$$= \int_0^y \sum_{k=1}^\infty \frac{\mu^{(2)}(\lambda^{(2)}\mu^{(2)}y^2)^{k-1}}{k!(k-1)!} e^{-(\lambda^{(2)}+\mu^{(2)})y} dy$$

Since the arrival of $A^{(2)}$ follows the Poisson process, we have that, for $z > 0$:

$$F_3(z) = Pr\{Z \leq z\} = 1 - e^{-\lambda^{(2)}z}$$

To illustrate performance of CADA in terms of the probability of correct detection ($E[P_{corr}]$) of sensed activities, we change the average message delay and obtain the numerical results, as shown in Fig. 10.6. We choose to vary the average message delay because it has the most significant impact on $E[P_{corr}]$. According to the numerical results, we find that $E[P_{corr}]$ remains near 100% when the message delay is not quite long. As the average message delay significantly increases, $E[P_{corr}]$ decreases quite slowly (note that the x-axis is the logarithm of message delay). This ensures that CADA achieves satisfying probability of correct detection of sensed activities in various pervasive computing environments with different message delay.

10.4.2.2   Probability of Early Detection

In context-aware applications, it is quite desirable, if not a must, to detect concurrent activities as early as possible. However, this issue was not sufficiently addressed in the existing work, e.g., in debugging of distributed programs [31,32,35]. In existing schemes, P_{che} only receives timestamps of a complete interval (with both lo and hi). Thus P_{che} detects concurrent activities no earlier than the latest hi among all the intervals [32]. CADA detects concurrent activities in a finer granularity. The timestamp of lo or hi is sent right after the $\uparrow$ or $\downarrow$ transitions of $A^{(i)}$. Thus, CADA has chances to detect concurrency earlier.

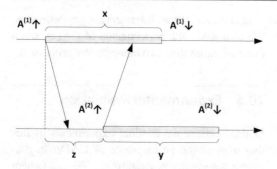

Fig. 10.7 CADA achieving early detection

We first discuss when and how CADA achieves early detection. As shown in Fig. 10.7, if concurrent activities are checked only when both lo and hi of the intervals are collected, we detect concurrent activities after $A^{(2)} \downarrow$. However, we can still detect that $A^{(1)}$ and $A^{(2)}$ overlap without the timestamp of $A^{(2)} \downarrow$. Observe that if we guarantee:

$$(A^{(1)}.lo \to A^{(2)}.lo) \wedge (A^{(2)}.lo \to A^{(1)}.hi)$$
$$\wedge (y > x - z)$$

we guarantee that Eq. (10.1) holds, thus guaranteeing $A^{(1)}$ and $A^{(2)}$ overlap. In this case, CADA has chances to detect concurrent activities after $A^{(1)}.hi$ is collected, not having to wait for $A^{(2)}.hi$.

Based on the analysis above, the probability of early detection is:

$$P_{early}(x, y, z)$$
$$= Pr\{msg^{(1)}.delay < z\}$$
$$Pr\{msg^{(2)}.delay < x - z\}Pr\{y > x - z\}$$
$$= (1 - e^{-\lambda z})(1 - e^{-\lambda(x-z)})(1 - F_2(x - z))$$

The expected probability of correct detection is:

$$E[P_{early}(x, y, z)] = \int_0^\infty \{\int_0^\infty [\int_0^x P_{early}(x, y, z)$$
$$dF_3(z)]dF_2(y)\}dF_1(x)$$
$$(10.7)$$

We also illustrate performance of CADA in terms of $E[P_{early}]$ by numerical results. From Fig. 10.6, we find that P_{early} is around half of

P_{corr} when the message delay is not quite long and both probabilities remain stable. Both probabilities decrease in a similar way as the average message delay significantly increases, i.e., $E[P_{early}]$ can also tolerate significant increase in the average message delay. Thus CADA achieves satisfying performance in terms of both probabilities in environments with different message delay.

10.4.3 Sensed and Physical Activities

As we discussed in Sect. 10.1, context collecting devices (often resource-constrained sensors) may delay the dissemination of context data to save energy. The interval between updating the context data is one of the primary sources of asynchrony [19]. The update interval may greatly increase the discrepancy between the physical activity and the sensed activity, and induce both false positive and false negative faults. Specifically,

- *false positive.* See the example in Fig. 10.8.[1] The ending of physical activity monitored by $P^{(2)}$ is not sensed until the next update of context data. Thus, the ending of the sensed activity $A^{(2)}$ is significantly "dragged behind". If $A^{(1)}$ is not significantly behind the corresponding physical activity, the sensed activities $A^{(1)}$ and $A^{(2)}$ may be false positively concurrent.
- *false negative.* In another example shown in Fig. 10.9, two physical activities actually over-

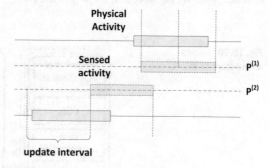

Fig. 10.8 False positive concurrency

---

[1]In our analysis, we only consider periodical updates of context data.

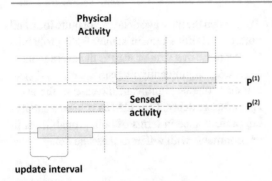

Fig. 10.9 False negative concurrency

sage delay and the update interval by experiments. We also study the performance of CADA when there are more than two non-checker processes.

10.5   Experimental Evaluation

In this section, we conduct experiments to further explore the performance of CADA in pervasive computing environments. We implement CADA over the open source middleware we developed [29]. We first outline the implementation of CADA. Then we describe the experiment setup. Finally, we discuss the evaluation results.

10.5.1   Implementation

lap. However, the beginning of $A^{(1)}$ is "dragged behind". Thus, the sensed activities $A^{(1)}$ and $A^{(2)}$ may be false negatively not concurrent.

10.4.4   Discussions

According to the discussions above, we have that: (i) when the context collecting devices update context data in time, the message delay has more impact on the accuracy of property detection. In this case, with high probability there are no false positive faults. There could be false negative faults with certain probability. (ii) when the context collecting devices delay the update of context data to save resource consumption, there could be both types of faults. Since the interval between context updates can be quite long, it may have more severe impact on the detection of contextual properties.

In reality, the causes of faults are a combination of both types. We further study impact of the mes-

The detection of contextual properties assumes the availability of an underlying context-aware middleware. We have implemented the middleware based on one of our research projects— *Middleware infrastructure for Predicate detection in Asynchronous Environments* (MIPA) [29]. The system architecture of MIPA is shown in Fig. 10.10.

From MIPA's point of view, the application achieves context-awareness by specifying contextual properties of its interest to MIPA. The checker process is implemented as a third-party service, plugged into MIPA. Non-checker processes are deployed to manipulate context collecting devices, monitoring different parts of the environment.

Fig. 10.10 System architecture of MIPA

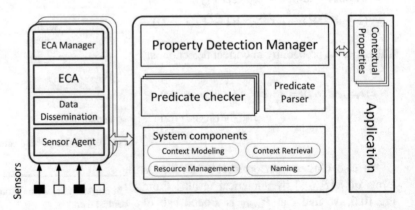

Table 10.2 Experiment configurations

Parameter	Value
Lifetime of experiment	500 h
Average sensing interval	1 min
Average stay in/out of the office	10 min/5 min
Average update interval	1–100 min
Average message delay	0–600 s
Average length of contextual activities	5–50 min
Number of non-checker processes	2–8

10.5.2 Experiment Setup

In the experimental evaluation, we simulate a smart-lock scenario, which is first investigated in our previous work [21,42]. In this scenario, a smart-lock application automatically locks the office when the user leaves. Obviously, the key problem here is to accurately detect the user's location.

In this scenario, the user's location is detected by RFID readers. However, the RFID data is intrinsically noisy and may often cause both false readings and cross readings [9,11,12]. To increase the accuracy of location detection, we also utilize the user's smart phone. When the smart phone connects to the access point inside/outof the office, the user's location is then decided.

Note that the RFID reader and the user's mobile phone do not necessarily have synchronized clocks. Moreover, the smart phone may delay the update of user's location data to save battery power. In order to accurately detect the user's location despite of the noisy context data and asynchronous interaction among context collecting devices, the application specifies the contextual property CP of its interest:

$$CP = Def(\phi_1 \wedge \phi_2),$$

where ϕ_1 = "the RFID reader inside the office detects the user's tag"; ϕ_2 = "the user's smart phone connects to the AP inside the office".[2]

User's stay inside and out of the office is generated following the queue discussed in Sect. 10.4. We model the message delay by exponential distribution, and set different update intervals for the smart phone. In the experiments, we study the probability of correct detection (P_{corr}) and early detection (P_{early}) of concurrent contextual activities. We first change the asynchrony (context update interval and message delay) of the environment. We also change the duration of contextual activities. Finally, we change the number of non-checker processes, which complements our analysis in Sect. 10.4.2. Detailed experiment configurations are listed in Table 10.2.

10.5.3 Effects of Tuning the Update Interval

In this experiment, we study how the interval between context updates affects the performance of CADA. To focus on the impact of update interval, the message delay is set to zero in this experiment.

We first study the impact when the update interval is no more than 10 m (average length of the contextual activities). We find that P_{early} is around half of P_{corr}. The increase in the update interval results in monotonic decrease in P_{corr} and P_{early} by 16.6% and 13.3% respectively, as shown in Fig. 10.11. This is in accordance with our analysis of how the increase of update interval adds to the asynchrony of the environment (Sect. 10.4), which affects the performance of CADA.

Then we greatly increase the update to 100 min and see how P_{corr} and P_{early} decrease as the

---

[2]When the user is outside the office, the location is detected similarly.

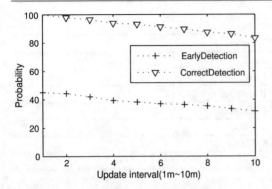

Fig. 10.11 Effects of tuning the update Interval

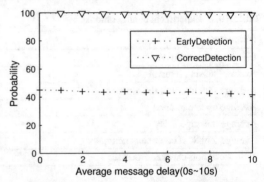

Fig. 10.13 Effects of tuning the message delay

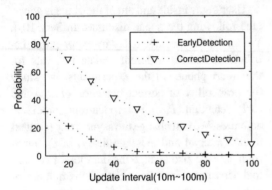

Fig. 10.12 Effects of tuning the update interval

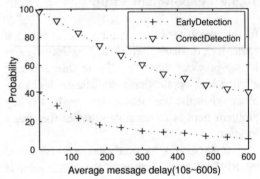

Fig. 10.14 Effects of tuning the message delay

update interval significantly increases. We find that both probabilities decrease quickly as the update interval greatly increases. When the update interval increases to 60 min, the decreases in both probabilities slow down. When we increase the update interval to around 100 min, P_{corr} decreases to around 10 % and P_{early} decreases to around zero, as shown in Fig. 10.12.

10.5.4   Effects of Tuning the Message Delay

In this experiment, we study how the message delay affects the performance of CADA. We fix the update interval to 1m. In our experiment, the sensor agent reports contextual events every 1m. Thus fixing the update interval to 1 min limits the impact of update interval.

We find that when encountered with reasonably long message delay (less than 10 s), P_{corr} is quite high (a little less than 100 %) and P_{early} is nearly half of P_{corr}, as shown in Fig. 10.13. Only when the delay goes up to more than 10 s, the probability begins to significantly decrease, as shown in Fig. 10.14. When we increase the delay to a large value (up to 10 min), P_{corr} may decrease to around 40 % and P_{early} may decrease to around 10 %. Note that though the message delay usually does not go up to several minutes, we increase the message delay to large values here to explore its impact on the performance of CADA.

Combining the results in Figs. 10.13 and 10.14, we also find that the message delay results in monotonic decrease of P_{corr} and P_{early}, mainly due to the increase in the asynchrony of the environment. However, the impact of the message delay is comparatively less than that of the update

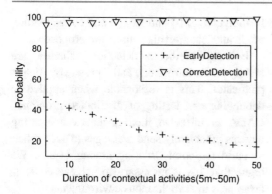

Fig. 10.15 Effects of tuning the duration of contextual activities

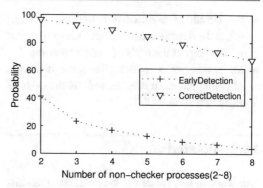

Fig. 10.16 Effects of tuning the number of non-checker processes

interval. This is in accordance with our analysis in Sect. 10.4.

10.5.5 Effects of Tuning the Duration of Contextual Activities

In this experiment, we study the impact of the average length of contextual activities. The average length of user's stay in the office is changed from 5 to 50 min. We set the update interval to be 3 min, and message delay to 0.5 s.

We find that P_{corr} slightly increases (by around 4.4 %), while P_{early} decreases (by around 31.6 %) when the duration increases, as shown in Fig. 10.15. P_{corr} increases mainly because with longer activities, the control messages have more chances to arrive in time, as shown in Fig. 10.3. As for P_{early}, duration of the activities do not impact whether $msg^{(1)}$ arrive in time, as shown in Fig. 10.7. Moreover, long activities ($x > z + y$) could reduce the chances of early detection. Thus P_{early} decreases.

This is in accordance with our analysis in Sect. 10.4. As shown in Eq. (10.6), when duration of user's stay in the office increases, values of both x and y increase, resulting in the increase in P_{corr}. The decrease in P_{early} mainly results from the increase in $F_2(x - z)$, as shown in Eq. (10.7). Since $F_2(x - z)$ is a probability function and is thus monotonically non-decreasing, increase in x results in the increase in $F_2(x - z)$.

Overall, impact of the average length of contextual activities on P_{corr} and P_{early} is not signif-

icant, which makes CADA widely applicable to detect concurrent activities of different length.

10.5.6 Effects of Tuning the Number of Non-checker Processes

We also study the impact of the number of non-checker processes, which complements our analysis in Sect. 10.4. We set the update interval and message delay to 3 min and 0.5 s respectively. We set average length of interval to 10 m.

As the number of non-checker processes increases, P_{corr} linearly decreases and P_{early} decreases a little faster. This is mainly because, for multiple activities, any activity which does not follow Eq. (10.1) will falsify $Def(\phi)$, i.e., the asynchrony of coordination among non-checker processes accumulates as the number of non-checker processes increases (Fig. 10.16).

10.5.7 Lessons Learned

Based on the experimental evaluation, we show that CADA is desirable for context-aware applications in asynchronous pervasive computing environments. In particular:

- CADA can tolerate a reasonably large amount of asynchrony (in terms of update interval and message delay), and update interval has more impact than message delay.

- the length of contextual activities does not affect the detection of concurrent activities, but it does impact the odds of early detection.
- the number of activities affects the detection of contextual activities, as well as the odds of early detection.

10.6   Related Work

Our work in this paper can be positioned against two areas of related work: context-aware computing and detection of global predicates in distributed computations.

As for context-aware computing, various schemes have been proposed for detection of contextual properties in the existing literature. In [13], properties were modeled by tuples, and property detection was based on comparison among elements in the tuples. In [30], contextual properties were expressed in first-order-logic, and an incremental property detection algorithm was proposed. In [15,16], an ontology was proposed to model context, and properties were expressed by assertions. In these existing work, temporal relations among the collected contexts are not sufficiently considered. It is implicitly assumed that the contexts being checked belong to the same snapshot of time. Such limitations make these schemes do not work in asynchronous environments.

In asynchronous distributed systems, the concept of time must be carefully reexamined [23,43]. In the seminal work of Lamport, causality was used to define the *happen-before* relation between events [23]. Based on the happen-before relation, logical clocks can be devised [24,25].

The problem of detecting global predicates mainly arises from the debugging and testing of distributed programs. In [35], Cooper et al. investigated the detection of general predicates, which brought combinatorial explosion of the state space. Conjunctive predicates play a key role in predicate detection and conjunctive predicates under both $Pos(\cdot)$ and $Def(\cdot)$ were studied in [31,32]. In [33,43], Kshemkalyani et al. give a refinement of the coarse-grained modality classi-

fication of $Def(\cdot)$ and $Pos(\cdot)$ and corresponding predicate detection algorithms are proposed.

Existing predicate detection schemes are mainly non-intrusive, and passively detect predicates. This is reasonable when applied to debugging and testing of distributed programs. CADA is intrusive, i.e., it makes computing devices proactively send messages to each other, to build temporal ordering among events. We argue that this is necessary to achieve context-awareness in asynchronous environments.

A constructive proof is presented in [32], which also builds the equivalence between $Def(\phi)$ and concurrency among contextual activities. Comparatively, our proof explores the geometrical/topological perspective and utilizes the lattice of CGSs. We argue that our proof is easier to understand. More importantly, it is more general and can be extended to prove results concerning other types of predicates. Our proof also well motivates us to consider possible improvements like early detection.

Moreover, it was not considered whether contextual properties were detected correctly and timely in the existing work. However, these issues are important for context-aware applications. We conduct both theoretical analysis and experimental evaluation to address these issues for CADA.

10.7   Conclusion

In this paper, we study how to detect contextual properties in asynchronous pervasive computing environments. Toward this objective, our contributions are: (i) we propose to detect contextual properties based on logical time in asynchronous pervasive computing environments; (ii) we propose the CADA algorithm to detect contextual properties at runtime; (iii) We evaluate CADA by both theoretical analysis and experimental evaluation.

Currently, the CADA algorithm still suffers from several limitations. In our future work, we need to study how to detect properties concerning behavioral patterns of the environment. We need to investigate how to explicitly and effectively maintain the lattice of CGSs at runtime and detect different types of contextual properties based on the lattice. It is also important to investigate how to reduce the message complexity of our proposed property detection schemes.

References

1. M. Weiser, The computer for the 21st century. Sci. Am. **265**(3), 66–75 (1991)
2. D. Garlan, D. Siewiorek, A. Smailagic, P. Steenkiste, Project aura: toward distraction-free pervasive computing. IEEE Pervasive Comput. **1**(2), 22–31 (2002)
3. M. Roman, C. Hess, R. Cerqueira, A. Ranganathan, R.H. Campbell, K. Nahrstedt, A middleware infrastructure for active spaces. IEEE Pervasive Comput. **1**(4), 74–83 (2002)
4. Y. Huang, J. Cao, B. Jin, X. Tao, J. Lu, Y. Feng, Flexible cache consistency maintenance over wireless ad hoc networks. IEEE Trans. Parallel Distrib. Syst. forthcoming
5. A. Dey, Providing architectural support for building context-aware applications. *Ph.D. Thesis, Georgia Institute of Technology* (2000)
6. K. Henricksen, J. Indulska, A software engineering framework for context-aware pervasive computing, in *Proceedings of IEEE International Conference on Pervasive Computing and Communications (PERCOM'04)*, Orlando, Florida, USA, March 2004, pp. 77–86
7. C. Julien, G.-C. Roman, Egospaces: facilitating rapid development of context-aware mobile applications. IEEE Trans. Softw. Eng. **32**(5), 281–298 (2006)
8. H.K. Pung, T. Gu, and W.X. et. al., Context-aware middleware for pervasive elderly homecare. IEEE J. Sel. Areas Commun. **27**(4), 510–524 (2009)
9. C. Xu, S.C. Cheung, W.K. Chan, C. Ye, Partial constraint checking for context consistency in pervasive computing. ACM Trans. Softw. Eng. Methodol. **19**(3), 1–61 (2010)
10. A.K. Dey, D. Salber, G.D. Abowd, M. Futakawa, The conference assistant: combining context-awareness with wearable computing, in *ISWC '99: Proceedings of the 3rd IEEE International Symposium on Wearable Computers*, Washington, DC, USA. IEEE Computer Society (1999), p. 21
11. S.R. Jeffery, M. Garofalakis, M.J. Franklin, Adaptive cleaning for rfid data streams, in *Proceedings of the International Conference on Very Large Data Bases (VLDB'06)*, Seoul, Korea, September 2006, pp. 163–174
12. J. Rao, S. Doraiswamy, H. Thakkar, L.S. Colby, A deferred cleansing method for rfid data analytics, in *Proceedings of the International Conference on Very Large Data Bases (VLDB'06)*, Seoul, Korea, Sept. 2006, pp. 175–186
13. C. Xu, S.C. Cheung, Inconsistency detection and resolution for context-aware middleware support, in *Proceedings of ACM SIGSOFT International Symposium on Foundations of Software Engineering (FSE'05)*, Lisbon, Portugal (2005), pp. 336–345
14. C. Xu, S. Cheung, W. Chan, C. Ye, Heuristics-based strategies for resolving context inconsistencies in pervasive computing applications, in *Proceedings of the International Conference on Distributed Computing Systems (ICDCS'08)*, Beijing, China, June 2008, pp. 713–721
15. Y. Bu, T. Gu, X. Tao, J. Li, S. Chen, J. Lu, Managing quality of context in pervasive computing, in *Proceedings of the International Conference on Quality Software (QSIC'06)*, Beijing, China, October 2006, pp. 193–200
16. Y. Bu, S. Chen, J. Li, X. Tao, J. Lu, Context consistency management using ontology based model, in *Proceedings of the Current Trends in Database Technology (EDBT'06)*, Munich, Germany, March 2006, pp. 741–755
17. Y. Huang, X. Ma, X. Tao, J. Cao, J. Lu, A probabilistic approach to consistency checking for pervasive context, in *Proceedings of the IEEE/IFIP International Conference on Embedded and Ubiquitous Computing (EUC'08)*, Shanghai, China, December 2008, pp. 387–393
18. E.A. Lee, Cyber-physical systems—are computing foundations adequate? in *NSF Workshop on Cyberphysical Systems: Research motivation (Techniques and Roadmap, Position Paper)*, Austin, Texas, USA (2006)
19. M. Sama, D.S. Rosenblum, Z. Wang, S. Elbaum, Model-based fault detection in context-aware adaptive applications, in *Proceedings of the 16th ACM SIGSOFT International Symposium on Foundations of software engineering (SIGSOFT'08/FSE-16)*. New York, NY, USA. ACM (2008), pp. 261–271
20. Y. Huang, X. Ma, J. Cao, X. Tao, J. Lu, Concurrent event detection for asynchronous consistency checking of pervasive context, in *Proceedings of the IEEE International Conference on Pervasive Computing and Communications (PERCOM'09)*, Galveston, Texas, USA, March 2009
21. Y. Huang, J. Yu, J. Cao, X. Ma, X. Tao, J. Lu, Checking behavioral consistency constraints for pervasive context in asynchronous environments, Technical Report, Institute of Computer Software, Nanjing University, November 2009, http://arxiv.org/abs/0911.0136
22. L. Kaveti, S. Pulluri, G. Singh, Event ordering in pervasive sensor networks, in *Proceedings of the IEEE International Conference on Pervasive Computing and Communications Workshops (PERCOMW'09)*, Galveston, US, March 2009, pp. 604–609
23. L. Lamport, Time, clocks, and the ordering of events in a distributed system. Commun. ACM **21**(7), 558–565 (1978)
24. C.J. Fidge, Partial orders for parallel debugging, in *Proceedings of ACM SIGPLAN and SIGOPS Workshop on Parallel and Distributed Debugging*, Madison, Wisconsin, US, May, 1988, pp. 183–194

25. F. Mattern, Virtual time and global states of distributed systems, in *Proceedings of the International Workshop on Parallel and Distributed Algorithms*, Holland (1989), pp. 215–226

26. O. Babaoğlu, K. Marzullo, Consistent global states of distributed systems: fundamental concepts and mechanisms, distributed systems (2nd ed.), chapter 4 (1993), pp. 55–96

27. R. Schwarz, F. Mattern, Detecting causal relationships in distributed computations: in search of the holy grail. Distrib. Comput. **7**(3), 149–174 (1994)

28. O. Babaoğlu, E. Fromentin, M. Raynal, A unified framework for the specification and run-time detection of dynamic properties in distributed computations. J. Syst. Softw. **33**(3), 287–298 (1996)

29. MIPA—Middleware Infrastructure for Predicate detection in asynchronous environments, http://mipa.googlecode.com/

30. C. Xu, S.C. Cheung, W.K. Chan, Incremental consistency checking for pervasive context, in *Proceedings of the International Conference on Software Engineering (ICSE'06)*, Shanghai, China, May 2006, pp. 292–301

31. V. Garg, B. Waldecker, Detection of weak unstable predicates in distributed programs. IEEE Trans. Parallel Distrib. Syst. **5**, 299–307 (1994)

32. V.K. Garg, B. Waldecker, Detection of strong unstable predicates in distributed programs. IEEE Trans. Parallel Distrib. Syst. **7**, 1323–1333 (1996)

33. P. Chandra, A.D. Kshemkalyani, Causality-based predicate detection across space and time. IEEE Trans. Comput. **54**(11), 1438–1453 (2005)

34. O. Babaoğlu, M. Raynal, Specification and verification of dynamic properties in distributed compu-tations. J. Parallel Distrib. Comput. **28**(2), 173–185 (1995)

35. R. Cooper, K. Marzullo, Consistent detection of global predicates, in *Proceedings of the ACM/ONR Workshop on Parallel and Distributed Debugging*, NY, USA (1991), pp. 167–174

36. B. Charron-Bost, C. Delporte-Gallet, H. Fauconnier, Local and temporal predicates in distributed systems. ACM Trans. Program. Lang. Syst. **17**(1), 157–179 (1995)

37. J.Y. Halpern, Y. Moses, Knowledge and common knowledge in a distributed environment. J. ACM **37**(3), 549–587 (1990)

38. P. Panangaden, K. Taylor, Concurrent common knowledge: defining agreement for asynchronous systems. Distrib. Comput. **6**(2), 73–93 (1992)

39. B. Bunday, *An Introduction to Queueing Theory* (A Hodder Arnold Publication, London, 1996)

40. Y. Tang, X. Tang, *Queuing Theory: Fundamentals and Analysis Techniques (in Chinese)* (Science Press, Beijing, China, 2006)

41. N. Duffield, F. Lo Presti, Multicast inference of packet delay variance at interior network links, in *Proceedings of the IEEE Conference on Computer Communications (INFOCOM'00)*, vol. 3, Tel Aviv, Israel, March 2000, pp. 1351–1360

42. Z. Wu, X. Tao, J. Lu, An ontology based dynamic context model. Front. Comput. Sci. Technol. **2**(4), 356–367 (2008)

43. A.D. Kshemkalyani, A fine-grained modality classification for global predicates. IEEE Trans. Parallel Distrib. Syst. **14**(8), 807–816 (2003)

From the architecture-centric technical framework proposed in Part 1, the Internetware paradigm needs to support HOW-TO-RUN (operating platform) and HOW-TO-DO (engineering approach). Part 3 introduces the operating platform with various supports such as online evolution and adaptation. This part introduces the Internetware engineering approach. It essentially follows the core and underlying principle of a software architecture with a whole-life cycle. This software architecture serves as a blueprint, and suggests or controls each stage in developing Internetware applications.

The Internetware engineering approach leverages the proposed methodology based on architecture-based component composition (ABC) in Chap. 11. ABC composes reusable software components under a single blueprint software architecture, and thus bridges the gap between high-level design and low-level implementation. ABC is capable of adaptation, which is a crucial ability for meeting changing requirements imposed by Internet computing. Its architecture allows for locating entities to be adapted, and recording what should be done at runtime in order for the adaptation to take place for the located entities. This architecture is capable of conducting the designed adaptation without stopping a running system. One may also integrate reasoning rules into ABC's software architecture to enable dynamic adaptation with a rule engine.

Internetware applications can be composed by aggregation of software entities in a bottom-up way to meet user requirements. This calls for the need of precise specifications to describe capabilities for Internetware entities. Chapter 12 proposes building such capability specifications based on an environmental ontology. This ontology includes a full conceptualization of interactive Internetware entities for a particular application domain.

With specified user requirements, a follow-up task is to derive corresponding design for target Internetware applications. This task concerns feature reuse and feature dependency analysis in software design. Chapter 13 introduces four kinds of dependency between features, namely, refinement, constraint, influence, and interaction, and three kinds of connection between these dependencies, namely, connections between refinement and constraint, between constraint and interaction, and between influence and interaction. The dependencies and connections are used to facilitate customizable reuse of user requirements, as well as how to employ dependency analysis results to design high-level software architectures.

Finally, Chap. 14 presents a mathematical characterization of object-oriented concepts used in engineering Internetware applications. An observation-oriented semantics is defined for a relational object-based language with a rich variety of features. These features include sub-types, visibility, inheritance, type casting, dynamic binding, and polymorphism. The language allows for practical use like specifying object-oriented designs or programs. The chapter also presents a calculus that supports both structural and behavioral refinement of object-oriented designs for Internetware applications.

A Software Architecture Centric Engineering Approach for Internetware 11

Abstract

As a new software paradigm evolved by the Internet, Internetware brings many challenges to traditional software development methods and techniques. Though Architecture-Based Component Composition (ABC) approach is originated in the traditional software paradigm, it can support the engineering of Internetware effectively due to its philosophy, rationales and mechanisms. In details, ABC does three major contributions to the engineering of Internetware. Firstly, the feature oriented domain modeling method can structure the "disordered" software to "ordered Internetware" bottom-up in the problem space. Secondly, the architecture centric design and analysis method can support the development of self-adaptive Internetware. Thirdly, the component operating platform is a reflective and self-adaptive middleware that not only provides Internetware with a powerful and flexible runtime infrastructure but also enables the self-adaptation of the structure and individual entities of Internetware.

Keywords

Internetware · Component · Software architecture · Feature model · Reflective middleware · Autonomous component

11.1 Introduction

The growing Internet brings new challenges to the information technology, requiring innovations on existing technologies. Some hotspots have

Parts of this chapter were reprinted with kind permission from Springer Science+Business Media: <Science in China Series F: Information Sciences, A software architecture centric engineering approach for Internetware, volume 49, 2006, 702–730, Hong Mei, Gang Huang, Haiyan Zhao and Wenpin Jiao., figure number(s), and any original (first) copyright notice displayed with material>.

emerged, in which many new ideas are proposed. For example, from the perspective of resource sharing and management, the grid computing discusses the appliance and construction of network applications in the future; from the perspective of human-computer interaction, the pervasive computing discusses how future network applications will be used and operated ubiquitously; the service computing emphasizes the idea of "software as a service" and proposes a new software paradigm that pays special attention to the coordination and dynamism of services; the model-driven development is based on domain-specific code generation and focuses on middleware-based development methods and techniques. Almost all of the work can be considered as attempts to review, rethink and evolve the information technology from some new perspectives. Similarly, Internetware grounds itself in the open, dynamic and ever-changing Internet and focuses on such new software paradigm that will be autonomous, evolutionary, cooperative, polymorphic, and context-aware [14]. Since traditional software engineering methods and techniques are originated from and more suited for a static and closed environment, they are not appropriate for open, dynamic, and ever-changing Internetware, which requires innovations to traditional software development methods and techniques.

Technically, Internetware spreads in the Internet and forms a Software Web [14] which is similar to existing information Web. Supported by software components and other technologies, the software entities constituting Internetware are distributed over the internet openly and autonomously. They are all published in an open environment, cooperating with each other in various manners. Due to the open, dynamic, and ever-changing Internet, as well as the various user preferences, Internetware is always evolving after it is developed and deployed. When an Internetware is published, it is capable of perceiving the dynamic changes of its environment and evolves according to its functionality, performance, trustworthiness, and so on, so that it can not only satisfy user requirements but also improve user experiences. Besides, the variation of user preferences and return of investment usually lead to a long lived and ever-evolving Internetware. The engineering of such Internetware as well as its supporting technologies is quite different from traditional ones.

Traditional software development processes are more suited for a platform that is relatively close, static and stable. Most of them adopt a common top-down approach, scoping the system border and using divide-and-conquer principles to make the whole process under control. However, the platform of Internetware has abundant resources and it is always open,

dynamic, and ever-changing. The development over this platform can be seen as the composition of various "disordere" resources into "ordered" software systems. As time elapses, changes of resources and environments may "disorder" existing software systems again, which will become "ordered" sooner or latter. The iterative transformation between "ordered" and "disordered" Internetware implies a bottom-up, and inside-out spiral development process. Besides, traditional software lifecycle emphasizes the importance of the whole development process; the software evolution is only managed by the phase of "software maintenance". This is appropriate for the development under a static and closed environment; however, it is not suitable for Internetware, because (1) for Internetware, new software entities are usually composed of existing ones. All entities are relatively independent and there is no central control over them. As a result, it is difficult to make sure that the developed Internetware does satisfy the desired functionalities and qualities until it is deployed and starts to run; (2) the open, dynamic, and ever-changing environment implies that the cooperation between Internetware may have to change as well. No matter whether these changes can be predicted, the Internetware is always evolving. As a result, software maintenance would become a relatively more important phase; (3) Internetware provides services to the worldwide users, as well as other Internetware. Furthermore, an Internetware is usually composed of software entities distributed over the Internet and then has no chance to be shut down completely after it is deployed and starts to run. This implies that all maintenance activities, including debugging, optimizing and upgrading, have to be performed online. All these activities also undergo the phase of analysis, design, implementation, testing and deployment, all of which cannot be well controlled by the concepts and techniques in traditional software maintenance.

Traditional software development methods pay little attention to how to make a software system autonomous, cooperative, context-aware, evolving and polymorphic. By autonomous, we mean that a software entity is relatively independent of others; it can perform operations as it will and adapt itself when necessary. Internetware is autonomous, because they are usually developed and managed independently; they run independently on distributed nodes. The goal as well as the services of an Internetware is determined by its owner; therefore, the Internetware behaves according to not only the composition or deployment strategies but also the owner's goal. Actually, an Internetware may collect information on environment change and adapt itself according to preset strategies in order to accommodate the ever-changing environment. By cooperative, we mean that software entities constituting an Internetware may cooperate with each other in static or dynamic manners. Comparatively, traditional software systems usually adopt a single and static connection mechanism; however, the connection mechanisms adopted by Internetware may also be changed if necessary. For example, communication protocols between Internetware may be switched, the security level can be increased or decreased at runtime, the availability of message passing may vary according to the changing environment. By context-aware, we mean an Internetware is capable of perceiving its runtime context, which includes both the underlying operating platform and other Internetware. Consequently, both the Internetware and the operating platform should expose their runtime states and behaviors. By evolving, we mean that the structure of an Internetware may change dynamically according to the requirements as well as its environment. Possible evolutions include the number of its constituents, the adjustment of its topologies, as well as dynamic configurations. This requires that the software architecture model for an Internetware should be able to change dynamically. By polymorphic, we mean that an Internetware may incarnate several compatible goals. Based on some basic cooperation principles, an Internetware may satisfy different but compatible goals in a dynamic environment. This requires the modeling of compatible goals. Besides, an Internetware should be able to determine its goal dynamically when the environment changes. In short, most characteristics an Internetware should have are related to its self-adaptability, including the self-adaptability

of single software entity as well as the software topology. A self-adaptable Internetware is capable of adapting itself according to specific changes at the right time, in the right place, such that it can satisfy the desired functionalities and qualities. Naturally, the degree of human intervention determines the degree of self-adaptability. Therefore, a real challenge for the engineering of Internetware is how to develop a self-adaptable Internetware, such that it can behave properly with as little human intervention as possible.

Traditional software development tools are usually targeted at one or several phases before the software is delivered; after delivery, the software is maintained by various management tools. As shown before, the emphasis of Internetware development is shifted from pre-delivery to the runtime. The runtime adaptation of Internetware (no matter by hand or automatically) usually depends on activities and artifacts produced in different development phases. Therefore, the software development tools for Internetware should not only cover the whole software lifecycle, but also be integrated with the runtime platform. Conversely, the above characteristics incarnated in Internetware challenges the runtime platform in various ways. Firstly, the runtime platform should not only be able to present its states and behaviors at runtime, but also facilitate the Internetware to present its runtime information. Secondly, the runtime platform should provide mechanisms to adapt the constituents of an Internetware as well as its topologies; otherwise, the Internetware cannot become self-adaptive.

In summary, the engineering of Internetware is quite different from that of traditional software. In particular, it follows a bottomup process, which composes "disordered" software entities into "ordered" software systems; it should pay special attention to the self-adaptability of the constituents and the structure of an Internetware; the supporting tools cover the whole lifecycle and are usually integrated with the operating platform, which provides required mechanisms to implement the self-adaptation of Internetware. In this chapter, we propose a software architecture centric engineering approach for Internetware, which is a natural extension of the Architecture Based

Component Composition (ABC) approach [8]. ABC uses software architectures as blueprints to develop middleware based software systems by assembling reusable components. To our point of view, the philosophy, rationales and mechanisms of ABC are compliant with the open, dynamic and ever-changing characteristics of Internetware, and in particular, the above three major issues of the engineering of Internetware can be efficiently handled by ABC.

The rest of this chapter is organized as follows: Sect. 11.2 introduces the core idea, design rationales as well as the process model of ABC; Sect. 11.3 discusses how to use feature models to organize and mange "disordered" Internetware resources; Sect. 11.4 presents how to design a self-adaptive software architecture for an Internetware; Sect. 11.5 introduces a reflective middleware that supports self-adaptation of software entities as well as software structures; Sect. 11.6 concludes this chapter and identifies the future work.

11.2   Overview of ABC Methodology

Originated in 1998 and formally proposed in 2000 [8], ABC is a combination of software architecture (SA) and component-based software development (CBSD) for supporting software reuse. SA provides a topdown approach to realizing component-based reuse. This approach uses architecture description languages (ADL) to abstract components, connectors as well as their interactions, which constitute the whole architecture model. However, SA doesn't pay enough attention to the refinement and implementation of the architectural descriptions, thus not fully able to automate the transformation or composition which results in an executable system. On the other hand, CBSD provides a bottomup way by using existing middleware infrastructures. It emphasizes how to reuse pre-fabricated components to build large-scale software systems. However, this method is mainly restricted to binary components (e.g., COM, CORBA, EJB); besides, it is not able to systematically guide the CBSD process, especially the component composition at higher abstract levels. To our

point of view, SA and CBSD are complementary and are able to be combined to realize effective component-based reuse.

ABC introduces software architectures into each phase of software life cycle, takes SA as the blueprint of system development, deployment and management, shortens the gap between high-level design and implementation by supporting tools and mapping mechanisms, realizes the automated system composition. The process model for ABC method is shown in Fig. 11.1, which includes the following phases:

- Requirement Analysis (Requirement View): SA is introduced into the requirement analysis phase to guide component composition at a high level. In this phase, the problem space, as well as the requirement specification, is structured in the way similar to SA [13]. ABC uses features to represent software requirements and relationships among features to represent relationships among requirements. In a word, feature is treated as a first class entity in the problem space. Features and static or dynamic relationships among features are organized as feature models. In particular, for the purpose of reuse, the feature model in ABC method uses variability mechanism to capture the commonality and variability of a set of similar requirements. The relationships among requirements are modeled by four relations in the feature model, including refinement, constraint, influence and interaction [13,16]. These relations can be used to validate the completeness and consistency of a feature model [18]. Based on feature models, an initial SA model can be designed by identifying responsibilities for each component and analyzing the dependencies among requirements [17]. This initial SA model is the input for the later phase of architecting, composition and maintenance.
- Architecting Phase (Design View): A complete SA model comes into being in this phase. The architect determines the global design decisions based on the requirement specification. In this phase, components and connectors in the initial SA model would be refined. New

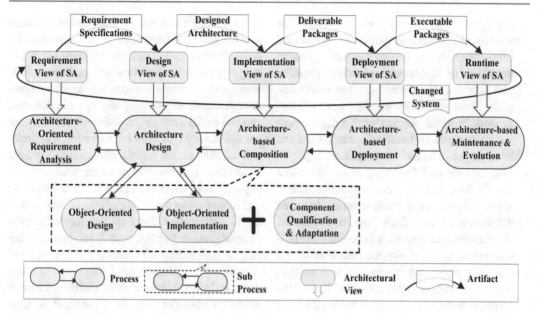

Fig. 11.1   Process and artifacts of ABC

components and connectors are created if necessary; different views (including type view, instance view and process view) may also be created. The relationships between the requirement specifications and SA models are set up in this phase [8,9]. Since reuse is emphasized in ABC method, the architects should take into account reusable components and connectors during the design. It should be noted that ABC method is not specific to a certain development paradigm. For example, object-oriented design (OOD) can also be adopted in this phase. The high-level OOD model can also be treated as an SA model, as long as the modeling elements in OOD model is encapsulated into those in the SA model (e.g., a set of classes may be encapsulated into a component according to their interaction frequency, the whole-part relation, the general-special relation, and so on.).

- Composition Phase (Implementation View): in ABC method, the SA-based composition implements a software system. In this phase, component implementations are qualified, selected or adapted according to the SA model. After all necessary component implementations are integrated, a deliverable software

package is produced [8,15]. However, in practice, there may be some components that have no reusable implementations. In that case, a detail design model (e.g., UML model) or some C++ or Java programming frameworks for those components would be generated in an automated manner [8]. These newly implemented components can be finally assembled into the target system as well.

- Deployment Phase (Deployment View): component-based software systems are usually specific to a certain middleware, such as Common Object Request Broker Architecture/CORBA Component Model (CORBA/CCM), Java 2 Platform Enterprise Edition/Enterprise JavaBeans (J2EE/EJB), Component Object Model (COM), Web Services, and so on. These software systems start to run only after they are deployed properly. Deployment-related information is usually given by hand, which is tedious and error-prone because such information is voluminous and trivial. In practice, most deployment-related information can be deduced from former views, including the design view and the implementation view. Therefore, an explicit deployment view is introduced in ABC. This view presents most information that is deduced from other views. It also supports intuitive operations on deployment-related information. The information on resources and workloads of the target environment is shown in real time as well. With the support of this deployment view, a component-based software system can be deployed in an automated manner [5].

- Maintenance and Evolution Phase (Runtime View): ABC can be seen as iterative refinement, mapping and transformation between different SA views. Each time the SA model is refined or transformed, it becomes more precise and complete. During the maintenance and evolution phase, the runtime view is used to depict the runtime states and behaviors of the software system. It is the view that has the most precise and complete information on the target system. Based on the support of reflective middleware, the runtime software architecture (RSA) embodied in the runtime view reflects the target system at runtime. The target system can then be maintained or updated at runtime by operations to the RSA [1,2].

To facilitate the above process, a set of tools are provided by ABC, including the feature modeling tool, SA modeling tool and middleware as component operating platform. In particular, the SA modeling tool supports visualized SA design, component composition, deployment, as well as online maintenance and evolution. To date, ABC has been applied to the development of several real applications experimentally, including the modeling of information system for Beijing Olympic 2008 and a loan management system in some commercial bank.

Though ABC is originated from traditional software systems, it can support the engineering of Internetware effectively because Internetware is an evolution of traditional software and ABC takes into account the support for the main characteristics brought by Internetware since 2002. In details, (1) Internetware shapes up from "disordered" resources to "ordered" software system. This process embodies a typical (and even ideal) paradigm for reuse. However, it still requires support for related technologies, which are also keys to ABC and have been already well supported by ABC. Definitely, there are some significant differences between Internetware and traditional software, such as reusable assets are distributed and decentralized, software entities are autonomous, and so on; (2) Though the autonomy of software entities is very typical in Internetware, it is under control to a certain degree. Otherwise, it is hard to form an "ordered" Internetware. Therefore, an explicit SA is still necessary to perform the global and loose control over Internetware. Compared to traditional software, some entities, as well as their connections, in the SA model for Internetware may be undetermined before runtime or changed continuously at runtime; (3) Different from traditional software, Internetware emphasizes the ever-evolution after delivery. As a result, it is difficult to split the development of Internetware from its execution. The development tools should then be integrated with the runtime platform. In ABC, SA model plays a central role in integrating tools for design, implementation, deployment, maintenance and evolution. In a word, the idea and process of ABC method are well suited to Internetware and ABC mechanisms can support the engineering of Internetware. In particular, ABC pays special attention to the following issues brought by the unique characteristics of Internetware. As to the engineering process, ABC cares about how to use feature-oriented requirement modeling to support the bottomup development process as well as the organization and management of "disordered" resources; after that, how SA models can be used to integrate the design, implementation, deployment, maintenance and evolution of Internetware. As to the engineering method, ABC cares about how to design a self-adaptive SA model for Internetware, especially when various qualities are taken into account. As to the supporting techniques, ABC cares about how to strengthen existing platforms that support EJB, Web Services and other main stream component models. The enhanced platform provides a reflective framework to support the monitoring and controlling on Internetware as well as the platform itself. It also provides mechanisms for rule-based autonomous components.

11.3   Feature Oriented Requirement Modeling for Internetware

Based on a platform with rich sets of software assets, the engineering of Internetware is usually in a bottomup fashion since new applications can be built by selecting and composing these existing assets according to user requirements. However, the platform is usually an open, dynamic and ever-changing framework and most of the existing assets in it are distributed, decentralized and heterogeneous. In that sense, the platform manifests itself "disordered" from a global perspective. Therefore, one challenge for the engineering of Internetware is how to conform these disordered assets into ordered and controllable ones, so as to allow the developers to employ mature software development methods, such as the traditional top-down, stepwise refinement method, in their construction of an Internetware.

As a systematic way to produce the reusable artifacts in a particular problem domain, domain engineering addresses the creation of domain models and architectures that abstract and represent a set of reusable assets within a domain through domain scoping, commonality and variability analysis and adaptable design construction based upon the study of existing systems, knowledge from domain experts, and emerging technology within a domain, taking the possible requirement changes, technology evolution, economic benefits and some limitation into consideration. In which, domain analysis is the process of identifying, collecting, organizing,

and representing the relevant information in a domain. In a sense, the domain analysis is a process in bottomup fashion coincided with the engineering of Internetware.

Therefore, ABC adopts the methods and techniques of domain engineering to coordinate the underlying resources, on which the engineering of Internetware is based, making the resources on the bottom sites into a set of ordered components, building the Internetware that fulfills some specific business goals.

As show in Fig. 11.2, we can first structure or organize the disordered resources distributed over the Internet into a domain model with variability representation mechanism, which embodies high level business goals for a bundle of Internetware, by domain scoping and analysis; and then build a new application by tailoring and extending the domain model according to the application-specific requirements. When time elapses, the new application may be scattered somewhere of the Internet as a service and then becomes a new disorder resource. In turn, these new disordered resources can be added into the domain model by further analysis, and therefore form the iterative process of disordered resources to ordered ones. The feature-oriented domain modeling method (abbr. to FODM [13,16–18]) in ABC provides an effective means to conform the building-block resources for Internetware.

Regarding features as basic elements in the problem space, ABC uses features, relationships (i.e. refinements and constraints) between features (called domain feature models) to structure the

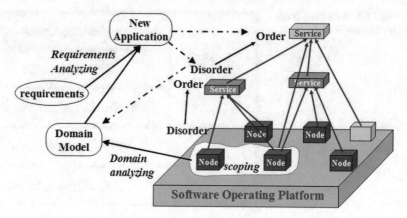

Fig. 11.2 Conforming the bottom resources by domain engineering

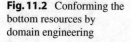

problem space, i.e., use features to group and organize the requirements, which supports modeling of domain requirements systematically. The relationship between features includes the refinement, constraint, influence and interaction. The former two are the static dependencies between features, which are significant to the commonality and variability modeling, while the latter two are dynamic ones which are important for the domain design based on feature models. Speaking concretely, (1) refinements are a kind of binary relationships between features. They integrate features at different levels of abstraction into hierarchical structures which provide an effective way to describe complex systems; (2) Constraints are a kind of static dependencies among features, provide a way to verify the results of requirement customization and release planning; (3) An influence between two features means one feature imposes additional responsibilities on the other, which depicts the dependencies between feature in the specification level; (4) Interactions reflect how features interact with each other at runtime. Figure 11.2 illustrates a concrete form of a feature model in ABC. Besides recording all the service features, function features, behavior characteristics features and use case features a system has, this model records the system's quality features and the constraint and interaction relationships between features explicitly. Features with different abstract levels and granularities (service, function and behavior characteristics) form a hierarchical structure via refinement relationships between them. The features in Use-Case Section are related to the service, func-

tion and behavior characteristics features through the dependencies between the features; while the quality features record the service, function and behavior characteristics features they may affect.

ABC's feature model is in nature a way to partition and organize the requirements since the features and their relationships depict the essential elements of the problem space. In the view of requirement's intension, a feature embodies a kind of capabilities or characteristics the system possesses, which reflect the requirement-enticer's understanding to the system; in the view of requirement types, a feature can be a functional requirement, a quality requirement, or some kind of environment constraints to the system (Fig. 11.3).

During the process of conforming and structuring the bottom resources on which to coordinate the Internetware, ABC uses features to represent and organize these resources, and relationships between features to depict the combination relationships between these resources. Consequently, to a set of Internetware with common requirements and certain variable requirements, ABC's feature model can depict their functions and services to be revealed, the system goals they need to achieve, and their adaptable requirements to environment. Furthermore, by identifying the responsibilities that features possess and analyzing the mutual dependencies between features, developers can get a high-level abstract architecture for this set of Internetware, which can be used as the basis for discriminating and filtering the bottom resources, and the guidelines for the later

Fig. 11.3 A concrete form for a feature model

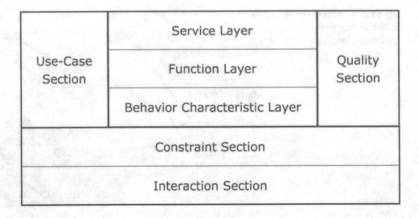

phases of design, composition and maintenance. If a set of Internetware with common and certain variable requirements is regarded as an application domain, the disordered bottom resources they depend on can be coordinated into ordered and controllable ones at a high level through the feature-oriented domain modeling method.

Figure 11.4 presents the feature modeling process of ABC. In which, the activity of Service Analysis identifies the service features that consist of Internetware to define their capabilities revealed to users or customers. The activity of Function Analysis identifies the functional features that a service possesses, which can derive what functions should be included to fulfill a specific service. The activity of Behavior Analysis is to identify the behavior characteristics of a function, such as the pre- and post-conditions of a function to be executed, and the control flow after the executing a function. Crossing the activities of service-function-behavior analysis, the activities of Domain Terminology analysis, commonality/variability analysis and Interaction analysis, Quality attribute analysis can be conducted simultaneously. That is, through analyzing the domain terminology, we can find the services it implies; through analyzing the commonality and variability in the service level, we can find the constraints between services; for each service, function and behavior, we can analyze their

related use cases and the commonalities and variabilities in use cases; and we can also find the quality attributes a service may have. The main task of the Use Case Analysis is to discover the features existing in the interaction between users and the Internetware systems, and by identifying the business process related with services, we can extract the commonalities and use cases that reflect the domain characteristics. The activity of Quality Attribute Analysis focuses on identifying the requirement for the quality attributes that this set of Internetware should be satisfied, and further make clear the system goals to achieve.

One practical approach to requirement reuse is the domain-specific and customization based reuse, that is, when the feature model in a specific domain has been constructed, the followed activity is how to reuse this feature model. One effective way to reuse the model is by customization to accommodate different applications in this domain. That is, we can get a set of features that interest the current application by tailoring the domain feature model. Since there are many dependencies between features, how to ensure the tailoring result consistent and integrated becomes very important. ABC proposes a tailoring process for feature models on the basis of the concept of atomic set, and the verification criteria to check the rationality of the tailoring result depends on the constraint relationship between features.

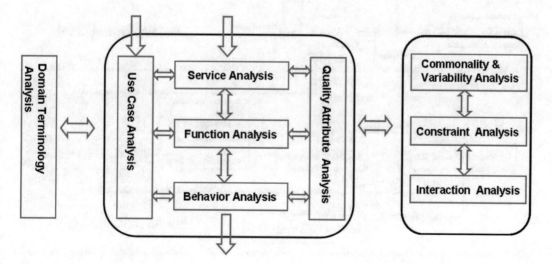

Fig. 11.4 The modeling process of feature model

To make the designer easy to discriminate and filter the suitable components from the bottom resources to build the new Internetware application, it is necessary to establish the corresponding mechanism between the features and their relationships identified in the phase of requirement analysis with the bottom resources and their relationships. Through the identification and assignment to the system responsibilities, ABC gives an approach to transforming a feature model to a high-level abstract software architecture (just acts as a draft model for architects).

There are two fundamental problems to be addressed for the model transformation. One is the traceability between the source model and the target model, which is the foundation of model transformation. The other is construction of the target model, which is the core of model transformation. The embodiment of these two problems in ABC is as the follows: the traceability between features and components; the software architecture construction based on feature model.

There exist n-n relations between features and components in nature. To trace this kind of complex relations, ABC introduces the concept of responsibility as the connector between features and components. A responsibility is a cohesive set of program specifications, and can be used as a basic unit for task assignment to software developers. Via the connection of responsibility, the complex n-n relation between features and components can be decoupled into two 1-n relations, that is, a feature can be operationalized into a set of responsibilities, and one component can implement multiple responsibilities. On this basis, the traceability between features and components can be established in two steps: operationalizing features to responsibilities; and assigning responsibilities to components.

An overview of the transformation from feature models to software architectures is depicted in Fig. 11.5. The concepts involved in the transformation can be divided into two levels. One is the Requirement Level of Internetware, on which the requirements can be structured as feature models. The other is the Specification Level. In this level, program specifications are first organized as a set of responsibilities, a set of resource containers, and interactions between them; and then responsibilities and resource containers are clustered into conceptual components, and the interactions between responsibilities or resource containers form the interactions between components by filtering and clustering. In fact, components can be considered as a kind of responsibility containers, so it can be constructed by responsibility clus-

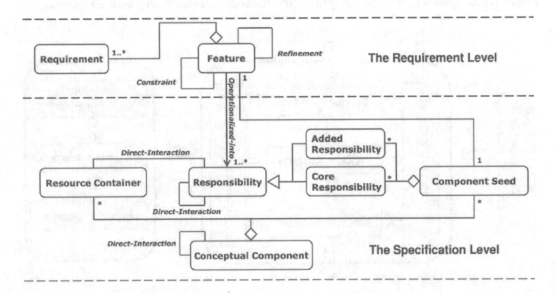

Fig. 11.5 An overview of transformation from feature model to software architecture

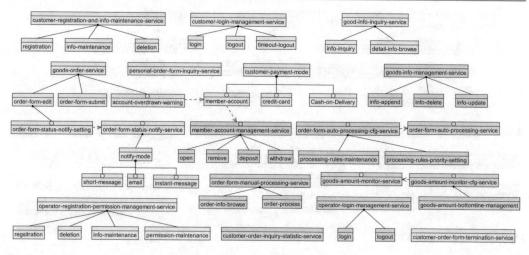

Fig. 11.6   Domain feature model for E-Shops

tering. The identification of interactions between components is guided by the following assumption: if two responsibilities are assigned to two different components, then any interaction between these two responsibilities will be developed into an interaction between components.

Using the forementioned ABC feature modeling method, we can model the Internetware's system goals, constituent capabilities and responsibilities naturally and clearly, so as to guide the discrimination of the bottom resources.

To better support the feature-oriented requirement modeling, ABC has developed a corresponding graphical supporting tool called FMTool, which provides means to model and edit the feature model easily. In addition to serving the traditional domain engineering and software product line, it is applicable to modeling complex software applications like Internetware.

To demonstrate, we use the Internet shops as the case study. There exist a lot of E-shopping sites today, and their portal software systems are generally disordered as "each does things in its own way". Here, by analyzing the requirements of this kind of software using feature modeling method, we can abstract their requirements as eight types of services. In which, the customer registration service, customer logging service, commodity information searching and browsing service, commodity ordering service are provided

to the customers; while the order form manual processing service, commodity information management service, automatic order form processing configuration service are provided to the shop assistants; the automatic order form processing service is provide as an extra intelligent service. Figure 11.6 presents the refinement view of the feature model for a class of Internet shop software systems.

The above feature model can be reused to get the feature model for a specific E-shop. For example, the feature model for an Internet Pet Shop[1] shown in Fig. 11.7 is a tailoring result of the model given in Fig. 11.6. In the process of customization, according to the JPS's specific requirements, some variation points in the Fig. 11.6 can be bound or removed, such as removing the feature of "short message" refined from the feature "notify mode".

On this basis, the responsibilities for each feature in the model can be further identified and assigned to the corresponding components so as to establish the traceability between the features

---

[1]Standard JPS is a traditional Web application. To illustrate ABC for the engineering of Internetware, we modify JPS to a certain degree, such as making it to satisfy some additional variable requirements. However, the source codes almost remain unchanged, because the additional requirements are mainly satisfied by the self-adaptation of Internetware supported by middleware.

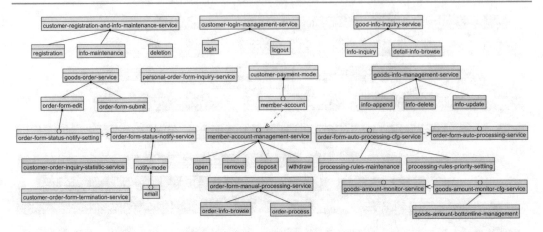

Fig. 11.7 Feature model for JPS

in the problem space with the components in the solution space. At the same time, the interactions between components can be found and established by analyzing the interactions between features and the interactions between responsibilities. Finally, the high level abstract architecture of JPS, shown in Fig. 11.8, has been constructed.

11.4   Architecture Modeling of Self-adaptive Internetware

Early research on self-adaptation concentrates on enabling the self-adaptability of a software system "physically". Most of these research leverages technologies that support self-adaptability, such as agents, design patterns and middleware. Recently, it is recognized that the key to self-adaptation research is to enable the self-adaptability of a software system "logically", that is, how to position the part that should be self-adaptive, how to determine the self-adaptation policies, and how to evaluate the self-adaptation. Considering that most self-adaptation is dedicated to the qualities of a software system, we argue that software qualities should play a central role in analyzing, designing and evaluating the self-adaptability. Meanwhile, SA is not only a blueprint for a software system, but also a carrier of system qualities. Most qualities are evaluated according to SA. The design decisions embodied in SA are almost restricted by quality constraints. Usually, a single design deci-

sion may influence several qualities; and in that sense, the design of SA can be seen as tradeoffs between different qualities. Furthermore, SA is also an important artifact for the management of runtime system changes, e.g. dynamic SA (DSA) records allowable system changes explicitly to guide the self-adaptation of a software system at runtime.

Although existing research provides direct support to the self-adaptability of software systems, there are still a lot of rooms for improvement. For example, most SA design and evaluation methods remain in a high level, not taking other development phases into account; therefore, the qualities can only be simulated or analyzed in a static way. For such qualities that are related to runtime (e.g., performance, availability), it is difficult to ensure the correctness and precision of their evaluation results. Some adaptation strategies for desired qualities may not be optimal or even wrong. Research on DSA introduces mechanisms to model allowable changes, such that the SA model can be used to guide the system maintenance and evolution at runtime. However, most DSA research concentrates on system evolution. It cares about how to add, delete or modify the system's functions, paying little attention to the system's qualities. Therefore, maintainers are required to adjust the qualities by hand and the system is not self-adaptive. Some techniques that support self-adaptation (e.g., reflective middleware) can be applied to implement self-adaptation

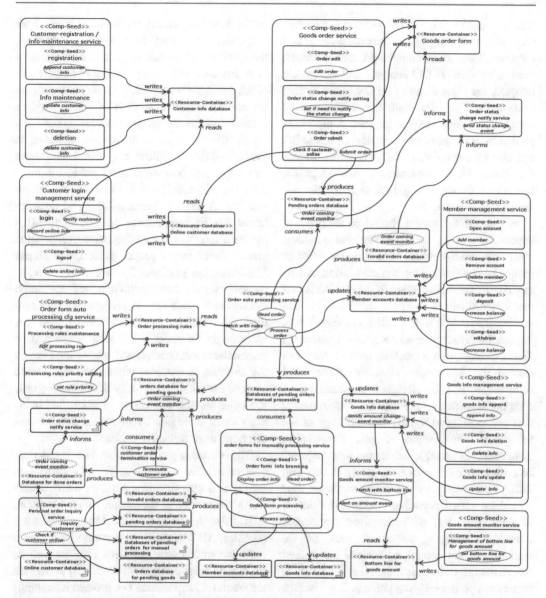

Fig. 11.8 High-level architecture for JPS

policies; however, they have no clue for "why", "when" and "what" to do to achieve the desired qualities.

As discussed before, self-adaptability is one of the most important capabilities of Internetware. And for enabling Internetware self-adaptable, ABC leverages existing efforts on self-adaptation in a systematic manner. Firstly, SA models are used to analyze expected qualities and the part of SA models that should be self-adapted is

located. Secondly, DSA records what should be done at runtime to achieve the desired qualities. Finally, proper self-adaptation mechanisms, like reflective middleware, will implement or execute the designed adaptation at runtime. ABC has no special restriction on the design of SA model according to requirement specifications. For example, a possible way to design an SA model is as follows. Developers can use the feature model based architecture derivation mentioned above, that is, organize features in a feature model into responsibilities, aggregate semantically related responsibilities into a component, and produce a draft SA model. If OO analysis and design are adopted, the class diagram for the target system is designed first; after that, the classes can be encapsulated into coarser grained components guided by some principles; finally, an initial SA can also be derived from OOD artifacts. Before the initial SA is implemented, we adopt the process as shown in Fig. 11.9 to make the SA model self-adaptive.

Firstly, the SA model should be analyzed to ensure the desired functionalities and qualities; otherwise, the SA model should be modified or refined before starting the self-adaptation modeling. During the modification, if the architects find that it is difficult to design a static SA that can achieve the desired functionalities or qualities, it implies the necessity of self-adaptation modeling. The self-adaptation modeling may or may not change the SA model violently. If involved components can be designed as autonomous component which can fulfill the requirements, it is unnecessary to modify the topology of the SA model. For example, if some autonomous component is capable of processing requests according to their priorities, surely it can also satisfy such requirement that the response time should be varied according to the priorities of requests. However, if the involved component cannot be designed as autonomous, or the autonomy is not enough to achieve the desired functionalities or qualities, then it is necessary to figure out a proper self-adaptation policy. Usually, there are two ways to design the self-adaptation

policy. One is to clarify what should be done for adaptation, including the triggering conditions, the addition or deletion of specified components or connectors. This is appropriate when only part of SA needs to be adapted. The other is to prepare several SA candidates, each of which satisfies certain functionalities or qualities. These SA candidates are switched at runtime according to the desired functionalities or qualities. The above two ways may be combined to produce a more complex self-adaptive SA. Once the SA model satisfies all desired functionalities and qualities (otherwise, the requirements may be modified), it can be implemented by component composition and deployed into a proper execution platform. The execution platform for self-adaptive Internetware should have sufficient self-adaptation mechanisms, such that it can monitor the runtime information and adapt the runtime SA accordingly. In short, ABC locates the part of Internetware that requires self-adaptation through SA analysis, determines when and what should be done for self-adaptation by SA design, records strategies for self-adaptation in DSA, and interprets these strategies by means of autonomous components or reflective middleware.

The modeling process in Fig. 11.9 is independent of specific techniques. To validate its feasibility and effectiveness, ABC currently adopts ATAM [4] to analyze the qualities of an SA model, ADD [6] to design an SA model in terms of given qualities, ABC/ADL [9] to describe DSA, and a reflective middleware, PKUAS [10], as well as the autonomous component model [3] to execute architectural adaptations. The process is exemplified as follows.

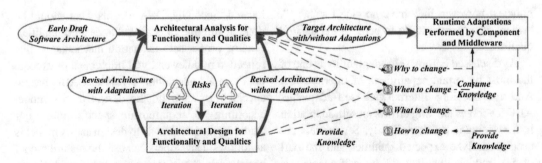

Fig. 11.9 SA-centric modeling of self-adaptive Internetware

ATAM is a systematic SA evaluation technique, which is proposed by CMU/SEI and put into practice for several years. All stakeholders are involved in ATAM to investigate whether a specified SA model does satisfy desired quality attributes. In ATAM, scenarios are used to capture requirements on qualities. These scenarios are prioritized and organized by a utility tree. Each quality attribute scenario uses six elements to identify a specific scenario: a source (some entity outside the system) generated a stimulus (a condition need to be considered when it arrives at a system) to some artifact (the stimulated artifact in the system) in a specific environment (the condition of the system when the stimulus occurs) and the artifact responses (the activity undertaken after the arrival of the stimulus) to the stimulus by some response measure (the response should be measurable in some fashion so that the requirement can be validated). After a careful analysis, sensitivity points and tradeoff points are identified, which are used to trade off different quality attributes. The ATAM in ABC is regulated to fit our needs; particularly, the semantics of some artifacts are specific to ABC, including the quality attribute scenario is used to analyze the time when self-adaptation is necessary, the source and stimulus are used to record the external conditions or events that trigger self-adaptation, all involved elements are recorded in environment and artifact, the threshold of quality attributes are recorded by response and response measure.

We illustrate the ATAM analysis by Java Pet Store (JPS). JPS is divided into four parts, namely the pet store (PS), order processing center (OPC), administration and supplier, respectively. The PS part interacts with end users directly, and sends order forms to OPC. OPC is responsible for the processing of order forms and sending order requests to the administration. The administrators approve (charging fees accordingly from the user's credit card) or reject (if the credit card has no enough money) the order forms through the administration part. The results are then sent back to OPC. For approved order forms, OPC forwards the order forms to the supplier, who ships the ordered pets to the end user and sends according invoices to OPC; for rejected order

forms, OPC sends a notification email to the end user. Table 11.1 shows part of quality attribute scenarios. These scenarios are analyzed with the utility tree, which prioritizes quality attribute scenarios according to the category of qualities. The importance as well as the difficulty to the support of each scenario is also determined. An important output of ATAM analysis is sensitivity points and tradeoff points derived from the quality attribute scenarios. A sensitivity point is a property of the architecture that is critical for the achievement of a particular quality attribute (e.g., using encryption to achieve confidentiality). A tradeoff point is a sensitivity point that is sensitive for multiple quality attributes (e.g., encryption improves security but increases latency). From ABC's perspective of self-adaptive analysis and design, the quality attribute scenarios imply when self-adaptation is necessary; the according sensitivity and tradeoff points show which part of the SA model should be adapted when some response measures are not satisfied. Based on quality attribute scenarios as shown in Table 11.1, we can find that the first 5 scenarios are concerned with performance. After evaluating the SA model of JPS, we can find that most components involved in these scenarios access databases. A performance sensitivity point of database access is then deduced. There are usually two ways to access a database, one is accessing databases each time data is read or written (in this case, less memories are required at the cost of longer response time), the other is buffering data and accessing databases only when data is written (in this case, shorter response time is acquired at the cost of more memories). As a result, components that access databases should compromise between performance and memory usage.

After the adaptation point is located, the according adaptation policy should be designed. There are three possible design decisions for the above example. One is to modify the SA model for JPS. For components (including Customer, Order, Catalog) that access databases, they are assigned two implementations (one uses data buffering, the other does not). Both implementations are composed into the target system. When there are

Table 11.1 Quality attribute scenarios for JPS

No	Source	Stimulus	Environment	Artifact	Response	Response measure
Scenario 1	End user	Detail pet information in the catalog	Runtime	Web site	The according pet information, including pictures	Response time is less than 5 s
Scenario 2	End user	Query of pets in the catalog	Runtime	Web site	Query result	Response time is less than 2 s
Scenario 3	Orders to be processed	Sending orders to OPC	Runtime with normal load	OPC	Order processing	More than 10 orders are processed in one minute
Scenario 4	End user	Order submission	Runtime with normal load	OPC	Notification to the end user (rejected or approved)	Response time is less than 5 min
Scenario 5	End user	Order submission	Runtime with heavy load	OPC	Notification to the end user (rejected or approved)	Response time is less than 6 min
Scenario 6	End user	Order submission	Runtime	The whole system	Detail information on orders	All shopping records
Scenario 7	Orders to be processed	Sending orders to OPC	Runtime	OPC	Order reception	The order should be encrypted
Scenario 8	Maintainer	Transporting to other databases	After delivery	The whole system	The transportation can be done easily	The transportation can be done within 12 h

enough memories, the implementation using data buffering is used for better performance; when available memories become limited, the other implementation will be used to ensure the stability of the whole software system. The switching between implementations can be implemented by the connection or disconnection to corresponding connectors. Another design decision is based on the self-adaptability of middleware. If those components leverage the data access services provided by middleware (e.g., entity EJB), the time when data buffering should be used is left to middleware. What middleware needs to know is the switching rules (for example, a possible rule may be data buffering should not be used when more than 80.

Similar to the above analysis, we can also find [19] that (1) the process control in OPC is

a tradeoff point for performance and security; accordingly, the design of process control should be revised to enable adaptability; (2) the encryption of order forms is also a tradeoff point for performance and security; we can design proper connectors to make it adaptable. All these designs for adaptability can be implemented, more details of which are discussed in the next section.

11.5 Reflective Middleware as Internetware Operating Platform

As shown before, the operating platform for Internetware should not only possess most capabilities in main stream platforms, such as interoperability, concurrency, security, transaction, persistency; but also provide mechanisms for self-adaptability, including that of runtime monitoring and management, rule-based reasoning. The operating platform for ABC is a software middleware, named PKUAS [1,10], which has been successfully applied in such fields as finance, communication, education and governance. It is one of the core products of Orientware, a middleware suite sponsored by National 863 high-tech program. PKUAS is a J2EE-compliant application server which is the platform including J2SE, common services and one or both of Web Container and EJB Container. It provides all functionalities required by J2EE v1.3 and EJB v2.0 in its componentized structure, as shown in Fig. 11.10. The characteristics of PKUAS include:

- Micro kernel based componentized platform: the design of PKUAS embodies the idea of componentization. It provides a registry and an invocation framework for the above platform components and other management entities, like class loading, relation, timer and monitor; and thus presenting a componentized architecture. This architecture is based on a set of fundamental functions, which forms the micro kernel. Other platform-related functions are encapsulated into independent modules (called system components); they can be customized or extended according to specific domains. When PKUAS starts up, the micro kernel is responsible for the organization of a domain-specific component operating platform. In this

way, PKUAS has great flexibility and extensibility.

- Container system supporting online evolution: a container provides a runtime space for the components in the deployed applications with lifecycle management and contract enforcement. PKUAS implements standard EJB containers for stateless session beans, stateful session beans, bean-managed entity beans, container-managed entity beans and message-driven beans. One instance of a container holds all instances of one EJB. And a container system consists of the instances of the containers holding all EJBs in a single application. The container system supports online evolution by adding, deleting, or replacing components at runtime. In this way, the applications can be debugged, upgraded, or optimized at runtime.
- Open interoperability framework: PKUAS supports most main stream interoperability protocols, including IIOP, JRMP, SOAP, and EJB Local. It even allows user-defined interoperability protocols. Which interoperability protocols are used are determined at deploy time; therefore, what protocols are used is transparent to the application developers.
- Standard and extensible service: PKUAS provides common services as specified in J2EE, including data, communication, security, and transaction. With the support of PKUAS, developers need to care about only business logics. Besides, PKUAS supports extended services, such as logging, clustering, and concurrency. Specifically, users are allowed to

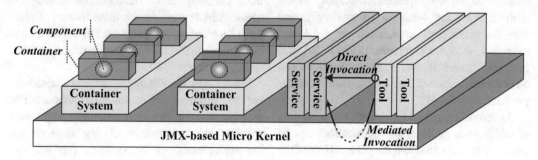

Fig. 11.10 Componentized structure in PKUAS

define specific services. For example, PKUAS supports a special data integration service that is targeted to software project management systems only.

- Rich tool support: PKUAS has provided a set of development, deployment and management tools for J2EE applications. For example, the deployment tool facilitates the composition, deployment, redeployment and un-deployment of J2EE applications at development and testing phases. It is also capable of modifying deployment descriptors or environment properties dynamically. Another example, a web-based management tool is capable of monitoring and managing J2EE applications as well as J2EE servers at runtime.

Based on the above characteristics, PKUAS supports SA-based reflection and the autonomous component, which can be used to support the self-adaptability of Internetware application structure and entities, respectively.

11.5.1   SA-Based Reflection

Being one of the hot topics in the researches and practices on next generation middleware, reflective middleware is considered as the fundamental approach to adaptable middleware. The users is allowed to access and operate on the runtime states and behaviors of middleware in a restrict way by the mechanism of reflection. By reflection, we mean a system can provide a self-representation on its states and behaviors. The self-representation is always consistent with the runtime states and behaviors, that is, changes to the self-representation apply to the runtime states and behaviors immediately, and vice versa. PKUAS implements an SA-based reflection, whose self-representation is SA and then middleware as well as its applications can be observed, reasoned, and manipulated from perspective of SA [1].

As shown in Fig. 11.11, the states and behaviors of middleware platform and applications can be observed and adapted from the perspectives of the platform RSA and application RSA respectively.

The platform RSA represents the implementation of middleware platform as components and connectors. Middleware applications are invisible or represented as the attributes of some components. For example, J2EE application server consists of containers and services and the J2EE application consists of EJBs or Servlets. In the platform RSA, the containers and services are represented as components; their interactions or dependencies are represented as connectors; and the EJBs or Servlets are represented as the attributes of the containers. For reflective middleware, the platform RSA is the representation of a set of platform specific meta entities, which are responsible for the reflection of base entities in the reflective middleware. On the other hand, the application RSA represents middleware application as components and connectors. Middleware platform details are typically represented as constraints or attributes of components and connectors. For example, J2EE security and transaction services are represented as the security and transaction constraints on the EJBs or Servlets. For reflective middleware, the application RSA is the representation of a set of application-specific meta entities, which are responsible for acquiring and maintaining the RSA of the application. In our implementation, the platform RSA is implemented as a set of meta entities, which collect the structural information on PKUAS componentized platform and monitor its states and behaviors. The platform will be adjusted as soon as its meta data changes. Similarly, the application RSA is implemented as a set of application-specific meta entities, which are built on top of meta entities of platform RSA. They are responsible for maintaining the application RSA as well as rich semantics from the SA in design time. The modification to application RSA is done by the meta entities of platform RSA indirectly. Users are allowed to access or manipulate the platform and application RSA through reflective API.

To our opinion, different structural adaptations require different reflection mechanisms. For example, the addition or deletion of components requires the mechanism of hot deployment, the replacement of components requires the mechanism of online evolution, the adjustment

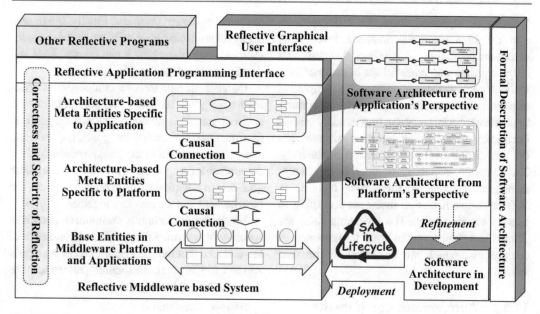

Fig. 11.11 Framework of SA-based reflective middleware

of connectors usually depends on the inter-operability framework, various constraints on components, connectors as well as SA (e.g., transaction, security, persistency, availability, etc.) require various services. More details can be found in [1,2,7,10–12]. For space limit, only the detail for component switching is discussed for illustrating the above adaptation sample of JPS.

As Fig. 11.12a shows, in a typical EJB container, the component interface, implementation, as well as its context are independent of each other. Each interface has an implementation, which may have several instances at runtime. Each instance

has its own context, which is used to maintain the instance's information on transaction, security, session, and so on. To support dynamic switching of component implementations, the above structure should be modified. As Fig. 11.12b shows, in PKUAS, the interface level presents the EJB managed by the container. The interface instances level presents multiple EJB instances for dealing with the concurrency. The implementation instances level presents the implementation instances in an EJB array. In the three-level management, an EJB instance still keeps an EJBContext, but the implementation

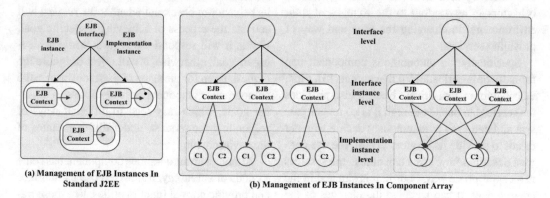

(a) Management of EJB Instances In Standard J2EE

(b) Management of EJB Instances In Component Array

Fig. 11.12 Automatic switching of component implementation in PKUAS

instance is separated from the EJB instance into the implementation instance level. This management makes it possible that an EJB keeps multiple implementations in the container without breaking the concurrency. If a component implementation is isomorphic, the according implementation instance can be shared by several interfaces; otherwise, an interface instance has its own implementation instance exclusively. The dynamic switching of component implementations is done by forwarding requests to different implementation instances according to preset switching rules. The switching rules are defined in a similar way to those for autonomous components, which are discussed in the next section.

11.5.2   Autonomous Components

Autonomous components retain the features and characteristics of traditional components on the one hand, and they have a conjunction with agents in possessing autonomous behavioral abilities on the other hand. However, autonomous components are neither traditional components nor agents. Like components, autonomous components have relatively independent functionalities, they provide specified services for outside use, and they can be reused and assembled into software systems. Nevertheless, autonomous components are software entities with autonomy. They are driven by their own goals and that they provide services is because doing so can help them to achieve their goals. Even when they are achieving their goals, they can adjust their behaviors in responding to the changes of their environment via changing the time and way of providing services.

Specifically, an autonomous component can formally be described from five aspects [3]. First, its behavior is goal-driven. Next, it also provides the services to outside though it is no longer passive and can even autonomously decide whether or not to provide its services. Third, the use contract describes how users can access the services in an appropriate way. Fourth, it is situated in the environment. It can perceive the changes of the environment and can adjust its behavior to adapt

to the changing environment. Finally, the dependency relationship between its goals and the environment determines how it can reason about and decide its behaviors to achieve its goals.

Because an autonomous component is specified mainly via its goals, the services, and the environment, it is crucial to reflect the interaction relationships among the goals, the services, and the environment in the implementation of the autonomous component. Therefore, we use the goal-driven rules and plans to relate the goals, the environment and the services together.

When the autonomous component perceives specific stimulus occurring in the environment and has deduced that the premise for achieving a goal appears, triggers the corresponding rule to activate the process of achieving the goal.

$$f(E) \rightarrow \text{Activate}(G)$$

Where f is a function of the environment and G is one of the goals of the autonomous component.

After the process of achieving a goal is activated, the autonomous component will plan the achievement of the goal, i.e., determine how to take actions to achieve the goal. Among the actions that the autonomous component takes to pursue the achievement of its goal, there may involve the activities of requesting or providing services.

$$\text{Plan} : G \rightarrow S*$$

Where a plan is a mapping from a goal to a sequence of actions (probably including activities of providing services).

When the autonomous component perceives a request for service from others, it will reason about its behavior to check out whether the request will activate the process of achieving a specific goal. If yes, it will respond the request while achieving its goal; otherwise, it will reject or ignore the request. Even for the same request for service, the autonomous component possibly activates different goals, which may lead to different ways of responding the request, under different states of the environment.

Although an autonomous component has some extends of autonomy, it must expose its interface and provide normal functionalities, like those traditional components, so that it could be assembled into software systems. Therefore, what makes an autonomous component different from traditional components is that the autonomous component takes a different way to implement its interface, i.e., it may adjust its behavior to provide services and implement its interface according to the states of the environment. However, for users, they always use the component and request its services through its interface and they care about neither how the autonomous component implements its interface nor how it adapts its behavior while providing services. We can say that the true difference between an autonomous component and a traditional component is the implementation structure and the runtime behavior. The implementation structure of an autonomous component is shown in Fig. 11.13.

In the figure, the environment information includes those environmental variables or data that the autonomous component cares and can perceive. The sensor is used to capture the states and changes of the environment and it is also responsible for maintaining the environment information according to the perceived information. The rule set specifies those rules driving and controlling the behavior of the autonomous component. A plan in the plan repository specifies the sequence of actions for the autonomous component to achieve a goal or implement a service. In order to simplify the implementation, we currently adopted an off-line way to define plans for the autonomous component.

The autonomous component will not take any actions unless a specific rule is triggered. The rule engine is responsible for deducing and triggering rules based on the environment information and the rule set. The plan engine will be actuated by some rules and is responsible for selecting appropriate plans to achieve goals.

The behavior mode that an autonomous component responds requests and provides services can be described as follows. (1) When the autonomous component receives a request for service, its rule engine will reason about its behavior based on the current environment and the rule set. If there is no such rule being able to be triggered, the autonomous component may not take any actions or directly rejects the request for service; otherwise, it may activate the plan engine to select and execute an appropriate plan to carry out the service. (2) In the execution of the selected plan, if all actions involved in the plan can be performed correctly and their executions do not violate any environment constraints, the requested service will be provided successfully; or else the autonomous component will report an exception of service failure. (3) Even if there is no an outside request for service, the rule engine may also trigger rules to carry out some actions according to the current environment states.

Since the usage of an autonomous component is like that of a traditional component, we add a new container into PKUAS to support the run of autonomous components. In the implementation, we integrated an open-source

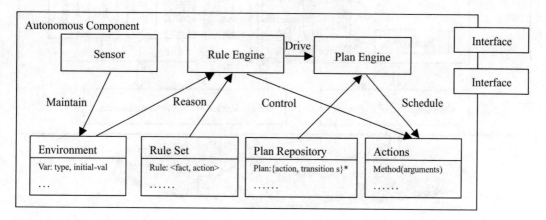

Fig. 11.13   The implementation structure of the autonomous component

rule engine called Drools and developed a plan engine to supply the capabilities of ruledriving and planning for autonomous components, as shown in Fig. 11.14. Just like the EJB containers in PKUAS, the autonomous component container provides the running space for the instance of an autonomous component, managing the life cycle of the autonomous component and the communications between the autonomous component and other components. The interceptor in the container implements the sensor of the autonomous component. The interceptor is responsible for intercepting communications between autonomous components and supports the interoperability of autonomous components. On the other hand, it captures the state information about the environment and maintains the environment information, which will be used by the rule engine to infer and trigger rules.

Considering that every instance of the autonomous component has a rule engine and a plan engine, we implement the rule engine and the plan engine as public services and put them into the public service management framework in the middleware. The autonomous component container will call those public services to control the behaviors of the autonomous component. When the autonomous component container receives a request for service, it will transfer the request to the interceptor, and then the interceptor will activate the rule engine and the plan engine to schedule the executions of the actions of the autonomous component.

For example, as mentioned above, when a JPS entity component (e.g., Customer) becomes the performance bottleneck of the system, it possibly needs to change the structure or the implementation of the entire system. In order to improve the structural and behavioral adaptabilities of the system, we can implement these components as autonomous components. We can customize specific behavior rules for the autonomous components to enable them to switch automatically between different service providing modes according to the runtime states of the environment and the system.

For example, for the Customer, it can provide its services in different ways when it uses different modes to access the database. Thus, we can specify behavior rules for the Customer to adopt different ways to perform its service as follows (Fig. 11.15). These rules specify that when the ratio between the amounts of occupied memory and the allocated memory is greater than 0.8, which implies that the request for the Customer's services has already become the performance bot-

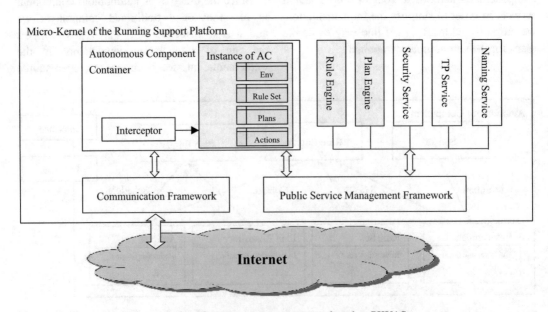

Fig. 11.14 The runtime support platform for autonomous components based on PKUAS

Fig. 11.15 Rules for the autonomous component to adjust its behaviors

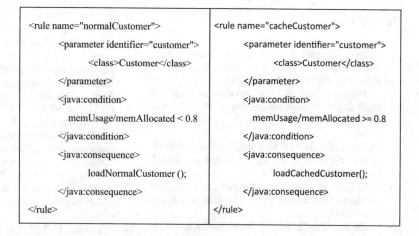

```
<rule name="normalCustomer">                      <rule name="cacheCustomer">
    <parameter identifier="customer">                <parameter identifier="customer">
        <class>Customer</class>                          <class>Customer</class>
    </parameter>                                      </parameter>
    <java:condition>                                  <java:condition>
        memUsage/memAllocated < 0.8                      memUsage/memAllocated >= 0.8
    </java:condition>                                 </java:condition>
    <java:consequence>                                <java:consequence>
        loadNormalCustomer ();                            loadCachedCustomer();
    </java:consequence>                               </java:consequence>
</rule>                                            </rule>
```

tleneck, the Customer will start the implementation version that uses the cache memory, otherwise it will start the normal version.

This kind of adaptation may influence the interaction relationships inside or among autonomous components. Under a specific circumstance, the changes of the interaction relationships among autonomous components may result in the reconfiguration of the software architecture.

11.6 Conclusion

In the past several decades, software technologies have experienced a series of development. The main line for this development is clear: the granularity of constituent software entities grows coarser; the software model fits our thinking better and better; as the power of software execution platform keeps increasing, more and more underlying complexities as well as those relating to software development are hidden; software techniques have been applied to more and more real world areas. As the Internet keeps rapid and continuous development, existing software technologies may confront more and more requirements and challenges. Typically, due to their static and close nature, traditional software technologies are not adequate and suited for the open, dynamic and ever-changing Internet; instead, a new software paradigm, Internetware,

appears naturally. It accommodates the open, dynamic and ever-changing Internet in a better way, manifesting itself as flexible, continually reactive software with multiple compatible goals. The engineering of Internetware requires innovations on traditional software development methods and techniques. In this chapter, we introduce a component oriented, architecture-centric and middleware-based approach, called ABC, to support the engineering of Internetware. ABC spans over all phases of software lifecycle, including the analysis, design, implementation, deployment, maintenance and evolution of Internetware. In particular, feature models are used to model, organize and manage "disordered" software resources; adaptive SA models are used to design a self-adaptive Internetware; reflective middleware is use to enforce the self-adaptation. Whatever, there are many open issues to be addressed, such as improving the automation of design for self-adaptability, incarnating cooperation among Internetware, refining component models dedicated to Internetware, and so on.

Acknowledgments This effort is sponsored by the National Basic Research Program of China (973) under Grant No. 2002CB31200003; the National Natural Science Foundation of China under Grant No. 60233010,90612011,90412011,60403030,60303004 and the Natural Science Foundation of Beijing under Grant No. 4052018.

References

1. G. Huang, H. Mei, F. Yang, Runtime software architecture based on reflective middleware. Sci. Chin. Ser. F: Inf. Sci. **47**(5), 555–576 (2004)
2. G. Huang, H. Mei, F. Yang, Runtime recovery and manipulation of software architecture of component-based systems. Autom. Softw. Eng. **13**(2), 257–281 (2006)
3. W. Jiao, P. Zhu, H. Mei, Modeling internet-based software systems using autonomous components. Chin. J. Electron. **15**(4), 593 (2006)
4. R. Kazman, M. Klein, P. Clements, Atam: method for architecture evaluation, Technical report, DTIC Document (2000)
5. L. Lan, G. Huang, L. Ma, M. Wang, H. Mei, L. Zhang, Y. Chen, Architecture based deployment of large-scale component based systems: the tool and principles, in *Component-Based Software Engineering, 8th International Symposium, CBSE 2005*, St. Louis, MO, USA, 14–15 May 2005, Proceedings (2005), pp. 123–138
6. B. Len, C. Paul, K. Rick, *Software Architecture in Practice* (Massachusetts Addison, Boston, 2003)
7. T. Liu, G. Huang, G. Fan, H. Mei, The coordinated recovery of data service and transaction service in J2EE, in *29th Annual International Computer Software and Applications Conference, COMPSAC 2005*, Edinburgh, Scotland, UK, 25–28 July 2005, vol. 1 (2005), pp. 485–490
8. H. Mei, J. Chang, F. Yang, Software component composition based on ADL and middleware. Sci Chin. Seri. F: Inf. Sci. **44**(2), 136–151 (2001)
9. H. Mei, F. Chen, Q. Wang, Y.-D. Feng, ABC/ADL: an ADL supporting component composition, in *Formal Methods and Software Engineering, 4th International Conference on Formal Engineering Methods, ICFEM 2002 Shanghai*, China, 21–25 Oct 2002, Proceedings (2002), pp. 38–47
10. H. Mei, G. Huang. PKUAS: an architecture-based reflective component operating platform, in *10th IEEE International Workshop on Future Trends of Distributed Computing Systems (FTDCS 2004)*, 26–28 May 2004, Suzhou, China (2004), pp. 163–169
11. J. Shen, X. Sun, G. Huang, W. Jiao, Y. Sun, H. Mei, Towards a unified formal model for supporting mechanisms of dynamic component update, in *Proceedings of the 10th European Software Engineering Conference held jointly with 13th ACM SIGSOFT International Symposium on Foundations of Software Engineering*, 2005, Lisbon, Portugal, 5–9 Sept 2005 (2005), pp. 80–89
12. T. Teng, G. Huang, R. Li, D. Zhao, H. Mei, Feature interactions induced by data dependencies among entity components, in *Feature Interactions in Telecommunications and Software Systems VIII, ICFI'05*, 28–30 June 2005, Leicester, UK (2005), pp. 252–269
13. Z. Wei, M. Hong, A feature-oriented domain model and its modeling process. J. Softw. **14**(8), 1345–1356 (2003)
14. F.Q. Yang, H. Mei, J. Lu, Z. Jin, Some thoughts on the development of software technologies. Acta Electronica Sinica (in Chin.) **26**(9), 1104–1115 (2003)
15. J. Yang, G. Huang, X. Chen, H. Mei, S.C. Cheung, Consistency assurance in flattening hierarchical architectural models. Ruan Jian Xue Bao/J. Softw. **17**(6), 1391 (2006)
16. W. Zhang, H. Mei, H. Zhao, A feature-oriented approach to modeling requirements dependencies, in *13th IEEE International Conference on Requirements Engineering (RE 2005)*, 29 Aug–2 Sept 2005, Paris, France (2005), pp. 273–284
17. W. Zhang, H. Mei, H. Zhao, J. Yang, Transformation from CIM to PIM: a feature-oriented component-based approach, in *Model Driven Engineering Languages and Systems, 8th International Conference, MoDELS 2005*, Montego Bay, Jamaica, 2–7 Oct 2005, Proceedings (2005), pp. 248–263
18. W. Zhang, H. Zhao, H. Mei, A propositional logic-based method for verification of feature models, in *Formal Methods and Software Engineering, 6th International Conference on Formal Engineering Methods, ICFEM 2004*, Seattle, WA, USA, 8–12 Nov 2004, Proceedings (2004), pp. 115–130
19. Y. Zhu, Modeling diverse and complex interactions enabled by middleware as connectors in software architectures, in *10th International Conference on Engineering of Complex Computer Systems (ICECCS 2005)*, 16–20 June 2005, Shanghai, China (2005), pp. 37–46

Toward Capability Specification of Internetware Entity Based on Environment Ontology

12

Abstract

Internetware can be formed by automated aggregation of Internetware entities in bottom-up way to satisfy user requirements. That requires Internetware entity capability specification of a high precision. Thus, semantic-based approach is more attractive. This chapter proposes to build capability specifications of Internetware entities based on environment ontology which includes full conceptualisation of the interactive environment entities of Internetware in a particular domain. Tree-like hierarchical state machine has been used to describe the stateful environment entities in which the states and the state transitions caused by external interactions of any environment entities have been explicitly captued. The assumption of this approach is the capability of an Internetware entity can be represented by the effects imposed by this entity on the environment entities. Algorithms for constructing the domain environment ontology and the matchmaking between capability descriptions of Internetware entities are presented to show how to support the automated discovery of Internetware entities. An example on On-line Education is given to illustrate this proposed approach.

Keywords

Ontology design · Intelligent web service languages

12.1 Introduction

Internetware is a new software paradigm which assume that the software are developed and run on the open, dynamic and changeable Internet. Internetware entities are the constituents of Internetware which are developed by different parties and are distributed on Internet. Internetware entities communicate and collaborate with each others in different ways for fulfilling the dynamically

Parts of this chapter were reprinted from © [2008] IEEE. Reprinted, with permission, from Puwei Wang, Zhi Jin, Lin Liu and Guangjun Cai. *Building toward capability specifications of web services based on an environment ontology*. In IEEE Transactions on Knowledge and Data Engineering (TKDE), Volume. 20, No. 4, pp. 547–561. April 2008. DOI: 10.1109/TKDE.2007.190719.

© Springer Science+Business Media Singapore 2016
H. Mei and J. Lü, *Internetware*, DOI 10.1007/978-981-10-2546-4_12

demanded users' requirements [1]. These features makes the development and execution of Internetware entity being different from the traditional software entity. Concretely, given a user requirement, the Internetware development is achieved by finding and aggregating some existed Internetware entities on Internet to satisfy this requirement, instead of starting from the scratch. That means, it follows a bottom-up process but not traditional top-down process. Moreover, the aggregation evolves dynamically in terms of changes of user requirement as well as the situation of the engaged Internetware entities. For example, when facing the changes of the user requirement, Internetware entity may evolve by changing its own configuration or asking new Internetware entities to join in the aggregation. Thus, it is very critical to precisely specify the capability of the Internetware entities to enable the automated discovery and aggregation.

In the area of the semantic Web services technology [2], researchers also paid many attentions to describe the Web services in an unambiguous and machine compatible way for enabling the intelligent interoperation of Web services. Ontology [37] has been widely used to enrich Web services with semantics [38,39], e.g., OWL-S (formerly DAML-S) [3], WSMO [4] and WSDL-S [5]. The earlier efforts on the semantic capability specifications of Web services assumed that the service capabilities can be modelled the inputs, the outputs, the preconditions and the results of Web services (henceforth referred to as IOPR).

Currently, Internet of Thing has widely been recognised as an innovative technology which is enabled by means of automatic identification technologies, sensors and actuators [6]. In IoT, physical entities are seamlessly integrated into the information network. And they are expected to become active participants in business processes where they are enabled to interact and communicate communicate among themselves and with the environment by exchanging data and information sensed about the environment, while reacting autonomously to the physical world events and influencing it by running processes that trigger actions [7]. So that the digital world can be seamlessly integrated with the physical world and enable things to serve people better.

When Internetware paradigm moves into the era of the Internet of Thing, the IOPE-based capability description is not enough. Through sensors and actuators, the Internetware entity can interact directly with its physical environment. As the physical environment may keep change autonomously or triggered by some events, the Internetware entity is be able to sense the changes and choose suitable behaviours as the response. In this sense, the capability of the Internetware entity needs to be specified as the adaption behaviours for dealing with the environmental changes. Based on our previous work [40–43], this chapter proposes an approach which specifies the capability of Internetware entity based on the effects which are to be achieved by this entity onto the environment. These effects are modelled as the state transitions of "real world" resource entities on which Internetware entity can operate, such as the physical devices in smart home applications. These "real world" resource entities are the environment entities to be modelled here. They are domain relevant and independent of the existence of any particular Internetware entity.

The environment-based view has its origin in the research area of requirements engineering. In this area, the requirements of a software system act as the meeting point between an inner world and an outer world, and this has been well-recognised. Here, the inner world refers to the "machine" (the software's inner construction) and the outer world refers to the "world" (the environment in which the software will operate on). In fact, this viewpoint can be traced back to David Parnas's famous Four-Variable Model [8]. In this model, two environment variables are used, i.e., the monitored and the controlled variables, to describe the system behaviours. This model has been successfully used in modelling control system requirements. Furthermore, Michael Jackson, in his foundation chapters [9,10], has pointed out that the semantics of a software system concerns the environment on which the system will operate instead of the system itself. In the Problem Frame approach [11], a context diagram is used to model requirements of software systems, which include domains in the "problem world", and interactions between the domains and systems. [12] also demonstrates that the meaning of the requirements of a desired software system can be depicted by the "to-be" environment of this system and the operative interactions between them.

In this chapter an Environment Modelling-based Capability specification Framework for Internetware entities (EMoCaS) is proposed as a way to obtain elaborated Internetware entity capability specification. It is motivated by the following considerations:

(1) *Environment exhibits the capabilities of Internetware entities.* The meaning of the requirements can be depicted by the operative interactions of the software system with its environment, as well as the causal relationships among these interactions [12]. Hence, the capabilities of Internetware entities can be expressed by the effects of the Internetware entities on the environment. The characteristics of and interconnections with the environment is what we need to know when specifying the capabilities of Internetware entities.

(2) *Environment entities are able to be shared among loosely coupled Internetware entities.* Internetware entities are loosely coupled, and they have sharable descriptions to support the entity discovery. In earlier efforts [13], service interfaces were modelled to contain sharable descriptions. A service is discovered when the service's interface description matches with the request. In contrast to the service interface description, the environment entities can play the role to obtain a more expressive sharable description. The environment entities are outside the boundary of Internetware entities. Internetware entities provided by different service providers can interact with some shared environment entities, and the expressive capability descriptions are obtained based on these environment entities.

(3) *It is very feasible, using an environment-based perspective, to specify the evolving capabilities of open Internetware entities.* In the systems theory, an open system is defined as a system that interacts with its environment [14]. The motivation for change in open Internetware entities is caused by the dynamic changing

requests. In other words, changes in the Internetware entities' desired effects on the environment cause the evolvement of service capabilities. To a particular Internetware entity, while its effects on the environment evolve with changing requests, the environment itself is comparatively stable.

The rest of this chapter is structured as follows: Sect. 12.2 introduces the structure of the environment ontology and a procedure of its construction. A running example is given for illustration. Section 12.3 describes the EMoCaS. Based on the EMoCaS, state machine-based capability specifications of Internetware entities are generated. Moreover, the matchmaking details between the capability specifications are presented to support the Internetware entity discovery. Section 12.4 analyses related works and compares them with the proposed approach. Finally, Sect. 12.5 concludes this chapter and discusses future work.

12.2 Environment Ontology

The environment of an Internetware entity is assumed to be a set of physical entities that will interact with this Internetware entity. To model the effects on the environment, an environment ontology is proposed which is featured by the conceptualisation of different environment entities.

12.2.1 Upper Environment Ontology

Environment ontology is the shared conceptualisation of the environment entities as well as the interactions between Internetware entity and the environment entities. Figure 12.1 is presented to show the conceptual hierarchy of the upper environment ontology. Following the assumptions about the software context in Problem Frame approach [11], we summarise three kinds of environment entities that have been conceptualised in the environment ontology: the autonomous entity; the symbolic entity; and the causal entity. They are the abstractions of all kinds of the interactors of Internetware entities. This upper ontology covers all aspects that the environment modelling based requirements engineering is taking care of.

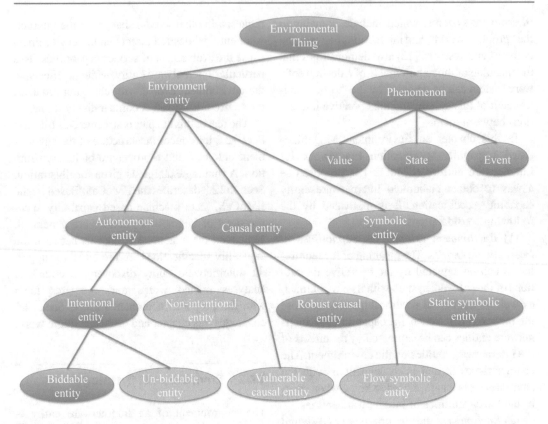

Fig. 12.1 Upper environment ontology

For example, taking care of non-intentional entity implies to allow the Internetware entity be adaptive, taking care of un-biddable entity implies to consider the security of Internetware entity, taking care of the un-determined causal entity means to ask for the fault-tolerance of Internetware entity based system, and taking care of flow symbolic entity is for considering the real timelity of Internetware entity.

This chapter only focuses on the normal functional capability specification. Thus, only the following three leaf concepts, i.e. the biddable entity, the robust causal entity and the static symbolic entity, will be considered. The phenomena are representing the potential interactions of environment entities with outside. The three kinds of the phenomena are value, state and event.

- value phenomenon: an individual that can not undergo change over time. The values we are interested in are such things as numbers and characters, represented by symbols.

- state phenomenon: an attribute-value pair of an causal entity that can be true at one time and false at another.

- event phenomenon: an individual that is an occurrence at some point in time, regard as atomic and instantaneous.

- biddable entity: any biddable entity is active to create itself and share its phenomena with others and is assumed to be able to follow shared phenomenon requests from others but there is no any predictable relationship between shared phenomena.

- symbolic entity: any symbolic entity is passive and normally is a repository of data.-Other entities can share with it the value phenomena.

- causal entity: Any causal entity is passive to shared phenomena from others. Some phenomena can trigger its change on its states in a predictable way followed by sharing its phenomena with others.

12.2.2 Domain Environment Ontology

In terms of the upper environment ontology, a set of environment entities can be identified and the domain environment ontology of Internetware entities in particular domain is structured by a set of environment entities and the phenomena relationship among these environment entities.

For capturing the causality of causal environment entities, it is assumed in our approach, the attributes of a causal environment entity are classified into two groups: (i) characteristic attributes (and their values which describe the states of this environment entity), and (ii) non-characteristic attributes. That is, for any environment entity $e \in Ent$, its characteristic attributes $CAtts(e) \subseteq Atts(e)$ define the set of states of e as

$$States(e) \overset{def}{=} \{\langle \alpha_i, v_j \rangle | \alpha_i \in CAtts(e), v_j \in value(\alpha_i)\}$$

That shows that the state of an environment entity is a pair of characteristic attributes of this environment entity and a certain value within its finite value range. For example, in the domain of travel agency, the environment entity "ticket" can be *"available"*, *"booked"*, and *"sold"* as its *'status'*. Thus, its *'(status)'* is a characteristic attribute that has three alternative values.

As we assume that the autonomous entities and symbolic entities are not modelled by internal causal structure. We use single-state machine as their models for unifying the representations of all environment entities. That means any autonomous entity can do anything that has been requested but always stay in its single state. So does the symbolic entity and it will stay in the same state after receiving/storing new data or sending out the available data. Hence, with a general domain ontology, the only burden of constructing the domain environment ontology is building the state machines of the causal entities. For supporting the different conceptualisation granularities, we use the hierarchical state machine. In the following, we will present how to construct the hierarchical state machines for causal environment entities.

First, we should define the basic state machine. Let $e \in Ent$ be an environment entity and $\alpha \in CAtts(e)$ be a characteristic attribute of e.

Definition 12.1 A Basic State Machine (BSM) of e is

$$< S, \Sigma, \delta, \lambda, q_0, F >$$

in which

- $S = \{\langle \alpha, v_j \rangle | v_j \in value(\alpha)\} \subseteq States(e)$ is a finite set of states of e;
- $\Sigma = \Sigma^{in} \cup \Sigma^{out}$. Σ^{in} is the set of input symbols and Σ^{out} is the set of output symbols;
- $\delta : S \times \Sigma^{in} \to S$ is the state transition function;
- $\lambda : S \to \Sigma^{out}$ is the output function;
- $q_0 \in S$ is the initial state.
- $F \subseteq S$ is the set of final states.

Then, hierarchy is added to the BSM. $\preccurlyeq$ is a tree-like partial order relation with a topmost point [15]. This relation defines the hierarchy on the states within $States(e)$ ($x \preccurlyeq y$ means that x is a descendant of y ($x \prec y$), or x and y are equal ($x = y$)). "Tree-like" means that $\preccurlyeq$ has the property: $\neg(a \preccurlyeq b \vee b \preccurlyeq a) \Rightarrow \neg\exists x : (x \preccurlyeq a \wedge x \preccurlyeq b)$. If the state x is a descendant of y ($x \prec y$), and there is no state z such that $x \prec z \prec y$, the state x is a child of y (x *child* y).

According to $\preccurlyeq$ on $States(e)$, the subdivision from a state s of e to a BSM N of e can be defined. If $s \notin S(N)$, for all $s' \in S(N)$ ($S(N)$ denotes the set of states in BSM N), such that $s'childs$, state s is a super-state of BSM N (or BSM N has a super-state s), and $\langle s, N \rangle$ is a *subdivision*. The initial state λ_0 in sub-BSM N is called the *"default child"* of super-state s. Since $\preccurlyeq$ is tree-like, the sub-BSM has no more than one super-state.

Definition 12.2 Let $e \in Ent$ be an environment entity, $BSM(e) = \{N_1, ..., N_n\}$ ($n \geqslant 1$) be the set of BSMs of e and let D be the set of subdivisions. A Tree-like Hierarchical State Machine (THSM) of e is defined as

$$< BSM(e), D >$$

in which,

- There is one and only one special BSM in $BSM(e)$ that called the *root* (denoted by $N_{root} \in BSM(e)$) of the HSM;

- Other BSMs are partitioned into $m > 0$ disjoint sets $B_1, \ldots, B_m$, where each of them also can constitute a THSM $\text{hsm}_i = \langle B_i, D_i \rangle$, $D_i \subseteq D, i \in [1, m]$, If $N_{root}^{B_i} \in B_i$ is the *root* of hsm_i, then there exists $s \in S(N_{root})$, such that $\langle s, N_{root}^{B_i} \rangle \in D$. hsm_i is also called a sub-THSM of s.

Definition 12.3 The environment ontology of Internetware entities in a particular domain is defined as a 6-tuple

$$< Ent, Rel, rel, H, hsm, Dep >$$

in which,

- *Ent* is a set of environment entities in this domain. An environment entity which can be abstract or concrete is described as $\langle id, Atts, Rans, value \rangle$, in which *id* is the name, $Atts = \{\alpha_1, \ldots, \alpha_n\}$ is a set of attributes, $Rans = \{v_1, \ldots, v_m\}$ is a set of values and $value : Atts \rightarrow 2^{Rans}$ is a function mapping attributes to value ranges;
- *Rel* is a set of relations, e.g. 'is-a', 'part-of', etc.;
- $r : Rel \rightarrow Ent \times Ent$ is a function, that relates environment entities;
- *H* is a set of Tree-like Hierarchical State Machines (THSMs). Each of which has a pair of finite sets of phenomena as its input and output symbols;
- $h : Ent \leftrightarrow H$ is a bijective function. For each environment entity $e \in Ent$, there is one and only one $hsm \in H$, such that $h(e) = hsm.hsm$ represents the causality of e in this domain;
- *Dep* is a set of phenomena pairs, each of which defines a desired relationship among the environment entities. These relationships are in fact representing the business assumptions in particular domain. There are three kinds of dependences:
  - Relationship represents that an entity instance is created when another entity instance initiates an event,

$$\text{entity.Phe} \rightarrow \text{entity.InitialState}$$

  - Relationship represents that an entity instance is eliminated when another entity instance initiates an event,

$$\text{entity.Phe} \rightarrow \text{entity.EndState}$$

  - Relationship represents that an entity instance is triggered to change its state along its hierarchical state machine when another entity instance initiates an event,

$$\text{entity.Phe} \rightarrow \text{entity.(StatePhe} \oplus \text{Phe)}$$

  - Relationship represents that an entity instance receive a value phenomenon that depends on shared value phenomena from other entities,

$$(\text{entity.ValuePhe})_1^n \rightarrow \text{entity.ValuePhe}$$

12.2.3 Construction of Domain Environment Ontology

Domain environment ontology is normally built by domain experts manually. The process for the construction is just like the process for developing the class hierarchy could be

- Identify and create the environment entities and let them be an instance of one atom type in the upper environment ontology. Define the attributes and the values of the attributes.
- For each causal entity, identify the characteristic attributes and define the state machine (if needed, the hierarchical state machine) including the states and the state transitions among states to represent the dynamical behaviour of the entity.
- Detect and define the 'is-a' and/or 'part-of' relationships between the entities of the same type by using the abstraction and division principles.
- Based on the business logics, declare the dependencies between phenomena aroused by environment entities.

Current general ontological structure [16] includes the concept declarations and the relations

Fig. 12.2 Fragment of a general domain ontology in education domain

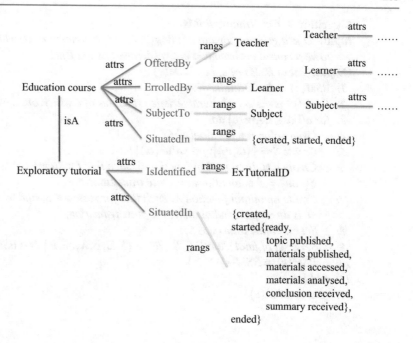

between them. We extend the general ontological structure in the following aspects. First, we extend the general ontological structure with state machines to include specifying those changeable environment entities with state transitions. Secondly, we use the hierarchical state machine [15] to support the different conceptualisation granularities for satisfying the demands of different abstraction levels.

The construction of the domain environment ontology can also be much easier as it can be semi-automatically built from the existing general domain ontology under the guidance of domain experts. Concretely, after the identification of the necessary environment entities, the static description of these entities can be extracted from the existing general domain ontology, as are the relations among them. The only extra effort is deriving the state machines for causal environment entities. We consider the following relations among environment entities as derived from the general domain ontology for constructing the THSMs of the environment entities.

- These relations represent the characteristics of concepts (called "characteristic relation"). For example, Fig. 12.2 is fragment of a general domain ontology in education domain. *Exploratory tutorial* is an environment entity, and the relations *SituatedIn* associated with it is a characteristic relation. Those values of this relation are used to the construction of the domain THSM of *Exploratory tutorial*.
- These relations are the components or the inheritance relations between concepts. For example, *isA* is an inheritance relation from *Exploratory tutorial* to *Education course*.

Without a loss of generality, we assume that $O = \{C, R, rel\}$ is an existing general domain ontology, in which C is a set of concepts, R is a set of relations and $rel : R \rightarrow C \times C$ is a relation. We identify the environment entities *Ent* from the concepts C ($Ent \subseteq C$) and the characteristic attributes of those causal environment entities from the relations R. After the environment entities and their characteristic attributes are

Algorithm 7 *ConstructingBSMs*

Input: *O is a general domain ontology, and e is a concept in O, which is identified*
       to be a causal environment entity (denoted as $e \in Ent$)

Output: *set of BSMs of e, i.e., BSM(e)*

  1:   $BSM(e) = \phi$; *//Initialisation*
  2:   *$CAtts(e)$ is the set of characteristic attributes of e which are derived from O;*
  3:   **for all** $\alpha \in CAtts(e)$ **do**
  4:      *Get a value range $value(\alpha)$;*
  5:      *Create $S = \{\langle \alpha, v_j \rangle | v_j \in value(\alpha)\}$;*
  6:      *Create a state transition function δ, such that for states $s, s' \in S$ and $m \in \Sigma^{in}$,*
         $\delta(s, m) = s'$ is an allowable state transition;
  7:      *Create an output function λ, such that for state $s \in S$, and $m' \in \Sigma^{out}$, $\lambda(s) =$*
         m' is an output symbol along the state transition;
  8:      *Set an initial state $q_0 \in S$;*
  9:      *Set a set of final state $F \subseteq S$; //$N = \{S, \Sigma, \delta, \lambda, q_0, F\}$ is a BSM of e*
10:      $BSM(e) = BSM(e) \cup \{N\}$;
11:   **end for**
12:   **return** $BSM(e)$

identified, the procedure of constructing the domain THSM of the causal environment entity can be executed. We first construct the BSMs of causal environment entity. The algorithm is given as follows.

After the BSMs of causal environment entities are constructed, we shift our focus to the component relation and the inheritance relation between environment entities. If there is an inheritance relation from one environment entity $e_1 \in Ent$ to another environment entity $e_2 \in Ent$, it means that e_1 inherits the attributes from e_2. For example, the environment entity *Education course* has three attributes {*OfferedBy*, *EnrolledBy*, and *SubjectTo*}. Therefore, the environment entity *Exploratory tutorial*, which has an inheritance relation to *Education course*, has also these three attributes plus its own attributes {*IsIdentified*, and *SituatedIn*}. Here, *SituatedIn* needs inherit and overiden. During the procedure of constructing

the HTSM of the child entities, the BSMs and the subdivisions in the HTSMs of the parent entity will be inherited. Similarly, if there is a component relation from e_2 to e_1, e_1 owns attributes of e_2 and the identifiers of these attributes are added with the identifier of e_2 as a prefix.

Algorithm 8 constructs the HSM of an environment entity $e \in Ent$ in terms of the inheritance relation. Let $e_1, \dots, e_n \in Ent$ be n environment entities. The domain HSMs of $e_1, \dots, e_n$ have been constructed, and e has the inheritance relation to $e_1, \dots, e_n$. The idea is that e inherits characteristic attributes of $e_1, \dots, e_n$, because e inherits $e_1, \dots, e_n$. Therefore, the domain THSMs $(hsm(e_1), \dots, hsm(e_n))$ are inherited during the construction of $hsm(e)$. The operation semantics of overloading and derivation in the algorithm are in order to create inheritance threads from the BSMs of e to its inherited BSMs from $e_1, \dots, e_n$.

Algorithm 8 *Constructing domain HSM in terms of the inheritance relation*

Input: HSMs $hsm(e_1), \cdots, hsm(e_n)$ and e has the inheritance relation to $e_1, \cdots, e_n$
Output: $hsm(e) = \{BSM_e, D_e\}$
1: $BSM_e = \phi;$
2: $\mathscr{D}_e = \phi;$ //Initialisation
3: $BSM_{own} = ConstructingBSMs(e, O);$ //Creating BSMs of e via ALGORITHM.7
4: $BSM_e = BSM_{own};$
5: **for all** $e' \in \{e_1, \cdots, e_n\}$ **do**
6:     $hsm(e') = \{BSM'_e, D'_e\}$ is the domain THSM of $e';$
7:     $BSM_e = BSM_e \cup BSM'_e;$
8:     $D_e = D_e \cup D'_e;$ //Inheriting domain THSMs of $e_1, \cdots, e_n$
9: **end for**
10: **for all** $N_i \in BSM_{own}$ **do**
11:     **while** $\exists N_j \in BSM_e - BSM_{own}$, N_i, N_j are constructed in terms of a same characteristic attribute **do**
12:        $Overridden(N_i, N_j);$
13:     **end while**
14:     **if** $\exists s$ is a state in BSM_e, $\langle s, N_i \rangle$ is a subdivision **then**
15:        $D_e = D_e \cup \{\langle s, N_i \rangle\};$ //Adding a subdivision
16:     **end if**
17: **end for**
18: **return** $hsm(e)$

Algorithm 9 constructs the HSM of an environment entity $e \in Ent$ in terms of the component relation. Let $e_1, \ldots, e_n \in Ent$ be n environment entities. The domain THSMs of $e_1, \ldots, e_n$ have been constructed, and $e_1, \ldots, e_n$ have the component relation to e. The algorithm is similar to Algorithm 8. The domain THSMs $(hsm(e_1), \ldots, hsm(e_n))$ are included during the construction of $hsm(e)$ except that it does not need to deal with the problem of overloading and derivation. During the procedure, the root BSMs which are constructed in terms of the characteristic attribute *inticond* of e and $e_1, \ldots, e_n$ are combined.

Algorithm 9 *Constructing domain THSM in terms of the component relation*

Input: Domain THSMs $hsm(e_1), \cdots, hsm(e_n)$ and $e_1, \cdots, e_n$ have the component relation to e
Output: $hsm(e) = \{BSM_e, D_e\}$
1: $BSM_e = \phi;$
2: $D_e = \phi;$ //Initialisation
3: $BSM_{own} = ConstructingBSMs(e, O);$ //Creating BSMs of e via ALGORITHM.7
4: $BSM_e = BSM_{own};$
5: **for all** $e' \in \{e_1, \cdots, e_n\}$ **do**
6:     $hsm(e') = \{BSM'_e, D'_e\}$ is the domain THSM of $e';$
7:     $BSM_e = BSM_e \cup BSM'_e;$
8:     $D_e = D_e \cup D'_e;$ //Including domain THSMs of $e_1, \cdots, e_n$
9: **end for**
10: **for all** $N_i \in BSM_{own}$ **do**
11:     **while** $\exists N_j \in BSM_e - BSM_{own}$, N_i, N_j are constructed in terms of characteristic attribute *initcond* **do**
12:        $Combine(N_i, N_j);$
13:     **end while**
14:     **if** $\exists s$ is a state in BSM_e, $\langle s, N_i \rangle$ is a subdivision **then**
15:        $D_e = D_e \cup \{\langle s, N_i \rangle\};$ //Adding a subdivision
16:     **end if**
17: **end for**
18: **return** $hsm(e)$

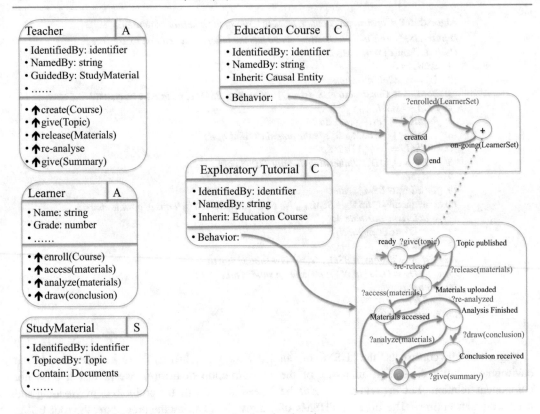

Fig. 12.3 Fragment of the environment ontology in education domain

Figure 12.3 shows the fragment of the environment ontology in education domain. In this figure, *Teacher, Learner, Study Materials, Education Course* and *Exploratory Tutorial* are the environment entities. There are inheritance relations among them: *Exploratory Tutorials* is a kind of *Education Course*. The dependency relationships among them are represented by the phenomena of the same names. The potential functionalities implied by the environment ontology corresponding to different study paths to the final state contain: (1) self-education exploratory course, in which learner can download the study materials; (2) exploratory course with supervised analysis, in which learner can obtain the supervision for study analysis; (3) exploratory course with supervised analysis and evaluation, in which learner can obtain the supervision for study analysis and result evaluation; and (4) fully supervised exploratory course, in which learner can obtain the supervision

for study analysis, result evaluation and advisers for further study.

12.3 Environment Ontology Based Capability Specification

Once the environment ontology is explicitly represented, we can then specify the capability of an Internetware entity. [12] demonstrates that the meaning of the requirements of a desired software system can be depicted by the "to-be" environment of the system and the operative interactions between the system and the environment as well as the causal constraints on these interactions. That is, the desired capabilities, of a software system act as the meeting point between an inner world and an outer world. Here, the inner world refers to the "software entities" (the inner construction of the software system) and the outer world refers to the "world" (the environment on which the software system will operate).

So, what is the capability of an Internetware entity? That is that an Internetware entity entity can only show its capability upon its interactive environment. That is, the essence of the capability of an Internetware entity is that this Internetware entity can impose effects onto its surroundings, i.e. enables the changes of its surroundings, by the mutual interactions between them.

12.3.1 Elements of EnOnCaS

The EnOnCaS mainly consists of the following elements.

Environment Ontology. The environment ontology is the fundamental layer for specifying Internetware entity capabilities. As stated in Sect. 12.2, it is a sharable knowledge base, constructed from the existing general domain ontology under the guidance of domain experts, and it is also maintained by them. In reality, these environment entities may belong to different environment ontologies. Ontological mapping and integration can be used to provide a common layer between them. Currently, various approaches of ontological mapping [17] and integration [18] have been investigated, such as the WSMO Mediators [19]. These ontological mediators allow the management of the variation in the environment ontology. In this chapter, we assume that there is only one environment ontology.

Capability Profile. The capability profile is designed to describe the capabilities of Internetware entities. To define the capability profile of an Internetware entity, we first define the effects that this Internetware entity can impose on its environment entities. Based on the effect-based view mentioned above, we consider the effects on the causal environment entity as its state sub-diagram with the message exchanges. For those autonomous entities and symbolic entities, the effects are only the message exchanges between them and the Internetware entity that can be 'enabled', but without any state changes.

Then how to define the capability profile? As it can only defined by the effects onto the envi-

ronment ontology, we need first to explore which kinds of the effects that the environment ontology can have. An intuitive idea is using the behaviours of the environment entities that can be caused. This will be formalised using the notion of *running paths* so that a running path describes a possible behaviour of an environment entity.

Definition 12.4 Let e be an environment entity, and $h(e)$ a THSM of e. A finite effect path ρ of e is an alternative sequence of states and shared/sharing phenomena[1] ending with a state

$$\rho \overset{\text{def}}{=} s_0 \frac{phe_1^{in}}{phe_1^{out}} s_1 \ldots s_{n-1} \frac{phe_n^{in}}{phe_n^{out}} s_n$$

such that in $h(e)$, $\delta(s_i, phe_{i+1}^{in}) = s_{i+1}$ and $\lambda(s_i, phe_{i+1}^{in}) = phs_i^{out}$ for all $0 \leq i \leq n$.

Note that, we can define the infinite effect path also in the same way. But in this chapter, for making things easy to understand, effect path represents only the finite effect path.

Definition 12.5 Let e be an environment entity, and $h(e)$ a THSM of e. An effect path ρ of e: $\rho = s_0 \frac{phe_1^{in}}{phe_1^{out}} s_1 \ldots s_{n-1} \frac{phe_n^{in}}{phe_n^{out}} s_n$ is complete if s_0 is an initial state and s_n is a final state.

Normally, a capability profile may refer more than one environment entity. Combined effect path has been introduced as follows.

Definition 12.6 Let $e_1, e_2, \ldots, e_n$ be n environment entities, and ρ_i be one of the effect paths of e_i ($0 \leq i \leq n$). A combined effect path $\Omega \overset{\text{def}}{=} \langle \rho_1, \ldots, \rho_n \rangle$. A combined effect path is complete when all of its individual effect paths are complete.

Furthermore, we need to introduce the feasible effect path as we know that only feasible effects can happen in reality. But in which sense the effect path can be feasible? As we know, it is the Internetware entities' duty to make these effects happen.

---

[1] A shared phenomenon is an input symbol and a sharing phenomenon is an output symbol.

That is the essence of the capability of Internetware entity. We are now in the step of defining the capability profile of Internetware entity.

Definition 12.7 Let $intE$ be an Internetware entity, $Ent = \{e_1, e_2, \ldots, e_n\}$ be the set of its environment entities, ρ_i be an effect paths of e_i $(0 \leq i \leq n)$, and $\Omega = \langle \rho_1, \ldots, \rho_n \rangle$ a combined effect path. Then

- For all i, $(1 \leq i \leq n)$, state $e_i.s_0$ in Ω is reachable by interacting with $IntE$; and
- For all i, $(1 \leq i \leq n)$, output phenomena $\lambda(e_i.s) = e_i.s.phe^{out}$ is enabled if state $e_i.s$ is reachable; and
- For all i, $(1 \leq i \leq n)$, state $e_i.s_j$ $(1 \leq j \leq i_n)$ in Ω is reachable by interacting with $IntE$ if
  - $e_i.s_{j-1}$ in Ω is reachable by interacting with $IntE$; and
  - There is a dependence relationships

$$e_{j_1}.s_{k_{j_1}}.phe^{out}, \ldots, e_{j_l}.s_{k_{j_l}}.phe^{out} \to e_i.phe$$

in which, $j \neq i$ and $k > 1$, $IntE$ can realise the transformation by interacting with the specified environment entities, and $e_{j_1}.s_{k_{j_1}}.phe^{out}, \ldots, e_{j_l}.s_{k_{j_l}}.phe^{out}$ are enabled; and
  - $\delta(e_i.s_{j-1}, phe) = e_i.s_j$.

Definition 12.8 Let $intE$ be an Internetware entity, $Ent = \{e_1, e_2, \ldots, e_n\}$ be the set of its environment entities, ρ_i be an effect paths of e_i $(0 \leq i \leq n)$, and $\Omega = \langle \rho_1, \ldots, \rho_n \rangle$ a combined effect path. An interaction sequence Φ of $IntE$ is a feasible and effective to a combined effect path Ω, if all the final states in Ω is reachable by interacting with $IntE$ by following the interaction sequence Φ. That is an effect imposed by $IntE$ upon Ent and can be written as $\Phi \odot \Omega$.

Definition 12.9 Let $IntE$ be an Internetware entity, $Env = \{e_1, e_2, \ldots, e_n\}$ be the environment that $IntE$ interacts with. Define

$$\text{effs}(IntE) \overset{\text{def}}{=} \{\Phi_1 \odot \Omega_1, \ldots, \Phi_m \odot \Omega_m\}$$

be the effect set that $IntE$ can impose onto its environment, in which, each Ω_i, $1 \leq i \leq m$, is a feasible combined effect path that can be realised by $IntE$ via interacting with its environment entities along feasible interaction sequence Φ_i.

Definition 12.10 The capability profile of an Internetware entity $IntE$ is defined as

$$\text{cap}(IntE) \overset{\text{def}}{=} \{\text{ent}(IntE), \text{effs}(IntE)\}$$

in which,

- $\text{ent}(IntE) = \{e_1, \ldots, e_n\}$ is a set of environment entities of $IntE$;
- $\text{effs}(IntE)$ is the effect set that $IntE$ can impose onto its environment.

Capability specification is generated by assigning the semantics (i.e., state transitions) automatically to the capability profile in the terms of the environment ontology.

Forest-Structured Hierarchical State Machine (FHSM). The capability of an Internetware entity is coordinating its environment entities by realising the dependencies among these environment entities to enable the behaviours (i.e. state transitions) of these environment entities. The capability specification of an Internetware entity $IntE$ is captured by a FHSM, which consists of a set of specific THSMs with those phenomenon pairs that can be enabled by these specific HSMs.

Any specific THSM is fragment of the domain THSM of one environment entity and each state transition in this fragmented domain THSM can be enabled by the Internetware entity. The fragmented domain THSM is representing the effect that the Internetware entity can impose on this environment entity. According to the principle of effect-based assumption, all the effects that the the Internetware entity can impose onto its environment entities represent the capability of the Internetware entity. That means that the Internetware entity can coordinate its environment entities to behave as desired. If we call each fragmented domain THSM that can be executed by interacting with a specific Internetware entity a specific

---

Capability Profile **IATM**
  Environment Entities:
    {ECO: teacher ; ECO: learner ; ECO: help−entity ; ECO: study−entity ;
    ECO: exploratory−tutorial}

  Dependences:{

    {teacher↑*create(exploratory-tutorial[name?Chinese-geography])*}
      ⊙{exploratory−tutorial [name?Chinese−geography]: null↦ready}
    {learner↑*enroll(exploratory-tutorial[name?Chinese-geography])*}
      ⊙{exploratory−tutorial [name?Chinese−geography].number++}

    {teacher↑*request(info)*,help−entity↓*request(info)*,
    help−entity↑*help(topic)*,teacher↓*help(topic)*,
    teacher↑*give(topic)*,exploratory−tutorial↓*give(topic)*}
      ⊙{help−entity:ready↦topic sent,
      exploratory−tutorial:ready↦topic published}

    {study−entity≫*(materials)*,teacher↓*(materials)*,
    teacher↑*give(materials)*,exploratory−tutorial↓*give(materials)*}
      ⊙{exploratory−tutorial:topic published↦materials published}

    {teacher↑*re-give*,exploratory−tutorial↓*re-give*}
      ⊙{exploratory−tutorial:materials published↦topic published}
  }

Listing 12.1 Capability Profile of IATM

THSM. A set of specific THSMs, and the dependencies among them that need to be enabled by the Internetware entity, constitute the capability specification, i.e. the FHSM, of the Internetware entity.

Definition 12.11 A Forest-structured Hierarchical State Machine is defined as

$$chm \overset{\text{def}}{=} \{\mathcal{K}, inter_{\mathcal{K}}\}$$

in which,

- $\mathcal{K} = \{k_1, \ldots, k_n\}$ is a set of specific THSMs corresponding to an effect set,
- $inter_{\mathcal{K}}$ is a set of phenomenon symbol dependencies among the specific HSMs in $\mathcal{K}$.

12.3.2 An Example Capability Profile

This section gives a capability profile of an Internetware entity to illustrate the environment ontology based capability description. The Internet-

ware entity (called "ISTM" for short) is able to configure topics and materials for an exploratory tutorial of Chinese geography. Its environment entities are *teacher*, *help entity*, *study entity*, and *exploratory tutorial[name?Chinese-geography]*. In an exploratory tutorial, help entity provides topics of Chinese geography for teacher, and teacher obtains materials from study entity.

In Fig. 12.3, the environment ontology for education course (ECO) is given. Based on this environment ontology, a capability description of the Internetware entity (IATM) is presented as in Listing 12.1.

We can see in this example that the capability profile captures the effects that need to be enabled (if describing the function request) or the effects that can be enabled (if describing the function providing) by an Internetware entity. The dependences among the environment entities describe what the Internetware entity needs to do or how to enable the desired effects. For example, dependences between teacher and exploratory tutorial are that: (1) teacher creates a new exploratory

Algorithm 10 *FHSM-Generation*

Input: *Environment Ontology* $\{Ent, Rel, rel, HSM, hsm, Dep\}$
   Capability Profile $\{ent(IntE), effs(IntE)\}$, *in which,*
   $ent(IntE) = \{e_1, ..., e_n\} \subseteq Ent,$
   $effs(IntE) = \{InterSet_1 \odot TranSet_1, \cdots, InterSet_m \odot TranSet_m\}.$

Output: *FHSM fhm* $= \{K, inter_K\}$

1: *Get* $hsm(e_1), \cdots, hsm(e_n)$ *which are domain HSMs of* $\{e_1, ..., e_n\}$ *from HSM respectively;*

2: *Let* $runhsms = \{hsm(e_1), \cdots, hsm(e_n)\};$ *//For depositing the original THSMs to be processed*

3: *Let* $readyhsms = \phi;$

4: **while** $(runhsms! = \phi)$ **do**

5:   $hsm(e) = GetFrom(runhsms);$//*Getting a tree-like hierarchical state machine* $hsm(e)$ *from runhsms*

6:   $runhsms = runhsms - \{hsm(e)\};$

7:   $Interaction(e) = GetInteractionFrom(e, EffectSet);$

8:   $Transition(e) = GetTransitionFrom(e, EffectSet);$ *//obtaining the set of inter- actions with causal entity e and the set of state changes of causal entity e from the set of effects*

9:   *Let* $k(e) = buildSpecificTHSM(hsm(e), Interaction(e), Transition(e));$
   //buildSpecificTHSM *is a procedure to build a specific THSM from origi- nal THSM according to the interaction set that e takes part in and the state transitions that e undergoes*

10:   $readyhsms = readyhsm \cup \{k(e)\};$

11:   *Let* $depIn(k(e)) = Interaction(e)$ *keep the set of interactions that e takes part in the specific THSM* $k(e);$

12: **end while**
   //*When runhsms is empty, the THSMs in readyhsms are the specific THSMs, and dependencies between these specific THSMs are also created*

13: *FCHM chm* $= \{K, inter_K\}$ *then is builded as:*
   $K = readyhsms = \{k(e_1), ..., k(e_n)\};$
   $inter_K = \{depIn(k(e_1)), ..., depIn(k(e_n))\};$

14: **return** *chm*

tutorial named '*Chinese Geography*'. As a result, an instance of exploratory tutorial is created; (2) teacher shares a phenomenon '*!give(topic)*', and state of exploratory tutorial changes from *ready* to *topic published*. This is a transition dependence; (3) teacher shares a phenomenon '*!give(materials)*', and state of exploratory tuto- rial changes from *topic published* to *materials published*. This is also a transition dependence; (4) teacher shares a phenomenon '*!re-give*', and state of exploratory tutorial changes from *materials published* to *topic published*.

12.3.3 Capability Specification Generation

The algorithm for generating the FHSM from a capability profile based on the environment ontol- ogy is described as follows.

Figure 12.4 is the screenshot showing the FHSM fhm_{IATM}, which is generated based on the capability profile of *IATM* and the environment ontology *ECO*.

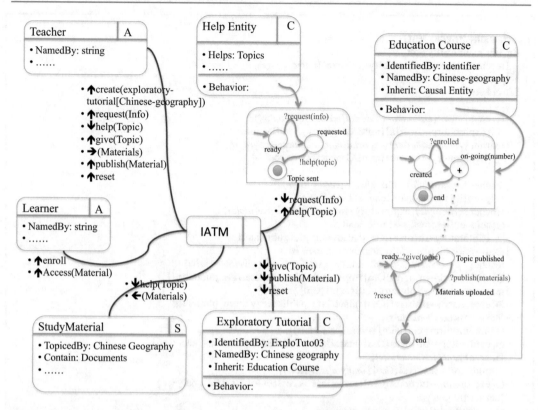

Fig. 12.4 Capability specification of IATM

12.3.4 Internetware Entity Discovery

According to environment-based view on software modelling, requirement is considered to be the desired effects on environment, and is not relevant to software implementation. In the framework of capability description of Internetware entity, the effects on environment are described to be a set of interactions with environment entities and state changes of causal entities in the environment entities. Requirement can be described in the same way. In other words, requirement is described to be a set desired environment entities, and desired interactions with these environment entities, and changes of these environment entities.

This section gives an example of requirement which requires an Internetware entity for Exploratory Tutorial of Geography (IETG). Desired environment entities are *teacher, learner, help entity, study entity* and *exploratory tutor-*ial[*name?geography*]. Desired capabilities are that: in an exploratory tutorial, teacher obtains topics of geography guided by help entity, and obtains study materials from study entity. Learner obtains these materials and analyses them to draw a conclusion. Finally, teacher summarises these conclusions and draws a summary. The requirement is described as Listing 12.2.

Based on the requirement description, required FHSM is generated by reasoning on the environment ontology for education course. Figure 12.5 shows the FHSM of the required capability.

Discovery is "the act of locating a machine-processable description of an Internetware entity which may have been previously unknown and which meets certain functional criteria"[20]. We use the environment ontology to represent the functional criteria, i.e., the goal, as provided by the requestor, as well as the machine-processable description of the Internetware entities that are to be provided by the provider.

Functionality Profile: IETG
  Environment Entity Set:
    {teacher, learner, exploratory–tutorial[*name?geography*
], help–entity, study–entity}
  Effect Set:{

    {teacher↑*create(exploratory-tutorial[name?Geography])*}
      ⊙{exploratory–tutorial[name?Geography]: null↦ready}
    {learner↑*enroll(exploratory-tutorial[name?Chinese-geography])*}
      ⊙{exploratory–tutorial[name?Geography].number++}

    {teacher↑*request(info)*, help–entity↓*request(info)*,
     help–entity↑*help(topic)*, teacher↓*help(topic)*,
     teacher↑*give(topic)*, exploratory–tutorial[Geo]↓*give(topic)*}
     ⊙{help–entity: ready↦topic sent,
        exploratory–tutorial[Geo]: ready↦topic published}
    {study–entity≫*(materials)*, teacher↓*(materials)*,
     teacher↑*give(materials)*, exploratory–tutorial[Geo]↓*give(materials)*}
     ⊙{exploratory–tutorial[Geo]: topic published↦materials published}
    {teacher↑*re-give*, exploratory–tutorial[Geo]↓*re-give*}
     ⊙{exploratory–tutorial[Geo]: materials published↦topic published}
    {learner↑*access(materials)*,
     exploratory–tutorial[Geo]↓*access(materials)*}
     ⊙{exploratory–tutorial[Geo]: materials published↦materials accessed}
    {learner↑*analyze(materials)*,
     exploratory–tutorial[Geo]↓*analyze(materials)*}
     ⊙{exploratory–tutorial[Geo]: materials accessed↦materials analyzed}
    {learner↑*re-analyze*,
     exploratory–tutorial[Geo]↓*re-analyze)*}
     ⊙{exploratory–tutorial[Geo]: materials analyzed↦materials published}
    {learner↑*draw(conclusion,learner.name.val)*,
     exploratory–tutorial[Geo]↓*draw(conclusion,*
     learner.name.val)}
     ⊙{exploratory–tutorial[Geo]: materials analyzed↦conclusion received}
    {teacher↑*give(summary,teacher.name.val)*,
     exploratory–tutorial[Geo]↓*give(summary, teacher.name.val)*}
     ⊙{exploratory–tutorial[Geo]: conclusion received↦summary received}

  }

Listing 12.2 Required Capability Description for IETG

Let $Cap(req) = \{ent(req), \mathrm{effs}(req)\}$ and $Cap(ava) = \{ent(ava), \mathrm{effs}(ava)\}$ be a goal profile and a capability profile of candidate Internetware entity respectively. The matchmaking process for the Internetware entity discovery includes the following two-step process:

Step 1. We first do the matchmaking between the sets of environment entities, i.e., Ent^{req} and Ent^{ava}. For two environment entities $e_1 = id_1[s\_attr_{11}?v_{11}, \ldots, s\_attr_{1n}?v_{1n}]$ $(s\_attr_{1i} \in NAttrs(e_1), i \in [1, n])$, $e_2 =$ $id_2[s\_attr_{21}?v_{21}, \ldots, s\_attr_{2m}?v_{2m}](s\_attr_{2j} \in NAttrs(e_2), j \in [1, m])$, $s\_attr_{1i} == s\_attr_{2j} \wedge v_{1i} \sqsubseteq v_{2j}$ means that v_{1i} and v_{2j} are values of a same non-characteristic attribute and v_{1i} is a subtype of v_{2j}. When values of non-characteristic attributes of environment entities are not designated here, the values are universal and denoted as $\top$ (for any value $v \sqsubseteq \top$). If e_1 and e_2 are a same environment entity, $id_1 == id_2$, or if e_1 is a subtype of e_2, $id_1 \sqsubseteq id_2$. Now, we can introduce three kinds of relations

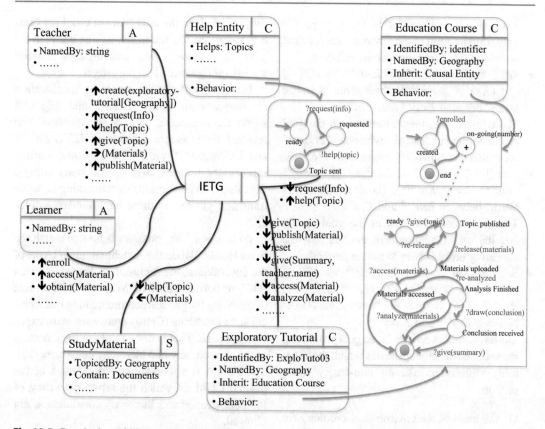

Fig. 12.5 Required capability specification of IETG

between the two environment entities e_1 and e_2 as follows:

1. (Subsumption) $e_1 \sqsubseteq e_2 \Leftrightarrow (id_1 \sqsubset id_2 \vee id_1 == id_2) \wedge \forall s\_attr_{1i} \in NAttrs(e_1), \exists s\_attr_{2j} \in NAttrs(e_2)(s\_attr_{1i} == s\_attr_{2j} \wedge (v_{1i} == v_{2j} \vee v_{1i} \sqsubset v_{2j}))$. e_1 is a subtype of e_2 or they are a same environment entity, and their non-characteristic attributes and values match inclusively;
2. (Equivalence)$e_1 == e_2 \Leftrightarrow e_1 \sqsubseteq e_2 \wedge e_1 \sqsupseteq e_2$. e_1 and e_2 are a same environment entity, and their non-characteristic attributes and values match exactly;
3. (Intersection)$e_1 \sqcap e_2 \Leftrightarrow (id_1 \sqsubset id_2 \vee id_1 == id_2) \wedge \exists s\_attr_{1i} \in NAttrs(e_1), \exists s\_attr_{2j} \in NAttrs(e_2)(s\_attr_{1i} == s\_attr_{2j} \wedge (v_{1i} == v_{2j} \vee v_{1i} \sqsubset v_{2j}))$. e_1 is a subtype of e_2 or they are a same environment entity, and they

have some equal values of non-characteristic attributes.

Then, the matchmaking between Ent^{req} and Ent^{ava}, in consideration of the inheritance relations, non-characteristic attributes and corresponding values, is given using a set-based approach in [21]:

- $\forall e^{req} \in Ent^{req}, \neg \exists e^{ava} \in Ent^{ava} \Rightarrow e^{req} \sqsubseteq e^{ava} \vee e^{req} \sqsupseteq e^{ava} \vee e^{req} \sqcap e^{ava}$ ($Ent^{req} \cap Ent^{ava} = \phi$), there is a non-match between Ent^{req} and Ent^{ava}.
  The environment entities in the goal profile and the environment entities that the capability profile refers to are irrelevant. In this situation, the matchmaking process terminates.
- $\forall e^{req} \in Ent^{req}, \exists e^{ava} \in Ent^{ava} \Rightarrow e^{req} \sqsubseteq e^{ava}$, ($Ent^{req} \subseteq Ent^{ava}$), there is the "Plug-In Match" between Ent^{req} and Ent^{ava}.

The environment entities in the goal profile only form a subset of the environment entities' set which that capability profile refers to.

- $\forall e^{ava} \in Ent^{ava}, \exists e^{req} \in Ent^{req} \Rightarrow e^{req} \sqsupseteq e^{ava}$ ($Ent^{req} \sqsupseteq Ent^{ava}$), there is the "Subsume Match" between Ent^{req} and Ent^{ava}.

The relevant environment entities in the goal profile form a superset of environment entities' set which that capability profile refers to.

- $Ent^{req} \sqsubseteq Ent^{ava} \wedge Ent^{req} \sqsupseteq Ent^{ava}$ ($Ent^{req} == Ent^{ava}$), there is the "Exact Match" between Ent^{req} and Ent^{ava}.

The environment entities in the goal profile and the set of environment entities that the capability profile refers to match perfectly.

- $\exists e^{req} \in Ent^{req}, \exists e^{ava} \in Ent^{ava} \Rightarrow e^{req} \sqsubseteq e^{ava} \vee e^{req} \sqsupseteq e^{ava} \vee e^{req} \sqcap e^{ava}$ ($Ent^{req} \cap Ent^{ava} \neq \phi$), there is the "Intersection Match" between Ent^{req} and Ent^{ava}.

The environment entities in the goal profile and the set of environment entities which the capability profile refers to have a "non-empty" intersection.

On the basis of the environment ontology for education course, matchmaking between the set of environment entities in the user requirement (IETG) and the Internetware entity for Acquisition of Topic and Materials (IATM) can be performed.

The environment entities in the requirement are IETG: {*teacher, learner, help entity, study entity, exploratory tutorial[name?geography]*}. The environment entities in the Internetware entity are IATM: {*teacher, exploratory tutorial[name?Chinese-geography], help entity, study entity*}. Moreover, Chinese-geography is a subclass of geography (Chinese-geography $\sqsubseteq$ geography). Therefore, IETG : $Ent^{req} \sqsupseteq$ IATM : Ent^{ava}. It means that there is a subsume match between the environment entities in requirement description and capability description the Internetware entity.

Step 2. If there is Relevancy (no non-match) between Ent^{req} and Ent^{ava}, they have some common or relevant environment entities. This step is to perform a matchmaking of their effects on the common or relevant environment entities. Because that FHSM is generated according to an effect

set grounded on the environment ontology (seeing Algorithm 10), the matchmaking between the effects is regarded as the matchmaking between the FHSMs generated on the effects.

Figure 12.4 shows the capability specification of Internetware entity IATM, and Fig. 12.5 shows the required capability specification. The relevant environment entities of IETG:Ent^{req} and IATM:Ent^{ava} are E^{ra} = {*teacher, learner, exploratory tutorial, help entity, study entity*}. This step is to perform the matchmaking between transition graphs on these environment entities E^{ra}.

At this point, the problem is how to match the two FHSMs. We do the matchmaking in terms of the equivalence, the inclusion or the intersection relations between the FCHMs [22]. The problem of matching the general communicating hierarchical state machines (CHM) consumes extra exponential space. This is due to the arbitrary nesting of the concurrency and hierarchy constructs [23]. The FCHM is a well-structured subclass of the general CHM, in which the arbitrary nesting of the concurrency and hierarchy constructs is not allowed.

Before describing the matchmaking of the FCHMs, some basic definitions are given [15]. Let $chm = \{\{k_1, \ldots, k_n\}, inter_K\}$ be a FCHM, $S(k_i)$ be the set of states in $k_i \in \{k_1, \ldots, k_n\}$ and $S(chm)$ be the set of all states in chm ($S(k_i) \subseteq S(chm)$).

Definition 12.12 States $a, b \in S(chm)$ are simultaneous ($a|b$), iff $a \in S(k_i), b \in S(k_j), i, j \in [1, n], i \neq j$.

The states a and b are simultaneous iff they are in different specific THSMs. For example, in Fig. 12.5, states *help entity-requested* and *exploratory tutorial-topic published* are simultaneously pairwise, because that they are in different tree-like hierarchical state machines respectively.

A set $A \in 2^{S(chm)}$ is said to be consistent iff $\forall a, b \in A : a|b$. It means that all elements of A are pairwise simultaneous. The set {*flight-ticket-sold, hotelroom-ordered*} is an example consistent set. A global state of FCHM is defined as a maximal consistent set of the FCHM.

Definition 12.13 The global state of FCHM chm is defined as a maximal consistent set $A \in 2^{S(chm)}$,

$$\forall x \in S(chm) - A : \neg consistent(A \cup \{x\})$$

For example, in Fig. 12.5, {*help entity-requested, exploratory tutorial-topic published*} is a consistent set, because that *exploratory tutorial-topic published* and *help entity-requested* are simultaneous states. After defining the global state, we then can define a next-state relation which is referred to as the global state transitions under triggers of FCHM.

Definition 12.14 The next-state relation of FCHM is defined as $F \subseteq G \times 2^{\Sigma^{in}} \times G$, in which G is the set of global states of the FCHM, Σ^{in} is the set of inputs to the FCHM.

For example, in Fig. 12.5, $g_1 = \{help$ *entity-requested, exploratory tutorial-ready*}, $g_2 = \{help$ *entity-topic sent, exploratory tutorial-topic published*} are global states. $\langle g_1, \{!help(topic), ?help(topic), !give(topic), ?give(topic)\}, g_2 \rangle$ is a global state transition. In which, help entity sends out a message *!help(topic)*, and its state changes from *requested* to *topic sent*. And then, teacher receives the message *?help(topic)*. It means that teacher obtains a topic about education course from help entity. Afterwards, teacher sends out a message *!give(topic)*. Exploratory tutorial receives this message, and its state changes from *ready* to *topic published*. It means that teacher confirms a topic about education course.

Given two FCHMs chm_1 and chm_2, and a binary relation $\varphi \subseteq G_1 \times G_2$ (G_1 is the set of global states of chm_1 and G_2 is the set of global states of chm_2). Let F_1 and F_2 be the next state relations of chm_1 and chm_2, $\Sigma^{in}(g)$ be the set of inputs to global state g. We give the following four conditions:

1. $\langle \sigma_1, \sigma_2 \rangle \in \varphi$, σ_1, σ_2 are the initial global states of chm_1 and chm_2 respectively;
2. $\langle g_1, g_2 \rangle \in \varphi \Rightarrow \forall i \in 2^{\Sigma^{in}(g_1)} g_1' \langle g_1, i, g_1' \rangle \in F_1 \Rightarrow \exists g_2' \langle g_2, i, g_2' \rangle \in F_2 \wedge \langle g_1', g_2' \rangle \in \varphi$;
3. $\langle g_1, g_2 \rangle \in \varphi \Rightarrow \forall i \in 2^{\Sigma^{in}(g_2)} g_2' \langle g_2, i, g_2' \rangle \in F_2 \Rightarrow \exists g_1' \langle g_1, i, g_1' \rangle \in F_1 \wedge \langle g_1', g_2' \rangle \in \varphi$;

Table 12.1 Match degree between chm_{req} and chm_{ava}

Degree	Meaning
Exact match	$chm_{req} =^{\varphi} chm_{ava}$
Plug-in match	$chm_{req} \sqsubseteq^{\varphi} chm_{ava}$
Subsume match	$chm_{req} \sqsupseteq^{\varphi} chm_{ava}$
Intersection match	$chm_{req} \sqcap^{\varphi} chm_{ava}$
Non-match	$chm_{req} \not\sim^{\varphi} chm_{ava}$

4. $\langle g_1, g_2 \rangle \in \varphi \Rightarrow \exists i \in 2^{\Sigma^{in}(g_1)} g_1' \langle g_1, i, g_1' \rangle \in F_1 \Rightarrow \exists g_2' \langle g_2, i, g_2' \rangle \in F_2 \wedge \langle g_1', g_2' \rangle \in \varphi$.

If φ satisfies conditions (1), (2) and does not satisfies condition (3), then φ is an inclusion relation and we say that chm_1 is included by chm_2 under φ, $chm_1 \sqsubseteq^{\varphi} chm_2$. Symmetrically, if φ satisfies conditions (1), (3) and does not satisfies condition (2), then we say that chm_1 includes chm_2 under φ, $chm_1 \sqsupseteq^{\varphi} chm_2$. If φ satisfies conditions (1), (2) and (3), then φ is an equivalence relation, chm_1 and chm_2 are equal under φ, $chm_1 =^{\varphi} chm_2$. If φ satisfies condition (4) and dose not satisfies condition (2), (3), then φ is an intersection relation and we say that chm_1 intersects with chm_2 under φ, $chm_1 \sqcap^{\varphi} chm_2$. If φ dose not satisfy any conditions above, then we say that chm_1 is irrelevant to chm_2 under φ, $chm_1 \not\sim^{\varphi} chm_2$. In summary, the matching degrees between two FCHMs chm_{req} and chm_{ava} are listed in Table 12.1.

The matchmaking between IETG:Eff^{req} and IATM: Eff^{ava} can be performed. According to Table 12.1, there is a subsume match between them. Moreover, in first step, there also is a subsume match between IETG:Ent^{req} and IATM:Ent^{ava}. In other words, the Internetware entity IATM only satisfies partially the requirement. To satisfy the requirement completely, the Internetware entity IATM needs to collaborate with other Internetware entities.

12.4 Related Work

Different from the traditional software which runs on centralized and close environment, Interneware is a new software paradigm running on open and dynamic Internet. This chapter focuses on how to describe Internetware entity semantically, and proposes capability description of Internetware entity based on environment ontology. This chapter also proposes a matchmaking process between requirement and capability descriptions to support discovery and aggregation of Internetware entity.

From the technical view, Internetware entities are to be autonomous software services which are distributed on various nodes in Internet. In this sense, this work is closely related to Web service description and capability specification. In this field, earlier efforts are mainly XML-based standards, such as Web Service Description Language (WSDL1.1) [24]. It is built on a Universal Description Discovery Integration (UDDI) [25], which provides a registry of Web services. Then, the keyword-based search is conducted against service profiles in WSDL1.1, which describes the Web services in terms of their physical attributes, such as name, address and services interface. Thus, service capabilities in WSDL1.1 are barely represented semantically.

Ontology-based Web service descriptions have made considerable progress on describing service capability from multiple perspectives. Major initiatives to be mentioned are OWL-S [3], and WSMO [4]. The OWL-S capability model is based on an one-step process, i.e., the IOPR schema. However, IOPR-based approaches fall short of logical relationships for underlying the inputs and the outputs [26]. The OWL-S process model and LARKS [27] are proposed to overcome such obstacles in order to achieve automated and intelligent service discovery. [28] proposes execution-related features which can be combined with OWL-S to provide richer semantic features. WSMO [4,29] differentiates from OWL-S, by specifying internal and external choreography by using abstract state machines. The external choreography also represents the service capabilities to some extent. Also the WSMO Mediator [19] handles heterogeneity among the requesters and providers.

There are also some lightweight approaches annotating WSDL documents with semantic descriptions, such as WSDL-S [5]. WSDL-S uses the semantic concepts analogous to those in OWL-S. However, similar to OWL-S, WSDL-S does not overcome the obstacles of IOPR schema mentioned above, either. [30] proposes to annotate WSDL documents by using pi-calculus to solve these problems.

Behaviour-based service description [31,32] aims to discover Web services by matching their behaviour descriptions. It is more expressive than the service interface-based description. Various behavioural models including extended finite-state automata, process algebraic notations, graph formalism and logic formalisms are studied. Web services are developed by different teams, and are described in different conceptual frameworks without prior agreement. Behaviours of Web services are described with semantic descriptions, such the efforts in [33].

Service contextual information has also been modelled with the purposes of coordinating and collaborating Web services in their actual implementation. WS-Resource [34] and WS-Context [35] are proposed to promote interoperability among Web services and their stateful interactions. [36] proposes an agent-based and context-oriented approach that supports the composition of Web services. Generally, these efforts emphasise the information on the actual execution of Web services. Descriptions of service capabilities at a higher-level of abstraction are not considered, either.

Our capability specification approach follows the environment-based "requirements engineering" to specify the Internetware entity capabilities. We give high regard to the effects which are to be achieved by the Internetware entity on its environment entities. The Internetware entity's capabilities are expressed by the effects that the Internetware entity can impose on the based on the environment entities, whose characteristics and logical interconnections are observable and applicable during discovery and composition. The environment entities play the role of bridging between Internetware entities. We follow the ontology-based approaches. The state-based mechanism, which is more expressive than the IOPR schema, is adopted in our capability model. Therefore, the set-based modelling [21] and matching of state machines [22] are combined to realise the automated Web service discovery.

12.5   Conclusion

This chapter proposes an approach for specifying Internetware entity capability based on an environment ontology. The main standpoint is that the capabilities of an Internetware entity can be grounded on the effects imposed by the Internetware entity onto its environment entities. We propose to build the environment ontology to supply the sharable understanding of those possible effects. The structure of the environment ontology has been presented. It is an extension of the general domain ontology, which associates THSM with each environment entity. The algorithm for constructing this kind of environment ontology from a general domain ontology has also been described, so that with the guidance of the domain experts, the environment ontology is constructed. After that, when a provider publishes Internetware entity, or a requester needs an Internetware entity, they can just provide the effects that the Internetware entity can impose on its environment entities. The algorithm has also been developed to transfer the effect-based profile into a capability specification (semi-) automatically.

The main contributions of this chapter include:

- An effect-based capability profile that makes the Internetware entity specification more accurate without exposing the its realisation details;
- The structured effects of the sharable environment entities modelled by FCHMs, which make the Internetware entity specifications more understandable with each other and make the Internetware entity capability expressive.

Furthermore, the sharable environment ontology allows the interoperability and the communication between Internetware entities to occur so that the automatic Internetware entity matchmaking of different degrees can be realised. The case study in the section III(D) has disclosed this kind of potential.

In the future, more "real world" cases will be studied to examine the validity, advantages and limitations of the environment-based approach. We also are developing a more efficient Internetware entity discovery support system, as well as an Internetware entity composition mechanism which is based on the environment's effects.

References

1. F. Yang, H. Mei, J. Lu, Z. Jin, Some discussion on the development of software technology. Acta Electronica Sinica **30**(12A), 1091–1096 (2002)
2. S.A. McIlraith, T.C. Son, H. Zeng, Semantic web services. IEEE Intell. Syst. **16**(2), 460–453 (2001)
3. D. Martin, M. Burstein, D. McDermott et al., OWL-S 1.2 Release, http://www.daml.org/services/owl-s/1.2/
4. J. Bruijn, C. Bussler, J. Domingue et al., Web Service Modeling Ontology (WSMO), http://www.wsmo.org
5. W3C, Web Service Semantics (WSDL-S), http://www.w3.org/Submission/WSDL-S/
6. D. Uckelmann, M. Harrison, F. Michahelles, *Architecting the Internet of Things* (Springer, Berlin, 2011)
7. O. Vermesan et al., Internet of things strategic research road map. European Commission-Information Society and Media DG, 1st edn. (2009)
8. D.L. Parnas, J. Madey, Functional documents for computer systems. Sci. Comput. Program. **25**(1), 41–61 (1995)
9. M. Jackson, The meaning of requirements. Annu. Softw. Eng. **3**(1), 5–21 (1997)
10. P. Zave, M. Jackson, Four dark corners of requirements engineering. ACM Trans. Softw. Eng. Methodol. **6**(1), 1–30 (1997)
11. M. Jackson, *Problem Frames: Analyzing and Structuring Software Development Problems* (Addison-Wesley, 2001)
12. Zhi Jin, Revisiting the meaning of requirements. J. Comput. Sci. Technol. **22**(1), 32–40 (2006)
13. M. Paolucci, T. Kawamura, T.R. Payne et al., Semantic matching of web services capabilities, in *Proceedings of International Semantic Web Conference (ISWC'02)*, (2002), pp. 333–347
14. L. Bertalanffy, *General System Theory: Essays on Its Foundation and Development* (George Braziller, New York, 1968)
15. M.P.E. Heimdahl, N.G. Leveson, Completeness and consistency in hierarchical state-based requirements. IEEE Trans. Softw. Eng. **22**(6) (1996)
16. A. Maedche, *Ontology Learning for the Semantic Web* (Kluwer Academic Publisher, 2002)
17. Y. Kalfoglou, M. Schorlemmer, Ontology mapping: the state of the art. Knowl. Eng. Rev. **18**(1) (2003)
18. A.B. Williams, A. Padmanabhan, M.B. Blake, Experimentation with local consensus ontologies with implications for automated service composition. IEEE Trans. Knowl. Data Eng. **17**(7), 969–981 (2005)

19. WSMO, WSMO Mediators (2005), http://www.wsmo.org/TR/d29/

20. W3C, Web Services Architecture (2004), http://www.w3.org/TR/ws-arch/

21. U. Keller, R. Lara, H. Lausen et al., Semantic web service discovery. WSMX Working Draft (2005), http://www.wsmo.org/TR/d10/v0.2/

22. M.D. Di Benedetto, A. Sangiovanni-Vincentelli, T. Villa, Model matching for finite-state machines. IEEE Trans. Autom. Control **46**(11) (2001)

23. R. Alur, R. Kannan, S. Yannakakis, M. Yannakakis, Communicating hierarchical state machines, in *Proceedings of International Colloquium on Automata, Languages and Programming (ICAL'99)*, LNCS 1644 (1999), pp. 169–178

24. E. Christensen, F. Curbera, G. Meredith et al., Web Services Description Language (WSDL) 1.1 Technical Report, W3C (2001), http://www.w3.org/TR/2001/NOTE-wsdl-20010315

25. L. Clement, A. Hately, C. von Riegen et al., UDDI version 3.0 (2004), http://uddi.org/pubs/uddi_v3.htm

26. S. Bansal, J.M. Vidal, Matchmaking of web services based on the DAML-S service model, in *Proceedings of International joint conference on Autonomous Agents and Multi-Agent Systems(AAMAS'03)* (2003)

27. K. Sycara, S. Widoff, M. Klusch et al., LARKS: dynamic matchmaking among heterogeneous software agents in cyberspace. Auton. Agents Multi-Agent Syst. **5**, 173–203 (2002)

28. B. Medjahed, A. Bouguettaya, A multilevel composability model for semantic web services. IEEE Trans. Knowl. Data Eng. **17**(7), 954–968 (2005)

29. D. Fensel, A. Polleres, J. Bruijn, Ontology-based choreography. WSMO Final Draft (2007), http://www.wsmo.org/TR/d14/v1.0/

30. S. Agarwal, R. Studer, Automatic matchmaking of web services, in *Proceedings of IEEE International Conference on Web Services (ICWS'06)* (2006), pp. 45–54

31. G. Salaun, L. Bordeaux, M. Schaerf, Describing and reasoning on web services using process algebra, in *Proceedings of IEEE International Conference on Web Services (ICWS'04)* (2004), pp. 43–50

32. A. Wombacher, P. Fankhauser, B. Mahleko, E.J. Neuhold, Matchmaking for business processes based on choreographies. Int. J. Web Serv. Res. **1**(4), 14–32 (2004)

33. Z. Shen, J. Su, Web service discovery based on behavior signatures in *Proceedings of IEEE International Conference on Services Computing(SCC'05)* (2005), pp. 279–286

34. I. Foster et al., Modeling Stateful Resources with Web Services, Version 1.1, http://www.ibm.com/developerworks/library/ws-resource/ws-modelingresources.pdf

35. M. Little, J. Webber, S. Parastatidis, Stateful interactions in web services: a comparison of WS-context and WS-resource framework. Web Serv. J. **4**(5) (2004)

36. Z. Maamar, S.K. Mostefaoui, H. Yahyaoui, Toward an agent-based and context-oriented approach for web services composition. IEEE Trans. Knowl. Data Eng. **17**(5), 686–697 (2005)

37. T.R. Gruber, A translation approach to portable ontology specifications. Knowl. Acquis. **5**(2), 199–220 (1993)

38. D. Martin, M. Burstein, D. McDermott et al., Bringing semantics to web services with OWL-S. World Wide Web J. **10**(3), 243–277 (2007)

39. M. Mrissa, D. Benslimane, Z. Maamar et al., Towards a semantic- and context-based approach for composing web services. Int. J. Web Grid Serv. **1**(3/4), 268–286 (2005)

40. P. Wang, Z. Jin, Web service composition: an approach using effect-based reasoning, in *Proceedings of International Workshop on Engineering Service-Oriented Applications: Design and Composition (WESOA'06)*, LNCS 4652 (2006), pp. 62–73

41. P. Wang, Z. Jin L. Liu, Environment ontology-based capability specification for web service discovery, in *Proceedings of International Conference on Formal Engineering Methods (ICFEM'06)*, LNCS 4260 (2006), pp. 185–205

42. P. Wang, Z. Jin, L. Liu, An approach for specifying capability of web services based on environment ontology, in *Proceedings of IEEE International Conference on Web Services (ICWS'06)* (2006), pp. 365–372

43. P. Wang, Z. Jin, L. Liu, On constructing environment ontology for semantic web services, in*Proceedings of International Conference on Knowledge Science, Engineering and Management (KSEM'06)*, LNAI 4092 (2006), pp. 490–503

Abstract

In this chapter, we introduce four kinds of dependency between features, namely *refinement, constraint, influence and interaction*, partly based on the observation of feature operationalization and assignment of responsibilities. Then, we explore three kinds of connection between these dependencies, that is, connections between refinement and constraint, between constraint and interaction, and between influence and interaction. We further show how to use the constraint dependencies to facilitate the customization-based reuse of requirements, and how to employ the result of feature dependency analysis to design high-level software architecture. A simple document editor and an email-client are used as running examples to illustrate the ideas introduced in this chapter.

Keywords

Feature-driven · Requirement dependency analysis · High-level · Software design

13.1 Introduction

Many researchers have recognized that individual requirements are seldom independent of each other, and various kinds of dependency exist among them [1–7]. Generally, dependencies are essential elements among the requirements of a real software system, because of the cohesion of a software system. Cohesion is a basic quality of a system, a quality that is necessary for a system to achieve certain customer-desired goals. At the same time, a software system must be described accurately and completely before it can be implemented. To serve the description purpose, we often need a set of requirements, since an individual requirement reflects only a partial fact of a system. Moreover, this set of requirements must possess intrinsic dependencies among them, otherwise these requirements denote only a set

Parts of this chapter were reprinted with kind permission from Springer Science+Business Media: <Requirements Engineering, Feature-driven requirement dependency analysis and high-level software design, volume 11, 2006, 205–220, Wei Zhang, Hong Mei and Haiyan Zhao, figure number(s), and any original (first) copyright notice displayed with material>.

of unrelated facts, and thus can never describe a system with enough cohesion.

One fundamental problem related to requirement dependencies is how these dependencies contribute to the development of software. This problem can further be refined into more explicit questions as to what benefits can be obtained if requirement dependencies are explicitly considered, which kinds of requirement dependency can help to get these benefits cost-effectively, and how to identify and specify these dependencies.

Much research on requirement dependencies has been done around these questions. Work by Robinson et al. [8] and van Lamsweerde et al. [9] represents a kind of research that focuses on how to eliminate negative dependencies among requirements at the phase of requirement analysis. Carlshamre et al. [1] provided an industrial survey of using requirement dependencies to plan releases of software products. Giesen and Volker [4] explored the problem of how requirement dependencies can help to satisfy stakeholders' preferences. Von Knethen et al. [10,11] showed an approach to requirement reuse and change analysis based on requirement dependencies.

However, most of the current research on requirement dependencies only focus their views on the requirement phase of software development (i.e. requirement analysis and reuse, release planning, requirement change analysis), and do not answer the question as to what are the possible roles of requirement dependencies in the solution space of software. If this question is not explicitly focused, we can never get a complete view of how requirement dependencies influence the whole process of software development. To answer this question, we may have to investigate which kinds of dependency have a significant effect on the design and implementation of software, and furthermore, how to identify these dependencies based on those commonly recognized dependencies in current research.

In this chapter, we present a feature-driven approach to analyzing requirement dependencies and designing high-level software architecture. The most important characteristic of this approach is that it does not use individual requirements but features as basic entities when exploring

requirement dependencies. We think that each feature essentially denotes a set of tight-related requirements from user/customer-views, and thus the feature-orientation provides a modular way to organize requirements and a proper granularity to analyze dependencies among them. In this approach, we not only care about static feature dependencies (i.e. *refinement* and *constraint*), but also attach importance to feature dependencies at the specification level (namely *influence*) and, furthermore, to dynamic dependencies between features (namely *interaction*) by which different software components can be connected with each other and be integrated into runnable software systems. Moreover, we also explore three possible connections between these feature dependencies. Through these connections, undiscovered feature dependencies can be more easily identified from those earlier identified. Based on these four kinds of feature dependency and their connections, we also provide two applications of them. One application shows how the constraint dependencies can be used to facilitate the customization-based reuse of requirements. The other points out a possible approach to high-level software architecture design using the result of feature dependency analysis.

The rest of this chapter is organized as follows. Section 13.2 gives some preliminary knowledge. Section 13.3 introduces four kinds of feature dependency. Three connections between these dependencies are clarified in Sect. 13.4. Section 13.5 shows how to use the constraint dependencies to verify requirement customization. Section 13.6 presents an approach to high-level software design based on feature dependencies. Related work is discussed in Sect. 13.7. Finally, Sect. 13.8 concludes this chapter with a short summary and future work.

13.2 The Preliminaries

In this section, we give some preliminaries to the analysis of feature dependencies, with the purpose of helping readers build a clear view on the concept of features and how features can be operationalized in the solution space of software.

13.2.1 Definition of Features

Generally, the definition of a concept can be considered from two aspects: intension and extension. The intension describes the intrinsic qualities of a concept, while the extension characterizes the external embodiment of a concept. Many researchers have given their definitions of features from either of the two aspects. For example, Turner et al. [12], Mehta and Heineman [13], and Wiegers [14] focus much on the intension aspect, defining a feature as a set of related requirements, while Kang et al. [15] and Griss [16] emphasize the extension aspect, stating that a feature is a software-characteristic from user or customer views. In our research, we do not introduce any novel understanding of features, but just combine these two aspects and give the following definition of features.

In intension, a feature is a cohesive set of individual requirements.

In extension, a feature is a user/customer-visible capability of a software system.

13.2.2 Basic Attributes of Features

Besides the intension and extension aspects, each feature also has some attributes for the purpose of specification. A concise explanation of these attributes is given in Table 13.1.

Name is the mnemonic of a feature. Any concise and meaningful character-string can be a feature's name. *Description* is the detailed presentation of the set of requirements denoted by a feature. According to different context, different kinds of technique (i.e. informal, semi-formal and formal) may be adopted for features' description. For example, Table 13.2 shows description of eight features in a simple document editor. We also use this document editor as a running example in the rest of this chapter.

Optionality describes whether a feature has the chance to be removed when its parent feature (if has) has been bound. Here, the parent-children relationship is imposed by refinements between features (see Sect. 13.3.1). Optionality has two

Table 13.1 Attributes of features

Attribute	Description	Values
Name	The mnemonic of a feature	Concise character strings
Description	The detailed presentation of a feature	{informal, semi-formal, formal}
Optionality	Whether a feature must be bound when its parent feature is bound	{mandatory, optional}
Binding-time	The phase when a feature must either be bound or removed	{reuse-time, compile-time, install-time, load-time, …}
Binding-state	Whether a feature has been bound or removed, or is waiting for being decided	{bound, removed, undecided}

Table 13.2 Description of features in a simple document editor

Feature	Description
Edit	The composition of features copy, cut and paste
Copy	Copy the selected text to the clipboard
Cut	Cut the selected text to the clipboard
Paste	Paste the text in the clipboard to the current position in the document
Un/re-do	The composition of features undo and redo
Undo	Undo unsaved edit operations (i.e. copy, cut, paste)
Redo	Redo unsaved edit operations (i.e. copy, cut, paste)
Save	Save a document into a disk

possible values, namely *mandatory* and *optional*. *Binding-time* is an attribute related to optional features. It describes the phase in the software life cycle when an optional feature must either be bound or removed. Typical binding-times include (but are not limit to) *reuse-time, compile-time, deploy-time, load-time,* and *run-time.* Different kinds of software system may have different sets of binding-times. The attribute *binding-state* has three values: *bound, removed* and *undecided.* A *bound* feature means that requirements denoted by this feature are activated in the current software system. A *removed* feature means that it will never be bound again. An *undecided* feature means that it is currently not in the *bound* or *removed* state, but still has the chance to be bound or removed in later binding-times.

In Sect. 13.5, we will show how to verify these binding and removing actions at each binding-time based on one kind of dependency between features, called *constraint.*

13.2.3   Operationalization of Features

To investigate the possible roles of feature dependencies in the solution space of software, we may have to consider how features are operationalized into program specifications and how their operationalization leads to the dependencies among them.

Currently, most software development methods encourage a modular way to the design and coding of software, for example, object-oriented software engineering (OOSE) and component-based software engineering (CBSE). A modular way has also been adopted at the requirement level of software development as presented in this chapter, that is, a feature serves as a module which encapsulates a set of related requirements. Based on these observations, we further apply such a modular approach to the level of program specifications and introduce the concept of *responsibilities.* Similar to features, we give the following definition of responsibilities from the intension and extension aspects.

In intension, a responsibility is a cohesive set of program specifications.

In extension, a responsibility is a basic unit for work assignment to software developers.

By introducing the concept of responsibilities, we can easily conclude the following basic property of feature operationalization.

A feature can be operationalized into a set of responsibilities.

UML defines a responsibility as "a contract or obligation of a classifier" [17]. This definition clarifies the fact that a responsibility will be assigned to a classifier, for example, to a component in the software architecture. However, it does not tell us where a responsibility comes from, nor does it tell us the intension of a responsibility. We define responsibilities as a concept at the level of program specifications and use it to partition program specifications for work assignment. We also think it is requirements that responsibilities come from, since the final purpose of building software is to satisfy requirements.

In the next section, we will show how these operationalized responsibilities are clustered for work assignment.

13.2.4   Responsibility Assignment

After responsibilities are identified, they should further be assigned to software developers. As a result, two responsibilities that are operationalized from a same feature may be assigned to different developers. Similarly, two responsibilities that are operationalized from different features may also be assigned to the same developer.

For example, *send-email* and *auto-save-email-copy* are two features in the email-client software. Table 13.3 shows the description and a possible operationalization of them. Table 13.4 shows the description of responsibilities operationalized from the two features. Figure 13.1 shows the result of responsibility assignment to two developers. As we can see, the two responsibilities *detection* and *send-email*, operationalized from two different features, are assigned to the same developer, since only the developer who is assigned the responsibility *send-email* has the capability to fulfill the responsibility *detection* (detecting email-sent-out events).

Based on this example, here, we show how to employ features as a kind of unit for work assignment, units that are larger than individual responsibilities.

Table 13.3 Feature operationalization (an example)

Feature	Description	Operationalization
Send-email[a]	Send-emails according to users' requests	Send-email
Auto-save-email-copy	When a email is sent out, save a copy of this email to the copy-box	Detection, save-copy

[a]Although the feature send-email is operationalized into one responsibility which has the same name, they do have different types: one denotes a feature, the other a responsibility

Table 13.4 Responsibility description (an example)

Responsibility	Description
Send-email	Send emails according to users' requests via SMTP
Detection	Detect events that indicate some email has been sent out
Save-copy	Save the email's copy to the copy-box

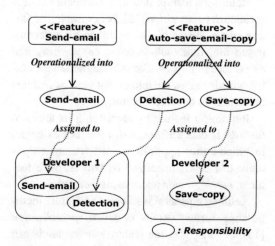

Fig. 13.1 Responsibility assignment to developers (an example)

First, we relate each feature F to a corresponding *responsibility container*, denoted by $F.RespC$. That is, there is a one-to-one relation between a set of features and their related responsibility containers.

Then, in the process of responsibility assignment, two kinds of responsibility are assigned to $F.RespC$. The first kind is the responsibilities that

are operationalized from F and also be assigned to $F.RespC$. We call them the *core-responsibilities* of F. The second kind is the responsibilities that are not operationalized from F but are assigned to $F.RespC$. We call them the *added-responsibilities* of F.

Figure 13.2 illustrates the process of feature operationalization and responsibility assignment. In this example, feature A is operationalized into three responsibilities: $AR1$, $AR2$, and $AR3$. $AR1$ and $AR2$ are assigned to $A.RespC$, and thus they are the core-responsibilities of A. $AR3$ is assigned to $B.RespC$, and thus it is one of the added responsibilities of feature B. The similar analysis is also to feature B.

After feature operationalization and responsibility assignment, to each feature F, we get the corresponding $F.RespC$, which now contains a set of responsibilities and can be used as a larger unit for work assignment than individual responsibilities.

In Sect. 13.3, we will further show how two kinds of feature dependency are identified based on the results of feature operationalization and responsibility assignment.

13.2.5 Resource Containers

Resource containers contain resources which are produced, consumed or accessed by features in their execution. The essential of resource containers is that they provide a way to structure resources used by features.

Resource containers can also be treated as a special kind of container of responsibilities, which passively accept features' requests for resource storing, querying, and retrieving. Thus, whether a resource container can fulfill its responsibilities is independent of features, but features often depend on the correct behavior of resource containers.

In the simple document editor, we have identified three resource containers from the description of features in Table 13.2. They are *clipboard, document,* and *storage*.

Resource containers often play the role of a medium of interaction between features. In

Fig. 13.2 Responsibility
assignment

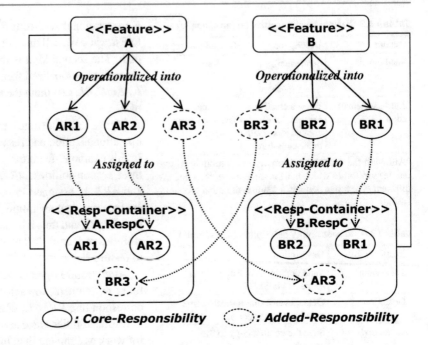

Sect. 13.3.4, we will discuss feature interaction
(as a kind of feature dependency) in detail.

13.3   Feature Dependencies

In this section, we introduce four kinds of dependency between features, namely *refinement, constraint, influence,* and *interaction.* As we will
see later, influence and interaction are dependencies originating from feature operationalization
and responsibility assignment, and play important
roles in the design of software.

13.3.1   Refinement

Refinement is a kind of binary relation among features, which integrate features at different levels of
abstraction into hierarchical structures. Hierarchical structures provide an effective way to describe
complex systems, since it is easier to understand a
complex system from general to specific and from
high levels to low levels.

Refinement can further be classified into three
more concrete subclasses: *decomposition, characterization*, and *specialization*.

Refining a feature into its constituent features
is called *decomposition* [15]. For example, the feature *edit* in the simple document editor is decomposed into three sub-features: *copy, paste,* and
delete (see Fig. 13.3). The sub-diagram in the dot-
ted box also gives the refinement view of features
in the simple document editor.

Refining a feature by identifying its attribute
features is called *characterization*. For example,
in graph-editor applications, the feature *graph-
move* can be characterized by two attribute features: *moving-mode* and *moving-constraint*.

Refining a general feature into a feature incorporating further details is called *specialization*
[15]. For instance, the feature *moving-mode* can
be specialized by more concrete features: *outline-
moving* and *content-moving*. Specialization is
often used to represent a set of variants of a
general feature. A general feature is also called a
variation point feature (vp-feature) in Griss [16].

The three kinds of refinement can be differenti-
ated by roles of features involved in them. Suppose
a and *b* are two features involved in a refinement,
we call the feature at a higher level of abstraction the *parent*, and the other feature the *child*.
Table 13.5 shows the different roles played by par-
ents and children in different kinds of refinement.

Fig. 13.3 Examples of refinement

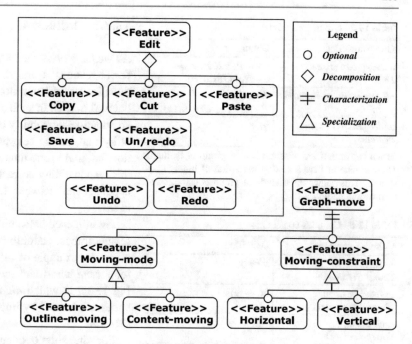

13.3.2   Constraint

Constraint is a kind of static dependency among features, and more strictly among binding-states of features. It provides a way to verify the results of requirement customization [18] and release planning [1,5]. Only those results that do not violate constraints on features can be treated as candidates of valid requirement subsets or releases.

We have identified three important constraint categories, namely *binary constraints, group constraints,* and *complex constraints.* Their formal definitions are given in Tables 13.6, 13.7, and 13.8, respectively.

It should be noticed that the three constraint categories are not entirely orthogonal. For example, all binary constraints in Table 13.6 can also be represented by complex constraints in Table 13.8.

Table 13.5 Roles in refinement

Refinement	Parent-role	Child-role
Decomposition	Whole	Part
Characterization	Entity	Attribute
Specialization	General-entity	Specialized-entity

Table 13.6 Binary constraints

Binary constraint	Definition
requires (a, b: Feature)	$bind(a) \rightarrow bind(b)$
m-requires (a, b: Feature)	*requires (a, b)* $\vee$ *requires (b, a)*
excludes (a, b: Feature)	$\neg\,(bind(a) \vee bind(b))$
Where: $bind(a : Feature) =_{def} (a.binding - state = bound)$	

Binary constraints are constraints on the binding-states of two features. This shows three kinds of basic binary constraint and their formal definitions

The reasons why we treat binary constraints as a separate category are twofold. First, binary constraints are the base of group and complex constraints. Second, in some cases, binary constraints can be used as the syntax sugar of complex constraints. For instance, the binary constraint "*a requires b*" is more concise than its complex form "*all-bind(a) requires all-bind(b)*".

In the simple document editor, we have identified the following four constraints on features:

[C1: multi-bind (copy, cut, paste) requires edit]
[C2: edit requires multi-bind (copy, cut, paste)]

Table 13.7 Group constraints

Group constraint	Definition
mutex-group (P: set Feature)	$\forall a \in P, b \in P, a \neq b \cdot excludes(a, b)$
all-group (P: set Feature)	$\forall a \in P, b \in P \cdot m - requires(a, b)$
undef-group (P: set Feature)	*true*

Group constraints are constraints on a group of features. These constraints are a kind of extension of binary constraints. This shows three kinds of group constraint and their formal definitions

Table 13.8 Complex constraints

Complex constraint	Definition
requires (x, y: Group-Predicate)	$x \rightarrow y$
m-requires (x, y: Group-Predicate)	$(x \rightarrow y) \vee \rightarrow (yx)$
excludes (x, y: Group-Predicate)	$\neg(x \vee y)$

Complex constraints are constraints between two feature sets, which extend the parameters of binary constraints to group predicates. This shows three kinds of complex constraint and their formal definitions. Typical group predicates are listed in Table 13.9

Table 13.9 Group predicates

Group predicate	Definition
single-bind (P: setFeature)	$\exists_{one} a \in P \cdot bind(a)$
all-bind (P: set Feature)	$\forall a \in P \cdot bind(a)$
multi-bind (P: set Feature)	$\exists_{some} a \in P \cdot bind(a)$
no-bind (P: set Feature)	$\forall a \in P \cdot \neg bind(a)$

Group predicates extend the parameter of the predicate *bind (a: Feature)* (see Table 13.6) to a feature set. This shows four kinds of group predicate and their formal definitions

[C3: all-group (un/re-do, undo, redo)]
[C4: un/re-do requires multi-bind (copy, cut, paste)]

The first three are refinement-imposed constraints (see Sect. 13.4.1). The fourth constraint means that "*un/re-do's* availability depends on at least one of the binding of *copy, cut, and paste*".

In Sect. 13.5, we will show how the constraint dependencies can be used to verify partially customized feature sets at different binding-times.

13.3.3 Influence

As we have observed in Sect. 13.2.4, for two different features *A* and *B*, a responsibility operationalized from A may not be assigned to *A.RespC*, but to *B.RespC*. In such a case, feature *A* imposes an added-responsibility on feature *B*, a responsibility that has no relevance to *B*'s implementation, but to *A*'s, and thus *A* depends on *B* to fulfill this responsibility correctly. In this chapter, such dependencies between features are called *influences*.

An influence between two features means one feature imposes additional responsibilities on the other. An example of influences is between features *send-email* and *auto-save-email-copy* (see Fig. 13.1), in which *auto-save-email-copy* influences *send-email* by imposing the responsibility *detection*.

For the simple document editor, we operationalize its eight features (see the result in Table 13.10) and assign these operationalized responsibilities to features' responsibility containers (see Fig. 13.4). In these two activities, we also identified an implicit resource container, called *un/re-doing info*, which contains the history information about *copy, cut*, and *paste*.

Then, we can easily identify the following influence dependencies between features:

[Inf1: un/re-do *influences copy by imposing "record copy-URI"*]
[Inf2: un/re-do *influences cut by imposing "record cut-URI"*]
[Inf3: un/re-do *influences paste by imposing "record paste-URI"*]
[Inf4: un/re-do *influences save by imposing "inform saved"*]

Influence is a kind of feature dependency at the specification level, which reflects the result of responsibility assignment. One possible use of influence is that it provides a way to analyze requirement changes. Influence is also one of the causes of another kind of dependency between features, namely *interaction*, which will be focused on in the next section.

Table 13.10 The result of feature operationaliztion

Feature	Operationalization (responsibilities)
Edit	Read-Selection, Remove-Selection, Read-Clipboard, Set-Clipboard, Write-Doc
Cooy	Read-Selection, Set-Clipboard
Cut	Remove-Selection, Set-Clipboard
Paste	Read-Clipboard, Write-Doc
Un/re-do	Undo, Redo, Clear-URI, Inform-Saved, Record Copy-URI, Record Cut-URI, Record Paste-URI
Undo	Undo
Redo	Redo
Save	Read-Doc, Write-Storage

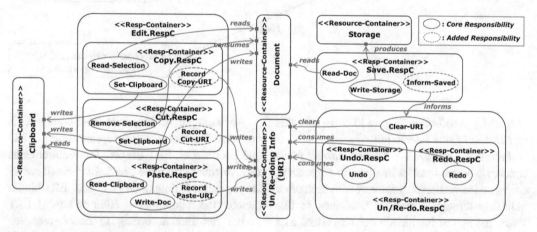

Fig. 13.4 The result of responsibility assignment

13.3.4   Interaction

Speaking generally, *interaction* is a kind of basic element in any system. It is by interaction that different components of a system can be connected with each other and be integrated into a whole. In this chapter, we use interaction to describe dynamic dependencies between features, dependencies that reflect how features interact with each other at run-time.

Following this section, we present four kinds of interaction, namely *inform, resource-configure, meta-level-configure*, and *flow*.

13.3.4.1   Inform

For features *A* and *B*, "*A informs B*" means that *A* sends *B* a piece of information to indicate that certain condition was achieved. An example of the *inform* interaction is between features *send-email*

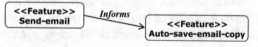

Fig. 13.5 An inform example

and *autosave-email-copy*, in which *send-email* sends *auto-save-email-copy* a piece of information to indicate that some email has been sent out. Figure 13.5 depicts this *inform* interaction.

13.3.4.2   Resource-Configure

For features *A* and *B*, "*A resource-configures B*" means that *A* configures *B*'s behavior by editing the resources that are accessed by *B*. An example of this kind of interaction is between features *filtering-rules-configurator* and *email-filter*, in which *filtering-rules-configurator* edits the resource container *filtering-rules* that

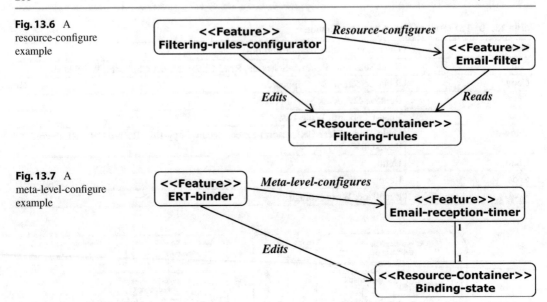

Fig. 13.6 A resource-configure example

Fig. 13.7 A meta-level-configure example

is read by *email-filter*. Figure 13.6 depicts this *resource-configure* interaction.

Resource-configure is a kind of *indirect* interaction, since two features involved in a *resource-configure* interaction only interact with each other indirectly through a resource container. In this sense, the *inform* interaction can be viewed as a kind of *direct* interaction.

If two features *a* and *b* interact through a resource container *c*, then this indirect interaction can be decomposed into two interactions between *a* and *c*, and between *b* and *c*. We can also introduce some meaningful names to characterize the interactions between features and resource containers, for example, *write, read, produce,* or *consume*.

13.3.4.3   Meta-level-Configure

Each run-time binding feature may be associated with a configurator feature which configures the feature's binding-state at run-time according to users' requests. We call this kind of interaction *meta-level-configure*, since the binding-state is a kind of meta-information of features. If we use a resource container to store a feature's binding-state, then, *meta-level-configure* can be viewed as a special case of the *resource-configure* interaction.

An example of the meta-level-configure is between features email-reception-timer (ERT) and ERT-binder. ERT denotes the requirements: receive emails from the pre-defined email server at pre-defined time intervals, and ERT-binder denotes the requirements: Bind or unbind ERT at the run-time according to users' requests. Figure 13.7 depicts this meta-level-configure interaction.

Resource-configure and *meta-level-configure* reflect the capability to modify a system's behavior. Buhr [19] calls such systems *self-modifying systems*. Anton and Potts [20] make a distinction between *core* features and *modulating* features.

13.3.4.4   Flow

Two features may also hold a data flow interaction between them. That is, data are processed in one feature, and then, flow to the other feature for further processing. Connected by *flow* interactions, a set of features can form a pipe-and-filter architectural style [21, 22]. Figure 13.8 depicts an example of *flow* interactions in the email-client software.

In the simple document editor, we have identified the following interactions between features:

[Int1: save *informs* un/re-do]
[Int2: copy *resource-configures* un/re-do]
[Int3: cut *resource-configures* un/re-do]

Fig. 13.8 A flow example

[Int4: paste *resource-configures* un/re-do]
[Int5: copy *resource-configures* paste]
[Int6: cut *resource-configures* paste]

13.4 Connections Between Dependencies

In Sect. 13.3, we have introduced four kinds of feature dependency. In this section, we further investigate the possible connections between these dependencies. One important function of these connections is that they facilitate the identification of feature dependencies, since unrecognized dependencies can be identified efficiently from those earlier identified through these connections.

13.4.1 Refinement-Imposed Constraints

Refinements implicitly impose constraints on features. We call these constraints *refinement-imposed constraints*. These constraints are caused by the following rules when binding or unbinding features.

(A) A pre-condition of binding a feature is that its parent must have been bound.

(B) A post-condition of binding a feature is that all its mandatory children must also be bound.

(C) A post-condition of binding a fully decomposed feature is that at least one of its constituent features must also be bound

(D) A pre-condition of unbinding a feature is that all its children must have been unbound.

(E) A post-condition of unbinding a mandatory feature is that its parent must also be unbound.

Based on these rules, Table 13.11 shows two examples of refinement scenarios, and refinement-imposed constraints identified from them.

13.4.2 Constraint and Interaction

In some cases, there are one-to-one relations between constraints and interactions. Table 13.12 shows three examples, in which, the interactions between features has been given in Sect. 13.3.

The explanation for the constraint "*auto-save-emailcopy (ASEC) requires send-email (SE)*" is that "*ASEC*'s availability depends on *SE*; if *SE* is not bound, the binding of *ASEC* will not be available to users". The explanation for "*filtering-rules-configurator (FRC) requires email-filter (EF)*" is that "*FRC*'s usability depends on *EF*; if *EF* is not bound, the binding of *FRC* will be of no value to users". And the explanation for "*email-filter (EF) requires decrypt-email (DE)*" is that "*EF* depends on *DE* when the current email is encrypted".

In these cases, constraints can be regarded as a static view of interactions, and interactions as a dynamic view of constraints.

13.4.3 Influence and Interaction

As we have concluded in Sect. 13.2.3, a feature can be operationalized into a set of responsibilities, but what we have not explicitly pointed out is that there are interactions between these responsibilities. And since *influence* causes some of these responsibilities to be assigned to other features' responsibility containers, some interactions between responsibilities are also interactions between features' responsibility containers at the same time. For simplicity, we just treat these interactions as interactions between features, since

Table 13.11 Refinement-imposed constraints

Refinement Scenario	Implied Constraints
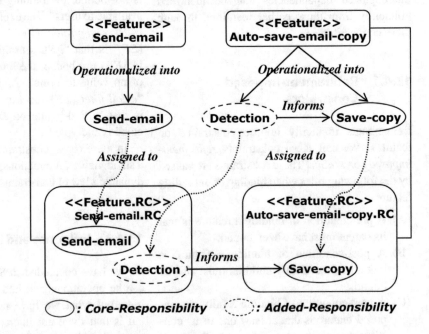	*all-group*(parent,mc-1, mc-n) *multi bind*(oc-1, oc-m) *requires* parent
	all-group(a,c), *all-group*(b,f,g), *all-group*(e,h,i), *multi bind*(b,d,e) *requires* a, j *requires* e

Table 13.12 Interaction-imposed constraint

Source	Interaction	Constraint
Figure 13.5	Send-email *informs* auto-save-email-copy	Auto-save-email-copy *requires* send-email
Figure 13.6	Filtering-rules-configurator *resource-configures* email-filter	Filtering-rules-configurator *requires* email-filter
Figure 13.8	Decrypt-email *flows* email-filter	Email-filter *requires* decrypt-email

Fig. 13.9 Influence and interaction

there is a one-to-one relation between a feature and its responsibility container.

To make the connection between influence and interaction more clear, let us review the example about features *send-email* and *auto-save-email-copy* (see Sects. 13.2.4 and 13.3.3 for the pre-vious description of this example, see Fig. 13.9 for its revision). We have operationalized *auto-save-email-copy* into two responsibilities *detec-tion* and *save-copy*. Now, we further point out the interaction between them: "*detection informs save-copy*", which means that once an *email-sent-*

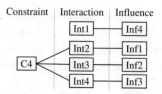

Fig. 13.10   Connections between dependencies

out event is detected, *detection* will inform *save-copy* of this event. We also have identified the influence dependency between these two features: "*auto-save-email-copy influences send-email by imposing the responsibility detection*". Then, we can notice that the *inform* interaction between responsibilities *detection* and *save-copy* also is an interaction between features *send-email* and *auto-save-email-copy*.

Figure 13.10 shows connections between these identified constraints, interactions, and influences in the simple document editor.

The influence dependency reflects the fact that responsibilities operationalized from the same feature are assigned to different features' responsibility containers, a fact that causes some interactions between responsibilities to become interactions between features. The earlier example shows how an influence instance relates to an instance of *direct* interactions. There may also be such cases in which the influence dependencies are related to *indirect* interactions.

13.5   Verification of Constraints and Customization

In this section, we show how the constraint dependencies can be employed to detect possible errors both in the constraints and in the binding resolutions on features.

13.5.1   Feature-Oriented Customization-Based Requirement Reuse

One practical approach to requirement reuse is the domain-specific customization-based reuse [23]. That is, first producing a set of reusable requirements in a specific software domain, and then cus-

tomizing them to accommodate different applications in this domain. To facilitate customization, requirements should be structured as a set of cohesive entities and dependencies between these entities should be identified and specified correctly.

Feature-oriented domain requirements modeling points out a possible way to implement the customization-based requirement reuse, since each feature denotes a cohesive set of individual requirements from users' or customers' views. However, it is often difficult to ensure that the constraint dependencies among features are identified completely and correctly [24], especially when there are a large number of features in a domain [25]. As a consequence of this problem, it is hard to say that a customization result is *consistent* and *complete* by simply checking the satisfaction of the set of identified constraints on features.

13.5.2   Customization Through a Series of Binding-Times

The purpose of customization is to get a subset of features suitable for the current application from the set of reusable features in a software domain. To get a suitable subset, we need to make a binding resolution to each element in the reusable feature set, that is, to select or remove it.

A real customization process is not a one-step action, but carried out through a series of stages or binding-times [26,27]. To facilitate customization, the set of binding resolutions made at a binding-time should be verified before their influence is transferred to the next binding-time. Otherwise, errors in the current stage will be spread implicitly to later stages, which decrease the efficiency of customization.

13.5.3   Three Verification Criteria

According to the values of binding-state, a feature set can further be partitioned into three subsets: the *undecided* subset, the *bound* subset, and the *removed* subset. *A binding resolution to an undecided* feature will move it to the *bound* or *removed* subsets.

Given a set of features and a set of constraints on the features, if the following three criteria are not satisfied, there must be some errors or deficiencies either in the constraints or in the binding resolutions on the features.

Criterion 1   there exists at least one set of binding resolutions to all features in the undecided subset, and after the set of resolutions are applied, all the constraints will not be violated.

Criterion 2   every feature in the undecided subset has a chance to be bound at later binding-times, without violating the constraints.

Criterion 3   every feature in the undecided subset has a chance to be removed at later binding-times, without violating the constraints.

Criterion 1 ensures the *consistency* of the binding resolutions have been made. That is, two conflicting features should not be in the *bound* state at the same time, and any features that are required by a *bound* feature should not be removed.

Criterion 1 can also help find the *inconsistency* of constraints. For example, suppose there are a bound feature *a* and two *undecided* features *b* and *c*, and three constraints on the three features: "*a requires b*", "*a excludes c*", and "*b requires c*". In this situation, *Criterion 1* is violated because of the inconsistency of the three constraints.

However, the inconsistency detecting function of *Criterion 1* only works well when some binding resolutions have been made. In the above example, if all the three features are in the *undecided* state, the inconsistency of the three constraints cannot cause the violation of *Criterion 1*, since the three constraints will be satisfied when all the three features are removed. In such a situation, we need *Criterion 2*.

Criterion 2 can be used to check the *consistency* of constraints before any binding resolution is made. In the earlier example, suppose feature *a* is *undecided* (no binding resolution is made to it), then *Criterion 2* will be violated by *a* because of the inconsistency of the three constraints. In addition, we can observe a fact that before the consistency of constraints is ensured, the use of constraint propagation algorithms (as suggested in [28,29]) in customization has a risk of making inconsistency unnoticed. In this example, if firstly

the bound subset contains only b, then a constraint propagation algorithm will automatically move c to the bound subset and a to the removed subset, neglecting the inconsistency of the three constraints.

The combination of *Criterion 2* and *3* can be used to check the completeness of the binding resolutions having been made. That is, if a feature is bound, then all its excluded features should be removed and all its required features be bound.

It should be pointed out that our purpose of the three criteria is not to propose some more efficient algorithms, but to provide a concise framework to help find any possible errors or deficiencies in constraints and binding resolutions on features as early as possible. Benavides et al. [30] have pointed out that the verification of a feature set is in the nature of a *constraint satisfaction problem* (CSP). Since the CSP is a very mature research field, we believe that the three criteria can be checked efficiently based on suitable CSP algorithms.

A formal description of the three criteria and their automatic verification by model checker SMV [31] can be found in Zhang et al. [18].

13.5.4   The Effectiveness of the Three Verification Criteria

Von der Maßen and Lichter [24] provided a detailed classification of possible deficiencies in constraints and in binding resolutions on features, and divided them into three categories: *redundancy, anomalies,* and *inconsistency.* We use the three verification criteria to detect all the 17 kinds of anomaly and inconsistency presented in von der Maßen and Lichter [24]. The results are shown in Table 13.13 (detailed information can be found in Appendix 1, 2, and 3).

In all the 10 kinds of anomaly and inconsistency of constraints, 8 are detected before any binding resolution is made. The verification results show that the three criteria can detect most kinds of anomaly and inconsistency of constraints at an early stage.

Table 13.13 Verification results of anomalies and inconsistency

Deficiency	Number of types	Result
Anomalies	6	All are detected: four types are detected before any binding resolution is made, and two types are detected after some binding resolutions are made
Inconsistency of constraints	4	All are detected before any binding resolution is made
Inconsistency of binding resolutions	7	All are detected

13.6   Design of High-Level Software Architecture

In software development, high-level design is one of the important activities after requirements analysis. In this section, we present an approach to designing high-level software architecture based on the result of feature dependency analysis.

13.6.1   An Overview

Through high-level design, a complex software system is decomposed into a set of computational elements and interactions between them [21]. These elements are also called components of a software system, and the decomposed structure is called the *software architecture*.

Here, we use the word 'high-level' before 'software architecture' to mean that we do not care for those *platform-specific* details, but only focus on the *platform-independent* aspect of software architecture.

An overview of this approach is depicted in Fig. 13.11. In this approach, components are constructed by clustering resource containers and component seeds. Interactions between components are identified by the following assumption: if two responsibilities are assigned to two different components, then any interactions between these two responsibilities will be developed into interactions between components. It should be noticed that the goal of this approach is not to make the transformation from features to the software architecture in a fully automatic way, but only in a disciplined way.

In the remaining section, four basic aspects of this approach are presented in four sections, respectively.

13.6.2   Resource Container Identification

In this approach, resource containers play important roles in component construction. A resource container itself may be developed into a single

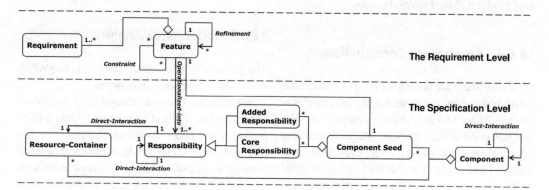

Fig. 13.11 An overview of feature-driven high-level software design

component, or sometimes is combined with responsibilities to form a component.

Resource containers can be identified in the following two ways. One way is by analyzing the description of features, since many resource containers have been explicitly mentioned in it. For instance, by analyzing the description of feature *copy* (see Table 13.2), a designer can easily find two resource containers: *clipboard* and *document*.

The other way is by analyzing constraints on features. Some resource containers are implied by constraints. For example, from the constraint *C4* in the simple document editor (see Sect. 13.3.2), an experienced designer should be able to identify the resource container that stores the history information about operations, although such a resource container is not mentioned by any features involved in the constraint.

13.6.3 Component Seed Creation

This activity is directly inherited from the activity of responsibility assignment which has been introduced in Sect. 13.2.4.

We think that those responsibility containers related to features can also serve as seeds to facilitate component construction because of the high cohesion of them in the solution space and the explicitly identified interactions between these units in feature dependency analysis. To express their meaning more directly, these units are called component seeds in the following. The component seed related to a feature f is still denoted by $f.RespC$. Inversely, the feature related to a component seed c will be denoted by $c.ftr$.

13.6.4 Component Construction

Generally, there are three heuristic rules to decide which component seeds and/or resource containers should be clustered into a component. The first rule is to consider the decomposition relationships between component seeds (inherited from features) and cluster a parent seed and all its children into a component. However, this rule pro-vides no support to further cluster these children into sub-components.

The second rule is to cluster component seeds with a same interaction context into a component. The interaction context of a component seed consists of all entities (component seeds or resource containers) that directly interact with it. For example, in Fig. 13.4, the three component seeds *copy.RespC*, *cut.RespC*, and *paste.RespC* have the same interaction context: {*clipboard, URI, document*}, and thus we cluster them into a component, called *edit*. In this example, the first and second rules indicate the same thing from two different viewpoints. In addition, the second rule can be used to cluster children seeds into sub-components.

The third rule is to cluster a resource container with component seeds that are consumers of the resources. For a resource container rc, and two component seeds p and c which play the producer and the consumer role, respectively, we prefer to cluster rc with c rather than p, since rc is only necessary to feature $c.ftr$'s implementation and has no contribution to $p.ftr$'s. According to this rule, the resource container *URI* (see Fig. 13.4) should be clustered with component seed *un/redo.RespC*, rather than *copy.RespC, cut.RespC* or *paste.RespC*.

There may also be such a situation, in which a resource container rc has several consumers, and these consumers cannot be clustered into one component. In this case, rc may need to be further decomposed. Otherwise, we can just transform rc into a single component without clustering it with other entities.

13.6.5 Interaction Analysis

The purpose of interaction analysis is to identify interactions between components.

Interactions between components are developed from two kinds of interaction related to component seeds and resource containers. The first kind is the direct interactions between component seeds. The second kind is the interactions between component seeds and resource containers. This

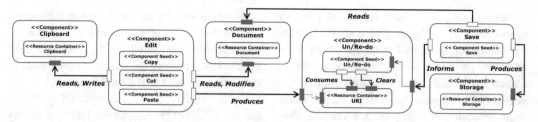

Fig. 13.12 The result of high-level software architecture design

kind of interaction can be obtained from the indirect interactions between features. Based on the two kinds of interaction, identifying interactions between components is relatively simple. If two entities (component seeds or resource containers) are clustered into the same component, then we can just exclude any interactions between the two entities from our consideration, since they have lost the chance to be developed into interactions between components. Similarly, if two entities are assigned to two different components, then interactions between the two entities should be developed into interactions between components correspondingly.

According to the rules for component construction and interaction identification, we construct six components and identify six sets of interactions between components from the result of feature dependency analysis to the simple document editor. The result is given in Fig. 13.12.

A more formal and detailed presentation of this feature-driven high-level software design method can be found in Zhang et al. [32].

13.7 Related Work

The interaction dependency in this chapter is not the same as the interaction in *Requirements Interaction Management* (RIM) [8], or the *Feature Interaction Problem* (FIP) in telecommunication systems [25]. RIM and FIP care much about the unexpected conflicts or interference among requirements or features (negative dependencies), while our work focuses on those interactions between features that are necessary for the final software to achieve certain customer-desired goals. These negative dependencies are caused

by the fact that requirements often originate from stake-holders with different or even conflicting viewpoints. Obviously, this research is a prerequisite for our work, since two requirements with an unrecognized conflict can never be satisfied in the final software at the same time. However, Robinson et al. [8] do propose to analyze unexpected interactions among requirements based on requirement subsets. This is similar to our work. In addition, researchers in the field of FIP also gradually realize the importance of positive interactions between features. One example is the DFC approach [22] proposed by Jackson and Zave. In DFC, flow interactions between various telecommunication features are systematically explored.

Feature-oriented domain analysis methods, such as FORM [15] and FeatuRSEB [33], also focus on the refinement and the constraint dependencies between features. However, these methods only identify two subclasses of the refinement: decomposition and specialization, and two basic binary constraints: requires and excludes. Our work further proposes a third subclass of the refinement, namely characterization, and two other kinds of constraint, namely group-constraints and complex-constraints. The constraint formalization based on propositional logic used in our method is partially inspired by the work of Fey et al. [34]. Cardinality-based feature modeling methods [27,35] use a general kind of group-constraint based on the cardinality notation, which provides a unified form of the three kinds of group-constraint used in our approach. Czarnecki and Kim [29] also propose an OCL-based approach to modeling constraints on features. But these methods seem to only pay attention to local constraints in single variation-points, partly because of the unsolved semantic conflict between global constraints and the feature-clone capability supported by these methods. Ferber et al. [3] focus on extracting feature interactions and constraints from legacy systems and separating them from feature refinement structures, but they do not make a clear distinction between interactions and constraints.

Dahlstedt and Persson [2] give a survey of the current research on requirement dependencies. In most of the existing research, the interaction dependencies are seldom focused, and little work recognizes the connections between different kinds of dependency. Lee and Kang [6] present an approach to reusable components design based on dynamic dependencies, but they fail to point out the connections between interactions and other kinds of dependency. Our work not only gives clear definitions of the four kinds of feature dependency, but also clarifies three kinds of connection between them. However, some research [1,5] also considers qualitative dependencies among requirements, which are not covered by our work.

Mannion [36] presents a first-order logic-based method to verify feature customization. This method does not make a distinction between undecided and removed features, and thus only has weak support for the verification of partially customized feature sets. Czarnecki et al. [26,27] propose the concept of staged configuration of feature models, but no explicit rule is presented to verify either the consistency of constraints or the binding resolutions performed at each stage. Recently, Batory [28] and Czarnecki and Kim [29] point out that the constraint propagation algorithms can be used to partly automate features' customization, which provides a more intelligent capability to ensure the completeness of binding resolutions than *Criterion 2* and *3* in our method which only detects possible incompleteness. However, constraint propagation algorithms help little to find inconsistency of constraints at an early stage, and only work well when there is no error in constraints. The three criteria proposed in our work provide more complete capabilities to detect both inconsistency in constraints at an early stage, and inconsistency

and incompleteness in binding resolutions. We believe that the combination of the three criteria and the debugging technique [28] gives a practical approach to ensuring the semantic correctness of constraints on a set of reusable features.

CRC cards [37], Responsibility-Driven Design (RDD) [38,39], General Responsibility Assignment Software Patterns (GRASP) [40] are three responsibility-driven object-oriented design methods, in which responsibilities are assigned to objects in a domain model. Although these methods implicitly acknowledge the tight relation between responsibilities and requirements, none of them provides enough capabilities to organize requirements, or to maintain traceability between requirements and responsibilities/objects. These methods also depend much on the correctness and completeness of a pre-created domain object model. Our approach to high-level software design adopts the concept of features to organize requirements, and uses responsibilities as the connector between requirements and design elements. Our approach focuses much on system functionality instead of object behavior, and is independent of any pre-created domain model. However, these methods do suggest an object-oriented way to implement the components in our approach.

13.8 Conclusions and Future Work

In this chapter, we presented a feature-oriented approach to analyzing dependencies among requirements by introducing four kinds of feature dependency, namely *refinement, constraint, influence*, and *interaction*, and pointing out three kinds of connection between them. We also gave two applications of these dependencies in software development.

Our future work will continually investigate the applicability of this approach by applying it to more complex software systems, and improve this approach based on the feedback of these case studies and by adding other important kinds of feature dependency and exploring the connections between them.

Acknowledgments This work is supported by the National Grand Fundamental Research 973 Program of China under Grant no. 2002CB312003, the National Natural Science Foundation of China under Grant no. 60233010, 60125206, and 90412011, and the Beijing Natural Science Foundation under Grant no. 4052018.

Appendix 1

ID	Scenario	Constraints	Binding-State	Verification Result
1		*all-group*(A, B), C *requires* A, B *requires* C.	*Undecided* = {A, B, C} *Bound* = {} *Removed* = {}	*Crit1*: Satisfied. *Crit2*: Satisfied. *Crit3*: Satisfied.
			Undecided = {C} *Bound* = {A, B} *Removed* = {}	*Crit1*: Satisfied. *Crit2*: Satisfied. *Crit3*: Violated by C.
2		*all-group*(A, B, C), *multi-bound*(D, E) *m-requires* C, D *excludes* E, B *requires* D.	*Undecided* = {A, B, C, D, E} *Bound* = {} *Removed* = {}	*Crit1*: Satisfied *Crit2*: Violated by E. *Crit3*: Satisfied.
			Undecided = {D, E} *Bound* = {A, B, C} *Removed* = {}	*Crit1*: Satisfied *Crit2*: Violated by E. *Crit3*: Violated by D.
3		*all-group*(A, B, C), *multi-bound*(D, E) *m-requires* C, B *requires* D.	*Undecided* = {A, B, C, D, E} *Bound* = {} *Removed* = {}	*Crit1*: Satisfied. *Crit2*: Satisfied. *Crit3*: Satisfied.
			Undecided = {D, E} *Bound* = {A, B, C} *Removed* = {}	*Crit1*: Satisfied. *Crit2*: Satisfied. *Crit3*: Violated by D.
4		*all-group*(A, B), C *requires* A, B *excludes* C.	*Undecided* = {A, B, C} *Bound* = {} *Removed* = {}	*Crit1*: Satisfied. *Crit2*: Violated by C. *Crit3*: Satisfied.
			Undecided = {C} *Bound* = {A, B} *Removed* = {}	*Crit1*: Satisfied. *Crit2*: Violated by C. *Crit3*: Satisfied.
5		*all-group*(A, B, C), *multi-bound*(D, E) *m-requires* C, D *excludes* E, B *excludes* D.	*Undecided* = {A, B, C, D, E} *Bound* = {} *Removed* = {}	*Crit1*: Satisfied. *Crit2*: Violated by D. *Crit3*: Satisfied.
			Undecided = {D, E} *Bound* = {A, B, C} *Removed* = {}	*Crit1*: Satisfied. *Crit2*: Violated by D. *Crit3*: Violated by E.
6		*all-group*(A, B, C), *multi-bound*(D, E) *m-requires* C, B *excludes* D.	*Undecided* = {A, B, C, D, E} *Bound* = {} *Removed* = {}	*Crit1*: Satisfied. *Crit2*: Violated by D *Crit3*: Satisfied.
			Undecided = {D, E} *Bound* = {A, B, C} *Removed* = {}	*Crit1*: Satisfied. *Crit2*: Violated by D *Crit3*: Violated by E.

Legend

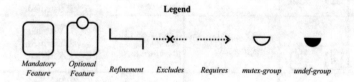

Mandatory Feature   Optional Feature   Refinement   Excludes   Requires   mutex-group   undef-group

Appendix 2

ID	Scenario	Constraints	Binding-State	Verification Result
1		*all-group*(A, B, C), B *excludes* C.	*Undecied* = {A, B, C} *Bound* = {} *Removed* = {}	*Crit1*: Satisfied. *Crit2*: Violated by A, B, C. *Crit3*: Satisfied.
2		*all-group*(A, B), A *excludes* B.	*Undecied* = {A, B} *Bound* = {} *Removed* = {}	*Crit1*: Satisfied. *Crit2*: Violated by A, B. *Crit3*: Satisfied.
3		*multi-bound*(B, C) *m-requires* A, B *excludes* C, B *requires* C.	*Undecied* = {A, B, C} *Bound* = {} *Removed* = {}	*Crit1*: Satisfied. *Crit2*: Violated by A, B, C. *Crit3*: Satisfied.
4		A *requires* B, A *excludes* B.	*Undecied* = {A, B} *Bound* = {} *Removed* = {}	*Crit1*: Satisfied. *Crit2*: Violated by A, B. *Crit3*: Satisfied.

Appendix 3

ID	Scenario	Constraints	Binding-State	Verification Result
1		*true requires all-bound*(A, B).	*Undecided* = {B} *Bound* = {A} *Removed* = {}	*Crit1*: Satisfied. *Crit2*: Satisfied. *Crit3*: Violated by B.
2		*all-group*(A, B, C)	*Undecided* = {C} *Bound* = {A, B} *Removed* = {}	*Crit1*: Satisfied. *Crit2*: Satisfied. *Crit3*: Violated by C.
3		*multi-bound*(B, C) *m-requires* A, B *excludes* C.	*Undecided* = { } *Bound* = {A} *Removed* = {B, C}	*Crit1*: Violated. *Crit2*: Satisfied. *Crit3*: Satisfied.
4			*Undecided* = { } *Bound* = {A, B, C} *Removed* = {}	*Crit1*: Violated. *Crit2*: Satisfied. *Crit3*: Satisfied.
5		*multi-bound*(B, C) *m-requires* A,	*Undecided* = { } *Bound* = {A} *Removed* = {B, C}	*Crit1*: Violated. *Crit2*: Satisfied. *Crit3*: Satisfied.
6		A *requires* B	*Undecided* = {B} *Bound* = {A} *Removed* = {}	*Crit1*: Satisfied. *Crit2*: Satisfied. *Crit3*: Violated by B.
7		A *excludes* B	*Undecided* = {B} *Bound* = {A} *Removed* = {}	*Crit1*: Satisfied. *Crit2*: Violated by B. *Crit3*: Satisfied.

References

1. P. Carlshamre, K. Sandahl, M. Lindvall, B. Regnell, et al., An industrial survey of requirements interdependencies in software product release planning, in *Fifth IEEE International Symposium on Requirements Engineering, 2001. Proceedings* (2001), pp. 84–91

2. A.G. Dahlstedt, A. Persson, Requirements interdependencies-moulding the state of research into a research agenda, in *9th International Workshop on Requirements Engineering–Foundation for Software Quality (REFSQ)* (2003), pp. 55–64

3. S. Ferber, J. Haag, J. Savolainen, Feature interaction and dependencies: modeling features for reengineering a legacy product line, in *Software Product Lines* (2002), pp. 235–256

4. J. Giesen, A. Völker, Requirements interdependencies and stakeholders preferences, in *IEEE Joint International Conference on Requirements Engineering, 2002. Proceedings.* (2002), pp. 206–209

5. J. Karlsson, S. Olsson, K. Ryan, Improved practical support for large-scale requirements prioritising. Requirements Eng. **2**(1), 51–60 (1997)

6. K. Lee, K.C. Kang, Feature dependency analysis for product line component design, in *Software Reuse: Methods, Techniques, and Tools* (2004), pp. 69–85

7. B. Ramesh, M. Jarke, Toward reference models for requirements traceability. IEEE Trans. Softw. Eng. **27**(1), 58–93 (2001)

8. W.N. Robinson, S.D. Pawlowski, V. Volkov, Requirements interaction management. ACM Comput. Surv. (CSUR) **35**(2), 132–190 (2003)

9. A. Van Lamsweerde, R. Darimont, E. Letier, Managing conflicts in goal-driven requirements engineering. IEEE TranS. Softw. Eng. **24**(11), 908–926 (1998)

10. A. von Knethen, A trace model for system requirements changes on embedded systems, in *Proceedings of the 4th international workshop on Principles of Software Evolution* (2001), pp. 17–26

11. A. Von Knethen, B. Paech, F. Kiedaisch, F. Houdek, Systematic requirements recycling through abstraction and traceability, in *IEEE Joint International Conference on Requirements Engineering, 2002. Proceedings* (2002), pp. 273–281

12. C.R. Turner, A. Fuggetta, L. Lavazza, A.L. Wolf, A conceptual basis for feature engineering. J. Syst. Softw. **49**(1), 3–15 (1999)

13. A. Mehta, G.T. Heineman, Evolving legacy system features into fine-grained components, in *Proceedings of the 24th international conference on Software Engineering* (2002), pp. 417–427

14. K.E. Wiegers, Practinal ways to manage-or participate in-the requirements engineering process. Softw. Requirements (1999)

15. K.C. Kang, S.G. Cohen, J.A. Hess, W.E. Novak, A.S. Peterson, Feature-oriented domain analysis (foda) feasibility study. Technical report, DTIC Document (1990)

16. M.L. Griss, Implementing product-line features with component reuse, in *Software Reuse: Advances in Software Reusability* (2000), pp. 137–152

17. UML 1.5 specification, http://www.uml.org/

18. W. Zhang, H. Zhao, H. Mei, A propositional logic-based method for verification of feature models, in *Formal Methods and Software Engineering* (2004), pp. 115–130

19. R.J.A. Buhr, Use case maps as architectural entities for complex systems. IEEE Trans. Softw. Eng. **24**(12), 1131–1155 (1998)

20. A. Antón, C. Potts et al., Functional paleontology: the evolution of user-visible system services. IEEE Trans. Softw. Eng. **29**(2), 151–166 (2003)

21. D. Garlan, M. Shaw, *An Introduction to Software Architecture* (1994)

22. M. Jackson, P. Zave, Distributed feature composition: a virtual architecture for telecommunications services. IEEE Trans. Softw. Eng. **24**(10), 831 (1998)

23. D. Barstow, G. Arango, Designing software for customization and evolution, in *Proceedings of the Sixth International Workshop on Software Specification and Design* (1991), pp. 250–255

24. T. von der Maßen, H. Lichter, Deficiencies in feature models, in *Workshop on Software Variability Management for Product Derivation-Towards Tool Support*, vol. 44 (2004)

25. D.O. Keck, P.J. Kuehn, The feature and service interaction problem in telecommunications systems: a survey. IEEE Trans. Softw. Eng. **24**(10), 779–796 (1998)

26. K. Czarnecki, S. Helsen, U. Eisenecker, Staged configuration using feature models, in *Software Product Lines* (2004), pp. 266–283

27. K. Czarnecki, S. Helsen, U. Eisenecker, Staged configuration through specialization and multilevel configuration of feature models. Softw. Process Improv. Pract. **10**(2), 143–169 (2005)

28. D. Batory, *Feature Models, Grammars, and Propositional Formulas* (2005)

29. K. Czarnecki, C.H.P. Kim, Cardinality-based feature modeling and constraints: A progress report, in *International Workshop on Software Factories* (2005), pp. 16–20

30. D. Benavides, P. Trinidad, A. Ruiz-Cortés, *Automated reasoning on feature models*, in Advanced Information, Systems Engineering (2005), pp. 491–503

31. Model checking @ CMU The SMV system, http://www.cs.cmu.edu/!modelcheck/smv.html

32. W. Zhang, H. Mei, H. Zhao, J. Yang, Transformation from cim to pim: a feature-oriented component-based approach, in *Model Driven Engineering Languages and Systems* (2005), pp. 248–263

33. M.L. Griss, J. Favaro, M.D. Alessandro, Integrating feature modeling with the rseb, in *Fifth International Conference on Software Reuse, 1998. Proceedings* (1998), pp. 76–85

34. D. Fey, R. Fajta, A. Boros, Feature modeling: A meta-model to enhance usability and usefulness, in *Software Product Lines* (2002), pp. 198–216

35. M. Riebisch, K. Böllert, D. Streitferdt, I. Philippow, Extending feature diagrams with uml multiplicities, in *6th World Conference on Integrated Design and Process Technology (IDPT2002)*, vol. 23 (2002)

36. M. Mannion, Using first-order logic for product line model validation, in *Software Product Lines* (2002), pp. 176–187

37. K. Beck, W. Cunningham, A laboratory for teaching object oriented thinking, in *ACM Sigplan Notices* (1989), pp. 1–6

38. R. Wirfs-Brock, A. McKean, *Object Design: Roles, Responsibilities, and Collaborations* (2003)

39. R. Wirfs-Brock, B. Wilkerson, Object-oriented design: a responsibility-driven approach, in *ACM SIGPLAN Notices* (1989), pp. 71–75

40. C. Larman, UML Applying. Patterns: an introduction to object-oriented analysis and design and the unified process (2001)

rCOS: A Refinement Calculus of Internetware Systems

14

Abstract

This article presents a mathematical characterization of object-oriented concepts by defining an observation-oriented semantics for a relational object-based language with a rich variety of features including subtypes, visibility, inheritance, type casting, dynamic binding and polymorphism. The language can be used to specify object-oriented designs as well as programs. We present a calculus that supports both structural and behavioral refinement of object-oriented designs. The design calculus is based on the predicate logic in Hoare and He's Unifying Theories of Programming (UTP).

Keywords

Object orientation · Refinement · Semantics · UTP

14.1 Introduction

Software engineering is mainly concerned with using techniques to systematically develop large and complex program suites. In the search for techniques for making software development more productive and software systems more reliable, object-oriented programming and formal methods are two important but largely independent approaches which have been influential in recent years.

The concept of *objects* is important concept in software development. Experimental languages of the 1970s provided various definitions of package, cluster, module, etc. They promote modularity and encapsulation, allowing the construction of software components which hide state representations and algorithmic mechanisms from users, and export only pertinent features. This produces components with a level of abstraction by separating the view of what a module does from the details of how it does them. It is clear that certain features of objects, particularly *inheritance* and the use of *object references* as part of the data stored by an object, could be used to construct large system *incrementally* and efficiently, as wellas making it

Parts of this chapter were reprinted from Jifeng He, Xiaoshan Li and Zhiming Liu. *rCOS: A refinement calculus of object systems.* Theoretical Computer Science, Vol. 365, Issues 1–2, pp. 109–142. © 2006 ACM, Inc. http://doi.acm.org/10.1016/j.tcs.2006.07.034.

possible to *reuse* objects in different contexts.

It is essential that software engineering is given the same basis in mathematics as other engineering disciplines. There has been good progress, resulting in three main paradigms: model-based, algebraic and process calculi. Practitioners of formal methods and experts in object technology have investigated how formal specification can supplement object-oriented development [1], and how it may help to clarify the semantics of object-oriented notations and concepts. Examples of such work include the formalization of the OMG's core object model [1] using Z.

Model-based formalisms have been used extensively in conjunction with object-oriented techniques, via languages such as Object-Z [1], VDM++ [2], and methods such as Syntropy [3] which uses the Z notation and Fusion [4] that is based on VDM. Whilst these formalisms are effective at modelling data structures as sets and relations between sets, they are are not designed for defining semantics of object-programs and thus do not deal with more sophisticated object-oriented mechanisms of object-oriented programming languages, such as dynamic binding and polymorphism.

Cavalcanti and Naumann defined an object-oriented programming language, called *ROOL*, with subtypes and polymorphism [5,6] using predicate transformers. Sekerinski [7,8] defined a rich object-oriented language by using a type system with subtyping and predicate transformers. However, neither reference types nor mutual dependency between classes are within the scope of these approaches. Because of complex flow of control, it is not feasible to calculate the weakest precondition of an object-oriented program for a given post condition. Thus semantic proofs of refinement rules in ROOL are quite hard and complex even without references. Without the inclusion of reference types, some interesting refinement rules can not be proved [9]. America and de Boer have given a logic for the parallel language POOL [10]. It applies to imperative programs with object sharing, but without subtyping and method overriding. Abadi and Leino have defined an axiomatic semantics for an imperative, object-oriented language with object sharing [11], but it does not permit recursive object types. Poetzsch-Heffter and Müller have defined a Hoare-style logic for object-oriented programs that relaxes many of the previous restrictions [12]. However, the specification of a method in the Poetzsch-Heffter and Müller logic is derived from the method's known implementation [13]. Leino has presented a logic in [13] with imperative features, subtyping, and recursive types. It allows the specification of methods, but inheritance is restricted and visibility is not considered.

In this article, we present part of a model and a refinement calculus (named as rCOS) for component and object systems. We focus on a mathematical characterization of object-oriented concepts, and provide a proper semantic basis essential for ensuring the correctness of programs and for developing tool support for formal techniques. We define an object-oriented language with subtypes, visibility, reference types, inheritance, type casting, dynamic binding and polymorphism. The language is similar to Java and C++. It has been used to develop meaningful case studies and to capture some of the central difficulties in modelling object-oriented designs and programs. However, we will not consider garbage collection, attribute hiding, multiple inheritance and exception handling.

rCOS is *class-based* and refinement is about making *correct* changes to the structure, methods of classes and the main program. The logic of rCOS is a *conservative extension* of standard predicate logic [14]. In our model, both commands and class declarations are identified as predicates whose alphabets include logic variables representing the initial and final values of program variables, as well as those variables representing contextual information of classes and their links. A variable of a built-in primitive type, such as the type Int of integers, stores data of the corresponding type whereas a variable of an object type holds the identity or reference and the current type information of an object as its value. We define the traditional programming constructs, such as conditional, sequential composition and recursion, in exactly the same way as their counterparts in an imperative programming language without reference types. This makes our approach more accessible to users who are already familiar with the existing imperative languages. All the laws about imperative commands remain valid without the need of reproving.

Another contribution of this work is to relate the notions of refinement and data refinement [15–17] in imperative programming to refactorings [18] and object-oriented design patterns for *responsibility assignments* [19,20]. Initial attempts to formalise refactorings in [21,22] are advanced by providing a formal justification of the soundness of the refactoring rules. The theories in [5,9,13,23] on object-oriented refinement are also advanced by dealing with large scale object-oriented program refinement with refactorings, functionality delegation, data encapsulation and class decomposition. Our refinement rules have been strongly motivated by the formal treatment of transformations of multi-view models, such as UML [24,25] and Rational Unified Process [26,27].

For simplicity, we do not consider attribute domain redefinition or attribute hiding. Our interest is in program requirement specification, design, verification and refinement; attribute domain redefinition and attribute hiding are language facilities mainly used for programming around defects in requirement specification or for the reuse of classes in a way that was not originally intended. For similar reasons, we ignore interfaces, throws clauses, concurrency, method name overloading, inner classes and method pointers. Some issues, such as concurrency and exception handling will be treated in a planned extension of this work.

The notion of *designs* in Unifying Theories of Programming [14] is introduced in Sect. 14.2. In Sect. 14.3 we define the syntax of rCOS. The semantics is given in Sect. 14.4, with a discussion about behavioral refinement of object-oriented designs (commands) under the same class declarations. The laws just extend the laws in UTP to object-oriented commands. In Sect. 14.5, we define a notion of object-oriented refinement that allows us to (i) refine both the class declarations and main methods, and (ii) explore structural refinement. In Sect. 14.6, we present refinement laws that capture the essence of object-oriented design and programming. We provide proofs for some of these laws. The semantic definition of rCOS is essential for the precise justification of these laws. We will draw conclusions and discuss related and future work in Sect. 14.7.

14.2   Semantic Basis

The execution of a program is modelled as a relation between *program states*. Here, the concept of state is more general than in a sequential language. For example, for a terminating sequential program, we are only interested in the initial inputs and final outputs. For a program which may not terminate, we need an observable by which we can describe whether or not the program terminates for its input. For concurrent and communicating programs, we observe the possible *traces* of interactions, *divergencies* and *refusals*, in order to verify if a program is deadlock free and livelock free. For real-time programs, we might observe time. Identifying what to observe in systems is one of the core ideas of UTP.

For a program P, we call what is to be observed the *observables* or *alphabet* of P, denoted by $\alpha(P)$ or simply α when there is no confusion. An observable of P may take different values for different executions or runs, but from the same value space called the *type* of the observable. Therefore, an observable is also a *variable*. Observables need not to appear in the program text but they are needed to define the semantics of the program.

Given an alphabet α, a *state* of α is a (well-typed) mapping from α to the value spaces of the observables. A program P with an alphabet α is then defined as a pair of predicates, called a *design*, represented as $Pre \vdash Post$, with free variables in α. It is generally interpreted as if the value of observables satisfies the *precondition Pre* at the beginning of the execution, the execution will *generate* observables satisfying the *postcondition Post*.

14.2.1   Programs as Designs

This subsection summarises how the basic programming constructs can be defined as designs.

For further details we refer the reader to the book on UTP [14].

For an imperative sequential program, we are interested in observing the values of the input variables $in\alpha$ and output variables $out\alpha$. Here we take the convention that for each input variable $x \in in\alpha$, its primed version x' is an output variable in $out\alpha$, that gives the final value of x after the execution of the program. We use a Boolean variable ok to denote whether a program is *started properly* and its primed version ok' to represent whether the execution has terminated. The alphabet α is defined as the union $in\alpha \cup out\alpha \cup \{ok, ok'\}$, while a design is of the form

$$(p(x) \vdash R(x, x')) \stackrel{def}{=} ok \wedge p(x) \Rightarrow ok' \wedge R(x, x')$$

where

- p is a predicate over $in\alpha$ and R is a predicate over $in\alpha \cup out\alpha$,
- p is the *precondition*, defining the initial states,
- R is the *postcondition*, relating the initial states to the final states,
- ok and ok' describe the initiation and termination of the program, respectively; they do not appear in the program texts.

The design represents a *contract* between the "user" and the program such that if the program has started properly in a state satisfying the precondition it will terminate in a state satisfying the postcondition R.

A design is often *framed* in the form

$$\beta : (p \vdash R) \stackrel{def}{=} p \vdash (R \wedge \underline{w}' = \underline{w})$$

where $\underline{w}$ contains all variables in $in\alpha$ except for those in β.

Before we define the semantics of a program, we first define some operations on designs.

- Given two designs such that the output alphabet of P is the same as primed version of the input alphabet of Q, the sequential composition

$$P(in\alpha_1, out\alpha_1); Q(in\alpha_2, out\alpha_2)$$
$$\stackrel{def}{=} \exists m \cdot P(in\alpha_1, m) \wedge Q(m, out\alpha_2)$$

- Conditional choice: $(d_1 \triangleleft b \triangleright d_2) \stackrel{def}{=} (b \wedge d_1) \vee (\neg b \wedge d_2)$
- Demonic and angelic choice operators:

$$d_1 \sqcap d_2 \stackrel{def}{=} d_1 \vee d_2 \quad d_1 \sqcup d_2 \stackrel{def}{=} d_1 \wedge d_2$$

- while b do d, also denoted by $b * c$, is defined as the worst fixed point of the relation expression $((d; X) \triangleleft b \triangleright skip)$, where the worst fixed point of $F(X)$ is the lest upper bound of $\{F^i(true) \mid i = 0, 1, \ldots\}$.

Some primitive programming commands as framed designs are given in in Table 14.1. Composite statements are then defined by semantics operations on designs.

In general, when giving a semantics, preconditions are usually strengthened with some *well-definedness* conditions of the commands. Thus, the semantics of a program or command c is generally of the form

$$[\![c]\!] \stackrel{def}{=} d(c) \Rightarrow Spec$$

Table 14.1 Basic commands as designs

Command: c	design: $[\![c]\!]$	Description
skip	$\{\} : true \vdash true$	Does not change anything, but terminates
chaos	$\{\} : false \vdash true$	Anything, including non-terminating, can happen
$x := e$	$\{x\} : true \vdash x' = val(e)$	Side-effect free assignment; updates x with the value of e
$m(e; v)$	$[\![\mathtt{var}\ in, out]\!]$; $[\![in := e]\!]$; $[\![body(m)]\!]$; $[\![v := out]\!]$; $[\![\mathtt{end}\ in, out]\!]$	$m(in; out)$ is the signature with input parameters in and output parameters out; $body(m)$ is the body command of the procedure/method

where *Spec* is a design and $D(c)$ is the well-definedness condition of c. Well definedness may be dynamic.

Strengthening preconditions by conjoining well-definedness conditions allows us to modify an ill-defined command to a well-formed one by means of a refinement. This approach supports incremental development as most cases of ill-definedness commands are due to insufficient data or services. The addition of data, services and components can thus be considered as refinements in our framework.

In this article, variables capturing aspects of dynamic typing, visibility, etc., are used to define the semantics of object-oriented programs. This ensures that the logic of rCOS is a conservative extension to that used for imperative programs. All the laws about imperative commands remain valid without the need of revision.

14.2.2 Refinement of Designs

The refinement relation between designs is defined to be logic implication.

Definition 14.1 A design $d_2 = (\alpha, P_2)$ is a *refinement* of design $d_1 = (\alpha, P_1)$, denoted by $d_1 \sqsubseteq d_2$, if P_2 entails P_1, that is

$$\forall x_1, \ldots, x_n, x_1', \ldots, x_n', ok, ok' \cdot (P_2 \Rightarrow P_1)$$

where $x_1, \ldots, x_n, x_1', \ldots, x_n'$ are the variables in α. $D_1 = d_2$ if $D_1 \sqsubseteq D_2 \wedge D_2 \sqsubseteq D_1$

♣

If the two designs do not have the same alphabet, we can use data refinement to relate their state spaces, as well as their behaviour

Definition 14.2 Let $\rho(\alpha_2, \alpha_1)$ be a many to one mapping from the state space of α_2 to the state space of α_1. Design $d_2 = (\alpha_2, P_2)$ is a *refinement* of design $d_1 = (\alpha_1, P_1)$ under ρ, denoted by $d_1 \sqsubseteq_\rho d_2$, if

$$((true \vdash \rho(\alpha_2, \alpha_1')); P_1) \sqsubseteq (P_2; (true \vdash \rho(\alpha_2, \alpha_1')))$$

Notice that both sides of the above refinement have the same alphabet $\alpha_1 \cup \alpha_2$.

♣

It is easy to prove that *chaos* is the worst program, i.e. *chaos* $\sqsubseteq P$ for any program P. For more algebraic laws of imperative programs, please see [14].

The following theorem establish that designs can be used for defining a semantics of programs.

Theorem 14.1 *The notion of designs is closed under programming constructors:*

$$((p_1 \vdash R_1); (p_2 \vdash R_2)) = ((p_1 \wedge \neg(R_1; \neg p_2)) \vdash (R_1; R_2))$$
$$(p_1 \vdash R_1) \sqcap (p_2 \vdash R_2) = (p_1 \wedge p_2) \vdash (R_1 \vee R_2)$$
$$(p_2 \vdash R_1) \sqcup (p_2 \vdash R_2) = (p_1 \vee p_2) \vdash ((p_1 \Rightarrow R_1) \wedge (p_2 \Rightarrow R_2))$$
$$((p_1 \vdash R_1) \triangleleft b \triangleright (p_2 \vdash R_2)) = ((p_1 \triangleleft b \triangleright p_2)) \vdash (R_1 \triangleleft b \triangleright R_2)$$

The proof can be found in [14].

14.3 Syntax of rcos

In rCOS, an object system (or program) S is of the form *Cdecls • Main*, consisting of class declaration section *Cdecls* and a main method *Main*. The main method is a pair $(extvar, c)$, where *extvar* is a finite set of *external variables declaration* and c is a command. The class declaration section *Cdecls* is a finite sequence of class declarations $cdecl_1; \ldots; cdecl_k$, where each class declaration $cdecl_i$ is of the form

```
[private] class M [extends N] {
         private    T_11 a_11 = d_11, ..., T_1m_1 a_1m_1 = d_1m_1;
         protected  T_21 a_21 = d_21, ..., T_2m_2 a_2m_2 = d_2m_2;
         public     T_31 a_31 = d_31, ..., T_3m_3 a_3m_3 = d_3m_3;
         method     m_1(T_11 x_1; T_12 y_1; T_13 z_1){c_1};
                    ...;
                    m_ℓ(T_ℓ1 x_ℓ; T_ℓ2 y_ℓ; T_ℓ3 z_ℓ){c_ℓ}
         }
```

where

- A class can be declared as *private* or *public* (the default is public). The class section is a *Java-like package* and *Main* an application program using the package. Only a public class or a primitive type can be used in the external variable declarations of *Main*.

- N and M are distinct names of classes, and N is called the *direct superclass* of M.
- Attributes annotated with *private, protected* and *public* are private, protected and public attributes to the class, respectively. The types and initial values of attributes are given in the declaration.
- A *method* declaration declares the method, its value parameters $(\underline{T}_{i1}\ \underline{x}_i)$, result parameters $(\underline{T}_{i2}\ \underline{y}_i)$, value-result parameters $(\underline{T}_{i3}\ z_i)$ and bodies (c_i).

We use the Java convention, and assume that an attribute is *protected* when it is not tagged with *private* or *public*. We assume, for simplicity, that all methods are public and can be inherited by a subclass. **Symbols.** We assume the following disjoint infinite sets of symbols,

- *CNAME* is used for the set of class names. We use C, d, M and N with possible subscripts to range over this set.
- *ANAME* is the set of symbols to be used as names of attributes, ranged over by a with possible subscripts.
- *VNAME* denotes the set of *simple variables* names. We use x, y, and z, etc. for simple variable names.

14.3.1   Commands

rCOS supports typical object-oriented programming constructs. It also provides some commands for the purpose of specification and refinement. The syntax of rCOS commands is:

$c ::= skip \mid chaos \mid \text{var } T\ x[=e] \mid \text{end } x \mid c; c \mid c \triangleleft b \triangleright c \mid c \sqcap c$
$\quad \mid b * c \mid le.m(\underline{e}; \underline{e}; \underline{e}) \mid le := e \mid C.new(le)$

where b is a Boolean expression, e a general expression, $\underline{e}$ a list of expressions and le an expression which may appear on the left hand side of an assignment, obeying the form

$$le ::= x \mid self \mid le.a$$

where

- x is a simple variable and a an attribute.
- $le.m(\underline{ve}; \underline{re}; \underline{vre})$ denotes a method m call within the object le. Expression lists $\underline{ve}$, $\underline{re}$ and $\underline{vre}$ are the actual value input parameters, result parameters and actual value-result parameters, respectively.
- The command $C.new(le)$ creates a new object of class C whose attributes have the initial values as declared in C and attaches the new object to le. When C has attributes whose types are classes, we allow nested object creation. For example, if $D\ a$ is an attribute of C, $C.new(le)[d.new(a)]$ creates a new object of class C and a new object of d attached to C's attribute a.
- Command $\text{var } T\ x = e$ declares a local variable x of type T with an initial value e; $\text{end } x$ ends the scope of the local variable x.
  A local variable can be declared a number of times with different types and values before it is undeclared. Thus a local variable x may have a sequence of declared types and it may takes sequence of values.

14.3.2   Expressions

Expressions, which can appear on the right hand side of an assignment, are constructed according to the rules below.

$$e ::= x \mid a \mid null \mid self \mid e.a \mid (C)e \mid f(e)$$

where *null* represents the special value (or object), *self* is used to denote the active object in the current scope (some object-oriented languages use *this*), *e.a* is the attribute a of e, $(C)e$ is type casting, and f is a built-in operation for a built-in primitive type.

14.4   Semantics

We now show how to use the basic model of the UTP to define the semantics of rCOS. We use $[\![\mathcal{E}]\!]$ to denote the semantics of an element $\mathcal{E}$, such as a command and a class declaration. The semantics takes into account the following features:

- A program operates not only on variables of primitive types, such as integers and Booleans, but also on variables of *object reference types*.
- To protect attributes from illegal accesses, the model addresses the problem of *visibility*.
- An object can be associated with any subclass of its original declaration. To validate expressions and commands in a dynamic binding environment, the model keeps track of the *current type* of each object.
- The dynamic type M of an object can be cast up to any superclass N and later cast down to any class which is a subclass of N and a superclass of M (or M itself). We record both the *cast type* N and the current type M of the object.

14.4.1 Structure, Value and Object

The class declaration section *Cdecls* of a program defines the types (value space) and static structure of the program.

14.4.1.1 Structure
We introduce the following *structural* variables:

- *pricname* = {$\texttt{private}\ C$ | C is declared in *Cdecls*}. We use *pubcname* to record the sets of names of the public classes in declared in *Cdecls*. Let *cname* be the union of these two sets.
- *superclass*: the partial function

$$\{M \mapsto N \mid [\texttt{private}]\, \texttt{class}\, M\, \texttt{extends}$$
$$N\ \text{is declared in } Cdecls\}$$

This function defines that N is a direct superclass of M. We define the general superclass class relation $\succ$ to be the transitive closure of *superclass*, and $N \succeq M$ if $N \succ M$ or $N = M$.

- *pri*, *prot*, and *pub*: these variables associate each class name $C \in cname$ to its private attributes *pri(C)*, protected attributes *prot(C)*, and public attributes *pub(C)*, respectively:

$$pri(C) \overset{def}{=} \{\langle a : T, d\rangle \mid T\, a = d \text{ is a private attribute of } C\}$$
$$prot(C) \overset{def}{=} \{\langle a : T, d\rangle \mid T\, a = d \text{ is a protected attribute of } C\}$$
$$pub(C) \overset{def}{=} \{\langle a : T, d\rangle \mid T\, a = d \text{ is a public attribute of } C\}$$

We define the following functions over attributes:

1. The function *attr* is the union of *pri*, *prot* and *pub*; for each C, *attr(C)* is the set of attributes declared in C itself.
2. The function *Attr* extends *attr(C)* for each C to include all the attributes that C inherited from its super classes.
3. *ATTR(Cdecls)* denotes the set of $\{C.a \mid C \in cname \land a \in Attr(C)\}$
4. *init(C.a)* denotes the initial value of attribute a of C.
5. *dtype(C.a)* denotes the *declared type* T if $\langle a : T, d\rangle \in Attr(C)$.
6. *ATTR(C)* is the set of all attributes that are associated to class C: it is the smallest set such that

   a. $Attr(C) \subseteq ATTR(C)$
   b. $Attr(dtype(N.a)) \subseteq ATTR(C)$ if $N.a \in ATTR(C)$ and *dtype(N.a)* is a class in *cname*.

- *op*: associates each class $C \in cname$ to its set of methods *(op)(C)*

$$op(C) \overset{def}{=} \{m \mapsto (\underline{x} : \underline{T}_1; \underline{y} : \underline{T}_2; \underline{z} : \underline{T}_3, c) \mid$$
$$m(\underline{x} : \underline{T}_1; \underline{y} : \underline{T}_2; \underline{z} : \underline{T}_3)\{c\}$$
$$\text{is declared as method of } C\}$$

The set of the above structural variables is denoted by Ω_{Cdecls}. A class declaration is a command that modifies these structural variables. However, the values of these variables remain unchanged during execution of the main method.

14.4.1.2 Attribute Expression
The set *eATTR(C)* of *attribute expressions* of class C is defined inductively below:

1. $\varepsilon \in eATTR(C)$,
2. $C.a \in eATTR(C)$ for each attribute a of C,
3. if $C.a \in eATTR(C)$ and $dtype(C.a) \in cname$, then $dtype(C.a).b \in eATTR(C)$ for any $b \in Attr(dtype(C.a))$.
4. if $e_i \in eATTR(C)$ for $i = 1, \ldots, n$, $dtype(e_i)$ are built-in primitive types and expres-

sion $f(x_1 : dtype(e_1), \ldots, x_n : dtype(e_n))$ is well-defined on these primitive types, then $f(e_1, \ldots, e_n) \in eATTR(C)$.

14.4.1.3   Value and Object

We assume a set $\mathcal{T}$ of *built-in primitive types*. We also assume an infinite set *REF* of *object identities* (or *references*), with *null* $\in$ *REF*. A *value* is either a member of a primitive type in $\mathcal{T}$ or an object identity in *REF* with its *dynamic typing information*. Let *VAL* be the set the set of values

$$VAL \stackrel{def}{=} \bigcup \mathcal{T} \cup (REF \times CNAME)$$

For a value $v = \langle r, C \rangle \in REF \times CNAME$, we use $ref(v)$ to denote r and $type(v)$ to denote C.

Definition 14.3 An *object o* is either the special object *null*, or a structure $\langle r, C, \sigma \rangle$, where

- reference r, denoted by $ref(o)$, is in *REF*,
- C, denoted by $type(o)$, is a class name.
- σ is called the *state* of o, denoted by $state(o)$, and it is a mapping that assigns each $a \in Attr(C)$ to a value in $dtype(a)$ if $dtype(a) \in \mathcal{T}$ and otherwise to an object o_1 (possibly *null*) such that $type(o_1) \preceq dtype(a)$. We use $o.a$ to denote $\sigma(a)$.
- the recursion is required to be finite.

♣

We extend *equality* to a relation over both values and objects

$$(v_1 = v_2) \stackrel{def}{=} \begin{pmatrix} (type(v_1) = type(v_2) \wedge \\ (type(v_1) \in \mathcal{T} \wedge (v_1 = v_2)) \vee \\ \forall a \in Attr(type(v_1)) \cdot (v_1.a = v_2.a) \end{pmatrix}$$

This equality ignores object references, but relating underlying primitive attributes. **Some notations.** Let $\mathcal{O}$ be the set of all objects, including *null*. The following notations are employed.

- For sets S and S_1, $S_1 > S$ is the set difference removing elements in S_1 from S. Let $>$ have higher associativity[1] than the normal set operators like $\cup$ and $\cap$.

- For a mapping $f : \text{d} \longrightarrow E$, $d \in \text{d}$ and $r \in E$,

$$f \oplus \{d \mapsto r\} \stackrel{def}{=} f' \quad \text{where } f'(b) \stackrel{def}{=} \begin{cases} r, & \text{if } b = d; \\ f(b), & \text{if } b \in \{d\} > \text{d}. \end{cases}$$

- For an object $o = \langle r, M, \sigma \rangle$, an attribute a of M and a value d,

$$o \oplus \{a \mapsto d\} \stackrel{def}{=} \langle r, M, \sigma \oplus \{a \mapsto d\} \rangle$$

- For a set $S \subseteq \mathcal{O}$ of objects,

$$S \uplus \{\langle r, M, \sigma \rangle\} \stackrel{def}{=} \{o \mid ref(o) = r\} > S \cup \{\langle r, M, \sigma \rangle\}$$
$$ref(S) \stackrel{def}{=} \{r \mid r = ref(o), o \in S\}$$

For a given class declaration section *Cdecls*, Σ_{Cdecls}, called the *object space* of *Cdecls*, denotes the set of all objects declared in *Cdecls*. The pair $(\Omega_{Cdecls}, \Sigma_{Cdecls})$ is called a *program context* and denote it by Ξ_{Cdecls}. When there is no confusion, we omit the subscript *Cdecls*. All dynamic semantic definitions are given under a fixed class declaration section. Therefore the evaluation $value(e)$ of an expression e is carried out in the context Ξ and the semantics $[\![c]\!]_\Xi$ defines the state change produced by execution of c in the context Ξ.

14.4.2   Static Semantics

We treat each class declaration as a command and its semantics is defined as a design. A class declaration changes the values of the structural variables *pricname*, *pubcname*, *cname*, *superclass*, *pri*, *prot*, *pub* and *op*. We first define the well-definedness of a class declaration.

Definition 14.4 A class declaration *cdecl* is *well-defined* if the following conditions hold.

1. M has not been declared before: $M \notin cname$.
2. N and M are distinct: $N \neq M$.
3. The attribute names in the class are distinct.
4. The method names in the class are distinct.
5. The parameters of every method are distinct.

We use $\mathcal{D}(cdecl)$ to denote the conjunction of the above conditions for the class declaration of *cdecl*.

♣

---

[1] This is the purpose of using this "strange" notation for set difference.

A well-defined private class declaration for M with a superclass N will modify the structural variables:

$$\llbracket cdecl \rrbracket \overset{def}{=} \{pricname, pubcname, superclass, pri, prot, pub, op\} : \mathscr{D}(cdecl) \vdash \begin{pmatrix} modifyPriCname \land modifyPubCname \land modifySuper \\ \land\ modifyPri \land modifyProt \land modidyPub \land modifyOp \end{pmatrix}$$

where

$$
\begin{aligned}
modifyPriCname &\overset{def}{=} pricname' = pricname \cup \{M\} \\
modifyPubCname &\overset{def}{=} pubcname' = pubcname \\
modifySuper &\overset{def}{=} superclass' = superclass \oplus \{M \mapsto N\} \\
modifyPri &\overset{def}{=} pri' = pri\oplus \\
&\qquad \{M \mapsto \{\langle a_{11} : T_{11}, d_{11}\rangle, \dots, \langle a_{1m_1} : T_{1m_1}, d_{1m_1}\rangle\}\} \\
modifyProt &\overset{def}{=} prot' = prot\oplus \\
&\qquad \{M \mapsto \{\langle a_{21} : T_{21}, d_{21}\rangle, \dots, \langle a_{2m_2} : T_{2m_2}, d_{2m_2}\rangle\}\} \\
modifyPub &\overset{def}{=} pub' = pub\oplus \\
&\qquad \{M \mapsto \{\langle a_{31} : T_{31}, d_{31}\rangle, \dots, \langle a_{3m_3} : T_{3m_3}, d_{3m_3}\rangle\}\} \\
modifyOp &\overset{def}{=} op' = op\oplus \\
&\qquad \{M \mapsto \{m_1 \mapsto ((\underline{x}_1 : \underline{T}_{11}; \underline{y}_1 : \underline{T}_{12}; \underline{z}_1 : \underline{T}_{13}), c_1), \dots, \\
&\qquad\qquad m_\ell \mapsto ((\underline{x}_\ell : \underline{T}_{\ell 1}; \underline{y}_\ell : \underline{T}_{\ell 2}; \underline{z}_\ell : \underline{T}_{\ell 3}), c_\ell)\}\}
\end{aligned}
$$

We can similarly define a class declaration for the cases when the class M is declared as a public class and when it is not declared as a subclass of another.

Definition 14.5 Let $Cdecls \equiv (cdecl_1; \dots; cdecl_n)$ be a class declaration section. Its *semantics* is defined by the sequential composition of the designs of the individual class declarations starting with all structural variables initialised to the empty set

$$\llbracket Cdecls \rrbracket \overset{def}{=} Empty; \llbracket cdecl_1 \rrbracket; \dots; \llbracket cdecl_n \rrbracket$$

where

$$Empty \overset{def}{=} true \vdash \begin{pmatrix} pricname' = \emptyset \land pubcname' = \emptyset \land superclass' = \emptyset \\ \land\ pri' = \emptyset \land prot' = \emptyset \land pub' = emptyset \land op' = \emptyset \end{pmatrix}$$

♣

Definition 14.6 A class declaration section *Cdecls* is *well-defined*, denoted $\mathscr{D}(Cdecls)$, if the following conditions hold

1. each class name $M \in cname$ and the name of its direct superclass N are distinct,
2. if $M \in cname$ and $superclass(M) = N$, then $N \in cname$,
3. any type used in declarations of attributes and parameters is either a built-in primitive type or a class in *cname*,

4. the superclass relation $\succ$ is acyclic,
5. any attribute of a class is not redeclared in its subclasses, i.e. we do not allow attribute hiding in a subclass,
6. the names of the attributes of each class are distinct,
7. the names of the methods of each class and the names of parameters of each method are distinct, respectively.

♣

A well-defined rCOS declaration section corresponds to a UML [28] class diagram. For related work on formal support to UML-based development, we refer to our work in [24,25,29].

Example 14.1 Consider a bank system illustrated by the UML class diagram in Fig. 14.1. *Account* has two subclasses: a current account *CA* and a savings account *SA*.

The declaration of public class *Bank* has three attributes: *name* and *address* are of primitive types, say `String`, and association *ac* which is of the power type $\mathbb{P}Account$ of class type `Account`. A specification of class declaration for *Bank* is given below.

```
class Bank {
private: String name, address;
private: PAccount ac = ∅;
method: withDraw(Int aID, Int amount){
        ∃a ∈ ac · a.aNo = aID ⊢
            ⋁        (a.balance' = a.balance − amount)
        a∈ac∧a.aNo=aId
        };
        getBalance(Int aID; Int res){
        ∃ac · a.aNo = aID ⊢
            ⋁        (res' = a.balance)
        a∈ac∧a.aNo=aId
        }
        openAcc(Int amount){
        var Account a = null;
                                   ⎛ Account.new(a);    ⎞
        ∃n, ∀b ∈ ac · n ≠ b.aNo ∧ ⎜ a.aNo := n;         ⎟
                                   ⎝ a.balance := amount ⎠
        }
}
```

Note designs can appear in the body of a method. We need to make a few remarks about the above specification

1. At the level of specification of the methods, we assume the attributes of class *Account*

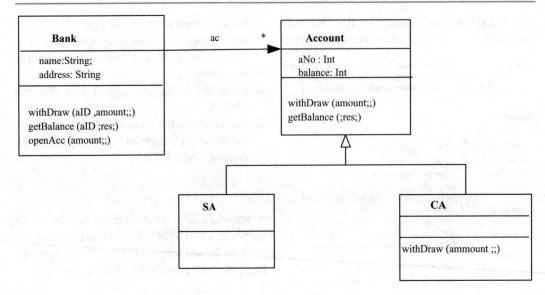

Fig. 14.1 A bank system

are all public and can be directly referred in the specification of the methods of call *Bank*.

2. In a later design stage, the specification of the these methods are refined into statement in which invocation of methods of *Account* are allowed, and after such refinements, the attributes of *Account* can be encapsulated and become protected.

3. To refine the specification of method *openAcc*, we need to add a method, say named by *openAc*, that implements the code in the big brackets.

The declaration of class *Account*, denoted by *declAccount*, is written as follows.

```
private class Account {
protected : Int aNo = 0, Int balance = 0;
method : getBalance(∅; Int b; ∅){b := balance};
         withDraw(Int x; ∅; ∅){balance ≥ x ⊢
balance′ = balance − x}
}
```

The declaration *declCA* of *CA* is given as

```
private class CA extends Account {
method : withDraw(Int x; ∅; ∅){balance := balance − x}
}
```

We can write the declarations of *SA* (in which method *withDraw* is inherited from *Account*) and *Bank* (which has a set of accounts associated with it) in a similar way.

It is easy to see that both *declAccount* and *declCA* are well-formed. The semantics of *declAccount* is defined by the following design, where unchanged variables are omitted.

$$
[\![declAccount]\!] = true \vdash
\left(
\begin{array}{l}
pricname' = \{Account\} \cup pricname \\
\wedge\ prof' = prot \oplus \{Account \mapsto \{\langle aNo : \text{Int}, 0\rangle, \langle balance : \text{Int}, 0\rangle\}\} \\
\wedge\ op' = op \oplus \{Account \mapsto \{getBalance \mapsto (\langle\emptyset; b : \text{Int}; \emptyset\rangle, b := balance), \\
\qquad\qquad withDraw \mapsto (\langle x : \text{Int}; \emptyset; \emptyset\rangle, \\
\qquad\qquad\qquad balance \geq x \vdash balance' = balance - x)\}\}
\end{array}
\right)
$$

The semantics of *declCA* is the following.

$$
[\![declCA]\!] = true \vdash
\left(
\begin{array}{l}
pricname' = \{CA\} \cup pricname \\
\wedge\ op' = op \oplus \{CA \mapsto \{withDraw \mapsto \\
\quad (\langle x : \text{Int}; \emptyset; \emptyset\rangle, balance := balance - x)\}\}
\end{array}
\right)
$$

The semantics of *declSA* and *declBank* for classes *SA* and *Bank* can be defined in the same way, but with *Bank* declared as public class. Their composition

$$[\![declAccount; declCA; declSA; declBank]\!]$$

combines the class names, attributes and methods together. The composition is well-defined.

♣

14.4.3 Dynamic Variables

Now consider the variables that can be changed during program execution.

14.4.3.1 System Configuration

First, we introduce a variable Π whose value is the set of objects created so far. We call Π the *current configuration* [30]. During the execution of the program, Π takes a value in the powerset 2^Σ that satisfies the following conditions:

1. *objects in Π are complete*: if $o \in \Pi$ and $a \in Attr(type(o))$ with a class type, then $o.a$ is either *null* or there is an object $o_1 \in \Pi$ and $ref(o.a) = ref(o_1)$, and
2. *objects are uniquely identified by their references:* for any objects o_1 and o_2 in Π if $ref(o_1) = ref(o_2)$ then

   a. $type(o_1) = type(o_2)$, and
   b. $ref(state(o_1)) = ref(state(o_2))$, where for each $a : T \in Attr(type(o))$

$$ref(state(o))(a) \overset{def}{=} \begin{cases} ref(o.a) & \text{if } T \in cname \\ o.a & \text{if } T \in \mathscr{T} \end{cases}$$

When a new object is created or the value of an attribute of an existing object is modified, the system configuration Π will be changed. For each class C, we use variable $\Pi(C)$ to denote the set of existing objects of class C.

14.4.3.2 External Variables

A set $extvar = \{x_1 : T_1, \ldots, x_k : T_k\}$ of variables with their types are declared in the main method of the program, where each type T_i is called the *declared type* of x_i, denoted as $dtype(x_i)$. A declared type is either a built-in primitive type or a public class in *pubcname*. Their values can be modified by methods and commands of the the main method containing them.

14.4.3.3 Local Variables

A set *localvar* identifies the local variables which are declared by local variable declaration commands. This set includes *self* (whose value

represents the current active object), and parameters of methods. The sets *localvar* and *extvar* are disjoint.

Method calls may be nested. Thus, *self* and a parameter of a method may be declared a number of times with possible different types before it is undeclared. A local variable x has a sequence of declared types represented as $(x : \langle T_1, \ldots, T_n \rangle)$. We use *TypeSeq* to denote the sequence of types of x, with T_1 being the most recently declared type $dtype(x_i)$.

We use $\bar{x}$ to denote the value of a local variable x. This value comprises a finite sequence of values, whose first (head) element, which is simply denoted by x itself, represents the current value of the variable. We use the conventions that $x : \langle T \rangle$ and $\bar{x}$ for x for an external variable $x : T \in extvar$.

14.4.3.4 Visibility

We introduce a variable *visibleattr* to hold the set of attributes which are visible to the command under execution. The value of *visibleattr* defines the current execution environment. A method of an object o sets *visibleattr* to $Attr(o)$ (the attributes of the current type of o) which including all the declared attributes of the class, the protected and public attributes of its superclasses and all public attributes of public classes; and the method resets *visibleattr* to the global environment (consisting of all the public attributes of the public classes) when exit its execution. Notice that the value space of *visibleattr* is the powerset of $\{C.a \mid C \in CNAME, a \in ANAME\}$.

We use

- *var* to denote the union of *extvar* and *localvar*,
- *VAR* is the set of *dynamic variables* consisting of the variables in *var* plus Π and *visibleattr*,
- *internalvar* is the set of elements of *VAR* excluding those of *extvar*.

14.4.4 Dynamic States

Definition 14.7 For a program $S = Cdecls \bullet Main$, a *(dynamic) state* of S is a mapping Γ from the variables *VAR* to their value spaces that satisfies the following conditions:

1. If $x \in VAR$ and $dtype(x) \in \mathscr{T}$ then $\Gamma(x)$ is a value in $dtype(x)$,
2. If $x \in VAR$ and $dtype(x) \in cname$ then $\Gamma(x)$ is

   a. either *null*, or
   b. a value in $v \in REF \times CNAME$ such that there exists an object $o \in \Gamma(\Pi)$ for which $ref(o) = ref(v)$ and $type(o) \preceq type(v)$.

   This attachment of an object o to a variable x provides the information about type casting: $type(o)$ is the *current* (base) type of x, denoted as $atype(x)$, and $type(v)$ is the *cast type* of x.

Two states Γ_1 and Γ_2 *are equal*, denoted by $\Gamma_1 = \Gamma_2$, if

1. $\Gamma_1(x) = \Gamma_2(x)$ for any $x \in VAR$ such that $dtype(x) \in \mathscr{T}$,
2. for any $x \in VAR$ and $dtype(x) \in cname$

   a. $\Gamma_1(x) = null$ if and only if $\Gamma_2(x) = null$, and
   b. if $o_i \in \Gamma_i(\Pi)$ and $ref(\Gamma_i(x)) = ref(o_i)$, where $1 \leq i \leq 2$, then $o_1 = o_2$ and $type(\Gamma_1(x)) = type(\Gamma_2(x))$.

♣

For state Γ and a subset $V \subseteq VAR$, $\Gamma(\Pi \downarrow_V)$ projects Π onto V and it is defined as follows:

1. if $x : C \in V$, $C \in cname$, $o \in \Gamma(\Pi)$ and $ref(\Gamma(x)) = ref(o)$, $o \in \Gamma(\Pi \downarrow_V)$
2. if $o \in \Gamma(\Pi \downarrow_V)$ and a is an attribute of $type(o)$ with a class type, $o_1 \in \Gamma(\Pi)$ and $ref(o.a) = ref(o_1)$, then $o_1 \in \Gamma(\Pi \downarrow_V)$
3. $\Gamma(\Pi \downarrow_V)$ only contains objects constructed from $\Gamma(\Pi)$ and the values of the external variables following the above two rules.

In particular, when we restrict a state Γ to the external variables *extvar* and project Π onto these variables, we obtain an *external state* in which all objects in the system configuration are attached to variables.

For a given state, each expression e, $visible(e)$ is true if and only if one of the following conditions holds:

1. e is a declared simple variable, i.e. e is x, where $x \in var$, or
2. $e \equiv self.a$ and there is a class name $N \in cname$ such that $N \succeq atype(self)$ and $N.a \in visibleattr$, or
3. e is of the form $e_1.a$ and e_1 is not *self* such that $visible(e_1)$, there exists a $N \succeq type(e_1)$ and $N.a \in visibleattr$.

Condition (2) says that if $type(self)$ is C and $atype(self)$ is d, then the attributes of d can be accessed in the method bodies of the methods of d which are inherited or overwritten from the casted class C. Condition (3) ensures an attribute of an object other than *self* can be directly accessed if and only if it is an attribute in the cast type, i.e. the type of the expression itself.

14.4.5   Evaluation of Expressions

The evaluation of an expression e under a given state determines its type $type(e)$ and its value that is a member of $type(e)$ if this type is a built-in primitive type, otherwise a value in $REF \times CNAME$. The evaluation makes use of the system configuration. Only well-defined expressions are evaluated. Well-definedness conditions can be static and dynamic dynamic. The evaluation results of expressions are given in Table 14.2.

14.4.6   Semantics of Commands

An important aspect of an execution of an object-oriented program is the attachment of objects to to program variables (or entities [31]). An attachment is made by an assignment, the creation of an object or passing a parameter in a method invocation. With the approach of UTP, these different cases are unified as an assignment of a value to a program variable. All other programming constructs are defined in exactly the same way as their counter-parts in a procedural language. We only define the object-oriented commands. The definition of other commands remains the same as in an imperative language. The semantics $[\![c]\!]$ of each command c has its well-defined condition

Table 14.2 Evaluation of expressions

Expression	Evaluation
null	$\mathscr{D}(null) \overset{def}{=} true, \quad type(null) \overset{def}{=} NULL, \quad ref(null) \overset{def}{=} null$
x	$\mathscr{D}(x) \overset{def}{=} visible(x) \wedge (dtype(x) \in \mathscr{T} \vee dtype(x) \in cname)$ $\wedge \quad dtype(x) \in \mathscr{T} \Rightarrow head(\overline{x}) \in dtype(x)$ $\wedge \quad dtype(x) \in cname \Rightarrow$ $ref(head(\overline{x})) \in ref(\Pi(dtype(x)))$ $type(x) \overset{def}{=} \begin{cases} dtype(x) & dtype(x) \in \mathscr{T} \\ type(head(\overline{x})) & \text{otherwise} \end{cases}$
self	$\mathscr{D}(self) \overset{def}{=} self \in locvar \wedge dtype(self) \in cname$ $\wedge \quad ref(head(\overline{self})) \in ref(\Pi(dtype(self)))$ $type(self) \overset{def}{=} type(head(\overline{self}))$
le.a	$\mathscr{D}(le.a) \overset{def}{=} \mathscr{D}(le) \wedge le \neq null$ $\wedge \quad dtype(le) \in cname \wedge visible(le.a)$ $type(le.a) \overset{def}{=} type(state(le)(a))$ $ref(le.a) \overset{def}{=} ref(state(le)(a))$
(C)e	$\mathscr{D}((C)e) \overset{def}{=} \mathscr{D}(e) \wedge type(e) \notin \mathscr{T} \wedge atype(e) \preceq C$ $type((C)e) \overset{def}{=} C$ $ref((C)e) \overset{def}{=} ref(e)$

$\mathscr{D}(c)$ as part of its precondition and thus has the form of $\mathscr{D}(c) \Rightarrow (p \vdash R)$.

14.4.6.1 Assignments

An assignment $le := e$ is well-defined if both le and e are well-defined and the current type of e matches the declared type of le

$$\mathscr{D}(le := e) \overset{def}{=} \mathscr{D}(le) \wedge \mathscr{D}(e) \wedge type(e) \in cname \Rightarrow$$
$$type(e) \preceq dtype(le))$$

Notice that this definition requires *dynamic type matching*. In fact the semantics ensures that if $dtype(e) \preceq dtype(le)$ then $type(e) \preceq dtype(le)$. When the value of e is an object $\mathscr{D}(le := e)$ ensures that $atype(e) \preceq dtype(le)$.

There are two cases of assignment. The first is to (re-)attach a value to a variable (i.e. change the current value of the variable). This can be done when the type of the object is consistent with the declared type of the variable. The attachment of values to other variables are not changed.

$$[\![x := e]\!] \overset{def}{=} \{x\} : \mathscr{D}(x := e) \vdash (\overline{x}' = \langle value(e) \rangle \cdot tail(\overline{x}))$$

As we do not allow attribute hiding or redefinition in subclasses, an assignment to a simple variable does not have side-effect. Thus the Hoare triple

$$\{o_2.a = 3\} \; o_1 := o_2 \; \{o_1.a = 3\}$$

is valid in our model, where $o_1 : C_1$ and $o_2 : C_2$ are variables, $C_2 \preceq C_1$ and $a :$ Int is protected attribute of C_1. These assumptions make the theory simpler than alternative Hoare-logic based semantics, e.g. [30].

The second case is the modification of the value of an attribute of an object attached to an expression. This is done by finding the attached object in the system configuration Π and modifying its state accordingly. All variables attached to the reference of this object are updated:

$$[\![le.a := e]\!] \overset{def}{=} \{\Pi(dtype(le))\} : \mathscr{D}(le.a := e) \vdash$$
$$\begin{pmatrix} \Pi(dtype(le))' = \Pi(dtype(le)) \uplus \\ \{o \oplus \{a \mapsto value(e)\} \mid o \in \Pi \wedge ref(o) = ref(le)\} \end{pmatrix}$$

For example, let x be a variable of type C such that C has an attribute d of d and d has an attribute a of integer type. $x.d.a := 4$ changes the state of $x = \langle r_1, C, \{d \mapsto r_2\}\rangle$, where reference r_2 is the identity of $\langle r_2, d, \{a \mapsto 3\}\rangle$ to the state $x = \langle r_1, C, \{d \mapsto r_2\}\rangle$, ehere x is as before but the underlying reference r_2 is modified and it is now the identity of the object $\langle r_2, d, \{a \mapsto 4\}\rangle$. This semantic definition also shows that an assignment can have side effects.

Law 1 $(le_1 := e_1; le_2 := e_2) = (le_2 := e_2; le_1 := e_1)$, *provided le_1 and le_2 are distinct simple names which do not occur in e_1 or e_2.*

Note that the law might not be valid if either le_1 le_2 is composite expressions. For instance, the following equation is not valid when x and y have the same reference:

$$(x.a := 1;\ y.a := 2) = (y.a = 2;\ x.a = 1)$$

14.4.6.2   Object Creation

The $C.new(le)$ is well-defined if

$$\mathscr{D}(C.new(le)) \overset{def}{=} C \in cname \wedge \mathscr{D}(le) \wedge dtype(le) \succeq C$$

The command creates a new object, attaches the object to le and sets the initial values of the attributes of class C to those of object le.

$$[\![C.new(le)]\!] \overset{def}{=} \{le, \Pi(C)\}{:}\mathrm{d}(C.new(le)) \vdash \exists r$$
$$\notin ref(\Pi) \cdot (AddNew(C, r) \wedge Modify(le))$$

where

$$AddNew(C, r) \overset{def}{=} \begin{array}{l} \Pi(C)' = \Pi(C) \\ \cup \{\langle r, C, \{a_i \mapsto init(C.a_i)\}\rangle \mid a_i \in Attr(C)\} \end{array}$$

$$Modify(le) \overset{def}{=} \left(\begin{array}{l} \overrightarrow{le}' = \langle r, C\rangle \cdot tail(\overrightarrow{le}) \wedge \\ TypeSeq'(le) = \langle C\rangle \cdot tail(TypeSeq(le)) \end{array} \right)$$

Here assume if $dtype(C.a_i) = M$, the assignment $a_i \mapsto init(C.a_i)$ is $a_i \mapsto M.new(C.a_i)$.

For creation of objects, we have the following laws

Law 2 $C_1.new(x); C_2.new(y) = C_2.new(y); C_1.new(x)$, *provided x and y are distinct.*

Law 3 *If x is not free in the Boolean expression b, then*

$C.new(x); (P \lhd b \rhd Q) = (C.new(x); P) \lhd b \rhd (C.new(x); Q)$

Local variable declaration and undeclaration
Command var $T\, x = e$ declares a variable and initialises it:

$$[\![\mathrm{var}\, T\, x = e]\!] \overset{def}{=} \{x\} : \mathscr{D}(\mathrm{var}\, T\, x = e) \vdash$$
$$(\overline{x}' = \langle value(e)\rangle \cdot \overline{x}) \wedge TypeSeq'(x)$$
$$= \langle T\rangle \cdot TypeSeq(x)$$

where

$$\mathscr{D}(\mathrm{var}\, T\, x = e) \overset{def}{=} (x \in localvar) \wedge \mathscr{D}(e)$$
$$\wedge type(e) \notin \mathscr{T} \Rightarrow type(e) \preceq T$$

We define $[\![\mathrm{var}\, T\, x]\!] \overset{def}{=} \sqcap_{d \in T}[\![\mathrm{var}\, T\, x = d]\!]$.

Command end x terminates the block (i.e. the current scope) of variable x:

$$[\![\mathrm{end}\, x]\!] \overset{def}{=} \{x\} : \mathscr{D}(\mathrm{end}\, x) \vdash \overline{x}'$$
$$= tail(\overline{x}) \wedge TypeSeq'(x) = tail(Tseq(x))$$

where $\mathscr{D}(\mathrm{end}\, x) \overset{def}{=} x \in localvar$. Please refer to [14] for the algebraic laws of declaration and undeclarartion.

14.4.6.3   Method Call

For a method signature $m(T_1\, x; T_2\, y; T_3\, z)$, let ve, re and vre be lists of expressions. Command $le.m(ve; re; vre)$ is well-defined if le is well-defined and it is a non-null object such that a method $m \mapsto (T_1\, x; T_2\, y; T_3\, z, c)$ is in the casted type $type(le)$ of le:

$$\mathscr{D}(le.m(ve; re; vre))$$
$$\overset{def}{=} \mathscr{D}(le) \wedge type(le) \in cname \wedge (le \neq null)$$
$$\wedge N \in cname \cdot N \succeq type(le)$$
$$\wedge \exists (m \mapsto (T_1\, x; T_2\, y; T_3\, z, c_1)) \in op(N)$$

The execution of this method invocation assigns the values of the actual parameters v and vr to the formal value and value-result parameters of the method m of the object o that le refers to, and then executes the body of m under the environment of the class owning method $m()$. Before termination, the value of the result and value-result parameters of m are passed back to the actual parameters r and vr.

$$\llbracket le.m(ve; re; vre)\rrbracket \overset{def}{=} \begin{array}{l}(\mathscr{D}(le.m(ve; re; vre)) \Rightarrow \\ \exists C \in cname \cdot (atype(le) = C) \\ \wedge \begin{pmatrix} \llbracket \text{var } T_1\ x = ve, T_2\ y, T_3\ z = vre\rrbracket; \\ \llbracket \text{var } C\ self = le\rrbracket; \\ \llbracket Execute(C.m)\rrbracket;\ \llbracket re, vre := y, z\rrbracket; \\ \llbracket \text{end } self, x, y, z\rrbracket \end{pmatrix}\end{array}$$

where $Execute(M.m)$ sets the execution environment, then executes the body and finally resets the environment. This is formalised by consider the following cases:

Case 1: If $m(T_1\ x; T_2\ y; T_3\ z)$ is not declared in C but in a superclass of C, i.e. there exists a command c such that $(m \mapsto (T_1\ x; T_2\ y; T_3\ z, c_1)) \in op(N)$ for some $N \succeq C$, then

$$Execute(C.m) \overset{def}{=} Execute(M.m)$$

where $M = superclass(C)$ is the direct superclass of C.

Case 2: If $m(T_1\ x; T_2\ y; T_3\ z)$ is declared in class C itself, i.e. there is a command c such that $(m \mapsto (T_1\ x; T_2\ y; T_3\ z, c_1)) \in op(C)$, then

$$Execute(C.m)$$
$$\overset{def}{=} Set(C); SELF_C(body(C.m)); Reset$$

where

- $body(C.m)$ is the body c of the method being called.
- The design $Set(C)$ determines those attributes visible to class M. $Reset$ resets the environment to the set of variables that are accessible by the main program:

$$Set(C) \overset{def}{=} \{\text{visibleattr}\} : true \vdash$$
$$\text{visibleattr}'$$
$$= \begin{pmatrix} \{C.a \mid a \in pri(C)\} \cup \\ \bigcup_{C \preceq N}\{N.a \mid a \in prot(N) \cup pub(N)\} \cup \\ \bigcup_{N \in pubcname}\{N.a \mid a \in pub(N)\} \end{pmatrix}$$

$$Reset \overset{def}{=} \{\text{visibleattr}\} : true \vdash$$
$$\text{visibleattr}' = \bigcup_{N \in pubcname}$$
$$\{N.a \mid a \in pub(N)\}$$

Set and $Reset$ are used to ensure data encapsulation is controlled by $visibleattr$ and the well-definedness condition of an expression.

- The transformation $SELF_C$ on a command is defined in Table 14.3, which adds a prefix $self$ to each attribute and each method in the

Fig. 14.2 Example 14.4

$Cdecls_1$	$Cdecls_2$

class C {
private $C_2\ o$;
method $get_a(\emptyset; \text{Int } x; \emptyset)\{o.get_a(\emptyset; x; \emptyset)\}$;
  $update_a(\text{Int } x; \emptyset; \emptyset)\{$
  $o.update_a(x; \emptyset; \emptyset)\}$
};
private class C_2 {
private $C_3\ o_3, C_4\ o_4, C_5\ o_5$;
method $get_a(\emptyset; \text{Int } x; \emptyset)\{$
  var Int $y; o_3.get(\emptyset; y; \emptyset)$;
  $o_4.get(\emptyset; x; \emptyset); x := x + y; \text{end } y\}$;
  $update_a(\text{Int } x; \emptyset; \emptyset)\{$
$o_3.update(x; \emptyset; \emptyset) \sqcap o_4.update(x; \emptyset; \emptyset)\}$
};
private class C_i {$/**i = 3, 4, 5$
private Int $a_i = 0$;
method $get(\emptyset; \text{Int } x; \emptyset)\{x := a_i\}$;
  $update(\text{Int } x; \emptyset; \emptyset)\{a_i := a_i + x\}$
}
	class C {
	private $C_1\ o$;
	method $get_a(\emptyset; \text{Int } x; \emptyset)\{$
	  $o.get_a(\emptyset; x; \emptyset)\}$;
	  $update_a(\text{Int } x; \emptyset; \emptyset)\{$
	  $o.update_a(x; \emptyset; \emptyset)\}$
	};
	private class C_1 {
	private Int $a = 0$, Int $b = 0$;
	method $get_a(\emptyset; \text{Int } x; \emptyset)\{$
	  $x := a\}$;
	  $update_a(\text{Int } x; \emptyset; \emptyset)\{$
	  $a := a + x\}$
	}

Table 14.3 The definition of *SELF*

c or e	$SELF_C(c)$ or $SELF_C(e)$
skip	*skip*
chaos	*chaos*
$c_1 \triangleleft b \triangleright c_2$	$SELF_C(c_1) \triangleleft SELF_M(b) \triangleright SELF_M(c_2)$
$c_1 \sqcap c_2$	$SELF_M(c_1) \sqcap SELF_M(c_2)$
var $T x = e$	T var $x = SELF_C(e)$
end x	end x
$C.new(x)$	$C.new(SELF_C(x))$
$le := e$	$SELF_C(le) := SELF_C(e)$
$le.m(ve; re; vre)$	$SELF_C(le).m(SELF_C(vr); SELF_C(re); SELF_C(vre))$
$m(ve; re; vre)$	$self.m(SELF_C(ve); SELF_C(re); SELF_C(vre))$
$c_1; c_2$	$SELF_C(c_1); Set(C); SELF_M(c_2)$
$b * c$	$SELF_C(b) * (SELF_M(c); Set(C))$
$le.a$	$SELF_C(le).a$
$f(e)$	$f(SELF_C(e))$
null	*null*
self	*self*
x	$\begin{cases} self.x, & x \in \bigcup_{C \le N} Attr(N) \\ x, & otherwise \end{cases}$

command. Notice that as a method call may occur in a command that will change the execution environment, therefore after the execution of the nested call is completed the environment needs to be set back to that of C.

Notice that semantics of a method call defines a method binding mechanism to ensure that

- only a method with a signature declared in the cast type or above the cast type in the inheritance hierarchy can be accessed, and
- the method executed is the lowest one in the inheritance hierarchy of the current type of the active object.

Example 14.2 We illustrate the semantics of method invocation. Consider the bank system in **Example** 14.1 again. We define $Execute(C.m)$ for the method $withDraw()$ in the classes CA and SA.

Assume all classes, except for *Bank*, are private classes. For class CA,

$Execute(CA.withDraw)$
$= Set(CA); SELF_{CA}(balance := balance - x); Reset$
$= visibleattr := \left\{ \begin{array}{l} CA.balance, CA.aNo, \\ Account.balance, Account.aNo \end{array} \right\};$
$self.balance := self.balance - x;$
$visibleattr := \emptyset$

Let o be an object of CA. The semantics of the method call $o.withDraw(e)$ attaches o to *self* and then performs $Execute(CA.withDraw)$ as defined above.

For the case of a saving account

$Execute(SA.withDraw)$
$= Set(SA); SELF_{SA}(Account.withDraw); Reset$
$= visibleattr := \left\{ \begin{array}{l} SA.balance, SA.aNo, \\ Account.balance, Account.aNo \end{array} \right\};$
$self.balance > x \vdash self.balance' = self.balance - x;$
$visibleattr := \emptyset$

Thus, the invocation to a *withDraw* method of a saving account is executed according to the definition of the method in the superclass *Account*.

♣

14.4.7 Semantics of a Program

Having defined the semantics of a class declaration section and a command, we combine them to define the semantics of an object program (*Cdecls • Main*).

Recall that *Main* consists of a set of external variables and a command c. For simplicity, we assume that any primitive command in c is in one of the following forms:

1. an assignment $x := e$ such that $x \in extvar$ and e does not contain sub-expressions of the form *le.a*. That is, we do not allow direct access to object attributes in the main method.
2. a creation of a new object *C.New(x)* for a variable $x \in extvar$,
3. a method call *x.m(ve; re; vre)*, where x is a variable in *extvar*.

Main is well-defined if the types of all variables in *extvar* are either built-in primitive types or public classes declared in *pubcname*:

$$\mathscr{D}(Main) \stackrel{def}{=} \bigwedge_{x \in extvar} (dtype(x)$$

$$\in pubcname \vee dtype(x) \in \mathscr{T})$$

The semantics of *Main* is then defined to be

$$[\![Main]\!] \stackrel{def}{=} \mathscr{D}(Main) \Rightarrow [\![c]\!]$$

Before *Main* is executed, the local variables have to be initialised to empty sequences:

$$Init \stackrel{def}{=} \mathscr{D}(Cdecls) \vdash visibleattr' = \emptyset \wedge (\Pi' = \emptyset)$$
$$\wedge \bigwedge_{x \in var} (\overline{x}' = <> \wedge TypeSeq'(x) = <>)$$

Definition 14.8 The *semantics of an object program Cdecls • Main* is defined as:

$$[\![Cdecls \bullet Main]\!] \stackrel{def}{=} \exists \, \Omega, \, \Omega', internalvar,$$
$$internalvar' \cdot ([\![Cdecls]\!]; Init; [\![Main]\!])$$

♣

This *black box* semantics hides the internal information, including the objects states of the external variables in the execution of a program, only observing the relation between the pre-state and post-state of the external variables. We cannot observe information about states of objects attached to these variables.

We define the *white box semantics* $[\![Cdecls \bullet Main]\!]_o$ as

$$\exists \{\Pi\} > internalvar, \{\Pi'\} > internalvar', \Omega, \Omega' \cdot$$
$$([\![Cdecls]\!]; Init; [\![Main]\!]; [\![\Pi' := \Pi \downarrow_{extvar}]\!])$$

The white box semantics allows us to observe all information about the external variables including the states of the objects that are attached to them. We can insert the command $\Pi' := \Pi \downarrow_{extvar}$ at any point of the main method without changing the white box and close box semantics of a program.

Lemma 14.1 *The white box semantics has the following properties. For any object program $S = Cdecls \bullet Main$ with main command c, we have*

1. $[\![Cdecls \bullet c]\!] = \exists \Pi, \Pi' \cdot [\![Cdecls \bullet c]\!]_o.$
2. $[\![Cdecls \bullet c_1; c_2]\!]_o = [\![Cdecls \bullet c_1; \Pi' := \Pi \downarrow_{extvar}; c_2]\!]_o$
3. $[\![Cdecls \bullet (c_1; b * (c_2; c_3); c_4)]\!]_o = [\![Cdecls \bullet c_1; b * (c_2; \Pi' := \Pi \downarrow_{extvar}; c_3); c_4]\!]_o$
4. $[\![Cdecls \bullet (c_1; (c_2; c_3) \lhd b \rhd c_4; c_5)]\!]_o = [\![Cdecls \bullet c_1; (c_2; \Pi':=\Pi \downarrow_{extvar}; c_3) \lhd b \rhd c_4); c_5]\!]_o$
5. $[\![Cdecls \bullet c_1; (c_2; c_3) \sqcap c_4]\!]_o = [\![Cdecls \bullet c_1; (c_2; \Pi' := \Pi \downarrow_{extvar}; c_3) \sqcap c_4]\!]_o$

14.5 Object-Oriented Refinement

We would like the refinement calculus to cover all stages of requirements analysis and specification. This section presents the results of our exploration on two kinds of refinement:

1. Refinement relation between object systems.
2. Refinement relation between declaration sections (*structural refinement*).

14.5.1   Object System Refinement

We define what we mean by a refinement between two object programs.

Definition 14.9 Let $S_i = Cdecls_i \bullet Main_i$, $i = 1, 2$, be object programs which have the same set of external variables *extvar*. S_1 is a *refinement* of S_2, denoted by $S_1 \sqsupseteq_{sys} S_2$, if the following implication holds:

$$\forall extvar, extvar', ok, ok' \cdot (\llbracket S_1 \rrbracket \Rightarrow \llbracket S_2 \rrbracket)$$

♣

Example 14.3 For any class declaration *Cdecls*, we have the following:

1. $S_1 = Cdecls \bullet (\{x : C\}, C.new(x))$ and
   $S_2 = Cdecls \bullet (\{x : C\}, C.new(x); C.new(x))$
   are equivalent.
2. Assume class $C \in pubcname$, $\langle a{:}\texttt{Int}, d\rangle \in attr(C)$, $get(\emptyset; \texttt{Int } z; \emptyset)\{z := a\}$ and $update()\{a := a + c\}$ in $op(C)$, then

   $Cdecls \bullet (\{x : C, y : \texttt{Int}\}, C.new(x); x.update(); x.get(y))$

   and

   $Cdecls \bullet (\{x : C, y : \texttt{Int}\}, C.new(x);$
   $x.update(); x.get(y); C.new(x))$

   are equivalent.

Proof We give a proof for item (2) of this example. We denote the first program by S_1 and the second by S_2. Assume the declaration section is well-defined. It is easy to check the main methods are both well-defined. The structural variables Ω are calculated according to the definition. Let d be

the initial value of attribute a of C and σ_0 denote the initial state of an object of C when it is created. We calculate the semantics of S_1:

$$\llbracket C.new(x); x.update(), x.get(y) \rrbracket$$
$$= \left(\begin{array}{l} true \vdash \exists r \in REF \cdot (\Pi' = \{\langle r, C, \sigma_0\rangle\} \wedge x' = \langle r, C\rangle); \\ \llbracket x.update(); x.get(y) \rrbracket \end{array} \right)$$
$$= \left(\begin{array}{l} true \vdash \exists r \in REF \cdot (\Pi' = \{\langle r, C, \sigma_0\rangle\} \wedge x' = \langle r, C\rangle) \wedge \\ self = <> \wedge \Pi' = \{\langle r, C, \sigma_0 \oplus \{a \mapsto d + c\}\rangle \mid r = ref(x)\}); \\ \llbracket x.get(y) \rrbracket \end{array} \right)$$
$$= \left(\begin{array}{l} true \vdash \exists r \in REF \cdot (\Pi' = \{\langle r, C, \sigma_0 \oplus \{a \mapsto d + c\}\rangle\} \wedge \\ x' = \langle r, C\rangle) \wedge self = <>); \\ \llbracket x.get(y) \rrbracket \end{array} \right)$$
$$= \left(\begin{array}{l} true \vdash \exists r \in REF \cdot (\Pi' = \{\langle r, C, \sigma_0 \oplus \{a \mapsto d + c\}\rangle\} \wedge \\ x' = \langle r, C\rangle) \wedge self = <>); \\ true \vdash self = <> \wedge z' = <> \wedge y' = d + c \wedge \\ visibleattr' = \{M.a \mid M \in pubname \wedge a \in pub(M)\} \end{array} \right)$$
$$= \left(\begin{array}{l} true \vdash \exists r \in REF \cdot (\Pi' = \{\langle r, C, \sigma_0 \oplus \{a \mapsto d + c\}\rangle\} \wedge \\ x' = \langle r, C\rangle) \wedge self = <> \wedge z' = <> \wedge y' = c + d \wedge \\ visibleattr' = \{M.a \mid M \in pubname \wedge a \in pub(M)\} \end{array} \right)$$

The semantics $\llbracket S_1 \rrbracket$ hides Ω, Π, *self* and z by existential quantification. Let $\llbracket Cdecls \rrbracket$ be $true \vdash \Omega = \emptyset \wedge \Omega' = \Omega_0$, we have $\llbracket S_1 \rrbracket$ equals to

$$\exists \left\{ \begin{array}{l} \Omega, \Omega', self, self', z, z', \\ visibleattr, visibleattr' \end{array} \right\}$$
$$\cdot (\llbracket Cdecls \rrbracket; Init; \llbracket C.new(x); x.update(), x.get(y)) \rrbracket \rrbracket)$$
$$= true \vdash \exists r \in REF \cdot x' = \langle r, C\rangle \wedge y' = c + d$$

The main method of S_2 is the main method of S_1 followed by command $C.new(x)$ and thus its semantics equals

$$\llbracket C.new(x); x.update(), x.get(y) \rrbracket; \llbracket C.new(x) \rrbracket$$
$$= \left(\begin{array}{l} true \vdash \exists r \in REF \cdot (\Pi' = \{\langle r, C, \sigma_0 \oplus \{a \mapsto d + c\}\rangle \wedge \\ x' = \langle r, C\rangle) \wedge self = <> \wedge z' = <> \wedge y' = c + d \wedge \\ visibleattr' = \{M.a \mid M \in pubname \wedge a \in pub(M)\}; \\ true \vdash \exists p \notin ref(\Pi) \cdot \Pi' = \Pi \cup \{\langle p, C, \sigma_0\rangle\} \wedge (x' = \langle p, C\rangle) \end{array} \right)$$
$$= \left(\begin{array}{l} true \vdash \exists r, p \in REF \cdot ((p \neq r) \wedge \\ \Pi' = \{\langle p, C, \sigma_0\rangle, \langle r, C, \sigma_0 \oplus \{a \mapsto d + c\}\rangle\} \wedge \\ x' = \langle p, C\rangle) \wedge self = <> \wedge z' = <> \wedge y' = c + d \wedge \\ visibleattr' = \{M.a \mid M \in pubname \wedge a \in pub(M)\} \end{array} \right)$$

After hiding the internal variables, $\llbracket S_2 \rrbracket$ is simplified to

$$true \vdash \exists p \in REF \cdot x' = \langle p, C\rangle \wedge y' = c + d$$

Thus, S_1 and S_2 refine each other. However, program $S_1; x.get(y)$ is not equivalent to $S_2; x.get(y)$. The final value of y for the first program remains will be still $d + c$. For the second program, the final value of y is d. On the other hand, if we take the white box semantics, S_1 and S_2 would not be equivalent in the first place.

♣

This example shows that program refinement is non-compositional. Given two main methods, $Main_i = (extvar, c_i)$, $i = 1, 2$,

$$Cdecls_1 \bullet Main_1 \sqsupseteq_{sys} Cdecls_2 \bullet Main_2$$

then it does not necessarily follow that

$$Cdecls \bullet (extvar, c_1; c) \sqsupseteq_{sys} Cdecls \bullet (extvar, c_2; c)$$

Non-compositionality is caused by the global internal variable Π being hidden in the semantics. However, if we define the refinement relation by the white box semantics, the above non-compositionality would hold disappear if s only refers to calls to methods of objects attached to the external variables. Therefore, refinement according to the white box is a sub-relation of the refinement according to the black box semantics and it is more compositional.

Theorem 14.2 *Let $Cdecls \bullet Main$, C be a public class declared in $Cdecls$ and $Cdecls_1$ be obtained from $Cdecls$ by changing C to a private class. Then if C is not referred in $Main$,*

$$Cdecls \bullet Main =_{sys} Cdecls_1 \bullet Main$$

where $=_{sys}$ is the equivalence relation $\sqsupseteq_{sys} \cap \sqsubseteq_{sys}$.

The relation $\sqsupseteq_{sys}$ is reflexive and transitive.

14.5.2   Structure Refinement

The proof in **Example** 14.3 shows that the local variables and *visibleattr* of a program are constants after each method invocation. When the main methods in the programs are syntactically identical, the relation between their system states is determined by the relation between the structure of these programs, i.e. their class names, attributes, sub-superclass relations, and methods in the classes.

An object-oriented program design is mainly about designing classes and their methods. A class declaration section can in fact support many different application main programs. The rest of this section focuses on *structural refinement*.

Definition 14.10 Let $Cdecls_1$ and $Cdecls_2$ be two declaration sections. $Cdecls_1$ is a *refinement* of $Cdecls_2$, denoted by $Cdecls_1 \sqsupseteq_{class} cdecls_2$, if the former can replace the later in any object system:

$$Cdecls_1 \sqsupseteq_{class} Cdecls_2 \overset{def}{=} \forall Main \cdot (Cdecls_1 \bullet Main \sqsupseteq_{sys} Cdecls_2 \bullet Main)$$

♣

Informally, $Cdecls_1$ supports at least as many services as $Cdecls_2$. It is obvious that $\sqsupseteq_{class}$ is reflexive and transitive. We use $=_{class}$ to denote the equivalence relation $\sqsupseteq_{class} \cap \sqsubseteq_{class}$. When there is no confusion, we omit the subscript.

A structural refinement does not change the main method. Every public class in $Cdecls_2$ has to be declared in the refined declaration section $Cdecls_1$, and every method signature in a public class of $Cdecls_2$ has to be declared in $Cdecls_1$. Recall that a main method only changes objects by method invocations to public classes.

When considering a refinement between $Cdecls_i$, $i = 1, 2$, we use Ω_i, Π_i, $cname_i$, etc. to denote the structural variables and configuration of $Cdecls_i$ and $[\![\mathscr{E}]\!]_i$ to denote the semantic definition of $\mathscr{E}$ under the declaration $Cdecls_i$. The notation of structural refinement is actually an extension to the notion of data refinement [14].

Definition 14.11 For $i = 1, 2$, let $Cdecls_i$ be two class declaration sections. A *structural transformation* from $Cdecls_1$ to $Cdecls_2$, is a relation between the object space Σ_1 of $Cdecls_1$ and the object space Σ_2 of $Cdecls_2$ that can be represented as a design $true \vdash \rho(\Omega_1, \Omega_2')$ such that the following conditions hold:

1. $Cdecls_1$ declares at least those public classes declared in $Cdecls_2$. That is ρ implies

$$true \vdash pubcname_2' \subseteq pubcname_1$$

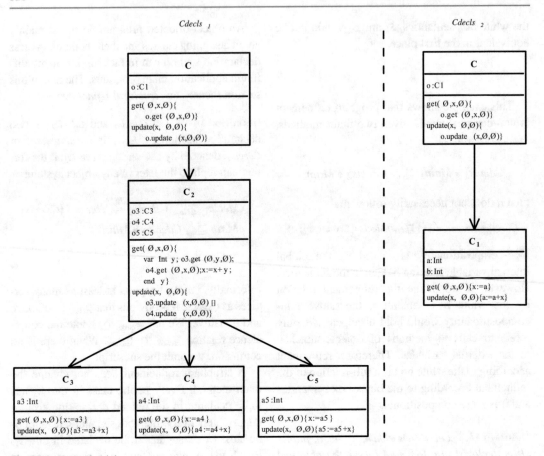

Fig. 14.3 Example 14.4

2. For each public class C declared in both $Cdecls_1$ and $Cdecls_2$, $Cdecls_1$ offers at least those methods offered by C than $Cdecls_2$. That is for every $C \in pubcname'$

$$Sig(op_2'(C)) \subseteq Sig(op_1(C))$$

where Sig returns the set of method signatures of a set of method declarations.

3. The restriction of ρ on the attributes $\rho(ATTR_1(C), ATTR_2'(C))$ for each public class C in both declaration sections can be described in terms of attribute expressions over $ATTR_1(C)$ in $Cdecls_1$ and $ATTR_2'(C)$ in $Cdecls_2$ that

a. the attributes' initial values $\rho(init(ATTR_1(C))$ $and init(ATTR_2(C)))$ are preserved

b. the operations on attribute expressions are preserved: if $\rho(\gamma_i, \beta_i)$ hold for all

$i = 1, \ldots, n$, then $\rho(\gamma_1 \cdot \gamma_2, \beta_1 \cdot \beta_2)$ and $\rho(f(\gamma_1, \ldots, \gamma_n), f(\beta_1, \ldots, \beta_n))$ hold.

♣

A structural transformation corresponds to a consistent transformation between the corresponding UML class diagrams [32].

Example 14.4 Figure 14.3 provides two class declaration sections, $Cdecls_1$ on the left and $Cdecls_2$ on the right. Figure 14.2 shows the class diagrams of the two declaration sections.

In the "abstract" version $Cdecls_2$ contains two classes, C and C_1. C_1 has two integer attributes a and b, and two methods: $get_a()$ which returns the value of attribute a and $update_a()$ which increments attributes a with the input value parameter.

Correspondingly, class C has an attribute o linked to C_1, and a method $get_a()$ which calls o's method $get_a()$ and a method $update_a()$ which simply calls the updating method of o.

Class declaration section $Cdecls_2$ implements C_1 using four classes in which

- C_2 acts as an interface to C as C_1 without storing or manipulating attributes. Each of C_3, C_4 and C_5 stores and manipulates an attribute.
- The attribute $C_1.a$ is implemented by the sum of $C_3.a_3$ and $C_4.a_4$
- The attribute $C_1.b$ is implemented by $C_5.a_5$
- The $get_a()$ method in in C_2 is implemented by getting each of the two attributes in C_3 and C_4 and then adding them together.
- The $update_a()$ in C_2 is implemented by nondeterministically updating and attribute of of C_3 and C_4.

We define a structural transformation ρ_1 from $Cdecls_1$ to $Cdecls_2$ as

$$true \vdash \left(\begin{array}{l} C.o' = C.o \\ \wedge\ C_1.a' = C_2.o_3.a_3 + C_2.o_4.a_4 \\ \wedge\ C_1.b' = C_2.o_5.a_5 \end{array} \right)$$

Note that the primed attributes of C and C_1 are about attributes in $Cdecls_2$.

♣

Consider a structural transformation ρ from $Cdecls_1$ to $Cdecls_2$. Let C be a public class in both declaration sections, $o_1 : C$ an object of $Cdecls_1$ and $o_2 : C$ an object of $Cdecls_2$. We say $\rho(o_1, o_2)$ holds if $\rho(ATTR_1(C)[o_1/C], ATTR'_2(C)[o_2/C])$ holds, where $ATTR_i(C)[o_i/C]$ is obtained from $ATTR_i(C)$ by replacing

1. $C.a$ with $o_i.a$ for each attribute a of C
2. $d.b$ with $o_i.a_1....a_k.b$ if there exists $a_1,...,a_k, b$ such that $C.a_1....a_k.b$ is an attribute expression over $ATTR_i(C)$ and D is the type of a_k.

We say that ρ is a *many-to-one* transformation if for each object $o_1 : C$ under $Cdecls_1$ there is only one $o_1 : C$ under $Cdecls_2$ such that $\rho(o_1, o_2)$.

Theorem 14.3 (*Upwards Simulation Implies Refinement*) $Cdecls_1$ *is a refinement of* $Cdecls_2$ *if there is a many-to-one structural transformation* $true \vdash \rho(\Omega_1, \Omega'_2)$ *such that for any public class name declared in both* $Cdecls_1$ *and* $Cdecls_2$, *any variable* $x : C$ *and any method* $m(\underline{x} : \underline{T}_1; \underline{y} : \underline{T}_2; \underline{z} : \underline{T}_3)\{c_1\}$ *in a public class* C *of* $Cdecls_1$ *and its corresponding method* $m(\underline{x} : \underline{T}_1; \underline{y} : \underline{T}_2; \underline{z} : \underline{T}_3)\{c_2\}$ *in* $Cdecls_2$,

$$([\![x.m(ve; re; vre)]\!]_1; [\![\Pi_1 := \Pi_1\downarrow_{\{x,re,rve\}}]\!];$$
$$\rho(\Pi_1, \Pi'_2)) \sqsupseteq (\rho(\Pi_1, \Pi'_2); [\![x.m(ve; re; vre)]\!]_2;$$
$$[\![\Pi_2 := \Pi_2\downarrow_{\{x,re,rve\}}]\!]) \qquad (14.1)$$

where $\rho(\Pi_1, \Pi'_2)$ *holds iff for each variable* y *and* $o_1 \in \Pi_1$ *such that* $ref(o_1) = ref(y)$ *there is exactly one* $o_2 \in \Pi'_2$ *and* $\rho(o_1, o_2)$.

Proof Let V be a set of variables and $Main = (V, c)$ be the main method for both $S_i = Cdecls_i \bullet Main$, $i = 1, 2$. From the general theory in UTP [14], we only need to prove there exists a many-to-one mapping $\hat{\rho}$ from the state space of $\{\Pi_1, visibleattr_1\}$ to that of $\{\Pi_2, visibleattr_2\}$ such that

$$[\![Init]\!]_1; [\![c]\!]_1; [\![\Pi_1 := \Pi_1\downarrow_V]\!]; \hat{\rho} \sqsupseteq \hat{\rho}; [\![Init]\!]_2; [\![c]\!]_2; [\![\Pi_2 := \Pi_2\downarrow_V]\!]$$
$$(14.2)$$

For this, we define

$$\hat{\rho}(\Pi_1, \Pi'_2) \overset{def}{=} \rho(\Pi_1, \Pi'_2)$$
$$\hat{\rho}(visibleattr_1, visibleattr'_2) \overset{def}{=} visibleattr'_2 = \{C.a \mid C \in pubcname_2 \wedge a \in pub(C)\}$$

Because of the syntactic definition of the main method of a program, if c is a well-defined primitive command, it can only be one of the following two cases:

1. It is a command that only involves variables of built-in primitive types. In this case, the theorem obviously holds.
2. It is an object creation $C.new(x)$ for some $x \in V$ and public class C.

In the case when c is an object creation, $C.new(x)$ does not change *visibleattr*. We also notice both $[\![Init]\!]_i$ set Π_i to be empty. So after the initialisation, $\rho(\Pi_1, \Pi_2)$ holds. We thus have for $i = 1, 2$

$$[\![C.new(x)]\!]_i ; [\![\Pi_i := \Pi_i \downarrow_V]\!]$$

$$= true \vdash \begin{pmatrix} \exists r \notin ref(\Pi_i) \cdot (\Pi_i' = \emptyset \cup \{\langle r, C, init_i(C)\rangle\} \wedge \\ (x' = \langle r, C\rangle)); [\![\Pi_i := \Pi_i \downarrow_V]\!] \end{pmatrix}$$

$$= true \vdash \exists r \notin ref(\Pi_i) \cdot (\Pi_i' = \Pi_i \downarrow_{\{x\} \gg V} \cup \{\langle r, C, init_i(C)\rangle\}) \wedge (x' = \langle r, C\rangle)$$

$$= true \vdash \exists r \in REF \cdot ((\Pi_i' = \{\langle r, C, init_i(C)\rangle\}) \wedge (x' = \langle r, C\rangle))$$

So we have

$$([\![C.new(x)]\!]_1 ; [\![\Pi_1 := \Pi_1 \downarrow_V]\!]; \rho(\Pi_1, \Pi_2')) \Rightarrow ([\![C.new(x)]\!]_2 ; [\![\Pi_2 := \Pi_2 \downarrow_V]\!])$$

Assume that Refinement (14.2) holds for command c, we need to prove it holds for command $c; c_1$. As the mapping on *visibleattr* is constant, we can ignore it in the proof. Furthermore, from Lemma 1, we can equivalently take c to be $c; \Pi' := \Pi \downarrow_V$. Let $[\![c]\!]_i = p_i \vdash R_i(V \cup \{\Pi_i\}, V' \cup \{\Pi_i'\})$ for $i = 1, 2$. The proof heavily use the definition of sequential composition of designs

$$(p_1(\alpha) \vdash R_1(\alpha, \alpha'); p_2(\alpha) \vdash R_2(\alpha, \alpha'))$$
$$\stackrel{def}{=} \exists s_m \cdot (p_1(\alpha) \vdash R_1(\alpha, s_m) \wedge p_2(s_m) \vdash R_2(s_m, \alpha'))$$

Case 1:   If c_1 only involves external variables of built-in primitive types, the refinement obviously holds as it does not change the system configuration.

Case 2:   Command c is an object creation $C.new(x)$. We have

$$[\![c; C.new(x)]\!]_i ; [\![\Pi_i := \Pi_i \downarrow_V]\!]$$

$$= [\![c]\!]_i ; true \vdash \begin{pmatrix} \exists r \notin ref(\Pi_i) \cdot ((\Pi_i' = \Pi_i \cup \{\langle r, C, init_i(C)\rangle\}) \wedge \\ (x' = \langle r, C\rangle)); [\![\Pi_i := \Pi_i \downarrow_V]\!] \end{pmatrix}$$

$$= \exists V_m, \Pi_i^{m_i} \cdot (p_i \vdash \begin{pmatrix} R_i(V \cup \{\Pi_i\}, V_m \cup \{\Pi_i^{m_i}\}) \wedge \\ \exists r \notin ref \Pi_i^{m_i} \cdot ((x' = \langle r, C\rangle) \wedge \\ (\Pi_i' = \Pi_i^{m_i} \downarrow_{\{x\} \gg V} \cup \{\langle r, C, init_i(C)\rangle\})) \end{pmatrix})$$

The induction assumption implies that for any $V, \Pi_1, \Pi_2, \Pi_1^{m_1}, \Pi_2^{m_2}$,

$$p_1 \vdash R_1(V \cup \{\Pi_1\}, V_m \cup \{\Pi_1^{m_1}\}) \wedge \rho(\Pi_1^{m_1}, \Pi_2^{m_2})$$
$$\Rightarrow p_2 \vdash R_2(V \cup \{\Pi_2\}, V_m \cup \{\Pi_2^{m_2}\})$$
$$(14.3)$$

Also the structural transformation ensures that $\rho(\Pi_1^{m_1}, \Pi_2^{m_2})$ implies

$$\rho(\Pi_1^{m_1} \downarrow_{\{x\} \gg V} \cup \{obj_1^0(C)\}, \Pi_2^{m_2} \downarrow_{\{x\} \gg V} \cup \{obj_2^0(C)\})$$

where $obj_i^0(C)$ is the object of C with its initials state defined in $Cdecls_i$ for $i = 1, 2$. This proves the refinement for this case.

Case 3: c_1 is $x.m(ve; re; vre)$. For $i = 1, 2$, let

$$[\![x.m(ve; re; vre)]\!]_i \stackrel{def}{=} p_1^i \vdash R_1^i(V \cup \{\Pi_i\}, V' \cup \{\Pi_i'\})$$

By   the   definition   of   composition, $[\![c; x.m(ve; re; vre)]\!]_i$ equals

$$\exists V_m, \Pi_i^{m_i} \cdot \begin{pmatrix} p_i \vdash R(V \cup \{\Pi_i\}, V_m \cup \{\Pi_i^{m_i}\}) \wedge \\ p_1^i(V_m \cup \Pi_i^{m_i}) \vdash R_1^i(V_m \cup \Pi_i^{m_i}, V' \cup \{\Pi_i'\}) \end{pmatrix}$$
$$(14.4)$$

Notice that the method class $x.m(ve; re; vre)$ only changes the object attached to x and those variables whose reference values are the same of x, and it may modify the objects attached to re and *vre* if they their types are classes.

The structural transformation ensures that if $\rho(\Pi_1^{m_1}, \Pi_2^{m_2})$ and $\rho(\Pi_1^{n_1} \downarrow_{V_1}, \Pi_2^{n_2} \downarrow_{V_1})$ for a subset V_1 of V, we then have

$$\rho(\Pi_1^{m_1} \oplus \Pi_1^{n_1} \downarrow_{V_1}, \Pi_2^{m_2} \oplus \Pi_2^{n_2} \downarrow_{V_1})$$
$$(14.5)$$

where $\oplus$ replace the objects in $\Pi_i^{m_i}$ that are attached to the variables in V_1 with those in $\Pi_i^{n_i}$.

From formula (14.4)

$$[\![c; x.m(ve; re; vre)]\!]; \Pi_i := \Pi_i \downarrow_V]\!]_1 ; \rho(\Pi_1, \Pi_2')$$
$$= \exists V_m, \Pi_i^{m_1}, \Pi_i^m \cdot \begin{pmatrix} p_i \vdash R(V \cup \{\Pi_1\}, V_m \cup \{\Pi_i^{m_1}\}) \wedge \\ p_1^i(V_m \cup \Pi_i^{m_1}) \vdash R_1^i(V_m \cup \Pi_i^{m_1}, V' \cup \{\Pi_i^m\}) \wedge \\ \rho(\Pi_1^m, \Pi_2') \end{pmatrix}$$

Notice that $\Pi_1^m = \Pi_1^{m_1} \oplus \Pi_1^m \downarrow_{\{x, re, vre\}}$. Property (14.5) of structural transformation together with Condition (14.1) and the induction assumption (14.3) proves the refinement for this case.

Case 4:   If c_1 is a command only involved in variables of built-in primitive types, the refinement obviously holds.

Case 5:   If c_1 is an assignment $x := y$ of one object variable to another, the execution of $\Pi_i := \Pi \downarrow_V$ after the execution of c_1 only removes from Π_i the object originally attached to y.

Case 6:   If c_1 is $x := (C)y$, it changes Π_i in the same way as in **Case 4**, but assign the value $\langle ref(y), C\rangle$ to x in both programs.

Case 7: Let c_1 be a conditional choice $c_{11} \triangleleft b \triangleright c_{12}$ and b an expression of variables of built-in primitive types (and constants). b is evaluated to *true* after the execution of c in S_1 if and only if it is evaluated to *true* after the execution of c in program S_2 because of the induction assumption. This case can then be proven for each c_{11} and c_{12} separately.

Case 8: If c_1 is a loop $b * c_{11}$, the refinement can then be proven by the induction and the properties of the weakest fixed point.

♣

Theorem 14.4 (*Downwards Simulation Implies Refinement*) $Cdecls_1$ is a refinement of $Cdecls_2$ if there is a one-to-many structural transformation $true \vdash \rho(\Omega_2, \Omega_1')$ such that for any public class name declared in both $Cdecls_1$ and $Cdecls_2$, any variable $x : C$ and any method $m(\underline{x} : \underline{T_1}; \underline{y} : \underline{T_2}; \underline{z} : \underline{T_3})\{c_1\}$ in a public class C of $Cdecls_1$ and its corresponding method $m(\underline{x} : \underline{T_1}; \underline{y} : \underline{T_2}; \underline{z} : \underline{T_3})\{c_2\}$ in $Cdecls_2$,

$$(\rho(\Pi_2, \Pi_1'); [\![x.m(ve; re; vre)]\!]_1; [\![\Pi_1 := \Pi_1 \downarrow_{\{x, re, rve\}}]\!])$$
$$\sqsupseteq ([\![x.m(ve; re; vre)]\!]_2; [\![\Pi_2 := \Pi_2 \downarrow_{\{x, re, rve\}}]\!]; \rho(\Pi_2, \Pi_1')) \tag{14.6}$$

Example 14.5 For the class declaration sections in **Example** 14.4, we can also define a structural transformation ρ_2 from $Cdecls_2$ to $Cdecls_1$:

$$true \vdash \left(\begin{array}{c} C.o = C.o' \wedge C_1.b = C_2.o_5.a_5' \\ \wedge\ C_1.a = C_2.o_3.a_3' + C_2.o_4.a_4' \end{array} \right)$$

It is a one-to-many transformation. With this transformation, we can check if $Cdecls_2$ is also a refinement of $Cdecls_1$.

♣

In the same way that we prove **Theorem** 14.3 we can prove the following theorem.

Theorem 14.5 *Let $Cdecls_1 \sqsupseteq Cdecls_2$ and $Cdecls$ be a class declaration such that if $a : C \in Attr(M)$ for some M in $Cdecls$ and C in $Cdecls_1$ then C is a public class. We have*

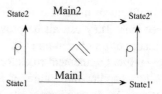

Fig. 14.4 Commuting diagram for class refinement

$$Cldecls_1; Cdecl \sqsubseteq Cdecls_2; Cdecls$$

The proof is similar to Theorem 14.3.
Remarks:

A structural refinement corresponds to a consistent transformation between the corresponding UML class diagrams, sequence diagrams and state diagrams [32]. A (upwards) structural refinement of a program under ρ is shown in Fig. 14.4.

Theorems 14.3 and 14.4 do not appear very helpful as refinement does not directly mention refinement of private classes. However, the theorems allow us to take a method m in a public class C as a "main method". This method may call methods of classes that are directly linked to C. Treating these classes as "'public classes" with respect to C and these classes together with their associated classes as a declaration section, the refinement Conditions (14.1) and (14.6) can be established for this sub-declaration section.

In general, finding and formulating a refinement mapping ρ is design step. It is easier to develop a system in a stepwise process in which each step is modest. This approach leads itself to establishing correctness in an incremental manner.

This framework suggests that a development process should first focus on structural refinement and then carries out further refinement of methods of classes and the main method of the program under a fixed class declaration, without the hiding the internal states. This can be done entirely within the classical theories of programming provided in UTP [14].

14.6 Refinement Rules

We have given some refinement laws for refining commands in Sect. 14.4.6. Those laws are about

command refinement under the same class declaration sections. They can all be proven in the
classical theory of programming [14].

We now present refinement rules for program
structures that capture the nature of *incremental* development in object-oriented programming.
Most of the laws are intuitively understandable.
Their proof are involves finding structural transformations and then using **Theorems** 14.3 and
14.4 (refinement by upwards or downwards simulations). The structural transformations are quite
obvious for the laws presented and we omit most
of the proofs.

We first introduce some notations. We use
$N[supclass, pri, prot, pub, op]$ to denote a well-formed
class declaration that declares the class N that has
supclass as its direct superclass; *pri*, *prot* and *pub* as
its sets of private, protected and public attributes;
and *op* as its set of methods. *supclass* is always of
either a class name M, when M is the direct superclass of N, or ∅ when N has no superclass. We may
only refer to some, or even none of M, *pri*, *prot*,
pub, *op* when we talk about a class declaration.
For example, N denotes a class declaration for N,
and $N[pri]$ a class declaration that declares the class
N that has *pri* as its private attributes.

Law 4 *The order of the class declarations in a
declaration section is not essential:*

$$N_1; \ldots; N_n = N_{i_1}; \ldots; N_{i_n}$$

*where N_i is a class declaration and $i_1, \ldots, i_n$ is a
permutation of* $\{1, \ldots, n\}$.

A law like this may look utterly trivial after we
formalise the structural variables Ω, but it is not
so obvious that a semantic definition of a class
declaration to guarantee this law. For example, if
the pre-condition of the class declaration requires
that the direct superclass be declared before this
class declaration, this law would not hold.

The next law says that more services may
become available after adding a class definition.

Law 5 *If a class name N is not in Cdecls, but M is
in Cdecls*

$$Cdecls \sqsubseteq N[M, pri, prot, pub, op]; Cdecls$$

provided the right hand side is well-defined

The structural transformation only extends the set
cname. The consequence is only that a command
c in the main method which is not well-defined in
the original declaration becomes well-formed in
the extended declaration.

The next law state that the introduction of a
private attribute has no effect.

Law 6 *If neither N nor any of its super classes and
subclasses in Cdecls has x as an attribute*

$$N[pri]; Cdecls \equiv N[pri \cup \{T\ x = d\}]; Cdecls$$

*provided d lies in T and either T is a primitive type,
or T is declared in Cdecls or $T = N$.*

Although adding an attribute has no effect, it will
allow more well-defined classes and methods to
be introduced using other laws.

Law 7 *Changing a private attribute into a protected one may support more services.*

$$N[pri \cup \{T\ x = d\}, prot]; Cdecls \sqsubseteq N[pri, prot \cup \{T\ x = d\}]; Cdecls$$

This refinement becomes equivalence if both
sides are well-defined. This condition is required
as we do not allow a protected attribute of a class
to be redeclared in its subclass.

Similarly, changing a protected attribute to a
public attribute refines the declaration too. This
together with the above two laws allow us to add
new attributes as long as the well-definedness is
not violated.

Law 8 *Adding a new method can refine a declaration. If m is not defined in N, let $m(paras)\{c\}$ be a
method with distinct parameters paras and a command c. Then*

$N[op]$; $Cdecls \sqsubseteq N[op \cup \{m(paras)\{c\}\}]$; $Cdecls$

The structural transformation only extends $op(N)$ in the new declaration section, and does not change the dynamic state variables.

Law 9 *We can refine a method. If* $c_1 \sqsubseteq c_2$,

$N[op \cup \{m(paras)\{c_1\}\}]$; $Cdecls \sqsubseteq N[op \cup \{m(paras)\{c_2\}\}]$; $Cdecls$

The refinement of the command is done under the same dynamic variables.

Law 10 *Inheritance introduces refinement. If none of the attributes of M is defined in N or any superclass of N in Cdecls,*

$M[\emptyset, pri, prot, pub, op]$; $Cdecls \sqsubseteq M[N, pri, prot, pub, op]$; $Cdecls$

provided the right hand side is well-formed.

Introducing an inheritance in this way in fact enlarges the set of attributes of N (and those of the subclasses of N). A structural transformation from the new declaration section just projects the enlarged set attribute back to the original attributes.

Law 11 *We can introduce a superclass. Let*

$$C_1 = M[\emptyset, pri \cup A, prot, pub, op]$$
$$C_2 = M[\{N\}, pri, prot, pub, op]$$

Assume N is not declared in Cdecls,

C_1; $Cdecls \sqsubseteq C_2$; $N[\emptyset, \emptyset, A, \emptyset, \emptyset]$; $Cdecls$

This can be in fact derived from adding a class and then introducing inheritance. After introducing a subclass this way, we can continue to apply other laws to introduce more attributes and methods.

Law 12 *We can move some attributes of a class to its superclass. If all the subclasses of N but M do not have attributes in A, then*

$N[prot_1]$; $M[\{N\}, prot \cup A]$; $Cdecls \sqsubseteq N[prot_1 \cup A]$; $M[\{N\}, prot]$; $Cdecls$

This only enlarges the set of attributes of N. This law and the law for promoting an attribute to a protected attribute allow us to move a private attribute to the superclass too. Repeated application of this law allows us to move the common attributes of the direct subclasses of a class to the class itself.

Law 13 *If N has* $M_1, \ldots, M_k$ *as its direct subclasses,*

$N[prot]$; $M_1[prot_i \cup A]$; $\ldots$; $M_k[prot_k \cup A]$; $Cdecls$
$\sqsubseteq N[prot \cup A]$; $M_1[prot_1]$; $\ldots$; $M_k[prot_k]$; $Cdecls$

Law 14 *We copy (but not remove) a method of a class to its superclass. Let* $m(paras)\{c\}$ *be a method of M, but not a method of its superclass N:*

$N[op]$; $M[\{N\}, op_1 \cup \{m(\underline{paras})\{c\}\}]$; $Cdecls$
$\sqsubseteq N[op \cup \{m(paras)\{c\}\}]$; $M[\{N\}, op_1 \cup \{m(\underline{paras})\{c\}\}]$; $Cdecls$

Copying a method to its direct superclass does not change any dynamic variable.

Law 15 *Let* $m(paras)\{c\}$ *be a method of N, then*

$N[op]$; $M[\{N\}, op_1]$; $Cdecls \sqsubseteq N[op]$; $M[\{N\}, op_1 \cup \{m(\underline{paras})\{c\}\}]$; $Cdecls$

We can remove a redundant method from a subclass.

Law 16 *Assume class N is the direct superclass of M,* $m(paras)\{c\} \in op \cap op_1$, *and c only involves in the protected attributes of N,*

$N[op]$; $M[\{N\}, op_1]$; $Cdecls \sqsubseteq N[op]$; $M[\{N\}, \{m(\underline{paras})\{c\}\} \gg op_1]$; $Cdecls$

Similarly, we can remove any unused private attributes.

Law 17 *If* $(T\,x)$ *is a private attribute of N[pri] that is not used in any command of N,*

$N[pri]$; $Cdecls \sqsubseteq N[\{T\,x = d\} \gg pri]$; $Cdecls$

We can also remove any unused protected attributes.

Law 18 *If* $(T\,x = d)$ *is a protected attribute of N[prot] that is not used in any command of N and any subclass of N,*

$N[prot]$; $Cdecls \sqsubseteq N[\{T\,x = d\} \gg prot]$; $Cdecls$

Law 19 *We can change a private class into a public class.*

`private` N; $Cdecls \sqsubseteq N$; $Cdecls$

A class is allowed to delegate some tasks to its associated classes.[2]

Law 20 (**Expert Pattern for Responsibility Assignment**) *Suppose $M[op_1]$ is declared in Cdecls, where Csecls has*

1. *an attribute x,*
2. *a method $m()\{c_1(x)\} \in op_1$ which may manipulate attribute x through execution of command c_1.*

Assume that $(M\ o)$ is an attribute of N, then

$$N[op \cup \{n(paras)\{c[c_1]\}\}];\ Cdecls \sqsubseteq N[op \cup \{n(paras)\{c[o.m()]\}\}];\ Cdecls$$

Here, c_1 is obtained from $\tilde{c}_1$ by replacing o.x with x, that is, $c_1 = \tilde{c}_1[x/o.x]$. Assume that $\tilde{c}_1$ does not refer to any attribute of N. While $c[\tilde{c}_1]$ denotes that $\tilde{c}_1$ occurs as part of command c, and $c[o.m]$ denotes that the command obtained from $c[\tilde{c}_1]$ by substituting o.m for $\tilde{c}_1$.

Proof Assume that M and N are public classes. It is easy to see there is a structural transformation that is identical except for $op(N)$. The dynamic state variables are the same in both declaration sections. For the left hand side declaration section to be well-defined, x has to be a public attribute of M.

Without losing any generality, assume that in the left hand side declaration section,

$$[\![c_1(o.x)]\!]_2 = p(y_1, y_3, o.x, \Pi) \vdash R(y_1, y_3, o.x, y_2', y_3', o.x', \Pi') \wedge (y_1' = y_1)$$

where y_1 does not appear in the left side of an assignment, the initial value of y_2 is not relevant in the execution of c_1 and y_3 is a general variable. We assume that they are not attributes of M. In this case y_1, y_2 and y_3 are the actual parameters of $o.M()$ in the declaration section on left hand side of the law. According to the semantics of a method call, we calculate the design for $[\![o.m()]\!]_2$ in the right hand side of the law.

$$
\begin{aligned}
[\![o.m()]\!]_1 &= \text{var } M\ self = o, T_1\ f_1 = y_1, T_2\ f_2, T_3\ f_3 = y_3;\ Set(M);\\
&\quad p(f_1;\ f_2;\ f_3, self.x, \Pi) \vdash R(f_1, f_3, self.x, f_1', f_2', f_3', self.x', \Pi');\\
&\quad y_2 := f_2;\ y_3 := f_3;\ \text{end } self, f_1;\ f_2;\ f_3;\ Reset\\
&\Rightarrow p(y_1; y_3, o.x, \Pi) \vdash R(y_1, y_3, o.x, y_2', y_3', o.x', \Pi') \wedge (y_1' = y_1)\\
&= [\![c_1(o.x)]\!]_2
\end{aligned}
$$

This implies that method $n()$ in class N satisfies the condition of **Theorem** 14.3 for the structural transformation. In case one or both of N and M are private, the refinement law holds because of **Theorem** 14.2.

♣

This law is illustrated by the UML class diagram in Fig. 14.5. It will become an equation if x is a public attribute of M.

To understand this law, let us consider the simple example from the aforementioned bank system in **Examples** 14.1 and 14.2.

Consider the method *getBalance* of class *Bank*. Initially, we might have the following design for it:

$$
\begin{aligned}
getBalance(&\texttt{Int } aID, \texttt{Int } res, \emptyset) \stackrel{def}{=}\\
&\exists a \in \Pi(Account) \cdot a.aNo = aID \vdash\\
&\exists a \in \Pi(Account) \cdot a.aNo = aID \Rightarrow res' = a.balance
\end{aligned}
$$

Note that it requires the attributes of class *Account* to be visible (public) to other classes (like *Bank*). Applying Law 20 to it, we can get the following design:

$$
\begin{aligned}
getBalance(&\texttt{Int } aID, \texttt{Int } res, \emptyset) \stackrel{def}{=}\\
&\exists a \in \Pi(Account) \cdot a.aNo = aID \vdash\\
&\exists a \in \Pi(Account) \cdot a.aNo = aID \Rightarrow a.getBalance(\emptyset; res; \emptyset)
\end{aligned}
$$

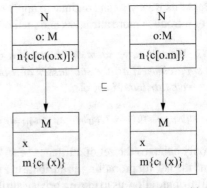

Fig. 14.5 Object-oriented functional decomposition

---

[2]This law is very useful in object-oriented system designs [20].

The refinement delegates the task of balance lookup to the *Account* class.

It is important to note that method invocation, or in other words, object interaction takes time. Therefore, this object-oriented refinement (and the one described in Law 22 later) usually exchanges efficiency for ease of reuse and maintainability, and data encapsulation.

After functionalities are delegated to associated classes, data encapsulation can be applied to increase security and maintainability. The visibility of an attribute can be changed from public to protected, or from protected to private under certain circumstances.

Law 21 (Data Encapsulation) *Suppose* $M[pri, prot, pub]$, *and* $(T_1\ a_1 = d_1) \in pub$, $(T_2\ a_2 = d_2) \in prot$.

1. *If no operations of other classes have expressions of the form le.a_1, except for those of subclasses of M, we have*

   $M[pri, prot, pub]; Cdecls$
   $\sqsubseteq M[pri, prot \cup \{T_1\ a_1 = d_1\}, \{T_1\ a_1 = d_1\} \rhd pub]; Cdecls$

2. *If no operations of any other classes have expressions of the form le.a_2, we have*

   $M[pri, prot, pub]; Cdecls$
   $\sqsubseteq M[pri \cup \{T_2\ a_2 = d_2\}, \{T_2\ a_2 = d_2\} \rhd prot, pub]; Cdecls$

The structural transformation only changes the different kind of attributes, it may thus affect visibility of attributes, and thus the well-definedness of commands. However, this will not happen because of the side conditions.

After applying Law 20 exhaustively to method *getBalance*, and applying Law 21) to the class diagram on the right hand side of Fig. 14.5, we achieve the encapsulation of the attribute *balance* of the class *Account*. The attribute *aNo* can be encapsulated in a similar way.

Another principle of object-oriented design is to make classes simple and highly cohesive. This means that the responsibilities (or functionalities) of a class, i.e. its methods, should be strongly related and focused. We therefore often need to decompose a complex class into a number of associated classes, so that the system will be

- easy to comprehend
- easy to reuse
- easy to maintain
- less delicate and less effected by changes

We capture the *High Cohesion* design pattern [20] by the following refinement rule.

Law 22 (High Cohesion Pattern) *Assume* $M[pri, op]$ *is a well-formed class declaration,* $pri = \{x, y\}$ *are (or are lists of) attributes of M,* $m_1(){c_1(x)} \in op$ *only contains attribute x, method* $m_2(){c_2[m_1]} \in op$ *can only change x by calling* m_1 *(or it does not have to change it at all). Then*

1. $M; Cdecls \sqsubseteq M[pri_{new}, op_{new}]; M_1[pri_1, op_1];$
   $M_2[pri_2, op_2]; Cdecls,$
   where

   - $pri_{new} = \{M_1\ o_1, M_2\ o_2\}$
   - $op_{new} = \{m_1(){o_1.m_1}, m_2(){o_2.m_2}\}$
   - $pri_1 = \{x\}, op_1 = \{m_1(){c_1(x)}\}$
   - $pri_2 = \{y, M_1\ o_1\}, op_2 = \{m_2(){c_2[o_1.m_1()]}\}$

   such that $\forall o : M \cdot (o.o_1 = o.o_2.o_1)$ *is an invariant of M. This invariant has to be established by the constructors of these three classes.*
   This refinement is illustrated by the diagram in Fig. 14.6.

2. $M; Cdecls \sqsubseteq M[pri_{new}, op_{new}]; M_1[pri_1, op_1];$
   $M_2[pri_2, op_2]; Cdecls,$ *where*

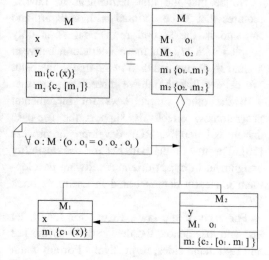

Fig. 14.6 Class decomposition (1)

Fig. 14.7 Class decomposition (2)

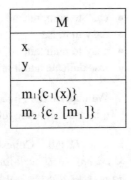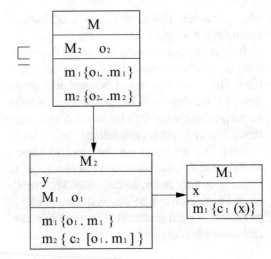

- $pri_{new} = \{M_2\ o_2\}$
- $op_{new} = \{m_1()\{o_1.m_1()\}, m_2()\{o_2.m_2()\}\}$
- $pri_1 = \{x\}$, $op_1 = \{m_1()\{c(x)\}\}$
- $pri_2 = \{y, M_1\ o_1\}$
- $op_2 = \{m_1()\{o_1.m_1()\}, m_2()\{c_2[o_1.m_1()]\}\}$

This refinement is illustrated by the diagram in Fig. 14.7.

The structural transformations for the two cases have
been nearly given in the law. The proofs of the two refinements in the law are similar to that for the expert pattern. First take M to be a public class and then use **Theorem** 14.2.

Notice that the first refinement in Law 22 requires that M be coupled with both M_1 and M_2; and in the second refinement M is only coupled with M_2, but more interaction between M_2 and M_1 are needed than in the first refinement. We believe that the above three laws, together with the other simple laws for incremental programming effectively support the use-case driven and iterative RUP development process [20]. The use of the patterns for responsibility assignment in object-oriented software development is clearly demonstrated in Larman's book [20].

For each of the laws, except for Law 9, let *LHS* and *RHS* denote the declarations on the left and right hand sides, respectively. For any main program *Main*, each refinement law becomes an equational law: *LHS • Main ≡ RHS • Main*, provided *LHS • Main* is well-defined.

14.7   Conclusions

We have shown how Hoare and He's design calculus [14] can be used to define an object-oriented language. A program or a command is represented as a predicate called a *design*, and the refinement relation between designs is defined as logic implication. Our model reflects most of the features of object-oriented designs [33]. For example, the model shows that inheritance with attribute hiding and method overriding makes system analysis difficult, while method invocation on an object may change external states. The good news is that we have been able to impose constraints on system development so that the "bad" features are not used.

14.7.1   Related Work

Formal techniques for object-orientation have been extensively studied [6,11,34–37]. The work there concerns programming languages. A large amount of work on operational semantics [36,37] supports methods of simulation and model checking. Our calculus is based on a relational model that supports state-based reasoning and stepwise (or incremental) refinement in system development.

There are a number of recent articles on Hoare Logics for object-oriented programming (see, e.g. [5,12,13,30,38,39]). The normal form of a program in our article is similarly to that of [5,30]. However, one major difference of our work is that we also provide a formal characterization and refinement of the contextual (or structural) features, i.e. the declaration section, of an object program. This is motivated by our work on the formalization of UML models [24,25]. This characterization has been proven to be very useful in defining semantics for integrated specification languages in general.

Class or object refinements are studied in [13,23]. A refinement object-oriented language (ROOL) and some general notions of refinement are defined in [5] using predicate transformers without treating reference types. The work in [9], also without treatment of reference types, describes a set of algebraic laws for ROOL, that can be used to derive refactorings [18,40]. Our initial version of rCOS (called OOL) with a relational semantics and the idea object-oriented refinement were presented in [41]. OOL does not have references types or nested variable declarations. In this article, we have revised OOL and its semantics. We have also provided refinement laws that reflect the characteristic aspects, functionality delegation, data encapsulation and class decomposition for high cohesion, of object-oriented design and the ideas of design patterns [20,42]. We also take a *weak semantic* approach meaning that when the pre-condition of a contract is not satisfied, the program will behave as *chaos*; any program modification made, such as adding exception handling, is a refinement. We also describe static well-formedness conditions in the pre-condition so that any correction of any static inconsistency in a program, such as static type mismatching, missing variables, missing methods, etc. can be treated as refinements too. This allows us to treat *refactoring* [40] as refinement and to combine it with *behavioural refinement*. This combination is important for composing different UML models and reasoning about their consistency [24,25,32].

Our work on formal support for object-oriented design using UML [24,25,32] has provided us with the insight of functional decomposition in the object-oriented setting and its relation with data encapsulation and class decomposition. The main ideas of those article are summarised in the following subsection.

14.7.2 Support UML-like Software Development

Consider the incremental and iterative Rational Unified Process (RUP) [27] and the use-case driven approach [26]. System requirements capture and analysis starts by identifying domain (or business) services and the domain structure that consists of the domain *classes* (or *concepts*) and their *associations*. Business services can be described by a UML use-case model and the domain structure is represented as a UML class diagram. The UML class diagram can be formally specified as a rCOS class declaration section, and each use case is declared as a set of methods of a *use-case controller* class. Then the application program is specified as a main method that uses the services, i.e. calls to the methods, provided in the use-case controller classes. Therefore, the normal requirement specification is of the form

$$(CM; Controller_1; \ldots; Controller_n) \bullet Main$$

where CM is a sequence of class declarations obtained from the class diagram (an association is also declared as a class). Each $Controller_i$ is a use-case controller class (following the facade controller pattern [20,42]) that contains the functional specifications (in terms of designs in rCOS) and formalizes the system sequence diagram of the corresponding use case. The *consistency* of the class diagram and the use cases (their sequence diagrams and functional specifications) has to ensure that the class diagram *fully supports* the use cases. Formally, this means that the declaration section $(CM; Controller_1; ...; Controller_n)$ of the program is well-formed and any invocation of a method in a use-case controller in P does not end with *chaos*. In case of any inconsistency, we can modify the class diagram or the use cases (or both) according to the refinement laws that allow us to change the UML model consistently.

We design each use case by applying Law 20 to delegate its partial responsibilities to other classes in the class diagram according to *what information a class maintains or knows via its associations with other classes*. In the mean time, we can decompose complex classes according to Law 22 and encapsulate data according to Law 21. Obviously, before applying Law 20 or 22, we have to add classes, attributes and methods. These design or refinement activities lead to incremental creation of the sequence diagrams and design class diagram of the system, and the refined laws will ensure that the design class diagram refines the requirement class diagram. For details about formalization of UML models of requirements and designs in rCOS, we refer the reader to [24,25, 32]. For detailed, but informal, application of the design patterns that have been formalized as refinement laws in this article, please see Larman's book [20].

rCOS captures the commonality and difference between structured functional development and object-oriented development. In the traditional structured approach, a software project starts with the identification of data and functions. A specification of a procedure defines how the data are manipulated in terms of precondition and postcondition: $\{Pre\}F\{Post\}$. The design is to decompose the functions step-by-step into subfunctions by applying the decomposition rule

$$\frac{\{Pre\}F_1\{Mid\}, \{Mid\}F_2\{Post\}}{F \sqsubseteq F_1; F_2}$$

The problem with this approach is that it is difficult to determine a suitable Mid, among many possibilities. In the object-oriented approach that we propose here, we use the *expert pattern* (Law 20) and High Cohesion pattern (Law 22) to decompose a use case according to the system structure modelled by the class diagram. As in the func-

tional approach, the decomposition has to preserve the functional specification of the use case, i.e. the pre- and post-condition relations. However, the decomposition is more pragmatic as its is supported by the known *structure*. In the structured approach, the design of the system has to be constructed by decomposition too.

The research of formal support for UML modelling is currently very active [43–45]. However, there is a large body of work in formalizing UML and providing tool support for UML focuses on models for a particular view (e.g. a class models, statecharts, and sequence diagrams), and the translation of them into an existing formal formalism (e.g. Z, VDM, B, and CSP). Very little work has been conducted as to how UML models can be *refined consistently*. In contrast, we are concerned with combinations of different UML models, the most *imprecise* part of UML. Our methodology is directed towards improved support for requirement analysis and transition from requirements to design models in RUP. Our choice of a Java-like syntax for the specification language is a pragmatic solution to the problems of representing name spaces and (the consequences of) inheritance in a notation such as CSP.

14.7.3   Limitation and Future Work

rCOS can be extended to deal with features of communication, interaction, real-time and resources. If we add variables for traces, refusals and divergence into the alphabet, the different kinds of semantics of communicating processes can be defined as designs [14]. By introducing clock variables in the alphabet [14,46–48], we can define real-time programs as designs and further extend our approach to support other aspects of object-oriented programming. Alternatively, one can also use temporal logic, such as [49], for the specification and verification of multithreading Java-like programs. However, we would like to deal with concurrency at a higher level [50–52].

In [33], Broy argued that the property of object identities is too low level and implementation oriented. The use of references does cause side-effects, making the semantics more complex. A preliminary version of the model without references can be found in [41]. This simplification is not significant. The complexity mainly affects reasoning about low level designs and implementations. With our approach, we can describe change of system state in terms of what objects are created or deleted, what modifications are made to an object and what links between objects are formed or broken. Low level features such as method overriding and attribute hiding are only useful to program around the requirement and design defects detected at the coding stage or even later when one tries to reuse a class with a similar template in a program that the class was not originally designed. These features cause problems in programming verification and the smooth application of the notion of program refinements.

Future work includes the study of the completeness of the refinement calculus and the applications of the method to more realistic case studies. We will also extend this work to deal with component systems [50–52]. Further challenges for formal object-oriented methods include the formal treatment of *patterns* [42] in general. We are also interested in studying the difference and relationship between our model and Separation Logic [53,54], that can be using for extending the calculus to multi-thread programming.

References

1. G. Smith, *The Object-Z Specification Language* (Kluwer Academic Publishers, 2000)
2. E. Dürr, E.M. Dusink, The role of VDM^{++} in the development of a real-time tracking and tracing system, in *Proceedings of FME'93*, eds. by J. Woodcock, P. Larsen. Lecture Notes in Computer Science 670 (Springer, 1993)
3. S. Cook, J. Daniels, *Designing Object Systems: Object-Oriented Modelling with Syntropy* (Prentice-Hall, 1994)
4. D. Coleman et al., *Object-Oriented Development: the FUSION Method* (Prentice-Hall, 1994)
5. A. Cavalcanti, D. Naumann, A weakest precondition semantics for an object-oriented language of refinement, in *Lecture Notes in Computer Science 1709* (Springer, 1999), pp. 1439–1460
6. D. Naumann, Predicate transformer semantics of an Oberon-like language, in *Proceedings of PRO-COMET'94*, ed. by E.-R. Olerog (North-Holland, 1994)
7. A. Mikhajlova, E. Sekerinski, Class refinement and interface refinement in object-orient programs, in *Proceedings of FME'97*. Lecture Notes in Computer Science (Springer, 1997)
8. E. Sekerinski, A type-theoretical basis for an object-oriented refinement calculus, in *Proceedigns of Formal Methods and Object Technology* (Springer, 1996)
9. P. Borba, A. Sampaio, M. Cornélio. A refinment algebra for object-oriented programming, in *Proceedigns of ECOOP03*, ed. by L. cardelli, Lecture Notes in Computer Science 2743 (Springer, 2003), pp. 457–482
10. P. America, F. de Boer, Reasoning about dynamically evolving process structures. Formal Aspects Comput. **6**(3), 269–316 (1994)
11. M. Abadi, R. Leino, A logic of object-oriented programs, in *TAPSOFT '97: Theory and Practice of Software Development, 7th International Joint Conference*, eds. by M. Bidoit, M. Dauchet (Springer, 1997), pp. 682–696
12. A. Poetzsch-Heffter, P. Muller, A programming logic for sequential Java, in *Proceedings of Programming Languages and Systems (ESOP'99)*, ed. by S.D. Swierstra. Lecture Notes in Computer Science 1576 (Springer, 1999), pp. 162–176
13. K. Rustan, M. Leino, Recursive object types in a logic of object-oriented programming, in *Lecture Notes in Computer Science 1381* (Springer, 1998)
14. C.A.R. Hoare, J. He, *Unifying Theories of Programming* (Prentice-Hall, 1998)
15. R. Back, J. von Wright, *Refinement Calculus* (Springer, 1998)
16. C.A.R. Hoare, Laws for programming. Commun. ACM **30**, 672–686 (1987)
17. C.C. Morgan, *Programming from Specifications*, 2nd edn. (Prentice Hall, 1994)
18. M. Fowler, *Refectoring, Improving the Design of Existing Code* (Addison-Wesley, 2000)
19. E. Gamma, R. Helm, R. Johnson, J. Vlissides, *Design Patterns, Elements of Reusable Object-Oriented Software* (Addlison Wesley, 1994)
20. C. Larman, *Applying UML and Patterns* (Prentice-Hall International, 2001)
21. D.B. Roberts, *Practical Analysis for Refactoring*. Ph.D. thesis, University of Illinois at Urbana Champain, 1999
22. L.A. Tokuda, *Evolving Object-Oriented Designs with Refactoring*. Ph.D. thesis, University of Texas at Austin, 1999
23. R. Back, A. Mikhajlova, J. von Wright, Class refinement as semantics of correct object substitutability. Formal Aspects Comput. **2**, 18–40 (2000)
24. Z. Liu, J. He, X. Li, Y. Chen, A relational model for formal requirements analysis in UML, in *Formal Methods and Software Engineering, ICFEM03*, eds. by J.S. Dong, J. Woodcock. Lecture Notes in Computer Science 2885 (Springer, 2003), pp. 641–664

25. Z. Liu, J. He, X. Li, J. Liu, Unifying views of UML. Electron. Notes Theor. Comput. Sci. (ENTCS) **101**, 95–127 (2004)

26. I. Jacobson, G. Booch, J. Rumbaugh, *The Unified Software Development Process* (Addison-Wesley, 1999)

27. P. Kruchten, *The Rational Unified Process—An Introduction* (2nd Edn.). (Addison-Wesly, 2000)

28. G. Booch, J. Rumbaugh, I. Jacobson, *The Unified Modelling Language User Guide* (Addison-Wesley, 1999)

29. J. Yang, Q. Long, Z. Liu, X. Li, A predicative semantic model for integrating UML models, in *Proceedings of 1st International Colloquium on Theoretical Aspects of Computing (ICTAC04)*. Lecture Notes in Computer Science, vol. 3407 (Springer, 2005), pp. 170–186

30. C. Pierik, F.S. de Boer, A syntax-directed hoare logic for object-oriented programming concepts. Technical report, UU-CS-2003-010, Institute of Information and Computing Science, Utrecht University, 2003

31. B. Meyer, From structured programming to object-oriented design: the road to Eiffel. Struct. Program. **10**(1), 19–39 (1989)

32. X. Li, Z. Liu, J. He, Q. Long, Generating prototypes from a UML model of requirements, in *International Conference on Distributed Computing and Internet Technology (ICDIT2004)*. Lecture Notes in Computer Science, Bhubaneswar, India, vol. 3347 (Springer, 2004)

33. M. Broy, Object-oriented programming and software development—a critical assessment, in *Programming Methodology*, eds. by A. McIver, C. Morgan (Springer, 2003)

34. P. America, Designing an object-oriented programming language with behavioural subtyping, in *REX Workshop*, eds. by J.W. de Bakker, I.P. de Roever, G. Rozenberg, Lecture Notes in Computer Science, vol. 489 (Springer, 1991), pp. 60–90

35. M.M. Bonsangue, J.N. Kok, K. Sere, An approach to object-orientation in action systems, in *Mathematics of Program Construction*, ed. by J. Jeuring. Lecture Notes in Computer Science 1422 (Springer, 1998), pp. 68–95

36. K. Bruce, J. Grabtre, G. Kanapathy, An operational semantics for TOOPLE: a statically-typed object-oriented programming language, in *Mathematical Foundations of Programming Semantics*, ed. by S. Brooks et al. Lecture Notes in Computer Science 802 (Springer, 1994), pp. 603–626

37. D. Walker, β-calculus semantics of object-oriented programming languages, in *Proceedings of TACAS'91*, Lecture Notes in Computer Science 526

38. M. Huisman, B. Jacobs, Java program verification via a Hoare logic with abrupt termination, in *FASE 2000, Lecture Notes in Computer Science 1783*, ed. by T. Maibaum (Springer, 2000), pp. 284–303

39. D. von Oheimb, Hoare logic for Java in Isabelle/HOL. Concurr. Comput. Pract. Exp. **13**(13), 1173–1214 (2001)

40. M. Fowler, K. Beck, J. Brant, W. Opdyke, D. Roberts, *Refactoring: Improving the Design of Existing Code* (Addison-Wesley, 1999)

41. J. He, Z. Liu, X. Li, Towards a refinement calculus for object-oriented systems (invited talk), in *Proceedigns of ICCI02, Alberta, Canada* (IEEE Computer Society, 2002)

42. E. Gamma et al., *Design Patterns* (Addison-Wesley, 1995)

43. R.J.R. Back, L. Petre, I.P. Paltor, Formalizing UML use cases in the refinement calculus, in *Proceedings of UML'99* (Springer, 1999)

44. D. Harel, B. Rumpe, Modeling languages: syntax, semantics and all that stuff—part I: the basic stuff. Technical report, MCS00-16, The Weizmann Institute of Science, Israel, Sept 2000

45. G. Reggio et al., Towards a rigorous semantics of UML supporting its multiview approach, in *Proceedings of FASE 2001*, ed. by H. Hussmann. Lecture Notes in Computer Science 2029 (Springer, 2001)

46. N. Jin, J. He, Resource models and pre-compiler specification for hardware/software, in *Proceedings of 2nd International Conference on Software Engineering and Formal Methods (SEFM'04)*, ed. by J.R. Cuellar, Z. Liu (IEEE Computer Society, Beijing, China, 28–30 Sept 2004)

47. A. Sherif, J. He, A. Cavalcanti, A. Sampaio, A framework for specification and validation of real-time systems using Circus actions, in *Proceedigns of 1st International Colloquium on Theoretical Aspects of Computing (ICTAC04)*. Lecture Notes in Computer Science 3407 (Springer, 2005), pp. 478–494

48. J.C.P. Woodcock, A.L.C. Cavalcanti, A semantics of circus, in *ZB 2002, Lecture Notes in Computer Science 2272* (Springer, 2002)

49. E. Abraham-Mumm, F.S. de Boer, W.P. de Roever, M. Steffen, Verification for Java's reentrant multithreading concept, in *Foundations of Software Science and Computation Structures*. Lecture Notes in Computer Science 2303 (Springer, 2002), pp. 5–20

50. J. He, X. Li, Z. Liu, Component-based software engineering, in *Proceedigns of 2nd International Colloquium on Theoretical Aspects of Computing (ICTAC05)* (Springer, 2005), pp. 70–95

51. J. He, Z. Liu, X. Li, A theories of reactive contracts. Technical report 327, United Nations University, the International Institute for Software Technology, Macao SAR, China, July 2005. To appear in Proceedings of 2nd International Workshop on Formal Aspects of Component Systems (FACS05), ENTCS

52. Z. Liu, J. He, X. Li, Contract-oriented development of component systems in *Proceedings of IFIP WCC-TCS2004*, Toulouse, France (Kulwer Academic Publishers, 2004), pp. 349–366

53. Y. Chen, J. Sanders, Compositional reasoning for pointer structures, in *8th International Conference on Mathematics of Program Construction* (Springer, 2006), pp. 115–139

54. J. Reynolds, Separation logic: a logic for a shared mutable data structure, in *Proceedings of IEEE Symposium Logic in Computer Science (LICS'02)* (IEEE Computer Sciety, 2002)

55. J. He, Z. Liu, X. Li, S. Qin, A relational model of object oriented programs, in *Proceedings of the Second ASIAN Symposium on Programming Languages and Systems (APLAS04)*. Lecture Notes in Computer Science 3302, Taiwan (Springer, Mar 2004), pp. 415–436

56. Z. Liu, J. He, X. Li, rCOS: Refinement of component and object systems, in *Proceedings of 3rd International Symposium on Formal Methods for Components and Objects (FMCO04)*. Lecture Notes in Computer Science 3657 (Springer, 2005), pp. 222–250

Guided by the software model (Part 1), operating platform and runtime supports (Part 2), and engineering approach (Part 3), this part describes how the Internetware paradigm is applied to real-world cloud and client applications. At the client side, applications on smartphones connect to the physical world and Internet by their built-in sensors and networking chips, respectively. At the cloud side, numerous computing platforms like virtual machines and middleware infrastructures are managed to run user tasks in a cost-effective way. We discuss how the Internetware paradigm is realized on the two sides, as well as how the two sides are connected and how applications can be diagnosed for energy efficiency.

Smartphone applications running at the client side expect a way to improve their performance and reduce their power cost. This incurs challenges on correctness, effectiveness, and adaptability. Chapter 15 proposes refactoring smartphone applications to be with the ability of on-demand computation offloading. This enables such applications to borrow computational capabilities from the cloud side.

At the cloud side, a major concern is the management cost in controlling various services on platforms like virtual machines and middleware infrastructures. Such controlling tasks are done by management programs, which are usually hard-coded by languages such as Java and C++. This brings enough capabilities and flexibility, but may also cause high programming efforts and costs. Chapter 16 proposes an architecture-based approach to developing management programs in a simple yet powerful manner. It brings many advantages on performance, interoperability, reusability, and simplicity.

For Internetware applications, software updates are common for coping with evolving user requirements. Distributing such software updates reliably to applications at the client side is a challenging task for ad hoc pervasive networks. Chapter 17 addresses this problem with storage and bandwidth constraints, and proposes an age-based approach. Mathematical models are derived to analyze the performance of various strategies.

Finally, it is observed that many smartphone applications can be subject to serious energy inefficiency problems. However, software developers lack handy tools for detecting such problems and identifying their root causes. This situation becomes even common for Internetware applications, no matter whether they run at the client side or the cloud side, as this relates to coding defects inside software. Chapter 18 proposes an automated approach to exploring an application's state space and monitoring its sensor and wake lock usage. It also analyzes whether sensory data are effectively utilized by state-sensitive data utilization measurement. This helps improve Internetware applications in their non-functional qualities.

Refactoring Android Java Code for On-Demand Computation Offloading

15

Abstract

Computation offloading is a promising way to improve the performance as well as reducing the battery power consumption of a smartphone application by executing some parts of the application on a remote server. Supporting such capability is not easy for smartphone application developers due to (1) correctness: some code, e.g., that for GPS, gravity, and other sensors, can run only on the smartphone so that developers have to identify which parts of the application cannot be offloaded; (2) effectiveness: the reduced execution time must be greater than the network delay caused by computation offloading so that developers need to calculate which parts are worth offloading; (3) adaptability: smartphone applications often face changes of user requirements and runtime environments so that developers need to implement the adaptation on offloading. More importantly, considering the large number of today's smartphone applications, solutions applicable for legacy applications will be much more valuable. In this paper, we present a tool, named DPartner, that automatically refactors Android applications to be the ones with computation offloading capability. For a given Android application, DPartner first analyzes its bytecode for discovering the parts worth offloading, then rewrites the bytecode to implement a special program structure supporting on-demand offloading, and finally generates two artifacts to be deployed onto an Android phone and the server, respectively. We evaluated DPartner on three real-world Android applications, demonstrating the reduction of execution time by 46–97 % and battery power consumption by 27–83 %.

Parts of this chapter were reprinted from Ying Zhang, Gang Huang, Xuanzhe Liu, Wei Zhang, Hong Mei and Shunxiang Yang. *Refactoring Android java code for on-demand computation offloading*, In Proceedings of the ACM International Conference on Object Oriented Programming Systems Languages and Applications © 2012 ACM, Inc. http://doi.acm.org/10.1145/2398857.2384634.

Keywords

Computation offloading · Bytecode refactoring · Energy · Android

15.1 Introduction

Android [1] is an open source mobile platform for smartphones, and it has gained more than 59 % of smartphone market share in the first quarter of 2012 [2]. Hundreds of thousands of developers have produced more than 490 thousands Android apps (a special kind of Java applications, app is short for application) since the platform was first released by Google in 2008 [3,4]. Following the fast improvement of smartphone hardware and increased user experience, Android apps try to provide more and more functionality and then they inevitably become so complex as to make the two most critical limits of smartphones worse.

The first limit is the battery power. Complex Android apps usually have intensive computations and consume a great deal of energy. For instance, the top 10 downloaded Android apps such as *Fruit Ninja* and *Angry Birds* on the Google Play [4] (formerly known as the Android Market) are all the complex ones that can drain the battery power in about 30 min if running on HTC G13 [5]. Although the battery capacity keeps growing continuously, it still cannot keep pace with the growing requirements of Android apps [6].

The second limit is the diversity of hardware configurations, which gives smartphone users very different experiences even running the same app. For example, among the best-selling HTC smartphones in 2011, G13 has a 600 MHz CPU, G11 and G12 have a 1 GHz CPU, and G14 has a 1.2 GHz CPU. The same *Fruit Ninja* app runs very slowly on G13, faster on G11 and G12, and the fastest on G14. Generally speaking, the lower hardware configuration of a phone implies the lower performance of the apps running on the phone. Users usually stop using the *slow* apps even if the root cause of the poor user experience is due to the low hardware configuration of the phone. Such factor can lead to a big loss of the app market for developers and vendors.

Computation offloading is a popular technique to help improve the performance of an Android-like smartphone app and meanwhile reduce its power consumption. Offloading, also referred to as *remote execution*, is to have some computation intensive code of an app executed on a nearby server (the so-called surrogate, e.g., a PC), so that the app can take advantage of the powerful hardware and the sufficient power supply of the server for increasing its responsiveness and decreasing its battery power consumption.

Computation offloading is usually implemented by a special program structure, or a design pattern, that enables a piece of code to execute locally or remotely and handles the interactions between the local and the remote code without impact on the correctness of the functionality. With respect to features of smartphones, three advanced issues have to be dealt with:

- Correctness: some code, e.g., that for GPS, gravity, and other sensors, can run only on the smartphone. Therefore developers have to identify which parts of the app cannot be offloaded;
- Effectiveness: the reduced execution time must be greater than the network delay caused by computation offloading. Therefore, developers have to calculate which parts are worth offloading;
- Adaptability: one of the most important natures of mobile computing is the diverse, frequent, and rapid changes of user requirements and runtime environments, which may lead to changes of computation offloading. For example, if the remote server becomes unavailable due to unstable network connection, the computation executed on the server should come back to the smartphone or go to another available server on the fly. Developers have to consider such changes in computation offloading.

The preceding issues are not easy to deal with and, more importantly in practice, a solution should be applied to legacy apps in a cost effective way considering the huge number of today's Android apps.

In this chapter, we present an automatic approach to realizing computation offloading of an Android app. Our chapter makes three major contributions:

- A well-designed pattern to enable an Android app to be computation offloaded on-demand. All Java classes of the app are able to interact with each other locally or remotely. The computations of a class can be offloaded dynamically and only the interactions between the smartphone and the server go through the network stack.

- A refactoring tool, named DPartner, to automatically transform the bytecode of an Android app to implement the proposed design pattern. DPartner first analyzes the bytecode for discovering the parts of an app that are worth offloading, then rewrites the bytecode to implement the design pattern, and finally generates two artifacts to be deployed onto the Android smartphone and the server, respectively. Refactoring is transparent to app developers and supports legacy apps without source code.

- A thorough evaluation on three real-world Android apps. The evaluation results show that our approach is effective. The offloaded apps execute much faster (reducing execution time by 46–97 %) and consume much less battery energy (reducing power consumption by 27–83 %) than the original ones.

We organize the rest of this chapter as follows. Section 15.2 presents the design pattern for computation offloading. Section 15.3 gives the implementation of DPartner. Section 15.4 reports the evaluation on Android apps. Section 15.5 discusses related work and we conclude the chapter in Sect. 15.6.

15.2 Design Pattern for Computation Offloading

An Android app is a Java program, whose building blocks are classes. Any meaningful computation is implemented as a method of a class, which uses the data and methods internal of the same class or invokes some methods of other classes. As a result, offloading computations can be implemented as remotely deploying and invoking a single class or a set of classes performing the computation. The goal of our approach is to automatically refactor Android apps into the ones implementing the design pattern for such deployment and invocation.

The principle of refactoring is to restructure the given code without altering the external functionality [7]. Generally speaking, refactoring is characterized by three aspects [7]: (1) the structure of the original code, i.e., source structure; (2) the structure of the target code, i.e., target structure; (3) a sequence of code refactoring steps that transform the original code to the functionally equivalent target code, so that the target code are finally able to take on the desired program structure. Thus, we introduce these aspects one by one in detail as follows.

15.2.1 The Source Structure and the Target Structure

In Java, the object reference determines whether two classes interact with each other locally or remotely. The source structure of the given code in any standalone Android app all take on the "local reference" program structure, i.e., the so-called "in-VM reference" program structure as shown in Fig. 15.1. Class X first gets the in-VM reference of class N and then invokes the methods of N. Such a structure does not support offloading any computation in class N because if N is offloaded to a remote server, N's in-VM reference held by X becomes invalid, i.e., it cannot help the VM pass

Fig. 15.1 Local invocation (source structure)

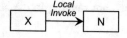

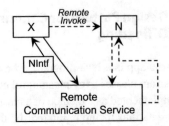

Fig. 15.2 Remote invocation (source structure)

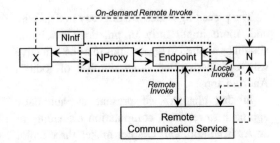

Fig. 15.3 On-Demand remote invocation (target structure)

the method invocations to N, and X will fail to obtain the new in-VM reference of N.

Figure 15.2 presents the typical code structure that enables class X to invoke the methods of a remote class N. That is, X gets a remote reference to N from a remote communication service, then uses the reference to interact with N remotely. The remote communication service is responsible to associate N's reference with N across the network. Take Android AIDL [8] as an example, its *ServiceConnection* can be seen as the main part of the remote communication service. X gets a reference to N in the *onServiceConnected* method of *ServiceConnection*, then uses the reference to invoke the methods of N. Such a structure can have the computations in N offloaded to a remote server, but suffer serious performance penalty if N and X are both in the same VM. As mentioned above, whether N is offloaded or not is determined dynamically and may change time to time. If N is not offloaded, all the interactions between X and N in such a structure will still go through the time-consuming network stack, which is contrary to the goal of computation offloading, i.e., improving performance and save energy. We have done an experiment on the standard Android SDK sample: net.learn2develop.Services [9]. X (*MainActivity*) uses the *ServiceConnection* to get the reference to N (*MyService*). After that it uses the reference to call N's methods. Compared with local interactions, such *remote interactions* in the same VM increase execution time by 680 % and battery power consumption by 287 %.

Figure 15.3 presents the target structure we propose for on-demand computation offloading, i.e., allowing X to effectively invoke N no matter the two are running in the same VM or in different

VMs across the network. The core of the structure is composed of two elements: *proxy* and *endpoint*.

A proxy, *NProxy* in Fig. 15.3, acts the same as the proxied class N except that it does not do any computation itself, but forwards the method invocations to the latter. If the location of the proxied class N is changed from local to remote, or from one remote server to another, *NProxy* keeps unchanged so that the caller, class X, will not get noticed.

The endpoint is responsible for determining the current location of N and for the truly crossing network communication from X to N. When N is running in a remote VM, the endpoint will take advantage of a given remote communication service to get a reference to N and pass it back to X, then X can use the reference to invoke N remotely. When X and N both run in the same VM, the endpoint will directly obtain the in-VM reference of N, so that X can invoke N without going through the network stack. The endpoint decouples the caller and the remote communication service. A smartphone can dynamically change its network connection with the same server among multiple protocols, e.g., Wi-Fi, and 3G. The endpoint automatically adapts to such changes so that the interacted app classes are unaware of them.

15.2.2   Refactoring Steps Overview

A sequence of refactoring steps will be performed on the Java bytecode of a given standalone Android app, so that the source structure of the code shown in Figs. 15.1 and 15.2 can be

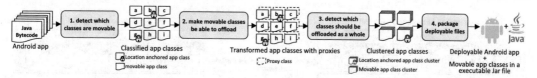

Fig. 15.4 Refactoring steps

transformed to the target structure shown in Fig. 15.3. We implement a tool, called DPartner [10], to automatically execute the refactoring steps, as shown in Fig. 15.4.

Step 1: detect which classes are movable. For a given app, DPartner automatically classifies the Java classes (i.e., bytecode files) into two categories: Anchored and Movable. The anchored classes must stay on the smartphone because they directly use some special resources available only on the phone, e.g., the GUI (Graphic User Interface) displaying, the gravity sensor, the acceleration sensor, and other sensors. If being offloaded to the server, these anchored classes cannot work because the required resources become unavailable. Besides those anchored classes, all other classes are movable, i.e., can execute either on the phone or on the server.

Step 2: make movable classes be able to offload. When a class is offloaded, the local invocation structure between this class and its interacted classes should be transformed to the on-demand remote invocation structure, e.g., generating the proxy of the callee class and rewriting the caller class to equip the proxy. Note that, if an anchored class is invoked by an offloaded class, the latter needs the former's proxy. Since which movable classes are offloaded is determined at runtime, we have to generate the proxies for all callee classes and rewrite the corresponding caller classes except that the caller and callee are both anchored. In our approach, a proxy class will be made to act exactly like its proxied app class. That is to say, these two classes will extend the same inheritance chain, implement the same interfaces, have the same method signatures, etc. In this way, class X will feel no difference when using the proxy of class N instead of N itself. The specific features of Java have to be considered when generating the proxies, which include the

static methods, final methods/classes, public fields, inner classes, arrays, etc. The details of proxy generation and class transformation will be presented in Sect. 15.3.

Step 3: detect which classes should be offloaded as a whole. There are numerous rules and algorithms to determine which movable classes should be offloaded [11]. As mentioned before, such a decision has to be made and changed at runtime due to the mobility of smartphones. Meanwhile, making decision at runtime inevitably consumes resources and therefore it is valuable to have done some pre-processing to simplify runtime decision. DPartner employs a well-known rationale for pre-processing based on class clustering [12], i.e., the frequently interacted classes should be offloaded as a whole. In this way, it cannot only avoid the time-consuming network communication between these classes, but also help accelerate runtime decision. For instance, if class X and class N interact with each other frequently, the endpoint only needs to profile the execution trace of X to determine offloading at runtime. When X is about to offload, N will then be profiled to decide whether it should be offloaded together. It is unnecessary to continuous profile N for reducing runtime overhead.

Step 4: package deployable files. The input of DPartner is the Java bytecode files of an Android app as well as the referenced resource files, e.g., images, xml files, and jar libs. After going through the above three steps, DPartner will package the files and then generate two artifacts. The first is the refactored Android app, i.e., an .apk file, which is ready to be installed on a phone. The second is an executable jar file, which contains the movable Java bytecode files cloned from the refactored app. Both artifacts include the code of the endpoint and the communication service.

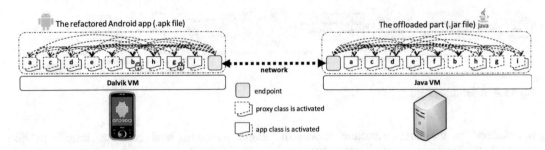

Fig. 15.5 The runtime architecture of an offloaded Android app

15.2.3 An Illustrative Example

Figure 15.5 shows an example of the runtime architecture of an offloaded Android app. This app is composed of six classes, with their names from *a* to *i*, respectively. In *Step 1*, DPartner finds that class *b* and *g* are both anchored classes, so that they should always run on the phone. All the other classes are movable. In *Step 2*, each app class is transformed and gotten its corresponding proxy class. In *Step 3*, DPartner finds that class *a*, *c*, *d*, *e*, and *f* are closely related to each other, and then clusters them for offloading as a whole. In *Step 4*, DPartner packages all the movable classes, the proxies, and the endpoint classes in to a jar file that will be deployed and executed on the server, and packages all the app classes, the proxies, and the endpoint classes as an Android apk file that will be deployed and executed on the phone.

At runtime, the endpoint predicts that offloading class *d* can improve the whole app performance, and then deactivates the *d* running on the phone and activates the *d* deployed on the server. The *d*'s proxy on the phone will forward the incoming method invocations to the *d* on the server. Since class *d* is clustered with class *a*, *c*, *e*, and *f* in *Step 3*, these classes will also be offloaded to the server when necessary by going through the deactivating, state synchronizing and activating procedures as class *d*. Any invocations to these app classes will be forwarded to the server by the endpoint. When the offloading-related conditions become unfavorable, e.g., the phone gets far away from the server which leads to a high network latency, the computations of *a*, *c*, *d*, *e*,

and *f* can get back to the phone by automatically deactivating them on the server and reactivating them on the phone. All invocations to these classes will be redirected to the phone by the endpoint.

15.3 Implementation of DPartner

15.3.1 Detect Movable Classes

DPartner classifies a Java class into anchored or movable via bytecode analysis. In an Android app, an anchored class must have one of the following features: (1) there are the "native" keyword existing in the class methods; (2) the class extends/implements/uses the Android system classes that are already regarded to be anchored by DPartner. For instance, the "android.view.View" class is used as the parent class for drawing the GUI of an Android app, so that it is classified to be the anchored class by DPartner. If a class is found to extend this class, it will also be anchored by DPartner. For another instance, the "android.hardware.*" classes are responsible for handling the camera and sensors of an Android smartphone. Therefore, they and the classes using them will be automatically anchored by DPartner. The rest of the classes will be classified as movable classes.

The above classification procedure may cause false positives and false negatives. A *false positive* means that a class is classified as a movable one, but the developer is unwilling to do this. For instance, the developer does not want the "cn.edu.pku.password" class be offloaded due to privacy concerns, although this class is classified as a movable one. A *false negative* means that a class is classified as an anchored one although it can actually be offloaded. For instance, as there are "native" keywords in its methods, the "cn.edu.pku.nativeCall" class will be classified as anchored automatically. However, such methods may never be invoked, so that this class can be offloaded. By analyzing the bytecode of an app, DPartner is able to tell whether an anchored class is invoked by the other classes of the same app. However, it cannot tell whether the class (acting as an Android service [13]) will be used by other apps, which may lead to false negatives of classification.

Therefore, we can see that DPartner takes a conservative approach to detecting movable classes, which can at least guarantee that a refactored app work correctly no matter being offloaded or not. To refine the classification results of anchored classes, DPartner provides a configuration file in which the naming patterns of anchored classes such as "android.hardware.usb.*" can be listed. In fact, the automatic classification procedure is carried out based on a predefined naming pattern list that takes effect just like the configuration file. At present, we have predefined 63 and 72 naming patterns for Android 2.1 and 2.2, respectively. Compared with Android 2.1, Android 2.2 has 96% naming patterns unchanged, 1% deleted, 1% revised, and 2% added. Developers can edit the configuration file to make the classification step adapt to the specific structures of each unique Android app and the platform. Of course, DPartner can force a movable class to be anchored by indicating it in the configuration file. For instance, developers can write "cn.edu.pku.password" in the file so that DPartner will automatically classify this class to be an anchored one.

15.3.2   Generate Proxies

One of the biggest challenge when generating proxies is to make a proxy act exactly like its proxied class. For instance, the app class X invokes the methods of another app class N. In the original code of X, a casting operation is done on N to N's parent *NParent*. If we just change N to *NProxy* in X's code, but not let *NProxy* extend class *NParent*, the casting operation will fail. Therefore, the proxy generated by DPartner will have the same program structure as the proxied class. Especially, the proxies themselves will maintain the same hierarchical structure as the proxied classes. For instance, N extends *NParent*, *NProxy* should also extend *NParent*'s proxy, so that any invocations to the inherited methods and constructors in N from *NParent*, can be forwarded first from *NProxy* to *NParent*'s proxy, and finally to *NParent*.

Java interface is used to separate the external representation and the internal implementation of a class. From the view of an interface, the proxy class and the proxied class are the same if they implement the same interface. Therefore, DPartner will automatically extract the interfaces to represent an app class and its proxy. For instance, there is an app class N, DPartner will (1) extract all the method signatures of N to form an *NIntf* interface; (2) make *NIntf* "extend" the *NParentIntf* interface of N's parent *NParent*, so as to maintain the inheritance hierarchy; (3) make N implement *NIntf*; and (4) make *NProxy* also implement *NIntf*. After that, DPartner will rewrite all the other classes (e.g., the class X) from using N to *NIntf*. However, to the static methods of N, as they are not allowed in Java interfaces, DPartner will directly use the corresponding static methods of *NProxy* to forward the method invocations.

15.3.3   Transform App Classes

The app classes should also be rewritten to adapt to the offloading requirements. Given an app class, DPartner will automatically transform it using the following transformers:

1. *Field2Method transformer*: The non-private fields of a class, i.e., with the *public*, *protected*, or *null* modifier, can be used by other classes outside of its class scope. However, if the class is offloaded, its callers can never get the reference to these fields. To solve this problem, the transformer will automatically generate the public getter/setter methods for the non-private fields of a given class X, and then change their modifier to

private. After that, the transformer will change all the classes that get/set the fields of X to use the corresponding getter/setter methods. In addition, to help state synchronization, the transformer also generates the getter/setter methods for the *private* fields. In this way, the inner states of a class instance can be collected and injected to enable state synchronization when the computations of a class instance are offloaded on-demand.

2. *Array transformer*: Given a class N that has an array type field being used by another class X, if X changes the element value of the array, N will see the changed value. That is because, in Java, an array is passed by reference. However, if X and N are running in different VMs, the array has to be passed by value between X and N, so that it can be transferred over the network. Under such a circumstance, X and N each have a copy of the array. If X changes the value of its copied array, but does not pass the array back, N will still use the old array, which makes the array value inconsistent. Therefore, the pass-by-reference feature of arrays should be kept. The array transformer wraps an array by using a functional equivalent class shown in Fig. 15.6, which encapsulates the get/set operations of an array.

For example, class N has a field *intArray* with the Integer array type. Class X changes the value of *intArray* as the following code:

```
n.intArray[5]=3;
```

Then the above code will be replaced by the following code:

```
Integer_Array_Dimension1_Intf
arrayIntf =
    n.getInteger_Array_Dimension1();
arrayIntf.aastore(5, new Integer(3));
```

```
//where n is an NProxy object
represented by NIntf.
//arrayIntf is an Integer_
  Array_Dimension1_Proxy
  object represented by Integer_
  Array_Dimension1_Intf.
```

In this way, the get/set operations in X on the *intArray* will be intercepted by the corresponding proxy class, and finally be forwarded to N. Otherwise, these operations will be done directly by using the aastore/aaload bytecode instructions that cannot be intercepted, which will lead to the value inconsistency of *intArray* in X and N. Transforming multi dimensional array is similar to single dimensional array. For example, Integer[][] will be wrapped as an Integer_Array_Dimension2 object. The type of the "_array" field will be changed to Integer_Array_Dimension1. The get/set operations on the one-dimensional elements will also be changed to the aaload/aastore methods of the Integer_Array_Dimension1.

3. *ServerObject transformer*: To make sure an invocation received by a proxy is correctly forwarded to the corresponding proxied class instance, this transformer will make an app class implement a specific *ServerObject* interface, which has two methods: *getID* and *getProxyForSerializing*. The *getID* method will return an Integer value to identify the app class instance, which is used to correlate this object with its proxy. The *getProxyForSerializing* method is used to handle the object serialization issue in the callback style method invocation described in Sect. 15.3.6.

Fig. 15.6 The treatment to (Integer) array type

```
public class Integer_Array_Dimension1 implements
                Integer_Array_Dimension1_Intf{
    private Integer[] _array;
    public Integer aaload(int position){
        return _array[position];
    }
    public void aastore(int position, Integer elem){
        _array[position] = elem;
    }
    ...
}
```

4. *Other transformers*: They handle the specific features of classes, including the anonymous constructor, inner class, "abstract" keyword, "final" keyword, etc. Their details are published on the website of DPartner [10].

15.3.4 Cluster App Classes

To improve the performance of runtime decision about which movable classes to offload, DPartner will cluster the frequently interacted classes and to offload them as a whole. It treats each app class as a node in the call-graph [14] of an Android app. The edge between two nodes means that the classes have one of the three relationships: *extend*, *implement*, and *use*. As shown in Fig. 15.7, class *A* extends *P*, implements *I*, and uses class *B*, *C*, and *D*. The call-value, i.e., edge weight, from *A* to *B* is ten, which means that by static bytecode analysis, it is found that *A* calls the methods of *B* ten times in its code. The call-value from *A* to *C* is six, which is less than that of *A* to *B*. It denotes that *A* depends on *B* more than on *C*. Class *P* is the parent of *A*, however, by code analysis, the method call from *A* to *P* may be less than that of *A* to *B*. In order to highlight the importance of *P*, DPartner will calculate the maximum call-value from *A* to other nodes, then assign this value to the edge from *A* to *P*. Thus in the following clustering procedure, *A* and its parent *P* will more likely be clustered together. DPartner will do the same thing on the edge of *A* to *I*.

DPartner treats the above call graph as $G = (V, E)$, where V is the set of nodes in the graph, and E is the set of edges. A cluster is defined as a sub-graph $G' = (V', E')$, where $V' \subseteq V$, and $E' \subseteq E$.

The nodes in V' has a much higher call-value with each other than with the nodes in $V - V'$. DPartner employs the Girvan and Newman [15] (shorten as G-N), a classical and often used clustering algorithm, to reveal the clusters in a graph. In the G-N algorithm, the "betweenness" of an edge is the number of shortest paths between all pairs of nodes that pass through the edge in graph *G*. The sum of the call-value of the edges on the shortest path between two nodes is smaller than that of all the other paths connecting the same nodes. The edges lying between clusters are expected to be those with the highest *betweenness* and the lowest call-value. Thus by removing such edges recursively, G-N algorithm can find a candidate cluster-separation of a graph.

DPartner uses static analysis to calculate the call-values. Comparing with dynamic analysis, the static one does not need extra auxiliary inputs such as test cases, thus can be carried out automatically. However, the call-value calculated by static code analysis may be imprecise because the number of method-calls lying between the *loop* and the *jump*-like instructions cannot be calculated precisely unless the code is actually executed. For instance, the method call from *A* to *D* in Fig. 15.7 is put in a while loop. By static code analysis, it is found that *A* calls *D* 3 times. When clustering, *A* and *C* will more likely be clustered together because they have a higher call-value than *A* to *D*. However, when the app is running, *A* will call *D* 3n times (n is the loop number). If *A* and *D* are not clustered together and are offloaded into different VMs, their in-between network communication will be very high.

Fortunately, some research projects show that the closely related classes often have highly similarity in semantics [16]. Thus, DPartner leverages the semantic similarity information to modify the call-value between each two classes for making the value more accurate. DPartner analyzes the names and contents of each two class files to decide their semantic similarity. It will segment the class name and the textual contents of a class file into a term vector: $T = < t_1, t_2, t_3, \ldots, t_m >$. The textual contents include the names and types of methods, local variables, etc. For simplicity, we use the class name as an example.

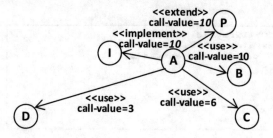

Fig. 15.7 The classes relationships in a call graph

There are two classes, $class_1$ with $name_1$: "insa.android.andgoid.strategy.Pattern", $class_2$ with $name_2$: "insa.android.andgoid.strategy. PatternStone". $name_1$ will be segmented as <insa, android, andgoid, strategy, pattern>; while $name_2$ will be segmented as <insa, android, andgoid, strategy, pattern, stone>. Then by using the Jaccard Coefficient, a classic term-vector based text matching algorithm [17], we can tell whether $name_1$ and $name_2$ have a high similarity in texts, which indicates the corresponding classes may be highly related. To make it more clear, the semantic similarity of these two classes is calculated as follows:

$$Semsim(class_i, class_j) = JacSim(T_i, T_j)$$
$$= \frac{N_{ij}}{N_i + N_j + N_{ij}}$$

In the above equation, N_{ij} represents the total number of terms contained in both T_i and T_j. For instance, the term "pattern" appears in both $name_1$ and $name_2$, so it will be counted in N_{12}. The term-containing check will be performed at the etyma level. That is to say, if "patterns" appears in T_i, and "patterned" appears in T_j, these two will be considered as the same one. N_i represents the total number of terms contained in T_i but not in T_j. N_j represents the total number of terms contained in T_j but not in T_i. DPartner will add such a $SemSim$ value to the call-value of each corresponding edge in an app's call-graph as below, so as to use the G-N algorithm to reveal the class clusters. The new call-value is calculated as follows:

$$CallValue_{A \rightarrow B} = a \times \frac{CallValue_{A \rightarrow B}}{\max(CallValue_{A \rightarrow X})}$$
$$+ \beta \times \frac{SemSim_{A \rightarrow B}}{\max(SemSim_{A \rightarrow X})},$$

$A, B, X \in V, and\ A \rightarrow X \in E$;

$\alpha\beta \in (0, 1),\ and\ \alpha + \beta = 1$

The whole clustering procedure is shown in Listing 15.1. The ranges of the $threshold$ are [1, N_{class_number}], where N_{class_number} is the number of classes in a given Android app. Therefore, the extreme cases of clustering are: (1) all the classes belong to a single cluster; (2) every single class belongs to its single class cluster. DPartner will iterate the values in [1, N_{class_number}] to get the clustering hierarchy graph of a given Android app as shown in Fig. 15.8.

For example, when $threshold$ is 2, the given app classes are clustered into two clusters. One cluster is composed of class a, c, d, e and f. The other is composed of b, g, h and i. As the second cluster contains anchored classes, i.e., b and g, thus this cluster is considered as an anchored class cluster, which means that the classes in such a cluster should never be offloaded together to execute on the server.

DPartner will store the above clustering information into the refactored Android app. Such information will be leveraged by the endpoint to decide which classes should be offloaded as a whole at runtime. To reduce the overhead of runtime decision, the endpoint leverages a selective monitoring strategy, i.e., it monitors only the execution trace of some of the most computation-intensive movable classes. If one monitored classes is predicted to be suitable for offloading, the other classes that are closely related to it will also be offloaded when necessary. For example, the most computation intensive class of an Android app is a. If the endpoint predicts that a should be offloaded, then it will search the clustering hierarchy graph from the top

```
1  c = inputApplicationClasses() g = buildCallGraph(c) callValue =
2  computeCallValue(g) SemSim = computeSemSim(c) callValue =
3  updateCallValue(callValue, semSim) b_set = computeBetweenness(g,
4  callValue) while (clusters_number < threshold)
5      b_maxSet = maxSet(b_set)
6      e_removedSet = removeEdges(b_maxSet)
7      g = g - e_removedSet ;
8      b_set = computeBetweenness(g, callValue)
9  clusters = disconnectedSubgraphs()
```

Listing 15.1 Class clustering

Fig. 15.8 The clustering hierarchy graph

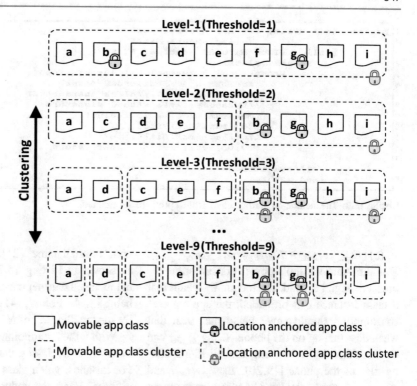

down to find the first movable cluster that contains a and meanwhile with all its classes being suitable for offloading. At first, the endpoint examines Level-1 in Fig. 15.8, and finds that the cluster at Level-1 is anchored. Therefore, the endpoint goes on to examine Level-2. The movable cluster at Level-2, i.e., the cluster $\{a, c, d, e, f\}$, happens to contain a. At this time, the endpoint will use the prediction algorithm presented in the next section to check whether the classes in the cluster are all suitable for offloading. Otherwise, it will go on to search the next level to find a cluster that can be offloaded as a whole. The extreme case of the end of searching is at Level-9, where the endpoint will surely find a cluster being suitable for offloading, i.e., the single class cluster with only class a.

15.3.5   Determine the Computations to Be Offloaded

As shown in [18], a class that has more byte-code instructions is usually the one that costs more

computing resources to run, e.g., CPU and memory. Therefore, DPartner calculates the instruction numbers of each movable app class to find the top n (e.g., $n = 3$) computation intensive classes. Then it will store these information into the refactored app. The endpoint will monitor only these top n classes to decide whether offloading is necessary by executing the following prediction algorithms at regular intervals (e.g., 1 s). The monitoring of the other classes is carried out as required, which helps reduce the runtime overhead on the smartphone.

A class instance must satisfy both the following two formulas when it is predicted to be suitable for offloading:

(a) $\forall$method m of class c, $t_{m\_phone}/t_{m\_offload}$ $= t_{m\_phone} / (d_{m\_input}/r + t_{m\_phone}/i + d_{m\_output}/r)$ $\geq \alpha$, where $\alpha \geq 1.5$. t_{m_phone} is the execution time when m is running on the phone, while $t_{m\_offload}$ is the total execution time when m is executed on the server; d_{m_input} is the method's input parameters in bytes; d_{m_output} is the method's return values in bytes; r is the data transmission rate over the network; $i = cpu_{server}/cpu_{phone}$ is the CPU cycle ratio between the server and the phone.

```
1  public class NProxy extends NParentProxy
2                      implements Nintf {
3         public  SIntf methodM(Sintf s, TIntf t) {
4            return (SIntf)
5               ProxyFacade.getEndpoint().invokeMethod(
6                  "foo.bar.N", //offloaded class
7                  this.serverobjID,//class instance ID
8                  //bytecode-level method signature
9                  "methodM(Lfoo/br/intf/SIntf;
10                 Lfoo/bar/intf/Tintf;)
11                 Lfoo/bar/intf/Sintf;",
12                 new Object[] {s, t} //parameters
13              );
14          }//end methodM
15       }//end NProxy
```

Listing 15.2 The method forwarding chain from a proxy to the endpoint

(b) $(E_{cpu\_offload} + E_{wifi\_or\_3G}) \leq E_{cpu\_local}$. E is the Android app's power consumption per time unit, e.g., 1 second. The inequality means that if class instance c is offloaded, the app's power consumption should never be greater than that when c is running on the phone. $E_{wifi\_or\_3G}$ can be calculated by monitoring the Wi-Fi/3G config files of the phone [19,20]. $E_{cpu\_offload}$ and E_{cpu_local} can be calculated by using the mapping algorithm between the bytecode instructions and energy consumption proposed in [18].

15.3.6 Offload Computations at Runtime

As shown in Fig. 15.5, its up to the endpoint to handle the actual crossing network communication between app classes. A method invocation from class X to class N is passed first from X to *NProxy* (which is represented as *NIntf*), then to the endpoint, and finally to N. An example of such method forwarding chain is shown in Listing 15.2. In a method body of *NProxy*, the "invokeMethod" method of the endpoint is used to forward the method invocation to the may-be-offloaded class N. The parameters of "invokeMethod" are: (1) the class N's full qualified class name; (2) the instance ID of class N. Each *NProxy* holds an ID of a class instance N. The ID is initialized when this proxy is created for the corresponding app class instance. Therefore, the endpoint can use the class name and ID to locate the N instance uniquely; (3) the bytecode-level method signature. Java bytecode

uses "internal name" [21] to represent a class type as shown in Listing 15.2. By using such internal names, DPartner can easily locate the method being invoked on N; (4) the parameters required for the "methodM" of N being actually executed.

With the endpoint, the communication between two classes can be easily optimized. For instance, when class A and B are located in different VMs, the endpoint has to pass method invocations through the network stack (e.g., TCP/IP). When A and B are both located in the same VM, the endpoint will use the in-VM local object reference to forward method invocations from A to B. In this way, the time-consuming network message transmission is avoided.

When invoking methods through the network stack, the method parameters have to be serialized. We should pay attention to the de/serialization mechanism of the caller object in the callback-style method invocation. For instance, the class instances of X run on the phone, and the class instance of N run on the server. An X instance calls the "handleCaller(XIntf)" method of *NIntf* (which represents an *NProxy* instance when the method is called) by passing itself as the method parameter. The invocation will cause the X instance be serialized on the phone side and then be deserialized on the server side. What should be noted is that after deserialization, there will be two X instances, one is the original X instance on the phone, and the other is the copied X instance on the server. If N processes the copied X on the server, the operations cannot be forwarded back to the X on the phone, which will make these two X

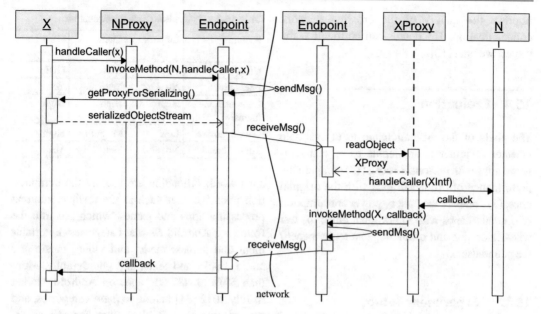

Fig. 15.9 Handling callback-style remote invocation

inconsistent. Additionally, if X is anchored, it cannot run on the server natively. To solve the above problems, the serialization of X should make an *XProxy* instance being serialized instead of the X instance itself. Any invocations on the *XProxy* instance will be called back to the X instance on the phone.

The serialization of the caller X to *XProxy* should not impact the normal serialization operation of X. For instance, when X is normally serialized, it may be designed to store its fields into the file system. To differentiate these two kinds of serialization operations, DPartner (1) first makes X implement a unique interface: *ServerObject* as described in Sect. 15.3.3; (2) then creates a unique method "getProxyForSerializing" in X through bytecode rewriting. In this method, an *XProxy* will be created and associated with the X object through instance ID. This proxy object will be used as the return value of the method; (3) the endpoint uses a specific ObjectStream for object serialization. If an object is an instance of *ServerObject*, the "getProxyForSerializing" method of the object will be invoked. The returned proxy object will finally be serialized and sent to the server. The procedure of such callback-style method invocation is shown in Fig. 15.9.

In addition to forwarding method invocations, the endpoint is also responsible for the context synchronization of class instances being offloaded. As described in Sect. 15.2.3, the general offloading procedure is to activate an object on the server/phone, deactivate its counterpart on the phone/server, and synchronize the object state from one side (e.g., phone) to another (e.g., server). The getter/setter methods of the offloaded object are used to collect and inject its states as described in Sect. 15.3.3. Dpartner collects class relationships using proxies, and tracks newly created objects using the "reflection" mechanism [22] together with a hashtable-like data structure. Additionally, the specific "SmartObjectInput/SmartOutputStream" are used to check whether a referred object of the offloaded one is serializable. If not, these streams will un/wrap the object using "NotSerializableObjWrapper", which tries to de/serialize the object's fields recursively, and send the serialized data to the other side to keep context synchronized.

Other communication related code, e.g., call-try, deadlock remover [23], and distributed garbage collection [24] are also implemented in the endpoint to form an interception chain for method invocation, which can greatly help improve the quality of the crossing network communication. The details can be found at the project website [10].

15.4   Evaluation

The goals of the evaluation are to (1) validate whether DPartner is applicable to offload real-world apps with reasonable costs; (2) compare the performance of offloaded apps with the original ones; (3) compare the battery power consumption of offloaded apps with the original ones; (4) test whether on-demand offloading can really benefit the phone users.

15.4.1   Experiment Setup

Currently, Wi-Fi is widespread in China for regions like schools, hospitals, malls, etc. For instance, The *China TeleCom corp.* has setup thousands of free Wi-Fi hotspots across the city of Beijing [25]. Therefore, we evaluate DPartner mainly with Wi-Fi connectivity. Moreover, we evaluate DPartner on smartphones that has less computing power as well as more computing power. The smartphone with less computing power is Samsung Galaxy S3 [26] with 1.4 GHz CPU, 1 GB RAM and Android 4.0. While the smartphone with more computingg power is LG Nexus 5 [27] with The server is a PC running Ubuntu 12.04 with 2.1 GHz dual-core CPU and 8 GB RAM. The phone and the server are connected by Wi-Fi with 50 ms RTT (Round Trip Time). The server uses "tc" [28] to add a controlled amount of queuing delay to the network path, which helps simulate different RTTs between the phone and the server for evaluating the offloading effects under different network conditions. We measure the battery power consumption of the phone by the Monsoon Power monitor [29], which gives the details of the power consumption for each targeted Android app.

We evaluate DPartner on three real-world Android apps and two computation-intensive apps implemented by the university of Florida as shown in Table 15.1. As described in [11,30], the

Table 15.1   The Android apps for evaluation

Features	Linpack	Chess game	Car game
UI	GUI	GUI	GUI
Interactive	No	Yes	Yes
Computation-Intensive	High	High	High
Data-Intensive	Low	Medium	High
Multi-Thread	No	Yes	Yes

apps worth offloading are usually the computation intensive ones such as the image/audio/text processing apps and games, which fall into the following Android Market categories: entertainment and games, media and video, music and audio, books and texts, and photography. More than 50 % of 487,601 apps on Android Market in July 2012 [31] belong to these categories, and we selected three typical ones for evaluation. Evaluations on other apps are available on the project website [10].

Table 15.1 shows the features of the five apps that are important to offloading. The first app is the Linpack benchmark [32] that carries out numerical linear algebra computations. The second is a chess game called Andgoid [33], an interactive app that allows a human player to place chess pieces by using the touch screen of the phone. The human and AI player each runs in a separate thread. It is more data-intensive than the Linpack app because when it is the turn of the AI player, all the chess piece positions on the chess board will be transferred to the AI class to compute the position of the next piece. The third is a 3D car game called XRace [34], a more interactive Android app. The car's direction and speed are controlled by the gravity sensor of the phone. It is also a multi-thread program. Comparing with the other two apps, the car game is the most data-intensive because it reads many data to form the 3D racing scenario, and its collision detection logic has to take in many car position data to check whether the car is running out of the road or colliding with the boundary fence. All the above three apps are computation-intensive, which means that they are much more suitable to be offloaded to take advantage of the powerful processing capability of the server.

Table 15.2 The refactoring performance of DPartner

Measurements	Linpack	Chess	Car
Original app size (KB) (.apk file)	75	233	12431
The app size after refactoring (KB)	107	306	13216
Size increased (KB)	32	73	785
# of classes in the original app (#: number)	36	43	72
# of classes after refactoring (excluding the classes that make up the app endpoint)	101	152	246
# of generated proxies	36	43	72
# of generated interfaces and other classes	29	66	102
# of classes that make up the app endpoint (using the TCP/IP communication service)	53	53	53
Total # of increased classes	118	162	227
Total # of methods in the original app	75	177	541
Total # of methods after refactoring	216	539	1642
Total # of bytecode instructions in the class methods of the original app	8219	16911	86524
Total # of bytecode instructions in the class methods of the refactored app	12982	28905	110538
# and % of movable classes	1 (2.8%)	31 (72.1%)	39 (42.2%)
Refactoring time (s)	20.2	43.7	219.8

15.4.2 Performance of Refactoring

Table 15.2 shows the refactoring performance of DPartner on the three Android apps. The size of the app after refactoring will be increased because DPartner rewrites each app class and generates proxies and interfaces for them. The endpoint code are also linked into the app. Since the size of smartphone's memory keeps growing and Android supports the "memory to SD card" app-installation feature, the increase of app size is acceptable. The refactoring time increases with the total number of bytecode instructions (just like the lines of code) of the Android app, which is also acceptable in practice because refactoring is performed before runtime.

To some extent, the percentage of movable classes implies the possibility and flexibility of computation offloading. In our experiment, the Linpack app has only 1 movable class, i.e., the Linpack.class, which performs algebra computations. The chess game has 31 movable classes, which are all used for different AI algorithms. The anchored classes of the above two apps all deal with UI interactions. The car game has 39 movable classes while its anchored classes control

the gravity sensor and draw images with Android OpenGL ES library [35].

In the movable classes, the most computation intensive one is *com.greenecomputing.linpack.Linpack* in Linpack, *insa.android.andgoid.strategy.MonteCarloAI* in the chess game, and *com.sa.xrace.collision.Line2f* in the car game. These three classes will be monitored by the endpoint at runtime as described in the last paragraph of Sect. 15.3.4. Table 15.3 shows the movable clusters containing the monitored classes. For each app, the movable clusters are arranged in the hierarchical structure just like Fig. 15.8. We manually checked the clustering results and found that all these classes were indeed closely related, which shows the correctness of clustering. Take the 3D car game as a example, the classes such as *Line2f*, *AABBbox*, and *MathUtil* are all used together for collision detection.

15.4.3 Comparison of App Performance

We compared the performance of the above three apps by running them in eight different scenarios.

Table 15.3 The movable cluster containing the monitored class

App	Cluster	Level	The classes in the movable cluster
Linpack	Linpack	Level-i (i ≥ 1)	{**Linpack**}
Chess	AI	Level-j (j ≥ 1)	{**MonteCarloAI**, UCTNode}
		Level-(j + 1)	{**MonteCarloAI**}
Car	Collision	Level-k (k ≥ 1)	{**Line2f**, AABBbox, Rectangle, MathUtil, Matrix4f, Point2f, Point3f, Plane3D, CollisionHandler}
		Level-(k + 1)	{**Line2f**, Rectangle, MathUtil, Matrix4f, Point2f, Point3f, Plane3D}
		Level-(k + 2)	{**Line2f**, Rectangle, MathUtil, Point2f}
		Level-(k + 3)	{**Line2f**}

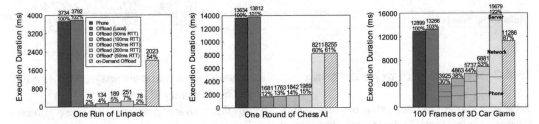

Fig. 15.10 The performance comparison of the Android apps running in different scenarios. Offload* is a special offloading test: we force apps to offload only the class that is the most computation intensive, and the RTT value of the test is 50 ms

In the first scenario, the original apps run entirely on the phone. In the next scenario, the refactored apps run entirely on the phone. In the following four scenarios, the clustered classes in Table 15.3 are offloaded to *always* execute on the server. The phone and the server are connected using Wi-Fi with different RTT values (50, 100, 150, and 200 ms). The exact clusters to be offloaded are at Level-i, Level-j, and Level-k for the three apps, respectively. In the seventh scenario, we force apps to offload only the monitored class, i.e., *Linpack*, *MonteCarloAI*, and *Line2f* executed on the server during the test with 50 ms RTT, so that we can test whether clustering can really help avoid the high overhead of the crossing network communication. The final scenario is for adapting the offloading and will be discussed in Sect. 15.4.5.

The performance comparison results are shown in Fig. 15.10. We can see that, running the refactored app entirely on the phone will increase the execution duration slightly compared with the original app. For instance, in the Linpack test, one run of the original Linpack costs 3.734 s, while the refactored Linpack costs 3.792 s, i.e., with an overhead of 0.058 s. For another instance, the time cost for drawing 100 frames of the refactored 3D car game running entirely on the phone is 0.367 s slower than the original app. The slight increase of execution time is due to that method invocations between local classes will be forwarded by the proxies and the endpoint.

However, offloading can really help improve the app performance. For instance, when offloading the Linpack cluster to the server, the execution time of the same test with 50 ms RTT is just

0.078 s or reduced by 98 %. The time for the AI to calculate the chess piece position in the original chess game is 13.63 s on average, while the time for the refactored chess game with the AI cluster being offloaded is just 1.681 s or reduced by 88 %. The execution time for drawing 100 frames in the car game is reduced by 70 %. The reason for the great performance improvement is that the computation intensive code is executed on a more powerful processor of the server other than the phone's own processor.

The quality of the network impacts the offloading effect significantly. If the RTT value becomes larger, the performance of the offloaded app will get decreased due to the fact that more time will be spent on network communication. For instance, when RTT is 50 ms, drawing 100 graph-frames in the 3D car game will cost 3.925 s. However, when RTT is 200 ms, this value is just 6.881 s or is increased by 75 %.

Offloading only the most computation intensive class but not the class cluster it belonged to will often put a negative impact on the app's performance, and even make offloading unworthy. For instance, in the "Offload*" test of the chess game, the time cost for the AI player to calculate the chess piece position is 8.211 s; while offloading the AI cluster (i.e., the cluster containing the *MonteCarloAI* and the *UCTNode* classes) can cost only 1.681 s to finish such a computation. For another instance, in the "Offload*" test of the 3D car game, drawing 100 frames will cost 15.679 s, which is even longer than that of the original app running on the phone. The total time can be divided into three parts: (1) *phone*, the time spent on the phone; (2) *network*, the time spent on the network; (3) *server*, the time spent on the server. The time spent on the network increases sharply in "Offload*" (accounting for 63 % of the total execution time of this test, as shown in Fig. 15.10). Thus we can see that offloading in the cluster unit can greatly improve the performance of an offloaded app, because it reduces the unnecessary network communication between the parts on the phone and the parts on the server.

15.4.4 Comparison of App Power Consumption

The power consumption results are shown in Fig. 15.11. When running the refactored app entirely on the phone, its power consumption will increase slightly compared with the original app, because the proxies and the endpoint in the refactored app cost energy to run. We can also see that, as offloading makes some computation intensive code be executed on the server, the energy consumption of an offloaded Android app is often reduced. For instance, in the Linpack test, running the benchmark one time will cost 3.28 J, while the result of the offloaded Linpack with 50 ms RTT is just 0.54 J or reduced by 83 %. What should be noted is that, the power of the Wi-Fi on the HTC smartphone we used is about 0.78 W [36], which may make the offloaded app's power consumption be greater than that of the original app. However, we get very small energy consumption (e.g., 0.54 J) in the offloaded tests because: (1) when the Wi-Fi device is not working, it will enter a sleep phase for saving energy. The power consumption in such a phase is about 30 mJ on the tested smartphone [36]; (2) In the Linpack app, one execution of the

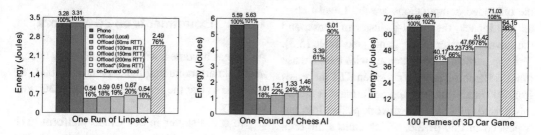

Fig. 15.11 The power consumption comparison of the Android apps running in different scenarios

benchmark will run the *Linpack* class instance 3 times to get the average test results. The number of runs (i.e., 3) will be sent as a parameter to the *Linpack* class. Therefore, in the offloaded app, the Wi-Fi channel will deliver the method request for linpack-calculation just once, and the server will execute the *Linpack* class instance three times before returning the average results. Thus the power consumption of the Wi-Fi is further reduced; (3) the time for sending one method request is very short, e.g., usually less than 10 ms. Therefore, the total power consumed by Wi-Fi will not be much when the number of the crossing network communication is relatively small. However, as shown by the "Offload*" test in Fig. 15.11, if the network communication becomes too frequent, the power consumption of Wi-Fi will increase. Thus the whole power consumption of the offloaded app will also increase. For instance, when offloading only the *Line2f* class of the 3D car game, the app will consume 30.86 more Joules than offloading the whole *Collision* class cluster. A lot of energy is wasted on the crossing network communication between the closely-related but not-together-offloaded classes.

15.4.5   The Effect of On-Demand Offloading

The last scenario in Figs. 15.10 and 15.11 shows the performance and power consumption of the three apps when offloading is adapted during the RTT value changing from 200 to 600 ms gradually in 120 s. The corresponding details are presented in Fig. 15.12 and Table 15.4. We can see that the performance plot of the apps can be divided into 3 regions. Region-1 is 0–30 s when RTT increases from 200 to 300 ms gradually. During this period, the offloaded computations are the Level-i cluster of Linpack, the Level-j cluster of chess, and the Level-k cluster of car game (see Table 15.3). The app performance decreases with the increase of RTT. Region-2 is 30–105 s when RTT increases from 300 to 550 ms. The app performances during this period fall sharply. Network packet loss has happened in this period, which causes the endpoint to retry method invocation several times.

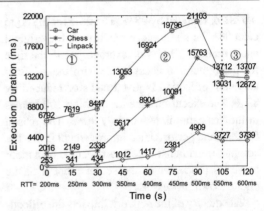

Fig. 15.12 The app performance during on-demand offloading

When found that the offloaded computations fail to satisfy the offloading requirements described in Sect. 15.3.5, the endpoint will draw these computations back to execute on the phone. For example, the endpoint of the car game will first draw back the computations of the classes in cluster (Level-k)–cluster (Level-(k + 1)), that is, the class instances belonging to cluster (Level-k) but not to cluster (Level-(k + 1)) will be drawn back to execute on the phone (see Tables 15.3 and 15.4). At this point, the offloaded computations are just the class instances of the cluster Level-(k + 1). As RTT increases continuously, the endpoint will change the contents of the offloaded computations to maintain the performance as described in Sect. 15.3.4. For example, the offloaded computations of the car game changes from Level-(k + 1) to Level-(k + 2), then to Level-(k + 3), and finally to none. In the 105th seconds, all the computations of the tested apps have come back to execute on the phone till the end of the test as shown in Region-3 of the plot.

15.4.6   Experiments on 3G Network

As 3G has become a widely accepted way to connect a smartphone and the servers in Cloud, we continue to test the refactored apps with 3G connectivity.

We use a server in our Cloud platform [37], which can be publicly accessed using 3G. The

Table 15.4 The on-demand offloaded computations in detail

Time (s)	RTT (ms)	Offloaded computations			Description
		Linpack	Chess	Car	
0	200	Level-i	Level-j	Level-k	Offloaded execution, performance decreases with the increase of RTT
15	250	Level-i	Level-j	Level-k	
30	300	Level-i	Level-j	Level-k	
45	350	Level-i	Level-j	Level-k	Network packet loss, invocation retry, from offloading only the suitable computations to offloading none
60	400	Level-i	Level-(j+1)	Level-(k+1)	
75	450	Level-i	Level-(j+1)	Level-(k+2)	
90	500	Level-i	Level-(j+1)	Level-(k+3)	
105	550	None	None	None	
120	600	None	None	None	Local execution

server is a Ubuntu 8.04 Xen VM [38] with 2.0 GHz four-core CPU and 1 GB RAM running on IBM blade HS22. We use the Chess app in the experiment with the experiment setup remained the same as previously, except that the offloaded cluster is accessed using 3G. The remained parts of the app on the phone use HTTP instead of TCP connections to interact with the offloaded parts of the app running on the server. The RTT value of the 3G test is about 360 ms, the upload speed is 23.4 kb/s, and the download speed is 28.9 kb/s.

Figures 15.13 and 15.14 present the performance and power consumption results, respectively. We have three observations from the results. First, offloading can really help improve the app performance a lot even if we connect the phone with the server using a relatively slower network connection of 3G instead of Wi-Fi. The average execution time of "one round of Chess AI" is 2.426 s or reduced by 82.2 % in 3G test compared with that of the original app running entirely on the phone. Second, The performance of the server greatly affects the offloading effects. The Cloud server we used in the experiment is much more powerful than the PC we used in the prior tests.

Therefore, the time delay brought by the slow network connection of 3G can be partly offset by the high computing capability of the Cloud server, and the finally obtained offloading effects are still very good. Third, 3G costs more energy than Wi-Fi. The power consumption of "one round of Chess AI" with Wi-Fi is 1.01 J on average. The consumed energy increases to 2.56 J in the 3G test. The above results indicate that offloading can save energy and improve performance for smartphone apps. However, this usually depends on the server's performance and the amounts of data exchanged through the network. Therefore, computation offloading is more suitable to offload computation-intensive apps with only a small amount of data exchanged between the server and the client [11], especially on 3G network.

15.5   Related Work

The idea of using a strong server to enhance the processing capabilities of a weak device (e.g., mobile phone) is not new [11]. Many early research projects have tried to automatically

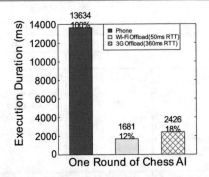

Fig. 15.13 The chess's performance in 3G test

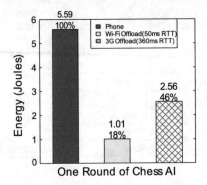

Fig. 15.14 The chess's power consumption in 3G test

partition a standalone desktop app to have some parts of it executed remotely on the server. The research on mobile computing then leverage such an idea to realize computation offloading on a smartphone.

Coign [39] is an early work on computation offloading. It takes the binary code of a Windows .COM application, then by using code interception and rewriting, it turns the app into a DCOM application with some COM components running on a common PC (i.e., a weak device) and the rest running on a powerful server (i.e., a strong surrogate). In this way, the performance of the original application can be improved. J-Orchestra [40] and JavaParty [41] are the early work on offloading standalone desktop Java applications. J-Orchestra works on the Java bytecode level, while Java-Party works on the source code level. They both require developers to manually tell the offloading tool about which class can be offloaded. For instance, J-Orchestra provides a GUI to ask developers to select the can-be-offloaded classes. Java-Party asks developers to annotate the source code

with the "Remote" keyword. Then the compiler provided by these tools will compile these selected classes to generate the RMI stubs/skeletons for them [42], so that the app is turned to be a client/server one by using RMI as the communication channel. The work of J-Orchestra and JavaParty cannot be directly used for offloading Android apps. One reason is that Android does not support RMI.

The research on mobile computing follows the above early work to offload computations running on the phone to run on the server. AIDE [43,44] can partition a mobile Java application at runtime through JVM instrumentation. It leverages a fuzzy control model to decide which class should be transferred to the server. The code on the phone and the code on the server can cooperate to work with the support of the modified JVM. Similarly, CloneCloud [45] augments the performance of Smartphone apps through *clone cloud execution*. It modifies the Android Dalvik VM to provide an application *partitioner* and an *execution runtime* to help apps running on the VM offload tasks to execute on a cloned VM hosted by a Cloud server. MAUI [46] requires developers to annotate the can-be-offloaded methods of a .Net mobile application by using the "Remoteable" annotation. Then the MAUI analyzer will decide which method should really be offloaded through runtime profiling. Cuckoo [30] is an offloading framework for Android apps. It requires developers to follow a specific programming model to make some parts of the app be offloaded. JDOP [47] mainly focuses on the algorithm of how to distribute objects among the phone and the server to achieve high app performance, and provides the request resolver and dispatcher facilities to make objects be able to offload. Spectra [48] requires developers to specify movable classes and modify the application. It then performs offloading at the granularity of methods. Puppeteer [49] targets at data adaptation via offloading when facing with limited bandwidth, and it is applicable for only COM/DCOM-like component-based applications.

Our offloading approach and the DPartner tool are different from the above work mainly in the aspects below. First, our approach is transparent to developers. We neither require them to annotate the code of an Android app to decide which class should be offloaded, nor require them to follow a specific programming model to redesign the whole app. Second, offloading at the granularity of class/object makes our approach be more suitable for object-oriented programs. Third, our approach can enable the on-demand offloading of an given Android app, while few of the above existing work can support such a feature. What should be noted is that, although the research projects such as AIDE, CloneCloud, and MAUI have tried to make offloading be on-demand. They all have some obvious drawbacks that can make them be impractical. For instance, AIDE and CloneCloud require using a modified JVM, and MAUI requires developers to annotate source code methods. DPartner does not impose such requirements. It can refactor any Android app into the one supporting on-demand offloading, no matter the app is newly designed or is already installed on a phone.

15.6   Conclusion and Future Work

In this chapter, we presented DPartner for automatically refactoring an Android app into one implementing the on-demand computation offloading design pattern, which can transfer some computation-intensive tasks from a smartphone to a server so that the task execution time and battery power consumption of the app can be reduced significantly. DPartner will be improved and further validated as follows. First, more experiments with real-world Android apps will be done, especially on 3G network. Second, to support refactoring and offloading obfuscated apps. DPartner leverages Dexmaker [50] and ASM [51] for bytecode refactoring. These libraries do not fully support obfuscated bytecode currently. Third, better measuring tools will be used. For example, we will use an external current meter to measure the power consumption of a phone much more accurately, and use routers to measure the amount of network packets transmitted. Fourth, more rules and algorithms will be explored and evaluated for deciding which class should be offloaded. We will put further

results on the website of DPartner: https://code. google.com/p/dpartner/.

Acknowledgments We thank Professor Lu Zhang of Peking University, Professor Tao Xie of North Carolina State University, Professor Zhendong Su of the University of California - Davis, and the anonymous reviewers for their valuable feedback on an earlier version of this paper. This work is supported by the National Basic Research Program of China (973) under Grant No. 2009CB320703; the National Natural Science Foundation of China under Grant No. 61121063, 60933003, 61003010; the European Commission Seventh Framework Programme under grant no. 231167; the IBM-University Joint Study and the NCET.

References

1. Android. http://www.android.com/
2. Smartphone market share. http://www.idc.com/getdoc.jsp?containerId=prUS23503312
3. The applications number of the google play. http://en.wikipedia.org/wiki/Google_Play
4. Google play. https://play.google.com/store
5. Apps drain battery power. http://www.droidforums.net/forum/droid-razr-support/216454-battery-drain.html
6. Android application requirements. http://www.netmite.com/android/mydroid/development/pdk/docs/system_requirements
7. M. Fowler, K. Beck, J. Brant, W. Opdyke, D. Roberts, *Refactoring: Improving the Design of Existing Code* (1999)
8. Android interface definition language (aidl). http://developer.android.com/guide/developing/tools/aidl.html
9. Android api demo. http://developer.android.com/resources/samples/ApiDemos/
10. Dpartner. http://code.google.com/p/dpartner/
11. K. Kumar, J. Liu, L. Yung-Hsiang, B. Bhargava, A survey of computation offloading for mobile systems. Mob. Netw. Appl. **18**(1), 129–140 (2013)
12. L. Zhang, J. Luo, H. Li, J. Sun, H. Mei, A biting-down approach to hierarchical decomposition of object-oriented systems based on structure analysis. Softw. Maint. Evol. Res. Pract. **22**(8), 567–596 (2010)
13. Android service. http://developer.android.com/reference/android/app/Service.html
14. Call graph. http://en.wikipedia.org/wiki/Call_graph
15. M. Girvan, M.E.J. Newman, Community structure in social and biological networks. Proc. Natl. Acad. Sci. **99**(12), 7821–7826 (2002)
16. J.I. Maletic, A. Marcus, Supporting program comprehension using semantic and structural information, in *Proceedings of the International Conference on Software Engineering, ICSE 2001* (2001), pp. 103–112

17. J. Han, J. Pei, M. Kamber, *Data Mining: Concepts and Techniques* (Elsevier, 2011)

18. W. Binder, J. Hulaas, Using bytecode instruction counting as portable CPU consumption metric. Electron. Notes Theor. Comput. Sci. **153**(2), 57–77 (2006)

19. Powertutor. http://powertutor.org/

20. L. Zhang, B. Tiwana, Z. Qian, Z. Wang, R.P. Dick, Z.M. Mao, L. Yang, Accurate online power estimation and automatic battery behavior based power model generation for smartphones. In: *Proceedings of the International Conference on Hardware/Software Codesign and System Synthesis, CODES 2010* (2010), pp. 105–114

21. The $java^{TM}$ virtual machine specification. http://docs.oracle.com/javase/specs/jvms/se7/html/index.html

22. Java reflection. http://java.sun.com/developer/technicalArticles/ALT/Reflection/

23. E. Tilevich, Y. Smaragdakis, Portable and efficient distributed threads for java, in *Proceedings of the ACM/IFIP/USENIX International Middleware Conference, Middleware 2004* (2004), pp. 478–492

24. S.E. Abdullahi, G.A. Ringwood, Garbage collecting the internet: a survey of distributed garbage collection. ACM Comput. Surv. (CSUR) **30**(3), 330–373 (1998)

25. Wi-fi hotspots in beijing. http://www.theregister.co.uk/2011/11/03/china_free_wifi/

26. Samsung galaxy s3. http://www.samsung.com/global/galaxys3/

27. LG Nexus 5

28. Traffic control settings,. http://manpages.ubuntu.com/manpages/lucid/man8/tc.8.html

29. Monsoon power monitor. https://www.msoon.com/LabEquipment/PowerMonitor/

30. R. Kemp, N. Palmer, T. Kielmann, H. Bal, Cuckoo: a computation offloading framework for smartphones. In: *Proceedings of the International Conference on Mobile Computing, Applications, and Services, MobiCase 2012* (2010), pp. 59–79

31. The android application categories. http://www.appbrain.com/stats/android-market-app-categories

32. Linpack. https://market.android.com/details?id=com.greenecomputing.linpack

33. Chess game. http://code.google.com/p/andgoid/

34. Car game. http://code.google.com/p/xrace-sa/

35. Android openGL ES. http://developer.android.com/guide/topics/graphics/opengl.html

36. HTC tattoo. http://www.htc.com/europe/product/tattoo/overview.html

37. Internetware testbed. http://icloud.internetware.org/

38. Xen. http://www.xen.org/

39. G.C. Hunt, M.L. Scott, The coign automatic distributed partitioning system, in *Proceedings of the USENIX Symposium on Operating Systems Design and Implementation, OSDI 1999* (1999), pp. 187–200

40. E. Tilevich, Y. Smaragdakis, J-Orchestra: enhancing java programs with distribution capabilities. ACM Trans. Softw. Eng. Methodol. **19**(1), 1–41 (2009)

41. M. Philippsen, M. Zenger, Javaparty: transparent remote objects in java. Concurr. Pract. Exp. **9**(11), 1225–1242 (1997)

42. Remote method invocation (RMI). http://docs.oracle.com/javase/tutorial/rmi/overview.html

43. G. Xiaohui, K. Nahrstedt, A. Messer, I. Greenberg, D. Milojicic, Adaptive offloading for pervasive computing. IEEE Perv. Comput. **3**(3), 66–73 (2004)

44. A. Messer, I. Greenberg, P. Bernadat, D. Milojieie, D. Chen, T.J. Giuli, X. Gu, Towards a distributed platform for resource-constrained devices, in *Proceedings of the International Conference on Distributed Computing Systems, ICDCS 2002* (2002), pp. 43–51

45. B.-G. Chun, S. Ihm, P. Maniatis, M. Naik, A. Patti, Clonecloud: elastic execution between mobile device and cloud, in *Proceedings of the European Conference on Computer Systems, EuroSys 2011* (2011), pp. 301–314

46. E. Cuervoy, A. Balasubramanianz, S. Saroiux, R. Chandrax, P. Bahlx, Maui: making smartphones last longer with code offload, in *Proceedings of the International Conference on Mobile Systems, Applications, and Services, MobiSys 2010* (2010), pp. 49–62

47. L. Wang, M. Franz, Automatic partitioning of object-oriented programs for resource-constrained mobile devices with multiple distribution objectives, in *Proceedings of the International Conference on Parallel and Distributed Systems, ICPADS 2008* (2008), pp. 369–376

48. J. Flinn, S.Y. Park, M. Satyanarayanan, Balancing performance, energy, and quality in pervasive computing, in *Proceedings of the IEEE International Conference on Distributed Computing Systems, ICDCS 2002* (2002), pp. 217–226

49. E. De Lara, D.S. Wallach, W. Zwaenepoel, Puppeteer: component-based adaptation for mobile computing. In: *Proceedings of the USENIX Symposium on Internet Technologies and Systems, USITS 2001* (2001), pp. 159–170

50. Dexmaker: Programmatic code generation for android. http://code.google.com/p/dexmaker/

51. ASM: A java bytecode engineering library. http://download.forge.objectweb.org/asm/asm4-guide.pdf

Towards Architecture-Based Management of Platforms in Cloud

16

Abstract

System management becomes increasingly complex and brings high costs, especially with the advent of Cloud Computing. In a Cloud, numerous platforms like Virtual Machines (VMs) and Middleware have to be managed to make the whole system work cost-effectively after an application is deployed. For controlling the management cost, in particular the manual management cost, many computer programs have been developed to take over manual management tasks or reduce their complexity and difficulty. These programs are usually hard-coded by languages like Java and C++, which bring enough capability and flexibility but also cause high programming effort and cost. This chapter proposes an architecture based approach to developing the management programs in a simple but powerful enough manner. First of all, the manageability (such as APIs, configuration files and scripts) of a given platform is abstracted as a runtime model of the platform's software architecture, which can automatically and immediately propagate any observable runtime changes of the target platforms to the corresponding architecture models, and vice versa. Then the management programs will be developed using modeling languages, instead of those relatively low-level programming languages. Such architecture-level management programs bring many advantages related to the performance, interoperability, reusability and simplicity. The experiment on a real-world cloud and the comparison with the programming language approach demonstrate the feasibility, effectiveness and benefits of the new approach for management program development.

Parts of this chapter were reprinted with kind permission from Springer Science+Business Media: <Frontiers of Computer Science, Towards architecture-based management of platforms in cloud, volume 6, 2012, 388–397, Gang Huang, Xing Chen, Ying Zhang and Xiaodong Zhang, figure number(s), and any original (first) copyright notice displayed with material>.

© Springer Science+Business Media Singapore 2016
H. Mei and J. Lü, *Internetware*, DOI 10.1007/978-981-10-2546-4_16

Keywords
Cloud management · Software architecture · Models at runtime

16.1   Introduction

Nowadays, more and more software applications are built or migrated to run in a cloud, with the goal of reducing IT costs and complexities. The layers of cloud computing can be divided into three kinds, including Infrastructure-as-a-Service, Platform-as-a-Service and Software-as-a-Service, which sit on top of one another. Other soft layers can be added on top of these layers as well, with elements like cost and security extending the size and flexibility of the cloud [1]. This trend brings unprecedented challenges to system management of Cloud. The increasingly efforts of platform (note that there's no consensus on the definition of platforms in cloud, while we consider the virtual machines, operating systems and middleware as platforms in this chapter) management mainly come from the following two aspects:

On one hand, the virtualization makes the physical resources easier to share and control but increases the complexity of management mainly because the virtualized resources are much more and less reliable than the physical ones. For instance, given an application that uses 10 nodes, cloud administrators have to manage the required 10 VMs as well as the physical nodes hosting these VMs. On the other hand, the service oriented natures of cloud make the management much more complex than the product centric natures of traditional datacenters because cloud applications can use different types of platforms and require resources on demand. For instance, a 3-tier JEE (Java Enterprise Edition) application typically has to use the web server, EJB server and DB server. These servers have different management mechanisms. An EJB server should comply with JMX management specification and rely on the JMX API, while a DB server is usually managed through the SQL-like scripts. In addition, the EJB server can usually sustain the running of several applications simultaneously. What's more, all of the platforms are in a resource sharing and competing environment. Administrators have to carefully coordinate each part to make the whole system work correctly and cost effectively.

To tame the complexity of manual system management, many programs are built to carry out management tasks automatically. Such a management program usually uses with the four-stage autonomic loop proposed by IBM [2]: monitor the runtime system and collect the critical data concerned, analyze the collected data to find if the system needs a reconfiguration, plan a proper reconfiguration procedure, and execute reconfigurations on the system. Such a management program is usually implemented in general purpose programming languages like Java and C/C++, which can bring enough power and flexibility but also cause high programming effort and cost. For instance, the existing VM and middleware platforms have already provided adequate proprietary APIs (e.g., JMX) to be used by monitoring and executing related codes. Administrators first have to be familiar with these APIs and then build programs upon them. Such a work is not easy due to the heterogeneity of platforms and the huge numbers of APIs provided. In a management program, proper APIs have to be chosen for use and different types of APIs (e.g., JMX and scripts) have to be made interoperable with each other. Such boring work is not the core of the management logics comprised by analyzing and planning related codes, but it has to be done to make the whole program run effectively. During this procedure, the irrelevant APIs as well as the collected low-level data can sometimes make administrators exhausted and frustrated. Furthermore, as the programs are built on the codes that directly connect with the runtime systems, they are not easy for reuse. Administrators have to write many different programs to manage different cloud applications and their platforms even the management mechanisms are the same. In addition, hard-coding the analyzing and planning related codes will also bring high costs. Although many advanced techniques such as model checking [3] can help to mitigate the complexity, administrators have to adapt the codes to the requirements of various model checkers. Therefore, the finally generated codes are very long and difficult to understand.

The fundamental challenge faced by the development of management tasks is the conceptual gap between the problem and the implementation domains [4]. To bridge the gap, using approaches that require extensive handcraft implementations such as hard-coding in general purpose programming languages like Java will give rise to the programming complexity. Software architecture acts as a bridge between requirements and implementations. It describes the gross structure of a software system with a collection of managed elements and it has been used to reduce the complexity and cost mainly resulted from the difficulties faced by understanding the large-scale and complex software system recently [5]. So it is a natural idea to understand management tasks through modeling the architecture of the cloud. Current research in the area of model driven engineering (MDE) supports systematic transformation of problem-level abstractions to software implementations [6]. The complexity of bridging the gap could be tackled through developing automated programs based on the model that describes the architecture of the cloud and through the automated support for transforming architectural models to running systems and vice versa. What's more, many model-centric analyzing and planning methods and mechanisms are already developed for use [6], such as architecture styles, constraints and model checkers. Programs based on models can benefit from these techniques to build their own analyzing and planning parts.

This chapter proposes a runtime architecture-based approach to managing the platforms such as middleware and VMs of the cloud. We construct an architecture-based model of the cloud for platform management and ensure the proper synchronization between the system and its model. Any change of the runtime model will be immediately propagated into the runtime system and vice versa. Then we evaluate our approach by comparing it to the hard-coding approach in terms of the performance, interoperability, reusability and simplicity. The evaluation results prove that the runtime architecture-based management is cost-effective and promising in the cloud environment.

The rest of this chapter is organized as follows: Sect. 16.2 presents an example to show the importance and necessity of architecture-based management of platforms in Cloud. Sections 16.3 and 16.4 describe our approach in detail. Sections 16.5 and 16.6 report the evaluation and related work of our approach. Section 16.7 concludes this chapter and identifies our future work.

16.2 Motivating Example

Many automated programs have been built to tame the complexity of manual management and most of them are hard-coded in general purpose languages like Java. However, it may result in several difficulties to develop management programs in such general purpose languages. For instance, platforms in the cloud consist of different types of resources which need to be managed collaboratively. Administrators have to be familiar with the management APIs and then build programs upon them. While developing a management program, they have to choose proper APIs for use and make different types of APIs interpretable with each other, as shown in Listing 16.1.

Such code fragments are not the core of management logics compared with the analyzing and planning related codes, but it has to be developed to make the whole program run effectively. Many similar code fragments are required for a simple task. As shown in Listing 16.1, the code fragment for fetching the value of the maxThreads attribute in a JOnAS (a popular open source Java application server) through JMX API is more than 20 LOC (Line of Code). What's more, administrators have to construct the adapters to invoke the different types of management interfaces such as JMX and Script.

```
1   /*
2   *JAVA: To get the value of the maxThreads of a JOnAS
3   *through the JMX.
4   */
5   public int getMaxThreads(String port)
6   {
7       //To prepare to invoke the interface
8       String objName = "jonas:type-Connector,port=" + port;
9       String attributeName = "maxThreads";
10      MBeanServerConnection mbeanServerConn = null;
11      try
12      {
13          JMXServiceURL connURL = new JMXServiceURL (
14          "service:jmx:rmi://localhost/jndi/rmi://localhost
15          :1099/jrmpconnector_jonas");
16          JMXConnector connector = JMXConnectorFactory.
17          newJMXConnector(connURL, null);
18          connector.connect(null);
19          mbeanServerConn = connector.getMBeanServerConnection();
20      }
21      ...
22      //To invoke the specific management interface
23      try
24      {
25          attributeValue = (Integer) mbeanServerConn;
26          getAttribute(obj, attributeName);
27      }
28      catch (AttributeNotFoundException e)
29      {
30      ...
31      /*
32      *JAVA: To set the value of the memory of a virtual machine
33      *through the script
34      */
35      public String setMem(String imgIp, String mem)
36      {
37          try
38          {
39              String[] args = new String[4];
40              args[0] = "sh";
41              args[1] = "/opt/xen/setMem.sh";
42              args[2] = imgIp;
43              args[3] = mem;
44              ProcessBuilder builder = new ProcessBuilder(args);
45              Process process = builder.start();
46          ...
```

Listing 16.1: An Example for Programming in Java

When using our approach, the programs become much simpler and shorter. Listing 16.2 shows the architecture-based program doing the similar management task, which is written in QVT [7], a widely adopted modeling language. The architecture-based model can shield programmers from the relatively low-level details of the managed platforms.

With the help of the runtime architecture-based model, administrators can focus on the manage-ment targets (e.g. VMs and middleware) and program in the architecture level, without developing code fragments to invoke management APIs. The architecture-based model is abstracted from the underlying infrastructure of Cloud as shown in Fig. 16.1, and the synchronization engine is needed to reflect the cloud into a model and ensures a bidirectional consistency between the system and the model. For instance, in this scenario, the synchronization engine must build a

```
1  /*
2  *QVT: To do memory allocation depending on
3  *the value of the thread pool
4  */
5  modeltype Cloud use "http://Cloud";
6  transformation Check(inout cloudModel:Cloud);
7  mapping Platform::check()
8     when {self.usedThreadPool > 300 and self.Memory < 2048;}
9     {
10        self.Memory := 2048;
11    }
12 main()
13 {
14    cloudModel.objectsOfType(Platform)->map check();
15 }
```

Listing 16.2: An Example for the Languages of QVT

model element for the JOnAS platform in the runtime model. When the management program deletes the model element of JOnAS, the synchronization engine must detect this change, identify which platform this removed element stands for and finally invoke the script to shut down the JOnAS platform.

16.3   An Architecture-Based Model for Platform Management in Cloud

16.3.1   Approach Overview

We provide an architecture-based runtime model for administrators to develop automated programs of platform management in the architecture level, and the correct synchronization between the model and the runtime system is ensured. The inputs of our approach include a meta-model for platform management specifying what kinds of elements can be managed in Cloud and an Access Model of the configurations specifying how to use the management APIs to monitor and modify those manageable elements. Then the runtime software architecture of the target system is automatically constructed by the code generated by SM@RT tool, which is proposed in [8].

The approach is applicable on the following premises. First, the SM@RT tool is not intrusive, that is, neither instructs non-manageable systems nor extends inadequate APIs. As a result, the man-

aged elements in Cloud such as virtual machines, operating systems and middleware should provide their own management mechanisms, API or script. This premise is feasible for the popular and well-developed platforms. Second, we reflect a direct model for the cloud (that means the model is homogeneous with the architecture of the cloud: each model element stands for one managed element in the runtime system). Note that SM@RT supports automatically just-in-time synchronization between two heterogeneous models [9] and then cloud administrators can define their own architectural models and the mapping to our built-in models.

16.3.2   The Architecture-Based Meta-Model

As shown in Fig. 16.1, physical nodes are the basic elements to compose the foundation of the cloud. The virtualization handles how images [1] of operating systems, middleware, and applications are pro-created and allocated to the given physical machines. The images could be moved around and put into production environment on demand. The virtual machines occupy resources such as computing power, memory and so on from physical machines. Upon them, different types of operating systems organize resources to support the basic environment for software running and network accessing. There is always only one middleware product in a virtual machine for the

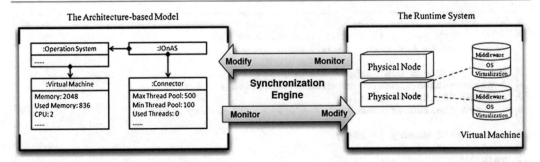

Fig. 16.1 A Common structure of the synchronization engine between the architectural model and runtime system

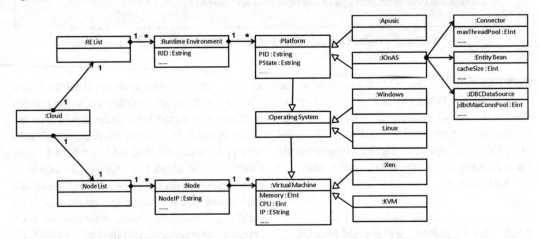

Fig. 16.2 The architecture-based meta-model for platform management in cloud

reason of isolation. The virtualized resources, operating system and middleware compose the platform and several platforms are organized properly to provide the runtime environment for a whole system. These elements above should be managed collaboratively. Therefore, we construct an architecture-based meta-model of the cloud for platform management as shown in Fig. 16.2, whose instantiation is the runtime model.

The *NodeList* class (lower left) represents the list of physical nodes in the cloud, which compose the shared infrastructure. The Node class and the *VirtualMachine* class separately represent physical nodes and virtual machines. Different types of virtualization products such as Xen and KVM are similar in management APIs, although they are different in implementations. So the *Xen* class and the *KVM* class (lower right) may be regarded as the subclasses of the *VirtualMachine* class. Therefore, the elements of nodes and virtual machines,

and the relations between them in the model reflect the working conditions of the shard infrastructure in the cloud.

The *RuntimeEnvironment* class (upper) represents the runtime environment for a whole system, which may contain more than one platform. The *Platform* class represents the platform which is the main managed element in the model. Platform, OS and VM consist of VM appliance [10] which may be regarded as one entire managed element. Therefore, the *Platform* class inherits the *OperatingSystem* class and the *VirtualMachine* class. Through the model elements of *Platform*, the attributes of the operating system and the virtualized resources may be accessed as well. And the subclasses of the *Platform* class represent different types of middleware products such as *JOnAS* and *Apusic*, whose architecture we have discussed in [8].

The architecture-based meta-model specifies what kinds of elements can be managed in Cloud and would help administrators understand their management tasks.

16.3.3 Runtime Changes

Given the architecture-based meta-model, we also need to identify the changes enabled by the model. Depending on the nature of the initiating agent, the changes can be classified as external changes (initiated by external entities) or internal changes (applied by the management system). For example, it is an external change that a node in the cloud does not work properly. Then the internal changes should be adopted to adjust it.

In this context, it becomes clear that for management purposes it is important to provide a comprehensive identification of the internal changes in Cloud, as they define the scope of potential actions that can be applied by the automated programs. The cloud platform can be managed at the levels of middleware, operating systems and virtualized resources. Table 16.1 provides a short list of the primitives which includes several main types of management operations. For each operation we detail the management operation names, the required arguments and the changes it causes to the configuration when applied (including value changes and the existence or not of the elements) and the management operations. It is possible to remove existing elements, and instantiate new runtime elements defined. The attributes of the existing units can also be adjusted, with controlling over their property configurations.

Although there are hundreds of management APIs in the cloud, we could model them into the Access Model [8] through specifying how to invoke the APIs to manipulate each type of elements. Where meta-element is the set of all the elements in the architecture-based meta-model (classes, attributes, etc.), the manipulation is the set of all types of manipulations, which are summarized in Table 16.2. The management operations in Table 16.1 are also classified according to the rules.

16.4 Implementations of the Runtime Architecture-Based Model

We define the architecture-based meta-model and the Manipulation on the Eclipse Modeling Framework (EMF) [11], and then generate the synchronization codes to maintain the causal links between model and system through our SM@RT tool [8]. The tool is an extension of EMF, and it generates the model listener, model proxy, and system proxy specific to the target system. Specifically, it generates a Java class for each of the MOF classes in the system meta-model, implementing the EObject interface defined by Ecore.

We have also constructed some architecture-based runtime model of virtualization products like Xen and JEE servers like JOnAS and Apusic, as shown in Table 16.3. It should be noted that the size of these models just reflects the manageability, not the size or functionality, of these products. Using these architecture-based models, administrators can cost-effectively develop automated programs in modeling languages for platform management in Cloud.

Table 16.1 Definition of some runtime changes

Name	Argument	Post condition
CreateAVM	Node rn, Image ri, Property[] props	$\exists$ VM rv, rv $\in$ rn.vms $\cap$ rv instanceof ri $\cap$ props $\subseteq$ rv.properties
ShutdownAVM	Node rn, VM rv	rv $\notin$ rn.vms
MigrateAVM	Node rnI, VM rv, Node rnO	rv $\notin$ rnI.vms $\cap$ rv $\in$ rnO.vms
PauseAVM	Node rn, VM rv	rv $\in$ rn.vms $\cap$ rv.state = STOPED
UnpauseAVM	Node rn, VM rv	rv $\in$ rn.vms $\cap$ rv.state = STARTED
ConfPProp	RuntimeUnit ru, Property[] props	props $\subseteq$ ru.properties

Table 16.2 All kinds of manipulations

Name	Meta element	Parameter	Description
Get	Property(1)	–	Get the value of the property
Set	Property(1)	newValue	Set the property as new Value
List	Property(*)	–	Get a list of values of this property
Add	Property(*)	toAdd	Add to Add into the value list of this property
Remove	Property(*)	toRemove	Remove to Remove from the list of this property
Lookfor	Class	Condition	Find an element according to condition
Identify	Class	Other	Check if this element equals to other
Auxiliary	Package	–	User-defined auxiliary operations
Internal Changes	Manipulation		
CreateAVM	Add		
ShutdownAVM	Remove		
MigrateAVM	Auxiliary		
PauseAVM	Set		
UnpauseAVM	Set		
ConfPProp	Set		

16.5　Evaluation

The previous sections have given the detailed description of our runtime model of the cloud. In this section, we present a set of experiments to evaluate our approach. The experiment is done on a cloud environment: Internetware Test Bed [12]. It is a research cloud project supported by the Nation Key Basic Research and Development Program of China. The Internetware Cloud provides on-demand VMs as well as middleware infrastructures (e.g. JEE server and DB server) for cloud users. We have applied the architecture-based model to the cloud and written a set of automated programs in QVT on the model.

We evaluate our approach by comparing it with the hand-coding approach in two scenarios. In the first experiment, we take anti-pattern detection [13] for example to prove that our approach has advantages related to the performance and the reusability. In the second experiment, we take VM states checking for example to validate the advan-

Table 16.3 Information about some architecture-based models

Runtime system	Number of elements	Number of manipulations
JOnAS	28	271
Apusic	26	351
Xen	8	33

tages of our approach on the interoperability and simplicity.

16.5.1　Anti-pattern Detection

A pattern is a kind of conclusion of well-known experience, which describes an effective solution to repeated problems. As an extension, an anti-pattern describes a commonly occurring solution that generates decidedly negative consequences. With the architecture-based model, administrators can easily develop programs of anti-pattern detec-

NO	Anti-pattern about JSP and Servlet	Ecperf	Executing Time(ms)			Line of Code		
			Java	QVT	Extra Time	Java	QVT	Reduced LOC
1	Ignoring Reality	√	46	91	98%	23	5	78%
2	Too Much Code	√	431	709	65%	22	5	77%
3	Embedded Navigational Information	√	293	453	55%	32	5	84%
4	Too Much Data in Session		775	1135	46%	26	5	81%
5	Ad Lib Taglib		735	1172	59%	25	5	80%
6	Accessing Entities Directly	√	53	87	64%	23	5	78%

//Programming in Java

```
1.  //JAVA: Too Much Data in Session
2.  EList<JSP> jsps;
3.  //To get the list of JSPs
4.  jsps = new EObjectResolvingEListForWrapping<JSP>(
5.      JSP.class, this,
6.      JOnASPackage.WEB_MODULE_JSPS,
7.      JOnASPackage.eINSTANCE.getJSP());
8.  /*
9.   * To count the number of the pattern of
10.  * "session.setAttribute"in each JSP
11.  */
12. ((EObjectResolvingEListForWrapping<JSP>) jsps)
13. .refreshWrap();
14. for(JSP j: jsps)
15. {
16.     java.util.regex.Pattern pattern = java.util.regex.
17.     Pattern.compile("session.setAttribute");
18.     java.util.regex.Matcher matcher = pattern.matcher(
19.         j.getCode());
20.     int count = 0;
21.     while(matcher.find())
22.         count ++;
23.     if(count > 10)
24.         return 0;
25. }
26. return 1;
```

```
1.  //JAVA: Ad Lib Taglib
2.  EList<JSP> jsps;
3.  //To get the list of JSPs
4.  jsps = new EObjectResolvingEListForWrapping<JSP>(
5.      JSP.class, this,
6.      JOnASPackage.WEB_MODULE_JSPS,
7.      JOnASPackage.eINSTANCE.getJSP());
8.  /*
9.   * To count the number of the pattern of
10.  * "taglib" in each JSP
11.  */
12. ((EObjectResolvingEListForWrapping<JSP>) jsps)
13. .refreshWrap();
14. for(JSP j: jsps){
15.     java.util.regex.Pattern pattern = java.util.regex.
16.     Pattern.compile("taglib");
17.     java.util.regex.Matcher matcher = pattern.matcher(
18.         j.getCode());
19.     int count = 0;
20.     while(matcher.find())
21.         count ++;
22.     if(count > 3)
23.         return 0;
24. }
25. return 1;
```

//Programming in QVT

	Ignoring Reality	`when(self.deploymentDescriptor.find("form-error-page") = 0)`
	Too Much Code	`when(self.jsps[JSP]->exists(jsp	jsp.code.length() > 5000))`
	Embedded Navigational Information	`when(self.jsps[JSP]->exists(jsp	jsp.code.find(".jsp") <> 0 or jsp.code.find(".JSP") <> 0))`
√	Too Much Data in Session	`when(self.jsps[JSP]->exists(jsp | jsp.sessionAttributeSize > 10))`
√	Ad Lib Taglib	`when(self.jsps[JSP]->exists(jsp|jsp.tagLibSize >= 3))`
	Accessing Entities Directly	`when(self.deploymentDescriptor.find("<ejb-ref-type>Entity</ejb-ref-type>") <> 0)`

Fig. 16.3 Programs of anti-pattern detection in the languages of Java and QVT

tion in a simple way compared with hard-coding in the languages like Java. As shown in Fig. 16.3, six classic anti-patterns about JSP and Servlet in JEE applications are concluded and classified. We separately develop management programs in Java and QVT to detect these anti-patterns in benchmark JEE application Ecperf. The results and the executing time are also shown in the figure.

The two groups of automated programs have the same results of anti-pattern detection. It is easy to see that the executing time of the Java programs is less than the QVT ones. The main reason for this is that the two sets of programs are based on the same management APIs and there are some extra operations in architecture-based approach, which are aimed to ensure the synchronization between the model and the runtime system. There are complex factors that affect the performance of synchronizers: first, the execution time of synchronization process is constituted of the time spent on QVT transformation and the API invocations. Second, the performance is affected by both the complexity and the scale of the runtime system architecture. However, their difference in executing time is very small and it could be ignored from the aspect of system management.

The logics to detect these anti-patterns are not complex, since they just check a few attributes of JSP or servlet in the system. For example, the automated program to detect the forth anti-pattern is aimed to check if there are too many codes about data processing in any JSP and it is just needed to count the times how many the pattern of session.setAttribute appears in one JSP. From the fragments of the Java program, it is easy to see that most of codes are aimed to deal with data accessing, which is not the core of the management logics, compared with less than 10 percent of codes to express management logics. What's more, the similar codes of data access have to be repeated in different automated programs, which make administrators exhausted. By contrast, the QVT programs reduce about 80 percent of LOC. The runtime architecture-based model is modeling those management APIs, which reuses the codes of data access. Then administrators can develop programs based on the architecture-based model and do not have to invoke specific management APIs any more, which reduces programming costs. It is easy to see that our approach has the advantages related to the reusability.

16.5.2   VM States Checking

Load balance management in the cloud requires resource provision (e.g., CPU and memory) to be both stable and reliable, which is an important problem and a challenge in system management. The fundamental solution to this issue is to integrate and coordinate the resources in a global view. Many automated programs are aimed for this problem [14]. One of the key challenges is to find if the current states of the cloud platform satisfy some specific conditions. In this experiment, we develop the automated program to check if there are physical nodes which are in a free or busy condition. Figure 16.4 describes some code fragments in Java and QVT programs.

As the figure shows, in the Java program, we traverse the list of physical nodes to check the conditions of each node in the first function, where the second function is invoked to count the memory utilization of a node. In the second function, a script is invoked to retrieve the information about memory allocation in a node and the result needs to be parsed. The administrators have to cope with the detailed implementations while hard-coding in Java, including the interaction between the Java program and the script, and the relatively low-level logics of data processing. Therefore, administrators need to understand the details of the managed system, which may make them exhausted.

By contrast, with the help of the architecture-based model, administrators focus on the logics of management tasks without handling the different types of APIs like scripts and low-level data processing. In addition, the modeling language provides operations in the model level, such as select, sum and so on, which make it simpler to do programming.

16.6   Related Work

Our architecture based runtime model is a general approach to platform management in Cloud. There are several industry cloud products to provide platform resources as a service, which are similar in architecture. For instance, Windows Azure [15] adopts Windows server to provide runtime environment to applications and relies on VM ware. Oracle Public Cloud [16] adopts the products of WebLogic Server and its infrastructure depends on Oracle VM. Though the products above support different types of applications, they all contain virtualization based infrastructure and middleware software products.

Platform management is a key problem in Cloud. Although there are some relative administrative tools, such as Tivoli [17] and Hyperic [18], which are aimed to the factors of heterogeneity and distribution; the management still costs a lot, for the infrastructure fundament and middleware software products should be managed collaboratively and there are too many metrics of different types to manage manually. But there are no effective administrator tools to do the management automatically at present and automated programs are needed.

Other efforts have been made to improve the development of automated management

```
//Fragment of Java Program                                 1.   /*
                                                           2.    * JAVA: To get a node's memory utilization
 //Object: To check if there are nodes whose memory        3.    * by invoking the management script.
 utilization is below 40 percents.                         4.    */
 //1st Function - getAMemFreeNode(): It contains the main   5.   public String getMemUtilizationOfNode()
 logic of the management task.                             6.   {
 //2nd Function − getMemUtilizationOfNode(): It deals with  7.       try{
 the detailed implements of the runtime system.            8.           String[] args = new String[2];
                                                           9.           args[0] = "/bin/sh";
 1.   /*                                                   10.           args[1] = "/opt/xen/getUsedMem.sh";
 2.    * JAVA: To get a node whose memory utilization is   11.           ProcessBuilder builder =
 3.    * less than 40%.                                    12.               new ProcessBuilder(args);
 4.    */                                                  13.           Process process = builder.start();
 5.   public String getAMemFreeNode()                      14.           BufferedReader br = new BufferedReader(
 6.   {                                                    15.               new InputStreamReader(process.
 7.       String[] nodes = getAllNodes().split(";");       16.                   getInputStream()));
 8.       int len = nodes.length;                          17.           String line;
 9.       // To check every node.                          18.           int usedMem = 0;
10.       for(int i = 0; i < len; i ++)                    19.           while((line = br.readLine()) != null)
11.       {                                                20.           {
12.           String nodeId = nodes[i];                    21.               //To get the value by parsing the string.
13.           String nodeIp = getNodeIp(nodeId);           22.               String[] tokens1 = line.split(" ");
14.           NodeClient nc = new NodeClient(nodeIp);       23.               if(!tokens[1].equals("ID"))
15.       /*                                               24.                   usedMem += Integer.parseInt(tokens[2]);
16.        * To get the nodes' memory utilization.         25.           }
17.        */                                              26.           process.waitFor();
18.           double memUltilization = Double.parseDouble(  27.           double memUtilization = usedMem / (double)mem;
19.               nc.getMemUtilizationOfNode());            28.           return String.valueOf(memUtilization);
20.           if(memUltilization < 0.4)                    29.       }
21.               return nodeId;                            30.       catch(Exception e){
22.       }                                                31.           return null;
23.       return null;                                     32.       }
24.   }                                                    33.   }
```

```
//Fragment of QVT Program
 //Operations in QVT Language: select() – To return a list of the objects which are in a certain condition.
 //To get the list of nodes in a free condition
 var freeNodes = cloudModel.objectsOfType(Node)->select(VM.Memory->sum() < Memory * 0.4);
 //To get the list of nodes in a busy condition
 var busyNodes = cloudModel.objectsOfType(Node)->select(VM.Memory->sum() > Memory * 0.8);
```

Fig. 16.4 Programs of load balance management in the languages of Java and QVT

programs. OpenStack Compute [19] is a cloud computing fabric controller. It is written in Python and utilizes many external libraries. It is easy to express management tasks in Python but programmers still need to be familiar with the management APIs and understand the architecture of runtime system. In previous work [20], we propose the solution of Management as a Service (MaaS) from the reuse point of view. We encapsulate functions, processes, rules and experiments in IT management into web services and regard them as reusable assets, which is to be presented, used and collaborate in a service-oriented style. However, programmers are hard to express complex management tasks in BPEL (Business Process Execution Language)

and still need to deal with the operations on attributes.

Architecture-based approach is usually used in system management. For example, they are applied for automatically obtaining valid configurations of network equipment such as routers and bridges [21]. By modeling the relevant characteristics of every manageable element and defining their restrictions using propositional logic, these engines can automatically find correct configurations for each element, or diagnose the correctness of a preset configuration. We will mention another interesting application of architecture-based approach, in this case for generating test cases of a complex system configuration [22]. This work highlights how this technique can be applied to find efficiently solutions to a search space where multiple constraints over the correct solution are defined. However, none of the analyzed initiatives addresses the problem of automating platform management in Cloud, although it has been successfully applied to some relative problems.

We have made many researches in the area of model driven engineering. For a given meta-model and a given set of management interfaces, SM@RT [8] can automatically generate the code for mapping models to interfaces with good enough runtime performance. If users change the meta-model, SM@RT can re-generate the mapping code. More details can be found in our previous works [23]. If the management interfaces support remote invocations, the RSA can invoke them. In our previous work [9], we encapsulate hundreds of management interfaces of WebSphere, JOnAS, Tomcat, MySQL, Apusic, etc. into SOAP-based web services for the remote management. In addition, for the situation of incomplete formalized of modeling languages, our previous work [24] has provided an MOF meta-model extension mechanism with support for upward compatibility and automatically generates a model transformation for model integration, and the work we implemented on architecture-level fault tolerance [25] can also compensate for this to a degree. Our RSA is also able to translate system logs into elements of RSA and users should analyze the root cause based on RSA. An example can be found in our previous work [26]. We translate JEE application server's system logs into sequence diagrams and then use the automata to detect anti-patterns that cause the poor performance. The approach in this chapter is built on our previous resources.

16.7   Conclusion and Future Work

Platform management in Cloud brings high costs. Many automated programs thus have been built to tame the complexity of management. Hard-coding these programs in languages like Java can bring enough power and flexibility but also cause high programming effort and cost. It is trivial for administrators to be familiar with different types of APIs and understand the detailed implementations of the cloud environment. This chapter proposes a runtime architecture-based approach to managing the platform facilities such as the middleware and VMs of Cloud. We construct an architecture-based model for administrators to develop automated programs of platform management at the architecture level, and the correct synchronization between the model and the runtime system is ensured. Then administrators may develop automated programs of management tasks in modeling languages. The cloud providers are the target users of our approach. Moreover, some cloud-based applications need to customize or even re-invent the management functions provided by the cloud. The developers of such applications can also use our approach to do their own management. We evaluate the approach by comparing it to the hard-coding approach in two management scenarios and the results prove that the architecture-based management is effective and promising in the performance, the interoperability, the reusability and the simplicity.

As future work, we plan to give more support for administrators to manage platforms in Cloud. At present, our approach has the bottle net of performance as other centralized management frameworks. We are searching the model-based solutions to this issue and have made some progress. We also plan to perform further analysis such as model checking to ensure a deeper correctness and completeness of the generated causal link between management tasks. In addition, our approach is an abstraction of any target system and supports any types of operations if there are corresponding management interfaces [27]. We will extend our architecture-based model to fulfill more requirements in cloud management, such as data storage managements and cloud application developments.

Acknowledgments This work is sponsored by the National Basic Research Program of China under grant no. 2009CB320703; the National Natural Science Foundation of China under grant no. 61121063, 60933003; the High-Tech Research and Development Program of China under Grant No. 2012AA011207; the European Commission Seventh Framework Programme under grant no. 231167; and NCET.

References

1. E. Kotsovinos, Virtualization: blessing or curse? Commun. ACM **54**(1), 61–65 (2011)
2. J.O. Kephart, D.M. Chessc, The vision of autonomic computing. IEEE Comput. **36**(1), 41–50 (2003)
3. J.M. Rushby, Model checking and other ways of automating formal methods, in *Position paper for panel on Model Checking for Concurrent Programs* (Software Quality Week, San Francisco, 1995)
4. D. Garlan, Software architecture: a roadmap, in *Proceedings of the Conference on the Future of Software Engineering*, pp. 91–101 (2000)
5. G. Huang, H. Mei, F.-Q. Yang, Runtime recovery and manipulation of software architecture of component-based systems. Autom. Soft. Eng. **13**(2), 257–281 (2006)
6. R. France, B. Rumpe, Model-driven development of complex software: a research roadmap, in *Future of, Software Engineering*, pp. 37–54 (2007)
7. Object management group. meta object facility (mof) 2.0 query/view/transformation (qvt). http://www.omg.org/spec/QVT
8. G. Huang, H. Song, M. Hong, Sm@ rt: applying architecture-based runtime management into internetware systems. Int. J. Soft. Inform. **3**(4), 439–464 (2009)
9. X. Chen, X. Liu, X. Zhang, Z. Liu, G. Huang, Service encapsulation for middleware management interfaces, in *2010 Fifth IEEE International Symposium on Service Oriented System Engineering (SOSE)*, pp. 272–279 (2010)
10. Wikipedia. virtual appliance. http://www.en.wikipedia.org/wiki/Virtual_appliance
11. Eclipse. eclipse modeling framework project (emf). http://www.eclipse.org/modeling/emf/
12. Peking university. internetware test bed. http://www.edu-icloud.internetware.org
13. L.A.N. Ling, G. Huang, W.-H. Wang, H. MeI, Anti-pattern based performance optimization for middleware applications. J. Soft. **19**(9), 2167–2180 (2008)
14. Y. Zhang, G. Huang, X. Liu, H. Mei, Integrating resource consumption and allocation for infrastructure resources on-demand, in *2010 IEEE 3rd International Conference on Cloud Computing*, pp. 75–82 (2010)
15. Microsoft. windows azure. http://www.windowsazure.com/
16. Oracle. oracle public cloud. http://www.cloud.oracle.com/
17. Ibm. ibm tivoli software. http://www-01.ibm.com/software/tivoli/
18. Springsource. hyperic. http://www.hyperic.com/
19. Openstack. the open source cloud operating system. http://www.openstack.org/projects/
20. X. Chen, X. Liu, F. Fang, X. Zhang, G. Huang, Management as a service: an empirical case study in the internetware cloud, in *2010 IEEE 7th International Conference on e-Business Engineering (ICEBE)*, pp. 470–473 (2010)
21. S. Hallé, É. Wenaas, R. Villemaire, O. Cherkaoui, Self-configuration of network devices with configuration logic, in *Autonomic Networking* (Springer, 2006), pp. 36–49
22. M.B. Cohen, M.B. Dwyer, J. Shi, Constructing interaction test suites for highly-configurable systems in the presence of constraints: a greedy approach. IEEE Trans. Soft. Eng. **34**(5), 633–650 (2008)
23. H. Song, G. Huang, F. Chauvel, Y. Xiong, H. Zhenjiang, Y. Sun, H. Mei, Supporting runtime software architecture: a bidirectional-transformation-based approach. J. Syst. Soft. **84**(5), 711–723 (2011)
24. X. Chen, G. Huang, F. Chauvel, Y. Sun, H. Mei, Integrating mof-compliant analysis results. Int. J. Softw. Inform. **4**(3), 383–400 (2010)
25. J. Li, X. Chen, G. Huang, H. Mei, F. Chauvel, Selecting fault tolerant styles for third-party components with model checking support, in *International Symposium on Component-Based, Software Engineering*, pp. 69–86 (2009)
26. W. Wang, G. Huang, Pattern-driven performance optimization at runtime: experiment on jee systems, in *Proceedings of the 9th International Workshop on Adaptive and Reflective Middleware*, pp. 39–45 (2010)
27. H. Song, G. Huang, F. Chauvel, W. Zhang, Y. Sun, W. Shao, H. Mei, Instant and incremental qvt transformation for runtime models, in *International Conference on Model Driven Engineering Languages and Systems*, pp. 273–288 (2011)

Golden Age: On Multi-source Software Update Propagation in Pervasive Networking Environments

17

Abstract

With the development of Internet technology, a large portion of computer softwares appear to run in a network-oriented, distributed-deployed, and self-evolving manner. The prevailing wireless communication technologies broaden the usage of Internetware in mobile platforms, enabling the pervasive computing paradigm where people can access information/service anytime and anywhere. In the pervasive networking environment where mobile devices operate on ad-hoc mode and communicate with each other opportunistically without wireless infrastructures, distributing the evolving software updates to a set of mobile terminals is a challenging task. In this chapter, we address the problem of distributing multiple software updates in pervasive networks with storage and bandwidth constraints, and propose age-based solutions to tackle this problem. The basic idea is to introduce different age-based priority mechanisms for propagation decision making in order to resolve the contention of wireless bandwidth and storage buffer. We investigate a number of update propagation strategies including random spread, youngest age, and golden age. Mathematical models are derived to analyze the performance of the proposed strategies. It is shown that the golden age strategy has the burst effect, which could be used to enhance the efficiency of software update distribution. The principles for choosing golden age values are proposed aiming to optimize different utility metrics. Extensive simulations under various network parameters show that the golden age strategy performs well for multi-source software synchronization in pervasive environments.

© Springer Science+Business Media Singapore 2016
H. Mei and J. Lü, *Internetware*, DOI 10.1007/978-981-10-2546-4_17

Keywords

Software synchronization · Content propagation · Pervasive network

17.1   Introduction

With the rapid development of Internet technology, more and more computer softwares
are network-oriented and operate in a distributed manner. Specifically, softwares integrate
decentralized computer resources, cooperate
on processing computational tasks, coordinate
communication among heterogeneous devices,
and provide service to users via Internet. Such
network-oriented software development is known
as the Internetware paradigm [1,2], which takes
into account the logical diagram of cloud computing [3,4], mobile computing and networks
to address undetermined software requirements
in dynamic Internet environment. In the recent
years, mobile devices such as smartphones and
tablets are quickly becoming the prominent computing and communication platform which allows
billions of people interact with each other and
get access to diverse resources and information
through wireless networks efficiently and ubiquitously [5]. To provide pervasive service, software
development in Internetware paradigm pays
special attention to the heterogeneous networking
environments, where software are installed in
diverse portable devices and work with various
of network standards including LAN, DSL, 3G,
WiFi, WiMax, and ad hoc communications.

Due to the increasing user demands and security reasons, software are evolving and are updated
online constantly to enhance their functionality
and reliability. For example, the release of software patches, the update of user profiles, and the
upgrade of virus database, among the others need
to be propagated to a set of end devices quickly
and effectively. Since most of mobile devices are
installed with a variety of softwares for daily
usage, there arises the problem of *multi-source
software update propagation*: when multiple software release their new versions simultaneously or
the upgrade of a platform causes the update of

multiple Apps timely, there is a need of propagating multiple updates to a set of mobile devices.
Especially in the pervasive computing environment where devices communicate via unstable
wireless links, achieving efficient multi-source
software update propagation is a challenging task.

Pervasive networking environments are characterized by *mobile, intermittent, diverse*, and
multi-hop. One of the important aspects of pervasive computing is to support the use of mobile
devices to access information from anywhere for
the convenience of people's daily life. As a consequence of user mobility, network connections are
intermittent due to the limitation of battery power
and the change of communication conditions such
as interference and handover. The communication
networks are diverse and heterogeneous: devices
can connect to Internet via wireless infrastructure
(e.g., 3G radio tower or WiFi access point), or they
can exchange information in the way of device-
to-device (D2D) communication (e.g., Bluetooth)
[6]. In many cases multi-hop wireless communication is employed to enable information access
in the suburbs without 3G or WiFi signals, where
mobile devices operate on the ad hoc mode and
forward message for each other forming a spon-
taneous network [7].

In this chapter, we address the multi-source
software update propagation problem in pervasive computing environments. When continuous
network connection is available, the problem
is similar to the traditional multicast problem
which could be solved by constructing multicast
trees for content delivery. However, in the case
of pervasive networks, the situation becomes
much more complicated. The mobility of users
and the ever-changing network topology make
the construction of multicast tree extremely hard.
Furthermore, nodes communication in the multi-
hop intermittent network typically employs a
store-carry-forward paradigm [6,8]: each device
stores undelivered messages (from itself and from
other devices) in the buffer, carries them as it

moves, and forwards the message to some nodes it encounters, until the destination is reached. In other words, the chance of communication depends on the *encounter* of mobile nodes, i.e., they form a communication link when they move into each other's communication range, which is opportunistic and intermittent. Thus software update propagation in pervasive computing environment takes into account a number of factors such as the opportunity of communication, the bandwidth of the wireless links, the capacity of storage of nodes, and their mobility to fulfill the task.

We propose age-based solutions to the multi-source software update propagation problem with storage and bandwidth constraints. Specifically, our attention is focused in a network with N mobile nodes and M updates, with the constraints that each node can only carry K $(K < M)$ updates and the network bandwidth is only enough for spreading one piece of update when two devices encounter. We define the age of an update item as the time duration elapsed since the update is made at the source. The priority of an update item is assigned as a function of their age, and the item with highest priority will be transferred on encountering of nodes. Targeting at efficient updates propagation, we explore a series of age-based priority mechanisms including *random*, *youngest age*, and *golden age* (where the highest priority is given to the item with a critical age value between 0 and the maximum number). We present mathematical models to analyze the efficiency of different age-based propagation strategies. We show that the golden age strategy has the property of *burst effect*: the number of copies of an update item grows slowly in the beginning, rises rapidly when approaching to the golden age, and drops quickly afterwards. Such a property will benefit the spread of multiple software updates simultaneously. By carefully choosing the golden ages for different update items, the multiple updates propagate alternately and orderly, which will reduce the contention of network resources and enhance the ratio of delivery. Three principles for choosing golden age values are discussed aiming to optimize

different utility metrics. Extensive simulations are conducted, which show that the golden age strategy achieves high delivery ratio over 95% with a decent delay time, substantially outperforming the other strategies for multi-source software synchronization in pervasive environments.

17.2 System Model

We consider the pervasive networking environment where devices operate in the ad hoc mode and there does not exist a constant communication path between any pair of nodes. Examples are vehicles running in the streets, mobile sensors collecting data in a battle field, and people with PDAs and cell phones moving in suburban areas without wireless infrastructure support. Two nodes can communication when they move into each other's communication range, which is called an *encounter* of nodes.

Assume there are a set of softwares in the system, which are evolving and generating updates dynamically for the purpose of releasing new patches, upgrading virus databases, and publishing content to subscribers. Let N be the total number of mobile nodes in the system. The set of software to be updated is denoted by S_M and the total number is $|S_M| = M$. Each node installs a subset of S_M, and each software is used by a number of nodes in the network.

When a software is updated, it generates *update items* and notifies the nearby mobile nodes. An update item contains the meta information such as the description of the update, the TS (timestamp), the SID (source identification) and the DIDs (destination identifications), and the update content. If any mobile node receives the update item, it will propagate the update item to other nodes who are using the same software in the network. Due to the intermittent nature of pervasive environment, the update item is propagated in the store-carry-forward manner. The updated item is stored in the buffer of a mobile node, and then it is spread to other nodes when communication opportunity is available, until the destination is reached. Since there could be multiple destinations and there is no efficient way to verify the update status of the nodes in the intermittent network environment, so the update propagation process is stopped when the update item is evicted from the buffer due to cache replacement, or when the updated item is expired, i.e., its life circle exceeds some predefined maximum threshold. The node initiating the update process is called a *source*, and the nodes needed to be synchronized with update are called *destinations*. In the pervasive networking environment, multiple software updates could occur at the same time. We consider the problem that M simultaneous update items are propagated in the network consisting of N mobile nodes, which is called *multi-source software update propagation problem*.

Now we put resource constraints and bandwidth capacity into consideration. Assume each mobile node has a limited buffer size which is used to store update items for other nodes. For the convenience of analysis, we further assume that the updates are chopped into items having the same size of one unit storage, and each node is capable of storing K ($K \ll M$) update items at most. When two nodes n_a and n_b encounter each other, assume they can exchange only one unit of information taking the encounter opportunity; that is, n_a can send an update item to n_b, and n_b can send an update item to n_a during the encounter.

In the context of multi-source update propagation, with the constraints of buffer size and bandwidth capacity, a propagation strategy needs to address several issues. First, when two nodes encounter, due to bandwidth limit, a node can only choose an update item out of the K items in the buffer to spread to the other node. Thus a *priority mechanism* is needed for propagation decision making. Second, when a node receives an update item, due to the buffer size limit, it has to evict an item from the buffer to make room for the new one. Thus a *replacement mechanism* is needed to decide the items to be evicted. In the next section, we will present propagation strategies to address these issues.

17.3   Update Propagation Strategies

In this section, we propose several propagation strategies which are called random spread, youngest age, and golden age.

When an update is generated, the update item is propagated to some relay nodes, and eventually reaches the destinations. We first introduce some definitions used in the rest of the chapter. Considering a software update process, the whole mobile nodes set $\mathscr{S}$ can be divided into 3 subsets: $\mathscr{U}$—the set of nodes containing a copy of the update item, which are called *updated nodes*; $\mathscr{W}$—the set of destinations waiting for the update item, which are called *non-update destinations*; and $\mathscr{V}$—the rest nodes neither having an update item nor being a destination, which are possible relays and are called *candidate nodes*. Notice that $\mathscr{S} = \mathscr{U} \cup \mathscr{W} \cup \mathscr{V}$.

We denote the event that node n_a encounters node n_b by $e(n_a, n_b)$. If $n_a \in \mathscr{U}$ and $n_b \in \mathscr{W}$, it is called a *crucial encounter*; if $n_a \in \mathscr{U}$ and $n_b \in \mathscr{V}$, it is called an *effective encounter*. In a crucial encounter, since n_b is a non-update destination, n_a will send the update item to n_b directly. On receiving the update item, n_b will store the update item in local storage (e.g., hard drive) permanently and become an updated node, which reduces the number of non-update destinations by one. In an effective encounter, n_a meets an intermediate node and it decides whether to spread the update item to n_b according to the propagation policies introduced in the following subsections. In pervasive networking environments, for lack of continuous connectivity and centralized infrastructure, there is no way to know when all the destinations are updated. So the update propagation process will last until all copies of the update item are evicted from the system or expired.

Define the *age* of an update item as the time duration since it is generated, which equals to current time minus its initial time. Denoted by $Age(I)$ the age of update item I.

At the beginning, the buffer of nodes are empty; thus an update item can spread freely to other node to occupy the vacant buffer. Since the buffer size K is smaller than the number of distinct update items M, after a warm up period, each node's buffer will be filled up with updated items. We say the system reaches a stable state. When the system is stable, the update items will be spread or replaced according to some strategies. Since the warm up period is only short-term, in the following sections, we only discuss the problem in the long-term stable situation. We propose a randomized strategy and several age-based strategies for update propagation.

17.3.1 Random Spread

The random spread strategy is simple yet intuitive. In this strategy, all update items have equal priority to be spread regardless of their ages. When two nodes meet, it is necessary to first check whether it is a crucial encounter. If yes, an update item will be sent to its destination. If it is an effective encounter, we will randomly choose an update item from the buffer to propagate and replace a random item of the other node. The details of the strategy are given as follows.

Strategy: Random Spread

When n_a and n_b encounter:

(1) If $e(n_a, n_b)$ is a crucial encounter, n_a sends the update item to n_b. If $e(n_b, n_a)$ is a crucial encounter, n_b will do the same thing

(2) If $e(n_a, n_b)$ is an effective encounter, n_a randomly chooses an item out of the K items in the local buffer and sends it to n_b, to replace a randomly chosen location in the buffer of n_b. Similarly, node n_b will take the same action

---

Random spread is simple and easy to implement. However, without considering the effect of ages, the random strategy provides equal chance for younger items and older items, which yields long delay and low delivery ratio in the system. The detailed analysis will be provided in Sect. 17.4.

17.3.2 Youngest Age

To improve the delay of update propagation, a simple idea is to give the younger items higher priority so that they can spread faster. The youngest age policy is to choose the youngest update item to spread and to choose the oldest item to replace, aiming at propagating the newest update as soon as possible. The details are described as follows.

Strategy: Youngest Age

When n_a and n_b encounter:

(1) If $e(n_a, n_b)$ or $e(n_b, n_a)$ is a crucial encounter, the update item will be sent to its destination directly

(2) If $e(n_a, n_b)$ is an effective encounter, n_a chooses the item with youngest age in its local buffer and sends it to n_b, to replace the item with oldest age in the buffer of n_b. Similarly, node n_b will take the same action. If equal ages exist, a random decision is made to break the ties

---

The youngest age policy is supposed to achieve fast update propagation by enhancing the chance of spreading newer items. However, it can affect the delivery ratio of the whole system since the older items can be easily replaced by the younger ones before they reach to their destinations. Furthermore, when multiple software updates occur at the same time, for the multiple update items with the same age, it is practically equal to random spread.

17.3.3 Golden Age

As mentioned above, both youngest age and oldest age strategies have disadvantages. To overcome such drawbacks, it is feasible to design a proper aging policy to achieve high delivery ratio and decent propagation delay. We propose the golden age policy to fulfill this objective.

The policy uses a golden age parameter Γ for propagation decision. It chooses the item whose age is closest to (but not larger than) Γ to spread, and evicts the older items. The mechanism is analogous to the process of human life. When a human being is very young, he/she is physically weak and mentally immature, and thus cannot carry out sophisticated tasks. With the age growing, he/she obtains more resources and becomes stronger and more capable. As a certain age, his/her strength and power reach a peak, which is known as the golden age of the life. The golden age may be different from person to person, but it represents the greatest successful chance in the period. As for software update propagation, when an update item approaches to its golden age Γ, it should be given higher chance of spread in the network. As a result, the propagation rate of an update item is growing over time, achieves the highest rate on its golden age, and drops down thereafter, which forms a burst effect to broaden the delivery range in a short period. The details of the strategy are given as follows.

Strategy: Golden Age

When n_a and n_b encounter:

(1) If $e(n_a, n_b)$ or $e(n_b, n_a)$ is a crucial encounter, the update item will be sent to its destination directly

(2) If $e(n_a, n_b)$ is an effective encounter, n_a sends I_a to n_b to replace I_b, where I_a is the item in n_a which satisfies: $0 < Age(I_a) < \Gamma$ and $|\Gamma - Age(I_a)|$ is the smallest; and I_b is the item in n_b which satisfies: $Age(I_b) > \Gamma$ and it is the oldest. If such I_a does not exist, it will choose the youngest item to propagate. If such I_b does not exist, it will choose the oldest item to replace. Similarly, node n_b will take the same action to n_a

---

Notice that youngest age is a special case of golden age when $\Gamma = 0$. Golden age achieves a trade-off between propagation delay and delivery ratio by choosing a proper aging priority. The principles of choosing the golden age value Γ are discussed in Sect. 17.4.3.

17.4   Performance Analysis

In this section, we propose mathematical models to analyze the performance of the proposed strategies, and discuss the principles of choosing golden age value.

Table 17.1 Notations

Notation	Meaning	Notation	Meaning
N	Number of mobile nodes	$\mathscr{S}$	The set of mobile nodes
M	Number of distinct update items	$\mathscr{U}$	The set of updated nodes
K	Buffer size of a mobile node	$\mathscr{W}$	The set of non-updated destinations
Γ	The golden age parameter	$\mathscr{V}$	The set of candidate nodes

17.4.1   Notations and Assumptions

We present the notations in Table 17.1 which are used in the rest of this chapter. The following assumptions are made:

- Assume time is slotted and denoted by discrete numbers 0, 1, 2, ...
- In each time slot, a node encounters some other nodes with probability p.
- The update of a software is assumed to be a Poisson process; thus the interarrival time of two consecutive updates follows an exponential distribution at a rate of λ. The Poisson process assumption is widely used in literature for evolving content [9, 10].

17.4.2   Number of Updated Nodes in the System

The efficiency of update propagation strategies can be evaluated by how fast the update reaches its destinations and how many nodes receives the newest updates. In this section, we use the number of updated nodes in the system as the performance metric to evaluate the proposed strategies. Assuming time equals 0 when an update item is generated, the number of updated nodes $u(t)$ is measured by the number of nodes having received the update item at time t. For a fixed time t, the larger the value of $u(t)$, the more nodes are updated to the newest software version.

The following theorem analyzes the value of $u(t)$ of different proposed propagation strategies, showing that the number of updated nodes in the system can be obtained by solving some differential equations.

Theorem 17.1 *Assume an update is generated at time 0. The total number of node is N, and the initial size of non-updated destinations $\mathcal{W}$ is $N_{\mathcal{W}}$. Let $u(t)$, $w(t)$ and $v(t)$ be the numbers of updated nodes, non-updated destinations and candidate nodes at time t accordingly. The following conclusions hold.*

(I) In the random spread strategy, the number of updated nodes at time t converges to

$$u(t) = \frac{(N_{\mathcal{W}} + 1)e^{\frac{(N_{\mathcal{W}}+1)p}{N-1}t}}{N_{\mathcal{W}} + e^{\frac{(N_{\mathcal{W}}+1)p}{N-1}t}}. \tag{17.1}$$

(II) In the youngest age strategy, the number of updated nodes at time t converges to the solution of the following differential equations;

$$\begin{cases} u' = \frac{p}{N-1}uw + \frac{p}{N-1}(e^{-\lambda t(K-1)} - (1 - e^{-\lambda t})^{K-1})uv \\ w' = -\frac{p}{N-1}uw \\ u(t) + w(t) + v(t) = N \\ u(0) = 1, w(0) = N_{\mathcal{W}}. \end{cases} \tag{17.2}$$

(III) In the golden age strategy, the number of updated nodes at time t converges to the solution of the following differential equations;

$$\begin{cases} u' = \frac{p}{N-1}uw + \frac{p}{N-1}(p_s - p_r)uv \\ w' = -\frac{p}{N-1}uw \\ u(t) + w(t) + v(t) = N \\ u(0) = 1, w(0) = N_{\mathcal{W}} \end{cases} \tag{17.3}$$

where

$$p_s(t) = \begin{cases} (1 - (e^{-\lambda t} - e^{-\lambda \Gamma}))^{K-1} &, t \leq \Gamma \\ e^{-\lambda t(K-1)} &, t > \Gamma \end{cases} \tag{17.4}$$

and

$$p_r(t) = \begin{cases} (e^{-\lambda t} - e^{-\lambda \Gamma})^{K-1} &, t \leq \Gamma \\ (1 - e^{-\lambda t})^{K-1} &, t > \Gamma. \end{cases} \tag{17.5}$$

Proof (I) In the random spread strategy, the update item is propagated with a fixed probability. The number of updated node is 1 at time 0. According to the assumption, each updated node has probability p meeting another node. With probability $\frac{w(t)}{N-1}$ it is a crucial encounter, and with probability $\frac{v(t)}{N-1}$ it is an effective encounter.

Consider the difference of the number of updated node $u(t)$ in time slot t, which is caused by the following events. (1) For a crucial encounter, the number of updated node is increased by one. The proportion of crucial encounter is $\frac{w(t)}{N-1}$; thus the total increase is $p\frac{w}{N-1}u$. (2) For effective encounters, if the update item is chosen to spread (with probability $\frac{1}{K}$), the number of updated node is increased, whose value is $p\frac{v}{N-1}u\frac{1}{K}$. (3) For effective encounters, if the update item is replaced (with probability $\frac{1}{K}$), the number of updated node is decreased, whose value is $-p\frac{v}{N-1}u\frac{1}{K}$. So the number of updated nodes in t converges to the following differential equation

$$\begin{aligned} \frac{du}{dt} &= p\frac{w}{N-1}u + p\frac{v}{N-1}u\frac{1}{K} - p\frac{v}{N-1}u\frac{1}{K} \\ &= p\frac{w}{N-1}u. \end{aligned} \tag{17.6}$$

Similar, since the probability of being spread and replaced are the same, the differential of $v(t)$ is zero

$$\frac{dv}{dt} = 0.$$

And $u(t)$, $w(t)$, $v(t)$ satisfy the following constraints

$$u(t) + w(t) + v(t) = N,$$

$$u(0) = 1, w(0) = N_{\mathcal{W}}.$$

This is similar to the disease infection model with a constant infection rate [11, 12]. According to the deduction in [11, 12], the solution of these equations is

$$u(t) = \frac{(N_{\mathcal{W}} + 1)e^{\frac{(N_{\mathcal{W}}+1)p}{N-1}t}}{N_{\mathcal{W}} + e^{\frac{(N_{\mathcal{W}}+1)p}{N-1}t}}.$$

(II) According to the assumption, data update follows an exponential distribution at a rate of λ; thus the age of a cache item also follows the same exponential distribution with λ.

Consider the difference of $u(t)$ in time t, which is caused by the following events. (1) For crucial encounters, similar to the analysis in (I), the total increase is $p\frac{w}{N-1}u$. (2) For an effective encounters, if the update item is the youngest, the number of updated node is increased by 1. The total increase is $p\frac{v}{N-1}u \cdot Pr\{the\ item\ is\ the\ youngest\}$. (3) For an effective encounters, if the update item is the oldest, it will be replaced, causing the number of updated node to be decreased by 1. The total decrease is $-p\frac{v}{N-1}u \cdot Pr\{the\ item\ is\ the\ oldest\}$.

Due to the properties of exponential distribution:

$Pr\{the\ item\ is\ the\ youngest\}$
$= Pr\{all\ other\ K - 1\ items\ are\ in\ the\ age\ of\,(t, \infty)\}$
$= e^{-\lambda t(K-1)}.$

$Pr\{the\ item\ is\ the\ oldest\}$
$= Pr\{all\ other\ K - 1\ items\ are\ in\ the\ age\ of\,(0, t)\}$
$= (1 - e^{-\lambda t})^{K-1}.$

So, $u(t)$ satisfies the following differential equation:

$$\begin{aligned}
\frac{du}{dt} &= p\frac{w}{N-1}u + p\frac{v}{N-1}ue^{-\lambda t(K-1)} \\
&\quad -p\frac{v}{N-1}u(1 - e^{-\lambda t})^{K-1} \\
&= \frac{p}{N-1}uw + \frac{p}{N-1}(e^{-\lambda t(K-1)} \\
&\quad -(1 - e^{-\lambda t})^{K-1})uv.
\end{aligned}$$

The differential of $w(t)$ satisfies

$$\frac{dw}{dt} = -p\frac{w}{N-1}u.$$

And $u(t)$, $w(t)$, $v(t)$ have the following constraints:

$$u(t) + w(t) + v(t) = N,$$

with their initial conditions:

$$u(0) = 1, w(0) = N_{\mathcal{W}}.$$

Above equations and conditions yield the conclusion of part (II) in the theorem. The solution of the equations is hard to be described as a mathematical expression, but it can be calculated by computer program if the parameters are determined.

(III) Consider the number of updated nodes increasing in time t for golden age. The probability of crucial encounter and effective encounter is exactly the same as the youngest age strategy. However, the spreading and replacing probability is different. Let p_s and p_t denote the probability of being spread and being replaced at time t in an effective encounter.

If $t \leq \Gamma$, according to the golden age policy, the item is spread if there are no other items ages in (t, Γ), whose probability is

$$Pr\{\ all\ other\ K - 1\ items\ are\ not\ in\ the$$
$$ages\ of\,(t, \Gamma)\} = (1 - (e^{-\lambda t} - e^{-\lambda \Gamma}))^{K-1}.$$

If $t > \Gamma$, the item is spread only when it is the youngest, whose probability is

$$Pr\{\ all\ other\ K - 1\ items\ are\ in\ the\ age\ of$$
$$(t, \infty)\} = e^{-\lambda t(K-1)}.$$

So

$$p_s(t) = \begin{cases} (1 - (e^{-\lambda t} - e^{-\lambda \Gamma}))^{K-1} &, t \leq \Gamma \\ e^{-\lambda t(K-1)} &, t > \Gamma \end{cases}$$

If $t \leq \Gamma$, the item is replaced if all other items are in the age of (t, Γ), whose probability is

$$Pr\{\ all\ other\ K - 1\ items\ are\ in\ the\ ages\ of$$
$$(t, \Gamma)\} = (e^{-\lambda t} - e^{-\lambda \Gamma})^{K-1}.$$

If $t > \Gamma$, the item is evicted only when it is the oldest, whose probability is

$$Pr\{all\ other\ K - 1\ items\ are\ in\ the\ age\ of$$
$$(0, t)\} = (1 - e^{-\lambda t})^{K-1}.$$

So,

$$p_r(t) = \begin{cases} (e^{-\lambda t} - e^{-\lambda \Gamma})^{K-1} & , \quad t \leq \Gamma \\ (1 - e^{-\lambda t})^{K-1} & , \quad t > \Gamma \end{cases}$$

Similar to the analysis of youngest age strategy, $u(t)$, $w(t)$ and $v(t)$ converge to the solution of the following differential equations:

$$\frac{du}{dt} = \frac{p}{N-1} uw + \frac{p}{N-1} (p_s(t) - p_r(t)) uv,$$

$$\frac{dw}{dt} = -\frac{p}{N-1} uw,$$

with the following constraints:

$$u(t) + w(t) + v(t) = N,$$
$$u(0) = 1, w(0) = N_{\mathscr{W}}.$$

These give the equations of part (III) in the theorem.

Theorem 17.1 shows that for the proposed random spread, youngest age and golden age strategies, the number of updated nodes at time t can be obtained by solving a number of differential equations. Although it is hard to derive a mathematical expression for the youngest age and the golden age strategies, their values can be calculated by computer programming when the parameters are given. Figure 17.1 shows the shape of $u(t)$ for the three strategies. As illustrated in the figure, in the random spread strategy, the population of updated nodes increases slowly in the system. Both youngest age and golden age increase faster than random spread. The population in golden age increases quickly and reaches the maximum value at its golden age. The peak value of the youngest age strategy is smaller than that of golden age. After the peak, populations of both youngest age and golden age decrease when ages get older.

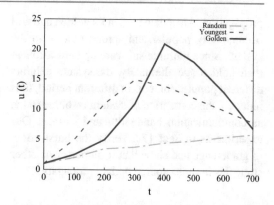

Fig. 17.1 Comparison of $u(t)$ on the proposed strategies

According to Eq. (17.6), the increasing rate of random spread strategy is very small. Since the probabilities of being spread and being replaced are equal, the expected number of updates propagated in an effective encounter is 0. So update is propagated only in crucial encounters. It is fair to treat all update items equally, but so doing suffers from long update process and poor performance. The age-based strategies seems to be a better idea by setting priorities to different ages. In the youngest age strategy, update is propagated rapidly at the beginning. As the age gets older, the chance of being chosen gets lower, and thus the propagation speed slows down. The golden age strategy, on the other hand, propagates slowly at the beginning. When the age grows to golden age, the propagation rate approaches to 1. The update process can be divided into two phases: the *spread phase* and the *shrinking phase*. In the spread phase, update is propagated to a number of nodes quickly. The number of update nodes reaches a maximum value at the golden age. After that, it enters the shrinking phase, where the population of updated nodes will decrease with age getting older.

It is worthwhile to note that golden age exhibits the *burst effect*. When a node is approaching to its golden age, it gains the highest priority to propagate update, while other nodes will step aside. At that moment, with a large base number and high propagation rate, the population of update items grows rapidly. Such an effect is also analogous to the phenomenon of population explosion in a society, which is very helpful for multi-source update propagation. An update item at its golden age will become very popular and spread rapidly in the system. Since multiple software updates arrive at their golden age alternately, the system exhibits different popular contents in different period, thus reducing the contention of system resources such as communication bandwidth and storage. Our experiments in Sect. 17.5 verify the burst effect of golden age and show that it outperforms other strategies in multi-source update propagation.

17.4.3 Principles for Choosing the Golden Age

The golden age parameter Γ has great influence on system performance. If Γ is too small, e.g., Γ approaches to 0, it is the youngest age strategy; if Γ is too large, it is the oldest age strategy. How to choose the best golden age value is still an open question. It is decided by different criterions, influence factors, and optimizing objectives. In the following, we propose three principles to choose the golden age.

17.4.3.1 Middle Age Rule

Since we do not hope the golden age is too small or too large, naturally we want it to be in the middle age. Specifically, consider a buffer with K items, when an item reaches its golden age Γ, we hope it is in the middle among all items' ages in the buffer. Consider a buffer item, the probability that its age is older than Γ is $1 - e^{-\lambda \Gamma}$. Letting the probability be $\frac{1}{2}$, we have $1 - e^{-\lambda \Gamma} = \frac{1}{2}$, which yields $\Gamma = -\frac{\ln \frac{1}{2}}{\lambda}$.

17.4.3.2 Maximum Population Rule

Since golden age strategy stops update propagation after Γ, if update interval is sufficiently long, choosing a larger Γ will result in a larger population of updated nodes in the system. However, a larger Γ will also decrease the update propagation rate at the beginning. We should consider the trade-off between population and propagation delay.

According to Eq. (17.3), in the spread phase ($t < \Gamma$), the propagation probability is

$$p_s(t) - p_r(t) = (1 - (e^{-\lambda t} - e^{-\lambda \Gamma}))^{K-1} - (e^{-\lambda t} - e^{-\lambda \Gamma})^{K-1}$$

It should be guaranteed that $p_s(t) - p_r(t)$ never be negative for $t = 1, 2, ..., \Gamma$, otherwise the item is more likely to be evicted instead of being propagated. Clearly it is an increasing function of t ($t \geq 1$). So, we only need to guarantee $p_s(1) - p_r(1) \geq 0$, that is,

$$(1 - (e^{-\lambda} - e^{-\lambda \Gamma}))^{K-1} - (e^{-\lambda} - e^{-\lambda \Gamma})^{K-1} \geq 0.$$

Solving this equation yields

$$\Gamma \leq -\frac{\ln(e^{-\lambda} - \frac{1}{2})}{\lambda}.$$

So if $e^{-\lambda} > \frac{1}{2}$, we can choose

$$\Gamma = -\frac{\ln(e^{-\lambda} - \frac{1}{2})}{\lambda} - \delta, \qquad (17.7)$$

where δ is a small positive number to break the tie at the beginning.

17.4.3.3 Percentage Rule

Assuming we hope that at the golden age Γ, the number of updated nodes achieves a percentage ρ of the total number of node N. So the expected number of non-updated destinations at Γ is $(1 - \rho)N_{\mathscr{W}}$. Considering the shrink phase of golden strategy, after Γ, the non-updated destinations are still able to be updated in crucial encounters. Consider a buffer with K items, the probability that an item is older than Γ is $\beta = 1 - e^{-\lambda \Gamma}$, and the probability that there are m items older than Γ is given by a binomial distribution $\binom{K+1}{m} \beta^m (1 - \beta)^{K-m}$. Therefore the expected number of items older than Γ is $K\beta = K(1 - e^{-\lambda \Gamma})$. Accordingly, if an item reaches its golden age, it is still expected to experience $K(1 - e^{-\lambda \Gamma})$ encounters before being replaced. There are ρN updated items, so the total expected number of encounters are $\rho N \cdot K(1 - e^{-\lambda \Gamma})$. Among them the probability of crucial encounter is $\frac{(1-\rho)N_{\mathscr{W}}}{N}$. Let the expected number of crucial encounter be equal to the number of non-updated destinations.

We have

$$\rho N \cdot K (1 - e^{-\lambda \Gamma}) \frac{(1 - \rho) N_{\mathcal{W}}}{N} = (1 - \rho) N_{\mathcal{W}}.$$

Solving this equation yields

$$\Gamma = -\frac{ln(1 - \frac{1}{\rho K})}{\lambda}. \qquad (17.8)$$

17.5 Numerical Results

17.5.1 Simulation Setup

We simulate a multi-hop wireless network with N nodes moving in a urban area. There exist M evolving softwares in the system, constituting the multiple source of updates. Update in a source follows an exponential distribution with rate λ. Each node has equal size of buffer K, which is a percentage of the number of sources. The golden age parameter Γ is chosen using the middle age rule by defaulting.

To mimic the movement of people and pervasive devices, we employ the City Section Mobility model which is presented in [13,14]. In the city section mobility model, the street network of a city or a suburb area is mapped to a grid road topology, and the node movement is constrained on the graph. All edges in the grid graph are bi-directional, double-lane roads with speed limits. Initially mobile nodes are randomly deployed in the street intersections. Then each mobile node randomly selects an intersection in the grid graph as its destination and move towards it with a constant speed. Upon reaching the destination, the mobile node pauses for a specified time and then randomly chooses another destination and repeats the process.

The major simulation parameters and default system settings are summarized in Table 17.2.

17.5.2 The Number of Updated Nodes

As mentioned before, we use the number of updated node in the system as the performance metric to evaluate the proposed strategies.

Table 17.2 Simulation parameters

Parameter	Meaning	Default value
N	Number of mobile nodes	300
M	Number of source	10–30 % of N
K	Buffer size	15–35 % of M
λ	Data update rate	$\frac{1}{700}$ to $\frac{1}{300}$
Γ	Golden age parameter	$-\frac{ln\frac{1}{2}}{\lambda}$

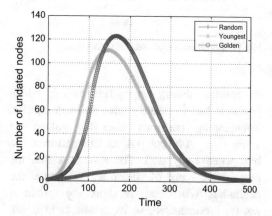

Fig. 17.2 Number of updated nodes versus time

Figure 17.2 shows the number of updated nodes versus time for the random spread, youngest age and golden age strategies.

As shown in the figure, the number of update node increases extremely slow for the random spread strategy. Both age-based strategies propagate much faster than random strategy. Youngest age increases faster than golden age at the beginning, reaches to the highest value about 110 at time 150, and then decreases with time. The golden age strategy, although it increases slow at first, bursts into a quick growth on approaching to its golden age. This verifies the phenomenon of burst effect, which matches our analysis in Sect. 17.4. Golden age reaches to its highest value 122 at time 180, which is about 12 % higher than that of youngest age. Since golden age spreads updates to more nodes, statistically it will update more destinations than the other strategies.

Figure 17.3 compares the percentages of updated destinations versus time. It shows that random spread only updates less than 30 %

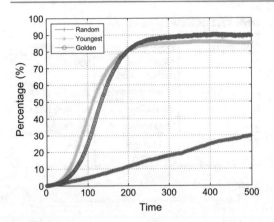

Fig. 17.3 Percentage of updated versus time

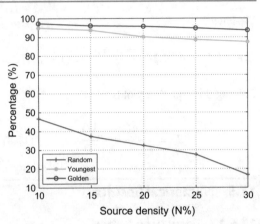

Fig. 17.4 Update percentage versus source density

destinations during an update period, which performs bad for multi-source software update. Youngest age performs better than golden age when $t < 200$, but golden age performs the best when $t \geq 200$. The reason is that the propagation speed of golden age is slow at the beginning. When time is short, the update is not fully propagated, so its update ratio is not comparable to that of youngest age. However, when approaching to Γ, the population of update nodes grows quickly in golden age and eventually exceeds that of youngest age, and thus the update ratio also increases. As shown in Fig. 17.3, at the end of update period, golden age achieves higher update percentage (also called delivery ratio) than the other strategies.

When time $t \leq \Gamma$, we call the percentage of updated destinations at t the *short term consistency*; when $t \leq \Gamma$, we called it *long term consistency*. It is clear that youngest age performs better in short term consistency. In comparison of long-term consistency, as indicated in Fig. 17.3, youngest age is lower than 85 %, while golden age is higher than 90 %. Golden age achieves the best performance in long term consistency.

17.5.3   Impact of Source Density

In this section, we investigate the update efficiency under different source densities. Figure 17.4 shows the long term consistency

when the number of source varies from 10 to 30 % that of the total nodes.

It can be seen that the performance of random spread decreases with the increase of source density. The update percentage drops from 48 to 18 %. The reason is that random strategy treats every update equally. The more the sources, the more updates are generated, and the less chance for an individual to be chosen to propagate. Thus the performance gets worse. The performance of youngest age decreases slightly. Golden age is the most stable among the three. It is barely affected by the density of source, thanks to the golden age property: when a node is at its golden age, it gains the highest priority to propagate update, while other nodes will step aside. So the increasing source density will not affect the performance of golden age.

17.5.4   Impact of Buffer Size

This section explores the influence of buffer size. Figure 17.5 shows the update percentage when the buffer size varies from 15 to 35 % of the number of source.

It is shown that performance of random spread decreases slowly with increasing buffer size. The reason is as follows. Although a single node can carry more updates when its buffer size increases, it also degrades the possibility an update to be chosen to spread, thus causing the difficulty of

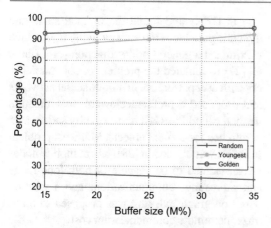

Fig. 17.5 Update percentage versus buffer size

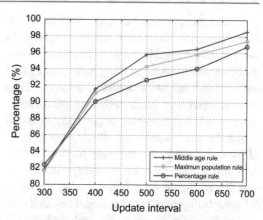

Fig. 17.7 Comparison of age choosing rules

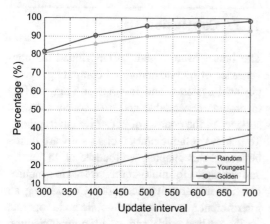

Fig. 17.6 Update percentage versus update interval

update propagation. As a result, the performance decreases slightly. Both youngest age and golden age are insensitive to the storage capacity and their performances improve slightly with the increasing buffer size. Again, golden age outperforms the other strategies.

17.5.5 Impact of Update Interval

Since update follows an exponential distribution with rate λ, the expected update interval is $\frac{1}{\lambda}$. By varying $\frac{1}{\lambda}$ from 300 to 700, Fig. 17.6 shows the update percentage of the three strategies.

As illustrated in the figure, the performances of all strategies get improved with the increasing update interval. The reason is that when update interval gets longer, there is more time to prop-

agate updates; thus the performances get better. Random spread still performs the worst, whose update percentage is less than 40 %. Golden age performs the best, whose performance approaches to 100 % at long update interval. Most of the time, golden age achieves about 10 % higher update percentage than youngest age.

17.5.6 Performance of Different Golden Age Parameter Choosing Rules

Figure 17.7 shows the performances of different golden age choosing rules with various update intervals (the parameter ρ of the percentage rule is set to 0.4 in the experiment). According to Fig. 17.7, there is no dramatic differences between their performances. The middle age rule and maximum population rule perform similarly, and most of the time their differences are less than 2 %. The percentage rule performs worse than the other rules. The middle age rule performs the best among the three principles.

17.6 Related Work

The related work include data routing strategies and content delivery service in pervasive networking environment.

Data routing is the basic function to enable communication in computer networks, which has been widely studied in the past. In pervasive networking environment, routing strategies can be summarized into two categories: the *single-copy* schemes and the *multi-copy* schemes. Direct transmission [15] is the simplest single-copy approach which let the source or a moving relay node (*DataMule*) carry the message to the destination directly. Spyropoulos et al. [8] studied several "smart" single-copy based routing strategies by using utility-based forwarding. They analyzed the performance theoretically and evaluated it by simulations. In [16], Yuan et al. presented a single-copy based routing protocol PER in intermittent networks where the nodes followed a semi-deterministic trajectory. The probability that two nodes will meet can be predicted and message is forwarded to a node with the highest probability that it can encounter the destination. Epidemic routing [17] is the most expensive and fastest multi-copy approach if resource is unlimited. It floods the message throughout the network to guarantee a shortest transmission path, but extremely wastes network resources. A number of approaches have been presented to reduce the overhead of epidemic routing for multi-hop networks [18–22]. Liu and Wu [19] presented a hop-count-limited forwarding scheme, in which every message had a maximum number of hops that can be forwarded by it. The history-based and utility-based routings were studied in [20]. In order to achieve both good delays and low transmissions, Spyropoulos et al. proposed two multiple-copy based routing protocols in [22]: *Spray and Wait* and *Spray and Focus*. Lin et al. [21] proposed a routing protocol based on network coding to reduce the number of bytes transmitted. Routing schemes based on the social properties of node mobility were discussed in [23,24].

In the context of data distribution service in DTN (delay tolerant network), Ioannidis et al. studied content updated over a mobile social network and proposed a strategy to optimize bandwidth allocation for service provider [25]. Altman et. al. considered single-source update propaga-

tion in DTNs and found the optimal static and dynamic policies to transmit evolving files, which maximized a general utility function [26]. Lin et al. [27] formulated the problem of content delivery with user preference in mobile social networks and proposed a preference-aware dissemination method called PrefCast to maximally satisfy user preference for content objects. Multicast problem in DTNs was studied in [28], where mobile nodes were assumed to be capable of both long-range and short-range communications and a solution based on graph indexing was proposed to minimize the remote communication cost.

17.7   Conclusion

The Internetware paradigm envisioned the convergence of mobile and cloud computing, cyber-physical systems, and Internet of Things (IOT) to provide dependable and trustworthy software services in the context of pervasive environment. To achieve reliable and efficient software distribution, in this chapter, we focused on the issues and strategies for multi-source software synchronization in pervasive networks. Considering an intermittent network where mobile nodes operate on the ad hoc mode and set up communication paths opportunistically, the objective is to propagate a number of update contents to their destinations efficiently, under the constraints of limited buffer size and narrow network bandwidth. We proposed age-based priority mechanisms for propagation decision making aiming to resolve the contention of system resources and enhance the probability of delivery. Based on the aging policies, we investigated several update propagation strategies including random spread, youngest age, and golden age. Theoretical analysis showed that the golden age strategy achieves rapid population growth at some critical age value, which is beneficial to enhancing update propagation efficiency. The principles of choosing the golden age value was discussed, and extensive simulations were conducted to show the effective of the proposed strategy. In the future, we will extends our multi-source software synchronization algorithms in a broader wireless and pervasive networking environments such as D2D communications and Vehicular Ad Hoc Networks (VANETs).

References

1. H. Mei, G. Huang, T. Xie, Internetware: a software paradigm for internet computing. IEEE Comput. **45**(6), 26–31 (2012)
2. H. Mei, Internetware: challenges and future direction of software paradigm for internet as a computer, in *IEEE 34th Annual Computer Software and Applications Conference (COMPSAC'10)*, Seoul, South Korea (2010), pp. 14–16
3. M. Armbrust, A. Fox, R. Griffith et al., A view of cloud computing. Commun. ACM **53**(4), 50–58 (2010)
4. L. Popa, A. Krishnamurthy, S. Ratnasamy, et al., Faircloud: sharing the network in cloud computing, in *Proceedings of the 10th ACM Workshop on Hot Topics in Networks (HotNets'11)*, New York, NY, USA (2011), pp. 1–6
5. R. Jain, J. Wullert, Challenges: environmental design for pervasive computing systems, in *Proceedings of the 8th Annual International Conference on Mobile Computing and Networking (MobiCom'02)*, New York, NY, USA (2002), pp. 263–270
6. K. Fall, A delay-tolerant network architecture for challenged internets, in *Annual Conference of the ACM Special Interest Group on Data Communication (Sigcomm'03)*, New York, NY, USA (2003), pp. 27–34
7. M. Pitkänen, T. Kärkkäinen, J. Ott et al., Scampi: service platform for social aware mobile and pervasive computing, in *Proceedings of the First Edition of the MCC Workshop on Mobile Cloud Computing (MCC '12)*, New York, NY, USA (2012), pp. 7–12
8. T. Spyropoulos, K. Psounis, C. Raghavendra, Efficient routing in intermittently connected mobile networks: the single-copy case. IEEE ACM Trans. Netw. **16**(1), 63–76 (2008)
9. D. Barbara, T. Imielinski, Sleepers and workaholics: caching strategies in mobile environments (extended version). VLDB J. **4**(4), 567–602 (1995)
10. G. Cao, A scalable low-latency cache invalidation strategy for mobile environments, in *The Annual International Conference on Mobile Computing and Networking (MobiCom'00)*, New York, NY, USA (2000), pp. 200–209
11. D. Daley, J. Gani, *Epidemic Modelling* (Cambridge University Press, Cambridge, 1999)
12. X. Zhang, G. Neglia, J. Kurose et al., Performance modeling of epidemic routing. Comput. Netw. **51**(10), 2867–2891 (2007)
13. V. Davies, Evaluating mobility models within an ad hoc networks. Master's thesis, Colorado, Colorado School of Mines (2000)
14. T. Camp, J. Belong, D. Davies, A survey of mobility models for ad hoc network research, in *Wireless Communication and Mobile Computing(WCMC): Special issue on Mobile Ad Hoc Networking: Research, Trends and Applications*, vol. 2(5) (2002), pp. 483–502
15. R. Shah, S. Roy, S. Jain, W. Brunette, Data mules: modeling and analysis of a three-tier architecture for sparse sensor networks. Ad Hoc Netw. **1**, 215–233 (2003)
16. I. Cardei, Q. Yuan, J. Wu, Predict and relay: an efficient routing in disruption-tolerant networks, in *The ACM International Symposium on Mobile Ad Hoc Networking and Computing (MobiHoc'09)*, New Orleans, Louisiana, USA (2009), pp. 95–104
17. A. Vahdat, D. Becker, Epidemic routing for partially connected ad hoc networks. Technical Report CS-200006, Duke University (2000)
18. J. Burgess, B. Gallagher, D. Jensen et al., Maxprop: routing for vehicle-based disruption-tolerant networks, in *Proceedings of IEEE International Conference on Computer Communications (INFOCOM'06)*, Barcelona, Spain (2006), pp. 1–11
19. C. Liu, J. Wu, An optimal probabilistic forwarding protocol in delay tolerant networks, in *The ACM International Symposium on Mobile Ad Hoc Networking and Computing (MobiHoc'09)*, New Orleans, Louisiana, USA (2009), pp. 105–114
20. J. Leguay, T. Friedman, V. Conan, DTN routing in a mobility pattern space, in *Proceedings of the ACM SIGCOMM Workshop on Delay-Tolerant Networking (WDTN'05)*, New York, NY, USA (2005), pp. 276–283
21. Y. Lin, B. Li, B. Liang, Efficient network coded data transmissions in disruption tolerant networks, in *Proceedings of IEEE International Conference on Computer Communications (INFOCOM'08)*, Phoenix, AZ, USA (2008), pp. 1508–1516
22. T. Spyropoulos, K. Psounis, C. Raghavendra, Efficient routing in intermittently connected mobile networks: the multiple-copy case. IEEE ACM Trans. Netw. **16**(1), 77–90 (2008)
23. E. Daly, M. Haahr, Social network analysis for routing in disconnected delay-tolerant manets, in *The ACM International Symposium on Mobile Ad Hoc Networking and Computing (MobiHoc'07)*, Montreal, Quebec, Canada (2007), pp. 32–40
24. P. Hui, J. Crowcroft, E. Yoneki, Bubble rap: social-based forwarding in delay tolerant networks, in *The ACM International Symposium on Mobile Ad Hoc Networking and Computing (MobiHoc'08)*, Hong Kong, China (2008), pp. 241–250

25. S. Ioannidis, A. Chaintreau, L. Massoulie, Optimal and scalable distribution of content updates over a mobile social network, in *Proceedings of IEEE International Conference on Computer Communications (INFOCOM'09)*, Rio de Janeiro, Brazil (2009), pp. 1422–1430

26. E. Altman, P. Nain, J. Bermond, Distributed storage management of evolving files in delay tolerant ad hoc networks, in *Proceedings of IEEE International Conference on Computer Communications (INFOCOM'09)*, Rio de Janeiro, Brazil (2009), pp. 1431–1439

27. K.C. Lin, C.W. Chen, C.F. Chou, Preference-aware content dissemination in opportunistic mobile social networks, in *Proceedings of IEEE International Conference on Computer Communications (INFOCOM'12)*, Orlando, USA (2012), pp. 1960–1968

28. M. Mongiovi, A.K. Singh, X. Yan, B. Zong et al., Efficient multicasting for delay tolerant networks using graph indexing, in *Proceedings of IEEE International Conference on Computer Communications (INFOCOM'12)*, Orlando, USA (2012), pp. 1386–1394

GreenDroid: Automated Diagnosis of Energy Inefficiency for Smartphone Applications

18

Abstract

Smartphone applications' energy efficiency is vital, but many Android applications suffer from serious energy inefficiency problems. Locating these problems is labor-intensive and automated diagnosis is highly desirable. However, a key challenge is the lack of a decidable criterion that facilitates automated judgment of such energy problems. Our work aims to address this challenge. We conducted an in-depth study of 173 open-source and 229 commercial Android applications, and observed two common causes of energy problems: missing deactivation of sensors or wake locks, and cost-ineffective use of sensory data. With these findings, we propose an automated approach to diagnosing energy problems in Android applications. Our approach explores an application's state space by systematically executing the application using Java PathFinder (JPF). It monitors sensor and wake lock operations to detect missing deactivation of sensors and wake locks. It also tracks the transformation and usage of sensory data and judges whether they are effectively utilized by the application using our state-sensitive data utilization metric. In this way, our approach can generate detailed reports with actionable information to assist developers in validating detected energy problems. We built our approach as a tool, GreenDroid, on top of JPF. Technically, we addressed the challenges of generating user interaction events and scheduling event handlers in extending JPF for analyzing Android applications. We evaluated GreenDroid using 14 real-world popular Android applications. GreenDroid completed energy efficiency diagnosis for these applications in a few minutes. It successfully located real energy problems in these applications, and additionally found new unreported energy problems that were later confirmed by developers.

Parts of this chapter were reprinted from © [2014] IEEE. Reprinted, with permission, from Yepang Liu, Chang Xu, Shi-Chi Cheung and Jian Lü. *GreenDroid: Automated diagnosis of energy inefficiency for smart-phone applications*. In IEEE Transactions on Software Engineering (TSE), Volume. 40, No. 9, pp. 911–940. September 2014. doi:10.1109/TSE.2014.2323982.

© Springer Science+Business Media Singapore 2016
H. Mei and J. Lü, *Internetware*, DOI 10.1007/978-981-10-2546-4_18

Keywords

Smartphone application · Energy inefficiency · Automated diagnosis · Sensory data utilization · Green computing

18.1 Introduction

The smartphone application market is growing rapidly. Up until July 2013, the one million Android applications on Google Play store had received more than 50 billion downloads [1]. Many of these applications leverage smartphones' rich features to provide desirable user experiences. For example, Google Maps can navigate users when they hike in the countryside by location sensing. However, sensing operations are usually energy consumptive, and limited battery capacity always restricts such an application's usage. As such, energy efficiency becomes a critical concern for smartphone users.

Existing studies show that many Android applications are not energy efficient due to two major reasons [2]. First, the Android framework exposes hardware operation APIs (e.g., APIs for controlling screen brightness) to developers. Although these APIs provide flexibility, developers have to be responsible for using them cautiously because hardware misuse could easily lead to unexpectedly large energy waste [3]. Second, Android applications are mostly developed by small teams without dedicated quality assurance efforts. Their developers rarely exercise due diligence in assuring energy savings.

Locating energy problems in Android applications is difficult. After studying 66 real bug reports concerning energy problems, we found that many of these problems are intermittent and only manifest themselves at certain application states (details are given later in Sect. 18.3). Reproducing these energy problems is labor-intensive. Developers have to extensively test their applications on different devices and perform detailed energy profiling. To figure out the root causes of energy problems, they have to instrument their programs with additional code to log execution traces for diagnosis. Such a process is typically time-consuming. This may explain why some notorious energy problems have failed to be fixed in a timely fashion [4–6].

In this work, we set out to mitigate this difficulty by automating the energy problem diagnosis process. A key research challenge for automation is the lack of a decidable criterion, which allows mechanical judgment of energy inefficiency problems. As such, we started by conducting a large-scale empirical study to understand how energy problems have occurred in real-world smartphone applications. We investigated 173 open-source and 229 commercial Android applications. By examining their bug reports, commit logs, bug-fixing patches, patch reviews and release logs, we made an interesting observation: *Although the root causes of energy problems can vary with different applications, many of them (over 60%) are closely related to two types of problematic coding phenomena:*

Missing sensor or wake lock deactivation. To use a smartphone sensor, an application needs to register a listener with the Android OS. The listener should be unregistered when the concerned sensor is no longer being used. Similarly, to make a phone stay awake for computation, an application has to acquire a wake lock from the Android OS. The acquired wake lock should also be released as soon as the computation completes. Forgetting to unregister sensor listeners or release wake locks could quickly deplete a fully charged phone battery [7,8].

Sensory data underutilization. Smartphone sensors probe their environments and collect sensory data. These data are obtained at high energy cost and therefore should be utilized effectively by applications. Poor sensory data utilization can also result in energy waste. For example, Osmdroid, a popular navigation application, may continually collect GPS data simply to render an invisible map [9]. This problem occurs occasionally at certain application states. Battery energy is thus consumed, but collected GPS data fail to produce any observable user benefits.

With these findings, we propose an approach to automatically diagnosing such energy problems in Android applications. Our approach explores an Android application's state space by systematically executing the application using Java PathFinder (JPF), a widely-used model checker for Java programs [10]. It analyzes how sensory data are utilized at each explored state, as well as monitoring whether sensors/wake locks are properly used and unregistered/released. We have implemented this approach as an 18 KLOC extension to JPF. The resulting tool is named GreenDroid. As we will show in our later evaluation, GreenDroid is able to analyze the utilization of location data for the aforementioned Osmdroid application over its 120 K states within three minutes, and successfully locate our discussed energy problem. To realize such efficient and effective analysis, we need to address two research issues and two major technical issues as follows.

Research issues. While existing techniques can be adapted to monitor sensor and wake lock operations to detect their missing deactivation, how to effectively identify energy problems arising from ineffective uses of sensory data is an outstanding challenge, which requires addressing two research issues. First, sensory data, once received by an application, would be transformed into various forms and used by different application components. Identifying program data that depend on these sensory data typically requires instrumentation of additional code to the original programs. Manual instrumentation is undesirable because it is labor-intensive and error-prone. Second, even if a program could be carefully instrumented, there is still no well-defined metric for judging ineffective utilization of sensory data automatically. To address these research issues, we propose to monitor an application's execution and perform dynamic data flow analysis at a bytecode instruction level. This allows sensory data usage to be continuously tracked without any need for instrumenting the concerned programs. We also propose a state-sensitive metric to enable automated analysis of sensory data utilization and identify those

application states whose sensory data have been underutilized.

Technical issues. JPF was originally designed for analyzing conventional Java programs with explicit control flows [10]. It executes the bytecode of a target Java program in its virtual machine. However, Android applications are event-driven and depend greatly on user interactions. Their program code comprises many loosely coupled event handlers, among which no explicit control flow is specified. At runtime, these event handlers are called by the Android framework, which builds on hundreds of native library classes. As such, applying JPF to analyze Android applications requires: (1) generating valid user interaction events, and (2) correctly scheduling event handlers. To address the first technical issue, we propose to analyze an Android application's GUI layout configuration files, and systematically enumerate all possible user interaction event sequences with a bounded length at runtime. We show that such a bounded length does not impair the effectiveness of our analysis, but instead helps quickly explore different application states and identify energy problems. To address the second technical issue, we present an application execution model (AEM) derived from Android specifications. This model captures application-generic temporal rules that specify calling relationships between event handlers. With this model, we are able to ensure an Android application to be exercised with correct control flows, rather than being randomly scheduled on its event handlers. As we will show in our later evaluation, the latter brings almost no benefit to the identification of energy problems in Android applications.

In summary, we make the following contributions in this work:

- We empirically study real energy problems from 402 Android applications. This study identifies two major types of coding phenomena that commonly cause energy problems. We make our empirical study data public for research purposes [11].
- We propose a state-based approach for diagnosing energy problems arising from sensory

data underutilization in Android applications. The approach systematically explores an application's state space for such diagnosis purpose.

- We present our ideas for extending JPF to analyze general Android applications. The analysis is based on a derived application execution model, which can also support other Android application analysis tasks.
- We implement our approach as a tool, GreenDroid, and evaluate it using 13 real-world popular Android applications. GreenDroid effectively detected 12 real energy problems that had been reported, and further found two new energy problems that were later confirmed by developers. We were also invited by developers to make a patch for one of the two new problems and the patch was accepted. These evaluation results confirm GreenDroid's effectiveness and practical usefulness.

The rest of this chapter is organized as follows. Section 18.2 introduces the basics of Android applications. Section 18.3 presents our empirical study of real energy problems found in Android applications. Section 18.4 elaborates on our energy efficiency diagnosis approach. Section 18.5 introduces our tool implementation and evaluates it with real application subjects. Section 18.6 discusses related work, and finally Sect. 18.7 concludes this article.

18.2   Background

We select the Android platform for our study because it is currently one of the most widely adopted smartphone platforms and it is open for research [12]. Applications running on Android are primarily written in Java programming language. An Android application is first compiled to Java virtual machine compatible .class files that contain Java bytecode instructions. These .class files are then converted to Dalvik virtual machine executable .dex files that contain Dalvik bytecode instructions. Finally, the .dex files are encapsulated into an Android application package file (i.e., an .apk file) for distribution and installation. For ease of presentation, we in the following may simply refer to "Android application" by "application" when there is no ambiguity. An Android application typically comprises four kinds of components as follows [12]:

Activities. Activities are the only components that allow graphical user interfaces (GUIs). An application may use multiple activities to provide cohesive user experiences. The GUI layout of each activity component is specified in the activity's layout configuration file.

Services. Services are components that run at background for conducting long-running tasks like sensor data reading. Activities can start and interact with services.

Broadcast receivers. Broadcast receivers define how an application responds to system-wide broadcasted messages. It can be statically registered in an application's configuration file (i.e., the `AndroidManifest.xml` file associated with each application), or dynamically registered at runtime by calling certain Android library APIs.

Content providers. Content providers manage shared application data, and provide an interface for other components or applications to query or modify these data.

Each application component is required to follow a prescribed lifecycle that defines how this component is created, used, and destroyed. Figure 18.1 shows an activity's lifecycle [13]. It starts with a call to `onCreate()` handler, and ends with a call to `onDestroy()` handler. An activity's foreground lifetime starts after a call to `onResume()` handler, and lasts until `onPause()` handler is called, when another activity comes to foreground. An activity can interact with its users only when it is at foreground. When it goes to background and becomes invisible, its `onStop()` handler would be called. When the users navigate back to a paused or stopped activity, that activity's `onResume()` or `onRestart()` handler would be called, and the activity would come to foreground again. In exceptional cases, a paused or stopped activity may be killed for releasing memory to other applications with higher priorities.

Fig. 18.1 An activity's lifecycle diagram

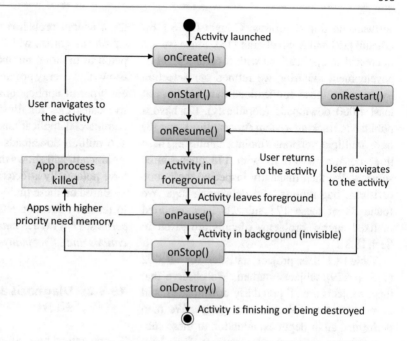

18.3 Empirical Study

In this section, we report our findings from an archival study of real energy problems in Android applications. For ease of presentation, we may use "energy problems" and "energy bugs" interchangeably in subsequent discussions. Our study aims to answer the following three research questions:

- **RQ1 (Problem magnitude)**: *Are energy problems in Android applications serious? Do the problems have a severe impact on smartphone users?*
- **RQ2 (Diagnosis and fixing efforts)**: *Are energy problems relatively more difficult to diagnose and fix than non-energy problems? What information do developers need in the energy problem diagnosis and fixing process?*
- **RQ3 (Common causes and patterns)**: *What are common causes of energy problems? What patterns can we distill from them to enable automated diagnosis of these problems?*

Subject selection. To study these research questions, we first selected a set of commercial

Android applications that suffered from energy problems. We randomly collected 608 candidates from Google Play store [14] using a web crawling tool [15]. These applications have release logs containing at least one of the following keywords: battery, energy, efficiency, consumption, power, and drain. We then performed a manual examination to ensure that these applications indeed had energy problems in the past and developers have fixed these problems in these applications' latest versions (note that we did not have access to the earlier versions containing energy problems). This left us with 229 commercial applications. By studying available information such as category, downloads and user comments, we can answer our research question RQ1. However, these commercial applications alone are not adequate enough for us to study the remaining two research questions. This is because to answer RQ2–3, we need to know all details about how developers fix energy problems (e.g., code revisions, the linkage between these revisions and their corresponding bug reports). As such, we also need to study real energy problems with source code available, i.e., from open-source subjects. To find interesting open-source subjects, we first randomly selected 250 candidates from three primary open-source software hosting platforms: Google Code [16], GitHub [17] and SourceForge [18]. Since we are interested in applications with a certain level of development maturity, we refined our selection by retaining those applications that: (1) have at least 1,000 downloads (popularity), (2) have a public bug tracking system (traceability), and (3) have multiple versions (maintainability). These three constraints left us with 173 open-source subjects. We then manually inspected their code revisions, bug reports, and debugging logs. We found 34 of these 173 subjects have reported or fixed energy problems (details are given in Sect. 18.3.1).

Table 18.1 lists project statistics for all 402 (173 + 229) subjects studied. We observe that these subjects are all popularly downloaded, and cover different application categories. We then performed an in-depth examination of these subjects to answer our research questions. The whole study involved one undergraduate student and four postgraduate students with a manual effort of about 35 person-weeks. We report our findings below.

18.3.1   Problem Magnitude

Our selected 173 open-source Android applications contain hundreds of bug reports and code revisions. From them, we identified a total of 66 bug reports on energy problems, which cover 34 applications. Among these 66 bug reports, 41 have been confirmed by developers. Most (32/41) confirmed bugs are considered to be serious bugs with a severity level ranging from medium to critical. Besides that, we found 30 of these confirmed bugs have been fixed by corresponding code revisions, and developers have verified that these code revisions have indeed solved corresponding energy problems.

On the other hand, regarding the 229 commercial Android applications that suffered from energy problems, we studied their user reviews and obtained three findings. First, we found from the reviews that hundreds of users complained that these applications drained their smartphone batteries too quickly and caused great inconvenience for them. Second, as shown in Table 18.1,

these energy problems cover 27 different application categories, which are quite broad as compared to the total number of 32 categories. This shows that energy problems are common to different types of applications. Table 18.2 lists the top five categories for illustration. Third, these 229 commercial applications have received more than 176 million downloads in total. This number is significant, and shows that their energy problems have potentially affected a vast number of users.

Based on these findings, we derive our answer to research question RQ1: *Energy problems are serious. They exist in many types of Android applications and affect many users.*

18.3.2   Diagnosis and Bug-Fixing Efforts

To understand how difficult the diagnosis and fixing of energy problems can be, we studied 25 out of the 30 fixed energy bugs in open-source applications. Five fixed bugs were ignored in our study because we failed to recover the links between their bug reports and corresponding code revisions.[1] Table 18.3 gives the basic information of our studied energy bugs, including: (1) bug ID, (2) severity level, (3) revision in which the bug was fixed, and (4) program size of the inefficient revision. Table 18.4 reports our study findings. For each fixed energy bug, Table 18.4 reports: (1) duration in which the bug report is open, (2) number of revisions for fixing the bug, and (3) number of classes and methods that were modified for fixing the bug. We also studied the 11 (= 41 − 30) confirmed but not fixed energy problems in open-source applications since four of the eight concerned applications are still actively maintained. We studied how long their bug reports stayed open as well as the duration of their related discussions. From these studies, we made the following three observations.

First, 24 out of the 25 energy problems listed in Tables 18.3 and 18.4 are serious problems whose

---

[1] Our manual examination of the commit logs around the bug fixing dates also failed to find the bug-fixing code revisions.

Table 18.1 Project statistics of our studied Android applications

Application type	Application availability				Application downloads			Covered categories
	Google Code	GitHub	Source Forge	Google Play	Min.	Max.	Avg.	
34 open-source ones (with energy problems)	27/34	8/34	0/34	29/34	1[a]–5 K	5[a]–10 M	0.49–1.68 M	15/32[b]
139 open-source ones (no reported energy problems)	108/139	26/139	10/139	102/139	1–5 K	50–100 M	0.50–1.22 M	24/32
229 commercial ones (with energy problems)	All apps are available on Google Play Store				1–5 K	50–100 M	0.77–2.02 M	27/32

[a] 1 K = 1,000 & 1 M = 1,000,000; [b] According to Google's classification, there were a total of 32 different categories of Android applications at our study time

Table 18.2 Top five categories of energy-inefficient commercial Android applications

Category	# of inefficient applications
Personalization	59 (25.8%)
Tools	34 (14.8%)
Brain and Puzzle	15 (6.6%)
Arcade and Action	13 (5.7%)
Travel and Local	11 (4.8%)

severity ranges from medium to critical. Developers take, on average, 54 work-days to diagnose and fix them. For comparison, we checked the remaining 1,967 non-energy bugs of similar severity (i.e., medium to critical) reported on these applications before March 2013. We found that these non-energy bugs were fixed, on average, within 43 work-days. Figure 18.2 gives a detailed box plot of open duration for the energy and non-energy bugs we studied. For example, the median open duration for non-energy bugs is five days while the median open duration for energy bugs is 11 days. Such comparison results suggest that energy problems are likely to take a longer time to fix. We further conducted a Mann-Whitney U-test [19] of the following two hypotheses:

- **Null hypothesis** H_0. Fixing energy problems does not take a significantly longer time than fixing non-energy problems.
- **Alternative hypothesis** H_1. Fixing energy problems takes a significantly longer time than fixing non-energy problems.

Our test results show that the p-value is 0.0327 (<0.05), indicating that the null hypothesis H_0 can be rejected with a confidence level of over 0.95. Therefore, we can conclude that energy problems take a relatively longer time to fix.

Second, for the 11 confirmed but not fixed energy problems, we found that developers closed five of them because they failed to reproduce corresponding problems and they did not receive user complaints after some seemingly irrelevant code revisions. For three of the remaining six problems, we found that developers are still working on fixing them without success [4–6]. Their three

associated bug reports have been remained open for more than two years. For example, CSipSimple is a popular application for video calls over the Internet. Developers have discussed its energy problem (issue 81) tens of times, trying to find the root cause, but failed to make any satisfactory progress so far. Due to this, some disappointed users uninstalled CSipSimple, as indicated from their comments on the bug report [4].

Third, as shown in Table 18.4, in 21 out of 25 cases, developers fixed the reported energy problems in one or two revisions. These fixes require non-trivial effort. For example, 16 out of these 25 fixes require modifying more than 5 methods. On average, developers fixed these 25 problems by modifying 2.6 classes and 7.8 methods.

We also looked into discussions on fixed energy bugs. We found that many of these bugs are intermittent. Developers generally consider these intermittent bugs as complex issues. In order to reproduce them, developers have to know details about how users interact with their applications before these problems occur. Developers often have to analyze debugging information logged at runtime in order to identify the root causes of these problems. For example, to facilitate energy waste diagnosis, K9Mail developers gave special instructions on how users could provide useful debugging logs [20]. This may become additional overhead for smartphone users when they report energy problems.

Based on these findings, we derive our answer to research question RQ2: *It is relatively more difficult to diagnose and fix energy problems, as compared to non-energy problems; user interaction contexts and debugging logs can help problem diagnosis, but they require additional user-reporting efforts, which may not be desirable.*

18.3.3   Common Patterns of Energy Bugs

Energy inefficiency is a non-functional issue whose causes can be complex and application-specific. For example, CSipSimple issue 1674 [21] happened because the application

Table 18.3 The studied energy bugs in open-source Android applications

Application name	Downloads	Issue information		Fixed revision	Inefficient revision size (LOC)
		Issue no.	Severity		
DroidAR[a]	5[c]–10 K	27*	Medium	207	18,106
Recycle Locator	1–5 K	33*	Medium	69	3,241
Sofia Public Transport Nav.	10–50 K	38*	Medium	156	1,443
Sofia Public Transport	10–50 K	76*	Critical	156	1,649
Google Voice Location[f]	10–50 K	4*	Medium	20	4,632
BitCoin Wallet	10–50 K	86	Medium	1bbc6295083c	27,220
Osmdroid	10–50 K	53*	Medium	751	13,385
Osmdroid	10–50 K	76*	Medium	315	8,636
Zmanim	10–50 K	50/56*	Critical	323	4,807
Transdroid	10–50 K	19*	Medium	Version 0.8.0	11,715
Geohash Droid	10–50 K	24*	Medium	6d8f0153a48	6,682
AndTweet[f]	10–50 K	29*	Medium	4a1ff9683f2	8,908
K9Mail	1[c]–5 M	574	Medium	933	72,723[e]
K9Mail	1–5 M	864	Medium	317	72,723
K9Mail	1–5 M	1031	Medium	1395	72,723
K9Mail	1–5 M	1643/1694	Medium	1731	72,723
K9Mail	1–5 M	N/A[d]	N/A	4542e64	72,723
Open-GPSTracker[f]	100–500 K	70	Critical	33f6e78aad9a	4,447
Open-GPSTracker[f]	100–500 K	128*	Low	3aa9fb4d4ffb	9,174
Ebookdroid	500 K–1 M	23*	Medium	138	14,351
CSipSimple	500–1 M	1674	Critical	1386	54,966
c:geo[b]	1–5 M	1709	Critical	cecda72	33,514
BableSink[f]	1–5 K	N/A*	N/A	9fbcbf01ce	1,718
CWAC-Wakeful	1–5 K	N/A*	N/A	c7d440fl5	896
Ushahidi[f]	10–50 K	N/A*	N/A	337b48f	10,186

[a] Applications from DroidAR to CSipSimple are hosted on Google Code

[b] Applications from c:geo to CommonsWare are hosted on GitHub

[c] 1 K = 1,000 & 1 M = 1,000,000

[d] The symbol "N/A" means "unknown", and the corresponding bugs are found by studying commit logs

[e] The size of K9Mail is based on revision fdfaf03b7a because we failed to access its original SVN repository after it switched to use Git

[f] All applications except Google Voice Location, AndTweet, Open-GPSTracker, BabbleSink and Ushahidi are still actively maintained (continuous code revisions)

Table 18.4 Diagnosis and fixing efforts of our studied energy bugs

| Application name | Issue no. | Diagnosis and fixing efforts | | | |
		Issue open duration (Days)	# of revisions to fix	# of changed classes	# of changed methods
DroidAR	27*	7	3	4	18
Recycle Locator	33*	1	1	1	5
Sofia Public Transport Nav.	38*	19	2	3	7
Sofia Public Transport Nav.	76*	1	1	1	1
Google Voice Location	4*	330	10	4	37
BitCoin Wallet	86	30	1	2	4
Osmdroid	53*	243	1	1	4
Osmdroid	76*	11	1	1	5
Zmanim	50/56*	35	1	6	14
Transdroid	19*	9	1	1	7
Geohash Droid	24*	3	1	1	6
AndTweet	29*	240	1	6	22
K9Mail	574	101	1	2	9
K9Mail	864	49	3	6	8
K9Mail	1031	20	1	1	1
K9Mail	1643/1694	6	2	3	2
K9Mail	N/A	N/A	1	1	2
Open-GPSTracker	70	2	1	3	9
Open-GPSTracker	128*	9	5	7	8
Ebookdroid	23*	2	1	4	5
CSipSimple	1674	6	1	1	1
c:geo	1709	16	1	2	9
BableSink	N/A*	N/A	1	1	1
CWAC-Wakeful	N/A*	N/A	1	1	1
Ushahidi	N/A*	N/A	1	2	9

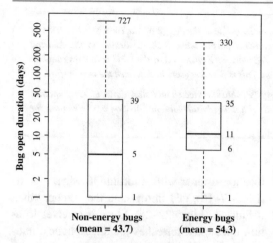

Fig. 18.2 Bug open duration of energy and non-energy bugs

monitored too many broadcasted messages, and its issue 744 was caused by unnecessary talking with a verbose server [22]. Nevertheless, by studying the bug-fixing patches and bug report comments of the earlier mentioned 25 fixed energy problems, we observe that 16 of them (64.0%) are due to misuse of sensors or wake locks. These problems are marked with "*" in Tables 18.3 and 18.4.

To confirm that misuse of sensors or wake locks can indeed lead to energy problems in Android applications, we analyzed the API usage of all 402 applications. On the Android platform, applications need to call certain APIs to invoke system functionalities. For example, an application needs to call the `PowerManager.Wake-Lock.acquire()` API to acquire a wake lock from Android OS so as to keep a device awake for computation. As such, API usage analysis can disclose which Android features are being used by an application. To analyze API usage of our 173 open-source applications, we compiled their source code to obtain Java bytecode. For commercial applications, we handled them differently. We first downloaded their .apk files from Google Play store using an open-source tool Real APKLeecher [23].[2] We then transformed their Dalvik bytecode (contained in the .apk files)

to Java bytecode using dex2jar [24], a popular Dalvik bytecode retargeting tool [25]. Finally, we scanned the Java bytecode of each application to analyze their API usage. From the analysis, we obtained two major findings. First, 46.7% (14/30) open-source applications that use sensors and 68.0% (17/25) open-source applications that acquire wake locks were confirmed to have energy problems. Second, 51.1% (117/229) energy inefficient commercial applications use sensors or wake lock. These findings suggest that misuse of sensors or wake locks could be closely associated with energy problems in Android applications.

Based on these findings, we further studied the discussions on fixed energy problems and their bug-fixing patches. We then observed two types of coding phenomena concerning sensor or wake lock misuse that can lead to serious energy waste in Android applications:

Pattern 1: Missing sensor or wake lock deactivation. To use a sensor, an application needs to register a listener with Android OS, and specify a sensing rate [7]. The listener defines how an application reacts to sensor value or status changes. When a sensor is no longer needed, its listener should be unregistered in time. As stated in Android documentation, forgetting to unregister sensor listeners can lead to unnecessary sensing operations that waste battery energy. Similarly, to keep a smartphone awake for computation, an application needs to acquire a wake lock from Android OS and specify a wake level. For example, a full wake lock can keep a phone's CPU awake and its screen on at full brightness. The acquired wake lock should be released as soon as the computation completes. Forgetting to release wake locks in time can quickly drain a phone's battery [8]. For example, Fig. 18.3 gives a developer's comment on an energy problem in AndTweet, a Twitter client [26]. AndTweet starts a background service `AndTweetService` right upon receiving a broadcast message indicating that Android OS has finished booting.

---

[2]The original Real APKLeecher is GUI-based. We modified it to support command line usage for study automation.

(Footnote 2 continued)
The modified version can be obtained at: http://sccpu2.cse.ust.hk/greendroid.

Fig. 18.3 Developers'
comments on energy bugs

> **AndTweet Issue 29:** *"Issue 29 is due to the design of AndTweetService: It starts right after boot and acquires a partial wake lock. According to the Android documentation, the acquired wake lock ensures that the CPU is always running. The screen might not be on. This is why few users had noticed the issue before."*
>
> **Geohash Droid Issue 24:** *"GeohashService should slow down its GPS updates to one every thirty seconds if nothing besides the notification bar is waiting for updates."*

When `AndTweetService` starts, it acquires a partial wake lock, which is not released until `AndTweetService` is destroyed. However, due to a design defect, `AndTweetService` keeps running at background, unless it encounters an external storage exception (e.g., SD card being un-mounted) or is killed explicitly by users, while such cases are rare. As a result, AndTweet can waste a surprisingly large amount of battery energy due to this missing wake lock deactivation problem.[3]

Pattern 2: Sensory data underutilization. Sensory data are acquired at the cost of battery energy. These data should be effectively used by applications to produce perceptible benefits to smartphone users. However, when an application's program logic becomes complex, sensory data may be "underutilized" in certain executions. In such executions, the energy cost for acquiring sensory data may outweigh the actual usages of these data. We call this phenomenon "sensory data underutilization". We observed that sensory data underutilization often suggests design or implementation defects that can cause energy waste. For example, Fig. 18.4a gives the concerned code snippet of a location data underutilization problem in an entertainment application Geohash Droid. This application is designed for users who like adventures. It randomly selects a location for users and navigates them there using GPS sensors. As the code in Fig. 18.4a shows, Geohash Droid maintains a long running `GeohashService` at background for location sensing. `GeohashService` registers a

location listener with Android OS when it starts (Lines 7–16), and unregisters the listener when it finishes (Lines 22–25). Once it receives location updates, it refreshes the smartphone's notification bar (Line 11), which provides users with quick access to their current locations. After that, it notifies remote listeners (e.g., the navigation map) to use updated location data (Lines 12, 27–36). Thus, location data are used to produce perceptible benefits to users when remote listeners are actively listening to such location updates. However, there are chances when no remote listeners are alive (e.g., the navigation map will not be alive when it loses user focus). When this happens, Geohash Droid would keep receiving the phone's GPS coordinates, simply for updating its notification bar [27]. Such updates do not reflect effective use of newly captured GPS coordinates, while the battery's energy is continuously consumed. Geohash Droid developers received a lot of user complaints for such battery drain. After intensive discussions, developers identified the cause of this problem and chose to reduce the GPS sensing rate when there is no active remote listener for such location updates. Figure 18.3 shows their comment after fixing this energy problem.

Another interesting example is the energy problem in Osmdroid, a popular map-based navigation application. Figure 18.4b gives a simplified version of the concerned code. The application has three components: (1) `MapActivity` for displaying a map to its users, (2) `GPSService` for location sensing and data processing in background, and (3) a broadcast receiver for handling location change messages (Lines 7–13). When `MapActivity` is launched, it starts `GPSService` (Lines 5–6), and registers its broadcast receiver (Lines 15–16). `GPSService`

---

[3] For more details, readers can refer to the following classes in package `com.xorcode.andtweet` of application AndTweet-0.2.4:
`AndTweetService`, `AndTweetServiceManager`, `TimelineActivity` and `TweetListActivity` [26].

```
1. public class GeohashService extends Service {        21.    //more code from GeohashService
2.    private ArrayList<RemoteListener> mListeners;     22.    public void onDestroy() {
3.    private LocationManager lm;                        23.      //GPS listener unregistration
4.    private LocationListener gpsListener;              24.      lm.removeUpdates(gpsListener);
5.    public void onStart(Intent intent, int StartId){  25.    }
6.      mListeners = new ArrayList<RemoteListener>();    26.    //notify alive remote listeners for loc change
7.      //get a reference to system location manager     27.    public void notifyRemoteListeners(Location loc){
8.      lm = getSystemService(LOCATION_SERVICE);         28.      final int N = mListeners.size();
9.      gpsListener = new LocationListener() {           29.      for(int i = 0; i < N; i++) {
10.        public void onLocationChanged(Location loc) { 30.        RemoteListener listener = mListeners.get(i);
11.          updateNotificationBar(loc);                 31.        if(listener.isAlive()){
12.          notifyRemoteListeners(loc);                 32.          //remote listeners consume location data
13.        }                                             33.          listener.locationUpdate(loc);
14.      };                                              34.        }
15.      //GPS listener registration                     35.      }
16.      lm.requestLocationUpdates(GPS, 0, 0, gpsListener); 36.    }
17.    }                                                 37. }
```

(a) Example from the Geohash Droid application (Issue 24)

```
1. public class MapActivity extends Activity {          31. public class GPSService extends Service {
2.    private Intent gpsIntent;                          32.    private LocationManager lm;
3.    private BroadcastReceiver myReceiver;              33.    private LocationListener gpsListener;
4.    public void onCreate(){                            34.    public void onCreate(){
5.      gpsIntent = new Intent(GPSService.class);        35.      //get a reference to system location manager
6.      startService(gpsIntent); //start GPSService     36.      lm = getSystemService(LOCATION_SERVICE);
7.      myReceiver = new BroadcastReceiver() {           37.      gpsListener = new LocationListener() {
8.        public void onReceive(Intent intent) {         38.        public void onLocationChanged(Location loc) {
9.          LocData loc = intent.getExtra();            39.          LocData formattedLoc = processLocation(loc);
10.         updateMap(loc);                              40.        //create and send a location change message
11.         if(trackingModeOn) persistToDatabase(loc);  41.        Intent intent = new Intent("loc_change");
12.       }                                              42.        intent.putExtra("data", formattedLoc);
13.     }                                                43.        sendBroadcast(intent);
14.     //register receiver for handling loc change messages 44.      }
15.     IntentFilter filter = new IntentFilter("loc_change"); 45.    };
16.     registerReceiver(myReceiver, filter);            46.      //GPS listener registration
17.   }                                                  47.      lm.requestLocationUpdates(GPS, 0, 0, gpsListener);
18.   public void onDestroy() {                          48.    }
19.     //stop GPSService and unregister broadcast receiver 49.    public void onDestroy() {
20.     stopService(gpsIntent);                          50.      //GPS listener unregistration
21.     unregisterReceiver(myReceiver);                  51.      lm.removeUpdates(gpsListener);
22.   }                                                  52.    }
23. }                                                    53. }
```

(b) Example from the Osmdroid application (Issue 53)

Fig. 18.4 Motivating examples for sensory data underutilization energy bugs

then registers a location listener with the Android OS when it starts (Lines 36–47). When the application's users change their locations (e.g., during a walk), GPSService would receive and process new location data (Line 39), and broadcast a message with the processed data (Lines 41–43). The broadcast receiver would then use the new location data to refresh a map (Line 10). If the users have enabled location tracking, these location data would also be stored to a database (Line 11). If the Android OS plans to destroy MapActivity (Lines 18–22),

GPSService would be stopped (Line 20), and both the location listener and broadcast receiver would be unregistered (Lines 21, 51). These all work seemingly smoothly. However, if Osmdroid's users switch from MapActivity to any other activity, MapActivity would be put to background (not destroyed), but GPSService would still keep running for location sensing. If the location tracking functionality is not enabled, all collected location data would be used to refresh an invisible map. Then, a huge amount of energy would be wasted [9]. To fix this problem, developers chose to disable the GPS sensing conditionally (e.g., according to whether the location tracking mode is enabled or not), when `MapActivity` goes to background.

From the preceding two examples of sensory data underutilization, we make three observations. First, locating sensory data underutilization problems can provide desirable opportunities for optimizing an application's energy consumption. When such problems occur, the concerned application can deactivate related sensors or tune down their sensing rates to avoid unnecessary energy cost. Second, to detect such sensory data underutilization problems, one should track how sensory data are transformed into different forms of program data and consumed in different ways. Third, sensory data underutilization problems may occur only at certain application states. For example, Geohash Droid wastes energy only when there is no active remote listener waiting for location updates. In Osmdroid, if its user has enabled the location tracking functionality before `MapActivity` goes to background, even if it is consuming non-trivial energy due to continuous GPS sensing, we cannot simply consider this as energy waste. This is because the collected location data could be stored for future uses, producing perceptible user benefits afterwards. These three observations motivate us to consider a state-based approach to analyzing sensory data utilization for Android applications. Such analysis can help developers judge whether their applications are using sensory data in a cost-effective way and provide optimization opportunities for energy efficiency if necessary.

18.3.4   Threats to Validity

The validity of our empirical study may be subject to some threats. One is the representativeness of our selected Android applications. To minimize this threat and avoid subject selection bias, we selected 173 open-source and 229 commercial Android applications spanning 27 different categories. These applications have been popularly downloaded and can be good representatives of real-world Android applications. Another poten-

tial threat is the manual inspection of our selected subjects. We understand that this manual process may be error-prone. To reduce this threat, we have all our data and findings independently inspected by at least two researchers. We cross-validated their inspection results for consistency.

18.4   Energy Efficiency Diagnosis

In this section, we elaborate on our energy efficiency analysis approach. We will begin with an overview of our approach.

18.4.1   Approach Overview

Our energy efficiency diagnosis is based on dynamic information flow analysis [28]. Figure 18.5 shows its high-level abstraction. It takes as inputs the Java bytecode and configuration files of an Android application. The Java bytecode defines the application's program logic, and can be obtained by compiling the application's source code or transforming its Dalvik bytecode [25]. The configuration files specify the application's components, GUI layouts, and so on. The general idea of our diagnosis approach is to execute an Android application using Java PathFinder (JPF) [10], a widely-used dynamic model checker for general Java programs (recall that Android applications are essentially Java programs), to systematically explore its application states. During the execution, our approach monitors all sensor registration/unregistration and wake lock acquisition/releasing operations. It feeds mock sensory data to the application when related sensor listeners are properly registered. It then tracks the propagation of these sensory data as the application executes, and analyzes how they are utilized at different application states. At the end of the execution, our approach compares sensory data utilization across explored states, and reports those states where sensory data are underutilized. It also checks which sensor listeners are forgotten to be unregistered, and which wake locks are forgotten to be released, and reports these anomalies.

Fig. 18.5 Overview of our energy efficiency analysis approach

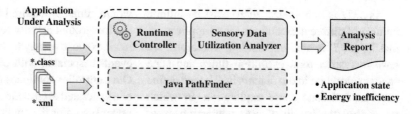

The above high-level abstraction looks straightforward, but contains some challenging questions: *How can one execute an Android application and systematically explore its states, especially in JPF? How can one identify those executions that involve sensory data? How can one measure and compare sensory data utilization at application states explored by these executions?* We answer these questions in the following subsections.

18.4.2 Application Execution and State Exploration

Android applications are mostly designed to interact with smartphone users. Their executions are often triggered by user interaction events. Typically, an Android application starts with its main activity, and ends after all its components are destroyed. During its execution, the application keeps handling received user interaction events and system events (e.g., broadcasted events) by "calling" their handlers according to Android specifications.[4] Each call to an event handler may change the application's state by modifying its components' local or global program data. As such, in order to execute an application and explore its state space in JPF, we need to: (1) generate user interaction events, and (2) guide JPF to schedule corresponding event handlers.

Before going into the technical details, we first formally define our problem domain and clarify

our concept of *bounded state space exploration*. We use P to denote the Android application under diagnosis, and E to denote the set of possible user interaction events for this application.

Definition 18.1 (*User interaction event sequence*): A *user interaction event sequence* $\overline{seq} = [e_1, e_2, \ldots, e_n]$, where each $e_i \in E$ is a user interaction event. Operation $len(\overline{seq})$ returns the length of the sequence $\overline{seq}$, and operation $head(\overline{seq}, k)$ returns a subsequence with the first k user interaction events in $\overline{seq}$. We denote the set of all possible user interaction event sequences as SEQ.

The SEQ set is theoretically unbounded as users can interact with an application in infinite ways.

Definition 18.2 (*Application execution*): An *execution* t of application P is triggered by a sequence of user interaction events $\overline{seq}$. We denote such an execution as $t = exec(P, \overline{seq})$. Then the set of all possible executions T for the application P is:

$$T = \{exec(P, \overline{seq}) \mid \overline{seq} \in SEQ\}.$$

Definition 18.3 (*State and state space*)[5]: During its execution, application P's state changes from s_0, which is P's initial state, to s' after it handles a sequence of user interaction events $\overline{seq}$, where $len(\overline{seq}) \geq 1$. We represent the new state s' as $\langle s_0, \overline{seq} \rangle$. Then we can define the state space explored for application P during its execution $t = exec(P, \overline{seq})$ as:

$$S_t = \{\langle s_0, head(\overline{seq}, k)\rangle \mid 1 \leq k \leq len(\overline{seq})\}.$$

---

[4]Android applications are event-driven. Their program code comprises many loosely coupled event handlers, among which no explicit control flow is specified. At runtime, these event handlers are in fact called by the Android framework, which builds upon hundreds of native library classes.

[5]We discuss state changes at an event handling level as users have control on that. We do not consider finer-grained state changes or state equivalence in our work.

As *SEQ* is unbounded, there exist an infinite number of different executions for an application, that is, set T is also unbounded. Therefore, we have to restrict total execution times and state space exploration in our diagnosis. We then define our bounded state space exploration, in which we control the length of user interaction event sequences.

Definition 18.4 (*Bounded state space exploration*): Given a bound value b (≥ 1) on the length of user interaction event sequences, our diagnosis examines the following executions for an Android application P:

$$T_b = \{exec(P, \overline{seq}) \mid \overline{seq} \in SEQ \ \& \ len(seq) \leq b\}.$$

For these executions, our diagnosis explores the following space of states:

$$S_b = \bigcup_{t \in T_b} S_t$$

After defining the bounded state space exploration concept, we proceed to introduce our diagnosis approach. To effectively explore an Android application's state space, we need to generate event sequences of user interactions and schedule corresponding event handlers. We address these two technical issues below.

Event sequence generation. Our runtime controller, as illustrated in Fig. 18.5, simulates user interactions by generating corresponding event sequences. Conceptually, the generation process contains two parts: static and dynamic. In the static part, i.e., before executing an application, we first analyze the application's configuration files to learn the GUI layouts of its activity components (recall that only activities have GUIs). Specifically, we map each GUI widget (e.g., a button) of an activity component to a set of possible user actions (e.g., button clicks). This constructs a *user event set* for each activity. In the dynamic part, i.e., when executing an application, our runtime controller monitors the application's execution history and current state. When the application waits for user interactions (e.g., after an activity's `onResume()` handler is called), our controller

would generate required events and feed them to the foreground activity for handling. This is done in an exhaustive way by enumerating all possible events associated with each activity component. Our controller continues doing so until the length of a generated event sequence reaches the required upper bound or the application exits. In this way, we generate all possible event sequences bounded by a length limit b, and explore its corresponding bounded state space S_b. For ease of understanding, we provide an example to illustrate the event sequence generation process.

The example application in Fig. 18.6 contains two activities: `MainActivity` and `AccountEditActivity`. When this application starts, `MainActivity` would appear first. Its users can click the "Edit account" button to edit their account information in another `AccountEditActivity`'s window (`MainActivity` would then be put to background). After editing, users can save the changes by clicking the "Save" button or discard the changes by clicking the "Cancel" button. This also brings users back to the previous `MainActivity`'s window (`AccountEditActivity` would then be destroyed). To exit the application, the users can click the "Exit app" button in the `MainActivity`'s window. For ease of presentation, suppose that: (1) we consider only button click events (our tool implementation can handle other types of events, e.g., filling textboxes and selecting from dropdown lists), (2) the event sequence length bound is set to four, and (3) each generated event is correctly handled (e.g., after clicking "Exit app", the application indeed exits).

Based on these assumptions, we consider generating event sequences for this example application. Our controller first constructs user event sets for the two activities. For instance, the user event set for `MainActivity` is {click "Edit account" button, click "Exit app" button}. At runtime, when `MainActivity` waits for user interactions, our controller can enumerate and generate all events in `MainActivity`'s user event set in turn. If it generates an "Edit account" button click event, `AccountEditActivity` would come to

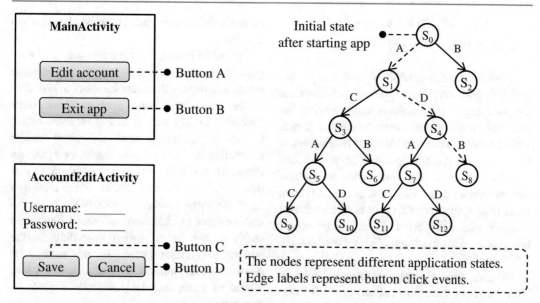

Fig. 18.6 Illustration of event sequence generation

foreground. When `AccountEditActivity` is ready for user interactions, our controller similarly enumerates and generates all events in `AccountEditActivity`'s user event set in turn. This event generation process continues until the length of a generated event sequence reaches four or the application exits (e.g., when the "Exit app" button is clicked). The tree on the right of Fig. 18.6 illustrates this event sequence generation process. The nodes on the tree represent different application states and the labels on edges that connect the nodes represent button click events. Each path from the root node to a leaf node corresponds to one user interaction event sequence. For example, the path with dashed edges represents an event sequence of length three (the first application starting event is not counted): starting the application, clicking "Edit account" button, clicking "Cancel" button, and finally clicking "Exit app" button.[6] Other sequences can be explained similarly.

Event handler scheduling. With event sequences generated to represent user interactions, we now consider how to schedule event handlers properly. As mentioned earlier, Android applications consist of a set of loosely-coupled event handlers, among which no explicit control flow is specified. Existing analysis techniques for Android applications commonly assume that developers should specify calling relationships between these event handlers [3]. However, this is not practical. Real-world Android applications typically contain hundreds of event handlers (e.g., the application DroidAR used in our evaluation has 149 event handlers). Manually specifying calling relationships between these event handlers is labor-intensive and error-prone. Therefore, in this work we do not make such an assumption. Instead, we propose to derive an application execution model (or AEM) from Android specifications, and leverage it to guide the runtime scheduling of event handlers. The extracted AEM model plays the role of enforcing calling relationships between event handlers. Specifically, the AEM model is a collection of temporal rules that are prescribed by the Android framework and followed by all Android applications (i.e., such rules are application-generic). We define the model as follows:

---

[6]In our implementation, the "start application" and "exit application" events are by defaults generated. That means each generated event sequence starts with the "start application" events and ends with the "exit application" events. Besides, there is no standard way to exit an Android application, our way is to destroy all active activity and service components.

$$AEM = \{R_i \mid R_i \text{ is a temporal rule of}$$
$$\text{form } [\psi], \quad [\phi] \Rightarrow \lambda\}$$

In each rule R_i, symbols ψ and λ represent two temporal formulae expressed in linear-time temporal logic. They make assertions about the past and future, respectively. Symbol ϕ represents a propositional logic formula making assertions about the present. Specifically, ψ describes what has happened in history during an application execution, ϕ evaluates the current situation (e.g., what system or user event is received), and λ claims what is expected. Therefore, the whole rule expresses the meaning: *If both ψ and ϕ hold, λ is expected.*

We give some examples of temporal rules in Table 18.5. For the entire collection of 29 rules, readers may refer to our research chapter [29].[7] In these example rules, propositional connectives like $\wedge$, $\Rightarrow$, and $\neg$ follow their traditional interpretations, i.e., conjunction, implication, and negation. For temporal connectives, we follow Etessami et al.'s notation [30], which is explained in the following. Unary temporal connective X means "next", and its past time analogue X^{-1} means "previously". Binary temporal connective S means "since". Specifically, a temporal formula "$F_1 \ S \ F_2$" means that F_2 held at some time in the past, and since then F_1 always holds.

We give explanation for the rules in Table 18.5. The first rule states that an activity's onStart() handler is to be called after its onCreate() handler completes as long as this activity is not forced to finish. The second rule states that a GUI widget's click event handler is to be called if: (1) the widget (e.g., a button) is clicked, (2) its enclosing activity is at foreground (i.e., the activity's onPause() handler has not been called since the last call to its onResume() handler), and (3) its click event listener is properly registered. The third rule disables the call to a message event handler before its registration and after its unregistration. The last rule states that a static message

event handler is to be called upon any broadcasted message.

Our AEM model, i.e., the collection of 29 temporal rules, is converted to a decision procedure which determines the event handlers to be called in the next step according to an application's execution history and its newly received events (events are handled in turn). This event handler scheduling is always deterministic, except when there are multiple receivers registered (either dynamically or statically) for broadcast messages from the same source.[8] If this is the case, the onReceive() handlers of those registered receivers are to be called according to the receiver registration orders. By this means, we can exercise an Android application in JPF's Java virtual machine, and systematically explore its state space.

18.4.3 Detecting Missing Sensor or Wake Lock Deactivation

We next discuss how to detect energy problems when exploring an application's state space. As mentioned earlier, missing sensor or wake lock deactivation is one common cause of energy problems. This shares some similarity with traditional resource leak problems, where a program fails to release its acquired system resources (e.g., memory blocks, file handles, etc.) [31]. Resource leak problems can cause system performance degradation (e.g., slower response), and similarly missing deactivation of sensors or wake locks can also waste valuable battery energy. Besides, according to Android process management policy [32], sensors and wake locks are not automatically deactivated even when the application components that activated them are destroyed (e.g., onDestroy() handler is called). We will give an example and details in Sect. 18.5.2.1. Based on the preceding state exploration efforts, we can now adapt existing

---

[7] We do not claim the completeness of the AEM model. We will show in our later evaluation that the current version of our AEM model already suffices for verifying many real-world Android applications.

[8] Although we did not observe such cases in our experiments, registering multiple receivers for broadcast messages from the same source is grammatically acceptable in Android applications.

Table 18.5 Example temporal rules in our AEM model

Rule 1: When should an activity's lifecycle handler act.onStart() be called?
$[X^{-1}act.onCreate()], [\neg ACT\_FINISH\_EVENT] \Rightarrow X\,act.onStart()$
Rule 2: When should GUI widget's click event handler view.onClick() be called?
$[(\neg act.onPause()\,S\,act.onResume()) \wedge (\neg view.reg(null)S\,view.reg(listener))], [VIEW\_CLICK\_EVENT] \Rightarrow X\,listener.onClick()$
Rule 3: When should a dynamic message handler rcv.onReceive() be called?
$[\neg rcv.unreg()\,S\,rcv.reg()], [MSG\_EVENT] \Rightarrow X\,rcv.onReceive()$
Rule 4: When should a static message handler Receiver.onReceive() be called?
$[True], [MSG\_EVENT] \Rightarrow X\,Receiver.onReceive()$

resource leak detection techniques [33,34] to detect missing sensor or wake lock deactivation bugs. In particular, our diagnosis monitors the execution of an Android application and keeps checking the violation of the following two policies:

- **Sensor management policy**: A sensor listener l, once registered, should be unregistered eventually before the application component that registered l is destroyed.
- **Wake lock management policy**: A wake lock wl, once acquired, should be released eventually before the application component that acquired wl is destroyed.

Note that such checking is feasible only after we have addressed the event sequence generation and event handler scheduling problems for Android applications.

18.4.4   Sensory Data Utilization Analysis

During an Android application's execution, its collected sensory data are transformed into different forms and consumed by different application components. We need to track these data usages for energy efficiency analysis. We do it at the byte-code instruction level by dynamic tainting. Our technique contains three phases: (1) tainting each collected sensory datum with a unique mark; (2) propagating taint marks as the application executes; (3) analyzing sensory data utilization at dif-

ferent application states. We elaborate on the three phases in the following.

18.4.4.1   Preparing and Ainting Sensory Data

In the first phase, we generate mock sensory data from an existing sensory data pool, which is controlled with different precision levels. They are then fed to the application under analysis after each event handler call. The object reference to each sensory datum is initialized with a unique taint mark before the datum is fed to the application. The taint mark will be propagated with the datum together for later analysis.

18.4.4.2   Propagating Taint Marks

At runtime, an Android application's collected sensory data are transformed into different forms by assignment, arithmetic, relational, and logical operations. For example, the Osmdroid application in Fig. 18.4b has its loc object (Line 38) transformed to another formattedLoc object (Line 39), which further affects the intent object (Line 42). Later, by message communication, this intent object is propagated to a broadcast receiver and converted back to the loc object (Line 9), which may or may not affect database content, depending on the variable trackingModeOn's value (Line 11). Such data flows need to be tracked to propagate taint marks so as to identify which program data depend on the collected sensory data. Based on this information, one is then able to analyze sensory data utilization.

Our technique intercepts the execution of a subset of Java bytecode instructions at runtime and propagates taint marks in JPF's Java virtual machine according to our tainting policy.[9] A key advantage of such an instruction-level taint propagation is that it does not require application-specific program instrumentation, which is often time-consuming and error-prone. Table 18.6 gives our tainting policy, which comprises 12 taint propagation rules. These rules handle taint propagations along data dependencies. They are expressed in the following form:

$$T(A) = T(B) \cup T(C)$$

This means that data B's and C's taint marks are merged to become data A's taint mark. Note that B and C can be optional. Each taint propagation rule in Table 18.6 is designed for a set of bytecode instructions with similar semantics (explained in the lower part of Table 18.6). For example, Rule 6 is for all binary calculation bytecode instructions (totally 37 instructions) such as fadd and iand. The instruction fadd adds two floating numbers popped from the operand stack in the current method call's frame, and pushes the addition result back into this operand stack. Similarly, the instruction iand performs a bitwise "and" operation on two integers popped from the operand stack in the current method call's frame, and pushes the operation result back into the stack. For all such binary calculation bytecode instructions, our taint propagation works as follows (Rule 6): the result (at the top of the operand stack after the calculation, represented by stack[0] in Table 18.6) would be tainted with the same marks if any operand (at the top of the operand stack before the calculation, represented by stack'[0] and stack'[1] in Table 18.6) is tainted before calculation. Other taint propagation rules can be explained similarly.[10]

We illustrate the taint propagation process by a concrete example. Figure 18.7 lists the code snippet from an application that uses accelerometer data to compute and display a phone's current acceleration status (Lines 21–28). The application also monitors whether the phone is being shuffled (Line 3), and if yes, it would change its background to a different color and notify its user (Lines 4–11). In this example, the initial taint mark is associated with an object reference event. The event object contains the sensory data from a smartphone's accelerometer. By object field access, the local array values of the isShuffled method get its assignment from the event object (Line 21). Since values is data dependent on the tainted object event, the taint mark is propagated to values according to Rule 8 (for handling object field reading instructions) and Rule 5 (for handling array element writing instructions). Then, by array element readings and local variable assignments, this taint mark is propagated to local variables x, y, and z (Lines 22–24) according to Rule 3 (for handling array element reading instructions) and Rule 4 (for handling local variable assignment instructions). Next, a local variable accelerationSquareRoot is calculated (Line 26–27). It is tainted according to Rule 6 (for handling binary calculation instructions) and Rule 4 since it is data dependent on the tainted local variables x, y, and z. Finally, method isShuffled's return value is tainted according to a special rule that handles control dependencies. The rule taints a method's return value if any of its arguments is tainted (to be further explained shortly). Later this return value is further assigned to local variable switchColor in method onSensorChanged (Line 3), and switchColor is also tainted with the same

---

[9]On real devices, an Android application runs in a register-based Dalvik virtual machine, while JPF's Java virtual machine is stack-based. This difference does not affect our analysis.

[10]Notes for Table 18.6: For Rule 8, we followed Taint-Droid's choice to propagate object reference's taint to retrieved object field values to avoid undertainting in

---

(Footnote 10 continued)
certain cases [35]. For example, we only taint the reference of sensory data objects (instead of tainting all object fields since the object can have complex structures) when taint propagation starts. Rule 8 can correctly help propagate taint marks when the sensory data object fields are read (see Fig. 18.7 for illustration). Rule 12 does not conflict with the rule for handling control dependencies (see the "propagation taint marks" part in Sect. 18.4.4). They can be applied together.

Table 18.6 Taint propagation policy

Index	Instruction type	# insns	Instruction semantics	Taint propagation rule
1	Const C	15	$stack[0] \leftarrow C$	$T(stack[0]) = \varnothing$
2	Load index	25	$stack[0] \leftarrow localVar_{index}$	$T(slack[0]) = T(localVar_{index})$
3	LoadArray arrayRef, index	8	$stack[0] \leftarrow arrayRef[index]$	$T(stack[0]) = T(arrayRef) \cup T(arrayRef[index])$
4	Store index	25	$localVar_{index} \leftarrow stack'[0]$	$T(localVar_{index}) = T(stack'[0])$
5	StoreArray arrayRef, index	8	$arrayRef[index] \leftarrow stack'[0]$	$T(arrayRef[index]) = T(stack'[0])$
6	Binary-op	37	$stack[0] \leftarrow stack'[1] \otimes stack'[0]$	$T(stack[0]) = T(stack'[0]) \cup T(stack'[1])$
7	Unary-op	20	$stack[0] \leftarrow \ominus stack'[0]$	$T(stack[0]) = T(stack'[0])$
8*	GetField index	1	$stack[0] \leftarrow stack'[0].instanceField$	$T(stack[0]) = T(stack'[0].instanceField) \cup T(stack'[0])$
9	GetStatic index	1	$stack[0] \leftarrow ClassName.staticField$	$T(stack[0]) = T(ClassName.staticField)$
10	PutField index	1	$stack'[1].instanceField \leftarrow stack'[0]$	$T(stack'[1].instanceField) = T(stack'[0])$
11	PutStatic index	1	$ClassName.staticField \leftarrow stack'[0]$	$T(ClassName.staticField) = T(stack'[0])$
12*	Return(non-void)	5	$callerStack[0] \leftarrow calleeStack'[0]$	$T(callerStack[0]) = T(calleeStack'[0])$

Index	Detailed instruction semantics (The semantics of the instructions whose index are underlined serve as examples)
1	Push a constant value C onto the Operand stack ($stack[0]$ represents the value at the stack top after an operation)
2, 3	Load the value of the #index local variable onto the Operand stack
4, 5	Pop and store the value at stack top to the #index local variable ($stack'[0]$ represents the value at the stack top before an operation)
6, 7	Perform the binary operation $\otimes$ on the two values popped from the Operand stack (i.e., $stack'[0]$ and $stack'[1]$) and push the result back onto the stack
8, 9	Get a field value of an object on the heap and push the value onto the Operand stack. The object reference is popped from the stack (i.e., $stack'[0]$). The object field's name and type can be found by referring to the #index slot of the constant pool
10, 11	Pop and store the value at the stack top (i.e., $stack'[0]$) to an object field on the heap. The object reference is popped from the stack (i.e., $stack'[1]$). The object field's name and type can be found by referring to the #index slot of the constant pool
12	Pop the value at the callee's Operand stack top (i.e., $calleeStack'[0]$), and push the value onto the caller's Operand stack

```
1. public void onSensorChanged(SensorEvent event){     20. public boolean isShuffled(SensorEvent event){
2.   if(event.sensor.getType() == ACCELEROMETER){       21.    float[] values = event.values;
3.     boolean switchColor = isShuffled(event);          22.    float x = values[0];
4.     if(switchColor){                                  23.    float y = values[1];
5.       showMessage("Device shuffled");                 24.    float z = values[2];
6.       if(getBackgroundColor() == RED){                25.    float g = SensorManager.GRAVITY_EARTH;
7.         setBackgroundColor(GREEN);                     26.    float accelerationSquareRoot
8.       } else{                                          27.        = (x * x + y * y + z * z) / (g * g);
9.         setBackgroundColor(RED);                       28.    updateAccTextView(accelerationSquareRoot);
10.      }                                                29.    if(accelerationSquareRoot >= 2){
11.    }                                                  30.        return true;
12.  }                                                    31.    }
13. }                                                     32.    return false;
                                                          33. }
```

Fig. 18.7 Example code to demonstrate taint propagation

mark (Rule 4). This completes the whole taint propagation process.

In our tainting process, we mainly consider data dependencies. Regarding control dependencies, we adopt a strategy similar to those studied in related work [36,37]. That is, we taint a method's return value if any of its arguments is tainted (including the method's implicit "this" argument if applicable). This strategy/rule is based on the assumption that a method's output (i.e., return value) should depend on its input in well-written programs. This is the only rule concerning control dependencies in our taint propagation process. We do it this way because tracking finer-grained control dependencies may incur significant performance overhead and even imprecision to analysis results [35,38]. Our taint propagation terminates when the application under analysis finishes its handling of sensor event.[11] This occurs in two situations. If the sensor event handler (e.g., onSensorChanged() in our example) does not start any worker thread to further handle the received sensor event, the propagation stops at the exit of this handler. Otherwise, the propagation has to continue until the sensor event handler returns and all worker threads terminate. Our taint propagation can thus identify the program data that depend on collected sensory data and trace their usages when an application executes. One thing that

deserves explanation is that there might be cases where an application starts worker threads in a special way, e.g., these threads are delayed in their running, periodically started by a timer or kept long-running for handling sensor events. Although we did not observe similar cases in our study, there is no restriction of using such multi-threading features in Android applications. When such cases occur, our taint propagation would theoretically have to continue until all worker threads end. However, in practice, this may compromise the tool's usability since it can perform taint propagation for very long time and fail to report analysis results in a timely fashion. Therefore, for practicality, one may wish to set a timeout value for restricting such long taint propagation. This is an implementation issue and we do not elaborate further.

18.4.4.3 Analyzing Sensory Data Utilization

With program data tainted with marks associated with sensory data, we can analyze how sensory data are used in an Android application and whether the uses are effective with respect to energy cost.

Consider an Android application's execution t_i, in which the application visits a set of states S_{t_i} by handling received events (user events, system events,[12] or sensory events), and finally termi-

---

[11]One can also track the usage of sensory data until an application exits or new sensory data arrive, but we did not observe any noticeable difference in our analysis results in experiments.

[12]In GreenDroid, system events are generated by monitoring API invocations. For example, a broadcast message event will be generated when GreenDroid observes the invocation of the corresponding message broadcast API.

nates with all its components destroyed. As mentioned earlier, when we fix an upper bound b for the length of user interaction event sequences, the space of explored states S_b for this application would be bounded (i.e., the total number of states in this space is finite). As such, we are able to analyze these states to understand how sensory data are used, and compare their usages across different states. For comparison purposes, we propose an analysis metric called *Data Utilization Coefficient* (*DUC* for short). It is defined by Eq. 18.1:

$$DUC(s, d) = \frac{usage(s, d)}{Max_{s' \in S_b, d' \in D}(usage(s', d'))}$$
$$(18.1)$$

The utilization coefficient of sensory data d at state s is defined as the ratio between d's usage at state s and the maximal usage of any sensory data from our data pool D at any state in S_b. A lower DUC value indicates a lower utilization of sensory data. The usage of sensory data d at state s is further defined by Eq. 18.2:

$$usage(s, d) = \sum_{i \in API\_Call(s,d)} eTest(i, d, s) \times noInst(i)$$
$$(18.2)$$

In this equation, $API\_Call(s, d)$ is the set of API call instructions executed since sensory data d are fed to the application at state s and until the data handling is finished. Function $eTest(i, d, s)$ is an effectiveness test to see whether the following two conditions both hold: (1) the API called by i uses program data dependent on sensory data d, and (2) the API's execution at state s produces perceptible benefits to users. When both conditions hold, the effectiveness test function returns 1. Otherwise, it returns 0. Function $noInst(i)$ returns the number of bytecode instructions executed by this API call. *The rationale behind our usage metric is that it reflects how many times and to what extent sensory data are used by an application at certain states to benefit its users.* This metric is designed based on our earlier study of 30 open-source Android applications that use sensors. These applications have called various Android or third-party APIs

(e.g., Google Maps APIs) to use sensory data to support phone users with various functionalities.

Now we explain how the effectiveness test function $eTest(i, d, s)$ is implemented. For its first condition, we check whether the concerned API is called with arguments (including its implicit "this" argument if applicable) having the same taint mark as sensory data d. For its second condition, we take an outcome-based strategy. The basic idea is that the API called by instruction i at state s passes the effectiveness test if and only if its execution produces perceptible outcomes/benefits to users (e.g., updating visible GUIs or writing to file systems). Specifically, our current strategy works as follows:

- If the API updates GUI elements, it passes the test as long as these GUI elements are visible at application state s, and fails otherwise.
- If the API: (1) stores any data to file systems, databases or network, (2) updates a phone's status (e.g., adjusting its screen brightness), or (3) passes any message for inter- or intra-application communication (e.g., broadcasting system-wide events), the API passes the test regardless of the application state. Here, we conservatively assume that the stored data or passed messages will eventually produce perceptible benefits to users.
- For all other cases, the API fails the test.

As such, our analysis can identify those application states where sensory data are underutilized based on calculated sensory data usage and cross-state comparisons. We give one example for illustration. Consider the three states in the Osmdroid example in Fig. 18.4b. They are also listed in Table 18.7. Take the third state $\langle s_0, [e_1, e_2, e_3] \rangle$ for example. It means that: Osmdroid's user starts the application by launching MapActivity (e_1), enables its location tracking functionality (e_2), and switches the application to another activity (e_3). We analyze sensory data utilization for these three states. For ease of presentation, we explain at a source code level (actual analysis is conducted at a bytecode instruction level), and assume that: (1) each method is a pre-defined

Table 18.7 GPS data utilization coefficients at three application states of Osmdroid

Application state	Method calls that consume GPS data	GPS data usage	GPS data utilization coefficient
$\langle s_0, [e_1, e_2] \rangle$	*ProcessLocation, putExtra, sendBroadcast*, getExtra, updateMap*, persistToDatabase**	$3n$	$3n/3n = 1.00$
$\langle s_0, [e_1, e_3] \rangle$	*ProcessLocation, putExtra, sendBroadcast*, getExtra, updateMap†*	n	$n/3n = 0.33$
$\langle s_0, [e_1, e_2, e_3] \rangle$	*ProcessLocation, putExtra, sendBroadcast*, getExtra, updateMap^f, persistToDatabase**	$2n$	$2n/3n = 0.66$

• e_1: users start Osmdroid and the map activity launches; e_2: users switch on the location tracking mode; e_3: users switch from map activity to another activity
• Method calls that can pass the effectiveness test are marked with the symbol "*"; method calls used to update invisible GUI elements are marked with the symbol "†"
• Please note that only method calls marked with the symbol * use GPS data and produce perceptible benefits to Osmdroid users

API, and (2) there are n bytecode instructions executed for each called API. Consider the second state, which is reached when the user switches to another activity from MapActivity directly. For this state, the location tracking functionality is not yet enabled. We observe that all external GPS data and internal program data depending on these GPS data are processed and used in turn by a set of APIs, namely, processLocation, putExtra, sendBroadcast, getExtra and updateMap. According to our usage metric, only the sendBroadcast API passes the effectiveness test. The other four APIs fail the test because none of them can produce perceptible benefits to users (note that the map is still invisible now). According to Eq. 18.2, the GPS data usage at this state is n. We can also calculate that GPS data would have a maximal usage of $3n$ at the first state, where updateMap is used to render a visible map, sendBroadcast spreads the GPS data to the entire system, and persistToDatabase method stores the GPS data to database. Therefore, the GPS data utilization coefficient for the second state is $0.33 (=n/3n)$. The coefficients for the other two states can be calculated similarly, as shown in Table 18.7. These results suggest that GPS data are clearly underutilized at the second state, as compared to the other two states.

Our GreenDroid implementation ranks sensory data utilization coefficients for different applica-

tion states such that energy problem reports can be prioritized and developers can then focus on the most serious energy problems. These reports contain two major pieces of information to ease energy problem diagnosis and fixing. First, Green-Droid reports how sensory data are consumed by different APIs at different application states, and highlights those APIs that ineffectively use sensory data. Second, GreenDroid provides concrete event handler calling traces (corresponding to user interaction event sequences). For ease of understanding, we give an example report in Fig. 18.8. It shows that GPS data are not well-utilized by Osmdroid at the second application state described in Table 18.7. In this example, GreenDroid reports that: (1) GPS data are used to render an invisible map (i.e., updateMap API invocation), and (2) an event handler calling trace to reach the problematic application state. Such reported information are actionable to developers. By examining reported event handler calling traces, developers will be able to construct concrete test cases (e.g., user interaction events) to reproduce the corresponding sensory data underutilization scenario. For instance, the event handler calling trace in our example report corresponds to the following two user interaction events: (1) launching the MapActivity, and (2) switching away from MapActivty (see Sect. 18.2 for the calling order of activity lifecycle event handlers). Besides, by examining reported sensory data usages, espe-

Fig. 18.8 Example
analysis report of
GreenDroid

===

Sensory Data Underutilization

===

[Sensory data usage]: *sendBroadcast, updateMap*†

[Sensory data utilization coefficient:] 0.33

[Event handler calling trace]:

MapActivity.onCreate (Line 4), *MapActivity.onStart, MapActivity.onResume, GPSService.onCreate* (Line 34), *MapActivity.onPause, MapActivity.onStop, gpsListener.onLocationChanged* (Line 38), *myReceiver.onReceive* (Line 8)

Notes: (1) "†" highlights APIs that ineffectively utilize sensory data. (2) For ease of understanding, we use class, variable and handler names to represent event handlers, while in real reports the event handlers are represented using object IDs and fully qualified Java method signatures. (3) Our tool will also output source file names and source line numbers if they are available.

cially ineffective data usages (e.g., `updateMap` in this example), developers can understand why an application consumes more energy than necessary. Such energy problem reports provide much richer information than pure complaints that can be commonly found in smartphone application forums [2]. Developers can thus pinpoint those problematic application states where energy is consumed unnecessarily due to ineffective use of sensory data. They can then take various actions for problem fixing, e.g., tuning down sensing rates or temporally disabling sensing as discussed in our earlier examples.

Finally, for detected missing sensor or wake lock deactivations, GreenDroid will also report similar information for energy problem diagnosis. Specifically, it will report: (1) those sensor listeners or wake locks that are forgotten to be properly unregistered or released before an application exits, and (2) event handler calling traces for reaching those problematic application states.

18.5 Experimental Evaluation

We implemented our energy diagnosis approach as a prototype tool named GreenDroid [11] on top of JPF [10]. GreenDroid consists of 18,367 lines of Java code, including 7,251 lines of code for energy diagnosis, and other 11,116 lines of code

for modeling Android APIs. We explain some details about GreenDroid's implementation. First, modeling Android APIs is necessary for our diagnosis because Android applications depend on a proprietary set of library classes that are not available outside real devices or emulators [39]. These library classes are mostly built on native code. Due to JPF's closed-world assumption [10], we have to model these library classes and their exposed APIs. Ignoring this modeling requirement would result in imprecision in the diagnosis results. For example, if GreenDroid does not properly model the Activity class's `startActivity()` API, it will not be able to analyze activity switches, which are very common in Android applications. However, Android exposes more than 8,000 public APIs to developers [40]. Fully modeling them is extremely labor-intensive and almost impossible for individual researchers like us. As such, in our current implementation, we took a pragmatic approach by manually modeling a subset of APIs that are commonly called in Android applications. Modeling these APIs is already sufficient for carrying out our evaluation with real application subjects. To be specific, we have carefully modeled 76 APIs using JPF's native peer and listener mechanisms [11,41]. These APIs either frequently get invoked in our experimental application subjects or have to be modeled as otherwise JPF will crash on their invocation (e.g., when they involve native calls). Modeling these APIs took us nearly three months. For remaining APIs, we provided stubs with simple logics. In these stubs, we basically ignored their corresponding APIs' side effect if any, and made them return a value selected from a reasonably bounded domain when necessary. Second, besides tracking standard JPF program state information (e.g., call stack of each thread, heap and scheduling information) [42], GreenDroid also tracks the following four types of information for analysis: (1) a stack of active activities, their lifecycle status, and visibility of their containing GUI elements, (2) a list of running services and their lifecycle status, (3) a list of registered broadcast receivers, and (4) a list of registered sensor listeners and wake locks. More tool implementation details can be found in our technical report [41] and research chapter [29].

In this section, we evaluate GreenDroid by controlled experiments and a case study. We aim to answer the following five research questions:

- **RQ4 (Effectiveness and efficiency)**: *Can GreenDroid effectively diagnose and detect energy problems in real-world Android applications? What is its diagnosis overhead?*
- **RQ5 (Necessity and usefulness of AEM model)**: *Can GreenDroid correctly schedule event handlers for Android applications with our AEM model? Can GreenDroid still conduct an effective diagnosis if it randomly schedules event handlers (i.e., with our AEM model disabled)?*
- **RQ6 (Impact of event sequence length limit)**: *How does the length limit of generated user interaction event sequences affect the thoroughness of our energy diagnosis in terms of code coverage?*
- **RQ7 (Comparison with resource leak detection work)**: *How is GreenDroid compared with existing resource leak detection work in terms of finding real missing sensor or wake lock deactivation problems?*
- **RQ8 (Energy saving)**: *How much energy can be potentially saved if our detected energy problems are fixed?*

18.5.1   Experimental Setup

We selected 14 open-source Android applications as our experimental subjects. Table 18.8 lists their basic information, which includes: (1) version number, (2) size of the selected version, (3) repository from which source code was obtained, (4) application category, and (5) number of downloads.[13] The first 12 applications were confirmed to have energy problems of our two identified patterns (Sect. 3.3). We use them to validate the effectiveness of our approach. We also selected two other subjects (Omnidroid and GPSLogger) from the open-source applications collected in our empirical study. Neither of these two applications have confirmed energy problem reports. However, from their project websites and user reviews, we judged that they heavily use GPS sensors in a very energy-consuming way and are susceptible to energy inefficiency problems. Thus we also selected them for our study to see whether our approach can identify energy optimization opportunities for them. We observe from Table 18.8 that our selected applications have been popularly downloaded (over five million downloads in total), and covered a variety of application categories (11 different categories). We obtained these applications' source code and compiled them on Android 2.3.3 for our experiments.[14] We conducted our experiments on a dual-core machine with Intel Core i5 CPU @2.60GHz and 8GB RAM, running Windows 7 Professional SP1. In the following we elaborate on our experiments with respect to the five research questions in turn.

---

[13]The number of application downloads reported here may slightly differ from what was reported in our empirical study due to the data update during the time gap between our empirical study and experiments.

[14]At our study time, we chose Android 2.3.3 because it was one of the most widely adopted Android platforms and is compatible with most applications on the market. Our approach is general and not restrictive to specific platform versions though.

Table 18.8 Experimental subject information and detected energy bugs

Application name	Version	LOC	Source code availability	Category	Download	Detected energy problem (severity level)
DroidAR	R-204[a]	18,106	Google Code	Tools	5–10 K	Missing sensor deactivation (Medium[c])
Recycle Locator	R-68	3,241	Google Code	Travel & Local	1–5 K	Missing sensor deactivation (Medium)
Ushahidi	R-9d0aa75	10,186	GitHub	Communication	10–50 K	Missing sensor deactivation (N/A)
AndTweet	V-0.2.4[b]	8,908	Google Code	Social	10–50 K	Missing wake lock deactivation (Medium)
Ebookdroid	R-137	14,351	Google Code	Productivity	1–5 M	Missing wake lock deactivation (Medium)
BableSink	R-12879a3	1,718	GitHub	Library & Demo	1–5 K	Missing wake lock deactivation (N/A)
CWAC-Wakeful	R-d984b89	896	GitHub	Education	1–5 K	Missing wake lock deactivation (N/A)
Sofia Public Transport Nav.	R-114	1,443	Google Code	Transportation	10–50 K	Sensory data underutilization (Critical)
Osmdroid	R-115	1,427	Google Code	Transportation	10–50 K	Missing sensor deactivation (Critical)
Zmanim	R-750	18,091	Google Code	Travel & Local	10–50 K	Sensory data underutilization (Medium)
Geohash Droid	R-322	4,893	Google Code	Books & References	10–50 K	Sensory data underutilization (Critical)
My Tracks	V-0.8.1-pre2	6,682	Google Code	Entertainment	10–50 K	Sensory data underutilization (Medium)
Omnidroid	R-7749d47	16,560	Google Code	Health & Fitness	5–10 M	Sensory data underutilization (N/A)
GPSLogger	R-863	12,427	Google Code	Productivity	1–5 K	Sensory data underutilization (Critical)
	R-15	659	Google Code	Travel & Local	1–5 K	Sensory data underutilization (Medium)

[a,b]Symbol "R" stands for "revision" and symbol "V" stands for "Version"
[c]We obtained the problem severities from corresponding applications' bug tracking systems. "N/A" means that developers did not explicitly label problem severities

18.5.2 Effectiveness and Efficiency

To answer research question RQ4 about Green-Droid's effectiveness and efficiency, we ran GreenDroid to diagnose each application listed in Table 18.8 and recorded its diagnosis overhead. In this set of experiments, we controlled Green-Droid to generate sequences of at most six user interaction events for each application execution (not including the first events for "launching entry activity" when our analysis starts and the last events for "finishing active activities and services" when our analysis ends). This is for cost-effectiveness and it already enabled GreenDroid to explore quite a large number of application states to expose energy problems as we will show later. We examined top ranked diagnosis reports, especially those with highlighted ineffective API calls, to see whether they can locate real energy problems in these applications.

We observed that GreenDroid successfully located 15 real energy problems in these applications, as listed in Table 18.8. Four of them are caused by missing sensor deactivation, four by missing wake lock deactivation, and the remaining seven by sensory data underutilization. The first 13 energy problems listed in Table 18.8 have been confirmed by developers prior to our experiments. In addition, GreenDroid successfully found two potential energy problems in Omnidroid and GPSLogger. These two problems were previously unknown. We submitted our bug reports to corresponding developers, and they were both confirmed. GPSLogger developers even invited us to join their team to help improve GPSLogger's energy efficiency. Besides, as shown in Table 18.8, the severity levels of our detected 15 problems range from "medium" to "critical". This indicates that such problems can cause serious energy waste. Indeed, we found many negative comments complaining about battery drain issues from the bug tracking systems and Google Play store user review pages of the concerned applications (e.g., Geohash Droid, AndTweet and Zmanim). We discuss some of these energy problems in detail below.

18.5.2.1 Missing Sensor or Wake Lock Deactivation

Android API documentation recommends developers to unregister sensor listeners and release wake locks when they are no longer needed [7,8]. However, we found that missing sensor or wake lock deactivation is common in Android applications. GreenDroid detected eight applications suffering such energy problems from our 14 subjects. These problems happened because developers either forgot to unregister sensor listeners or release wake locks, or performed these operations incorrectly. For example, the code snippets in Fig. 18.9 demonstrate how Ushahidi developers wrongly unregistered a GPS listener. We observe in the buggy version that, developers registered a GPS listener gpsListener in the onCreate() handler of the CheckInMap activity (Lines 3–6), and then tried to unregister the listener in the onDestroy() handler of CheckInMap (Lines 10–11). However, instead of passing previously registered gpsListener to the sensor listener unregistration API removeUpdate(), developers wrongly created a new GPS listener instance and passed its reference to removeUpdate(). The consequence is that the previously registered sensor listener gpsListener was not properly unregistered.

For performance considerations, the Android OS keeps an application process alive as long as possible, until the system runs low on resources (e.g., memory). According to this policy, even a dummy process that hosts no application component is not guaranteed to be terminated in a timely fashion [32]. Therefore, in the buggy version, the gpsListener instance would remain in memory for a long time even if the activity it belongs to has been destroyed. The activity instance could also remain in memory after its onDestroy() handler is called. As a result, valuable battery energy can be wasted by unnecessary GPS sensing. Ushahidi's developers later realized this problem from bug reports and fixed it. Figure 18.9 also gives the correct version for comparison.

Fig. 18.9 The energy bug
in Ushahidi application

```
/**buggy version of the CheckInMap class**/
1.  public class CheckinMap extends MapActivity {
2.    public void onCreate(){
3.      MyGPSListener gpsListener = new MyGPSListener();
4.      LocationManager lm = getSystemService(LOCATION_SERVICE);
5.      //GPS listener registration
6.      lm.requestLocationUpdates(GPS, 0, 0, gpsListener);
7.    }
8.    public void onDestroy() {
9.      //unregister GPS listener
10.     getSystemService(LOCATION_SERVICE)
11.           .removeUpdates(new MyGPSListener());
12.   }
13.   //location listener class
14.   public class MyGPSListener implements LocationListener {
15.     public void onLocationChanged(Location loc) {
16.       //utilize location data
17.     }
18.   }
19. }


/**correct version of the CheckInMap class**/
20. public class CheckinMap extends MapActivity {
21.   private MyGPSListener gpsListener;
22.   private LocationManager lm;
22.   public void onCreate(){
23.     gpsListener = new MyGPSListener();
24.     lm = getSystemService(LOCATION_SERVICE);
25.     //GPS listener registration
26.     lm.requestLocationUpdates(GPS, 0, 0, gpsListener);
27.   }
28.   public void onDestroy() {
29.     //unregister GPS listener
30.     lm.removeUpdates(gpsListener);
31.   }
32. }
```

18.5.2.2 Sensory Data Underutilization

GreenDroid also detected seven applications suffering from sensory data underutilization problems out of our 14 subjects. Among these detected problems, three (Table 18.8) are critical ones that can cause massive energy waste. We discuss these seven problems in detail below.

Osmdroid. Osmdroid is a navigation application similar to Google Maps. After diagnosis, GreenDroid reported that Osmdroid's location data utilization coefficient is no more than 0.2239 for 30.51 % explored states, but close to 1 for other

states, as shown in Fig. 18.10a.[15] This strongly suggests that Osmdroid poorly utilizes location

[15]Notes of the Fig. 18.10 and Fig. 18.11: (1) In the figures, the location utilization coefficient is accurate to four decimal places. (2) Two states with indistinguishable utilization coefficients (i.e., cannot be distinguished by four decimal places) are shown in the same bar. (3) Utilization coefficients with very few occurrences (i.e., less than 0.5 %) are not shown in the figures for ease of presentation, so the percentages in each figure may not add up to 100 %. (4) The total number of states for each application does not equal the number of explored states reported later because the location sensing is not enabled in some explored states.

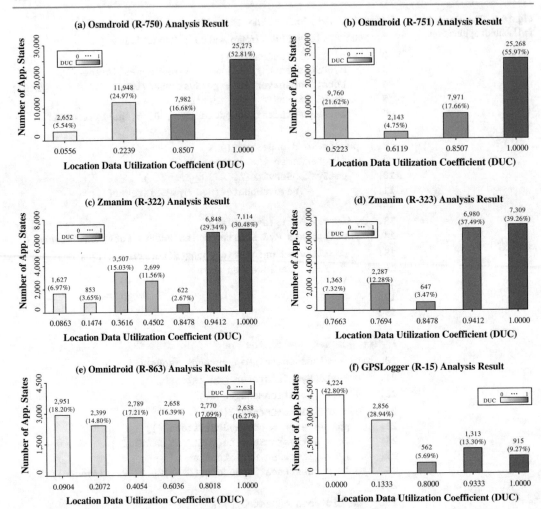

Fig. 18.10 Sensory data utilization analysis results (part 1)

data at certain states. We examined the reports generated by GreenDroid and quickly found that if users switch from `MapActivity` to other activities without enabling location tracking, location data would be used to render an invisible map (recall that GreenDroid can highlight ineffective API calls). This greatly wastes valuable battery energy as reported by users [9]. To fix this problem, developers later disabled GPS sensing if users leave `MapActivity` without the location tracking functionality enabled. Figure 18.10b gives the new version's location data utilization analysis result. We can observe that location data are now much better utilized with a utilization coefficient above 0.5223.

Zmanim. Zmanim is a location-aware application for reminding Jewish people about prayer time during the day (i.e., zmanim). The application generates zmanim according to users' locations and corresponding time zones. Interestingly, developers already realized that location sensing could be energy-consuming, and they made the application stop location sensing once its required locations are obtained. However, as Fig. 18.10c shows, GreenDroid still reported that for 37.37 % explored states, Zmanim's location data utilization coefficient is no more than 0.4502, but close to 1 for other states. This energy problem is similar to what we found in Osmdroid. If users switch from the location sensing activity to other activ-

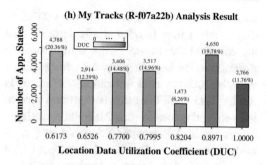

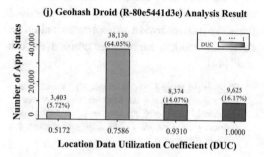

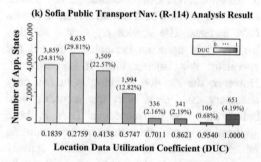

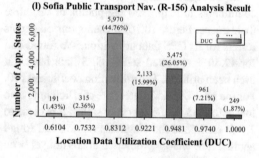

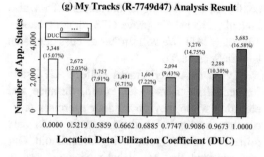

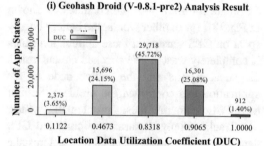

Fig. 18.11 Sensory data utilization analysis results (part 2)

ities before the required locations are successfully obtained, battery energy would keep being wasted to update invisible GUI elements. In scenarios where GPS signals are rather weak, users frequently complained that Zmanim caused huge battery drain [43]. We give an example of such complaints below. Similar to Osmdroid, Zmanim developers also later disabled location sensing in such problematic cases, and we give the new version's location data utilization analysis result in Fig. 18.10d for comparison (much improved utilization).

Zmanim Issue 56: *"I should see GPS icon only until a location is obtained. After that, GPS should be turned off. However, even if turning off GPS once a fix is obtained, this issue remains as a bug, since a*

user could hit home button before the fix is obtained, therefore leaving GPS on. These bugs quickly kill my battery."

Omnidroid. Omnidroid helps automate system functionalities based on user contexts. For example, Omnidroid can help users automatically send a reply message such as "busy in a meeting" when they receive a phone call during an important meeting. When Omnidroid runs, it maintains a background service to periodically check location updates. If any location update satisfies a pre-specified condition, its corresponding action would be executed as a response. Our diagnosis results in Fig. 18.10e show that 18.2% explored states have a location data utilization coefficient of no more than 0.0904. We found that at these states, users have not specified any condition or chosen any action. In other words, location data are collected for no use except being stored to a database for logging purposes (this explains why the location data utilization coefficient is not 0). Then why does this background service keep collecting location data? It could cause huge energy waste. We reported this problem (previously unknown) to Omnidroid developers, and suggested enabling location sensing only when there are conditions/rules concerning user locations. We then received a prompt confirmation and developers marked our reported problem as "critical" [44]:

> **Omnidroid Issue 179**: *"Completely true, and your suggestion is a great idea and you're correct Omnidroid does suck up way more energy than necessary as a result. I'd be happy to accept a patch in this regard."*

GPSLogger. GPSLogger collects users' GPS coordinates to help them tag photos or visualize their traces. Figure 18.10f presents our diagnosis results for its GPS data utilization. We found that for 42.80 % explored states, GPS data have not even been utilized. The utilization coefficient is 0. For the next 28.94 % states, the coefficient is also low at 0.1333, while for other states, it is close to 1. We examined the diagnosis reports and found another new energy problem that has not yet been reported. Similar to Omnidroid, GPSLogger also maintains a background service to collect GPS data. It continually evaluates whether collected GPS data satisfy certain precision requirements. If yes, the data are processed and stored to a database, and GPSLogger would then update its GUI to notify users. Otherwise, the data are discarded. However, when GPS signals are weak, GPS sensors may keep collecting noisy data. These data mostly do not satisfy precision requirements and are actually discarded. This produces no benefits to users, and explains why GPS data have a very low utilization coefficient at some states. This problem can be common when users enter an area where the GPS reception is bad. We submitted a bug report [45] to suggest temporarily slowing down or disabling location sensing when the application continuously finds its collected GPS data of low quality. Our bug report was

confirmed by GPSLogger developers. They also invited us to help improve GPSLogger's energy efficiency [45]. We will further discuss our patch later in Sect. 18.5.6.

My Tracks. My Tracks collects GPS data for recording users' path, speed, distance and elevation while they do outdoor exercises (e.g., running, cycling). We diagnosed the GPS data utilization of My Tracks using GreenDroid. Our tool reported that My Tracks does not utilize GPS data for 15.07 % explored states, as shown in Fig. 18.11g. In other words, the battery energy spent on GPS sensing at these application states is completely wasted. We checked GreenDroid's diagnosis reports and the source code of the application and confirmed the problem. Similar to GPSLogger, at these problematic states, My Tracks simply discards any collected GPS data. The energy waste occurred due to a mistake in the application's implementation. My Tracks uses a long running background service to handle GPS updates. The service registers a location listener right upon its launching and will not unregister this listener until it is destroyed. However, the location listening is in fact only necessary after users start the recording and before they stop the recording. Then in those application states when there is no recording initiated by users but the service is actively running, the obtained location data will not be processed and stored (discarded instead), leading to energy waste. Developers later realized this problem and fixed it eventually by registering location listener after users start recording, and unregistering the listener after the recording is stopped [6] (revision f07a22b). For comparison, we further analyzed the GPS location utilization of the application after developers fixed the problem. As Fig. 18.11h shows, there are no application states where GPS data are not utilized in the fixed version.

Geohash Droid. Geohash Droid is an entertainment application for adventure enthusiasts. It randomly picks up a location for adventure, and navigates its users to that location using GPS data. We diagnosed Geohash Droid and found that its utilization coefficient is no more than 0.4673 for 27.80 % explored states, as shown in Fig. 18.11i.

We studied the diagnosis reports and found that at these states, GPS data were used only to show the users' current locations in an icon on the phone's notification bar (a phone's notification bar is a GUI element container that is outside an application's normal GUI and is always visible when the phone's screen is on). However, in other states, GPS data were also used to update the navigation map as well as computing detailed travel information (e.g., distance to destination). This comparison shows that GPS data were not well utilized in those 27.80 % explored states, and this could cause energy waste. After realizing this, Geohash Droid's developers made a patch to slow down the application's GPS sensing rate to every 30 s to save energy when GPS data are only used for updating the notification bar [27]. Figure 18.3 shows their comment after patching, and both their own testing and user feedbacks confirmed that there is indeed a significant improvement in Geohash Droid's energy efficiency [27]. Besides, in later revisions to Geohash Droid, developers redesigned the application by completely removing this notification icon. They chose to automatically switch off GPS updates when the navigation map and detailed information screen become invisible (see revision 80e5441d3e for details). We analyzed this new version and present the result in Fig. 18.11j for comparison. The result shows that in 94.29 % explored states, the GPS data are now effectively utilized.

Sofia Public Transport Nav. Sofia Public Transport Nav. uses its collected GPS data to locate the nearest bus stops for its users, and provides arrival time estimation for concerned buses by querying a remote server. GreenDroid diagnosed its GPS data utilization, and reported that GPS data were poorly utilized for 24.81 % explored states, and for the next 52.38 % states, the utilization coefficient was also below 0.4138, as shown in Fig. 18.11k. We examined the diagnosis reports and confirmed this energy problem. In Sofia Public Transport Nav., GPS data are mainly used to update a map that shows nearby bus stops. However, for many states, the dialog box showing bus arrival time is at fore-

ground,[16] hiding the map that shows nearby bus stops. Then because users may keep refreshing the dialog box to check bus arrival time, GPS data during this period will be used mainly to update the map hidden by the dialog. This is a waste of energy. The application developers later found this problem, and disabled its GPS update for states where the bus arrival time estimation dialog is at foreground. Interestingly, although developers closed the corresponding bug report [46] soon after creating this patch, they mistakenly introduced another missing sensor deactivation problem. In later development and communications with users, they realized this new problem and eventually fixed it [47]. This story suggests that: (1) developers lack easy-to-use and effective tools to help detect energy problems in their applications, and (2) fixing sensory data underutilization problems is non-trivial and may instead introduce new energy problems. For comparison, we also analyzed the application after developers eventually fixed all energy problems including this new one. As the result in Fig. 18.11l shows, there are now no application states whose GPS data utilization coefficient is significantly lower than others.

From the above discussions, we can see how automated sensory data utilization analysis can help diagnose energy problems for Android applications. When developers find that sensory data are clearly underutilized at certain states of their applications, they can consider whether their applications can reach these problematic states frequently and stay there for long time (e.g., an activity can be left to background until users explicitly switch back to it). If yes, developers may have to tune down the concerned sensors' sensing rates or even disable them, as otherwise energy cost can be very high, but produced benefits can be marginal instead. Besides, we also find that in large-scale application subjects like Omnidroid and Zmanim, their sensory data

---

[16]GreenDroid models pop-up windows like dialog boxes by this strategy: (1) If a pop-up window is being displayed, GreenDroid considers all GUI elements underneath invisible; (2) If a pop-up window is dismissed, GreenDroid considers the GUI elements underneath visible again.

usage is very complex, involving hundreds of method/API calls. In such subjects, manually examining how sensory data are utilized can be extremely labor-intensive and error-prone. This justifies the great need for an automated diagnosis tool like our GreenDroid to help locate potential energy problems caused by sensory data underutilization. To reduce developers' efforts in reading diagnosis reports, GreenDroid prioritizes these reports according to their sensory data utilization coefficients, and highlights ineffective API calls (e.g., those for updating invisible GUIs). This can help developers quickly figure out the causes of some subtle energy wastes.

18.5.2.3 Analysis Overhead

Table 18.9 presents GreenDroid's diagnosis overhead. For each of our 14 subjects, it reports: (1) the number of application states GreenDroid explored, (2) the average number of event handlers GreenDroid executed during each application execution, including those handlers for system events,[17] (3) diagnosis time, and (4) the amount of memory GreenDroid consumed. For each subject, we conducted experiments three times to obtain these results. The number of application states explored and event handlers executed in different runs remained the same. The diagnosis time and memory consumption slightly varied in different runs and Table 18.9 reports the averaged results.

We observe that GreenDroid could quickly explore thousands of application states and perform energy inefficiency diagnosis. For example, for the two largest subjects My Tracks (over 16K LOC) and DroidAR (over 18K LOC), GreenDroid explored over 80 K states during its diagnosis and executed over 40 event handlers in each application execution (recall that GreenDroid executes each subject many times). It finished diagnosis within five minutes. The memory cost was less than 350 MB. Such overhead can be well supported by modern PCs, and compares favorably

---

[17] System events could result in several consecutive handler calls. For example, an activity-destroying event may trigger the concerned activity's `onPause()`, `onStop()`, and `onDestroy()` handlers in turn.

with state-of-the-art testing or debugging techniques, which typically take hours to explore up to 100 K states [48]. This suggests that GreenDroid is a practical tool for diagnosing energy problems in real-world Android applications.

18.5.3 Necessity and Usefulness of AEM Model

To answer research question RQ5 about the usefulness of our proposed AEM model, we conducted two comparison experiments. First, we ran GreenDroid to diagnose our experimental subjects with the AEM model disabled, assuming that event handlers can be randomly scheduled. We examined whether GreenDroid could still locate energy problems in such a setting. Second, to study whether the executions of our experimental subjects in GreenDroid (with AEM model enabled) resemble real executions, we instrumented all 149 event handlers defined in our largest subject DroidAR, and conducted the following experiment. We randomly selected 50 execution traces of DroidAR generated by GreenDroid. These executions on average involve 54 event handler calls (not necessarily distinct). We extracted from them corresponding user interaction event sequences. We then ran DroidAR in the Android emulator [12], which is included in the Android Software Development Kit, and manually provided the same user interactions (i.e., the same event sequences). We logged real event handler calling traces, and compared them with those from GreenDroid. We discuss the results of these experiments below.

First experiment. We observe that without AEM model (i.e., scheduling event handlers randomly), GreenDroid (actually JPF) already encountered great challenges in executing Android applications, not to mention diagnosing any of their energy problems. The last column of Table 18.9 lists these execution results. Among 100 application executions, we observed many runtime exceptions. For example, 79 out of 100 executions of Osmdroid failed because of runtime exceptions, and these exceptions also crashed JPF. We manually studied these

Table 18.9 GreenDroid diagnosis overhead and random execution result

Application name	Diagnosis information and overhead				Random event handler scheduling results (runtime exceptions)
	Explored states	Avg. number of handlers executed during each application execution	Diagnosis time (seconds)	Memory consumption (MB)	
DroidAR	91,170	60	284	233	67/100
Recycle Locator	114,709	44	46	162	4/100
Ushahidi	55,269	75	32	175	58/100
AndTweet	98,410	33	47	192	82/100
Ebookdroid	57,330	42	22	149	86/100
BableSink	42,987	63	15	154	17/100
CWAC-Wakeful	30,705	46	11	118	11/100
Sofia Public Transport Nav.	57,316	50	17	204	62/100
Osmdroid	120,189	43	159	575	79/100
Zmanim	54,270	34	114	237	31/100
Geohash Droid	144,710	60	185	229	71/100
My Tracks	82,137	45	207	341	74/100
Omnidroid	52,805	78	242	396	22/100
GPSLogger	58,824	28	41	153	9/100

exceptions, and found that most of them arose from ignoring data flow dependencies between event handlers. For instance, it is quite often that developers initialize a GUI widget instance in an activity's onCreate() handler, and later use this instance in other handlers. In random handler scheduling, if other handlers are wrongly scheduled before onCreate(), a null pointer exception may be thrown. Such exceptions cannot be easily addressed, and can cause termination of our energy diagnosis. For two small-sized subjects Recycle-locator and GPSLogger, fewer exceptions (4 and 9) were observed since their data flow dependencies between event handlers are relatively simple. Still, these exceptions seriously prevented GreenDroid from diagnosing our experimental subjects. Besides, even for cases where no exceptions occurred, we found that the diagnosis reports contain many meaningless handler calling traces that offer little information to help developers pinpoint energy

problems. This suggests that our AEM model is indeed necessary for an effective diagnosis of energy problems in Android applications. In addition, since our AEM model is essentially an abstraction of event handler scheduling policies for the Android platform, it can easily be adapted and used in other analysis techniques for Android applications.

Second experiment. We observe that in 39 out of 50 executions, GreenDroid generated exactly the same handler calling traces as real executions. In the remaining 11 cases, GreenDroid failed to schedule event handlers in the same way as real executions did due to two major reasons. First, we did not consider dynamic GUI updates when implementing GreenDroid. This could make GreenDroid generate some user interaction events that are impossible in an Android emulator (and also in real devices), because they are invalid due to runtime GUI updates (4 cases). Second, Green-Droid did not model concurrency adequately in its current implementation because JPF did not fully model Java concurrency programming constructs (e.g., `java.util.concurrent.Executor` was not modeled). This caused GreenDroid to fail to handle some system events (e.g., broadcast events) that were triggered in some worker threads (7 cases). Although these two problems did not cause noticeable consequences on the effectiveness of our diagnosis, we will still consider addressing them in future releases of our GreenDroid. This requires non-trivial engineering effort.

18.5.4   Impact of Event Sequence Length Limit

Our research question RQ6 studies how the thoroughness of our energy diagnosis can be affected by the length limits on generated user interaction event sequences. To answer this question, we applied GreenDroid to analyze each of our application subjects multiple times and studied how the code coverage would change accordingly. Specifically, GreenDroid analyzed each application nine times. For these nine runs, we gradually increased the length limit from zero to eight and measured the percentage of source code lines that were executed (i.e., statement coverage). We chose statement coverage as the metric for measuring the thoroughness of our diagnosis for two reasons. First, to the best of our knowledge, we are not aware of any existing metrics that are designed for assessing the thoroughness of energy diagnosis. Second, statement coverage has been widely used for measuring code coverage for general purposes because it strikes a good balance between utility and collection overheads [49,50]. Table 18.10 reports our study results and from them we obtain two major findings as discussed in the following.

Coverage saturation. We observe that for all application subjects, the statement coverage increases quickly at the beginning with the growth in the length of generated event sequences. The coverage gradually saturates at certain points and stops increasing when the length limit further grows. Take Osmdroid as an example.

Its statement coverage increases from 1.01 to 24.68 % when the length limit grows from zero to four. When the length limit reaches five, the statement coverage saturates at 30.15 %, with no further increase even if the length limit grows to a larger value. Other applications are similar. To understand why, we inspected all these applications. We found that many of these applications contain only a small number of activity components (with GUI). As listed in the second column of Table 18.10, 8 of our 14 applications contain no more than six activity components. Although the applications Ushahidi and Omnidroid contain relatively larger number of activity components, we found that many of these activity components are actually designed only for displaying information. Besides, for user friendliness, developers have made their applications' GUIs intuitive. This means that users do not have to perform very long sequences of interactions from an application's entry GUI to reach other GUIs for using their designed major functionalities. This explains why the statement coverage measurement can quickly saturate for our studied applications.

Difficulties in achieving high coverage. We also observe that even if our event sequence generation enumerates all possible combinations of user interaction events, GreenDroid can still achieve only low statement coverage for some applications. For example, for DroidAR, AndTweet, My Tracks and Omnidroid, Green-Droid covers less than 25 % statements. We thus inspected these applications and found three major difficulties in achieving higher code coverage. These findings can benefit related research such as automated Android application testing [49,51]. We discuss these findings in the following:

- **Sophisticated external stimulus**. Achieving high code coverage may require sophisticated external stimulus for certain Android applications. For example, Omnidroid registers a broadcast receiver with Android OS to monitor 26 different system broadcast events (e.g., "missing phone call" and "phone connected to a physical dock" broadcast events). A large

Table 18.10 Statement coverage with respect to different event sequence length limits

Application name	# activities	Statement coverage (%) w.r.t different event sequence length limits (0–8)								
		0	1	2	3	4	5	6	7	8
DroidAR	6	0.54[a]	2.28	11.99	11.99	**12.54**	12.54	12.54	12.54[b]	12.54
Recycle Locator	3	1.23	16.11	23.76	28.17	32.18	**36.96**	36.96	36.96	36.96
Ushahidi	17	1.47	4.06	10.97	15.17	19.87	25.35	**25.39**	25.39	25.39
AndTweet	6	1.74	10.25	12.07	**15.94**	15.94	15.94	15.94	15.94	15.94
Ebookdroid	8	0.20	2.02	2.79	12.72	**25.81**	25.81	25.81	25.81	25.81
BableSink	1	2.68	24.39	30.33	**30.38**	30.38	30.38	30.38	30.38	30.38
CWAC-Wakeful	1	1.12	10.27	32.37	**42.30**	42.30	42.30	42.30	42.30	42.30
Sofia Public Transport Nav.	3	3.47	9.70	24.67	37.91	**38.12**	38.12	38.12	38.12	38.12
Osmdroid	8	1.01	11.36	18.09	18.93	24.68	**30.15**	30.15	30.15	30.15
Zmanim	3	1.72	11.81	27.71	27.96	28.04	**28.08**	28.08	28.08	28.08
Geohash Droid	9	2.96	10.31	19.87	22.94	25.58	**25.62**	25.62	25.62	25.62
My Tracks	12	1.06	5.30	12.72	20.17	**23.56**	23.56	23.56	23.56	23.56
Omnidroid	16	0.45	8.64	17.91	18.25	**20.88**	20.88	20.88	20.88	20.88
GPSLogger	1	4.86	14.11	44.31	**46.13**	46.13	46.13	46.13	46.13	46.13

[a] Statement coverage is not 0 because in our implementation we do not count "launch the entry activity (when analysis starts)" and "finish all active activities and services (when analysis ends)" when generating user interaction event sequences

[b] Underlined runs took more than one hour to finish. Memory consumption (maximum heap size set to 4GB) did not increase much when we relaxed the length limits

proportion of its code is used for handling such broadcasted system events, while our Green-Droid currently cannot actively generate such events. This suggests that in order to cover such code, systematic simulation of external stimulus would be necessary.

- **Complex inputs and non-standard user interactions**. Achieving high code coverage may require complex inputs and non-standard user interactions for certain Android applications. Take DroidAR, an augmented reality application on Android, for example. It presents its user a live view of real-world objects that are augmented with various sensory inputs, and allows the user to interact with these objects digitally. In many cases, DroidAR requires video input from phone cameras for recognizing and rendering augmented objects accordingly. It contains two types of GUI elements: (1) standard GUI elements defined in Android libraries (e.g., buttons), and (2) augmented objects rendered by native graphics libraries. Both types of GUI elements can be dynamically updated. Therefore, covering a high proportion of DroidAR code would require its user not only to interact with standard GUI elements (e.g., clicking buttons), but also to interact with the non-standard GUI elements (e.g., rotating augmented objects). However, our GreenDroid currently cannot support video inputs or user interactions with non-standard GUI elements. This explains why GreenDroid achieves low code coverage when diagnosing DroidAR.

- **Special running environment**. Achieving high code coverage may require special running environments for certain Android applications. For example, AndTweet is a light-weight Twitter chat client. Covering most of its code requires: (1) a valid Twitter account, (2) network connectivity, and (3) meaningful data (e.g., tweets and followers) associated with this account. Failing to satisfy any of these requirements would make the application run meaninglessly, leading to low

code coverage. Our GreenDroid currently does not know how to satisfy such application-specific requirements and this deserves further research.

From the above discussions, we can make two observations. First, similar to related studies [52], it is practical to limit the length of generated event sequences in program analysis due to the combinatorial explosion problem. In our case, setting the length limit to six is a cost-effective choice. This is because a larger length limit does not further improve code coverage, but instead results in much longer diagnosis time (as in a magnitude of hours), as reported by our experiments. In practice, such settings should be made on a case by case basis as different applications may have different characteristics. Therefore, tools like our GreenDroid should allow its users to customize their required depth of diagnosis and provide a time budget [39]. Second, we observed that for some application subjects, GreenDroid located their energy problems even with low statement coverage. This can be explained. As discussed earlier (Sect. 18.3), energy problems typically only occur at certain application states reached by handling corresponding user interactions. For example, the energy problem in Zmanim can be exposed by the following four steps: (1) switching on GPS, (2) configuring Zmanim to use current location, (3) starting Zmanim's main activity, and (4) hitting the "Home" button when GPS is acquiring a location. Therefore, generating user interactions in a certain order is a prerequisite for exposing such problems. GreenDroid essentially enumerates all possible combinations of different types of user interaction events (e.g., button click events and checkbox selection events) and provides appropriate event values when generating these events. This explains why it can systematically explore an application's state space to locate potential energy problems. This also suggests that although statement coverage can be used for measuring the code coverage achieved by a certain energy diagnosis approach, it may not be a good metric for assessing the effectiveness of such energy diagnosis.

18.5.5 Comparison with Resource Leak Detection Work

Our work shares some similarity with existing resource leak detection work [31,33,34,53] since sensor listeners and wake locks are considered as valuable resources in Android OS and applications. Our research question RQ7 studies how our GreenDroid compares to such work in terms of detecting real missing sensor or wake lock deactivation problems. To answer this question, we chose Relda for comparison [53]. Relda is the latest resource leak detection work dedicated for Android applications. It is a fully automated static analysis tool for Android applications and supports detecting leak of 65 types of system resources, which also include sensor listeners and wake locks as studied in our work. Therefore, it would be interesting to know whether Relda can also effectively help detect missing sensor or wake lock deactivation problems in our studied Android application subjects. With the help of Relda's authors, we conducted experiments using their original tool (not our implementation, which can otherwise lead to bias in the comparison). In the experiments, we successfully applied Relda on 13 of our application subjects listed in Table 18.8 (except My Tracks). Relda reported 36 resource leak warnings, out of which 15 are related to sensors and wake locks, while the remaining 21 are related to other seven types of resources (e.g., phone cameras), which are outside the scope of our study. We further invited Relda's authors to manually validate these raw data and remove duplicate and false warnings as they did in their publication [53] (we did not do it by ourselves in order to avoid bias). Finally, they confirmed that Relda detected two real resource leak problems in DroidAR and one in Ebookdroid out of the 13 application subjects. By analyzing the experimental results, we obtained several findings as discussed below.

First, the two problems Relda detected in DroidAR happened because developers forgot to unregister a sensor listener and to disable a phone vibrator after usage, respectively. The other problem Relda detected in Ebookdroid happened because developers forgot to recycle a velocity tracker (it tracks the velocity of touch events for detecting gestures like flinging) back to the Android OS after using it. From these results, we can see that Relda can indeed detect more types of resource leaks than GreenDroid since it has a much wider focus. However, two of the three detected real problems are not related to sensors or wake locks. Within the scope of our study, Relda actually detected only one real problem of our interest (i.e., the missing sensor deactivation problem in DroidAR). As a comparison, our GreenDroid detected eight missing sensor or wake lock deactivation problems in these 13 application subjects as we discussed earlier. All these eight problems (including the one detected by Relda) are real problems as confirmed by developers.

Second, we carefully studied Relda to understand why it cannot effectively detect the other seven real missing sensor or wake lock deactivation problems that can be detected by GreenDroid in our studied Android applications. Based on our study results and our communications with Relda's authors, we identified four major reasons: (1) Relda does not conduct intra-procedural flow analysis. To avoid false positives, which can be a major concern for static analysis, Relda does not report any resource leak problem as long as a concerned resource can possibly be released at any program path. Due to this conservative nature, Relda did not effectively detect missing wake lock deactivation problems in BabbleSink and AndTweet. For example, the wake lock acquired by AndTweet might be released in certain program paths, but such paths could only be executed in exceptional cases that are not feasible during normal running (see Sect. 18.3.3 for more details). As such, AndTweet can constantly drain a phone's batter energy during its normal usage, but this problem cannot be reported by Relda. (2) Relda does not conduct points-to analysis. Thus it cannot figure out what object(s) a reference is pointing to, and this is a common limitation of static analysis techniques without points-to analysis. Due to this reason, Relda did not effectively detect the missing sensor deactivation problem in Ushahidi, where its developers mistakenly passed a newly created GPS sensor listener to the unregistration API (Line 11 in Fig. 18.9) instead of passing the listener that has been registered earlier (Line 6 in Fig. 18.9). (3) Relda does not properly model or consider event handler scheduling as we studied in this work. Thus it cannot handle message passing and receiving well. Due to this reason, it did not detect the missing wake lock deactivation problem in CWAC-Wakeful. The reason is that CWAC-Wakeful acquires a wake lock from the Android OS only when it receives a message that asks it to perform some long running task at background. (4) Relda did not detect missing sensor or wake lock deactivation problems in Recycle Locator, Sofia Public Transport Nav. and Ebookdroid due to its incomplete resource operation table. These applications use sensors or wake locks by calling compound APIs that wrap basic sensor listener registration/unregistration APIs or basic wake lock acquisition/releasing APIs. For example, Sofia Public Transport Nav. calls Google Maps APIs to use a phone's GPS sensor, and Ebook-Droid calls the `setKeepScreenOn()` API in the `android.view.SurfaceView` class to acquire wake locks. Our GreenDroid does not have these discussed issues. It systematically executes an Android application. Its dynamic analysis is naturally flow-sensitive and does not need points-to analysis. Besides, it relies on our AEM model to ensure reasonable scheduling of event handlers so that it can handle messaging passing and receiving properly. Moreover, Green-Droid only focuses on two types of resources, i.e., sensor listeners and wake locks, so that we could prepare a more complete operation table for them with affordable effort. This explains why Relda missed some missing sensor or wake lock deactivation problems but GreenDroid could still detect them.

Third, although Relda can detect energy problems caused by missing sensor or wake lock deactivation as a form of resource leak, it cannot help diagnose energy problems caused by sensory data underutilization. These problems are more complicated as discussed throughout this chapter. Our GreenDroid supports automated analysis of sensory data utilization and can help developers diag-nose energy problems caused by cost-ineffective use of sensory data.

From the above discussions, we can observe that both Relda and GreenDroid have their own scopes and strengths. Relda can detect a much wider range of resource leak problems and some of them may lead to serious energy waste. On the other hand, GreenDroid's scope is more focused (sensor and wake lock related energy problems) and its energy problem detection capability is sat-isfactory. In terms of detecting energy problems caused by missing sensor or wake lock deacti-vation, GreenDroid performs better than Relda. We did not compare GreenDroid to other resource leak detection work due to various reasons includ-ing tool availability and applicability (some work are for conventional Java programs, e.g., Tor-lak et al.'s work [31]). The above comparisons and discussions confirm that GreenDroid is useful and effective for diagnosing energy problems in Android applications, and its idea may also com-plement and contribute to existing resource leak detection work on the Android platform.

18.5.6   Energy Saving Case Study

To answer research question RQ8 about potential energy saving if our detected energy problems can be fixed, we conducted a real case study. In prac-tice, users may interact with an application in dif-ferent ways, and this could affect the application's energy consumption quite significantly [54]. To minimize the effect of such user interactions, we selected the application GPSLogger as our case study subject because it requires almost no human intervention after initial setup. We prepared two versions of GPSLogger: one with energy prob-lem (will be referred to as GPSLogger-r15) and the other with our patch (will be referred to as GPSLogger-clean). We built this patch conserva-tively by slightly modifying the GPS sensing part of GPSLogger. To be realistic, we built this patch by following Geohash Droid's real patch on fix-ing its energy problem (issue 24) [27]. Specifi-cally, the patched GPSLogger would slow down its GPS sensing rate to every 30 s when it finds its collected GPS data keep being of low quality (e.g., after five consecutive imprecise readings), and set the sensing rate immediately back to the original value when it finds that GPS data have become precise again (e.g., after two consecutive precise readings). In fact, one can also do it in an aggressive way by disabling GPS sensing or setting a longer slow-sensing period if the application keeps receiving imprecise GPS data. Although this may save more energy, we took the previous conservative strategy for making our best efforts in avoiding potential effect on the application's functionality.

Table 18.11 compares the energy consumption between the two versions of GPSLogger. We conducted the case study for six consecutive days. On each day, our study participant, a postgraduate student, who was unaware of our experimental setup and purpose, strictly followed the same pre-specified activity pattern: (1) walking from his office to canteen and having lunch there (from 1:00 to 1:45 pm), (2) walking back to his office and then studying (from 1:45 to 3:30 pm), (3) walking to library and read some newspapers or magazines (from 3:30 to 4:15 pm), and (4) finally going to gym for physical exercises (from 4:15 to 5:00 pm). This activity pattern is common for a postgraduate student. We had this participant carry the same smartphone, Samsung Galaxy S3 (with Android 4.1.2), with different versions of GPSLogger installed on different days (he is unaware of this difference), as shown in Table 18.11. For each version, we arranged three days for experiments, to minimize effects of unpredictable and uncontrollable physical environment (e.g., GPS signal strength may be subject to change for unknown reasons). At the end of each day, we collected the following information from the smartphone: (1) number of precise GPS points collected, (2) number of imprecise GPS points discarded, and (3) energy consumed by GPSLogger during the experiment. We measured energy consumption by PowerTutor [55], which is a highly rated tool for measuring real energy consumption (in Joules) for selected Android applications or components.

Table 18.11 reports our study results. We give energy consumption data only for CPU and GPS sensor in each day's experiment. This is because

GPSLogger ran at background and thus battery energy was mostly consumed by its CPU computing and GPS sensing. We can make two observations from Table 18.11. First, in six experiments, the two versions of GPSLogger collected comparable numbers of GPS data points, ranging from 230 to 304 with a mean of 270. Since GPSLogger is mainly designed for recording its user's location traces, such small difference has little effect on the application's functionality. In fact, our participant also did not notice any difference in terms of user experience while using the two versions of this application. Second, we observe a large drop in GPS data discarding rate for the patched version GPSLogger-clean. On average, GPSLogger-clean discarded 18.2 % of GPS data, while GPSLogger-r15 discarded 32.6 % of GPS data (79.1 % more). Accordingly, GPSLogger-clean consumed 635.7 J in CPU computing and 4410.8 J in GPS sensing. For GPSLogger-r15, the energy consumption became 768.8 J in CPU computing (20.9 % more) and 5162.8 J in GPS sensing (17.0 % more). Note that this comparison is based on a conservative strategy, and in practice, the difference can be even larger (e.g., if the patch adopts an aggressive strategy). This shows that fixing GreenDroid's detected energy problem can indeed save much energy consumption on real smartphones.

With these promising results, we submitted our patch to GPSLogger developers. The patch was recently accepted. We also helped release it online for trial downloads for interested users.[18] So far, this patch has received around 1,000 downloads. This indicates that developers indeed acknowledge and accept our efforts in helping defend their Android applications from energy inefficiency.

18.5.7 Discussions

Tool implementation. Our energy diagnosis approach is independent of its underlying program analysis framework. Currently, we implemented it on top of JPF because JPF is a highly extensible Java program verification framework with internal support for dynamic tainting. However,

---

[18]https://code.google.com/p/gpslogger/downloads/list.

Table 18.11 Energy saving case study result

Experiment time	Application version	Collected GPS points	Discarded GPS points	Discarding rate (%)	Energy consumption (Joule)
Day 1 (1–5 pm)	GPSLogger-r15	266	127	32.3	CPU: 709.7J; GPS: 4842.6J
Day 3 (1–5 pm)	GPSLogger-r15	304	135	30.8	CPU: 835.2J; GPS: 5626.5J
Day 5 (1–5 pm)	GPSLogger-r15	272	144	34.6	CPU: 761.4J; GPS: 5019.3J
Day 2 (1–5 pm)	GPSLogger-clean	230	51	18.1	CPU: 601.4J; GPS: 4217.1J
Day 4 (1–5 pm)	GPSLogger-clean	253	63	19.9	CPU: 625.3J; GPS: 4354.6J
Day 6 (1–5 pm)	GPSLogger-clean	293	58	16.5	CPU: 680.5J; GPS: 4660.7J

analyzing Android applications using JPF is still challenging as discussed throughout this chapter. We have to carefully address the problems of event sequence generation and event handler scheduling, as well as Android library modeling. In particular, modeling Android libraries is known to be a tedious and error-prone task [39]. This is why our current implementation only modeled a partial, but critical, set of library classes and concerned APIs. Extending our tool to support more Android APIs is possible, but would require more engineering effort, and our GreenDroid is evolving along this direction. Besides, in GreenDroid's current implementation, all temporal rules in our AEM model have been translated into code for ease of use. We are considering building a more general execution engine that can take these rules as inputs to schedule Android event handlers reasonably. This would make our GreenDroid more extensible to new rules. To realize this, we need: (1) a new domain language to specify these rules, and (2) a mechanism that automatically interprets and enforces these rules at runtime. Moreover, we are also considering integrating our diagnosis approach into Android framework by modifying the Dalvik virtual machine much the same as Enck et al. did [35]. This can bring two benefits. First, it enables real-time energy inefficiency diagnosis. Second, modeling Android libraries is no longer necessary, such that the imprecision

caused by inadequate library modeling can also be alleviated or avoided. Lastly, GreenDroid can be designed to be interactive, providing its users visualizations of sensory data usage details. This would help developers quickly figure out the root causes for a wide range of domain-specific energy problems.

Tainting quality. Our sensory data utilization analysis relies on dynamic tainting for tracking propagation of sensory data. It is well known that designing precise dynamic tainting is challenging [37]. Researchers have found that ignoring control dependencies in taint propagation can cause *undertainting* (i.e., failing to taint some data derived from taint sources), but considering control dependencies can also cause *overtainting* (i.e., tainting some data that are not derived from taint sources) [38]. It is therefore suggested that the tainting policy should be designed according to its application scenarios [37]. In our case, we need to track propagation of sensory data and identify program data that are derived from such sensory data. For this purpose, we adapted TaintDroid's tainting policy [35] and added a special rule for handling control dependencies (ignoring control dependencies is one of TaintDroid's limitations). While this rule may potentially result in overtainting in theory, we did not observe any evident impact on our sensory data utilization analysis results. We made some analysis of our studied application subjects. We found that unlike user privacy data (e.g., phone number) handled by TaintDroid, sensory data in our studied applications are typically updated frequently. These data can be quickly replaced with new data. Their consumption is thus short-term, implying that they are unlikely to affect a large volume of program data in Android applications. This explains why our control dependency handling does not introduce evident overtainting problems.

Limitations. Our current GreenDroid implementation has some limitations. First, GreenDroid cannot generate complex inputs (e.g., video inputs or user gestures). Thus, there can be application states not reachable by GreenDroid. If any energy problem is associated with these states, GreenDroid would not be able to detect them (i.e., the analysis may be incomplete, leading to false negatives in bug detection). Second, GreenDroid's event sequence generation belongs to the category of model-based approaches [39,51,56]. One common problem with these approaches is that they rely on a statically extracted model and lack runtime information. For example, GreenDroid relies on a GUI model extracted by statically analyzing an application's layout configurations. It cannot cope with dynamic GUI updates (e.g., news reading applications can dynamically load a new list of items). Therefore, we found in our evaluation that GreenDroid sometimes generated infeasible user interaction event sequences (e.g., a sequence containing a click event on a GUI element that has been removed). For our largest subject DroidAR, GreenDroid generated around 8 % infeasible event sequences due to its inability to handle dynamic GUI updates. Because of this limitation in event sequence generation, our analysis may be unsound in certain cases, leading to false positives in bug detection. Third, GreenDroid cannot systematically simulate different sensory data as this requires a comprehensive characteristic study of real-world sensory data. Currently, we randomly picked up mock sensory data from a pre-prepared data pool controlled by different precision levels. It could be possible that the selection of sensory data has an impact on a program's control flow (e.g., an execution path that requires specific data values cannot be explored). Although we did not observe the above three issues affecting GreenDroid's effectiveness

in diagnosing our application subjects, we are investigating them and plan to come up with more complete solutions in future. For example, the second limitation may be addressed by integrating GreenDroid's energy inefficiency diagnosis into the Android framework. Then its event sequence generation no longer needs pre-extracted GUI models for Android applications under diagnosis. Instead, one can analyze an application's GUI layout at runtime and adapt automated testing tools like Robotium [48] for generating user interaction events. This limitation may also be addressed by adding event sequence feasibility validation to GreenDroid (e.g., using Jensen et al.'s work [51]). Then GreenDroid can first validate the feasibility of its generated event sequences before presenting them to developers for reproducing its detected energy problems. We leave these potential improvements to our future work.

Alternative analysis approach. Our current sensory data utilization analysis is only one possible approach. It analyzes how many times and to what extent sensory data are utilized by an application at certain states. We believe that there can also be other good designs for effective analysis of sensory data utilization. We discuss one possible alternative here. For example, instead of accumulating sensory data consumptions (i.e., analyzing how many times sensory data are utilized; see Eq. 18.2) in the analysis, we can also consider that as long as sensory data are effectively utilized once, the battery energy for collecting the data is well spent. Besides, when designing the "data usage" metric, we can also choose not to distinguish different APIs that utilize sensory data. Specifically, we can choose not to scale the usage metric value by the number of bytecode instructions executed during the invocation of an API that utilizes sensory data (i.e., not analyzing to what extent the sensory data are utilized). Such a design may also help locate energy problems. For instance, although we cannot distinguish how many times sensory data are utilized in different application states, we can still identify application states that totally do not utilize sensory data. In our experiments, we found that such "complete energy waste" cases indeed exist (i.e., GPSLogger's energy problem). However, for most of our studied energy problems, the concerned applications do not totally discard collected sensory data. For example, Geohash Droid always uses location data to update a phone's notification bar (see Fig. 18.4a), but still its developers consider that if other remote listeners are not actively monitoring location updates, then only updating phone notification bar is a waste of valuable battery energy. In such cases, the alternative design might not be able to locate such energy problems. As a comparison, our approach can not only help locate application states that totally do not utilize sensory data, but also help locate those that do not utilize sensory data in a fully effective manner. Therefore, it can generally provide finer-grained information for energy diagnosis and optimization. Of course, our design allows GreenDroid to report more energy problems than the alternative design. This is why we also propose a prioritization strategy to help developers focus on the potentially most serious energy problems, i.e., those have the lowest data utilization coefficients.

Fixing detected energy bugs. Our GreenDroid can help detect three common patterns of energy bugs. To fix the detected missing sensor or wake lock deactivation bugs, developers can simply add sensor listener unregistration and wake lock releasing operations in the corresponding program locations. However, fixing sensory data underutilization bugs is a non-trivial task for developers. In our empirical study, we observed two commonly-used strategies: (1) temporarily reducing sensing frequency when sensory data are not utilized in a fully-effective manner, and (2) temporarily deactivating sensors when sensory data are completely not useful. Based on this observation, GreenDroid would suggest developers to consider the two optimization strategies when it detects energy bugs caused by sensory data underutilization. Nevertheless, how to fix detected sensory data underutilization bugs should be application-specific. In particular, if developers choose to follow the second strategy, which is more aggressive than the first one, they should take into account that activating and deactivating sensors have energy overhead. In other words, developers need to carefully judge whether the energy consumed by the useless sensing operations in the inefficient ver-

sion of their application outweighs the energy cost of deactivation (when the sensory data are completely not useful) and reactivation of sensors (when the application reaches a state where sensory data will be effectively utilized). If yes, the optimization can bring overall energy saving. Otherwise, they should consider to optimize their application using other strategies.

18.6   Related Work

Our GreenDroid work relates to several research topics, which include energy efficiency analysis, energy consumption estimation, resource leak detection, and information flow tracking. Some of them particularly focus on smartphone applications. In this section, we discuss representative pieces of work in recent years.

18.6.1   Energy Efficiency Analysis

Smartphone applications' energy efficiency is vital. In past several years, researchers have worked on this topic mostly from two perspectives. First, various design strategies have been proposed to reduce energy consumption for smartphone applications. For example, MAUI [57] helped offload "energy-consuming" tasks to resource-rich infrastructures such as remote servers. EnTracked [58] and RAPS [59] adopted different heuristics to guide an application to use GPS sensors in a smart way. Little Rock [60] suggested a dedicated low power processor for energy-consuming sensing operations. SALSA [61] helped select optimal data links for saving energy in large data transmissions. Second, different techniques have been proposed to diagnose energy problems in smartphone applications. Kim et al. proposed to use power signatures based on system hardware states to detect energy-greedy malware [62]. Pathak et al. conducted the first study of energy bugs in smartphone applications, and proposed to use reaching-definition dataflow analysis algorithms to detect no-sleep energy bugs, which can arise from mishandling of power control

APIs in Android applications (e.g., wake lock acquisition/releasing APIs) [2,3]. Zhang et al. proposed a taint-tracking technique for the Android platform to detect energy wastes caused by unnecessary network communications [63]. To help end users troubleshoot energy problems on their smartphones, Ma et al. built a tool to monitor smartphones' resource usage behavior as well as system or user events (e.g., configuration changes in certain applications) [64]. Their tool can help identify triggering events that cause abnormally high energy consumption, and suggest corresponding repair solutions (e.g., reverting configuration changes) to users.

Our work shares a similar goal with these pieces of work, in particular, recent work in the second category discussed above [3,63,64]. Nevertheless, our work differs from them on several aspects. Regarding Pathak et al.'s work [63], our work has two distinct differences. First, we found that detecting no-sleep bugs like missing wake lock deactivation is not difficult. One can always adapt existing resource leak detection (as we did in our work) or classic reaching-definition data flow analysis (as they did in their work) techniques for this purpose. However, our empirical study revealed more subtle energy problems caused by sensory data underutilization. As discussed earlier, effectively detecting sensory data underutilization problems is non-trivial. It requires a systematic exploration of an application's state space and a precise analysis of sensory data utilization. Second, to conduct data flow analysis, Pathak et al. assumed that control flows between event handlers were already available from application developers. This is not a practical assumption for Android applications. Asking developers to manually derive program control flow information is unrealistic, especially when applications contain hundreds of event handlers (e.g., our experimental subjects DroidAR and Omnidroid). As such, we chose to formulate handler scheduling policies extracted from Android specifications as an AEM model so that it can be reusable across different applications for correctly scheduling event handlers during program analysis. Our experimental results have confirmed that this model is necessary and useful

for effectively diagnosing energy problems in Android applications.

Zhang et al.'s work also makes a similar observation to ours, i.e., using network data to update invisible GUIs can be an energy waste [63]. However, our work differs from theirs in three ways. First, we focus on energy problems caused by cost-ineffective uses of sensory data instead of network data, as our empirical study reveals that ineffective use of sensory data has often caused massive energy waste. Second, besides analyzing how sensory data are utilized by Android applications, we also studied ways of systematically generating event sequences to exercise an application, while their work may require extra testing effort for effective analysis (they did not study how to automate an application's execution for analysis). Third, we proposed a state-based analysis of sensory data utilization. It effectively distinguishes different usage scenarios of sensory data, while Zhang et al.'s work only supports distinguishing two types of scenarios, i.e., network data used to update visible or invisible GUIs, respectively. As a result, our work can provide richer information to help diagnose energy problems with a wider scope.

Our work also has a different objective from Ma et al.'s work [64]. Their work does not analyze an application's program code. Instead, it monitors a device's energy consumption as well as system or user events to help identify those events that have likely caused abnormally high energy consumption. By reverting the effect of these events (e.g., uninstalling a suspicious application), users can potentially suffer less battery drain. On the other hand, our work directly diagnoses causes of energy problems in an application's program code and helps fix them by providing concrete problem-triggering conditions.

18.6.2   Energy Consumption Estimation

One major reason why so many smartphone applications are not energy efficient is that developers lack viable tools to estimate energy consumption for their applications. Extensive research has been conducted to address this topic. PowerTutor [55] uses system-level power-consumption models to estimate the energy consumed by major system components (e.g., display) during the execution of Android applications. Such models are a function of selected system features (e.g., CPU utilization) and obtained by direct measurements during the controlling of the device's power state. Sesame [65] shares the same goal as PowerTutor, but can perform energy estimation for much smaller time intervals (e.g., as small as 10 ms). eProf [66] is another estimation tool. Instead of estimating energy consumption at a system level like PowerTutor and Sesame, eProf estimates energy consumption at an application level by tracing system calls made by applications when they run on smartphones. WattsOn [67] further extends eProf's idea by enabling developers to estimate their applications' energy consumption on their workstations, rather than real smartphones. The most recent work is eLens [68]. It combines program analysis and per-instruction energy modeling to enable much finer-grained energy consumption estimation. However, eLens assumes that smartphone manufacturers should provide platform-dependent energy models for each instruction. This is not a common practice as both the hardware and software of a smartphone platform can evolve quickly. Requiring manufacturers to provide a new set of instruction-level energy models for each platform update is impractical. Regarding this, eLens provides a hardware-based technical solution to help obtain such energy models. Still, power measurement hardware may not generally be accessible for real-world developers.

Typical scenarios for the techniques discussed above are to identify hotspots (software components that consume the most energy) in smartphone applications, such that developers can perform energy consumption optimization. However, simply knowing the energy cost of a certain software component is not adequate for an effective optimization task. The missing key information is whether this energy consumption is necessary or not. Consider an application component that continually uses collected GPS data to render a map for navigation. This com-

ponent can consume a lot of energy and thus be identified as a hotspot. However, although the energy cost can be high, this component is evitable in that it produces great benefits for its users by smart navigation. As such, developers may not have to optimize it. Based on this observation, our GreenDroid work helps diagnose whether certain energy consumed by sensing operations can produce corresponding benefits (i.e., high sensory data utilization). This can help developers make wise decisions when they face the choice of whether or not to optimize energy consumption for certain application components. For example, if they find that at some states, sensing operations are performed frequently, but thus collected sensory data are not effectively utilized, then they can consider optimizing such sensing mechanisms to save energy as Geohash Droid developers did [27].

18.6.3 Resource Leak Detection

System resources are finite and usually valuable. Developers are required to release acquired resources in a timely fashion for their applications when these resources are no longer needed. However, tasks for realizing this requirement are often error-prone due to a variety of human mistakes. Empirical evidence shows that resource leaks commonly occur in practice [34]. To prevent resource leaks, researchers proposed language-level mechanisms and automated management techniques [69]. Various tools were also developed to detect resource leaks [31,33]. For example, QVM [33] is a specialized runtime environment for detecting defects in Java programs. It monitors application executions and checks for violations of resource safety policies. TRACKER [31] is an industrial-strength tool for finding resource leaks in Java programs. It conducts inter-procedural static analysis to ensure no resource safety policy is violated on any execution path. Besides, Guo et al. recently collected a nearly complete table of system resources in the Android framework that require explicit release operations after usage [53]. Similar to our work, they also adapted the general idea of resource safety policy checking discussed in QVM [33] and TRACKER [31] for problem detection. The major differences between our work and these pieces of work are two-fold. First, we proposed to systematically explore an Android application's state space for energy problem detection. This requires addressing technical challenges in generating user inter-action event sequences and scheduling event handlers. Second, we also focused on studying more complex energy problems, i.e., sensory data underutilization. As discussed throughout this chapter, detecting these energy problems requires precise tracking of sensory data propagation and careful analysis of sensory data usage. Regarding this, we have proposed analysis algorithms and automated problem detection in this work, and they have not been covered by these pieces of existing work.

18.6.4 Information Flow Tracking

Dynamic information flow tracking (DFT for short) observes interesting data as they propagate in a program execution [28]. DFT has many use-ful applications. For example, TaintCheck [70] uses DFT to protect commodity software from memory corruption attacks such as buffer over-flows. It taints input data from untrustworthy sources and ensures that they are never used in a dangerous way. TaintDroid [35] prevents Android applications from leaking users' private data. It tracks such data from privacy-sensitive sources, and warns users when these data leave the system. LEAKPOINT [71] leverages DFT to pinpoint memory leaks in C and C++ programs. It taints dynamically allocated memory blocks and monitors them in case their release might be forgotten. Our GreenDroid work demonstrates another application of DFT. We showed that DFT can help track propagation of sensory data, such that their utilization analysis against energy consumption can be conducted to detect potential energy problems in smartphone applications.

18.7 Concluding Remarks

In this chapter, we presented an empirical study of real energy problems in 402 Android applications, and identified two types of coding phenomena that commonly cause energy waste: missing sensor or wake lock deactivation, and sensory data underutilization. Based on these findings, we proposed an approach for automated energy problem diagnosis in Android applica-tions. Our approach systematically explores an application's state space, automatically analyzes its sensory data utilization, and monitors the usage of sensors and wake locks. It helps developers locate energy problems in their applications and generates actionable reports, which can greatly ease the task of reproducing energy problems as well as fixing them for energy optimization. We implemented our approach into a tool GreenDroid on top of JPF, and evaluated it using 14 real-world popular Android applications. Our experimental results confirmed the effectiveness and practical usefulness of GreenDroid.

Acknowledgments This research was partially funded by Research Grants Council (General Research Fund 611813, 611811) of Hong Kong, and National Basic Research 973 Program (Grant No. 2015CB352202), and National Nat-ural Science Foundation (Grant Nos. 61472174, 91318301, 61321491) of China.

References

1. *Google Play Wiki Page.* https://code.google.com/p/gpslogger/issues/detail?id=7
2. A. Pathak, Y.C. Hu, M. Zhang, Bootstrapping energy debugging on smartphones: a first look at energy bugs in mobile devices, in *Proceedings of the 10th ACM Workshop on Hot Topics in Networks (Hotnets'11)* (ACM, 2011), pp. 5:1–5:6
3. A. Pathak, A. Jindal, Y.C. Hu, S.P. Midkiff, What is keeping my phone awake? Characterizing and detecting no-sleep energy bugs in smartphone apps, in *Proceeding of the 10th International Confer-ence on Mobile Systems, Applications, and Services (MobiSys'12)* (2012), pp. 267–280

4. *CSipSimple Issue 81*. https://code.google.com/p/csipsimple/issues/detail?id=81
5. *K9Mail Issue 3348*. https://code.google.com/p/k9mail/issues/detail?id=3348
6. *MyTracks Issue 520*. https://code.google.com/p/mytracks/issues/detail?id=520
7. *Android Sensor Management*. http://developer.android.com/reference/android/hard-ware/SensorManager.html
8. *Android Power Management*. http://developer.android.com/reference/android/os/Power-Manager.html
9. *Osmdroid issue 53*. https://code.google.com/p/osmdroid/issues/detail?id=53
10. W. Visser, K. Havelund, G. Brat, S. Park, Model checking programs, in *Proceedings of the 15th International Conference on Automated Software Engineering* (2000), pp. 3–11
11. *GreenDroid Project Website*. http://sccpu2.cse.ust.hk/greendroid
12. *Android Developer Website*. http://developer.android.com/index.html
13. *Android Activity Lifecycle*. http://developer.android.com/guide/components/activities.html
14. *Google Play Store*. https://play.google.com/store
15. *Crawler4j*. https://code.google.com/p/crawler4j/
16. *Google Code*. http://code.google.com/
17. *GitHub*. https://github.com/
18. *SourceForge*. http://sourceforge.net/
19. H.B. Mann, D.R. Whitney, On a test of whether one of two random variables is stochastically larger than the other. Ann. Math. Stat. **18**, 50–60 (1947)
20. *K9Mail issue 1986*. https://code.google.com/p/k9mail/issues/detail?id=1986
21. *CSipSimple Issue 1674*. https://code.google.com/p/csipsimple/issues/detail?id=1674
22. *CSipSimple Issue 744*. https://code.google.com/p/csipsimple/issues/detail?id=744
23. *Real APKLeecher*. https://code.google.com/p/real-apk-leecher
24. *Dex2jar*. https://code.google.com/p/dex2jar/
25. D. Octeau, S. Jha, P. McDaniel, Retargeting Android applications to Java bytecode, in *Proceedings of the 20th ACM SIGSOFT International Symposium on Foundations of Software Engineering (FSE'12)* (ACM, 2012), pp. 6:1–6:11
26. *AndTweet issue 29*. https://code.google.com/p/andtweet/issues/detail?id=29
27. *Geohash Droid issue 24*. https://code.google.com/p/geohashdroid/issues/detail?id=24
28. V.P. Kemerlis, G. Portokalidis, K. Jee, A.D. Keromytis, Libdft: practical dynamic data flow tracking for commodity systems, in *Proceedings of the 8th International Conference on Virtual Execution Environments (VEE'12)* (2012), pp. 121–132
29. Y. Liu, C. Xu, S.C. Cheung, W. Yang, CHECKERDROID: Automated quality assurance for smartphone applications. Int. J. Softw. Inf. (IJSI), **8**(1), 21–41 (2014)
30. K. Etessami, T. Wilke, An Until hierarchy for temporal logic, in *Proceedings of the 11th Annual IEEE Symposium on Logic in Computer Science (LICS'96)* (1996), pp. 108–117
31. E. Torlak, S. Chandra, Effective interprocedural resource leak detection, in *Proceedings of the 32nd International Conference on Software Engineering (ICSE'10)* (2010), pp. 535–544
32. *Android Process Lifecycle*. http://developer.android.com/reference/android/app/Activity.html
33. M. Arnold, M. Vechev, E. Yahav, QVM: an efficient runtime for detecting defects in deployed systems, in *ACM Transactions on Software Engineering and Methodology*, vol. 21 (2011), pp. 2:1–2:35
34. W. Weimer, G.C. Necula, Finding and preventing runtime error handling mistakes, in *Proceedings of the 19th Annual ACM Conference on Object-Oriented Programming, Systems, Languages, and Applications (OOPSLA'04)* (2004), pp. 419–431
35. W. Enck, P. Gilbert, B.G. Chun, L.P. Cox, J. Jung, P. McDaniel, A.N. Sheth, TaintDroid: an information-flow tracking system for realtime privacy monitoring on smartphones, in *Proceedings of the 9th USENIX Symposium on Operating Systems Design and Implementation (OSDI'10)* (2010), pp. 393–407
36. J. Clause, W. Li, A. Orso, Dytan: a generic dynamic taint analysis framework, in *Proceedings of the International Sympoisum on Software Testing and Analysis (ISSTA'07)* (2007), pp. 196–206
37. E.J. Schwartz, T. Avgerinos, D. Brumley, All you ever wanted to know about dynamic taint analysis and forward symbolic execution, in *Proceedings of the 31st IEEE Symposium on Security and Privacy* (2010), pp. 317–331
38. D. King, B. Hicks, M. Hicks, T. Jaeger, Implicit Flows: Can't Live with 'Em, Can't Live without 'Em, in *Proceedings of the 4th International Conference on Information Systems Security (ICISS'08)* (2008), pp. 56–70
39. N. Mirzaei, S. Malek, C.S. PǍCsǍČreanu, N. Esfahani, R. Mahmood, Testing android apps through symbolic execution. SIGSOFT Softw. Eng. Notes **37**, 1–5 (2012)
40. A.P. Felt, E. Chin, S. Hanna, D. Song, D. Wagner, Android permissions demystified, in *Proceedings of the 18th ACM Conference on Computer and Communications Security (CCS'11)* (2011), pp. 627–638
41. Y. Liu, C. Xu, S.C. Cheung, Verifying Android applications Using Java Pathfinder, Technical Report HKUST-CS-12-03
42. C.S. Pǎsǎreanu, P.C. Mehlitz, D.H. Bushnell, K. Gundy-Burlet, M. Lowry, S. Person, M. Pape, Combining unit-level symbolic execution and system-level concrete execution for testing NASA software, in *Proceedings of the International Symposium on Software Testing and Analysis (ISSTA'08)* (ACM, 2008), pp. 15–26
43. *Zmanim Issue 50/56*. https://code.google.com/p/android-zmanim/issues/detail?id=50/56
44. *Omnidroid Issue 179*. https://code.google.com/p/omnidroid/issues/detail?id=179

45. *GPSLogger Issue 7.* https://code.google.com/p/gpslogger/issues/detail?id=7

46. *Sofia Public Transport Nav issue 38.* https://code.google.com/p/sofia-public-transport-navigator/issues/detail?id=38

47. *Sofia Public Transport Nav issue 76.* https://code.google.com/p/sofia-public-transport-navigator/issues/detail?id=76

48. *Robotium, a testing framework for Android applications.* http://code.google.com/p/robotium/

49. T. Azim, I. Neamtiu, Targeted and depth-first exploration for systematic testing of android apps, in *Proceedings of the ACM SIGPLAN International Conference on Object-Oriented Programming Systems Languages and Applications (OOPSLA'13)*, ACM, pp. 641–660

50. S. Park, B.M.M. Hossain, I. Hussain, C. Csallner, M. Grechanik, K. Taneja, C. Fu, Q. Xie, CarFast: achieving higher statement coverage faster, in *Proceedings of the 20th ACM SIGSOFT International Symposium on Foundations of Software Engineering (FSE'12)* (ACM, 2012), pp. 35:1–35:11

51. C.S. Jensen, M.R. Prasad, A. Mÿller, Automated testing with targeted event sequence generation, in *Proceedings of the International Symposium on Software Testing and Analysis (ISSTA'13)* (2013), pp. 67–77

52. S. Anand, M. Naik, M.J. Harrold, H. Yang, Automated concolic testing of smartphone apps, in *Proceedings of the 20th ACM SIGSOFT International Symposium on Foundations of Software Engineering (FSE'12)* (ACM, 2012), pp. 59:1–59:11

53. C. Guo, J. Zhang, J. Yan, Z. Zhang, Y. Zhang, Characterizing and detecting resource leaks in Android applications, in *Proceedings of the 28th ACM/IEEE International Conference on Automated Software Engineering (ASE'13)* (2013), pp. 389–398

54. T. Dao, I. Singh, H.V. Madhyastha, Tide: A user-centric tool for identifying energy hungrey applications on smartphones, in *Proceedings of the 35th IEEE International Conference on Distributed Computing Systems (ICDCS'15)* (Columbus, Ohio, USA, June 2015)

55. L. Zhang, B. Tiwana, Z. Qian, Z. Wang, R. Dick, Z.M. Mao, L. Yang, Accurate online power estimation and automatic battery behavior based power model generation for smartphones, in *Proceedings of the 8th IEEE/ACM/IFIP International Conference on Hardware/Software Codesign and System Synthesis (CODES+ISSS'10)* (2010), pp. 105–114

56. W. Yang, M.R. Prasad, T. Xie, *A grey-box approach for automated GUI-model generation of mobile applications,* Lecture Notes in Computer Science (2013), pp. 250–265

57. E. Cuervo, A. Balasubramanian, D. Cho, A. Wolman, S. Saroiu, R. Chandra, P. Bahl, MAUI: Making smartphones last longer with code offload, in *Proceedings of the 8th International Conference on Mobile Systems, Applications, and Services (MobiSys'10)* (ACM, 2010), pp. 49–62

58. M.B. Kjærgaard, J. Langdal, T. Godsk, T. Toftkjær, EnTracked: energy-efficient robust position tracking for mobile devices, in *Proceedings of the 7th International Conference on Mobile Systems, Applications, and Services (MobiSys'09)* (ACM, 2009), pp. 221–234

59. J. Paek, J. Kim, R. Govindan, Energy-efficient rate-adaptive GPS-based positioning for smartphones, in *Proceedings of the 8th International Conference on Mobile Systems, Applications, and Services (MobiSys'10)* (ACM, 2010), pp. 299–314

60. B. Priyantha, D. Lymberopoulos, J. Liu, Little-Rock: Enabling energy-efficient continuous sensing on mobile phones. IEEE Pervasive Comput. **10**, 12–15 (2011)

61. M. Ra, J. Paek, A.B. Sharma, R. Govindan, M.H. Krieger, M.J. Neely, Energy-delay tradeoffs in smartphone applications, in *Proceedings of the 8th International Conference on Mobile Systems, Applications, and Services (MobiSys'10)* (ACM, 2010), pp. 255–270

62. H. Kim, J. Smith, K.G. Shin, Detecting energy-greedy anomalies and mobile malware variants, in *Proceedings of the 6th International Conference on Mobile Systems, Applications, and Services (MobiSys'08)* (2008), pp. 239–252

63. L. Zhang, M.S. Gordon, R.P. Dick, Z.M. Mao, P. Dinda, L. Yang, ADEL: an automatic detector of energy leaks for smartphone applications, in *Proceedings of the 10th IEEE/ACM/IFIP International Conference on Hardware/Software Codesign and System Synthesis (CODES+ISSS'12)* (2012), pp. 363–372

64. X. Ma, P. Huang, X. Jin, P. Wang, S. Park, D. Shen, Y. Zhou, L.K. Saul, G.M. Voelker, eDoctor: Automatically diagnosing abnormal battery drain issues on smartphones, in *Proceedings of the 10th ACM/USENIX Symposium on Networked Systems Design and Implementation (NSDI'13)* (April 2013), pp. 57–70

65. M. Dong, L. Zhong, Sesame: Self-constructive high-rate system energy modeling for battery-powered mobile systems, in *Proceedings of the 9th International Conference on Mobile Systems, Applications, and Services (Mobisys'11)* (ACM, 2011), pp. 335–348

66. A. Pathak, Y.C. Hu, M. Zhang, Where is the energy spent inside my app? Fine grained energy accounting on smartphones with Eprof, in *Proceedings of the 7th ACM European Conference on Computer Systems (EuroSys'12)* (2012), pp. 29–42

67. R. Mittal, A. Kansal, R. Chandra, Empowering developers to estimate app energy consumption, in *Proceedings of the 18th International Conference on Mobile Computing and Networking (Mobicom'12)* (2012), pp. 317–328

68. S. Hao, D. Li, W.G.J. Halfond, R. Govindan, Estimating mobile application energy consumption using program analysis, in *Proceedings of the 35th International Conference on Software Engineering (ICSE'13)*, pp. 92–101

69. I. Dillig, T. Dillig, E. Yahav, S. Chandra, The
    CLOSER: automating resource management in Java,
    in *Proceedings of the 7th International Symposium on
    Memory Management (ISMM'08)* (ACM, 2008), pp.
    1–10
70. J. Newsome, D. Song, Dynamic Taint Analysis for
    Automatic Detection, Analysis, and Signature Gen-
    eration of Exploits on Commodity Software, in *Pro-
    ceedings of the 12th Network and Distributed System
    Security Symposium (NDSS'05)* (2005)
71. J. Clause, A. Orso, LEAKPOINT: pinpointing the
    causes of memory leaks, in *Proceedings of the 32nd
    International Conference on Software Engineering
    (ICSE'10)*, pp. 515–524

Part VI
Conclusion and Future Outlook

Conclusion and Future Outlook

To be sure, there is no silver bullet in software engineering, but we hope the work presented in previous chapters can pave the way for pursuing a systematic and disciplined software methodology for Internet computing. In particular, the proposed Internetware software paradigm covers three main aspects:

- Software model (WHAT-IS). The Internetware software model concerns with entities, collaborations, and environments, as well as their relationships. We have discussed the environment model, software architecture model and requirement model for Internetware, as well as their enabling techniques. Collectively, these models define not only how autonomous software entities distributed in the open Internet environment are dynamically coordinated and federated to form Internetware application systems, but also how these systems flexibly adapt to the constant changes in the environment they are situated and the requirement they must satisfy.
- Software operating platform (HOW-TO-RUN). The runtime support for Internetware application systems covers various aspects of the execution and adaptation of software situated in the open and dynamic Internet environment. Runtime Software Architectures (RSA) are employed to govern on-demand collaborations. Leveraging autonomic computing for management, the Internetware middleware supports the self-organization and self-adaptation of Internetware software applications, and promises high quality-of-services (such as reliability and performance) at runtime. In particular, the structure of the Internetware middleware is open and extensible, so new capabilities and services can be on-demand loaded or customized. Besides the middleware system, Internetware runtime support also include facilities for dynamic software updating and distributed event monitoring.
- Engineering approach (HOW-TO-DO). The Internetware engineering approach follows the core principle of "Software Architecture of the Whole Lifecycle". A software architecture acts as the blueprint and controls every stage of software development with Internetware. To support online self-organization and self-adaptation of Internetware software applications, the software architecture is used to implement and govern Internetware software entities and their on-demand collaborations. To better control the development process, domain modeling techniques are employed for organizing heterogeneous distributed resources of a specific domain. The engineering approach also involves capability specification based on environment ontology and feature-driven analysis of requirement dependencies. Moreover, a mathematical characterization of object-oriented concepts and a calculus that supports both structural and behavioral refinement of object-oriented designs is proposed for Internetware applications.

© Springer Science+Business Media Singapore 2016
H. Mei and J. Lü, *Internetware*, DOI 10.1007/978-981-10-2546-4_19

The aspect on quality assurance, i.e., HOW-WELL, crosscuts the above described aspects. In addition, to materialize the ideas and principles of the Internetware paradigm in mainstream software application scenarios, we have further specialized Internetware techniques for and experiment them with cloud and client applications. We have shown how dynamic adaptation to the changing environment and how non-functional requirements such as performance and energy efficiency are achieved with novel techniques beyond conventional software practices.

A number of new research issues in Internetware are under investigation to accommodate recent trends of networked computing environments.

First, Internetware needs to be extended to cope with the software-defined cyberspace built upon converging heterogeneous networks. Telecom network, mobile network, sensor network, and other *ad hoc* networks are now capable of connecting and collaborating via the Internet. This phenomenon results in a hybrid complex network environment. The Internet is playing an increasingly essential role of connecting the cyber world, physical world, and social world as a new complex *cyberspace*. Computing devices, human society, and physical objects will be seamlessly integrated together. In such a cyberspace, software systems will orchestrate the information, process, decision, and interactions among the cyber world, physical world, and social world. The cyberspace will be where *software defines everything*. Correspondingly, the systems in the cyberspace might have larger scale and higher complexity. Internetware needs to be extended to support such a "software-defined" cyberspace, i.e., enabling the deep sensing and governance as well as the real-time and precise control of all objects.

Second, the Internetware paradigm should take into account the ever-increasing volume and value of data from millions of systems, billions of users, and zillions of sensors, of the emerging application domains. The Internetware software model should carefully re-examine the relationships between the business logics and their processed data, and incorporate new data structure and algorithms to support the increasing complexity, variety, and velocity of data. For Interntware engineering approach, mining and synthesizing various data assets such as open-source code, documentations, bug reports, user reviews and feedbacks, etc. should be better leveraged in the development process and toolkits, or further support the Dev-Ops of Internet-based systems. Some new development fashions such as crowd-sourcing or collective intelligence should be considered as well. For Internetware operating platform, new capabilities should be developed, such as efficient parallel data processing and online analytic and diagnosis of runtime system behaviors.

Last but not the least, the Internetware paradigm needs to be extended to accommodate shifted focuses on software quality. In the cyberspace, software systems can directly serve millions or even billions of users with various online services. The diversity of network environments, devices, and user preferences make the quality assurance more challenging and complex. Internetware software applications as well as the Internetware operating platform should be of *high-confidence*, which is more *user-centric and user-oriented*. Quality in real use needs to be assured but its measurement is relatively subjective, since it significantly relies on individual users' preferences and experiences. In addition, high confidence has to be gained by comprehensively measuring a set of quality attributes and making tradeoffs among them.

Printed in the United States
By Bookmasters